THE BACK DOOR GUIDE TO

SHORT-TERM JOB

ADVENTURES

THE BACK DOOR GUIDE TO

SHORT-TERM JOB

ADVENTURES

INTERNSHIPS, SUMMER JOBS, SEASONAL WORK, VOLUNTEER VACATIONS, AND TRANSITIONS ABROAD

FOURTH EDITION

MICHAEL LANDES

TEN SPEED PRESS

BERKELEY/TORONTO

DEDICATION

To my mom and dad, who not only opened my eyes to so many things while I was growing up but who also provided me with the tools I needed to develop into the person I am today. I feel very fortunate—it's comforting to know that someone encourages you and has faith in your abilities no matter what.

10

Ten Speed Press
Box 7123
Berkeley, California 94707
www.tenspeed.com

Distributed in Australia by Simon and Schuster Australia, in Canada by Ten Speed Press Canada, in New Zealand by Southern Publishers Group, in South Africa by Real Books, and in the United Kingdom and Europe by Airlift Book Company.

Cover and text design by Ed Anderson
Text production by Bonnie Monohan, FlashType

Library of Congress Cataloging-in-Publication Data
Landes, Michael.
  The back door guide to short-term job adventures : internships, summer jobs, seasonal work, volunteer vacations, and transitions abroad / Michael Landes.—4th ed.
    p. cm
    Includes bibliographical references and indexes.
  ISBN-10: 1-58008-669-1 (pbk. : alk. paper)
  ISBN-13: 978-1-58008-669-1 (pbk. : alk. paper)
  1. Job hunting. 2. Interns. 3. Volunteers. I. Title: Short-term job adventures. II. Title.

HF5382.7.L352 2005
650.14—dc22   2005001226

Printed in the United States of America
First printing, 2005

1 2 3 4 5 6 7 8 9 10 — 09 08 07 06 05

CONTENTS

OPENING THE BACK DOOR TO YOUR FUTURE

Remember when you thought about "what I want to be when I grow up"? Not there now? Well, think about it again, because you still have plenty of options to choose from. At first glance, you may think this book is solely an encyclopedia of unique short-term job opportunities. Undoubtedly, this may be the most alluring ingredient—especially since there are roughly five hundred pages worth of life-changing opportunities. However, I don't believe that a book of opportunities makes much sense without first questioning your existence and your purpose—you know, the who, what, where, how, and why. That's why the first three sections of your guide—the self-help component—focus solely on the philosophies that will help to bring happiness, meaning, passion, and lifelong learning. And that's exciting stuff.

So what is the secret to discovering your passion, achieving your dream career, pursuing a lifelong interest, or just doing something different (whether or not it relates to your career)? Simply ask yourself, "Does the opportunity have heart?" If not, what could you do that does? In other words, begin your journey by doing things that naturally harmonize with your values, skills, abilities, and God-given talents. Create a vision—your game plan for your personal path through life—then map out how you'll get there. If you haven't found out already, you'll learn that the things you do right now affect who you will become in the future.

Although "discovering your passion" and "achieving your dream career" sound like far-fetched goals, remember that every journey starts with one step. Think about your path step-by-step. Yes, it's a long process, but it will also be filled with exploration, adventure, and fulfillment that you can feel with each step, knowing you're on your way. It's also important to realize that every new path you take is an opportunity to create, learn, grow, and stretch while exploring life's possibilities—whether or not it leads to a dream career.

> *Too often we decide to follow a path that is not really our own; one that others have set for us. We forget that whichever way we go, the price is the same: in both cases we will pass through both difficult and happy moments. But when we are living our dream, the difficulties we encounter make sense.*
>
> —PAULO COELHO

When you try something new, your mind, body, and soul stretch and never go back to their original shape. Opening the back door to your future is really about growing and gravitating toward something that brings meaning to your life. Each experience will move you in new directions that you never imagined before you came up with the idea. You'll also find that these experiences are shaping your life—pushing and pulling you in different directions—until eventually you find something that really rocks your world. Just like getting on a train and picking up momentum—your life will gain momentum and get better and better. That is, if you work hard at it.

Look at your current situation. Does it fit in with your vision? If not, change it! (Again, the best place to start is with the heart.) And don't be afraid to do what feels natural for you, even if these things sound totally far-out. If it interests you and excites you and attracts you, it's a pretty good bet. Societal norms dictate many people's lives. Creating your own path means becoming a pioneer and explorer, discovering new places, exploring new ideas, meeting new people, and, most of all, uncovering the unique gifts that you were born with. Since no one blatantly tells us what these gifts are, we have to challenge ourselves to bring them out. Fortunately, you'll find that these gifts always direct you to your place in the world.

> *Start by doing what's necessary, then what's possible . . . and suddenly you are doing the impossible.*
>
> —SAINT FRANCIS

It's also about finding your zone space. Do you know that feeling—the zone you get into when everything feels right? Some figure out their zone space right away, others take a lifetime to get there, and, unfortunately, many give up when success is just around the corner (so please, please don't give up!). It may take a lot of work on your part, but you can carve out the path that's right for you. You'll know it right away. It will be a path with heart and it will energize your existence on earth.

In a recent short-term job adventure as a farm apprentice, I learned about the art of farming—just one of many experiences tucked away on my life's list of things to accomplish (have you created yours?). While at the farm, I participated in a series of classes focusing on the spiritual component of farming and life (just one of the benefits of a short-term job adventure). One class of particular interest centered on the influences from Saint Francis—insights that have resonated with my very own work. Read through the following insights and see what each means to you (I've also included corresponding feature stories throughout this guide for further understanding).

- To find your calling, put silence in your life. (Food for the Soul, page 325)

- Open yourself up to who you really are. (Open Yourself Up to the Possibilities, page 81)

- Let go, so something greater can come forth. (Open Letter to a Friend, page 18)

- Understand your path of conversion—the natural growth that takes place when you stay on your path, no matter how hard it may become. (Finding a Place in the World, page 519)

- Keep developing your gifts one step at a time. This work will take you (and keep you) on the right path. (In Search of a Mission—A Deeper Calling, page 433)

- See the beauty in everything and everyone through the eyes of faith. (A Whole New Way to Move through the World, page 465)

My hope is that the many "voices" that speak to you throughout the pages of your guide will not only encourage you to find your place in the world, but also allow you to realize that life is truly a miraculous event.

AT THE HEART OF THIS GUIDE

In 1996 a dream of mine finally came to fruition—the creation of the very guidebook you're holding. Much has changed since these early roots; however, the heart of your guide has not—it's still a tool that can change lives.

You must not let your life run in the ordinary way; do something that nobody else has done, something that will dazzle the world. Show that God's creative principle works in you.
—PARAMAHANSA YOGANANDA

That's why your guidebook goes beyond a directory of different opportunities to explore. It features seven unique components so you can make the most of your new journey:

- Three sections of self-help material (so you can discover who you are, what you want to do, and where you want to go).

- Eight topic-specific sections of program reviews (with organizations that provide thousands and thousands of short-term job opportunities season after season and year after year—in the U.S. and all over the world).

- Five specialized indexes (so you can quickly locate the material you need).

- More than 300 inspirational quotes peppered throughout (I suggest pulling out your favorites and posting them on the walls of your home for inspiration).

- Hundreds of recommended resources, books, and websites (for further research).

- Thirty feature stories from experts and short-term job adventurers in the field as well as countless "insider tips" from *Back Door* readers and program directors (you'll really enjoy these!).

- Over one hundred photos (so you can begin to visualize your dreams!).

Most of all, I have worked very hard at making the content playful, inspirational, and fun to read—with a design that's fresh and engaging.

With each new edition, every word, fact, philosophy, program, resource, quote, and visual is looked at with discriminating eyes—and dramatic changes occur. Just as I'm growing and learning and exploring, so is this book. Writing, carefully researching, updating, and revising a guidebook involves an enormous amount of information gathering and exacting attention to the nitty-gritty. Each year I'm presented with new programs, new resources, new ideas, new stories, and new quotes—many make it into your guide and many do not. In the process of writing and updating this book, I am fortunate to be able to communicate with thousands of people and programs. However, the real joy of my work is the process of going "undercover"—actually visiting the programs in your guide, then writing from these experiences. I encourage you to do the same. Visit a prospective organization whenever possible prior to inking the deal. This small adventure will not only impress the hiring team, but will allow you make a sound decision based on the big picture. (And if it doesn't work out, think of all the learning that took place!)

You will recognize your own path when you come upon it,
because you will suddenly have all the energy and imagination
you will ever need.

—JERRY GILLIES

This book evolves by my gathering of information, talking with people, showing up at their back door, and finding out what really goes on. One thing leads to the next. You can do the same. Beyond my own research, *Back Door* readers have proved to be a valuable asset by providing me with the realities of working for a particular program. Any comments I receive from readers on their experiences, I try to integrate into the respective listing. Many times you'll find a direct quote at the bottom of the listing that captures a participant's experience.

Whatever the way I've uncovered the information, every fact is verified with the program directors prior to inclusion in the guide. The updating process (which I do through mail, email, and phone) also serves as my weeding-out process. The challenge is to sift through all the important stuff and present you with a unique blend of information and inspiration. I spend thousands and thousands of hours writing and rewriting each listing so that it conveys the spirit and soul of each adventure. My formative years taught me that you should do a job to the best of your ability or not do it all. I hope you will find that my work reflects this very philosophy.

A CALLING UNIQUE TO ME

As I reflect on a handful of experiences in my lifetime—landing my first internship with Gallo Winery while in college; learning to "think different" as an intern at Apple Computer; traveling coast-to-coast with MTV; counseling and inspiring college students about the importance of internships at a university; venturing to Europe on a solo backpacking and cycling adventure; experiencing the beauty of Yellowstone National Park while working as a recreation manager; connecting more with the earth as an apprentice at a farm; or teaching elementary school children—I realize that all of these experiences, no matter how unrelated they were, have made me the person I am today. By looking at the world with curious eyes and exploring what's on the other side of the mountain, I now can see this incredible place we live in from many perspectives. Amazingly, I've seen my calling in life develop through this extraordinary sojourn that I've experienced. Fortunately, I can now share my insights, tumbles, adventures, and philosophies with you through this book (which I'm very thankful for).

ABOUT THE AUTHOR

With over fifteen years of experience in the career and life-planning field (and considered an internship guru in job adventure circles), Michael Landes believes there is room for every person to "find their place in the world" and meaning in their work. At age forty (and a kid at heart), Landes has worked in literally hundreds of short-term job experiences over the course of his life.

CONNECTING WITH THE AUTHOR

 Simply stated, I'd love to hear from you. Your adventurous (and not-so-adventurous) tales, experiences, suggestions, and feedback help to fuel my passion and make each edition better than the last. Since my journeys take me to different locales throughout the year, the best way to contact me is through email. Send me a note at mlandes@backdoorjobs.com or visit my companion website at www.backdoorjobs.com.

Happy adventures!

ACKNOWLEDGMENTS

The amazing journey of creating your guidebook has boiled down to two key ingredients—people and place—ingredients that have colored every aspect of my writing. The very nature of this guidebook has allowed me to transplant myself to many new environments; however, this component has also challenged me in many ways. Leading an adventurous life is definitely invigorating, but I have also been challenged with balancing transition and stability. This means creating a home base that I could find comfort in and an environment that would allow me to explore and take part in all the world has to offer—a factor that you must look at very carefully as you begin your own adventurous pursuits. While revising and rewriting the pages of this fourth edition, I've been very fortunate to have dear friends and family who helped me to balance this sense of place.

Beyond the sense of place that was created and nurtured, it was my connections with an amazing group of people (my "back door" team) that helped my words come alive. I feel very blessed for the hundreds of people who have influenced and added their gifts to this book: my team of contributing writers; readers who have shared their experiences with me; all the program directors and staff members who year after year provide me with information and invaluable insights about their short-term job opportunities; my talented team at Ten Speed Press, who amazingly turned my words into this beautiful book; and finally, many, many thanks go to each of you for believing in and supporting all my hard work. Thank you for keeping my passion alive!

Reach for the highest

Strive for the best . . .

Live day by day

And to God leave the rest.

The Climb

A small boy heard the mountain speak,
"There are secrets on my highest peak;
but beware, my boy, the passing of time.
Wait not too long to start the climb."

CHAPTER 1

BEGINNING THE CLIMB

So quickly come and go the years,
and a young man stands below—with fears.
"Come on—come on," the mountain cussed.
"Time presses on—on, climb you must."

Now he's busied in middle-aged prime,
and maybe tomorrow he'll take the climb.
Now is too soon—it's raining today;
Gone all gone—years are eaten away.

An old man looks up—still feeling the lure.
Yet, he'll suffer the pain—not climb for the cure.
The hair is white—the step is slow.
And it's safer and warmer to stay here below.

So all too soon the secrets are buried,
along with him and regrets he carried.
And it's not for loss of secrets he'd cried,
But rather because he'd never tried.

—PHYLLIS TRUSSIER

For those who already know they want to excavate an archaeological dig in Peru or teach kids about the wonders of the Atlantic Ocean and don't need to do extensive soul-searching, taking a peek at this chapter can't hurt. Finding yourself, deciding what brings meaning to your life, and determining your destiny all take time. This chapter will give you some creative ideas about the bigger picture in life and start your climb off on the right foot.

> *How can you get very far,*
> *If you don't know who you are?*
> *How can you do what you ought,*
> *If you don't know what you've got?*
> *And if you don't know which to do*
> *Of all the things in front of you,*
> *Then what you'll have when you are through*
> *Is just a mess without a clue*
> *Of all the best that can come true*
> *If you know what and which and who.*
>
> —WINNIE THE POOH

THIS CHAPTER WILL HELP YOU TO

- Uncover who you are and what naturally motivates you.

- Find balance in your life.

- Map out the big picture of your life.

- Understand the power of people and place.

- Begin the decision-making process.

WHO ARE YOU?

If you want to become an extraordinary, happy, fulfilled, and balanced person, it's time to stop being nebulous. Now is the time to take inventory of your talents, your personal quirks, and the careers that might resonate with your skills and abilities. With the work you are about to engage in, you will gain the ability to promote your uniqueness with passion and vigor when the time comes. Think of your life as a long, never-ending pathway stretching out ahead of you, with many pathways leading off to either side. The path you are on now represents the lifestyle you are now living (whether it be good or challenging); the offshoots from this pathway represent new directions you might

Knowing where you are is the first step toward knowing where you want to go.

take—new jobs, new places to live, new relationships, and new experiences. However, in giving yourself many options, you'll always come to a signpost on the road presenting you with two or three (or four . . .) attractive possibilities. Which one should you take? Which one in the short run will help you with your long-term goals? Of course, some of these paths might have huge doors in front of them, and to get through these doors, you must do certain things before they swing open for you. A particular door might need a certain skill, a degree, a well-connected friend or family member, a unique personal characteristic, or a past experience as a key. So, let's start from the beginning and uncover the unique you.

> *We could all use an emptying out of identity every now and then. Considering who we are not, we may find the surprising revelation of who we are.*
>
> —THOMAS MOORE

> *Everyone has his own specific vocation or mission in life to carry out a concrete assignment which demands fulfillment. Therein he cannot be replaced, nor can his life be repeated. Thus, everyone's task is as unique as is his specific opportunity to implement it.*
>
> —VIKTOR FRANKL

SETTING THE STAGE

Have you ever been to a play? If not, make plans to see a production for the sheer enjoyment of it. Now, take a few minutes and ponder all the things that went into the play's production: the directors, producers, writers, cast, set designers, musicians, costuming, acting, rehearsals, development, fundraising, program design, publicity, and so forth. It's amazing to think of all the steps necessary to create one production. Have you thought about what will make your very own "production" incredible? Have you thought about the things you want to (or may want to) accomplish to create an incredible

> *I've learned that everyone wants to live on top of the mountain, but all the happiness and growth occurs while you're climbing it.* —ANDY ROONEY

story for yourself? Are you the director and author of your story, or are you letting societal norms or others dictate or shape your story? Are you actively taking the time to develop your plot and create the things that are the most important? Think of all the players who are involved in your story: the scenery, the things that happen on a daily basis, the decisions that are made, the highs and the lows.

I dare you to think differently and to take your potential seriously. It's time to call on all your resources—to stretch them and challenge them. It's time to trade in your days of getting by and begin to work toward a life that brings fulfillment in everything you do. Today is the day. This journey must begin with an understanding of what's happening in your life right now—behind the scenes and on center stage. A powerful way to visualize the big picture of your life is by explicitly writing out all the important details—the fabric that will give you something to work with and something to act upon.

> *It's very important to fall in love with what you're doing. To be able to get out of bed and do what you love for the rest of your day is beyond words. It'll keep you around for a long time.*
>
> —GEORGE BURNS

JOURNAL WORK

- What kind of person do you want to be?

- What (and whom) do you gravitate toward naturally?

- What are your values?

- What are your unique qualities?

- What are your passions?

- What are five skills you enjoy using?

- What three words best describe you?

- What are your dreams and fears?

- Where do you need improvement?

- What do your friends say you are good at?

- Whom do you admire?

- What traits of those you admire would you make your own?

- Putting money aside, what job would give you the most satisfaction?

- If you could begin any hobby, what would that be?

SAMPLE

What are my passions? I can play the piano. I speak two languages. I can juggle. I love teaching kids about the wonders of the world. I hate snakes. I love frogs. I'm a so-so painter. I love thunderstorms and crazy weather. I'm afraid of not having enough money, going into debt, or being dependent on my parents or another person. I'm a pretty good cook. I'm a rotten city driver and really don't care for big cities. I really want to be a writer, photographer, teacher, and speaker! I'm not very organized. I love Italian music and food. A lot of money is not important to me. I want to travel in my work. I enjoy helping others out. I want to be settled somewhere. I just want to goof off for a couple of months. I'd like to try living on a boat or on a remote island. One day I'd like to have my own business—maybe open a coffee shop. I want to work on an organic farm in another country. I like a lot of change and stimulation. I've always wanted to visit every national park in the U.S. (and even work at one!).

JOURNAL ENTRY

Working through these questions (and additional ones you might have) will set the tone for the events and experiences that are now taking shape. You might also uncover some very interesting facts about yourself. But don't be alarmed if you don't. You might just need to think, explore, and do more. Once you begin to understand who you are and what is unfolding in your life, it will be easier to set goals, make decisions, and push past any barriers that might come your way. If you don't know yourself and the tools you have to work with, you'll certainly have a "mess without a clue" (as Pooh suggests). It's important not to overlook this important step in your journey.

TIPS ON REACHING YOUR GOALS

- Memorize your favorite motivating phrases in this guide and say them every day!

- Make little signs (or huge obnoxious ones that demand your attention) that point toward what you want in your life and put them all over your home. These will serve as reminders of where you want your life to go. Don't take them down until you have actually succeeded in your efforts.

- If you can articulate your top goals without having to sit down and think about them, you're closer to reaching them than you realize.

You are today where your thoughts have brought you;   5
you will be tomorrow where your thoughts take you. —JAMES ALLEN

FEELING GROOVY— THE BALANCING ACT

As you uncover who you are, it's equally important to strive for balance in all you do. This means stimulating your mind, exercising your body, viewing the world as an integrated whole, and understanding that life is not a series of random, meaningless events. When you strive to reach this balance in your life, you'll harmonize your actions with the way life is and make the will of nature your own. Remember, it's not what you do once in a while that will shape your life, it's what you do on a consistent basis. Make the time each day to work on the whole you!

⚓ INSIDER TIP: The importance of the whole—the balance of the mind, body, and spirit—is essential for anyone who wants to make a personal commitment to self-exploration and growth. Explore your options at various holistic retreat centers found in the Food for the Soul section on page 325.

Nurture your mind with great thoughts, for you will never go any higher than you think.

—BENJAMIN DISRAELI

MENTALLY

Becoming mentally active means becoming aware of the world around you. Every relationship, experience, mishap, or good fortune in your life is making an impact on who you become. The information you take into your mind, whether it be from a conversation with a stranger, news on television, concepts you learned from a workshop, or an idea from a book, is a continual process. Although some experiences are beyond your control, you must realize that you have the ability to influence what you decide to take into your mind or not. Are the turmoil and mishaps from the evening news helping to shape your life or detracting from it? Are the people you interact with on a daily basis adding a positive component to your life or inhibiting it? Since we generally find ourselves in other people and events, it's important to be aware of these associations.

What, then, are ways to include positive stimuli in your mind? For instance, make a list of friends and colleagues who make you feel more alive, happier, and more positive about life. Make it a point to spend more time with these people. Pay close attention to the book recommendations I have made throughout this guide (as well as recommendations from other friends). The words found in books will help you to think better and to become a more discerning and reflective person. Books will help you exercise your mind—learn a new skill, uncover new places to explore, be introduced to a new philosophy, and open your world to new concepts and ideas that will help to shape your life. In addition to reading the words of others, you might decide to create your own. I've had an ongoing journal for most of my life, which has included my thoughts, insights, experiences, or lessons I've learned. I generally carry my journal everywhere I go—you never know when a great idea might come your way! My journal has also served as the basis for much of the writing that has been included in this guide.

KEEPING A JOURNAL

Make time in your life to reflect upon your experiences. You don't have to start a new job or partake in a new experience to begin. Start today! Journals can help you discover new ideas, take action on these ideas, sort out difficulties with others, invent new ways of seeing things, plan new adventures, and help you to relive your experiences later in life. Books with blank pages seem to work the best. It's up to you to fill them with pictures, inspiring quotes, collages, or whatever is on your mind. You might just find the answers you were looking for.

The best of all things is to learn. Money can be lost or stolen, health and strength may fail, but what you have committed to your mind is yours forever.

—LOUIS L'AMOUR

PHYSICALLY

All right, put this guide down and give me fifty—fifty push-ups, that is. Being physically balanced means making a commitment to taking care of your body. For one, this means adding positive behaviors that promote good health, as well as strengthening habits you've already created for yourself. It also means making a commitment to exercise every day. You'll find that when you look and feel your best, you tend to be a happier person, with more confidence propelling everything you do.

For some it will take breaking old habits and starting out fresh. Changing habits is especially hard at first, because it requires determined efforts and time to make the changes stick. If you are just beginning your journey with exercise, walking is truly the best activity because it provides you with a complete workout. My preference is to walk in beautiful surroundings during the

The body is the soul's house. Shouldn't we therefore take care of our house so that it doesn't fall into ruin? —PHILO JUDAEUS

morning hours (there is something magical about the world waking up). I either walk with a companion to converse with, or by myself so I can be alone with my thoughts and nature. Begin with twenty minutes each day; then gradually increase the duration so that you are walking at least thirty to forty minutes per day. Daily stretching, which improves the flexibility of your body, is another healthful component to include in your exercise program. The more flexible your body is, the better it can meet the demands of life. You might also explore yoga as a formal way of stretching your body (and mind). Yoga helps to tone every muscle in your body and will assist in balancing all parts of your body, along with helping you to relax.

☞ **INSIDER TIP: Spend at least ten minutes a day meditating on how you can become a better person.**

• •

If you stuff yourself full of poems, essays, plays, stories, novels, films, comic strips, magazines, and music, you automatically explode every morning like Old Faithful. I have never had a dry spell in my life, mainly because I feed myself well, to the point of bursting. I wake early and hear my morning voices leaping around in my head like jumping beans. I get out of bed to trap them before they escape.

—RAY BRADBURY

We are what we repeatedly do. Excellence, then, is not an act, but a habit.

—ARISTOTLE

• •

Make exercise a daily ritual and vary it every so often so you find it refreshing and invigorating. Those who are more active can find a variety of pursuits that can help get the heart going, along with sweating out all the daily toxins of life. If you're not a fan of active sports, such as mountain biking, sea kayaking, or surfing, joining a fitness center will provide varied activities to keep your routine fresh. I especially like the energy that comes from step aerobics or a spinning class, or the spiritual connection that yoga provides. One key to exercise is making time for it, but the most important key is listening to your body. It will tell you if you've had too much or too little, so don't overdo. Sometimes curling up with a good book is all you really need to recharge your batteries. So listen. Getting sufficient sleep and relaxation is just as important as pushing your body.

Along with your exercise prescription, healthy eating habits are just as important. Those who are creating and eating well-balanced and healthful meals that include whole grains, fresh vegetables and fruits, fish, and minimal amounts of meat are off to a great start. It's especially beneficial to seek out people whose lifestyle promotes healthier eating habits, as you are more apt to mirror their habits. What you take into your body will largely affect how you feel throughout the day. It takes time to figure out your balance. Because we need food to sustain us, it's exciting to explore the possibilities that will not only bring ample energy to all we do, but will also enhance and protect our healing abilities. Those of you who work hard at maintaining a healthful diet, daily exercise, and proper relaxation will find an energy that will invigorate everything you do.

☞ INSIDER TIP: **Before you indulge in your next meal, take a moment and feel gratitude for the food you are about to eat. This will help to raise your spiritual awareness and provide a firmer sense of your dependence on other living things.**

OPTIMUM HEALTH

It's about creating healthy habits for eating, exercising, breathing, using your mind, and nourishing your spirit. It's about wholeness and balance. It's about making health choices on a daily basis that allow you to meet the demands of living without being overwhelmed. Holistic guru Dr. Andrew Weil, with his book *Eight Weeks to Optimum Health* (Ballantine Books, $13.95), provides a week-by-week program that will help shape and strengthen behaviors for becoming naturally healthy throughout your life. To explore other resources and advice from Dr. Weil, check out his companion website at www.drweil.com.

SPIRITUALLY

The point of bringing a spiritual perspective into your life is a simple reminder that you are more than just your physical body. I also believe it's accepting in childlike faith that a Supreme Being exists. I was born and raised Catholic, so my parents provided a solid foundation for my spiritual growth. It was not until college that I questioned just about everything—especially my existence and the meaning of life. I took classes on Buddhism and existentialism and began exploring different types of organized religions. After years of agonizing over this area in my life, I realized it didn't really matter what everyone called this Being from above, so long as I reaffirmed that "he" did exist and that I needed to live my life with this knowledge. Life didn't really get any easier with this knowledge; however, my existence has become more meaningful, more magical, and more heartfelt by nourishing this spiritual side.

☞ INSIDER TIP: **The secret to enjoying life is to be thankful for what each day brings.**

Don't be weary in prayer, keep at it; watch for God's answers and remember to be thankful when they come. —COLOSSIANS 4:2

The way we spiritually connect to the world will be different for each of us, but once you find this connection, everyday problems of life (when we feel helpless, confused, or resentful) become more tolerable, and everyday occurrences become more purposeful. Nourishing your spirituality might include reading inspirational quotes, immersing yourself in nature, listening to the rhythms of a particular song, bringing fresh flowers into your home, lighting candles and being silent, praying, meditating, or listening to a sermon each Sunday. Whatever you do to get in touch with your core, it's very important to view the world as an integrated whole and live your life with faith. Religious leader David McKay taught, "The greatest battles of life are fought out daily in the silent chambers of the soul." Once you work with these inward battles (and realize you cannot anticipate or control events), you will find that life is not a series of random, meaningless episodes. Set aside a small part of your day to spiritually connect and become familiar with the complexities of your inner life.

📛 **INSIDER TIP: Building a deeper life of spirituality often begins with the development of a personal prayer life.** *Beginning to Pray* **by Anthony Bloom (Paulist Press, $7.95) offers practical guidelines on the power of prayer for people at all spiritual levels.**

> *Slow me down, God, and inspire me to send my roots down deep into the soil of life's enduring values, so I may grow toward the stars and unfold my destiny.*
>
> —WILFRED PETERSON

EMOTIONALLY

Life is continually filled with emotions tied to daily occurrences in your life. What happens in these everyday situations can also affect the way you feel. Staying emotionally balanced entails the ability to be secure enough within yourself to handle life's ups and downs and not allow these things to control your life. Realize some things are within your control and others are not. You always have a choice about the content and integrity of your own life; however, external events and circumstances are beyond your control. When things don't go as you planned or people don't react the way you had hoped, you have the choice to allow feelings of hurt, anger, and inner turmoil to spread throughout your body or not.

You also have the choice to fill yourself with thoughts and actions that make you feel inspired, happy, excited, passionate, magical, energized, and enthusiastic. Positive results generally follow positive actions. Even though you may find yourself in challenging or difficult situations, these occurrences, approached with positive eyes, all help to make you a stronger and happier person. Tom Dennard, in his book *Discovering Life's Trails*, puts it this way: "We all have a tendency to want to label events in our lives as being good or bad because that's how we perceive them at the time. But bad can blend into good and good can blend into bad. We need to alter our perception of life's happenings as being good or bad and realize that every occurrence is necessary to make us who we are."

As you begin to understand your emotions, I encourage you to enjoy life's simple pleasures: compliment a stranger, hug a friend, laugh hysterically, scream at the top of your lungs, cry until the tears run dry. Remember you're human; do what you need to balance your emotions.

INSIDER TIP: Inspiration, self-improvement, and motivation. Need some? With Josh Hinds behind the inspiration wheel, GetMotivation.com will provide you with ideas and insights on leading a more successful, fulfilling life. Sign up for the inspiration a day—a daily eNewsletter including motivational quotes, an inspiring story, and engaging commentary by Josh.

INSIDER TIP: Are you looking for a regular dose of inspiration and information to live a more fulfilling life of doing what you love? Check out ChangingCourse.com—and be sure to sign up for the bi-monthly eNewsletter *It's Your Life*.

DREAMS

Listen to yourself and listen through your dreams. Dreams can help you understand your inner workings, solve life's problems, and see what your unconscious mind is working on at the moment. Dreams can point you in the right direction, whether you are lost or on the right track. You'll also find that your unconscious mind loves to guide you and answer questions you're not ready to ask your conscious mind.

If you can dream it, you can do it.
WALT DISNEY

Often people attempt to live their lives backwards: they try to have more things, or more money, in order to do more of what they want so that they will be happier. The way it actually works is the reverse. You must first be who you really are, then, do what you need to do, in order to have what you want.

—MARGARET YOUNG

CREATE A HAPPY BOX

Find an old shoe box and fill it with your favorite quotes. When you're feeling dispirited, pull one out at random and see what words of wisdom will help to inspire you, change your way of thinking, and move you in a new direction.

Each day comes to me with both hands full of possibilities, and in its brief course I discern all the verities and realities of my existence: the bliss of growth, the glory of action, the spirit of beauty.
—HELEN KELLER

BRINGING IT ALL TOGETHER

Now that you have a better picture of who you are, your desires, and how to maintain balance in all you do, it's time to focus on your needs. The most basic of human needs are food, shelter, and the ability to make enough income to meet your financial obligations. Once these essentials have been fulfilled, you can take strides to include more in your life—the path of self-actualization. Everyone will have different levels of each need as well as different ways to meet them. Up to this point, much of the focus has been on your wants. Wants are, well, anything. If you can figure out what you really want to do and what your basic needs are, you can be creative and resourceful about meeting both of them.

MASLOW'S HIERARCHY OF NEEDS

SELF-ACTUALIZATION

Step 5: Beauty, Truth, Goodness, Aliveness, Individuality, Perfection, Necessity, Completion, Creativity, Simplicity, Playfulness, Self-Sufficiency, Significance

GROWTH NEEDS

Step 4: Self-Esteem, Status, Ego, a Feeling of Importance
Step 3: Belonging, Companionship, Love
Step 2: Safety, Security, Risk Avoidance

BASIC NEEDS

Step 1: Health and the Preservation of Life, Air and Water, Food, Shelter, Sleep, Sex, Clothing

EXPLORE SIMPLICITY

To explore simplicity involves thinking about how your actions affect the earth, yourself, and others in this world. Simplifying your lifestyle is a continual process of choosing to focus on what is most important mentally, physically, spiritually, and emotionally. This may mean learning to become more self-reliant (such as planting your own garden or learning a new skill), seeking out entertainment that involves creativity and community growth, cooking from scratch to minimize waste, or volunteering your skills for a cause that helps to make the world a better place. The process of simplifying enables you to re-examine your wants and needs, and to shed the burdens of the unnecessary. You might also be pleasantly surprised that happiness goes beyond the material things in life.

🐦 INSIDER TIP: **Living simply need not translate into becoming poor, but rather making the wisest use of time and resources to live a richer and more joyful life.** *The Simple Living Guide* **by Janet Luhrs (Broadway Books, $21.95) brings all the key elements together—from money, working, and travel to exercising, housing, and health—and is rich in resources and real-life examples to help you explore the possibilities of a simpler lifestyle.**

PEOPLE AND PLACE

Your connections with people and places, which have provided a definition of who you are, are now changing. Change requires a release of these connections. Times of transition—changing jobs, changing eating habits, changing partners, changing where you live—all require you to give something up in order to gain. Definitely not an easy process! When you hold onto what used to be, it inevitably blurs your reasons for change in the first place. The only way you can grow is by pushing past your old way of thinking to create the things that are important to you.

THE HUMAN CONNECTION

Once you've focused on what is important, whether this means becoming a more balanced person or turning your dream job into a reality, that "fire in your belly" will take hold and bring energy and enthusiasm to everything you do. The things you thought you could not do become visions of the past. Undoubtedly you will have periods of discouragement or times when progress appears to be at a standstill. To push past these fleeting moments, it is important to seek out people, teachers, and mentors who will not only encourage you but who will also enable you to develop your initial enthusiasm over the long haul.

We are a product of the choices we make, not the circumstances that we face.   13
—ROGER CRAWFORD

I believe in the old adage "When the student is ready, the teacher will come." Of course, this does not mean that someone will appear at your back door or your phone will magically ring with your teacher ready to guide you. However, it does mean that your commitment, your hard work, and your enthusiasm toward your passion will promote this ability to uncover people who will take your passions to a new level. For instance, when I made the decision to write this book, I began calling other like-minded authors who could provide me with insights from their journeys. Over a period of a couple years, I soon developed a network of people whom I could bounce ideas off and share my enthusiasm with, and people who would keep me focused when I had lost momentum or felt discouraged. With their support and words of wisdom, I have been able to grow in ways I never thought imaginable when I first started out. The key to developing relationships such as these was putting myself out there, with the realization that some people would be willing to help and others would not. Those who did have made all the difference in the world.

LESSONS FROM GEESE
(based on the work of Milton Olson)

Fact: As each goose flaps its wings, it creates an uplift for the bird that follows. By flying in a V formation, the whole flock adds 72 percent greater flying range than if each bird flew alone.

Lesson: People who share a common direction and sense of community can get where they are going quicker and easier because they are traveling on the thrust of one another.

Fact: When a goose falls out of formation, it suddenly feels the drag and resistance of flying alone. It quickly moves back into the formation to take advantage of the lifting power of the bird immediately in front of it.

Lesson: If we have as much sense as a goose, we stay in formation with those headed where we want to go. We are willing to accept their help and give our help to others.

Fact: When the lead goose tires, it rotates back in the formation and another goose flies to the point position.

Lesson: It pays to take turns doing the hard tasks and sharing leadership. As with geese, people are interdependent on each other's skills, capabilities, and unique arrangement of gifts, talents, and resources.

Fact: The geese flying in formation honk to encourage those up front to keep up the speed.

Lesson: We need to make sure our honking is encouraging. In groups where there is encouragement, the production is greater. The power of encouragement (to stand by one's heart or core values and encourage the heart and core values of others) is the quality of honking we seek.

• •

The people I consider successful are so because of how they handle their responsibilities to other people, how they approach the future—people that have a full sense of the value of their lives and what they want to do with it. —RALPH FIENNES

During your life, everything you do and everyone you meet rubs off in some way. Some bit of everything you experience stays with everyone you've ever known, and nothing is lost. That's what's eternal, these little specks of experience in a great and enormous river that has no end. —HARRIET DOERR

• •

CREATING A SENSE OF PLACE

Along with the importance of people, our surroundings also shape our thoughts, emotions, and actions. We need places that support, rather than fragment, our lives. Many times your growth is limited by sitting around in your old haunts, which promotes the way things used to be. Again, it's important to break past these associations so you may respond to the positive stimulation of new things and places, which, in turn, promotes new directions and possibilities. When you're in an environment that offers few distractions and allows you to experience things you weren't sure you could do, it's much easier to figure out what matters and what doesn't, and to make the necessary changes in your life.

On the other hand, the current home environment that many of you have created often provides structure, a connection to family and friends, and familiar surroundings. There is also a certain aspect of yourself that resides in this place and that needs to be embraced. But, like it or not, we all have to leave home to find ourselves. The self you may be seeking is not "out there" in the literal sense but always within; often it reveals itself through your journey. To leave is to grow through adventure, risk taking, and excitement. Understand that "coming home" can also provide you with stability and strength. As you stumble in your quest for self-discovery and growth, you will find that leaving and staying are necessary components. The secret is to heed the wisdom that emanates from your soul and find the balance between each path.

🐟 **INSIDER TIP: Why is it that some people thrive in the hustle and bustle of city life while others choose to find comfort in the quiet of the countryside? In *The Power of Place* (Perennial, $13), Winifred Gallagher takes a hard look at how our physical place can delight us, deprive us, alter our moods, confine us, or influence everything we do. Revealing the complexities between people and the places in which they live, work, and enjoy, this book is highly recommended for those searching for a place that brings a sense of home.**

If we are always arriving and departing, it is also true that we are eternally anchored. One's destination is never a place, but rather a new way of looking at things. —HENRY MILLER 15

🐟 INSIDER TIP: Do you like a lot of sunny weather? Do you want to live near a college? FindYourSpot.com provides an online quiz that focuses on the issues that are really important to you—from climate and recreational activities to religion and community resources. Once you've completed the quiz, a tailored list of the best cities and small towns is displayed, complete with photos and information on demographics, median housing costs, and education. Dig deeper with colorful reports, job listings, and more for a small fee.

MAKING CHOICES

As you begin to take action in your new beginning, you will be faced with many choices that will lay the foundation for your adventure and how you live your life. When you face the difficulties of making conscious choices, you will grow stronger, more capable, and more responsible to yourself. Choices are never easy; however, with a little planning, you can map out a tentative

AUTOBIOGRAPHY IN FIVE SHORT CHAPTERS
by Portia Nelson

ONE
I walk down the street. There is a deep hole in the sidewalk. I fall in. I am lost. I am helpless. It isn't my fault. It takes forever to find a way out.

TWO
I walk down the same street. There is a deep hole in the sidewalk. I pretend I don't see it. I fall in again. I can't believe I am in the same place. But it isn't my fault. It still takes a long time to get out.

THREE
I walk down the same street. There is a deep hole in the sidewalk. I see it is there. I still fall in. It's a habit. My eyes are open. I know where I am. It is my fault. I get out immediately.

FOUR
I walk down the same street. There is a deep hole in the sidewalk. I walk around it.

FIVE
I walk down another street.

course of action, realizing that the outcome may or may not work. By understanding that either a positive or a negative outcome may result, you'll save yourself a lot of grief when unforeseen or unwanted consequences follow. That's why choices must first begin with a commitment attached to your choices. Tentative efforts always lead to tentative outcomes. Consider the real nature of your aspirations, begin making decisions based on these aspirations, then fully give yourself to these endeavors. It's only when you fully commit that the world responds in magical ways.

FIRST STEPS TO A BETTER LIFE

In what unique way can you make your life better right now?

- Create a life's list. I want to work on an organic farm, lead an adventure trip in Nepal, climb Mount Fuji, write a book, turn that hobby into a business, live on a boat . . . got the picture? See how many you can check off your list this year. (And see how many more you can add to it!)

- Indulge in three books to start your new adventure off right. That's right, for every idea you have about landing a cool job, there's a book to help you with your pursuits. See what changes happen because of it!

- Connect with the right person. Whether your dream is to work at a national park or to volunteer in Africa, there is someone who has "been there, done that." Make it a goal to find that person and pick their brain. Offering to buy them lunch is a good starting point.

- Listen to the Zen inside. Sound silly? Not really. Your inner light will always guide you on the right path if you stop and listen. Journalize these thoughts.

- Thank everyone who helps you in your pursuits. Not only does humanity need more acts of kindness, you never know how this "helping hand" will change your life.

A happy person is not one with a certain set of circumstances,
but rather a person with a certain set of attitudes. —HUGH DOWNS

OPEN LETTER TO A FRIEND

My friend:

Your life is now. I tell you this from the bottom of my heart. It is not what you did yesterday. It is not what you will do tomorrow or in your future. It is now. Today is your opportunity to live the real life. Today is your time to get out of the swamp of the status quo. You need to be different on purpose:

- Don't sit around your house and watch TV.

- Don't sell your soul for a great benefits package.

- Don't buy things to have a cooler image.

- Don't hang around with people aiming low in their lives.

- Don't chase money and stuff.

- Don't let the majority shape you.

You are a great-spirited person; it shows in your ambitions and dreams. However, you are not taking your potential seriously. You're trading invaluable days for mere "good times" and "getting by," because you're letting your fears get the best of you. You fear the time is not right, the resources aren't there, you don't have what it takes. And now, your fear is slowing you down like an anchor that slips overboard and drags along the bottom.

The only fear you need is the fear that you might continue living a life much smaller than your spirit and awake someday to find yourself a shell of a person, a product of a hundred small mediocre choices. Or worse yet, you might die unexpectedly tomorrow, next week, or next month with your music still in you. Your life is now. Your life is now, or never.

- You can't choose money over your real dreams without a negative consequence on your spirit.

- You can't keep putting your true talents on hold without ending up talentless.

- You can't keep putting off your big move without, bit by bit, killing off your desire to make a move.

- You can't go on trading away your true power for comfort without someday ending up weak.

Call on your tremendous mental and physical resources. They want to be stretched, exercised, and challenged. They demand to be used to their full capacity. Your reward for doing so will be greatness and excellence.

Let me be blunt, in hopes of making my true point: Every day you do not commit yourself to greatness, you are falling asleep, allowing yourself to suffocate on an atmosphere of mediocrity. Is the spirit-killing atmosphere I reference real? You only need to look at the newspaper or TV to know we are surrounded by negativity that cares little about inspiring greatness. We are often exposed to people who care nothing about being different, trying harder, or aiming higher. And you are barraged by a constant stream of products and services and efforts where average makes the grade. Yes indeed, you live in an atmosphere of mediocrity, and like poison gas it will dull you, bore you, disillusion you, and lessen you if you don't wake up and do something about it.

My friend, your life is now. Make the best of it.

Sincerely,

Patrick

—Contributed by Patrick Combs, who spends much of his time inspiring people from coast to coast as a motivational speaker. After paying his

way through college by managing a rock band, he became one of the youngest managers at Levi Strauss & Co. At twenty-six, he walked away from corporate America to help students succeed. While supporting himself by testing video games, he became a published author (*Major in Success: Make College Easier, Fire Up Your Dreams, and Get a Very Cool Job*) and a fixture on the college speaking circuit. Patrick lives in San Diego with his wife and daughter. For more inspirational insights from Patrick, explore the Good Thinking website (www.goodthink.com), or contact him at pcombs@goodthink.com.

Patrick Combs with his daughter Alyssa.

The greatest secret of success in life is for a person to be ready when their opportunity comes.
—BENJAMIN DISRAELI

Each path is only one of a million paths. Therefore, you must always keep in mind that a path is only a path. If you feel that you must now follow it, you need not stay with it under any circumstances. Any path is only a path. There is no affront to yourself or others in dropping it if that is what your heart tells you to do. But your decision to keep on the path or to leave it must be free of fear and ambition. I warn you—look at every path closely and deliberately. Try it as many times as you think necessary. Then ask yourself and yourself alone one question. It is this—does this path have a heart? If it does, then the path is good. If it doesn't, it is of no use.

—CARLOS CASTANEDA, *THE TEACHINGS OF DON JUAN*

CHAPTER **2**

YOUR PATH

The work you have done in chapter 1—understanding who you are, accepting yourself at every level, becoming your best, and uncovering what motivates you—has provided the foundation and structure for building your path. With this foundation, you will be able to uncover your passions more easily and make choices that affect the bigger picture of your life. This process takes time and will undoubtedly change as your life evolves. Chapter 2 is about putting your ideas into action, knocking on the right doors, and making your dreams a reality.

THIS CHAPTER WILL HELP YOU TO

- Explore your options and gather information.

- Be successful in getting the right job based on your passions.

- Fund your adventure and think about money.

- Make the most of your short-term job adventure.

THE TOP TEN SECRETS
TO ACHIEVING YOUR DREAM CAREER

10. What would you attempt to do if you knew you could not fail?

9. "Whatever you can do, or dream you can, begin it. Boldness has genius, power, and magic in it. Begin it now." —attributed to Johann von Goethe

8. Plan ahead! It wasn't raining when Noah built the ark.

7. Don't spend a lifetime exploring possibilities and do nothing. Action requires courage.

6. Don't put all your eggs in one basket. Always have an alternate plan.

5. To get what you want in life, you've got to ask others for help.

4. The shortest route to your life's work is not necessarily a straight line.

3. "Never let the fear of striking out get in your way." —Babe Ruth

2. "Perseverance is a great element of success. If you only knock long enough and loud enough at the gate, you are sure to wake up somebody." —Henry Wadsworth Longfellow

1. "Never, never, never give up!" —Winston Churchill

GATHERING INFORMATION AND TAKING THE NEXT STEP

You have options—and lots of them! What will it be for you? Interning at an environmental education center? Seasonal work at Yellowstone? Leading raft trips on the jungle rivers of Costa Rica? Inspiring kids at a summer camp? Becoming an apprentice at an organic farm? Playing the life of a cowboy at a dude ranch? Preparing for a career in theatre? Helping those with mental illness? Patrolling a remote island wilderness in Alaska by kayak? Raising the sails on a fifty-foot schooner every day? Playing the role of a historic resident at a living history museum?

Enter phase two of your journey—gathering information and connecting with the right people. If you haven't done so already, take time to read through this entire guide and highlight programs, resources, and ideas that will assist you with your dream. And that's just for starters. Realize that this book is only one of many, many resources that will help you along on your journey. A recommended book or web link just might turn into hundreds of other leads for you. Don't cut any corners at this stage. Make an investment in every resource that piques your interest. Join an association, attend their national conference, and connect with like-minded people in your field. By immersing yourself completely in this information-gathering stage, you will be able to make sound decisions on the direction of your life.

. . . .

Never look down to test the ground before taking your next step. Only he who keeps his eye fixed on the far horizon will find the right road.

—DAG HAMMARSKJÖLD

Profound joy of the heart is like a magnet that indicates the path of life. One has to follow it, even though one enters into a way full of difficulties.

—MOTHER TERESA

. . . .

Collecting information also means talking to anybody and everybody who might help you to see more clearly and present you with ideas to fuel your fire. Think of all the possibilities: family and friends, career counselors and professors, colleagues, and even strangers. One of the best ways to get more information about a career that you are exploring is to talk to someone who is actually in the job you desire. For instance, if you want to write a book, talk to authors; if you want to be a raft guide, talk to raft guides; if you want to work for the Peace Corps, talk to volunteers. Find role models who

In the path of life, don't try to cover your footsteps. Instead look back on them to see where you have grown.
—COLT WYNN

are acting in ways you are gravitating toward; then, make time in your day to talk to these people.

So where do you start? You might begin your efforts by calling a friend who has participated in a life-changing work experience and asking what steps he or she took. Or, depending on your situation, you might make an appointment with a career counselor at school or through work and pick his or her brain. These initial strides will help to broaden your comfort zone, so you will be able to approach just about anyone. The worst-case scenario in asking for help is rejection. This just means you made contact with the wrong person, so you move on to the next person until you find someone who will help.

INSIDER TIP: Attention college students and alumni: Don't forget to take advantage of your career services office. Besides being filled with hundreds of resources and job opportunities to explore, you'll also get to bounce ideas off professional counselors at no cost!

. . . .

Don't follow the path. Go where there is no path and begin the trail. When you start a new trail equipped with courage, strength, and conviction, the only thing that can stop you is you!

—RUBY BRIDGES

You will never change your life until you change something you do daily.

—MIKE MURDOCK

. . . .

YOUR CHALLENGE

Over the next couple of weeks, I challenge you to seek out one person who might help you in your pursuits. For those who are extroverts, this might be a simple task; however, for others, pushing yourself out of your comfort zone can be quite a daunting exercise. Enter risk taking. Risking is about moving from the fear of the unknown to the excitement of what is about to happen. Without risks, you'd never move away from home, find a great job, make a new friend, or fall in love. By learning how to take small risks, you'll begin to feel more comfortable about asking for anything that you want to help you in your journey.

CONNECTIONS

After you have uncovered strong work possibilities with specific organizations in this guide or through your conversations with others, narrow down your prospective leads to about ten (so you don't get overwhelmed at first). Out of this ten, pick the one program that interests you the *least,* and call them for more information. This call serves as your training ground, allowing you to get all your phone-talk kinks worked out prior to conversing with the program that is on top of your list. With time, you will feel more comfortable and confident about talking with program directors and asking the right questions.

This guide includes contact names for many of the programs listed, so be sure to ask for this person. However, sometimes you'll find that the contact has changed. Don't let that throw you off. Generally, someone will just transfer you to the right person; other times you'll have to explain who and what you're after. Eventually, you will talk to the right person.

This initial call is the first impression you will make on both the program director and the organization, so make sure it is a good one. Something that happens in this conversation just may be the link that eventually gets you the job. Some program contacts are receptive to talking; others don't have the time. At this point, you are mainly gathering information and promoting your enthusiasm as a potential candidate. During your conversation, you might ask for program brochures and an application, inquire about upcoming deadlines or the number of applicants that are hired, and uncover what they are specifically looking for in a candidate. Most of the information can be gathered through this guide and the organization's website, but it's also a good idea to verify any specific facts with the person you are talking to (largely because the nitty-gritty details can change from year to year).

🠖 INSIDER TIP: **Never be scared to ask. Ask and keep asking. Communicate your needs to others. Call people out of the blue. Take people to lunch. Open yourself up to others. You'll find success is usually a team effort. Asking is powerful. It can work magic. It sure isn't easy and it doesn't work every time. It will, however, if you persist. So ask, and it shall be given to you!**

> *Go around asking a lot of damn fool questions and taking chances. Only through curiosity can we discover opportunities, and only by risking can we take advantage of them.*
>
> —CLARENCE BIRDSEYE

Half the time you won't speak to a real person; you'll talk to their voice mail. Be prepared. If you stumble here, there's no way to erase what you've said. Prior to calling, it's a good idea to loosely script out what you want to

> *And the day came when the risk to remain tight in a bud was more painful than the risk it took to blossom.*
> —ANAÏS NIN

say. It might go something like this: "Hello, my name is Max Kean and I read in *The Back Door Guide to Short-Term Job Adventures* that you offer a summer internship program. Could you please send me an informational brochure and application?" At this point, give your mailing address, email address, and phone number. It's also important to speak slowly and clearly, and spell out any words that are difficult to understand. Remember, someone is writing down your message to get you the information you need. Conclude with any enthusiasm you may have about the possibility of joining their program.

Many of you will request information through a simple email note. Although email seems to be the most efficient way to get the information you need, many programs are generally bogged down by all the notes they receive in a day's time. So be patient in receiving a response. Prior to clicking on your send button, be sure you have crafted a professionally written letter that has been spell-checked, grammar-checked, and proofread several times. Remember, you are not emailing a friend to say hello. Think of this note as your initial cover letter to the program, which means putting effort into what you write. Although email serves as an easy way to communicate, keep in mind that it also lacks the human ingredient. Anytime I want to make an impression on a new client or am seeking out a new work assignment, I either call the person over the phone or schedule a meeting in person. Never overlook the power of the human connection.

INSIDER TIP: Send short, handwritten thank-you notes to all who help you in your quest. Not only will you realize at a later point how important these people were in getting you where you are today, this small note of appreciation can also lead to lifelong connections and friendships with exciting possibilities.

STAYING ORGANIZED

What works best for you? Whether it be with index cards or a computer database, you need to keep track of all the information you'll be collecting. For starters, create a notes log of all your correspondence. Write down everything, from the date of your initial phone call to the details of your conversation. This is especially beneficial if you are applying to several programs—your log will keep you focused on the needs of each. Make notes of important dates: deadlines, dates to make follow-up phone calls, or when you need to send off a thank-you letter. I also jot down personal tidbits about the person after talking with them. These tidbits serve as great conversation starters the next time you talk with the person, as they generally are surprised you remembered something so personal.

THE APPLICATION PROCESS

Once you receive the program's application packet in the mail, act upon it right away. Many times positions are filled as soon as applications have been reviewed. The saying "the early bird gets the worm" generally holds true when applying for seasonal-type jobs. Although each program wants the best person for a specific job, many directors are concerned about filling the position before it is too late.

You'll also find that putting together your application seems to take longer than you anticipate, especially if the program has a four-page form to fill out and desires a couple of short essays and three letters of recommendation (along with a personalized cover letter and your updated resume). Yes, many programs ask a lot from you, but this is their first opportunity to weed out candidates who haven't taken this step seriously. Keep in mind the payoff for all your hard work: the possibility of working with a program that will forever change your life. Whatever you're asked to do in the application process, be sure that your skills, interests, and abilities are very apparent in the packet you send them.

INSIDER TIP: Don't just randomly apply to every job you're remotely qualified for or interested in. Put together a list of all the aspects of your ideal job, taking into account your personality, skills you enjoy using, what's important to you, the work environment, and your talents. Then go after it with complete determination and optimism. You have the power to make it happen!

INSIDER TIP: Before sending off your completed application, make a copy of it. In case it gets lost in the mail, you'll have a spare copy. This will also serve as your master for doing other applications.

YOUR RESUME AND COVER LETTER

Your resume might be the most important document to assist you in your job search. The resume is your marketing brochure and selling tool—information that will hopefully paint a very clear picture of your talents and abilities. What kind of person are you? What kind of skills do you have? What are some of your life experiences? What do you do in your spare time? What hobbies do you have? What are some major things that you have accomplished? If you've done your homework in chapter 1, answering these questions will come easily and naturally.

The best resumes are those that are filled with the entire you. Along with your academic record and work experiences, be sure to include your skills, accomplishments, volunteer service, and any other unique attributes that make you stand out. I even put my favorite quote at the bottom of my resume.

Originality is not doing something no one else has ever done,
but doing what has been done countless times with new life, new breath.
—MARIE CHAPIAN

As you create and develop your resume, it's very helpful if a team of people looks it over for ideas, spelling errors, and areas you could improve on. If at all possible, have a career counselor or program director provide you with feedback; otherwise, there are plenty of resume books that are filled with great ideas. No matter what advice is given, the beauty of creating your resume is that anything goes—you get to make all final decisions!

Set your resume aside for a few days before you come back to it for revisions. This will give you time to work on a personalized cover letter (also known as a letter of interest or intent). Many people think that a cover letter is the same as a Post-it note that says: "Hey, check this out—I'd really like to work for you!" Unfortunately, you'll find these cover letters lying in the bottom of recycle bins. Your cover letter is the icing on the cake and is just possibly as important as the resume itself. It serves as an expansion of your resume and answers these key questions: what you are applying for, why you want to work for this particular organization, how your skills and abilities relate to the job opportunity, and why they should hire you.

Your cover letter also describes your potential to the employer. Let your personality shine in your writing. You might not have all the necessary skills, but your cover letter can demonstrate that you're trainable for the job. Remember, many applicants are hired not necessarily based on skill, but more so for enthusiasm and energy. Job-specific skills and responsibilities, in general, can always be taught.

🖙 **INSIDER TIP: Good hiring managers always smell a form letter before you lick the stamp. Bring out your inner child and make it personal!**

LETTERS OF RECOMMENDATION

Unless you've planned ahead and already have copies of letters of recommendation from former bosses, professors, or colleagues, this task might take some work on your part. First off, I need to emphasize how important it is to develop relationships with your professors or people who might serve as mentors in your career development. This means reaching out to others, asking for help, and seeing what develops and what doesn't. These people will serve as allies in all you do, especially when it comes to developing your future.

🖙 **INSIDER TIP: Even though a program might not ask for letters of recommendation, include them anyway. They will make your application packet stand out.**

For those who haven't developed a network of support and "sideline cheerleaders," it's best to ask former bosses, teachers, or anyone who can provide a sincere impression of your talents and abilities. Query your list of possible candidates to see who is comfortable in sharing with others about your skills and abilities. To help the person in writing your letter, provide them with information about the program, the position you are applying for, and strengths that should be highlighted. Another nice touch is to provide them with a postage-paid envelope so they can either send it to you or directly to the employer. After all is said and done, be sure to thank these people who have taken time out of their lives to help you along in your path. A handwritten letter always makes a nice touch.

FOLLOW-UP

Although each step in getting your dream job is important in itself, following up on your application might make the difference in who gets the job and who does not. One to three weeks after sending in your application materials, pleasantly surprise your contact with a phone call. In this phone call, verify that they have received your application, and at the same time, ask if there is anything else you can provide as well as any other questions that concern you. Once again, promote your enthusiasm about the program and job prior to ending your conversation.

YOUR INTERVIEW

Congratulations! Once you've made it this far, all your preliminary hard work has paid off (and impressed the hiring team). The interview, the final step of landing the job, is where you get to show off what you're all about and how you'll make a difference in their program. Whether you are interviewing in person or over the phone, it's best to prepare a loose script prior to your interview. Your script should include various trigger words that will help your brain connect your thoughts. These words are simply reminders of items (skills, unique stories, and strengths) you need to cover as you talk about yourself and the position. Moreover, if the work you want to do is really something you believe in, your feeling of enthusiasm will come across naturally.

To grapple with any uneasiness prior to your interview, I suggest working with a friend who can act as your interviewer. Come up with a list of typical interview-type questions and challenge yourself to answer them out loud. By speaking out your answers, you are connecting your thoughts and ideas with actual words and stories. With practice, you'll be able to answer any question that comes your way. Remember, your goal is to paint a very real and sincere picture of who you are, what skills you have obtained over the years, and your potential for future growth. You should have the ability to talk about anything mentioned in your resume, along with supporting examples. If a question ever catches you off guard, don't be afraid to pause while you think about the question posed—the advantages of organizing your mind as opposed to blurting out anything outweigh any perceived disadvantages of a few seconds of silence. Those who have successful interviews are those who have done plenty of preparation and anticipate what questions the interviewer might ask. Just like anything, the more you interview, the better you will become.

Just be what you are and speak from your guts and heart—it's all a man has.
—HUBERT HUMPHREY

That which we persist in doing becomes easier—not that the nature of the task has changed, but our ability to do so has increased.

—RALPH WALDO EMERSON

✄ **INSIDER TIP: Practice interviewing in front of your cat, dog, or goldfish. Pets are always a supportive audience and will definitely build your confidence. (Be sure to thank your critter with a treat or two!)**

THOSE PESKY INTERVIEW QUESTIONS

You never know what will be asked of you in your interview. However, these questions and ideas will help you to prepare for anything asked of you:

- How would you describe yourself to someone who didn't know you?

- What qualities do you most admire (and dislike) about yourself?

- Explain your creative side.

- Describe yourself in one word.

- Give three specific examples of your strengths.

- What things come easily to you? What's more difficult?

- What have you learned about yourself in the last year?

- What's important to you in life?

- Describe a role model in your life.

- Write five reasons why you shouldn't be hired. Come up with rebuttals for each and memorize them. Alternately, come up with five specific reasons why you should be hired.

Your interview also serves as your time to ask those all-so-important questions that will help you make decisions about your future. Just as your prospective employer is studying everything about you during the interview, you should be doing the same. You're each sizing the other up to see if you are compatible for a budding work relationship. Think of it in the same light as dating. Here are some key questions that you want to ask of your prospective employer.

- **What investment will the program make in directing and enhancing your natural learning process in exchange for your work and energy?**

On-the-job training is inherent in every position that you will be considering; however, the amount of training you will receive is an important consideration—especially if this is your first job in the field. Those that offer intensive training programs, informal and formal discussions, workshops, seminars, or lectures as part of your learning experience may be much more desirable.

- **What staff members will you be working with and what are their backgrounds?**

The permanent staff will serve as your mentors, your teachers, and your guides. These people will also help you network in the field and connect you to possibilities that will enhance your career. You must decide whether you'll get the guidance you need given the staffing arrangement that exists.

- **What are the criteria for hiring short-term staff members?**

You'll find that your peers will provide some of the best sources of inspiration, learning, sharing, and friendship during your experience. Will your peers be likely to have a level of schooling and experience that will ensure that you are surrounded by a strong support group?

- **What kind of living conditions will be provided?**

A nice benefit for short-term work opportunities is that many offer room and board as part of your compensation package. If not, be sure to ask what type of housing assistance they provide, if any. Don't be the person that arrives at their new job only to find out that they will be sharing a room with three others and eating meals that don't do much for a healthy lifestyle. Will you have a private room? Will you share a bathroom? What types of meals are served? Are there kitchen facilities available for your use? Find out the details about any of these issues that are important to you.

- **What kind of experience did past seasonal staff members have with the program?**

I always suggest talking candidly to others who have participated in the program to get their impression of the experience. You'll find that many programs also provide the names and phone numbers of past participants, so be sure to ask. In addition to talking with former participants, you might find it to your advantage to schedule an on-site interview (if one isn't provided), so you can talk with various staff members and interns who are currently working there, along with getting a feel for your work environment.

It's a funny thing about life; if you refuse to accept anything but the best,
you very often get it.
—W. SOMERSET MAUGHAM

- **What kind of job opportunities will exist after completion of your assignment?**

The beauty of a short-term work opportunity is that it can naturally evolve into a lifelong career with the organization. Many times the permanent staff is made up of former interns. It's important to see if there will be opportunities for future growth within the organization or if any career assistance will be provided upon the conclusion of your experience.

• •

You have a unique message to deliver, a unique song to sing, a unique act of love to bestow. This message, this song, and this act of love have been entrusted exclusively to the one and only you.

—JOHN POWELL

If a man is called to be a street sweeper, he should sweep streets even as Michelangelo painted, or Beethoven composed music, or Shakespeare wrote poetry. He should sweep streets so well that all the hosts of heaven and earth will pause to say, here lived a great street sweeper who did his job well.

—DR. MARTIN LUTHER KING, JR.

• •

ASK AND YOU SHALL RECEIVE!

If you have gathered enough information during your interview to make a sound decision about joining an organization, be sure to tell the recruiter so. Many applicants leave this open-ended as their interview comes to a close, allowing the recruiter to make his or her own judgment. If you feel that you can make an impact on their program and that they offer an experience that will enhance your talents and abilities, let them know! Most often, you won't get a job offer on the spot, but your enthusiasm will definitely leave an impression.

After you've had a chance to digest your interview, take the time to send a handwritten letter to the person who interviewed you. Reiterate your enthusiasm for the program (and position), expand on anything that you felt was left open-ended in the interview, and again, let them know that you want the job. Often, recruiters interview a handful of super applicants for only one position. Your persistence will often help influence their decision to hire you!

Life is not easy for any of us. But what of that? We must have perseverance and above all confidence in ourselves. We must believe that we are gifted for something, and that this thing, at whatever cost, must be attained.

—MARIE CURIE

REJECTION SHOCK

After all the hard work, time, and energy that you put into landing what you thought was the ideal job, there may be a time when the mail brings a thin letter that states (in so many nice words) that you will not be offered a position. Enthusiasm and excitement quickly turn to feelings of failure. Nobody likes rejection; however, you must realize that this component will be part of your life no matter how hard you try. In fact, what has been thought of as a failure often turns into a blessing in disguise, even though it's not very apparent at the time. It's like falling off your bike for the first time. You simply get on it and try again. Life is constantly like this—especially for those who are willing to risk and go after what they truly believe in.

That's why it's very important not to put all your eggs in one basket. It's easier to set yourself up for success by opening yourself up to many opportunities. By applying to many programs that pique your interest, you are bound to receive an offer or two—many times, more than you anticipated!

• •

If you're not rejected ten times a day, you're not trying hard enough.

—ANTHONY COLEMAN

Everyone has a talent. What is rare is the courage to follow that talent to the dark place where it leads.

—ERICA JONG

• •

APPROACH YOUR LIFE
WITH A LONG-HAUL MENTALITY

As I'm sure you are well aware, it takes time for careers, opportunities, and relationships to develop in your life. There is a process to everything you do. Again, try to think of what you are doing right now as your never-ending journey.

A long-haul mentality approach will help you understand that the things you do now entirely affect the opportunities that are presented in your future. Overnight success is rare (and is usually because of the hard work that led up to that point). Don't rush the process. Each step in your journey takes time.

Those who have planted a vegetable garden or have spent time on a farm know that there are certain steps that are necessary to turn a seed into something life sustaining. Mother Nature will also challenge this process every step of the way. That's why life should be approached with a long-haul mentality. Enjoy every good and challenging step along the way. Good things come to

Ask, and it shall be given to you; seek, and ye shall find; knock, and it shall be opened unto you.
—MATTHEW 7:7

people who work hard to get what they're after. You might not see the results today or next week or even a month from now, but they'll hit you when you least expect it, and you'll be very happy to know that all your hard work has paid off.

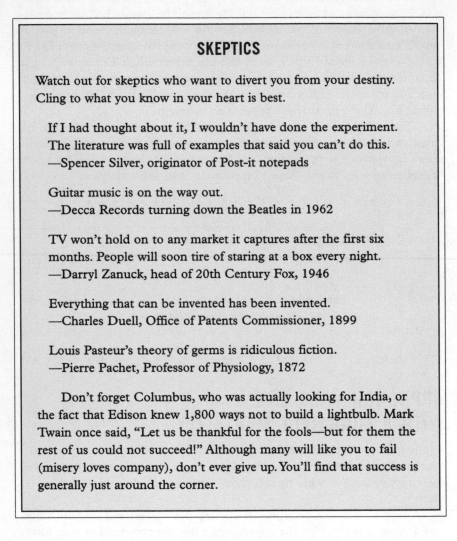

SKEPTICS

Watch out for skeptics who want to divert you from your destiny. Cling to what you know in your heart is best.

If I had thought about it, I wouldn't have done the experiment. The literature was full of examples that said you can't do this.
—Spencer Silver, originator of Post-it notepads

Guitar music is on the way out.
—Decca Records turning down the Beatles in 1962

TV won't hold on to any market it captures after the first six months. People will soon tire of staring at a box every night.
—Darryl Zanuck, head of 20th Century Fox, 1946

Everything that can be invented has been invented.
—Charles Duell, Office of Patents Commissioner, 1899

Louis Pasteur's theory of germs is ridiculous fiction.
—Pierre Pachet, Professor of Physiology, 1872

Don't forget Columbus, who was actually looking for India, or the fact that Edison knew 1,800 ways not to build a lightbulb. Mark Twain once said, "Let us be thankful for the fools—but for them the rest of us could not succeed!" Although many will like you to fail (misery loves company), don't ever give up. You'll find that success is generally just around the corner.

DON'T QUIT

When things go wrong, as they sometimes will; when the road you're trudging seems all uphill; when the funds are low and the debts are high, and you want to smile, but you have to sigh; when care is pressing you down a bit—rest if you must but don't you quit.

Life is queer with its twists and turns, as every one of us sometimes learns; and many a fellow turns about when he might have won had he stuck it out. Don't give up though the pace seems slow—you may succeed with another blow.

Often the goal is nearer than it seems to a faint and faltering man; often the struggler has given up when he might have captured the victor's cup; and he learned too late when the night came down, how close he was to the golden crown.

Success is failure turned inside out—the silver tint of the clouds of doubt; and you never can tell how close you are. It may be near when it seems afar; so stick to the fight when you're hardest hit—it's when things seem worst that you mustn't quit.

DON'T TRAVEL DOWN THAT BIG RIVER IN EGYPT

• •

I was raised to sense what someone wanted me to be and be that kind of person. It took me a long time not to judge myself through someone else's eyes.

—SALLY FIELD

The college years—a time of exploration, excitement, discovery, and learning. Should I study architecture or maybe engage in the field of psychology? Like many of us navigating through this period in our life, Craig Dunkin was presented with a handful of tough questions—questions he had to answer without much direction. At that age, who among us really is aware of what we want our life to develop into? Unfortunately, most of us opt for the easy route, allowing the hand of society to push us in certain directions instead of making the big decisions for ourselves. Craig was really interested in sports broadcasting; however, smart people go to law school, so that's what he did.

Twelve years later, Craig sat in his office at a very reputable law firm in Los Angeles. He was very successful and made good money, but on this day, mindless lawyer tasks were par for the course. Then, the epiphany hit: "There is more to life than what I'm doing." This thought consumed him for the rest of the day. The "Inner Craig" whispered, "What are you doing practicing law? What are you working toward?" This day changed his life.

While still acting as a lawyer, Craig decided to take a class at a local community college on sports broadcasting. A professor soon became his mentor, helping him to answer many of the tough questions he ignored in college. With excitement and passion as his guides, Craig spent the next few years revitalizing his inborn talents. He spent his evenings and weekends at any sporting event he had time to experience. However, he didn't sit there like any other ordinary fan, he was there on a mission. Positioning himself in the centerfield bleachers or away from the crowds, a sports broadcaster was soon born.

Using a microphone and tape recorder as his tools of the trade, he began giving play-by-play action of the games. Although he did not actually engage an audience on the details of the event (except for a few fans sitting near him), these demo tapes soon doubled as a key component of his sports broadcasting portfolio. Shortly thereafter, he began scouting out ball teams so he might expose his talents to the world. "I called every minor league baseball team across the nation and asked if they needed a broadcaster. If they said yes or maybe, I sent those tapes."

Months (which seemed like years) went by until he finally got a break from a ball team in the South who thought he had potential. A deal was made, and this ex-California lawyer made his way to the small town of Clarksville, Tennessee.

Although he would spend extra time on weekends and at night figuring out the small details that make a ball game exciting, the extra work became a labor of love, rather than just laboring (as he had done as a lawyer). "That's what drew me to it all. This was my chance to be really good at something." He looks back at all his lawyer years as "floating down that big river in Egypt." To clarify what he meant, he continued, "You know, the Nile?" You see, the Nile was a constant reminder that he had been living in a world of denial—denial of what he really felt and wanted to do with his life.

Craig's thoughtful advice for anyone looking to make sense of their career is this: "If you don't like being a lawyer, but it allows you to have season tickets to the opera or a beautiful home on five acres—and that's what brings meaning to your life—then so be it. But if that's not enough for you, then why do it? You have to figure out what's important and then fill that aspect in your life. No matter how difficult it is to get into something, don't let that stop you. If you feel you are a talented actor, go do that. But, most importantly, just don't visit that river out in Egypt."

With broadcasting passion in his eyes, Craig stops for a quick photo op in between innings of a ball game.

The significant problems we face cannot be solved at the same level of thinking we were at when we created them. —ALBERT EINSTEIN

MONEY AND FUNDING YOUR ADVENTURE

Once you realize that your self-worth has nothing to do with your net worth, money will not be the only source of richness and fulfillment in your life. Obviously a lack of money can constrain us from doing the things we really want to do, especially if we're burdened by school loans, credit card debts, or making just enough to meet our daily financial obligations. Those in this situation will learn to become resourceful; there is always another way to make your dreams come alive, no matter what roadblocks lie ahead. Once you've committed to a goal, whether it be working as a seasonal employee at a national park, starting a business, participating in a service learning adventure, or funding an experience abroad, opportunities will start taking shape. By broadcasting your intentions to the world, the world usually responds back in amazing ways (and if it doesn't, this might tell you that you've walked down the wrong path or perhaps you just need to try a little harder).

So how do you survive in the world while funding your passion in life? Although some of the ideas below might seem ludicrous, being resourceful and creative will help you create a livelihood that will blossom over time.

• •

One of the main reasons wealth makes people unhappy is that it gives them too much control over what they experience. They try to translate their own fantasies into reality instead of tasting what reality itself has to offer.

—PHILIP SLATER

We are very short on people who know how to do anything. So please don't set out to make money. Set out to make something and hope you get rich in the process.

—ANDY ROONEY

• •

SELL LEMONADE!

Many of us had the chance to become young entrepreneurs as we grew up—selling lemonade, mowing lawns, washing cars—experiences that taught us the value of money. Apply this same philosophy to your current situation. What skill do you have that could benefit others and, at the same time, bring in some extra cash? Are you a budding artist? Perhaps a local business in town might need your help in designing a few brochures for a fee. Or possibly the local health club wouldn't mind offering you a membership in their club for your creativity. How about writing an article in your field of expertise and finding a website willing to publish the content for its readers? (Even though you might not get paid, this is a great way to attract attention to yourself.) Whatever your goal, bartering your unique skills will definitely help in funding your passion.

TEMP JOBS

This is a great way to provide structure in your life while searching out what really matters and, at the same time, keeping a steady stream of income to meet your financial obligations. Many people have developed a complete lifestyle engaged in temporary work because of the diversity in job assignments and varied time commitments. You'll also find that more and more temp agencies are offering health insurance and other services, which are benefits you don't want to overlook. Once you've built a reputation with a few organizations who like your work, many turn mundane work assignments into challenging work projects. Often this leads into permanent or consulting work that pays more and provides more freedom. Temp agencies abound in urban and suburban areas. Kelly Services (www.kellyservices.com) and Manpower (www.manpower.com) are two agencies that you might check out as you explore this option.

SUBSTITUTE TEACHING

If you have a college degree and like children, substitute teaching in an elementary, middle, or high school is a perfect in-between job—and just possibly, the start of a new career. Not only does it pay fairly well and offer a flexible schedule, you'll learn just as much from the children as they will from you. It's also a chance to work on your speaking skills and connect more with people in your community.

POSSESSION DOWNSIZING

Most of us have garages or closets filled with possessions that have been sitting around for years—these make up all the key ingredients in conducting a profitable garage sale. The old adage "one man's trash is another man's treasure" can bring you enough money to make a dent in your fund-raising efforts. A successful garage sale takes planning on your part: all your items should be priced, an ad should go in the local paper, and huge signs should

The pessimist sees difficulty in every opportunity. **39**
The optimist sees opportunity in every difficulty. —WINSTON CHURCHILL

be put up around the neighborhood the night before. I even conduct a pre-garage-sale for neighbors and friends the night before. Many people who know you are fund-raising to support your passion might even provide a monetary donation. Whatever the case, it's a good way to clear out clutter and make some extra cash on the side.

✒ **INSIDER TIP:** Spreading the "frugal gospel," Amy Dacyczyn's *The Complete Tightwad Gazette* (Villard Books, $19.99) includes nine hundred pages worth of sensible advice, recipes, tips, tricks, and strategies to save money.

• •

The man who does not work for the love of work but only for money is not likely to make money nor find much fun in life.

—CHARLES SCHWAB

Life is change.

Growth is optional.

Choose wisely.

—KAREN KAISER CLARK

• •

GRANTS AND LOANS

Many seeking to participate in worthy causes can raise money through phil-anthropic groups (like Kiwanis), campus and alumni groups, community organizations, civic and religious groups, local businesses, colleagues, or even your current coworkers. There are also plenty of grants that major non-profits give out each year. (Check out your library's reference area for books that cover grant possibilities.) In addition, don't be afraid to ask your family for help. A small loan might be the helping hand you need until you get on your feet.

SPARKLETT'S JUG THEORY

Find yourself an old Sparklett's jug at your local thrift store. Set it somewhere in your house and start dropping in your spare change. I find that it's more exciting if you attach a goal to the money you're saving prior to putting in your first coin.

DO WITHOUT

Simply stated, live within your means. The next time you go shopping, ask yourself, "Do I really need this?" More than likely, you don't. Remember the financial goal you've set up for yourself and don't stray from that path.

☞ **INSIDER TIP: For other fund-raising ideas, be sure to check out the tips offered on page 510 in the chapter on Transitions Abroad.**

MAKING THE MOST OF YOUR EXPERIENCE

The day will come when you've packed your car and your short-term job adventure begins. It will undoubtedly bring you a wealth of experience, a firmer sense of who you are and where your career is going, and a supportive network of friends and colleagues in the field. Before you rush off, here are some ideas to help you make the most of your new adventure:

- Make alliances with the administrative support team right away. That's right, secretaries are the eyes and ears of the organization and can really enhance your experience. Smile, sincerely get to know them, make friends with them, and ask for their helping hand.

- Doesn't it feel good when someone remembers your name? Make an effort to learn people's names right away. This is a great first step at building relationships and paying your coworkers a subtle compliment. Practice by repeating a person's name several times in conversation and associating the name with their expressions or appearance.

- Be prepared to work in areas not related to your main responsibility, have a can-do attitude, and chip in wherever needed. Look at every job you're given as an opportunity to learn more about the field you've chosen and a chance to contribute to the overall success of the program.

- Make it a goal to acquire as many skills, in as many areas, as you can. Attend every class and seminar that is offered and immerse yourself in every aspect of the program.

- Hard work is not the only key to success—enjoy yourself and have fun!

Far away there in the sunshine are my highest aspirations.
I may not reach them, but I can look up and see their beauty. Believe in them and try to follow
where they lead. —LOUISA MAY ALCOTT

- Enthusiasm and a positive spirit are contagious—bring these traits with you to work every day. Not only will your coworkers appreciate your "happy" energy, your supervisor will undoubtedly take note and give you more responsibilities. On the same note, stay clear from the troublemakers—you'll find out who they are right away. Don't let the negativity, complaining, or disrespect of others become your reality. Rise above and always focus on the positive—it will carry you far!

- Throughout the course of your adventure, talk to fellow staff members about their careers and lives. You'll be surprised at how much your peers enjoy giving advice and sharing their story with you. It's also flattering (to most) to be asked one's opinion—another person's insights might help you make better decisions in your life and further develop your career.

- Show a sincere interest in others and try to develop as many friendships as possible. Not only is it important to create a support group for yourself, you never know when a newfound alliance will have the opportunity to help you with your path at a future point!

- Finally, follow those hunches, take risks, be flexible, make plans, bend with life's twists and turns, and look at each day as an exciting learning adventure that you can make happen!

☞ **INSIDER TIP: Happiness is like a butterfly. The more you chase it, the more it will elude you. But if you turn your attention to other things, it comes and softly sits on your shoulder.**

> *Work is about daily meaning as well as daily bread. For recognition as well as cash; for astonishment rather than torpor; in short, for a sort of life rather than a Monday through Friday sort of dying. . . . We have a right to ask of work that it include meaning, recognition, astonishment, and life.*
>
> —STUDS TERKEL

TIPS FOR YOUR JOURNEY

As you venture down the path of life, keep these tips in your back pocket:

Find your own retreat (and use it often).

Give support, encouragement, and praise to others; and learn to accept them in return.

Change your routine often and your tasks when you can.

Focus on a good thing that happened during your day.

Be creative and try new approaches.

Use the "buddy system" regularly as a source of support, assurance, and redirection.

Surprise someone with something.

Find the child inside.

Laugh, play, and smile.

Be gentle with yourself and do the best job you can do.

Purchase a book that you've been meaning to get; then lose yourself completely in the words.

Reflect on the gifts you've been given from "Above." Write about this awareness.

Think different.

See how many colors you can incorporate into a meal.

Think of something you're grateful for, then call or write to thank the person responsible.

Treat yourself to a massage or a day at a spa.

Feel the beauty in your life as you fall asleep.

Tape a favorite quote to your computer. Read it every day this week.

Say something nice to a person you've never met. See what happens.

Create a list of places you want to visit, things you want to do, and people you want to meet. See how many you can cross off your list this year.

Fill the pages of your life with wonder and imperfection.

The grand essentials to happiness in this life are something to do, something to love, and something to hope for. —JOSEPH ADDISON

Choose a job you love and you will never have to work a day in your life.
—CONFUCIUS

CHAPTER 3

FINDING YOUR WAY

As you begin to map out the big picture of your life (and turn your inspiration into action!), you'll definitely need some tools to help you navigate through the twists and turns of your adventures. Fortunately, for every idea you have, there's a resource that can provide you with the information and enlightenment to build upon your dreams. To help you in "finding your way," this chapter offers reviews of my favorite books, publications, resources, and websites that have helped supercharge, guide, invigorate, and shape my career and life—and I know many of these will do the same for you!

USING THIS GUIDE

With so many short-term opportunities presented throughout the pages of this guide, the challenge may well be in picking one to do. To ease this challenge, each section introduction provides an overview of what's tucked inside. This introductory material also includes information on a variety of opportunities in the chapter, along with special stories and other insights that you don't want to miss. Each chapter concludes with my recommendations on other resources—books, newsletters, websites, associations—for further exploration.

UNDERSTANDING THE LISTINGS

Each listing is visually laid out in the same fashion, so at first glance you can get the bigger picture of the program. The header information includes important facts about the program—the category (or "buzzword") it represents, the specific state or country where you will work, and the time commitment that is needed from you. These three elements also make up three of the five indexes found at the end of this guide. Note that when an organization has its work assignments evenly spread throughout many states, it is listed as USA. On the same note, if the program covers many regions throughout the world, it is listed as Worldwide. The header information also contains up to four icons that represent compensation or fees, if housing is offered or provided, and eligibility requirements.

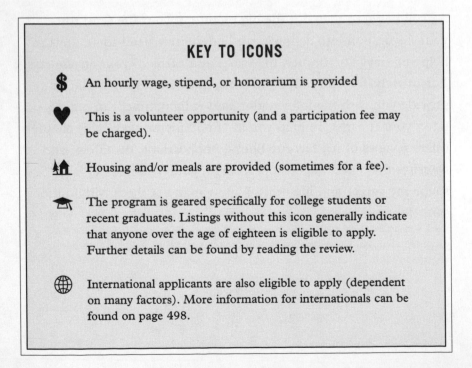

KEY TO ICONS

$ An hourly wage, stipend, or honorarium is provided

♥   This is a volunteer opportunity (and a participation fee may be charged).

⌂   Housing and/or meals are provided (sometimes for a fee).

   The program is geared specifically for college students or recent graduates. Listings without this icon generally indicate that anyone over the age of eighteen is eligible to apply. Further details can be found by reading the review.

⊕   International applicants are also eligible to apply (dependent on many factors). More information for internationals can be found on page 498.

SAMPLE

BIG BEND RIVER TOURS

Outfitter • Texas • 1–6 Months
www.bigbendrivertours.com

$

Tucked away in a remote corner of southwestern Texas lies a colorful, majestic, and sparsely populated area called Big Bend. The river gave this piece of Texas its name by bending like an elbow while cradling the desert, sheer-walled canyons, deep gorges, and Chisos Mountains. The river is also home to Big Bend River Tours, offering year-round adventures by paddle, oar, foot, or vehicle. Seasonal guides lead groups on rafting, canoeing, hiking, and interpretive tours throughout the region and into Mexico. Guides must complete a training program before leading trips. All applicants must be CPR and advanced first aid (forty hours) certified as well as hardworking and willing to go the extra mile. Pay is on a per-trip basis, with camping available at local campgrounds. New trainees must commit to six months, while experienced guides must commit to a minimum of three months (year-round applicants are given preference). Call, write, or email for an information packet and application. Details can also be found online.

THE ESSENTIALS: The ideal candidate has great people skills and previous river guiding and natural/cultural history interpretation experience. Those who play a musical instrument for campfire entertainment are also preferred.

YOUR FIRST MOVE: Initial contact is preferred through email.

FOR MORE INFORMATION: Jan Forté, General Manager, Big Bend River Tours, P.O. Box 317, Terlingua, TX 79852-0317 • (800) 545-4240 • (915) 432-3033 (915) 432-3034 (fax) • rapids317@hotmail.com

INSIDER TIP: Trip leaders are experienced, talented, high-energy, and supportive people. We only select leaders who have extensive experience and the sensitivity and maturity to handle the needs of teenagers.

LISTING

RECOMMENDED BOOKS, RESOURCES, AND WEBSITES

There is more treasure in books than in all the pirates' loot on Treasure Island . . . and best of all, you can enjoy these riches every day of your life.

—WALT DISNEY

I am truly amazed at all the resources that people are continually creating to help us with our very own journey (thank goodness they have taken the time to share their secrets with the world!). Whether you need a resource to enrich your soul, a book to offer a fresh perspective, or perhaps a website that offers a directory of great job resources, the following section is a compilation of my favorites. Any books included here can also be found at the bookshop on my companion website, Backdoorjobs.com (with direct links to Amazon.com). Additional topic-specific resources can also be found at the end of each chapter of this guide. Read through and see what resources might help in shaping your life!

BOOKS TO ENRICH THE SOUL

Treat yourself to a mind-stretching book or two that will certainly change the way you look at life.

Santiago, a shepherd boy searching for his treasure, teaches us about listening to our heart, acting upon the omens strewn along life's path, and realizing one's destiny is a person's only real obligation. Full of adventure, magic, and wisdom, *The Alchemist* by Paulo Coelho (HarperSanFrancisco, $13) shares with us that the possibility of having a dream come true is what makes life interesting!

You can become blind by seeing each day as a similar one. Each day is a different one; each day brings a miracle of its own. It's just a matter of paying attention to this miracle.

—PAULO COELHO

Richard Bode's lifelong love affair with sailing provides a vivid metaphor on living life to the fullest. *First You Have to Row a Little Boat* (Warner Books, $10) is a wonderful book that teaches us to maneuver with patience around the obstacles we encounter in our own passage through life.

I come now, at the late juncture of my life, to this sudden realiza-
tion: I have no destination, no real destination in the literal sense.
The destination, the place toward which my life is tending, is the
journey itself and not the final stopping place. How I get there is
more important than whether I arrive, although I know I will
arrive.

—RICHARD BODE

What would it be like if we were each given a life assignment? *The Giver* by
Lois Lowry (Laurel Leaf, $6.50) provides a somewhat eerie look at the way
we might live someday. The story takes place in a utopian community where
there is no hunger, no disease, no pollution, no fear—until a twelve-year-old
boy rebels against the choices that have been denied him.

Hope for the Flowers . . . The rush to get to the top will take on new meaning after you read this touching and thought-provoking story about two
caterpillars. Author Trina Paulus challenges us to believe in the butterfly
inside. (Paulist Press, $14.95, splurge for the hardcover.)

"I command that you be happy in the world, as long as you live!" What
if someone demanded that of you? And is it really possible? A wonderful
story (and a quick read), Richard Bach's *Illusions: The Adventures of a*
Reluctant Messiah (Dell, $7.50) takes you on a journey that just possibly
answers the question of why we exist. And if you like *Illusions,* you'll also
want to read *Jonathan Livingston Seagull* (Avon, $6.50), a unique fable
about a bird's journey of freedom and flight. Through the eyes of Jonathan,
you'll learn that there's much more to life than searching for food and flying
with the flock. Both of these classics can be found at most used bookstores
across the country.

While lying in a hospital bed some ten years ago, a dear friend of mine gave
me a small book called *The Little Prince,* by Antoine de Saint-Exupéry
(Harcourt Brace, $18, splurge for the hardcover). Within a few hours my
entire perspective of life changed. Yours will too, as "what is essential is
invisible to the eye." Also check out the animated claymation video, which
is superb!

The important thing is to strive toward a goal that is not imme-
diately visible. That goal is not the concern of the mind, but of the
spirit.

—ANTOINE DE SAINT-EXUPÉRY

We read books to find out who we are.
What other people, real or imaginary, do, think, and feel is an essential guide to our
understanding of what we ourselves are and may become. —URSULA K. LEGUIN

Dr. Seuss opens the door to all the exciting possibilities that lie ahead and earnestly warns of the potential pitfalls. You'll find *Oh, the Places You'll Go!* (Random House, $17, splurge for the hardcover) to be the perfect send-off for your new adventure.

> *I like nonsense, it wakes up the brain cells. Fantasy is a necessary ingredient in living; it's a way of looking at life through the wrong end of a telescope. Which is what I do, and that enables you to laugh at life's realities.*
>
> —DR. SEUSS

Benjamin Hoff's *The Tao of Pooh* (Penguin Books, $11.95) is the perfect read for anyone wanting to learn the basic principles of Taoism, but through the eyes of the beloved character Winnie the Pooh, who "wanders around asking silly questions, making up songs, and going through all kinds of adventures, without ever accumulating any amount of intellectual knowledge or losing his simpleminded sort of happiness." Maybe Pooh has something, huh?

> *Everything has its own place and function. That applies to people, although many don't seem to realize it, stuck as they are in the wrong job, the wrong marriage, or the wrong house. When you know and respect your own Inner Nature, you know where you belong. You also know where you don't belong.*
>
> —BENJAMIN HOFF

FRESH PERSPECTIVES

These resources will help you to look at yourself in a whole new way.

How do I live a happy, meaningful, and flourishing life? How can I be both a noble and effective person? Answering these fundamental questions was the single-minded passion of Epictetus, the revered philosopher who was born a slave about A.D. 55 in the eastern outreaches of the Roman Empire. *The Art of Living* (HarperSanFrancisco, $11.95), provides guidance on how to live a day-by-day, down-to-earth life of virtue.

"Excitement wears orange socks, faith lives in the same apartment building as doubt. . . ." *The Book of Qualities* by Ruth Gendler (Perennial, $12) challenges you to look at your emotions and unique character in new and inspiring ways.

Do you need a whack on the side of the head . . . or maybe just a kick in the pants? Then indulge in Roger von Oech's *Creative Whack Pack* (U.S. Games Systems, $16), a deck of cards (sixty-four in all); each provides a brief story, hint, or insight that will keep your mind spinning for days to come.

How many times have you talked yourself out of something because of self-sabotaging fears? *Feel the Fear and Do It Anyway* by Susan Jeffers (Ballantine Books, $14) will teach you to push past the negative chatter in your head, risk a little every day, and turn every decision into a "no-lose" situation.

FIVE TRUTHS ABOUT FEAR
by Susan Jeffers

1. The fear will never go away as long as I continue to grow.

2. The only way to get rid of the fear of doing something is to go out and do it.

3. The only way to feel better about myself is to go out and do it.

4. Not only am I going to experience fear whenever I'm on unfamiliar territory, but so is everyone else.

5. Pushing through fear is less frightening than living with the underlying fear that comes from a feeling of helplessness.

Wouldn't it be nice to live a happier, more successful, and more peaceful life? *Happiness Is a Choice* (Ballantine Books, $10.95) is about believing in ourselves, having a positive attitude, and being hopeful about the events that shape our lives. And after reading Barry Kaufman's book, you might also want to take part in one of the many educational programs he (and his happy staff) offer through the Option Institute (see their listing on page 337). Whether you want to improve the quality of your life or overcome a challenging adversity, the program will help you actively explore a new way to live your life.

Based on the Myers-Briggs personality test, *Lifetypes* by Sandra Krebs Hirsh and Jean Kummerow (Warner Books, $13.95) gives you the tools to develop a psychological self-portrait. After completing a series of questions (which is great fun with a group of friends), your "lifetype" emerges. The book then provides you with examples of each personality type as it relates to careers, relationships, and recreational activities that you should choose or avoid—and discusses how to get the most out of your life by gaining a better understanding of yourself.

The way we choose to see the world creates the world we see. 51
—BARRY NEIL KAUFMAN

Leo Buscaglia has to be one of my all-time favorite authors. His writings teach us to be human—to be who we are and what we feel—and how we can learn to be loving individuals and get the most out of life through love. Known for getting his students to hug trees (and each other) at the University of Southern California while teaching a class on love, Dr. Buscaglia will guide you to new levels of happiness (on this fantastic journey we're all on). *Love* and ***Living, Loving, and Learning*** (Ballantine Books, $12.95/$13.95) are my favorites.

> *If you go around doing your thing without expectation, then you already have everything you need. If you receive something in return, you take it with open arms. It should always come as a surprise. But if you expect a response and it comes, it's a bore. Cease expecting and you have all things.*
>
> —LEO BUSCAGLIA

How is it that we can find meaning in life when confronted with a hopeless situation? This is the very premise in Dr. Viktor Frankl's reflective and inspiring writings. Born out of the years he spent as a prisoner in concentration camps—and what kept him going—***Man's Search for Meaning*** (Pocket, $6.99) explores the basis of human potential and how we can rise above any situation that causes suffering.

> *Everything can be taken from us but one thing: the last of our human freedoms—to choose one's attitude in any given set of circumstances, to choose one's own way.*
>
> —VIKTOR FRANKL

Self-doubt and negative thoughts seem to be the most devastating handicaps for many. But it doesn't have to be this way—and ***The Power of Positive Thinking*** (Ballantine Books, $12.95) will help you to climb above those old habits and unleash your true potential. Dr. Norman Vincent Peale offers powerful tips, prayerful exercises, and "filling your mind full of God" each day to positively master those challenges of everyday living. For positive thinking tune-ups, turn to Guideposts (www.dailyguideposts.com) or get in touch with the Peale Center for Positive Thinking at (845) 855-5000.

> *The greatest power we have is the power of choice. It's an actual fact that if you've been moping in unhappiness, you can choose to be joyous instead and, by effort, lift yourself into joy. If you tend to be fearful, you can overcome that misery by choosing to have courage. Even in darkest grief you have a choice. The whole trend and quality of anyone's life is determined in the long run by the choices that are made.*
>
> —NORMAN VINCENT PEALE

Stroll down the path of life with SARK and learn about her 250 jobs, how to relax about money, making friends with freedom and uncertainty, living juicy, drawing on the walls, and making your life an adventure. SARK's *Inspiration Sandwich* (Celestial Arts, $14.95) will inspire your creative freedom, and *Living Juicy: Daily Morsels for Your Creative Soul* (Celestial Arts, $15.95) will challenge the way you look at your life and bring a refreshing new approach to "daily meditation." Planet SARK, her companion website (www.planetsark.com), provides all the details—including some of her latest books (twelve in all). For those who need a quick dose of inspiration, call her Inspiration Hotline at (415) 546-3742 for a five-minute recorded message.

Work, love, friendship, spirituality, living fully . . . how do we make sense of life's daily challenges as friends or parents or of leading a balanced lifestyle *and* achieving our best? *Touchstones: A Book of Daily Meditations for Men* by David Spohn and *Each Day a New Beginning: Daily Meditations for Women* by Karen Casey (Hazelden, each $12) are great companions for beginning each day with a thought-provoking meditation, helping you to ignite new possibilities and strengthen you on your path.

POSITIVE STEPS TO CAREER CHANGE

If you need some career insights from the experts, you've come to the right place!

Career counselor Rick Jarow challenges each of us "to create a life work that will reflect our own nature, and to develop the courage and wisdom to bring it into form." *Creating the Work You Love* (Inner Traditions, $14.95) offers a step-by-step and self-reflective process based on the seven chakras (the body's energy centers) that will challenge you to move past the daily struggles of life and push toward making your life a work of art. Also, visit Rick's "anticareer" website at www.anticareer.com for more spirited words.

Are your life and career a little foggy? Barbara Sher—motivational specialist, therapist, and career counselor—has a handful of books to help you lift this fog, gain momentum, and get your life on the right path. *Live the Life You Love* (Dell, $12.95) provides ten step-by-step lessons to create a meaningful, rewarding life, with exercises that are quite fun. *I Could Do Anything If I Only Knew What It Was* (Dell, $14.95) explores the basic fact that each of us really does know what we want. Through creative exercises and fresh perspectives, Sher will definitely help you to create your own luck, push past your fears of success, and make your dreams come alive. Check out www.barbarasher.com for an overview of all her books.

Joy increases as you give it and diminishes as you try to keep it for yourself.
In giving it, you will accumulate a deposit of joy greater than you ever believed possible.
—NORMAN VINCENT PEALE

The 7 Habits of Highly Effective People, by Stephen Covey (Free Press, $15), provides a step-by-step pathway for living principles that give us the security to adapt to change, and the wisdom and power to take advantage of the opportunities that change creates.

> *It's incredibly easy to get caught up in an activity trap, in the busy-ness of life, to work harder and harder at climbing the ladder of success only to discover it's leaning against the wrong wall. Thus every step we take just gets us to the wrong place faster. We may be very busy, we may be very efficient, but we also will be truly effective only when we begin with the end in mind.*
>
> —STEPHEN COVEY

If you're going through a transition, whether it be a breakup, career change, or ending something, and are unsure about your next step, I highly recommend ***Transitions*** (Perseus Press, $16.50). William Bridges takes you through the three stages of transition: endings (that difficult process of letting go of an old situation), the neutral zone (that seemingly unproductive and confusing nowhere of in-betweenness), and the new beginning (launching forth again in a new situation). To guide you through this transitional path, see his companion website at www.wmbridges.com.

What Color Is Your Parachute? (Ten Speed Press, $17.95). Just the title of this book intrigues me. After reading it from cover to cover (and working through a dozen of Richard Bolles's flower exercises), I realized that it should be required reading for anyone who wants to successfully carve out their own career niche. Revised and updated annually, *Parachute* (a metaphor coined by the author when he was referring to career transitions back in the late 1960s) is about taking chances, gaining confidence, and making changes in your career and life. Complete with exercises on self-assessment and career planning, it is perhaps most valuable to those who are securely employed but unhappy with what they're doing. As a companion for his wit, words, and wisdom, Richard Bolles has also crafted a magnificent website—JobHuntersBible.com—replete with many, many job-hunting and career links and advice.

> *Though we might think God will yell out our mission in life from some mountain top, we find ourselves in the valley, where God softly speaks "take one step at a time," even when you don't see where it all is leading or where your mission is going. The path of life and the moments of decision. . . . Take the one that leads to more gratitude, more kindness, more love in the world.*
>
> —RICHARD BOLLES (FROM THE BOOK *HOW TO FIND YOUR MISSION IN LIFE*)

BECOMING YOUR OWN BOSS

If you're ready to start that business you've always dreamed of doing, these books will fuel your fire!

Do you have the urge to strike out on your own and develop a career path that just might have the greatest job satisfaction and personal development? Let Paul Hawken show you the way. *Growing a Business* (Simon & Schuster, $13) provides straight talk on what works and what doesn't, and why. You'll also learn that being in business is not about making money. It is a way to become who you are.

> *Most successful new businesspeople do not start out in life thinking that this is what they want to do. Their idea springs from a deep immersion in some occupation, hobby, or other pursuit, spurred by something missing in the world.*
>
> —PAUL HAWKEN

For some reason, we have been brainwashed by the idea that the more we work, the better off we become. *The Joy of Not Working* (Ten Speed Press, $16.95) teaches us how we can create a paradise away from the workplace—and develop our world of leisure (while making a living). Ernie Zelinski's down-to-earth writing is filled with great stories, cartoons, quotes, and plenty of exercises—all of which provide insights on how to get that zest back into your life and become excited about everything you do.

Got the urge to throw in the towel at what you're currently doing and become joyfully jobless? Barbara Winter's book *Making a Living without a Job* (Bantam Books, $15) is for anyone who has always dreamed of becoming their own boss (and creating the work they love). She'll take you on a step-by-step journey that integrates the things you like to do with the things you're good at doing. She also self-publishes *Winning Ways,* a brilliant newsletter (six issues per year for $36), which is designed to share creative ideas about successful self-employment, along with thoughts on personal development. By the way, if you're ready to become an entrepreneurial gypsy, she also teaches a unique seminar, How to Support Your Wanderlust, in various locales throughout the country. Check out all the "goings-on" on her companion website, www.barbarawinter.com.

Every job should be looked at as an education and an adventure. The satisfaction must come from your work. —RICHARD BOLLES

CAMPUS CROWD

Whether you're in high school or college or are a student of life, these resources will jump-start your journey!

Are you in the search for a college education that will support your values while providing you with the tools to make a better world? Miriam Weinstein's *Making a Difference College and Graduate Guide* (SCB Distributors, $18.50) profiles hundreds of alternative and innovative colleges that range from sustainable development and earth literacy to experiential-based international programs. To fund your new vision in life, Weinstein also offers information on college scholarships, fellowships, and other funding options in her companion guide—*Making a Difference Scholarships for a Better World* (SCB Distributors, $14). More information can be found at www.making-a-difference.com.

If you are searching out a path to greatness, you definitely want to check out what Patrick Combs has to say. Geared mainly to the college crowd, although helpful to people of all ages, *Major in Success* (Ten Speed Press, $12.95) will walk you through an inspirational journey, helping you to take a fresh look at your life and explore how to uncover your dream job. Once you've absorbed the information in his book, turn to his website at www.goodthink.com for more motivation, inspiration, and life-changing stories. (In fact, you can read one on page 201.) Good Thinking Hot Tips can also be received through email by signing up online.

Are you craving real-world experiences and learning opportunities beyond the standard fare in high school? Then come explore the possibilities presented in Rebecca Greene's *The Teenagers' Guide to School Outside the Box* (Free Spirit Publishing, $15.95), and you'll definitely be armed with the tools to plot out your own alternative learning adventure. For other books that promote positive self-esteem in teens (written by experts in the field), check out Free Spirit on the Web at www.freespirit.com.

Are you "navigating" through your first year in college? **First Year Focus** (www.abacon.com/firstyearfocus) provides support, information, and tips that will help get you on the right path. Included are some great ideas on internships and careers.

Ever wanted to learn more about being a marine biologist or a screenwriter? With **GetThatGig.com,** you can find heaps of information and links in a very informative and playful way. Targeted to high school students looking for a cool summer job or internship or those in college about to make their first career decision, twenty categories highlight a variety of interesting and unique programs with additional links, resources, and stories to kick-start your career.

Jobweb.com provides a comprehensive website for college students and graduates seeking information on careers and jobs, including short-term work and internship experiences, career fairs, professional associations, career library resources, and employment centers.

UNIQUE JOB SITES AND RESOURCES

To explore some of the best job and career links on the Web—from cool jobs to international internships—check out **About.com's Guide to Job Searching** (www.jobsearch.about.com), hosted by career guru Alison Doyle. Along with spotlight articles and hundreds of hot job-seeking tips, be sure to sign up for her weekly newsletter, which includes information on upcoming features and updates to the website.

The **Aboutjobs.com** network provides a variety of job venues—including summer, resort, overseas, and intern jobs—for the adventure seeker, complete with a database searchable by location or keyword.

What's it like to be a postal worker, a McDonald's team player, or a clown? **AboutMyJob.com** provides a place for ordinary people to share their stories of exciting and not-so-exciting jobs and places. You definitely can't believe everything you read, but it just may help you decide whether you should learn to cope better with your current situation or head out to greener pastures!

If you were to start from scratch on finding a job on the Internet, you might start with the **Riley Guide** (www.rileyguide.com). It's filled with link upon link of job resources, listings, and information guides. The site's "webmistress," Margaret Dikel, is also the author of the *Guide to Internet Job Searching* (McGraw Hill, $14.95), which is published every other year. The guidebook offers expert advice and information for bulletin boards, recruiter information, job listings, discussion groups, resume-posting services, and more—if it's career-related, you'll find the links in this book.

For heaps of career resource links, job hunting sites, career articles, and cover letter and resume advice, explore the gems offered by **Quintessential Careers** (www.quintcareers.com). Be sure to sign up for *QuintZine,* their biweekly newsletter filled with career advice, job information, and the latest website news.

> *The important thing is not to stop questioning. Curiosity has its own reason for existing. One cannot help but be in awe when he contemplates the mysteries of eternity, of life, of the marvelous structure of reality. It is enough if one tries merely to comprehend a little of this mystery every day. Never lose a holy curiosity.*
>
> —ALBERT EINSTEIN

Life never presents us with anything which may not be looked upon as a fresh starting point. **57**
—ANDRE GIDE

I learned early that the richness of life is adventure. Adventure calls on all faculties of mind and spirit. It develops self-reliance and independence. Life then teems with excitement. But you are not ready for adventure unless you are rid of fear. For fear confines you and limits your scope. You stay tethered by strings of doubt and indecision and have only a small and narrow world to explore.
—WILLIAM O. DOUGLAS

CHAPTER 4

ADVENTURE JOBS

An adventurous lifestyle means to grow through excitement, challenge, and risk taking. It's about learning to look at the world through curious eyes—to wonder what's on the other side of the mountain—and allowing wanderlust to become your guide. The intimacy of your adventurous pursuits will allow you to see, hear, taste, and smell more intensely. You'll work hard and you'll play hard; however, by exploring your options in this chapter, you'll learn that work and play become the same thing. Push past any fears and let your journey to adventure begin!

UNIQUE OPPORTUNITIES TO EXPLORE IN THIS CHAPTER

- Looking for excitement, risk, unique experiences, education, and fun? Learn what an expert river guide has to say about the outdoor adventure field, her experiences, and why she loves her job so much in a special "day-in-a-life" story. And if this story sends chills up your back, you'll want to explore the details for a handful of river outfitters who are awaiting your job application (page 61).

- Is it true that the more risk you take, the more you can open yourself up to new adventures? Find out how Michael and Dorrie Williams left their Corporate America jobs and experienced an adventure of a lifetime by pedaling their bikes across America. The special cycling section beginning on page 81 also features seasonal employment opportunities with some of the best biking adventure programs in the U.S.

- Experience the four pillars of self-reliance, fitness, craftsmanship, and compassion taught at Outward Bound by participating in one of their rugged adventure programs or becoming a seasonal staff member at one of their four wilderness schools (page 104).

- Road Trip USA? If you're about to hit the road for a cross-country adventure and are looking for a budget-conscious housing option with a spirited twist, staying at a youth hostel might be your answer. Read more about hostel-style travel, working options, and unique lodging arrangements in a special section beginning on page 127.

A seasonal raft guide with Alaska Wildland Adventures (page 69) leading a trip in the Kenai Peninsula.

ALASKA WILDLAND ADVENTURES

PLAYING FOR A LIVING

A RIVER GUIDE'S PERSPECTIVE ON THE OUTDOOR ADVENTURE FIELD

There is no denying that outdoor adventure has come into its own. I still remember the days when people would look at me sideways with that "you are a bright girl, don't you think you should have a real job" look on their faces when I told them that I was an adventure tourism guide. But these days the responses are very different indeed. Now, a little light shines in their eyes and they ask me which rivers I have guided and if I can give them any advice in planning their next trip. How things change.

Adventure travel and ecotourism form one of the world's fastest-growing tourism sectors, with outdoor adventure programming at the heart of this growth. Consumers of these programs are looking for excitement, a level of risk, unique experiences, education, and fun. With the growth of the industry has also come a need for professionals to be on the front line to deliver these programs—and a well-qualified professional is a sought-after commodity worldwide in adventure travel. Many colleges and universities have keyed into this need and are now offering excellent programs that provide students with a solid foundation in the outdoor adventure tourism industry. Although employers value postsecondary education, most programs do not hire solely on industry-recognized skills certification. It is the combination of attitude, knowledge, skills certification, and experience that will make you marketable in this field.

I always tell people starting out in this industry that what I do, I do because I love it, and what I get paid for is having the judgment and decision-making skills necessary to lead a successful trip. By that I mean, your goal as a river guide is to make sure people have a great time—that they are fed amazing food, hit all the big rapids, and learn things about the new places they have visited. But I am more than a river hostess: I have years of experience behind every decision I make; I have specialized training in rescue and wilderness medicine; I have studied the places I work in and respect the inherent risks of my working environment; I have planned every detail of the trip beforehand and drawn up contingency plans; and I understand both the strengths of my group and my own limitations.

Adventure can be an end in itself. **61**
Self-discovery is the secret ingredient that fuels daring. —GRACE LICHENSTEIN

This is not a job for everyone. It is not for people who do not want to take responsibility. This is a job for leaders—which doesn't mean someone who is a control freak. It is someone who is well organized, cares about people, and puts group and guest needs ahead of their own. It is someone who is flexible, has a sense of humor, and is so passionate about what they do that their professionalism and pride in their work shows through in their every action. Though I cannot remember who said it, the words ring in my ears: A good leader is one who, at the end of the day and when all the goals have been met, will have the group say, "We did it ourselves." Many times I have guided trips with corporate executives who have told me that if ever I get tired of "playing for a living" I would be welcome in their human resources department or in a managerial position. Needless to say, I have never taken any of them up on their offers.

I have now been "playing for a living" for over ten years and I am not prepared to quit any time soon. Why would I? I love my office, the casual dress (and the need not to worry about how my hair looks), all the wild and wonderful places of the earth that I get to experience, the fabulous people I meet, and the new inspirations that come forth each day because of the variety of my job.

A typical day may involve waking up in some spectacular place, making coffee, and packing your gear before anyone else is out of their tents. After breakfast, perhaps a hike or a paddle on the river—and if you see something wonderful, you stop and check it out. Maybe it's a herd of caribou or young golden eagles in their nest; maybe it's a stream that meanders to a waterfall just perfect for swimming under; or perhaps it's the artwork of a people who traveled the same way thousands of years before you.

All day long you play, you discover, and you explore the places around you. You learn, you teach, and you soothe your tired and happy body with a soak in a natural hot spring. It is hard work, but you will truly love your job. You're also guaranteed to hear these words from almost every one of your guests at one time or another: "Boy, it must be great to get paid for what you do!" and you will heave a big sigh and say "yeah . . . it is."

· ·

—Contributed by Jill Baxter, who has been a working professional in the outdoor adventure industry for over fourteen years, with teaching at the heart of her passion. She has guided extended river expeditions from the awe-inspiring Grand Canyon of the Colorado River to the legendary Nahanni River in Canada's Northwest Territories. Currently she is the owner/operator of Bear Creek Outdoor Centre (www.bearcreekoutdoor.com), located near Canada's capital city of Ottawa. Bear Creek runs a ten-week intensive summer leadership training and certification in outdoor adventure, with activities including white-water canoeing, kayaking, rafting, mountain biking, climbing, wilderness first aid, swift-water rescue, riverboarding, leadership development, team building, and a wilderness canoe expedition. Contact Jill at jill@bearcreekoutdoor.com or by calling (888) 453-5099.

If you want to play for a living on the white waters of North America, here's a handful of outfitters that specialize in river guiding. Unless you're an experienced guide, it will be necessary to participate in a preseason certificate training workshop in the spring. No need to worry, because most outfitters offer this training for a fee—and some at no cost! In addition to river guides, many outfitters hire base camp staff, cooks, reservationists, and shuttle drivers.

BIG BEND RIVER TOURS

Outfitter • Texas • 1–6 Months
www.bigbendrivertours.com
$ ⊕

Tucked away in a remote corner of southwestern Texas lies a colorful, majestic, and sparsely populated area called Big Bend. The river gave this piece of Texas its name by bending like an elbow while cradling the desert, sheer-walled canyons, deep gorges, and Chisos Mountains. The river is also home to Big Bend River Tours, offering year-round adventures by paddle, oar, foot, or vehicle. Seasonal guides lead groups on rafting, canoeing, hiking, and interpretive tours throughout the region and into Mexico. Guides must complete a training program before leading trips. All applicants must be CPR and advanced first aid (forty hours) certified as well as hardworking and willing to go the extra mile. Pay is on a per-trip basis, with camping available at local campgrounds. New trainees must commit to six months, while experienced guides must commit to a minimum of three months (year-round applicants are given preference). Call, write, or email for an information packet and application. Details can also be found online.

FOR MORE INFORMATION:
Jan Forté, General Manager
Big Bend River Tours
P.O. Box 317
Terlingua, TX 79852-0317
(800) 545-4240 • (915) 432-3033
(915) 432-3034 (fax)
rapids317@hotmail.com

River guides set up base camp
on the spectacular Rio Grande
with Big Bend River Tours.

BIG BEND RIVER TOURS

Without exploration, there are no discoveries. **63**
—DENG MING-DAO

CHUCK RICHARDS' WHITEWATER

River Outfitter • California • Summer
www.chuckrichards.com

$ 🏕

Here's rafting Southern California style—blazing hot days, balmy starlit evenings, sizzling barbecues, great grins, no bugs, and no goose bumps. Raft guides will take adventure seekers on the Kern River, which provides class three to class five rapids. In order to be a summer guide, applicants need to participate in three to five successive weekends of training in March and April (for a fee of $350). Along with lodging in their bunkhouse, guides receive $55 to $70 per day (plus tips).

FOR MORE INFORMATION: Chuck Richards, President, Chuck Richards' Whitewater, Box W.W. Whitewater, Lake Isabella, CA 93240 • (760) 379-4444 (760) 379-4685 (fax) • chuck@chuckrichards.com

DENALI RAFT ADVENTURES

River Outfitter • Alaska • Seasonal
www.denaliraft.com

$ 🏕 ⊕

Denali Raft Adventures offers two-hour, four-hour, and full-day raft trips on the mighty Nenana River, which forms the eastern border of Denali National Park. The season runs from mid-May through mid-September, and seasonal staff work as reservations clerks, bus drivers, and river guides. Dormitory-style rooms run $80 per month, and everyone gets a roommate. Ideal applicants are those who enjoy the outdoors and are punctual, friendly, outgoing, hardworking, energetic, enthusiastic, and guest oriented. Send a cover letter and resume to begin the application process.

FOR MORE INFORMATION: Jim and Val Raisis, Directors, Denali Raft Adventures, Drawer 190, Denali Park, AK 99755 • (888) 683-2234 • (907) 683-2234 (907) 683-1281 (fax) • denraft@mtaonline.net

OUTDOOR ADVENTURE RIVER SPECIALISTS

River Outfitter · California · Seasonal
www.oars.com

$ 🏠 🎓 ⛺

Outdoor Adventure River Specialists, also known as OARS, has been recognized worldwide as the industry model for river outfitters. They operate river trips on over twenty-five rivers in the western U.S., as well as on Canadian and international waters. Choose the challenge of class five rapids or gentler trips with an "oar" option, meaning the guide does all the rowing while guests sit back and enjoy the ride. Internships are available in marketing, customer service, interpretation, and Internet development. Pay is $200 per week, with basic housing. Free trips are also available during days off.

FOR MORE INFORMATION: General Manager, Outdoor Adventure River Specialists, P.O. Box 67, Angels Camp, CA 95222 · (800) 346-6277 · (209) 736-4677 (209) 736-2902 (fax) · info@oars.com

RIVER ODYSSEYS WEST

River Outfitter · Idaho/Montana · Summer
www.rowinc.com

$ 🏠

River Odysseys West, commonly known as ROW, leads wilderness rafting and walking trips in Idaho, Oregon, and Montana, as well as voyageur canoe trips, rafting adventures, and yachting and barge trips throughout the world. With the chance to run spectacular rapids, sleep under the stars, meet interesting people, make new friends, and be surrounded by nature's beauty, being a river guide is a dream job for many. But make no mistake about it, being a river guide is hard work and physically demanding.

WHAT YOU'LL BE DOING: If you don't have any previous white-water or guiding experience but want to experience a great summer in the outdoors, becoming a swamper or river jester (ROW's term for guide assistants) may be your ticket. Swampers travel in cargo boats ahead of the river group to set up camp and greet the guests. In addition to swamper duties, river jesters lead family activities and games geared toward learning about nature. Guide positions are the most sought after at ROW. Those who have experience will lead one- to six-day white-water trips on the rivers of northern and central Idaho. Some trips paddle through deep gorges; others through beautiful valleys.

COMMITMENT: Bear in mind that guiding is physically demanding work with long hours. During the peak season in July and August, guides may be asked to work six days a week.

PERKS AND REWARDS: Meals, housing, and a daily wage are provided for all.

THE ESSENTIALS: The ideal candidate has great people skills and previous river guiding and natural/cultural history interpretation experience. Those who play a musical instrument for campfire entertainment are also preferred.

YOUR FIRST MOVE: Initial contact is preferred through email.

FOR MORE INFORMATION: Peter Grubb, Owner, River Odysseys West, P.O. Box 579, Coeur d'Alene, ID 83816-0579 • (800) 451-6034 (208) 765-0841 • (208) 667-6506 (fax) • info@rowinc.com

INSIDER TIP: Any guide who has little or no white-water experience and is seeking employment for our two-month Clark Fork season is required to attend our guide school in late June. In this five-day clinic, experienced guides will demonstrate the camping, food preparation, and organizational and rafting techniques that we use on our trips. By the end of the clinic, our goal is to have you ready to guide. We do not necessarily seek people who have previous experience; rather we seek those with strong people skills, intelligence, humor, organizational aptitude, attention to detail, and a strong work ethic. Cost for this five-day clinic, including instruction and meals, is $350.

WILDWATER LTD. RAFTING

River Outfitter • Carolinas/Tennessee • Seasonal
www.wildwaterrafting.com

$ ⛺ 🌐

Beginning at the base of Whitesides Mountain in North Carolina and flowing along the Sumter and Chattahoochee National Forests to the border of South Carolina and Georgia, the Chattooga River is definitely one of the wildest and most beautiful white-water rivers in the country. The Chattooga is also home to Wildwater, the oldest outfitter on the river. In addition to white-water rafting on three other rivers in the Carolinas and Tennessee, Wildwater offers canoe and kayak clinics, raft and rail excursions, team-building retreats, and a variety of lodging facilities.

WHAT YOU'LL BE DOING: With a main office and four rafting centers, Wildwater has plenty of seasonal work opportunities to explore. Guide and trip leader positions are the most numerous and the most sought after; however, if you love people (and don't have the desire to play in water all day), you might consider a land-based position. Reservations personnel take that first phone call from guests (and also provide that first impression of Wildwater); front desk/retail management staff are the first smiling faces guests see while assisting in the retail shop; marketing staff are responsible for the entire marketing effort in the local area; transportation drivers keep guests coming and going; and food service team members prepare and serve meals to guests and employees.

COMMITMENT: The white-water season runs from March through October; and consequently, preference is given to those who can work the entire season (however, opportunities do exist for the summer months, their busiest time).

PERKS AND REWARDS: In addition to competitive wages, free staff housing (bunkhouse and dormitory-style), and meal options (for a small fee) at some locations, you can also expect a lot of benefits: unlimited river trips, complimentary tickets and lodging discounts for family and friends, pro deals with various equipment vendors—and working with like-minded and adventurous people.

THE ESSENTIALS: Since guests and seasonal staff are Wildwater's lifeblood, applicants who are willing to go out of their way to meet or exceed expectations (and have a positive attitude, good work ethic, and friendly personality) are always at the top of the hiring list. Previous experience is not necessary but can be helpful in obtaining the position you want. Guides must be eighteen years of age, certified in first aid and CPR, and be able to participate in the guide school during the spring. Guide training is unpaid but is provided at no cost (except for food and supplies).

FOR MORE INFORMATION: Staffing Director, Wildwater Ltd. Rafting, P.O. Box 309, Long Creek, SC 29658 • (800) 451-9972 • (864) 647-9587 (864) 647-5361 (fax) • wwltd@nuvox.net

A wise man will make more opportunities than he finds.
—FRANCIS BACON

ADVENTURES CROSS-COUNTRY

Adventure Education • USA/Worldwide • Summer
www.adventurescrosscountry.com

$ 🏕

Imagine backpacking through Yosemite, sea kayaking in Alaska's Glacier Bay, surfing on the beaches of Hawaii, rafting jungle rivers in Costa Rica, sailing in the aqua blue waters of the Caribbean, or scuba diving the Great Barrier Reef in Australia. With Adventures Cross-Country, teenagers have the opportunity to participate in mentally and physically challenging wilderness adventure travel programs in unique places in the western U.S., Hawaii, Alaska, and British Columbia, and overseas in Australia, Belize, the Caribbean, Costa Rica, Fiji, France, Italy, New Zealand, Spain, Switzerland, Tahiti, and Thailand.

WHAT YOU'LL BE DOING: Guides lead a group of up to thirteen teenagers, with a coleader of the opposite sex, through a rigorous adventure trip, with activities that may include backpacking, rock climbing, mountain biking, rafting, kayaking, mountaineering, sailing, scuba diving, and snow skiing. The trips are both mentally and physically challenging for guides and participants, with adventures ranging from fifteen to forty days (twenty-four hours a day).

COMMITMENT: Guides must be available starting in mid-June and typically finish their assignments sometime between mid-July and late August.

PERKS AND REWARDS: Wages for first-year staff members range from $920 to $1,550 depending on the number and length of trips led. In addition, leaders enjoy the added benefits of pro deals from well-known companies and a discounted Wilderness First Responder (WFR) course, as well as a ten-day staff training at the beginning of the summer season. All leader living and travel expenses are provided while working.

THE ESSENTIALS: Applicants must be at least twenty-one years of age, possess strong wilderness and backpacking skills, and have experience working with teenagers, along with current certification in WFR. (For those who are not WFR certified, a WFR course is offered in early June.) Those who are charismatic, fun, flexible, and easygoing will thrive in this environment. Applicants with scuba or sailing experience or qualifications are encouraged to apply.

YOUR FIRST MOVE: Leader details and applications can be obtained online. If Web access is not available, an application may be requested via phone or email.

FOR MORE INFORMATION: Jon Davies, Staffing Coordinator, Adventures Cross-Country, 242 Redwood Hwy., Mill Valley, CA 94941-9769 (800) 767-2722 • (415) 332-5075, ext. 221 • (415) 332-2130 (fax) employment@adventurescrosscountry.com

ALASKA MOUNTAIN GUIDES

Outdoor Education • Alaska • Summer
www.alaskamountainguides.com

$ 🏕

As a comprehensive guide service, climbing school, and outdoor education center, Alaska Mountain Guides and Climbing School offers high quality instruction and adventures throughout Alaska and the world. Programs range from challenging expeditions on the world's highest mountains to wilderness and cultural adventures in some of our planet's most remote and fascinating areas. Summer opportunities are available in Skagway, Alaska, for rock climbing guides, drivers, and administration staff. Benefits include a $9-per-hour wage ($13.50-per-hour overtime), a $1-per-hour bonus (if you work through season end in September), tips, pro-deal purchases, training, and shared housing for $150 per month. Successful applicants have a can-do attitude and are friendly, outgoing team players who love to spend time outside. First aid certification is required and climbing experience is helpful, but not required. Send off your resume to begin the application process, or call for more information.

FOR MORE INFORMATION: Darsie Culbeck, Director, Alaska Mountain Guides, P.O. Box 1081, Haines, AK 99827 • (800) 766-3396 • (907) 766-3366 (907) 766-3393 (fax) • climb@alaskamountainguides.com

ALASKA WILDLAND ADVENTURES

Ecotourism • Alaska • Seasonal
www.awasummerjobs.com

$ 🏕

Are you looking to experience Alaska this summer as a spirited adventurer with a cool job? With a commitment to ecotourism, Alaska Wildland Adventures offers wilderness lodge–based travel, tours, and adventure in Alaska's Kenai Peninsula and Denali National Park. Those with a passion for outdoor adventure can work as a natural history, fishing, or river guide or as a safari apprentice/intern. Is behind-the-scenes work your strength? Plenty of options to choose from here including cooks, hospitality staffers, trip packers, maintenance workers, and office staff. Salaries range from $800 to $2,000 per month, plus any gratuities. Rustic cabin-tent housing (with staff kitchen and lounge) is provided along with a payroll deduction for meals. Most positions run from mid-May through mid-September; however, some positions have flexible start and end dates. Essential requirements for each position and a downloadable application can be found online. Hiring is conducted through the end of April, with interviews most often conducted by phone.

A safari guide with Alaska Wildland Adventures spots an eagle (or could it be a moose, bear, or caribou?) with participants on a mountain adventure.

FOR MORE INFORMATION: Program Director, Alaska Wildland Adventures, P.O. Box 389, Girdwood, AK 99587 • (800) 478-4100 • (907) 783-2928 (907) 783-2130 (fax) • summerjobs@alaska-wildland.com

BOMBARD BALLOON ADVENTURES

Ballooning • Europe • Seasonal
www.bombardsociety.com/jobs

$ 🏠 🌐

Bombard Balloon Adventures engages guests in hot-air ballooning adventures throughout Europe each May through October as well as in Switzerland during the months of January and February. Along with balloon pilots, chefs, and guides, the ground crew facilitates all the details of each ballooning adventure—from preparing each trip to mapping out and retrieving the balloon once it has landed (and it's noted that there is a lot of driving over the course of a workday). Applicants must have a clean driving record and, for those who reside outside of Europe, must have a valid work permit prior to application. (See InterExchange on page 523 or CIEE on page 506 for more information on obtaining a work permit.) While fluency is not required, working knowledge of spoken French, Italian, or German is definitely helpful. Benefits include a small wage along with lodging and meals. Send a resume, a copy of your driver's license, dates of availability, and your height and weight.

FOR MORE INFORMATION: Mike Lincicome, Staffing Director, Bombard Balloon
Adventures, Château de Laborde, 21200 Beaune, France • (011) 33 380 26 63 30
mike@bombardsociety.com

BOOJUM INSTITUTE FOR EXPERIENTIAL EDUCATION

Experiential Education • California • 4 Months
www.boojum.org

$ 🏕 🌐

Founded in 1975, the Boojum Institute is a nonprofit educational organization dedicated to personal and organizational development through unlocking
potential, promoting self-discovery, and inspiring growth. The institute operates
courses designed for school outdoor education programs and disadvantaged
youth organizations. In addition to multiday base camp and wilderness programs with backpacking, rock climbing, canoeing, sea kayaking, and hiking,
Boojum offers challenge courses focused on team building and leadership
development.

YOUR SURROUNDINGS: You'll have the opportunity to travel to some of the
most remote and beautiful areas of the southwestern U.S., including Joshua
Tree National Park, the Sierra Nevada, the Colorado River, Yosemite National
Park, Channel Islands National Park, San Jacinto Mountains, and Point
Reyes National Seashore.

WHAT YOU'LL BE DOING: Boojum instructors provide facilitation and instruction
in outdoor skills, natural history, environmental awareness, challenge-course
activities, and life skills in order to "unlock potential, promote self-discovery,
and inspire growth" in their students. The internship program is designed to
expose participants to program operations behind the scenes, including logistics, training and support, the development of learning and teaching curricula,
as well as the delivery and evaluation of field programs. All staff kick off the
season with intensive training that includes familiarization with team challenge
courses, experiential education techniques, natural history overviews, and
group process and facilitation skills.

COMMITMENT: Positions are available from March through June and August
through November. Instructors can expect to work weekends and some holidays depending on course load.

PERKS AND REWARDS: Instructors start at $80 per day, plus room and board
while on programs and access to housing on days off. Interns receive a stipend

of $150 per month, housing, and expenses paid while in the field. Additional benefits to all are a 403(b) retirement plan and extensive pro-deal benefits.

THE ESSENTIALS: All applicants must be at least twenty-one years old, hold current Wilderness First Responder and CPR certification, and have an excellent driving record. At least one year of leadership experience in the outdoor education field is required, and a college degree is preferred. Instructors should have balanced proficiency in communication and technical skills, including minimum impact techniques, rock climbing, canoeing, kayaking, backpacking, and backcountry travel and navigation.

YOUR FIRST MOVE: Applications and reference forms are available online. Send your completed application along with a cover letter and resume well in advance of the position start date. (Boojum hires early for upcoming seasons!)

FOR MORE INFORMATION: David Kostial, Program Director, Boojum Institute for Experiential Education, P.O. Box 687, Idyllwild, CA 92549-0687 (951) 659-6250, ext. 19 • (951) 659-6251 (fax) • employment@boojum.org

INSIDER TIP: These are base-level positions in the organization with room for advancement. We are looking for folks who are open, honest, have a sense of humor, like working with young people, and have a desire to learn and grow professionally.

BOSTON UNIVERSITY SARGENT CENTER FOR OUTDOOR EDUCATION

Outdoor Education • New Hampshire • 3–9 Months
www.bu.edu/outdoor

$ ♠ ⊕

Intensive staff training. Extensive work experience. Community living. Recreation wonderland. Professional contacts in the field. Future long-term employment opportunities. These benefits form the foundation for seasonal teaching opportunities at Boston University Sargent Center and their residential outdoor education program. Instructors will learn how to create compelling lesson plans, then instruct groups of ten to twelve students (primarily grades five through eight) in all aspects of environmental education, outdoor skills, and adventure challenge activities. Benefits include a weekly stipend starting at $150 for first-season instructors, room in one of two housing facilities, meals, Internet and outdoor equipment access, and temporary health and accident insurance assistance. Applicants must be at least eighteen years of age and comfortable working long hours outdoors. A college degree in a related field is preferred, as is experience working with children. Three-, six-, and nine-month positions are available (however, nine-month applicants are preferred). Check out their website for other short-term opportunities, including summer positions at their adventure camp.

FOR MORE INFORMATION: Kelly Meyer, School Program Coordinator, Boston University Sargent Center for Outdoor Education, 36 Sargent Camp Rd., Hancock, NH 03449 • (603) 525-3311, ext. 18 • (603) 525-4151 (fax) school_program@busc.mv.com

BRECKENRIDGE OUTDOOR EDUCATION CENTER

Outdoor Education/Therapeutic Recreation • Colorado • 4–6 Months
www.boec.org

$ 🏠 ⊕

Since 1976, Breckenridge Outdoor Education Center (BOEC) has offered quality outdoor adventure expeditions and trips, therapeutic adventure programs, team building and leadership development, and adaptive-skiing experiences to people of all abilities, including those with disabilities and special needs. The center's goal is to provide students and guests with the opportunity to learn new skills, experience natural areas, challenge themselves, and work together to enhance the health and self-confidence necessary to explore their full potential.

WHAT YOU'LL BE DOING: Because BOEC courses rely primarily on interns, the internship program offers its participants the chance to play an integral role in empowering people of all abilities through outdoor experiences. A unique aspect of the BOEC internship is that it gives the interns an unlimited amount of responsibility. After an intense monthlong training, winter interns become an integral part of the Adaptive Ski Program, working first as assistant instructors and quickly advancing to primary instructors for people with various disabilities and special needs, along with facilitating wilderness courses. The life of a winter intern is not all skiing, as some days are spent doing administrative duties at the ski office. Summer interns participate in a three-week intensive training, then become staff members of the Wilderness Program. Responsibilities include planning, implementing, facilitating, and evaluating one- to ten-day courses that are held at the BOEC wilderness site or in a mobile format (camping, canoeing, or rafting trips). Participants in these programs range from children with traumatic brain injuries, epilepsy, or cancer, to adjudicated or "high-risk" youth.

COMMITMENT: Applicants must commit to working full-time for an entire season. The winter season runs from early November to May 1, and the summer season from mid-May to mid-September. Expect few days off and long workdays.

PERKS AND REWARDS: A monthly stipend of $50 is provided, along with meals and housing in rustic and peaceful cabins. Perks include a ski pass during the winter and, of course, the invaluable training and great experience that come from participation in the internship. Interns are able to trade some of their time and wilderness expertise for membership at the Breckenridge Recreation Center, which has an indoor climbing wall and track, hot tubs, swimming pools, and workout equipment.

THE ESSENTIALS: Group facilitation and strong supervisory skills are important. Other qualities, such as flexibility, willingness to work long hours, and the ability to live harmoniously with others in a community setting are just as important. However, they have hired interns with a limited experiential education background, basing their decisions largely on the applicant's commitment, good attitude, and enthusiasm for the BOEC and its mission. Applicants must be over twenty-one years of age and have advanced first aid and CPR certification.

YOUR FIRST MOVE: Applications can be found online. Along with a completed application, a cover letter, resume, and one letter of reference are recommended. Application deadlines: summer—March 1; winter—September 1.

FOR MORE INFORMATION: Robyn Graber, Internship Director, Breckenridge Outdoor Education Center, P.O. Box 697, Breckenridge, CO 80424 (800) 383-2632 • (970) 453-0146 • (970) 453-3845 (fax) • internship@boec.org

CANADIAN BORDER OUTFITTERS

Canoe Outfitter • Minnesota • Summer
www.canoetrip.com

$ 🏕

Located where the air is clear, lakes are deep, fishing is excellent, hiking trails are well marked, and wildlife is abundant, Canadian Border Outfitters is a full-service wilderness canoe trip outfitter located in the northeast corner of Minnesota just a few miles from the Ontario border. Most staff are hired not to work in one specific job but rather in an area of the business. Assignments may include work in the pack house, restaurant, or store, or in cleaning/maintenance, dock/canoe handling, or wilderness instruction. While the canoe outfitting season is short (May through September), a great deal of site maintenance, ordering, customer service, and marketing goes on during the whole year. Six permanent staff work year-round, while fifteen to twenty staff members work seasonally during the summer months. Hourly wages range from $5.75 to $6.50. Limited lodging is available for staff at the base on Moose Lake, and some choose to rent apartments in the Ely area, share expenses, and commute to Moose Lake. Meals can be purchased at the base camp at a discount. Applications are available online; the hiring process involves two job interviews in person or over the phone, along with reference checks.

FOR MORE INFORMATION: Deb Florer, Owner, Canadian Border Outfitters, 14635 Canadian Border Rd., Ely, MN 55731 • (800) 247-7530 • (218) 365-5847 (218) 365-5847 (fax) • cbo@cbo-ely.com

CHILKAT GUIDES

Outdoor Outfitter • Alaska • Summer
www.raftalaska.com

$ 🏕

As a stepping-stone to the greater world of guiding and backcountry recreation, Chilkat Guides (based in the picturesque town of Haines, Alaska) will teach anyone with the aptitude and interest how to guide themselves and others safely in and out of the wild. Whether engaged in trail hikes, float trips, wilderness safaris, or river expeditions, summer guides, trip leaders, and

With a look of determination and confidence, this Chilkat Guides trip leader prepares his group for a paddling adventure on Alaska's Alsek River, commonly known as the "Grand Canyon of the North."

RUSTIN GOODIN

Be not the slave of your own past. Plunge into the sublime seas, dive deep, and swim far, so you shall come back with self-respect, with new power, with an advanced experience, that shall explain and overlook the old. —RALPH WALDO EMERSON

naturalists get participants excited about the great outdoors. Their annual guide school (beginning in mid-April for those without guiding experience) is by invitation only and is free of charge to accepted applicants. All participants successfully completing the guide school are offered employment as guides from May through the end of September. Some fees are required for additional classes, such as Swiftwater Rescue Tech I and Wilderness Advanced First Aid. Pay is $9 per hour for straight guiding, with added incentives for trip leaders and naturalists (expect overtime, which is paid at time and a half). Applicants must have the desire to work long and hard (usually six to twelve hours per day) in sometimes unpleasant conditions, be athletic, and have a love for people. Active seniors are also needed to work as commercial bus drivers (with training provided). Applications are available online.

FOR MORE INFORMATION: Andy Hedden, Operations Manager, Chilkat Guides, P.O. Box 170, Haines, AK 99827 • (888) 292-7789 • (907) 766-2491 (907) 766-2409 (fax) • raftalaska@chilkatguides.com

CLEARWATER

Sailing • New York • 1 Week–4 Months
www.clearwater.org

$ ⚓ 🌐

With the mission to protect and restore the Hudson River (and its tributaries and related waterways), Clearwater conducts environmental education, advocacy programs, and celebrations—simple reminders that the vitality of the region is tied to the health of the environment. The sloop *Clearwater* (a magnificent 106-foot replica of boats that sailed the Hudson over one hundred years ago), serves as its classroom of waves, providing unique programs on ecology, history, awareness, and teamwork to nearly twenty thousand adults and children every year.

WHAT YOU'LL BE DOING: Crew for the sloop is made up of six paid professionals, including first and second mates, a third mate (deckhand), a bosun (who does odd jobs), an engineer, and a cook. Two sailing apprentices, one education intern, and six volunteers join the crew each week. After intensive training by professional educators, everyone will participate in all aspects of the sloop, including sailing, educational activities, and maintenance, so you'll have the opportunity to contribute your own special talents to the overall effort.

Sailing apprentices and their classroom of waves aboard Clearwater's flagship sloop.

CHRIS BOWSER

COMMITMENT: The sailing season begins in early April and ends in early November, although positions are available year-round. Crew positions run four months; education assistants—one to two months; sailing apprentices—one month; and interns/volunteers—at least one week. Between November and March, there are also opportunities for winter crew who are interested in maintenance (woodworking, engineering, and finish work).

PERKS AND REWARDS: All crew, apprentices, and interns receive room and board. Crew salaries range from $180 to $360 per week, while apprentices and interns receive a stipend of $50 per week ($75 per week during the winter). Weekly volunteers first must become Clearwater members ($35 per year) and also contribute a small fee for food. The living quarters are rustic, featuring open bunks, no showers (although some docks have facilities), composting, and unique toilets.

THE ESSENTIALS: Candidates must be sixteen years or older and willing and able to work outdoors eight to ten hours per day. Strength and sailing skill are not as important as coordination, common sense, and an enthusiasm for learning. The ability to deal intelligently with the sloop's hundreds of passengers and casual visitors, and to live and work cooperatively in a close and sometimes stressful environment, is critical.

YOUR FIRST MOVE: Call for application materials and current deadlines. It's recommended you volunteer for one week to see what it's like before you commit to other positions.

FOR MORE INFORMATION: Sloop Liaison, Clearwater, 112 Market St., Poughkeepsie, NY 12601-4095 • (845) 454-7673 • (845) 454-7953 (fax) office@clearwater.org

The pessimist complains about the wind; the optimist expects it to change; and the realist adjusts the sails. —WILLIAM ARTHUR WARD

CLIPPER CRUISE LINE

The yachtlike *Clipper Odyssey* travels to remote corners of the Pacific.

CLIPPER CRUISE LINE

Sailing • Worldwide • 1 Year
www.clippercruise.com

$ 🏠

Clipper Cruise Line's fleet of small ships leads passengers and crew on several itineraries throughout the world. Like many birds, their ships are migratory and follow the sun—northbound in the summer and southbound in the winter. Each ship is equipped with a motorized inflatable landing craft that can be launched in minutes for spontaneous landings on small islands and deserted beaches. Onboard crew members typically begin their assignments in entry-level positions, which include housekeepers/servers, galley assistants, and deckhands. Applicants must commit for one year, be at least twenty-one years of age, pass a pre-employment drug screen and merchant marine physical, have a clear criminal background (due to international travel), have U.S. citizenship or a green card, be friendly and outgoing, and have the stamina to work long hours—seventy-two to seventy-five hours per week! In addition to a salary and tips, crew members receive room (in shared crew cabins with private bath), meals, transportation to and from the ship, and a full-benefit medical package. This is a unique opportunity to travel to places around the world while saving money. A generous bonus is also awarded at the completion of twelve months of service. Applications are available online, or call for more information.

FOR MORE INFORMATION: Captain Scott Will, Global HR Services, Clipper Cruise Line, 11969 Westline Industrial Dr., Suite 300, St. Louis, MO 63146-3221
(800) 234-9625 • (314) 655-3924 • (314) 655-3882 (job hotline)
(314) 655-3960 (fax) • employment.global@nwship.com

CONTIKI HOLIDAYS

Educational Travel • USA • 2–7 Months
www.contiki.com

$ 🏕

In 1961, a young New Zealander named John Anderson arrived in London to tour Europe. He didn't want to go alone and didn't have much money, so he put a deposit on a minibus and gathered a group of travelers who spent twelve weeks exploring Europe. At the end of the trip, John tried to sell the minibus but no one wanted it. So in the spring of 1962, he advertised his Europe tour again. This time, he was able to fit two trips into the summer season and doubled his business. Over thirty years later, Contiki has become the world's largest travel company for eighteen- to thirty-five-year-olds, taking participants on adventurous trips to all corners of the world. Note that Contiki in the U.S. only runs tours in North America.

WHAT YOU'LL BE DOING: Tour managers with Contiki conduct city tours, give historical and practical information talks, and organize each day of a tour, including stops en route, meals, and excursions. Coach drivers work with a tour manager on most tours and are responsible for driving motor coaches seating up to fifty-four passengers.

COMMITMENT: Tours, which all depart from Anaheim, range in duration from three to twenty-four days and generally are conducted May through October. Tour managers are responsible for their clients twenty-four hours per day.

PERKS AND REWARDS: Tour managers receive a weekly salary (based on performance), while drivers receive a daily wage (based on length of tour and seniority). Accommodations, food, and some expenses are covered while on tour; however, the biggest perk is the places you'll go!

THE ESSENTIALS: It's preferred that tour manager applicants have a college degree, a couple years of work experience, knowledge of U.S. history and geography, and a great personality. Mandatory training for tour managers begins in mid-March for three to four weeks. A fee of $500 is charged to attend the school (which includes accommodation, breakfast, dinner, and transportation), although you may be reimbursed based on performance after four tours. Drivers can be trained at any time to receive their Class B Commercial Driver's License, free of charge. This particular office runs North American tours only and legal U.S. working status is required.

YOUR FIRST MOVE: Applications are accepted beginning in November. Interviews are generally conducted mid-January through March.

Life isn't about finding yourself. Life is about creating yourself. **79**
—GEORGE BERNARD SHAW

FOR MORE INFORMATION: Kelly Camps Pitre, Director of Operations, Contiki Holidays, 801 E. Katella Ave., 3rd Floor, Anaheim, CA 92805 (714) 935-0808 • (714) 940-1715 (fax) • info@contiki.com

CRUISE WEST

Sailing/Outdoor Education • Alaska • 3–9 Months
www.cruisewest.com

$ 🏠

Up close, casual, and personal. That's what Cruise West delivers for guests onboard their fleet of small ships—the largest holding just 114 guests—and that's where the work of their sea crew truly shines. Whether you lead nature walks in the wilds of Alaska, bring iced tea to a guest on the beaches of Mexico, or perform in the "No-Talent" night onboard a ship bound for British Columbia, your job is to ensure a perfect vacation for each guest. Having fun may be at the cornerstone of your job, but there's also a lot of hard work. The pace is quick, the hours are long, and you can't go home at the end of the day. All vessel positions (from galley assistants to deckhands) work on a "rotation schedule." This means you'll be scheduled to work on board from four to six weeks at a time, with a daily shift of twelve hours. During this period, you'll receive meals, shared crew quarters (with up to four other crew members), and competitive pay and gratuities. After each rotation, a time-off period of two weeks is provided (although you'll be responsible for your own room and board). Applicants must be at least eighteen years of age and most positions require a commitment from March through November. Midseason openings in May, June, and July are possible, as are a limited number of winter positions. Applications are available online.

If working onboard one of Cruise West's small ships is not for you, you might consider seasonal opportunities with their land-tour division. Exploration leaders and driver/guides greet guests, handle luggage, and conduct sightseeing/narrative tours that explore the gold country of Fairbanks, the Mendenhall Glacier near Juneau, Denali National Park's wildlife and wilderness, the mountain town of Ketchikan (a place only accessible by ship or plane), the small fishing village of Petersburg, and Alaska's largest city, Anchorage. In addition, guest services representatives provide guests with general information and orientation to the local area. The majority of positions typically begin in May and end in early September. Plan on working eight to twelve hours per day. All guides go through a paid comprehensive training program in early April.

FOR MORE INFORMATION: People Care & Development, Cruise West, 2301 Fifth Ave., Suite 401, Seattle, WA 98121 • (888) 842-8029 (206) 733-5676 • (206) 733-5654 (fax) • resume@cruisewest.com

CYCLING ADVENTURES

. . . .

OPEN YOURSELF UP TO THE POSSIBILITIES

It's those who take the risk and make that "left-hand turn in the road" who get the most from life.

—MICHAEL WILLIAMS

Michael and Dorrie Williams were living the American Dream—well-paying corporate jobs, benefits, a beautiful two-story home, security, and all the possessions that a lifestyle like this can bring. Yet there was a downside to the world the Williamses created for themselves. They were married to their jobs, Uncle Sam was taking most of their loot, and another snow-filled winter in Philadelphia wasn't helping their mental state. All they could think of was a week's vacation that would recharge their batteries.

However, their plan for a one-week vacation soon turned into two weeks, and then kept lengthening the more they talked about it. "We got to thinking. Why are we living this sort of lifestyle? What were we really working toward? What would we do if we put all our responsibilities aside?" Finally, it was an overnight decision. An overwhelming realization consumed them. Now was the time for them to walk away from the things that society dictated as being the right things to do. Their decision? To adventure around the U.S. on their bikes for not a week or two—but a whole year.

That night they talked about their trip. The next morning they worked out the details. Just like that. They soon broke the news of the new direction in their life to coworkers, family, and friends. At the same time, they started sifting through the material possessions in their home, soon to be peddled off

Michael and Dorrie Williams conquer the top of their third pass while crossing the Rockies on their bike adventure across America.

Either you let your life slip away by not doing the things you want to do, or you get up and do them. —CARL ALLY

and turned into funds for their trip. "It was the biggest garage sale we ever had. We sold everything except for the things that meant the world to us (and a couple bikes)."

What about security? What about money? What about the future? "That's why a lot of people don't want to make a change. They're scared about starting over, that they're not going to find a job again." Quite the contrary for Michael and Dorrie—"There will always be jobs out there. If you want something bad enough, you'll get it eventually."

And the adventure began! They hopped on their bikes and took off across America—from the hills of Kentucky, through the flatlands of the Midwest (milking a few cows along the way), across the perilous Rockies (conquering the tops of three mountain passes), all the way to the Pacific Ocean. To help them on their 3,700-mile journey, they used maps and guides purchased through the Adventure Cycling Association (page 88), which provided information on hostels, campgrounds, bike shops, where to get food, and distances between landmarks on the Trans-America Bike Trail.

For the Williamses, the trip wasn't about covering a certain distance each day. Their philosophy? Open yourself up to the experience and other people, and let anything happen; then deal with it, learn from it, and experience it as it comes to you. "We knew nothing about what to expect, and that's why we had such a great time. Without setting up a structure or any restrictions, you won't set yourself up for a letdown. Some days we rode just a few miles because we loved where we were or the company we were with." The key—the more risk they took, the more they opened themselves up to new adventures.

What do you do when you finish a cycling adventure like this? Michael and Dorrie found themselves back in the small college town where they first met and created jobs that resonate with the simple things that are most important to them. Their trappings are fewer, and they live on less, but they live more happily and at a better pace. "It's nice to plant some roots, have a circle of friends, and balance adventure with the grounding we've created."

It's amazing how much more mental a long journey on a bicycle is than physical! It can be a group journey, but there is plenty of time on one's own, pedaling away. There's a lot of time to think and grow and look into yourself.

—SARAH WAGONER

Are you thinking about creating your own cycling adventure? Not only can you pedal anywhere in the world, you might also consider leading others on a cycling trip by working seasonally for a bike adventure organization. Here's a handful of programs based in the U.S. that offer riding adventures and other work opportunities that will take you to all corners of the earth.

BACKROADS

Cycling · Worldwide · Seasonal
www.backroads.com

$ 🏕 🌐

Backroads offers more than 150 different active-travel vacations, including bicycling, walking, hiking, and multisport journeys in more than eighty-five destinations around the world. Traveling actively means traveling under your own power and at your own pace—not watching the world go by from behind the window of a car or tour bus. It means getting out there by foot, bicycle, water, or ski—seeing, touching, feeling, and experiencing. It means trying out the native greetings, meeting the locals, making new friends, and having a whole lot of fun.

WHAT YOU'LL BE DOING: As a leader, you're the catalyst for a fun, interesting, safe, and personally rewarding experience for your guests. This means being able to think on your feet and display total confidence when unusual situations arise. It also means displaying infinite compassion and patience at all times and maintaining a positive attitude and sense of humor. You'll become involved in every aspect of the adventure, ensuring that all equipment is in optimal working condition; buying and preparing food; delivering luggage at each night's accommodations; acting as a representative at hotels, restaurants, campgrounds, and with the general public; and keeping accurate financial records and complete written reports.

PERKS AND REWARDS: First-year leaders receive a daily stipend of $55 to $73, plus gourmet meals, accommodations in some of the best inns or campgrounds the region has to offer, and transportation costs. The pay scale and benefits increase in recognition of each year's experience. Backroads requests that you be at least a temporary resident of the Bay Area during the trip-leading season. All leaders are flown to and from trips out of either the San Francisco or Oakland airport. If you are not living in the area, you are responsible for getting yourself to the Bay Area prior to your flight. All leaders are expected to attend events at Backroads' Berkeley headquarters to launch the summer season in April and celebrate its end in October.

Opportunity never knocks; it lies there waiting for somebody to pick it up.
—JOEL WELDON

THE ESSENTIALS: The staff is composed of high-energy individuals with varied backgrounds who enjoy people, travel, and the outdoors. To become a leader, candidates must be a minimum of twenty-one years of age and have a valid driver's license and an excellent driving record. The ideal candidate is a master problem solver, effective public speaker, chef, area expert, translator (on trips to Europe), skilled driver, meticulous record keeper, a motivating force in group dynamics while being sensitive to individual needs, and in great physical shape. Foreign applicants must be citizens of the European Community.

YOUR FIRST MOVE: Write to request a detailed application packet or call the Backroads Job Hotline at (510) 527-1889, extension 560, for voice-recorded information twenty-four hours a day. Leader applications are evaluated starting in January, with interviews conducted from February through April. The application deadline is April 1; however, it is to your advantage to submit your application as early as possible.

FOR MORE INFORMATION: Leader Applications—BDG, Backroads, 801 Cedar St., Berkeley, CA 94710-1800 • (800) 462-2848 • (510) 527-1889, ext. 560 (510) 527-1444 (fax) • humanresources@backroads.com

BIKE-AID

Cycling • USA • 2 Months
www.globalexchange.org/bikeaid

♥ ⛺ 🌐

A unique program of Global Exchange, Bike-Aid is a vibrant, innovative cycling adventure that combines physical challenge, community interaction, education, leadership, fund-raising, and community service in the empowering experience of a lifetime. With departures from San Francisco and Seattle beginning in mid-June, eighty individuals from around the world will cycle to Washington, D.C., over a two-month period. Cyclists will raise $1 for every mile ridden, totaling $3,800 (and Bike-Aid will provide an endless source of creative ideas to help with your efforts). Three scholarships are also offered for those who are able to spend time organizing the ride during the spring prior to participation. Overnight lodging is donated by community organizations, schools, and individuals, and will include some camping. Beginners to prizewinning racers have participated in Bike-Aid, and riders from the ages of sixteen to sixty have met the challenge. It is not a race, and it encourages the participation of people from all backgrounds, ages, and abilities. Cyclists are advised to apply by April 1 to save on registration fees.

FOR MORE INFORMATION: Program Director, Bike-Aid, Global Exchange, 2017 Mission St., #303, San Francisco, CA 94110 • (800) 743-3808 (415) 575-5544

🐟 INSIDER TIP: Bike-Aid satisfied my quest for community. My interests lay in the cause—promoting environmental solutions—rather than in the physical challenge of the ride itself. To me, the group dynamics were more of a challenge than the actual pedaling. Each of us is part of the solution: it takes too much wasted energy to blame others for things that don't work right in our world. —*Alona Jasik, participant*

CICLISMO CLASSICO

Cycling • USA/Italy • Seasonal
www.ciclismoclassico.com

$ 🏠 ⊕

Experience Italy's hidden treasures by pedaling, walking, or skiing with Ciclismo Classico. These cultural adventures offer educational and dreamy itineraries that celebrate the Italian landscape, art, language, music, folklore, and its beloved cuisine. As cultural liaisons, bicycling and walking leaders take small groups on nine- to fifteen-day tours from April through October. Leaders engage participants in musical evenings, Italian lessons, wine tastings, cooking demonstrations, and other authentic experiences with their extensive network of Italian friends and families. For those who want to experience the U.S. before heading on over to Italy, Ciclismo now offers adventure trips throughout New England. Applicants must be at least twenty-three years of age, fluent in Italian (for Italy tours), and have travel and group-leader experience, bike mechanic skills, and boundless energy. Benefits include all trip expenses, along with a $400 (and up) per week salary plus bonuses and tips. Call or email for an application packet.

LAUREN HEFFERON

FOR MORE INFORMATION:
Staffing Director
Ciclismo Classico
30 Marathon St
Arlington, MA 02474
(800) 866-7314
(781) 646-3377
(781) 641-1512 (fax)
jobs@ciclismoclassico.com

Bicycle leaders with
Ciclismo Classico introduce
participants to Italy's hidden
treasures.

Life does not have to be perfect to be wonderful.
—ANNETTE FUNICELLO

85

SOCKEYE CYCLE

Cycling · Alaska · Summer
www.cyclealaska.com

$ 🏕

Located at the upper end of the sixteen-million-acre Tongass National Forest in Alaska, Sockeye Cycle offers cycling adventures along local roads and trails that are home to grizzly bears, moose, mountain goats, black-tailed deer, and bald eagles. From May through the end of September, Sockeye hires a variety of seasonal employees, including guides, van drivers, bicycle mechanics, and managers. At minimum, applicants must be twenty-three years old with a clean driving record. Wages run from $9 to $12 per hour, plus tips (managers are paid a salary); and limited employee housing is available for $200 per month. Applications are available online or send off your resume and cover letter. Interviews begin in September with positions filled by March 1.

FOR MORE INFORMATION: Thomas Ely, President, Sockeye Cycle, P.O. Box 829, Haines, AK 99827-0829 · (907) 766-2869 · (907) 766-2851 (fax) sockeye@cyclealaska.com

STUDENT HOSTELING PROGRAM

Cycling · USA/Canada/Europe · Summer
www.bicycletrips.com

$ 🏕 🌐

Since 1969, the Student Hosteling Program (SHP) has been offering teenagers two- to eight-week bicycle touring trips through the countrysides and cultural centers of the U.S., Canada, and Europe. SHP trips provide adventure, fun, outdoor education, and the opportunity for emotional growth, while providing one of the safest and most wholesome youth environments available. Their groups are small, usually eight to twelve participants (ages thirteen to seventeen) and two to three leaders, making possible a close and rewarding group experience. SHP groups travel by bicycle, at their own pace and close to the land, using public and private transportation when necessary. Groups live simply, using campsites, hostels, and other modest facilities. In the countryside, groups buy food at local markets and cook their own meals.

WHAT YOU'LL BE DOING: Prior to hitting the road, leaders will complete a five-day training course that focuses on cycling and camping, with sessions covering bike repair, SHP policies, groups, kids, finances, and problems that may occur on a trip as well as group and trip assignment. From there, all leaders receive further training for their particular trip during a four-day preparation and orientation period just before their trip departure date. The senior leader is in charge of the trip, enforces rules and bike safety, makes all final decisions, and is expected to be the central personality within the group. The assistant leader is the back-up person (acting as an extra set of eyes, ears, hands, and feet) and assists the senior leader whenever necessary and wherever possible.

COMMITMENT: The minimum leadership time commitment is four weeks. This includes four days of pre-trip logistics and preparation and three days of post-trip activities. You may lead one trip (from three to six weeks), two short trips, or one long and one short trip. Employment begins in late June for part or all of the summer.

PERKS AND REWARDS: Senior leaders earn $1,040 to $2,640 depending upon the length of the work period; assistant leaders earn from $780 to $1,980. In addition, all trip-related expenses are paid, including transportation, meals, and accommodations. Leaders can borrow rear panniers and handlebar bags, but must provide all other cycling equipment (which can be purchased new at cost from SHP).

THE ESSENTIALS: Senior leaders must be at least twenty-one years of age (the average is about twenty-five) and are typically teachers, graduate students, and college seniors. Assistants must be at least eighteen years old and are usually college sophomores and juniors. Many are former SHP trip participants. All leaders must hold a valid Red Cross first aid certificate and many have advanced first aid training as well. Most importantly, the leader's personality is the most critical element in making a trip work.

YOUR FIRST MOVE: After a lengthy screening process, leaders are selected to complete one of the five-day training courses in Massachusetts before being assigned a trip. Applications are available online.

FOR MORE INFORMATION: Ted Lefkowitz, Director, Student Hosteling Program, 1356 Ashfield Rd., P.O. Box 419, Conway, MA 01341 • (800) 343-6132 (413) 369-4275 • (413) 369-4257 (fax) • shpbike@aol.com

🐾 **INSIDER TIP: Leading an SHP trip can be a unique opportunity for a rewarding and wonderful experience. The small groups that become so close-knit, the physical exercise, the beauty of the country-side, the excitement of new places, and the emotional ties and joys that you'll develop with the kids—it's an unbeatable combination.**
—*Ted Lefkowitz, Director*

The price of not following your dream is the same as paying for it.
—PAULO COELHO

RECOMMENDED RESOURCES

The **Adventure Cycling Association** (www.adventurecycling.org) is America's largest nonprofit recreational bicycling organization. Since 1973 they have been helping members use their bicycles for adventure, exploration, and discovery. They publish detailed bike maps for over thirty-two thousand miles of scenic backroads and mountain trails in North America, which allow you to travel cross-country without ever seeing an interstate highway. The maps include information on bicycling conditions, local history, and services that cyclists need (such as locations of bike shops, campgrounds, motels, and grocery stores). Membership ($33 per year; students/seniors—$28) provides discounts on all sorts of resources, and includes *Adventure Cyclist* (their member-only magazine published nine times a year) and *The Cyclist's Yellow Pages*, its annual guide to bicycle maps, books, routes, and organizations (also available online).

If you want to lead tours of your own, you may considering taking part in Adventure Cycling's three-day leadership training course, designed to teach the fundamentals of leading a self-contained bicycle expedition. There's a fee of $399 and training takes place in various spots throughout the U.S. from January through May. For more information contact the Adventure Cycling Association, P.O. Box 8308, Missoula, MT 59807-8308; (800) 755-2453, info@adventurecycling.org.

Are you looking for a community that encourages its residents to cycle for recreation, fitness, and transportation to work or the local market? The **Bicycle Friendly Community Campaign** (www.bicyclefriendlycommunity.org) offers community profiles of the best cities in the U.S.—including the bicycle capital of the U.S.—Davis, California.

The **International Bicycle Fund** (www.ibike.org) is dedicated to promoting sustainable transport and international understanding, with major areas of activity including nonmotorized urban planning, economic development, bike safety education, and responsible travel and cycle tourism. In addition, they provide cross-cultural, educational bicycle tours that allow Westerners to learn more about Africa, Asia, Cuba, Ecuador, Guyana, and the U.S. at a person-to-person level not usually available to tourists. Itineraries highlight the cultural, historical, economic, and physical diversity of the area. Tours are generally two or four weeks long, with costs ranging from $990 to $1,490, not including airfare. Unpaid internships are also available at their office in Seattle, Washington, with a majority of the work focused on grant writing, fund-raising, administration, and supporting bicycle advocacy organizations around the world. Call for the free newsletter, *IBF News* (or check it out at www.ibike.org/ibfnews.htm), which includes information on grassroots cycling programs all over the world. For more information contact the International Bicycle Fund, 4887 Columbia Dr., South, Seattle, WA 98108-1919; (206) 767-0848, ibike@ibike.org.

ENVIRONMENTAL TRAVELING COMPANIONS

Therapeutic Recreation · California · Seasonal
www.etctrips.org

$ 🏕 ⊕

Founded in 1971, Environmental Traveling Companions (ETC) is a non-profit organization that provides outdoor adventure and environmental education experiences for disadvantaged youth and people with special needs. The populations they serve are diverse—many of their participants have visual and hearing impairments or physical and/or developmental disabilities, and some are disadvantaged inner-city youth. ETC's primary goal is to provide access to the wilderness to people of all abilities and promote self-esteem, self-sufficiency, and a greater appreciation for the environment. Annually, they serve over two thousand participants in three outdoor programs—white-water rafting, sea kayaking, and cross-country skiing—with destinations primarily in Northern California.

WHAT YOU'LL BE DOING: White-water rafting field interns assist or guide white-water rafting trips and outdoor activities and games as well as aid in logistical planning, coordination of volunteers, program development, maintenance of the site, and repair of equipment. White-water guide school takes place in early spring and is mandatory for prospective interns without solid class three rafting skills. Cross-country skiing guide interns live in the beautiful Sierra Nevadas and lead adaptive ski trips for people with special needs. Interns aid in trip coordination and logistics, maintenance of the site and equipment, and program development. Mandatory intern guide training takes place in mid-January. Sea kayaking office and field interns work in the San Francisco headquarters and guide one- to two-day sea kayaking trips on San Francisco Bay. ETC also has salaried, short-term management and administration positions (call for details on these).

COMMITMENT: Positions are offered seasonally throughout the year (thirty to forty hours per week), with the exception of sea kayaking positions, which are only available from April through October (twenty to forty hours per week).

PERKS AND REWARDS: Intern benefits include a small stipend of $200 per month, room, partial board, and rafting, skiing, and sea kayaking privileges. One of the biggest perks is the intensive training each intern receives. Training focuses on instruction in their specialty, disability and diversity awareness, working with special populations, and outdoor leadership skills. Management position wages range from $1,000 to $1,700 per month, along with room and partial board.

THE ESSENTIALS: Applicants must have a desire to develop leadership skills; be enthusiastic about wilderness adventure; be comfortable in the outdoors;

be self-starters and able to work independently; enjoy working with people; and be certified in CPR and first aid. Experience in desired positions and work with special populations is preferred but not necessary. ETC guides represent a diversity of cultures, abilities, and backgrounds—including teachers, engineers, counselors, carpenters, lawyers, and university interns.

YOUR FIRST MOVE: Write or call for application details. Deadlines: Nordic Skiing Program—October 15; Rafting/Sea Kayaking Programs—February 28.

FOR MORE INFORMATION: Dana Talise, Office Manager, Environmental Traveling Companions, Fort Mason Center, Building C, San Francisco, CA 94123 (415) 474-7662, ext. 10 • (415) 474-3919 (fax) • info@etctrips.org

⤞ INSIDER TIP: The pool of over four hundred volunteer-guides makes up an incredibly enthusiastic, eclectic, and fun community. Once introduced, most folks get sucked into the ETC whirlpool and stay involved for years to come!

FOUR CORNERS SCHOOL
OF OUTDOOR EDUCATION

Adventure Travel • Utah • 3–6 Months
www.fourcornersschool.org

$ 🏠 ⊕

Here in the rugged terrain of the "four corners," where Arizona, Colorado, New Mexico, and Utah meet, participants join Four Corners School of Outdoor Education on unique educational vacations. Programs are by foot, van, and raft, and explore areas such as wilderness advocacy, archaeology, and research with the Bureau of Land Management, National Park Service, and U.S. Forest Service. The school's goal is low-impact adventures with a very healthy dose of education.

WHAT YOU'LL BE DOING: Internships vary with the season, program content, special projects, and office load. Four Corners School is very conscious about maintaining a balance between office work and fieldwork. Special skills may be put to use, such as public relations, computer programming, painting, and carpentry.

COMMITMENT: Internships generally run in three sessions, with start dates in March, mid-June, and mid-August.

PERKS AND REWARDS: A small stipend and primitive housing is provided. Interns are also in the unique position to go on a number of outdoor field programs, which generally last five days. Their programs are so diverse that one week you may be out backpacking, the next on the San Juan River. You'll also have access to their world-class experts.

THE ESSENTIALS: Applicants must be at least eighteen years of age. No area of experience supersedes another, but some prior knowledge of the outdoors is very helpful.

YOUR FIRST MOVE: Call for application materials (which must be received by January 15). Phone interviews will be conducted.

FOR MORE INFORMATION: Janet Ross, Executive Director, Four Corners School of Outdoor Education, Southwest Ed-Ventures, P.O. Box 1029, Monticello, UT 84535 • (800) 525-4456 • (435) 587-2156 • (435) 587-2193 (fax) fcs@fourcornersschool.org

INSIDER TIP: We like applicants who are excited about the outdoors and make good ambassadors for the school. Our participants like friendly, knowledgeable people. We all have to work hard, so it helps to have an intern who doesn't mind the work. It doesn't hurt to know about the office environment, as duties will include some office time.

GENESEE VALLEY OUTDOOR LEARNING CENTER

Experiential Education • Maryland • 3–9 Months
www.geneseevalley.org

$ 🏕

Spread over three hundred acres of farmland, Genesee Valley Outdoor Learning Center (GVOLC) is host to one of the East Coast's largest ropes courses and specializes in youth development, outdoor education, environmental studies, and team-building retreats. During the spring and fall seasons, a majority of programs last for one day. Facilitators are challenged by various participants, including school groups, college organizations, community groups, at-risk youth, emotionally disturbed youth, and corporate groups. The summer season expands beyond the one-day programs, and includes four different adventure camps for seven- to fifteen-year-olds.

WHAT YOU'LL BE DOING: Adventure. Growth. Self-discovery. Got you interested? GVOLC hires ropes-course facilitators and interns during the spring through fall and counselors-in-training. Interns participate in a two-week training program where they will learn the "ropes"—theory, facilitation, and technical skills—then co-facilitate groups before doing solo facilitating.

To achieve the marvelous, you must do the unthinkable . . . the answer will hit, 91
like a big psychic orgasm, if you listen to your dreams. They never lie. —E. JEAN CARROLL

Ongoing training in ropes-course maintenance and administration is also provided. Counselors-in-training get involved in activities including environmental studies, outdoor skills, canoeing, rock climbing, introductory ropes course, swimming, arts and crafts, fishing, farm life, and gardening.

PERKS AND REWARDS: Wages vary with the length of contract and experience (usually around $180 to $250 per week); health insurance assistance and a contributory retirement plan are also provided. All staff live in rustic, dormitory-style housing and enjoy meals together with vegetarian and meat options. GVOLC also fosters a strong, supportive community where your safety, individuality, growth, and happiness are important.

THE ESSENTIALS: Instructors and interns must be at least eighteen years of age as well as interested in and dedicated to the experiential education field. Those who are flexible, committed to excellence, willing to take the initiative, team players, and sensitive toward others' needs will thrive here.

YOUR FIRST MOVE: Send a resume and cover letter to begin the application process. Job opportunities and application materials can also be found online.

FOR MORE INFORMATION: Steve Malbrough, Director of New Staff and Programs, Genesee Valley Outdoor Learning Center, 1717 Rayville Rd., Parkton, MD 21120 (410) 343-0101 • (410) 343-1451 (fax) • info@geneseevalley.org

GLOBAL WORKS

Service Adventures • USA/Worldwide • Summer
www.globalworksinc.com

$ ⚑ ⊕

Global Works is an environmental and community service–based travel program (with language immersion and homestay options) for students ages fourteen to eighteen. Leaders and staff provide the backbone for these four-week summer adventures that take participants to places that range from small villages in the mountains of Fiji to castle ruins in Spain. With a work hard, play hard mentality, the program fills the students' days with meaningful projects, travel, and exposure to different cultures. Life-changing community projects may include building a new water system, constructing a playground, educating children about wolves, or rebuilding castles in ruins—all in the hope of positively affecting the community. Working conditions are excellent and the pay quite good (a salary, living expenses during the program, and airfare to and from the country of the program being served are provided). Applicants must be at least twenty-three years old and have experience in leading groups and working with kids. Immersion program applicants must have a true language proficiency. Leaders must be available for a training session held during the Memorial Day weekend and for service throughout the duration of the program (usually one month from late June to early August). Applications are available online.

FOR MORE INFORMATION: Biff Houldin, Director, Global Works, 1113 S. Allen St., State College, PA 16801 • (814) 867-7000 • (814) 867-2717 (fax) staffapp@globalworksinc.com

GREENBRIER RIVER OUTDOOR ADVENTURES

Adventure Education • West Virginia • 2–12 Weeks
www.groa.com

$ 🏕

Greenbrier River Outdoor Adventures offers a wide variety of programs for young people between the ages of ten and seventeen. Programs are based on the development of self-esteem and leadership through adventure, challenge, and small-group experiences, including community service projects. Everything—playing, cooking, eating, and sleeping—is done outdoors. While not a survival program, a large part of the program is learning how to live comfortably outdoors while taking time to enjoy the experience.

YOUR SURROUNDINGS: The base camp is located on a 250-acre site nestled in the West Virginian mountains of the Monongahela National Forest, home to top-rated rock climbing and mountain biking along with white-water rafting, caving, and backpacking. Their New England programs explore the White Mountain National Forest, Acadia National Park, and other beautiful areas of northern New England.

WHAT YOU'LL BE DOING: Staff members kick off the summer by participating in a weeklong intensive training session in West Virginia. Group leaders and activity instructors, along with interns, provide supervision (and general safety) of participants, oversee program logistics and itinerary, teach outdoor living skills and adventure activities, and facilitate and develop group dynamics.

COMMITMENT: Since some staff members might be looking for a full summer of employment (June through August) while others are only interested in leading programs for just a few weeks, positions are available from two to twelve weeks (with most positions available from six to twelve weeks).

PERKS AND REWARDS: A competitive salary is provided along with room, board, and pro deals on outdoor clothing and equipment.

When we are motivated by goals that have deep meaning, by dreams that need completion, by pure love that needs expressing, then we truly live life. —GREG ANDERSON

THE ESSENTIALS: All candidates must be at least eighteen and have certification in CPR and first aid. A sincere interest in working with youth in the outdoors, experience in the field, and competency in outdoor living are traits found in their staff.

YOUR FIRST MOVE: Printable applications can be found online; otherwise, send your resume and a cover letter requesting an application.

FOR MORE INFORMATION: Thomas Bryant, Staffing Director, Greenbrier River Outdoor Adventures, HC 77, Box 117, Bartow, WV 24920 • (800) 600-4752 (304) 456-5191 • (304) 456-5572 (fax) • groa@groa.com

HIOBS—OUTREACH PROGRAMS

Wilderness Education • Florida/South Carolina • 3 Months
www.members.tripod.com/outward.bound

$ 🏠

The Hurricane Island Outward Bound School's (HIOBS) Outreach Programs offer the Outward Bound experience and philosophy to both delinquent and at-risk youth throughout Florida and in Charleston, South Carolina. The U.S. Department of Justice reported HIOBS as one of the five most successful programs in the nation. The program serves over one thousand youths per year and is a leader in community service.

WHAT YOU'LL BE DOING: The Outreach Programs teach the four pillars of Outward Bound (self-reliance, craftsmanship, physical fitness, and compassion) to young adults between the ages of twelve and eighteen. Programs are either exclusively wilderness based or a combination of wilderness and residential programming. Courses range from 20 to 180 days, and all programs work with teams of instructors and teachers. The internship experience includes an eleven-day orientation/expedition along with up to two and a half months of experiential work in two program areas. Interns will undertake lots of draining, exhausting, feel-good work that will train them to become wilderness instructors.

COMMITMENT: The Adolescent Instructor Practicum ends when participants attain a recommendation as an assistant instructor for HIOBS, which can take one to two months. Seasonal and full-time work is available following the program.

PERKS AND REWARDS: There is a cost of $500 per participant for the orientation, which includes all food and lodging for ten days. During the internship, a daily stipend of $15 to $35, food, lodging, and travel between bases is provided. Interns also have access to HIOBS staff trainings and pro-deal purchases.

THE ESSENTIALS: At the minimum, applicants must be at least twenty-one years of age, be U.S. citizens, and have current CPR and first aid certification. Preference is given to those who have participated in an Outward Bound course as a student, have experience working with teenagers, and have enthusiasm and interest in impacting young adults.

YOUR FIRST MOVE: Email or call to request an applicant packet. For more information on HIOBS, check out www.hurricaneisland.org.

FOR MORE INFORMATION: Alyse Ostreicher, Staff Developer/Recruiter, Adolescent Instructor Practicum, HIOBS—Outreach Programs, 177 Salem Ct., Tallahassee, FL 32301 • (850) 414-8816 • (850) 922-6721 (fax) flrecruit@hurricaneisland.org

HULBERT OUTDOOR CENTER

Experiential Education • Vermont • 3–11 Months
www.alohafoundation.org/hulbert

$ 🏠 ⊕

Established in 1978, the Hulbert Outdoor Center is a nonprofit educational institution that serves six thousand participants annually through programs designed to foster personal growth, self-reliance, cooperation, confidence, and a sense of community in people of all ages. Year-round programs range from school programs, wilderness trips, Elderhostel experiences, and a unique leadership training program that includes certifications in everything from Wilderness First Responder and backcountry search and rescue to lifeguard training and the ACA Canoe Instructor's Course (which are available to staff members).

YOUR SURROUNDINGS: The Center is located in Vermont's Upper Connecticut River Valley on the shores of Lake Morey, surrounded by over five hundred acres of young forests, bluffs, and rolling countryside. Recreation opportunities include miles of mountain biking, hiking, backcountry skiing, and access to water sports and developed ski areas.

WHAT YOU'LL BE DOING: Hulbert provides unique opportunities that combine elements of wilderness travel, outdoor skill development, teamwork, sensitivity to the environment, and personal growth experiences. The prime responsibility

Trust in yourself. Your perceptions are often more accurate than you are willing to believe.
—CLAUDIA BLACK

95

of school program staff is to work with middle-school children in programs emphasizing team building, the ropes course, natural history, and other curriculum areas. Trip leaders guide extended wilderness experiences for groups of eight to ten participants.

COMMITMENT: During the summer, a three-month commitment is ideal; trip staff are contracted per course. During the spring and fall, a five-month commitment is necessary, and some positions have the option of continuing on for nine or eleven months.

PERKS AND REWARDS: Dependent upon experience, wages begin at $45 to $55 per day. You'll also receive room, board, and paid staff training.

THE ESSENTIALS: Applicants must be at least twenty-one years of age and have a bachelor's degree, certification in first aid and CPR (Wilderness First Responder or higher preferred), a valid driver's license, the ability to work long hours in the outdoors, and demonstrated experience teaching (preferably in the experiential education field).

YOUR FIRST MOVE: Send a cover letter and resume. An application packet will be mailed upon receipt.

FOR MORE INFORMATION: Greg Auch, Wilderness Trips Director, Hulbert Outdoor Center, The Aloha Foundation, 2968 Lake Morey Rd., Fairlee, VT 05045-9400 • (802) 333-3405, ext. 121 • (802) 333-3404 (fax) greg_auch@alohafoundation.org

✄ **INSIDER TIP: The staff at Hulbert form a unique community of educators that values dedication, creative problem solving, and hard work. In the course of our work, we put in long hours and fill diverse roles. Throughout, in work and in the residential environment, we strive to create and to maintain a positive sense of community.**

INTERNATIONAL FIELD STUDIES

Marine Science/Sailing • The Bahamas • 1 Year+
www.intlfieldstudies.com

$ 🏠 🌐

International Field Studies (IFS) is a nonprofit organization that operates Forfar Field Station and a sailing program on Andros Island in the Bahamas (where you can find the world's third-largest barrier reef).

WHAT YOU'LL BE DOING: Staff at the field station educate and lead high school and college groups in natural science activities and perform routine maintenance on boats, vehicles, and the facility. As a captain or first mate in the sailing program, staff live on the boat (and are responsible for maintaining it), as well as running trips and sailing.

COMMITMENT: A minimum one-year commitment is required.

PERKS AND REWARDS: Benefits include a monthly stipend beginning at $200, along with meals, rustic housing on the beach or on board sailboats, travel between Florida and the Bahamas, educational courses, permits, training, licenses in scuba and outboards, four weeks' paid vacation, and two complimentary one-week trips to the station for family members.

THE ESSENTIALS: Applicants must be able to withstand bugs, heat, and the lack of a U.S.–style civilization. Especially needed are applicants who are hardworking, eager to learn, self-motivated, positive, patient, flexible, and great with people from all walks of life. Mechanical aptitude and a knowledge and love of nature are also highly desirable.

YOUR FIRST MOVE: Download an application from their website, then send the completed application, your resume, and a letter of intent either through regular mail or email. Selected applicants will be scheduled for an interview week in the Bahamas. The only way IFS can get serious applicants is to charge $620 for the interview week (which will be reimbursed after a year of service).

FOR MORE INFORMATION: Lisa Forbes, Program Coordinator, International Field Studies, 30 Public Square, P.O. Box 428, Nelsonville, OH 45764 (800) 962-3805 • (740) 753-9231 • (740) 753-5100 (fax) office@intlfieldstudies.com

KIEVE LEADERSHIP DECISIONS INSTITUTE

Experiential Education • Maine • 4–10 Months
www.kieve.org

$ 🏕

Kieve's Leadership Decisions Institute (LDI), a leader in adventure-based, experiential education and prevention, works with over nine thousand students each year from over 120 school systems all over Maine and New England. Throughout the spring and fall seasons, middle school students

I cannot predict the wind but I can have my sail ready.
—E. F. SCHUMACHER

travel to their camp facility on Damariscotta Lake and spend up to five days working on skills in teamwork, conflict resolution, relationships, communication, decision making, leadership, and positive risk taking. During the winter months, Kieve staff travel to schools to deliver outreach programs based on the same curriculum.

WHAT YOU'LL BE DOING: Ten-month interns are integrated closely into all aspects of the Kieve programming, including classroom management, curriculum development, peer mediation, conflict resolution, and adventure-based instruction. During the fall and spring programs, most of the time is spent on-site. The schedule guarantees a mix of observation, one-on-one and group discussion, and, as the intern's experience grows, in-class facilitation. During the winter months, interns have the opportunity to accompany and assist the teaching staff in delivering outreach programs at schools. Responsibilities of seasonal Peer Resident Overseers (PROs) include organizing and supervising students during out-of-class time along with supervision of a cabin of fifteen boys or girls, operation of the ropes course and climbing wall, waterfront and other recreational activities, and performing in an interactive theatre skit.

COMMITMENT: The ten-month intern program runs from late August until early June or March through December. Seasonal PRO positions are available either during the spring (February through mid-June) or the fall (late August through early December). Kieve is flexible with start and end dates.

PERKS AND REWARDS: Ten-month interns will receive a stipend of $8,000 (with health benefits available), while seasonal employees receive $175 per week. Benefits include housing in cabins, meals, laundry facilities, computer and Internet access, a health club membership, access to their recreational building, and a spectacular waterfront location.

THE ESSENTIALS: Intern applicants must be college graduates seriously considering a career in education who feel they would benefit from a year of hands-on training; at the minimum, seasonal employees must be at least eighteen years of age. All staff must be compassionate, caring people with lots of energy to work within a residential program.

YOUR FIRST MOVE: Call or email for additional information. Applications are accepted continually throughout the year.

FOR MORE INFORMATION: Bob Grant, Director, Kieve Leadership Decisions Institute, 42 Kieve Rd., P.O. Box 169, Nobleboro, ME 04555 • (207) 563-6212 (207) 563-5833 (fax) • ldi@kieve.org

LINDBLAD EXPEDITIONS

Sailing • USA/Canada/Mexico • 6 Months
www.expeditions.com

$ 🏕

Known for their expedition travel voyages, Lindblad Expeditions places a strong emphasis on in-depth exploration and discovery, where guests (and crew) learn about the environment, ecology, and natural history of a region through lectures, slide presentations, and guided walks. The vessels are small (just 152 feet in length), so the twenty-four crew members and sixty guests are able to travel where the big ships cannot. Destinations include the Sea of Cortez and Baja California, the Columbia and Snake Rivers (Oregon and Washington), British Columbia, and southeast Alaska. Most shipboard staff work year-round; however, stewards and deckhands can work over a six-month period. The work is demanding—averaging twelve hours a day—but time off is often filled with the chance to go hiking, snorkeling, kayaking, or whale watching. Crew members earn on average $2,700 per month and receive room and board. Along with having a positive attitude, adventurous spirit, and outgoing personality, applicants must be at least eighteen years of age (positions that serve alcohol must be twenty-one).

FOR MORE INFORMATION: Human Resources Department, Lindblad Expeditions, 1415 Western Ave., Suite 700, Seattle, WA 98101 • (206) 403-1501 (fax) crewus@expeditions.com

LONGACRE EXPEDITIONS

Adventure Travel • Worldwide • Summer
www.longacreexpeditions.com

$ 🏕 🌐

Each summer Longacre Expeditions leaders and groups of ten to sixteen teenagers bicycle, backpack, rock climb, sea kayak, mountain climb, whitewater raft, snowboard, snorkel, scuba dive, explore caves, and canoe across miles of the most beautiful territory in North and Central America as well as Iceland. Trips focus on group living, wilderness skills, cooperation, independence, and fun.

WHAT YOU'LL BE DOING: Whether backpacking in primitive environments, repairing a bicycle on the road, or setting up a campsite, Longacre leaders challenge their team, nurture relationships, and, of course, have a lot of fun in the process. In addition to trip leaders, other staff positions include assistant trip leaders, support and logistics people, an equipment manager, a base camp cook, and specialists for rock climbing and sea kayaking. All seasonal staff are required to attend an eight- to nine-day training period, which begins around June 15.

COMMITMENT: Seasonal staff have various work schedules to choose from, including leading a trip for four weeks, then acting as support staff for two to five additional weeks; working a two- to six-week trip; or arriving a few weeks early to help open the base camp before staff week, as well as scouting new routes and campsites.

PERKS AND REWARDS: Adventure leaders are paid $46 and up per day; base camp staff are paid $1,050 to $2,500 per season depending on position and length of contract; and staffers who hold current certificates in EMT or Wilderness EMT are compensated an additional $100. There is no compensation for the staff training period; however, room and board are supplied. Perks include pro-deal purchases.

THE ESSENTIALS: Applicants must be twenty-one years of age, have a good driving record, and have Wilderness First Responder certification, lifeguard training, and CPR. Common traits include ability to communicate and be comfortable with teenagers, competence in a variety of outdoor activities, great physical condition, the ability to embrace Longacre's trip-leading philosophy, and commitment to the group. Staffers come from all over the country and are often graduate students or college juniors or seniors who have taken a few years off to take a job or tour the world. Others are teachers who see the summer as an opportunity to be with kids in a nonclassroom setting. Still others join Longacre each year from seasonal positions at ski resorts, environmental centers, and other wilderness programs.

YOUR FIRST MOVE: Applications must be received by June 15. A personal interview is highly recommended.

FOR MORE INFORMATION: Meredith Schuler, Program Director, Longacre Expeditions, 4030 Middle Ridge Rd., Newport, PA 17074 (800) 433-0127 • (717) 567-6790 • (717) 567-3955 (fax) longacre@longacreexpeditions.com

This Mountain Institute group sets out for their one-week adventure into the woods of West Virginia.

THE MOUNTAIN INSTITUTE

Environmental Education • West Virginia • 1 Week–8 Months
www.mountain.org

$ ♠♠

Since the early 1970s, the Mountain Institute has been running environmental education programming for a variety of schools and students, private organizations, and universities, with courses that highlight physical, emotional, and intellectual challenges, as well as discovery, growth, and the learning of new outdoor skills. Many programs work with ten to fifteen students in an extended, field-based setting, either at their four-hundred-acre Spruce Knob facility, in yurts (circular domed tents of skins or felt stretched over a collapsible lattice framework), or in the national forest. Since programs are taught experientially, participants and the field staff can't help but wander into group dynamics and leadership quite a bit.

WHAT YOU'LL BE DOING: The course instructor team works together to create a dynamic, educational week utilizing the surrounding landscape, with programming that covers the general topics of ecology, mountain geology, and biodiversity. Interns assist the staff with the delivery of all educational programs, including group handling, logistical planning and preparation, and field skills instruction.

COMMITMENT: Course instructor positions are seasonal and on a contract basis from mid-April to June and mid-September to mid-October. There are

Joy comes from using your potential. **101**
—WILL SHULTZ

a limited number of opportunities in the summer, with the majority of staff working in the spring and fall. Interns generally work during the spring, summer, or fall for ten consecutive weeks. During the winter months, internships are administration focused.

PERKS AND REWARDS: Wages for field staff start at $65 per day, and meals and tent housing are provided. Interns are provided with room and board at the Mountain Center campus and receive a weekly stipend of $100.

THE ESSENTIALS: Field staff must be at least twenty-one years of age and have experience working with youth in the outdoors. CPR and Wilderness First Responder (WFR) certifications are required. (However, the institute hosts a WFR and CPR training in the spring for those who don't have current certification.) Interns must be at least nineteen years old with an interest in working for an environmentally friendly nonprofit organization.

YOUR FIRST MOVE: Send a resume, references, and a cover letter explaining why you would like to work for the institute.

FOR MORE INFORMATION: Matthew Tate, Program Officer, The Mountain Institute, HC 75, Box 24, Circleville, WV 26804 • (800) 874-3050 (304) 567-2632 • (304) 567-2666 (fax) • learning@mountain.org

NATIONAL OUTDOOR LEADERSHIP SCHOOL

Wilderness Education • Worldwide • 1–3 Months
www.nols.edu

♥ 🏠 ⊕

The National Outdoor Leadership School (commonly known as NOLS) is an educational organization with its roots in extended wilderness expeditions— believing that long stays in wild places are vital to understanding both the natural world and ourselves. Courses take students away from the distractions of civilization and into the mountains, deserts, and oceans to learn the skills they need to run their own expeditions. NOLS graduates are leaders who have an understanding of environmental ethics, a sense of teamwork, an appreciation of natural history, and overall competence and good judgment. NOLS operates nine branch schools in Alaska, the Pacific Northwest, the Rocky Mountains, the Southwest, Teton Valley, Mexico, and the Yukon in North America, as well as in Kenya and Patagonia (Chile).

WHAT YOU'LL BE DOING: Prior to working at NOLS as a seasonal staff member or instructor, it's virtually necessary to have participated in a NOLS course (these vary in length from ten to ninety-four days). Most folks select their

Instructor and students line boats in the Yukon Territory, home to the NOLS canoe program.

DEBORAH SUSSEX

course by concentrating on either location or skills. Terrain, weather, expedition length, and specialized skills vary, but every course includes a core curriculum emphasizing leadership through the development of judgment and decision-making skills. Your choice will depend on your interests, experience, and time constraints. Course types include mountaineering, wilderness backpacking, ocean (sea kayaking and sailing), river (kayaking, rafting, and canoeing), winter (backcountry skiing and dogsledding), semester (a variety of skills over three months), outdoor educators (for practicing or potential outdoor educators), and shorter courses for people twenty-five and older.

Once you've graduated, there are over one hundred temporary and seasonal positions at NOLS that you may consider. These include everything from managers to kitchen workers. In addition, there are over five hundred active NOLS instructors throughout the world. New instructors generally work only two summer courses during their first two years at the school (with 50 percent of the work available in the summer).

PERKS AND REWARDS: For participation in a NOLS course, fees range from $750 to $10,300 depending on the location and the length of the educational expedition. Pay for seasonal employment is usually entry-level with benefits varying from branch to branch.

THE ESSENTIALS: Successful students come willing to learn and develop leadership skills and wilderness ethics. Prior outdoor experience is not a prerequisite for most NOLS courses, although being in good shape and having a positive attitude and the desire to learn wilderness skills in locations of incredible beauty are musts.

YOUR FIRST MOVE: For more information on employment opportunities, contact the human resources director, or for participating in a NOLS course, call or send an email note to admissions@nols.edu.

FOR MORE INFORMATION: Human Resources Director, National Outdoor Leadership School, 284 Lincoln St., Lander, WY 82520-2848
(800) 710-6657 • (307) 332-5300 • (307) 332-1220 (fax)
human_resources@nols.edu

That is what learning is.
You suddenly understand something you've understood all your life, but in a new way.
—DORIS LESSING

THE OUTWARD BOUND EXPERIENCE

. . . .

> *There is more in us than we know. If we can be made to see it,*
> *perhaps, for the rest of our lives we will be unwilling to settle*
> *for less.*
>
> —KURT HAHN, FOUNDER OF OUTWARD BOUND

As a nonprofit education organization with five core programs that change lives, build teams, and transform schools, Outward Bound USA delivers action, adventure, and challenge in the wilderness, urban settings, workrooms, and classrooms to help students achieve their possibilities, and to inspire them to serve others and to care for the world around them. Outward Bound Wilderness, one of the five Outward Bound USA programs, is comprised of four wilderness schools that together offer over 750 wilderness-based courses—from backpacking and mountaineering to sailing and dogsledding— spanning twenty states across the nation.

Since the first wilderness school in the U.S. was established in 1961, over half a million people of all ages have participated in Outward Bound programs. Courses are designed to help people develop confidence, compassion, an appreciation for service to others, and a lasting relationship with the natural environment. Outward Bound is not a survival school. They do offer, however, a rugged adventure in the wilderness during which you will receive unparalleled training in wilderness skills. They provide a unique, rigorous curriculum, in which you will learn by doing and put your learning to the test daily. The four pillars of self-reliance, fitness, craftsmanship, and compassion are central to the Outward Bound experience.

Outward Bound will challenge you, both individually and as a member of a team, by taking you into unfamiliar territory and allowing you to apply your newfound knowledge and skills. Sometimes you may fail in your efforts. Facing failure and learning to overcome it through reasonable, responsible action is an essential part of the Outward Bound experience. Teammates and instructors provide the emotional support for you to try and, if you fail, to try again. Perseverance is the basis for the Outward Bound motto, "To serve, to strive, and not to yield."

WORKING FOR OUTWARD BOUND

Many factors influence the quality and success of a group's Outward Bound experience, but none is more important than the quality of the staff. Staff members are sensitive, highly skilled, energetic outdoor leaders who are committed to the Outward Bound philosophy. The majority of staff are educators who are also climbers, hikers, mountaineers, paddlers, and sailors with solid life experience. Although some staff work year-round; the majority of staff work seasonally while maintaining other careers. Above all, staff members possess one important outdoor skill—good judgment, or the ability to make sound, safe decisions under challenging circumstances.

TERRY MOORE

Positions include instructional staff, support staff, and volunteer positions. Instructors are paid on a per diem basis in the range of $40 to $125 per day (dependent on the position and wilderness school); support staff are paid hourly rates in the range of $7 to $12 per hour. Room and board are often available, and all staff may receive discounts on brand-name outdoor equipment and clothing. Most of the schools also have programs for corporate clientele. Facilitators are recruited to deliver these programs, some of which are classroom based, while others are more wilderness oriented.

Taking a course prior to working for Outward Bound is strongly encouraged and may be required, depending on the program to which you are applying. Some schools offer instructor development courses or internships that give you the skills you need to become an Outward Bound instructor. Below you'll find opportunities available at each school.

GENERAL INFORMATION: Outward Bound Wilderness, 910 Jackson St., Golden, CO 80401 • (866) 467-7640 • www.outwardboundwilderness.org

You gain strength, courage, and confidence by every experience in which you really stop to look fear in the face.
—ELEANOR ROOSEVELT

WILDERNESS SCHOOLS

HURRICANE ISLAND OUTWARD BOUND SCHOOL

Established initially as Outward Bound's landmark sailing program, the school now includes canoeing, backpacking, sea kayaking, rock climbing, and programs on a schooner, along with corporate, urban, and educational programs that provide challenge-course activities and expeditions. Seasonal opportunities are available in Maine and Maryland; Florida offers year-round opportunities working with at-risk and adjudicated youth, as well as a three-month internship program. See HIOBS—Outreach Programs on page 94 for details.

A kayaker learns about the four pillars of self-reliance, fitness, craftsmanship, and compassion taught at Outward Bound.

FOR MORE INFORMATION: Josie Howard, Human Resources Specialist, Hurricane Island Outward Bound School, 75 Mechanic St., Rockland, ME 04841 (866) 746-9771 • (207) 594-5548, ext. 388 • employment@hurricaneisland.org www.hiobs.org

NORTH CAROLINA OUTWARD BOUND SCHOOL

Since its beginnings in the rugged mountains of southern Appalachia, the school has expanded its programming to the North Carolina Outer Banks, Florida Ten Thousand Islands, Exumas Bahamas, and Patagonia. Students choose from a range of activities that include rock climbing, mountaineering, whitewater paddling, sea kayaking, and backpacking. The classic (and most popular) Outward Bound course is a twenty-one- to twenty-eight-day multi-activity program, although courses range in length from four to seventy-eight days.

Experienced wilderness instructors are hired to deliver challenging, adventure-based courses aimed at skill development and individual growth. People with experience rock climbing, white-water canoeing, sea kayaking, and leading wilderness trips are hired to oversee the operation of these program activities. Logistics staff and cooks work to keep the base camps running while providing support to instructors. The selection of new applicants begins in November, with most contracts offered in February or March. Most people work for the majority of the summer in their first season, with opportunities for additional off-season work that becomes available in late summer.

North Carolina Outward Bound also offers two training programs for people interested in getting into the outdoor field. The Outdoor Leader Course is designed for those over eighteen who would like to develop technical, leadership, and teaching skills to gain a position with a camp or outdoor organization. The more selective Instructor Apprenticeship Program is geared for those over twenty-one with diverse life skills and previous teaching experience. This program is designed to provide the necessary training and skills to begin working for North Carolina Outward Bound School. An instructor job application and interview are required to be considered for this program.

FOR MORE INFORMATION: Cameron Richardson, Staffing Director, North Carolina Outward Bound School, 2582 Riceville Rd., Asheville, NC 28805 (800) 850-7823 • (828) 299-3366, ext. 142 • staffing@ncobs.org www.ncoutwardbound.org/jobs

OUTWARD BOUND WEST

At the first Outward Bound School in the U.S., premier mountaineers, rock climbers, white-water boaters, desert "rats," and sea kayakers teach students the skills to tackle the rugged challenges of backcountry travel (with a focus on personal development through exceptional wilderness education) in Baja California and the western U.S. (including Alaska, California, Colorado, Idaho, New Mexico, Oregon, Utah, Washington, and Wyoming).

FOR MORE INFORMATION: Scott Joy, HR Coordinator, Outward Bound West, 910 Jackson St., Golden, CO 80401 • (888) 837-5209 • (720) 497-2394 sjoy@outwardboundwest.org • www.obwest.org/staff

VOYAGEUR OUTWARD BOUND SCHOOL

From the remote wilderness of Minnesota and Manitoba to the deserts and rivers of Texas and the Big Sky country of Montana, border-to-border adventures abound with Voyageur. With course areas in four states, Canada, and Mexico, Voyageur was also the first Outward Bound school to run women's, youth, and Life Career Renewal courses. Internships, which are offered in most of their program areas, begin with a training expedition in the given course area with a senior staff trainer. Interns are then involved in a variety of support roles in rock climbing, ropes courses, driving, logistics, and general base camp maintenance. Great training, room, board, a weekly stipend, and

Growth means change and change involves risks, stepping from the known to the unknown.
—GEORGE SHINN

pro-deal purchases are offered. Positions vary in length from five to nine weeks (generally from May through August) and are base camp focused. Assistant instructor positions are also available for those with a strong base of experience. Although positions are available in the fall, winter, and spring, these positions are generally filled by their summer pool (translation: work for them in the summer first!). All applicants must be at least twenty-one and very excited about working with both motivated youth and struggling teens.

FOR MORE INFORMATION: Staffing Director, Voyageur Outward Bound School, 101 E. Chapman St., Ely, MN 55731 • (800) 328-2943 • (218) 365-7790 staffing@vobs.com • www.vobs.org

BEYOND THE UNITED STATES

COSTA RICA RAINFOREST OUTWARD BOUND SCHOOL

Costa Rica Outward Bound has various staff and administration positions available throughout the year, including field instructor, surf instructor, student administrator, marketing positions, and webmaster. Candidates must have general outdoor education and leadership experiences or knowledge and make a commitment of eight to twelve months depending on position (although shorter-term possibilities may be available). Spanish fluency is definitely a plus. Send your resume and philosophy statement to begin the application process. As a nonprofit foundation, they are able to obtain volunteer visas for foreign staff. This type of visa prevents them from paying volunteers a salary; however, it does allow the school to cover airfare, room, board, and a cash stipend. Health insurance is provided under the ISIC card that is purchased for all foreign staff.

FOR MORE INFORMATION: Staffing Director,
Costa Rica Rainforest Outward Bound School,
SJO 829, Box 025216, Miami, FL 33102-5216 • (506) 777-1222
In Costa Rica: CRROBS, P.O. Box 243, Quepos, Costa Rica
info@crrobs.org • www.crrobs.org/employment

PACIFIC WHALE FOUNDATION

Ecotourism/Marine Science • Hawaii • Seasonal
www.pacificwhale.org

$

On behalf of the ocean and all of its life, the Pacific Whale Foundation is on the scene supporting and conducting responsible marine research while addressing marine conservation issues through activism and education. Millions of people have learned about whales, dolphins, and the marine environment through the foundation's environmental education programs, which include ecotourism cruises, comprehensive programs for grades K–12 in Hawaii's schools, and an Ocean Science Discovery Center on Maui's Ma'alaea Harbor.

WHAT YOU'LL BE DOING: Aboard one of the many ecotourism boat adventures, seasonal staff are the backbone of providing educational interpretation and respectful and appropriate encounters with marine life. Captains are responsible for the vessel, crew, and passengers while providing vessel maintenance, maritime training, line handling, and navigation. Ocean naturalists provide comprehensive presentations about local marine life to passengers on board, facilitate marine education programs, locate and observe marine life, and help passengers connect with the sea. Finally, pursers are responsible for food and beverage service, merchandise sales, and assisting with the passenger experience.

COMMITMENT: Positions are available throughout the year; however, April and November are peak hiring times.

PERKS AND REWARDS: Along with the benefits of experiencing intensive marine life, Hawaiian culture, and interpretive training courses, hourly wages start at $8 per hour for pursers and $10 per hour for ocean naturalists. The captain's wage is dependent on experience.

THE ESSENTIALS: Successful applicants must have excellent people skills, a positive attitude, and a team player mind-set. Due to the rigorous duties on a boat, applicants must also be able-bodied with the ability to lift fifty pounds. First aid and CPR certification and lifeguard training is a plus. Captains must hold a U.S. Coast Guard Master of Vessels 100-ton license from the State of Hawaii; ocean naturalists must have a four-year college degree in a scientific or natural science discipline.

The right time is anytime one is so lucky as to be alive.
—HENRY JAMES

YOUR FIRST MOVE: Send off an email to begin the application process; resumes are accepted year-round.

FOR MORE INFORMATION: Deserie Donae, Director of Naturalists, Pacific Whale Foundation, 300 Ma'alaea Rd., Suite 211, Wailuku, HI 96793 (808) 249-8811 • (808) 243-9021 (fax) • deserie@pacificwhale.org

PUTNEY STUDENT TRAVEL

Educational Travel • Worldwide • Summer
www.goputney.com

$ 🏕

Nicaragua. The Caribbean. Tanzania. Brazil. The U.S. . . . These are just a few of the locales you might venture off to this summer as an adventure travel guide for Putney Student Travel. Providing unusual education opportunities for small groups of secondary school students, Putney trip leaders focus either on cultural exploration, language learning, or community service trips over a four- to five-week period during the summer months. Applicants must be energetic, fun, creative, active, knowledgeable about the area they are visiting, and excited about spending time with high school students. Proficiency in the language of the host country is required, but there are no foreign language requirements for trips to the Caribbean and the U.S. Leaders will receive a stipend along with all their expenses paid (including round-trip airfare, housing, and meals). If you are excited about the prospect of helping students learn about a different culture this summer, send a resume (with the phone numbers and/or email addresses of three references) and a cover letter that addresses the following topics: language proficiency; travel experience and/or knowledge of host country; experience in leadership/organization, working with teenagers, and community service (if applicable); and personal strengths or skills that make you an exceptional leader.

FOR MORE INFORMATION: Kelsey Burns, Leadership Coordinator, Putney Student Travel, 345 Hickory Ridge Rd., Putney, VT 05346 • (802) 387-5885 (802) 387-4276 (fax) • kelsey@goputney.com

🐾 **INSIDER TIP: In addition to travel guide opportunities, Putney also recruits qualified instructors and residential staff for their summer Excel program at campuses in the U.S., Europe, and Cuba. These nontraditional enrichment programs provide high school students with insights into college life in an informal campus environment while fostering a balance of personal and intellectual growth. Salaries are competitive and all living expenses are paid.**

THE ROAD LESS TRAVELED

Adventure Travel • USA/Worldwide • Summer
www.theroadlesstraveled.com

$ 🏠 🌐

The Road Less Traveled encompasses summer wilderness adventure, community service programs, cultural awareness, and challenging coast-to-coast expeditions for teenagers. Participants venture to unique and culturally rich spots in Alaska, Australia, British Columbia, Costa Rica, Ecuador, Guatemala, India, Norway, Panama, and Peru. Trip leaders begin their summer with ten days of staff training in Larkspur, Colorado, then guide and engage participants in backpacking, ice and snow mountaineering, rock climbing, kayaking, white-water rafting, and desert hiking. Candidates must be at least twenty-one years of age, Wilderness First Responder (WFR) or Wilderness EMT (WEMT) certified, have experience working with teenagers, and have solid wilderness skills. Along with a salary (dependent upon experience), benefits include all living expenses during time of employment, full payment of WFR, WEMT, or EMT recertification (or $300 toward upgrade certification) upon successful completion of employment, pro-deal purchases for gear and clothing, and the opportunity to work with world-renowned and expert guides. Send off a cover letter and resume via fax, mail, or email to begin the application process. A personal interview and references are required.

FOR MORE INFORMATION: Jim Stein, Director, The Road Less Traveled, 2331 N. Elston Ave., Chicago, IL 60614-2907 • (800) 939-9839 (773) 342-5200 • (773) 342-5703 (fax) • employment@theroadlesstraveled.com

SAIL CARIBBEAN

Sailing/Diving/Marine Science • The Caribbean • Summer
www.sailcaribbean.com

$ 🏠 🌐

Voyaging throughout the British Virgin, Leeward, and Windward Islands in the Caribbean, Sail Caribbean leads groups of teenagers from around the globe on sailing and diving adventures. Students develop leadership skills and self-confidence by taking turns reading charts, hauling in the sails, chopping vegetables, or just getting to know one another aboard fifty-one-foot sailboats with teens of their own age group. Summer staff opportunities include captains, mates, marine biology teachers, dive masters, or scuba instructors, and activities range from instruction in curriculum and shipboard life to land activities and group dynamics. Applicants must have extensive sailing or diving credentials along with a strong background in working with teenagers. One full week of intensive training is provided in leadership skills, teaching methods, and safety techniques specific to Sail Caribbean. Benefits include a salary, room and board, and, of course, life in the Caribbean.

FOR MORE INFORMATION: Mike Liese, Director, Sail Caribbean, 79 Church St., Northport, NY 11768 • (800) 321-0994 • (631) 754-2202 • (631) 754-3362 (fax) info@sailcaribbean.com

SAN JUAN SAFARIS

Ecotourism • Washington • Summer
www.sanjuansafaris.com

$ 🏕

Destination San Juan Islands—a spectacular area of Washington where you might catch a glimpse of wild orca whales, see bald eagles soaring high overhead, or watch sea lions frolicking in a cove. That is, if you have the right guide. San Juan Safaris exposes small groups to wildlife through boating and sea kayaking tours where participants not only view wildlife in their natural habitat, but also gain a deeper understanding and appreciation for the habitat. Whether giving talks as a naturalist, leading sea kayaking lessons for guests, or working the docks or appointment desk, those who are hardworking, responsible, drug free, and outdoorsy thrive in this environment. Wages range from $8 to $12 per hour (plus tips!), along with a season-end bonus based on $2 per every hour worked. At the minimum, applicants must have a strong ecological awareness and first aid certification and be able to work long days. Send off a cover letter and resume to begin the application process.

FOR MORE INFORMATION: Colleen Johansen, Seasonal Employment Director, San Juan Safaris, P.O. Box 2749, Friday Harbor, WA 98250 • (800) 450-6858 (360) 378-1323 • (360) 378-6546 (fax) • fun@sanjuansafaris.com

SEMESTER AT SEA

Educational Travel • Worldwide • 3–4 Months
www.semesteratsea.com

$ 🏕 🌐

With Semester at Sea, you'll watch twenty-foot waves hit the bow of your "campus" (the MV *Explorer*), live with Chinese students in a dorm at the University of Beijing, stay at an "untouchable" village in India, learn about the life of the Masai while on safari in Kenya, attend an Afro-Venezuelan drum workshop, or study tropical rain forests while canoeing down the Amazon River. These international field experiences, coupled with a stimulating onboard classroom environment, make Semester at Sea an exceptional opportunity for learning for both staff and participants alike.

WHAT YOU'LL BE DOING: Staff positions are available as administrative assistant, assistant dean, AV/media coordinator (and assistant), bursar (financial operations), director of student life, field office coordinator (and assistant), information technology coordinator, librarian (and assistant), mental health professional, nurse, photographer, physician, resident director, secretary, security officer, and senior adult coordinator. In addition to regularly assigned duties, you'll be an integral part of the shipboard community, participating in all aspects of the program as your shipboard work schedule permits, as well as working on a limited number of in-port duty assignments, which may include serving as a trip leader for some of the field practicums.

COMMITMENT: Spring voyages depart from Vancouver in late January and return mid-May to Florida; summer voyages depart from Canada in early June and return mid-August to Florida; and fall voyages depart from the Bahamas in mid-September and return just before Christmas to Seattle.

PERKS AND REWARDS: A small stipend of $1,500 to $4,000 is provided along with room and board while on the ship. In addition, a $600 travel allowance is offered to help defray the cost of travel to and from the ports of embarkation and debarkation. Staff members are responsible for the cost of a passport, required visas (approximately $80 for U.S. citizens), and any required inoculations. Note that a spouse and/or dependent children may be able to accompany staff on the voyage for a fee of $2,000.

THE ESSENTIALS: The ideal applicants are those who support the concept of academic and personal enrichment through travel and education. Maximum flexibility, cooperation, and adaptability are essential traits of all applicants.

YOUR FIRST MOVE: Visit their website to view the most current information and to download an application (accepted on an ongoing basis). Applying for a single, specific voyage and expecting to be hired is not realistic. While personally it might be the best time for an individual's own needs, applicants are rarely hired right away. For most positions, there are between forty and sixty applications on file; thus, competition is very high. Some applicants wait several years before receiving an interview and applications remain active for three years.

FOR MORE INFORMATION: Staff Selection, Semester at Sea, 811 William Pitt Union, University of Pittsburgh, Pittsburgh, PA 15260 (800) 854-0195 • (412) 648-7490 • (412) 648-2298 (fax) info@semesteratsea.pitt.edu

Optimism is the faith that leads to achievement.
Nothing can be done without hope and confidence.
—HELEN KELLER

SUNTREK TOURS

Adventure Travel • USA/Canada/Mexico • 4–6 Months
www.suntrek.com

$ 🏕 ⊕

Have you ever wanted to adventure across North America with a small group of independent-minded and "young at heart" people like the old pioneers once did by tent and wagon? With Suntrek, trip leaders will have the opportunity to travel in fifteen-passenger maxi-vans (stocked with camping gear) while exploring isolated Indian villages and carved rock canyons, visiting famous national parks and frontier towns, and seeking out wilderness, wildlife, and western nightlife with their group. Leaders will arrange daily itineraries and activities, facilitate daily camp set-up and break-down, load and unload camping gear, work with local vendors to arrange activities, organize food shopping and cleaning, and proactively handle the varying dynamics and personalities of each group. Qualified applicants are asked to join one of Suntrek's training camps beginning in mid-April (operating every three weeks through July) and must be available for work through mid-October. In addition to extensive training, all leaders will receive a monthly stipend starting at $1,200 and accommodations. Along with having an interest in meeting and working with a diverse group of travelers as well as excellent organization and leadership skills, all applicants must be at least twenty-one with a clean driving record. Applications can be filled out online.

FOR MORE INFORMATION: Tiffani Lopez, Personnel Manager, Suntrek Tours, 77 W. 3rd St., Santa Rosa, CA 95401 • (800) 786-8735 • (707) 523-1800 (707) 523-1911 (fax) • personnel@suntrek.com

Prior to hitting the road in fifteen-passenger vans, Suntrek leaders take time to arrange daily itineraries and activities for their group.

TOUCH OF NATURE ENVIRONMENTAL CENTER

Wilderness Education • Illinois • Seasonal
www.pso.siu.edu/tonec

$ 🏕 ⊕

Since 1969, Touch of Nature's wilderness programs have provided outdoor education and recreation experiences for a wide variety of groups. Through wilderness settings, initiative courses, and adventure activities, the Spectrum Wilderness Program helps participants achieve self-confidence, self-reliance, cooperation, trust, and appreciation of the outdoors. Interns work and learn in most aspects of outdoor adventure programming, including backpacking, initiative courses, rock climbing, caving, and canoeing, including a thirty-day wilderness course with at-risk youth. A monthly stipend along with basic living quarters is provided. College graduates (or those nearing completion) who have wilderness training, first aid and CPR certification, and experience working with at-risk youth are encouraged to apply. This program works with a very challenging population in a wilderness setting. A strong desire to work with at-risk youth is important. Detailed information and applications are available online.

FOR MORE INFORMATION: Lisa Wait, Spectrum Wilderness Program Coordinator, Touch of Nature Environmental Center, Southern Illinois University, Mail Code 6888, Carbondale, IL 62901 6888 • (618) 453-1121, ext. 255 (618) 453-1188 (fax) • tonec@tonec.siu.edu

TRAILMARK OUTDOOR ADVENTURES

Adventure Education • USA • Summer
www.trailmark.com

$ 🏕

Throughout New England, Colorado, and the Northern Rockies, Trailmark runs summer adventure trips for teens ages eleven to sixteen—programs that foster a genuine family-like atmosphere. Three-leader teams will guide twelve to eighteen participants in activities that encompass rafting, biking, backpacking, horse packing, climbing, sailing, sea kayaking, and canoeing over a two- to three-week period. Well before the Trailmark summer begins, leaders participate in an intensive precamp training session to prepare and review the summer's activities and itineraries, and learn about teen-counseling issues. All leaders, who average twenty-five years of age, must have first aid,

CPR, and safety training. Many have been trained at Outward Bound and National Outdoor Leadership School (NOLS). Benefits include room, meals, and a competitive salary during the training period, while in the field, and between trips. Gear discounts and internships are also available. Additional compensation is provided for those who have Wilderness First Responder, Wilderness First Aid, or lifeguard certification. Staff applications can be downloaded online.

FOR MORE INFORMATION: Rusty and Donna Pedersen, Directors, Trailmark Outdoor Adventures, 16 Schuyler Rd., Nyack, NY 10960 • (800) 229-0262 (845) 358-0262 • (845) 348-0437 (fax) • staff@trailmark.com

✎ **INSIDER TIP: Trip leaders are experienced, talented, high-energy, and supportive people. We only select leaders who have extensive experience and the sensitivity and maturity to handle the needs of teenagers.**

TREKAMERICA

Adventure Travel • USA/Canada/Mexico • Summer
www.trekamerica.com
$ ⌂ ⊕

With over seventy itineraries, TrekAmerica offers active, small-group camping tours to foreign travelers (usually between the ages of eighteen and thirty-eight) that cover most of North America, including Canada, Alaska, and Mexico.

WHAT YOU'LL BE DOING: Tour leaders take their group in fifteen-passenger vehicles to national parks, cities, small towns, and everything in between. In a day's work, leaders must be prepared for driving, organizing activities, providing briefings and commentary, and leading a safe and enjoyable holiday for their passengers.

COMMITMENT: First-year leaders can normally expect to work from April through mid-September; longer seasons are possible in subsequent years. Each tour lasts from one to nine weeks, with a two- to three-day break between trips.

PERKS AND REWARDS: The base pay for first-year leaders is $1,100 per month, and all accommodation is provided during the season. The biggest perk, perhaps, is meeting interesting people from around the world and participating in a variety of adventure activities ranging from jeep tours to water sports on a complimentary basis.

THE ESSENTIALS: Applicants must be at least twenty-three with a clean driving record. The best applicants are outgoing, adventurous, and flexible, and have a considerable knowledge of North American history, geography, and culture. Knowledge of a foreign language is helpful, but not required. Leaders must participate in a three-week training process before leading any tours. While training, half wages are paid and all accommodations are provided.

YOUR FIRST MOVE: Call for application materials. Applications are accepted throughout the winter, spring, and early summer. Training takes place from April until the end of July with various start dates.

FOR MORE INFORMATION: Tavis Moses, Tour Leader Recruitment, TrekAmerica, Premiere International, P.O. Box 1338, Gardena, CA 90249 • (800) 345-8777 (310) 719-9877 • (310) 719-1478 (fax) • personnel@premiereops.com

U.S. NAVY MWR TRAINING BRANCH

Recreation • Worldwide • 3 Months
www.mwr.navy.mil/mwrprgms/intern.html

$ 🏠 🎓

The Morale, Welfare, and Recreation (MWR) Division of the U.S. Navy provides a variety of recreational and leisure programs and services to the worldwide navy community of sailors, their families, military reservists, and retired personnel. With the goal of offering programs that contribute to the "retention, readiness, and mental, physical, and emotional well-being of their sailors," MWR operates in twenty-four states in the U.S. and in thirteen countries abroad (including Bahrain, Iceland, Italy, Japan, Korea, and Spain). Students in their senior year of college (or grad students) have the opportunity to participate in MWR's intern program, with programs focusing on aquatics, child care and development, food and beverage, recreation, young adult programs, sports and fitness, and teen/youth activities. Applicants must have programming experience (paid or volunteer), be earning credit for an internship, have basic first aid and CPR certification, be mature and independent, and be an American citizen. Programs are offered for three months starting in January, May, and September. Housing and a weekly stipend of $150 to $250 are provided, and overseas interns also receive round-trip airfare. Application materials and a complete listing of opportunities can be found online.

FOR MORE INFORMATION: Robin McCord, Intern Program Manager, U.S. Navy MWR Training Branch, 5720 Integrity Dr. (P654C3), Millington, TN 38055-6540 • (901) 874-6726 • p654c3@persnet.navy.mil

If I were to begin life again, I should want it as it was.
I would only open my eyes a little more.
—JULES RENARD

U.S. OLYMPIC COMMITTEE

Sports • California/Colorado/New York • 10–16 Weeks
www.usolympicteam.com

$ ♨ 🎓 ✈

The U.S. Olympic Committee is a nonprofit organization dedicated to providing opportunities for American athletes as well as preparing and training those athletes for challenges that range from domestic competitions to the Olympic Games.

WHAT YOU'LL BE DOING: The internship program is designed to provide a quality work experience and a unique opportunity for exposure to the Olympic movement and spirit of Olympism in the U.S. The program offers internships in the areas of accounting, broadcasting, journalism, marketing, sports administration, and sport science (strength, conditioning, and performance). The majority of internships are at their headquarters in Colorado Springs; however, interns also might work at Lake Placid, New York, or Chula Vista, California.

COMMITMENT: Ten- to sixteen-week internships are available each season.

PERKS AND REWARDS: A stipend plus housing and meals at Olympic training centers (where the athletes live) on a double-occupancy basis equal an hourly wage of $8.50. Interns have free use of the strength and conditioning gym and other athletic facilities.

THE ESSENTIALS: Applicants must be enrolled in an undergraduate or graduate program and have completed at least two years of college before the start of their internship. Most who get accepted into the program have a GPA of 3.0 or higher and have good writing skills. Work experience, volunteer experience, and college extracurricular activities are seriously considered in the selection process. Internships are very competitive.

YOUR FIRST MOVE: Send off an email to have an application packet mailed to you. Applications must be received by these dates: winter/spring—October 1; summer—February 15; and fall—June 1. Late or incomplete applications will not be considered. You will be notified four to eight weeks after submitting your application.

FOR MORE INFORMATION: Student Intern Program, U.S. Olympic Committee, 1 Olympic Plaza, Colorado Springs, CO 80909-5760 • (719) 632-2597 (719) 866-4817 (fax) • internprog@usoc.org

VISIONS SERVICE ADVENTURES

Combining outdoor adventure with community service, a VISIONS Service Adventures team works with locals on a construction project in Peru.

VISIONS SERVICE ADVENTURES

Service Adventures • Worldwide • 6–10 Weeks
www.visionsserviceadventures.com

$ 🏠 ⊕

VISIONS Service Adventures offers teens a summer service experience in Australia, the British Virgin Islands, Dominica, the Dominican Republic, Ecuador, Guadeloupe, Peru, and the U.S. (Alaska Athabaskan villages, Montana Plains Indian reservations, and the Sea Islands in South Carolina). A VISIONS summer integrates construction-based community service and cross-cultural living and learning (including language immersion and a home-stay in selected sites) in coed residential programs of up to twenty-five high school students and six staff. Students and staff live in schools or other local buildings in the heart of the host community.

WHAT YOU'LL BE DOING: Are you ready to be challenged physically, mentally and emotionally? Serving as mentors, summer trip leaders and specialists supervise groups of teens in a residential living setting and during commu-nity-service projects. You may teach participants building techniques, basic carpentry or masonry skills, and outdoor activities such as backpacking, rock climbing, and rafting, and introduce them to and facilitate cross-cultural activities and experiences.

Fear is an emotion indispensable for survival.
—HANNAH ARENDT

COMMITMENT: Staff positions are available for six, seven, or ten weeks during the summer months.

PERKS AND REWARDS: Stipends for staff positions start at $245 per week (dependent on position and experience) with benefits that include housing, meals, and travel to and from the program site.

THE ESSENTIALS: All staff applicants must be at least twenty-two years old and have current first aid and CPR certification, experience leading or teaching teenagers, a safe driving record, solid interpersonal skills, enthusiasm for working with teens, and a sense of humor. Carpentry or masonry skills and/or advanced first aid certification are also sought for some positions. Spanish fluency is required for the Dominican Republic, Ecuador, and Peru; French fluency for Guadeloupe. VISIONS typically employs teachers, graduate students and Ph.D. candidates, returned Peace Corps volunteers, and experiential outdoor educators.

YOUR FIRST MOVE: Send in your application (which can be downloaded online), cover letter, and resume (including three work references). Applications are accepted starting in November for the following season.

FOR MORE INFORMATION: Joanne Pinaire and Teena Beutel, Directors, VISIONS Service Adventures, P.O. Box 220, Newport, PA 17074-0220 (800) 813-9283 • (717) 567-7313 • (717) 567-7853 (fax) info@visionsserviceadventures.com

WESTCOAST CONNECTION

Adventure Travel • USA/Australia/Canada/Europe • Summer
www.westcoastconnection.com

$ 🏕

White-water raft the Colorado river . . . catch a ball game in San Francisco . . . tour the famous Las Vegas strip . . . snowboard the Swiss Alps. Got your attention? Since 1982, Westcoast Connection has been providing three- to six-week summer travel experiences for teenagers (ages thirteen to nineteen) across the U.S., Australia, Canada, and Europe. With the goal of providing each tour group the "summer of a lifetime," the summer staff consists of a tour director, a food director, and up to five tour leaders/specialists. Duties for all positions include tour member supervision, meal/snack preparation and cleanup, itinerary management, coordination of various sports and programs, and a multitude of other camp counselor–type duties. Lodging, meals, transportation, activities, and a weekly stipend of $100 to $400 are provided. If you are motivated, hardworking, energetic, and have experience working with young people, grab an application today.

FOR MORE INFORMATION: Alli Kaye, Assistant Director, Westcoast Connection, 154 E. Boston Post Rd., Mamaroneck, NY 10543 • (800) 550-0905 (914) 835-0905 • (914) 835-0798 (fax) • staff@westcoastconnection.com

WHITE PASS & YUKON ROUTE RAILROAD

Train • Alaska • Summer
www.whitepassrailroad.com

$ 🏠 ⊕

All Aboard! Born in the scramble of the 1898 gold rush, the White Pass & Yukon Route (WP&YR) remains a rare nugget in the annals of railroad history. Prior to its golden beginnings, a mountain range—huge and looming—stood between a prospector and his fortune. But with a will, there's always a way,

and soon enough, construction began on a narrow gauge railroad—an engineering marvel that traverses some of the world's most breathtaking terrain. Through the years, the WP&YR has enjoyed a rich and colorful history, and today, modern-day "prospectors" get to enjoy an unforgettable trip through gold rush history with the help of the WP&YR summer staff team. By far, becoming a tour guide is the most interesting of positions (unless you don't enjoy making an entertaining presentation to over five hundred people).

With snowcapped mountain peaks in the background, summer staff aboard the White Pass & Yukon Route Railroad have the opportunity to view and explore some of Alaska's incredible terrain.

CHRISTIAN RACICH

If you wait to do everything until you're sure it's right, you'll probably never do much of anything.
—WIN BORDEN

Other positions include gift shop clerks, baristas (can you make a "triple dry cap"?), stockers, shuttle drivers, and ticket agents. Along with competitive wages, reasonably priced housing is provided. Applicants must be available for work from May 1 through late September. Applications are available online or call for more information.

FOR MORE INFORMATION: Beth Cline, Assistant Manager, White Pass & Yukon Route Railroad, P.O. Box 435, Skagway, AK 99840-0435 • (800) 343-7373 (907) 983-2217 (907) 983-2734 (fax) info@whitepass.net

WILDERNESS ADVENTURE AT EAGLE LANDING

Adventure Education • USA/Worldwide • 3 Months+
www.wilderness-adventure.com

$ 🏠

With a focus on developing leadership, confidence, self-esteem, and teamwork for its participants (ages nine to eighteen), Wilderness Adventure offers one- to four-week courses that involve everything from rock climbing and kayaking to cultural immersion and environmental education. After a mandatory orientation and staff training beginning in mid-May, trip leaders guide their group (twelve participants and two leaders) by foot, canoe, bike, or kayak and engage them in a variety of adventurous activities from site to site each day. First-year leaders are based out of Virginia, although there are future opportunities to lead trips in West Virginia, Alaska, British Columbia, Ecuador, Puerto Rico, and Vietnam. Additional seasonal positions include activity instructors and a variety of base camp support staff. A typical summer wage is $2,400, with benefits that include room and board, training and trip experience, discounted wilderness medical courses and gear purchases, and the opportunity to extend seasonal contracts through November (or year-round!). Senior trip leaders must be at least twenty-one years of age (nineteen for other positions), have backpacking or camping experience and their own gear, and a desire to teach children in the wild. Applications are available online.

FOR MORE INFORMATION: Pete Eshelman, Director of Operations, Wilderness Adventure at Eagle Landing, P.O. Box 760, New Castle, VA 24127 (800) 782-0779 • (540) 864-6792 • (540) 864-6800 (fax) info@wilderness-adventure.com

WILDERNESS INQUIRY

Adventure Travel · Worldwide · 3–5 Months
www.wildernessinquiry.org

$ 🏕 ⊕

Wilderness Inquiry is a nonprofit organization that focuses on getting individuals of all ages, backgrounds, and abilities to experience the natural world in destinations throughout the world. Whether by canoe, sea kayak, dogsled, horse pack, or backpack, trips are integrated to include lots of different folks. It's the unique mix of people and places that makes each trip a special experience.

WHAT YOU'LL BE DOING: Trail leaders and assistant leaders are responsible for organizing and leading trips primarily throughout North America, with the chance to travel to Costa Rica or Australia. Rigorous adventures are par for the course, with groups usually traveling five to twenty miles per day. Over the course of a single trip, trail leaders may fill the roles of pack horse, teacher, rehabilitation specialist, folksinger, chef, personal-relationship counselor, storyteller, disciplinarian, dishwasher, and bush doctor. Canoe workshop staff either teach the basics of canoeing at community festivals across Minnesota and Wisconsin or lead three-hour Mississippi River trips. Internships are also available in outdoor recreation and experiential education, outreach and public relations, training, and fund-raising and development.

COMMITMENT: Trip leader positions are seasonal, from December through April and June through September; canoe workshop staff must make a time commitment ranging from three to twenty days per month; and internships are offered year-round, from twenty to forty hours per week for a minimum of six weeks.

PERKS AND REWARDS: Depending on the position, staff members can earn anywhere from $35 up to $140 per day, along with meals while working and staff housing between trips. Full-timers also receive full benefits. The best perk has to be the opportunity to participate in outdoor adventures in locations around the globe.

THE ESSENTIALS: Individuals with previous experience working outdoors and with people with disabilities are desired. Leaders and canoe staff must have certain certifications (Wilderness First Responder, lifeguard training, CPR,

There's magic in you. Let it out. **123**
—DAVID BROWER

and current driver's license) and be sensitive and responsible, have good judgment and a sense of humor, and be competent in providing training in all aspects of wilderness travel and living.

YOUR FIRST MOVE: Send a resume, cover letter, three references, and application. Application materials are available for download (in PDF format) through their website.

FOR MORE INFORMATION: Stephanie Schmit, Administration Director, Wilderness Inquiry, 808 14th Ave. SE, Minneapolis, MN 55414-1516 (800) 728-0719 • (612) 676-9400 • (612) 676-9401 (fax) stephschmit@wildernessinquiry.org

WILDERNESS VENTURES

Adventure Travel • Worldwide • Summer
www.wildernessventures.com

$ 🏕

Since the early 1970s, Wilderness Ventures has been leading wilderness travel adventures in a variety of environments for students between the ages of thirteen and twenty. Each summer, trip leaders hit the road and take groups of up to thirteen students on backpacking, climbing, canoeing, rafting, biking, mountaineering, kayaking, sailing, and service project trips to places all across the U.S. and as far away as Australia, Costa Rica, Ecuador, and Europe. Responsibilities include teaching outdoor skills, minimum-impact camping, environmental awareness, and natural and cultural history. Applicants should have experience and an interest in the outdoors, but it is even more important to value working with teenagers. If your goal is to climb the Grand Teton, this is not the job for you. Your goal should be helping teenagers get up the Grand Teton, and helping them to learn about themselves and others at the same time. All applicants must be at least twenty-one and have valid CPR and Wilderness First Responder certifications. A nice wage and all trip expenses are provided. Applications can be downloaded from their website or send off your resume to begin the application process.

FOR MORE INFORMATION: Personnel Coordinator, Wilderness Ventures, P.O. Box 2768, Jackson Hole, WY 83001 • (800) 533-2281 • (307) 733-2122 (307) 739-1934 (fax) • staff@wildernessventures.com

WINDSOR MOUNTAIN INTERNATIONAL

Adventure Travel/General Camp • New Hampshire • Summer
www.windsormountain.org

$ ⚐ ⊕

Since 1961, more than ten thousand young people have explored the world Windsor Mountain style. Whether participants join the residential summer camp in New Hampshire or participate in a community service or travel program throughout the world, Windsor Mountain campers and students learn by doing. They enrich their lives with lasting friendships, new skills, self-discoveries, and increased environmental and cultural awareness.

WHAT YOU'LL BE DOING: The International Summer Camp is a creative community of 180 boys and girls (ages nine to fifteen) and 60 staff members from all over the world. Counselor opportunities abound at Windsor Mountain—from outdoor adventures and land sports to dance, woodworking, and gardening. Travel leaders take to the road with small groups of twelve to sixteen students and explore new and unusual environments, learn new skills, and challenge themselves physically and intellectually. These programs focus on a traveling theatre performance show, adventure or wilderness experiences, coastal environmental studies, cycling, horsemanship, leadership training, and community service in the U.S. and abroad.

COMMITMENT: Camp counselors must make a ten-week commitment beginning in early June; travel leaders can opt for either a three-week or six-week program.

PERKS AND REWARDS: Camp position wages range from $1,300 to $2,200 for the summer; travel leader wages range from $1,500 to $3,125. All staff members receive room, board, pro-deal purchases, and extensive training.

THE ESSENTIALS: Summer camp applicants must be at least twenty years of age and have finished one year of college as well as have experience teaching children and expertise in one of the many activities Windsor Mountain provides. Travel leader applicants must be at least twenty-four years of age, with expertise in teaching theatre, visual arts, outdoor adventure, language (French or Spanish), or environmental education, along with the ability to work with small groups of teenagers.

YOUR FIRST MOVE: Send your resume and a cover letter requesting a staff application packet (or you can download an application online). It's best to apply by January.

FOR MORE INFORMATION: David Love, Staffing Manager, Windsor Mountain International, One World Way, Windsor, NH 03244 • (603) 478-3166, ext. 17 (603) 478-5260 (fax) • mail@windsormountain.org

Things don't change, only the way you look at them.   **125**
—CARLOS CASTANEDA

THE WORLD OUTDOORS

Adventure Travel • USA/Worldwide • Seasonal
www.theworldoutdoors.com

$ ⚑ ⊕

Since 1988, the World Outdoors has been offering high-quality services to individuals seeking adventure in the outdoors while learning the skills necessary to enjoy these activities. Sampler and multisport adventures combine hiking, sea kayaking, rock climbing, canyoneering, white-water rafting, horseback riding, or mountain biking all over the Rockies and the Southwest, as well as escapes to Alaska and Hawaii, Australia, Belize, Canada, Costa Rica, Cuba, the Dominican Repulic, Mexico, and New Zealand.

WHAT YOU'LL BE DOING: Tour leaders guide groups in backcountry biking, hiking, and multisport adventures, which feature both inn-to-inn and camping retreats over a six- to eight-day period. Yes, this means you might pedal along the shores of glacier-fed lakes, hike through an ancient rain forest, paddle the white water of a raging river, and sea kayak among sea lions all in the same trip! Internships are also available for those who are interested in the programming aspects of their activities.

COMMITMENT: In-depth guide training is held each April. Most leaders spend two to four weeks per month on tour, with time off between trips, through October. A first-year leader can expect to work six to ten trips.

PERKS AND REWARDS: Tour leader wages begin at $60 per day (on up to $100 per day), along with room and board during each trip. Tips from guests can also be expected, ranging from $200 to $400 per trip. All staff are expected to find their own living arrangements between trips.

THE ESSENTIALS: Work as a tour leader is exciting and demanding. Those who have excellent people skills, thorough regional knowledge, and thrive in social situations fit the basic profile of their guides. Applicants must be at least twenty-one years old and, at a minimum, have Wilderness First Responder or equivalent certification. Leaders must also provide their own mountain bikes, helmets, first aid kits, bike racks, and other personal gear (which can be purchased through a discount program).

FOR MORE INFORMATION: Greg Jones, Director of Operations, The World Outdoors, 2840 Wilderness Place, Boulder, CO 80301
(800) 488-8483 • (303) 413-0938 • (303) 413-0926 (fax)
gregj@theworldoutdoors.com

HOSTEL-STYLE ADVENTURES

Suppose that the thoughtful young people of all countries could be provided with suitable meeting places where they could get to know each other. That could and must be the role of our youth hostels, not only in Germany, but throughout the world, building a bridge of peace from nation to nation.

—RICHARD SCHIRRMANN,
FATHER OF THE HOSTELING MOVEMENT

Short of camping on the roadside, hostels are by far the least expensive places to rest your weary head for the night, with costs ranging from $5 to $50 per night. The six thousand hostels scattered across the globe vary widely, from lighthouses, tree forts, and home hostels to ranch bunkhouses, Victorian buildings, mountain huts, and medieval castles—each with a personality and charm of its own.

One thing is certain about hostels: they are usually crammed with other budget-conscious folks and happy wanderers who are looking for the same things that you are—adventure and excitement. Many hostels are dormitory-style and separated by gender, while others offer private rooms (for a few dollars more) for those traveling together or if you desire a good night's rest. Hostels generally supply a bed and a blanket; you just need to bring your own sleepsack (or sleeping bag). Many provide do-it-yourself kitchens, lockers, laundry facilities, and common areas where you can discuss global events with people from the world over.

Hosteling is perhaps best described as traveling cheaply with an adventurous spirit. You see the world from a perspective that the average tourist will never see. You meet local people, learn customs, eat local food, and often have opportunities to do things you never imagined. Budget hotels, pensions (family-owned inns), university dorms, and bed-and-breakfasts provide alternatives to hostels for the same or slightly higher costs.

FINDING OUT MORE

Been there, done that? If you've explored the world hostel-style, you can now share your enthusiasm with others by volunteering at one of the many

hostels throughout the U.S. with the help of Hostelling International–USA (HI-USA). Positions range from travel workshop presenters and information center specialists to community service leaders and event hosts. If you have a skill, there's a good chance they'll have a position for you. Beyond meeting fellow volunteers and hostelers from around

If you always do what you've done, you'll always get what you've always got. **127**
—LARRY WILSON

the world, you can accrue hours toward free hostel overnights, free memberships, and travel service discounts. The national office has a searchable database of current opportunities. Visit www.hiusa.org/about/employment.cfm or contact Hostelling International–USA, 8401 Colesville Rd., Suite 6000, Silver Spring, MD 20910; (301) 495-1240, members@hiusa.org, www.hiusa.org.

➤ **INSIDER TIP: An investment in a HI-USA membership will help get you connected to the hosteling movement. A one-year membership card is $28, which includes a complimentary guide to HI-USA hostels in Canada and the U.S., plus newsletters from a regional office. Membership also allows you to receive discounts while staying at HI-USA sponsored hostels.**

> *The word hostel does not describe a place; it describes an attitude, a philosophy, a coming together of culturally diverse people sharing the wonders, high and low, of the traveling adventure.*
> —JANET THOMAS, AUTHOR OF
> *AT HOME IN HOSTEL TERRITORY*
> (ALASKA NORTHWEST BOOKS; $12.95)

Many travelers have also turned their short stay at a hostel into a three- to six-month work experience. For instance, the Malta Youth Hostels Association operates a year-round work camp and focuses on helping people who come in need of shelter. Volunteers, aged sixteen to thirty, may receive free lodging and use of the kitchen for two weeks to three months in exchange for three hours of work per day on various projects including hostel maintenance and administration. To apply, send three international reply coupons (which you can get at a local post office) or $2, and detailed information and an application form will be sent to you. Your completed application should be received at least three months prior to your arrival date. Malta Youth Hostels Association Workcamp, 17, Triq Tal-Borg, Pawla, PLA 06, Malta; (011) 356 2169 3957, myha@keyworld.net.

> *For a moment we smile, striving to pull down barriers quickly. Strangers becoming friends, we only have a small amount of time. Tomorrow . . . you go north, I go south. Adventures in travel, seeking new experiences. This moment is special. Our lives were meant to touch, to share. My life is richer because I have met you. There have been so many people like you in the youth hostels of the world.*
> —REDWOOD NATIONAL PARK
> YOUTH HOSTEL JOURNAL

GATHERING MORE INFO

Everything you ever wanted to know about hosteling and the hostel movement can be found at Hostels.com. Along with advice, stories, budget travel resources, and a backpacker bookstore, visitors can search for information on any hostel in the world.

A must for information on cheap places to sleep in the U.S. and Canada is Jim Williams's *The Hostel Handbook* (www.hostelhandbook.com). This guide provides contact information and prices for more than six hundred Hostelling International hostels, independent hostels, and backpacker's bungalows. The information is extremely fresh, with a new edition of this pocket-sized guide released early every year (usually in March). A lifelong traveler and incredible cook, the author keeps busy by running his own hostel, the Sugar Hill International House, in New York City (which is conveniently located off the A-train express near 145th Street). If you do stay at his hostel, be sure to ask about the "six barstool" Texas Star, which serves up great food at 1950s prices. His handbook is available at independent hostels, bookstores, or by sending a check or money order for $6 (which includes shipping) directly to the author: Jim Williams, 730 St. Nicholas Ave., New York, NY 10031; (212) 926-7030, infohostel@aol.com.

From hostels that provide a real family spirit to those you might want to bypass altogether, *Hostels USA* (Globe Pequot Press, $15.95) details more than three hundred hostels throughout the country. With a new edition released every other year, this comprehensive and witty guide provides engaging descriptions, stories, and guest comments that will assist everyone from the "serious" hosteler to those who might want a romantic getaway. Author Paul Karr also has an entourage of other hostel guides that will take you beyond North America.

Are you headed to Canada? Backpackers Hostels Canada (www.backpackers.ca) provides links to hostels, retreat centers, campgrounds, guest houses, college residences, and hostel farms throughout North America (including the U.S. and Mexico). Accommodations generally run about CAN$17 to CAN$22 per person.

BEYOND HOSTELS—
UNIQUE LODGING ARRANGEMENTS

While driving through Arizona, plan on a side trip to Arcosanti (details on page 316), an experimental town in the high desert, just seventy miles north of Phoenix. Learn about Paolo Soleri's concept of arcology (the synthesis of architecture and ecology), tour the grounds, or purchase one of the world-famous Soleri Bells. Concerts and other events in the Colly Soleri Music Center also allow visitors to experience Arcosanti. Shows include dinner and are often followed by a light show on the opposite mesa. Limited overnight

Never take a step backward, not even to gain momentum.
—ANDY GARCIA

guest accommodations are available by reservation. The simple guest rooms, beginning at $20 a night, provide no-frills accommodations. The Sky Suite, at $75 a night, includes a kitchenette and a panoramic view of this beautiful valley.

If you ever imagined stepping into a simpler lifestyle, without worry of rent or making a living, you might check out the opportunities listed in *The Caretaker Gazette* (www.caretaker.org). Each issue of this unique bimonthly newsletter (with weekly email updates) lists more than 150 caretaker and house-sitting positions throughout the U.S. and as far away as Australia and Costa Rica, at properties including estates, farms, ranches, resort homes, or even a private island. Yes, that's over one thousand opportunities per year! Duties range from general house and property upkeep to land restoration, cooking, and organic farming. Caretakers are provided with free housing and some positions include meals and salaries. A one-year subscription is available for $29.95. Visit the Gazette online or call (830) 336-3939.

Looking to rejuvenate the spirit and soul or possibly just an unconventional lodging arrangement on your next journey? *Sanctuaries: The Complete United States* by Marcia and Jack Kelly (Bell Tower, $18) features over 1,200 monasteries, abbeys, and retreat centers. Although the guide focuses mainly on Catholic and Episcopalian havens, it's also filled with Buddhist, Hindu, Sufi, and other faith-based places to find quiet and seclusion.

INSIDER TIP: For a longer-term hiatus to rejuvenate the soul, you might consider spending some time at a retreat center. Work-study programs are offered at a variety of ecovillages, monasteries, yoga institutes, and Zen centers throughout the world. Explore your options in the Food for the Soul section on page 325.

To the full-time RVer, home is where you park it. In years past, RVers were synonymous with retired folks, but there is a growing trend of people of all ages taking to the road in search of recreation, friendships, new opportunities, and exciting jobs, while traveling around in motor homes and travel trailers. *Workamper News,* published bimonthly, provides information on short-term jobs and opportunities in places all around the country specifically for those who travel RV-style. Yearly subscriptions run $25, and a sampler of listings is provided on their website (which includes a bookshop with other pertinent RV resources and guides). For an extra $1 per month, you can also view the online Workamper Hotline, which consists of immediate job openings from coast to coast. Greg and Debbie Robus, Workamper News, 709 W. Searcy St., Heber Springs, AR 72543-3761; (800) 446-5627, info@workamper.com, www.workamper.com.

RECOMMENDED RESOURCES

Attention aspiring sailors—with the **American Sailing Association** (ASA) you can obtain online information for over 250 ASA schools (many of which offer weeklong courses), sailing clubs, and charter companies throughout the world. For more information contact the American Sailing Association, P.O. Box 12079, Marina del Rey, CA 90295; (310) 822-7171, info@american-sailing.com, www.american-sailing.com.

The **Association for Experiential Education** (AEE) is a great way to begin your journey in experiential/outdoor education, and their website (www.aee.org) will fill in all the details. You'll learn about the benefits of becoming a member ($55 for students) or how to get involved in their next regional or international conference (a great way to network). In addition, AEE's Jobs Clearinghouse Online will provide you with information on hundreds of current seasonal, internship, and career jobs in the field. AEE can also be reached by calling (303) 440-8844.

If you're on a starboard tack and the wind veers, will you get lifted or headed? You'll learn the answer to this question and much more by enrolling in **Offshore's Learn to Sail** program. This adventure-based vacation offers invaluable lessons and satisfying experiences on the ABCs of sailing. In less than a week, you will be able to handle a sailboat of up to thirty feet without an instructor or paid skipper. The curriculum is based on seeing it, learning it, and then going out and doing it. Eleven school locations can be found in Florida, New Jersey, New York, Rhode Island, and the Bahamas, St. Martins, and Tortola in the Caribbean. For more information contact the Offshore Sailing School, 16731 McGregor Blvd., Fort Myers, FL 33908; (800) 221-4326, sail@offshore-sailing.com, www.offshore-sailing.com.

Are you building an adventurous career? **Wilderdom** (which refers to "natural living") provides career advice and job listings in the outdoor, environmental, and adventure education fields (www.wilderdom.com/joblistings.html).

Avoiding danger is no safer in the long run than outright exposure.
Life is either a daring adveture or nothing.
—HELEN KELLER

The luckiest people in the world are those who get to do all year round what they most like to do during their summer vacation.
—MARK TWAIN

CHAPTER 5

CAMPS, RANCHES, AND RESORT JOBS

Getting paid for what you love to do is the common theme within the pages of this chapter. Whether you're guiding kids at a summer camp, teaching adults how to ski at a resort, or strumming your guitar at the nightly campfire of a dude ranch, this chapter will provide you with insights and options for taking part in unique opportunities in enticing places.

UNIQUE OPPORTUNITIES TO EXPLORE IN THIS CHAPTER

- Are you ready to feel like a kid again—but with a lot more responsibility? Thousands of camp counselors travel to unique places each summer to share their skills, talents, and zest for life while mentoring, inspiring, and teaching kids in the pursuit of adventure and fun. Whether teaching surf classes (page 203) or academic and personal growth skills (page 200), or perhaps leading global awareness workshops (page 166) or making musical instruments (page 153), you'll have plenty of exciting programs to explore in this chapter.

- Participation in meditation, yoga, and a Native American pipe and sweat-lodge ceremony are just a few of the unique opportunities that lie within a special place called Hidden Creek Ranch (page 161).

- Explore the wonders of the Florida Keys, a place once inhabited by Indians and pirates, and minutes from the most extensive living coral reef in North America. Instructors and camp counselors at Seacamp help participants gain a better understanding of the natural features of the ocean and its ecosystems, along with instructing them in activities ranging from sailing to scuba (page 174).

- Are you looking for a winter filled with glades, half-pipes, parks, bowls, and cruisers? What's that, you ask? Yes, skiers and snowboarders have a jargon of their own—just one of the many things you'll learn by working at a ski resort. A special section beginning on page 176 profiles some of the best ski resorts in the U.S. along with details on the work, the rewards, and landing the job.

EAGLE'S NEST FOUNDATION

Fresh air, mountain music, laughter, love, and unique learning experiences abound at Eagle's Nest Camp (page 153). This summer counselor demonstrates the art of raku firing to a camper at the natural arts arena.

This is just one of twenty-three pools interns can enjoy on their time off at Amelia Island Plantation.

AMELIA ISLAND PLANTATION

AMELIA ISLAND PLANTATION

Resort • Florida • 4–12 Months
www.aipfl.com

$ 🎓

Amelia Island Plantation (AIP), a 1,350-acre resort and private residential community in Florida, offers miles of sandy beach in a preserved natural setting and many amenities—just imagine twenty-three swimming pools and three eighteen-hole golf courses at one locale! Four- to twelve-month internships for college juniors and seniors are available throughout the year, and a sixteen-week minimum commitment is preferred. Positions are offered in a variety of resort areas, including accommodations, aquatics, conference services, culinary, environmental interpretation, food and beverage, golf, human resources and staff development, marketing, recreation, and tennis. A weekly housing stipend of $250 and two meals per workday are provided for most positions; others are paid an hourly wage. Perks include assistance in locating housing, extensive training, use of the resort's amenities, and discounts on just about everything. Previous related experience, paid or unpaid, is a plus; a clean driving record is a requirement for most positions; and all candidates must be receiving school credit for their experience, be fluent in conversational English, and provide their own transportation. Further information and applications can be obtained online, through email, or by calling. Along with a completed application, a cover letter and resume are also necessary. Be sure to indicate your area of interest and when you are available. It's best to apply at least two months before the start date.

FOR MORE INFORMATION: Amei Hugo, Internship/International Coordinator, Amelia Island Plantation, P.O. Box 3000, Amelia Island, FL 32035-3000 (904) 277-5904 • (904) 491-4345 (fax) • intern@aipfl.com

It doesn't happen all at once. . . . You become.
It takes a long time. —MARGERY WILLIAMS

> INSIDER TIP: We have over twenty years experience in offering internships, and many interns have stayed on full-time with AIP afterward. AIP's former interns include our recreation director, human resources director, training manager, golf pros, guest services supervisors, conference services managers, assistant spa director, and many more. We'd love to add you to our list!

AMERICAN CAMP ASSOCIATION— NEW YORK

General Camp • Northeast • Summer
www.acampjob4u.org

$ 🏕

Are you looking for the perfect summer camp job? The American Camp Association—New York can assist you in finding a summer camp job with one of their member camps throughout the Northeast, from Pennsylvania to Maine. Camps typically operate from mid-June through late August, with job opportunities that include general counselors, activity specialists, outdoor adventure leaders, support staff, and many more. Room, board, and a salary are always provided for residential-camp positions. Day camp applicants must live within commuting distance; thus room and board are not provided. If you are at least eighteen years of age, have a love for the great outdoors, enjoy

working with children, and want to experience a memorable summer, apply online and get ready for the summer of a lifetime.

FOR MORE INFORMATION:

Robin Katz Wenczl
Camp Staffing Services Director
American Camp Association—New York
1375 Broadway, 4th Floor
New York, NY 10018
(800) 777-2267 • (212) 391-5208
(212) 391-5207 (fax)
robin@aca-ny.org

Challenging campers to make it to the top of a climbing wall is just one of the many activities for an American Camp Association summer staff member.

ASPEN RANCH

Therapeutic Community • Utah • 3 Months+
www.aspenranch.com

$ 🏠

Located in rural Utah next to Capitol Reef National Park, Aspen Ranch is a residential treatment center for troubled teens between the ages of thirteen and seventeen who need to make positive changes in their lives. Experiential learning happens constantly on the ranch—whether the students are in school, participating in the therapeutic horse program, on the ropes course, or in their dormitories. Along with offering a variety of flexible short- and long-term job opportunities, the ranch hires residential staff members who are responsible for supervision, activities, homework help, and experiential and therapeutic groups, including the therapeutic horse program and ropes course. Benefits include competitive pay, full-coverage health and dental insurance (after ninety days), and meals while on shift. While housing is not provided, it is available for a fee. Those who are over twenty-one years of age, self-motivated, physically active enough to work in a ranch environment, and interested in helping teenagers will thrive at the ranch. Contact the ranch for application details.

FOR MORE INFORMATION: Ramola Harding, Human Resources, Aspen Ranch, 2000 West Dry Valley, Loa, UT 84747 • (877) 231-0734 • (435) 836-1104 (435) 836-2277 (fax) • rharding@theaspenranch.com

BEAVER RUN RESORT

Resort • Colorado • Seasonal
www.beaverrun.com

$ 🏠 ⊕

With skiing at Breckenridge Ski Resort out your back door during the winter months and hiking, mountain biking, fly-fishing, white-water rafting, and outdoor music festivals during the summer, Beaver Run Resort is the perfect destination for the outdoor enthusiast. A variety of hospitality, guest services, and lodging positions, as well as college internships, are offered seasonally. Wages start at $8.50 per hour and limited employee housing in shared, fully furnished apartments (two to three people per room) is available for $300 to $350 per person per month. The latest openings, along with application materials, can be found online. Applicants are encouraged to stop in for a personal interview.

It is good to realize that if love and peace can prevail on earth, and if we can teach our children to honor nature's gifts, the joys and beauties of the outdoors will be here forever **137**
. —JIMMY CARTER

FOR MORE INFORMATION: Emily Preslar, Human Resources Assistant Manager, Beaver Run Resort, P.O. Box 2115, Breckenridge, CO 80424-2115 (800) 288-1282, ext. 8737 • (970) 453-8737 • (970) 453-9351 (fax) work@beaverrun.com

C LAZY U RANCH

Guest Ranch • Colorado • Seasonal
www.clazyu.com

$ 🏕 ⊕

At C Lazy U Ranch, there's still plenty of room to stretch out. Time to relax. A range to ride. Mountains to explore. Fish to catch. All simple pleasures to experience.

WHAT YOU'LL BE DOING: Working at C Lazy U is a great opportunity for folks who want hands-on experience in a resort setting. A large seasonal staff is hired each summer and winter with positions including wranglers, counselors (kid wranglers), housekeepers, kitchen help, waitstaff, bartenders, ranch hands, gardeners, office help, and, in winter, a cross-country ski instructor.

COMMITMENT: The summer season runs from mid-May through mid-October, although the core season is from late May through Labor Day. The winter season is short—one month from mid-December to mid-January—and is ideal for college students looking for work during their holiday break.

C LAZY U RANCH

Come experience the American West with C Lazy U Ranch, where the lifestyle of the American cowboy still lingers.

PERKS AND REWARDS: Compensation consists of a base pay of $800 per month, along with meals and bunkhouse-style accommodations (two to four people per room). The biggest perk is joining guests in activities and entertainment during time off.

THE ESSENTIALS: Good people skills are a must for all positions. Those who are enthusiastic, considerate, and genuinely friendly as well as hardworking and service-minded make the best staff members. Being a self-starter who can work with minimum supervision is also an asset. Counselors and wranglers must have riding experience. Applicants must be at least eighteen years of age, and for summer empolyment, preference is given to those who can work at least through Labor Day.

YOUR FIRST MOVE: Applications are accepted for summer jobs beginning January 1; for winter, starting September 1. It's noted that you should give careful consideration to the dates of availability you list; these are instrumental in the decision-making process. You'll find applications on their website.

FOR MORE INFORMATION: Guest Services Director, C Lazy U Ranch, 3640 Colorado Hwy. 125, P.O. Box 379, Granby, CO 80446 • (970) 887-3344 (970) 887-3917 (fax) • ranch@clazyu.com

CAMP CHATUGA

General Camp • South Carolina • Summer
www.campchatuga.com

$ 🏠 ⊕

Camp Chatuga is a small, independent camp for boys and girls from six to sixteen, with a focus on developing their potential intellectually, emotionally, spiritually, and physically in a fun and relaxed natural environment. A job at Chatuga is not a summer vacation—it is work. It is mentally and physically exhausting, but unbelievably rewarding. Can you live without alcohol, tobacco, perfect hair, privacy, a Walkman, air-conditioning, a VCR, a predictable schedule, and lots of money? If you answered yes, then this may be the job for you. Eight-week summer positions include counselors as well as waterfront, horseback, outdoor program, and health supervisors. Precamp training helps staff members earn or renew certifications. Staff members receive $180 per week, plus room, board, free trips, and a staff T-shirt. Salaries go up based on education, experience, and certifications.

FOR MORE INFORMATION: Kelly Moxley, Personnel Director, Camp Chatuga, 291 Camp Chatuga Rd., Mountain Rest, SC 29664 • (864) 638-3728 (864) 638-0898 (fax) • mail@campchatuga.com

CAMP COURAGEOUS OF IOWA

Therapeutic Camp • Iowa • 1–4 Months
www.campcourageous.org

$ 🏕 ⊕

Camp Courageous of Iowa, surrounded by hundreds of acres of state and
county land, is a year-round camp founded on the belief that children
and adults with disabilities have the right to opportunities found in the world
around them. Campers with mental and physical disabilities, hearing and
visual impairments, autism, and brain injuries are served, along with other
distinct groups. Counselors supervise the health, well-being, and personal
care of groups of campers and ensure that they have a successful and enjoyable time. Activity specialists develop and implement programs in everything
from canoeing, camping, crafts, and nature activities to rock climbing, rappel-
ling, caving, and the high- and low-ropes course. Full-time positions of one to
four months are offered throughout the year, and the hours are long (generally sixty to eighty hours per week). Interns and volunteers receive a salary of
$100 per month; seasonal staff receive $250 per week; and year-round staff
receive up to $360 per week. All receive room and board. Candidates should
have flexibility and patience. A genuine desire to give your time, energy, and
enthusiasm to others is a must.

FOR MORE INFORMATION: Jeanne Muellerleile, Camp Director, Camp Courageous
of Iowa, P.O. Box 418, Monticello, IA 52310-0418 • (319) 465-5916, ext. 206
(319) 465-5919 (fax) • jmuellerleile@campcourageous.org

🦌 **INSIDER TIP: Working with children and adults with disabilities is
an experience you will never forget.**

CAMP HIGH ROCKS

General Camp • North Carolina • Summer
www.highrocks.com

$ 🏕

Camp High Rocks is a relatively small boys' camp with a staff-to-camper ratio
of approximately one to three, insuring a high degree of individual attention
for each boy. Activities include hiking, backpacking, mountain biking, rock
climbing, English horseback riding, and water activities (from swimming to
an extensive river canoeing and kayaking program). Counselors must have
completed one year of college, be competent in their teaching field, and have
an understanding of and interest in children. An extensive counselor training

program is offered to staff before the camp begins. Counselor salaries range from $1,800 to $2,700 for the nine-week season, depending on qualifications. Benefits include room, board, laundry, and a two-day Wilderness Medical Associates Wilderness First Aid course.

FOR MORE INFORMATION: Hank Birdsong, Camp Director, Camp High Rocks, P.O. Box 210, Cedar Mountain, NC 28718-0210 • (828) 885-2153 (828) 884-4612 (fax) • staffinfo@highrocks.com

CAMP HIGHLAND
OUTDOOR SCIENCE SCHOOL

Science School • California • Seasonal
www.camphighland.net

$ 🏠 🌐

With a unique blend of science, the environment, team building, and personal growth, Camp Highland Outdoor Science School is an innovative residential grade-school science program in the foothills of the San Bernardino Mountains, just fifty miles from Joshua Tree National Park. During the spring and fall, outdoor education instructors have the opportunity to teach over twenty classes, including archaeology, botany, ecology (wildlife, forest, mountain, and desert), entomology, canoeing, climbing, archery, ropes course, team building, and outdoor living skills. Creative and energetic individuals who love working in the outdoors and want to make a positive impression on today's youth are preferred. Wages start at $45 per day, plus room and board. To begin the application process, send a resume, cover letter, and three references.

FOR MORE INFORMATION: Brett Tillman, Program Director, Camp Highland Outdoor Science School, 10600 Highland Springs Ave., Cherry Valley, CA 92223 (909) 572-2020 • (909) 845-8090 (fax) • info@camphighland.net

CAMP SOUTHWOODS

General Camp • New York • Summer
www.southwoods.com

$ 🏠 🌐

Come experience a meaningful and rewarding summer with Camp Southwoods in the beautiful Adirondack Mountains of New York. With traditional programs including land and waterfront sports and the creative arts, Southwoods also offers an exciting outdoor adventure trek program. "Trekkie" staff will work

If you take any activity, any art, any discipline, any skill, take it and push it as far as it will go, push it beyond where it has ever been before, push it to the wildest edge of edges, then you force it into the realm of magic. —TOM ROBBINS

with children in a variety of outdoor pursuits—climbing, facilitating high and low ropes, tripping (camping, hiking, canoeing, caving, and more!)—and are trained in all program areas. Benefits include a salary, housing, meals, professional certification and training, laundry, and Internet access, just to name a few. Positions begin in mid-June and continue through mid-August. If you are dedicated, flexible, able to work in a team environment, and, most importantly, want to positively impact the life of a child, fill out the online application.

FOR MORE INFORMATION: Justin Dockswell, Staff Coordinator, Camp Southwoods, P.O. Box 459, White Plains, NY 10603 • (888) 449-3357 (914) 524-9200 • (914) 524-0773 (fax) • info@southwoods.com

CAMP WAKONDA

General Camp • New York • Summer
www.homesforthehomeless.com

$ 🏠

Are you flexible, fun, caring, and responsible? Do you have a love for children and the outdoors and a craving to do something different? Then come explore your summer job opportunities with Camp Wakonda. Nestled in the foothills of Bear Mountain (about an hour north of New York City), Camp Wakonda provides homeless children a place to learn, grow, explore, and belong—free of charge. Staff members (from unit leaders to activity specialists and general counselors) work together to promote the development of self-esteem, provide a role model for healthy group living, and get campers excited about life (whether learning to paddle a canoe or gazing at the Big Dipper for the first time). Housing, meals, and a stipend are provided.

FOR MORE INFORMATION: Staffing Director, Camp Wakonda, 9 Baileytown Rd., LT4 Lower Twin Lake, Central Valley, NY 10917 • (845) 928-1333

CENTER FOR TALENTED YOUTH

Teaching • USA • Summer
www.cty.jhu.edu/summer

$ 🏠

The Center for Talented Youth at Johns Hopkins University is a comprehensive, university-based initiative that promotes the academic ability of children and youth throughout the world. Each summer, the center holds residential and commuter programs that provide the opportunity for participants to take rigorous courses in the humanities (music/art, history, social sciences/philosophy, history/politics, language, and writing) and math/science (lab science, computer science, and mathematics). Residential programs are offered at twenty-three sites around the country and held on beautiful college campuses in Arizona, California, Hawaii, Maryland/Washington, D.C., Massachusetts, New York, Pennsylvania, and Rhode Island.

WHAT YOU'LL BE DOING: This is a wonderful opportunity to work with unique and highly able youngsters in a dynamic setting. Positions include instructional (instructors, teaching assistants, laboratory assistants, and program assistants), residential assistants (similar to a college residential assistant), and administrative (residential program assistants, health assistants, site nurses, office managers, academic counselors, academic deans, dean of residential life, and site directors).

COMMITMENT: Applicants must commit to two three-week sessions beginning in late June and ending in early August.

PERKS AND REWARDS: The starting salary for instructors ranges from $1,800 to $2,800 per three-week session, while instructional assistants earn $950, and residential assistants earn $1,050. All staff members receive a private room in a college dormitory and meals.

THE ESSENTIALS: Applicants are generally in college or are recent graduates. All candidates must be creative, energetic, and dynamic, and have the desire to work with children in an academic setting.

YOUR FIRST MOVE: Candidates whose application materials are completed by the end of January will be considered first. Some openings occur late in the hiring process, so qualified candidates are encouraged to submit their applications through June.

FOR MORE INFORMATION: CTY Summer Employment, Center for Talented Youth, Johns Hopkins University, 3400 N. Charles St., Baltimore, MD 21218 (410) 516-0053 • (410) 516-0093 (fax) • ctysummer@jhu.edu

CHELEY COLORADO CAMPS

General Camp • Colorado • Summer
www.cheley.com

$ 🏔 🌐

Since 1921, family-owned Cheley Colorado Camps has been welcoming young people for an enriching, adventurous, and value-centered camp experience during the summer months. Cheley facilities include five horseback

If you want to be successful, know what you are doing, love what you are doing, and believe in what you are doing.
—WILL ROGERS

riding rings, a climbing wall and ropes course, a gymnasium and weight room, a grassy amphitheater with a lighted stage, a soccer field beside an aspen grove, a fishing pond, a fleet of forty mountain bikes, and facilities for working with leather, paints, fibers, and wood.

WHAT YOU'LL BE DOING: Whether as a support staff member (from camp cooks and barn crew to photographers and nurses) or as a counselor (from challenge course facilitators to crafts counselors), over two hundred seasonal workers are hired each year. The summer kicks off with an eight- to ten-day staff training period, with exposure to professionals in the fields of child development, forests and parks, psychology, and wilderness medicine.

COMMITMENT: A nine-week commitment beginning in June and continuing until the middle of August is necessary. There are also opportunities to start as early as mid-May and continue on through the end of October.

PERKS AND REWARDS: Room, board, a base salary of about $1,500, and an end-of-season travel allowance are provided.

THE ESSENTIALS: Those who enjoy working with children and making a difference in the world are essential traits of Cheley staff. All counseling staff must have a current CPR and basic first aid certification; backpacking, hiking, and horseback riding counselors are required to have Wilderness First Aid certification. Staff members range in age from nineteen (the minimum age requirement) to eighty-something!

YOUR FIRST MOVE: Application materials can be found online or call the toll free number for more information. In-person or telephone interviews are conducted.

FOR MORE INFORMATION: Program Director, Cheley Colorado Camps, P.O. Box 6525, Denver, CO 80206-0525 • (800) 226-7386 • (303) 377-3616 (303) 377-3605 (fax) • office@cheley.com

CHINGACHGOOK YMCA OUTDOOR CENTER AND CAMP

Outdoor Education • New York • 3–9 Months
www.chingachgook.org

$ 🏠

Chingachgook (pronounced chin-ja-cook), located on spectacular Lake George in the New York Adirondacks, provides year-round programs for over thirteen thousand children and young adults each year. More than 150 interns and seasonal staff keep things hopping at its outdoor education school and summer camp, where they teach environmental, recreational, and outdoor education as well as lead teen adventure trips (which focus on hiking, canoeing, rock climbing, mountaineering, rafting, ice climbing, kayaking, and camping). Most positions are available from March through November, with various time commitments. Benefits include an hourly wage, housing, meals, and extensive training. The biggest perk, however, may be working at Lake George! Preferred applicants are at least twenty-one years of age with experience in the outdoor adventure field. Send off your resume, cover letter, and three references with contact information to start the application process.

FOR MORE INFORMATION: Matt Fisher, Senior Program Director, Chingachgook YMCA Outdoor Center and Camp, 1872 Pilot Knob Rd., Kattskill Bay, NY 12844 • (518) 656-9462, ext. 14 • (518) 656-9362 (fax) mfisher@cdymca.org

CHRISTODORA— MANICE EDUCATION CENTER

Wilderness Education • Massachusetts/New York • 3–12 Months
www.christodora.org

$ 🏠 ⊕

Coordinating camping programs since 1908, Christodora provides challenging and rewarding environmental learning experiences to motivate urban youths who generally come from economically or experientially disadvantaged families in New York City. The center is a small, high-quality residential center in the Berkshire Mountains of Massachusetts and has a strong emphasis on environmental education and adventure programs.

WHAT YOU'LL BE DOING: Field teachers educate and facilitate the growth, understanding, and development of students (ages eleven to eighteen) in program areas such as environmental sciences, wilderness, group initiatives, and leadership training. This might also include supervision of overnight trips and wilderness expeditions. Outdoor education interns assist field teachers in program areas while developing skills to teach their own lessons in a supervised setting. Wilderness leadership interns supervise and co-lead six- to nineteen-day courses with field teachers. Interns working through AmeriCorps will spend three months teaching environmental education in New York City and six months in Massachusetts teaching at the Manice Education Center.

PERKS AND REWARDS: Field teachers receive a minimum stipend of $325 per week, while interns receive a minimum of $200 per week. Room, board,

Do not try to do extraordinary things, but ordinary things with intensity.
—EMILY CARR

equipment discounts, and insurance coverage are also provided. There is an AmeriCorps educational award for a nine- to twelve-month commitment.

THE ESSENTIALS: Field teacher applicants must have a college degree; outdoor education interns must have completed one year of college; and wilderness leadership positions require a minimum of two years of college. All candidates must have a strong interest in the wilderness, interpretation, and experiential education. CPR, first aid, and lifeguard certifications are preferred.

YOUR FIRST MOVE: Submit your resume, cover letter, and three references.

FOR MORE INFORMATION: Michael Vecchiarelli, Director, Christodora—Manice Education Center, 68 Savoy Rd., Florida, MA 01247 (413) 663-8463, mikev@christodora.org

In New York: One E. 53rd St., 14th Floor, New York, NY 10022; (212) 371-5225 (212) 371-2111 (fax), info@christodora.org

CLEARWATER CANOE OUTFITTERS AND LODGE

Lodge • Minnesota • Summer
www.clearwateroutfitters.com

$ 🏠 ⊕

The main lodge of Clearwater Canoe Outfitters and Lodge was completed in 1926 and is listed on the National Register of Historic Places. The largest remaining whole-log structure in northeastern Minnesota, it has retained the look and feel of the pioneer days. A few secluded cabins and bed-and-breakfast rooms in the lodge itself offer an alternative to camping. The business prides itself on its wilderness preservation ethic and consists of six to eight staff members. Seasonal positions include front desk, housekeeping, waterfront, maintenance, cook, naturalist, and outfitting packer. (Most staff work in more than one position.) A salary along with room and board are provided.

FOR MORE INFORMATION: Mike, Peggy, and Lynn, Directors, Clearwater Canoe Outfitters and Lodge, 774 Clearwater Rd., Grand Marais, MN 55604 • (800) 527-0554 • (218) 388-2254 (218) 388-2254 (fax) • info@clearwateroutfitters.com

CLUB MED—NORTH AMERICA

Adventure Travel • USA/The Bahamas/The Caribbean/Mexico
6 Months+
www.clubmedjobs.com

$ ⚑ ⊕

Known for its great locations, interesting architecture, and carefree lifestyle, Club Med is the pioneer of the all-inclusive resort, attracting thousands of adventurous singles and families each year. Whether guests are snorkeling, indulging in a gourmet meal, or being entertained, the "voice of Club Med" is their team of ten thousand GOs (*gentils organisateurs*)—those "energetic, fun, and innovative" men and women from all around the world who do everything they can to make their enthusiasm contagious to the flock of GMs (*gentils membres*)—the guests!

WHAT YOU'LL BE DOING: Each year Club Med recruits over 3,500 new GOs in all areas of expertise. GOs work hard giving sports instruction, being sociable, leading group activities and tours, or putting on evening entertainment. Basically, from the moment the GMs arrive until their farewell cocktail party, their Club Med experience is defined by the GOs they meet along the way.

COMMITMENT: GOs must commit to at least six months; the summer season starts in May and the winter season begins in November.

PERKS AND REWARDS: You don't work at Club Med to become a millionaire, but rather to explore a different lifestyle—and to have some fun! Still, you should be able to save most of your salary since Club Med covers almost all your expenses, including transportation from your home to the village, room and board (GOs are generally lodged two to a room), health care coverage, and full use of the village's amenities.

THE ESSENTIALS: In order to qualify for a job, you'll need a lot of energy and a love of entertaining. Ideal applicants have knowledge of a second language and must speak English.

YOUR FIRST MOVE: All applicants must complete an online application. A few commonsense tips: pay careful attention to the qualifications requested (language requirements, degrees, experience, and availability) and, most importantly, be sure you communicate all your enthusiasm and energy in the interview.

FOR MORE INFORMATION: GO Recruiter, Club Med—North America, 75 Valencia Ave., Coral Gables, FL 33134 • (888) 233-0362 • (305) 925-9217 (305) 476-4100 (fax) • resumes@clubmed.com

We must be willing to get rid of the life we've planned, so as to have the life that is waiting for us. **147**
—JOSEPH CAMPBELL

COFFEE CREEK RANCH

Guest Ranch • California • Seasonal
www.coffeecreekranch.com

$ ⚑ ⊕

Located on 367 acres surrounded by national forest and the Trinity Alps
Wilderness Area in Northern California, Coffee Creek Ranch guests experience trout fishing, hiking, horseback riding, kayaking, wilderness pack trips,
Nordic skiing, gold panning, and use of the health spa and rifle range.
Seasonal staff members are needed in the office, the front desk, accounting,
and the kitchen, including prep chefs and bakers. Pay depends upon the position and season chosen, but generally runs $1,100 to $1,800 per month.
Room, board, and use of the facilities at the ranch (including the exercise
room and hot tub) are provided.

FOR MORE INFORMATION: Alicia and Shane Ryan, Owners, Coffee Creek Ranch,
HC2, Box 4940, Trinity Center, CA 96091-9502 • (800) 624-4480
(530) 266-3343 • (530) 266-3597 (fax) • ccranch@tds.net

🐾 **INSIDER TIP:** The more versatile you are the better. We are looking
for people who never say, "That's not my job!"

THE COLLEGE SETTLEMENT OF PHILADELPHIA

General Camp • Pennsylvania • Seasonal
www.collegesettlement.org

$ ⚑ ⊕

The College Settlement of Philadelphia operates a day and resident summer
camp and a residential outdoor school, mostly for seven- to fourteen-year-
olds from economically disadvantaged families. Many of these children live in
difficult situations and face challenging problems in their daily lives. The Teen
Adventure Program offers a once-in-a-lifetime chance for urban youth to
experience the thrill of camping, hiking, and adventuring on the East Coast.
Summer adventure trip leaders plan custom trips and activities and take their
groups by van to various locations in Pennsylvania, New York, Maryland, and
West Virginia. Summer camp staff—from counselors to activity leaders—
teach and share experiences with children in a fun and caring environment.
Finally, spring and fall teacher/naturalists teach science and team-building
activities. Summer wages for trip leaders start at $3,000 for the season ($225
per week for spring and fall staff), along with a $100 stipend, meals, and
housing. Applicants should have experience in outdoor pursuits (climbing,

backpacking, rafting, or kayaking preferred), be enthusiastic, work well with others, and have a sense of fun mixed with a great dose of common sense. Those who are open-minded and enjoy making a difference in others' lives are strongly encouraged to apply.

FOR MORE INFORMATION: Penny Mimmo, Program Director, The College Settlement of Philadelphia, 600 Witmer Rd., Horsham, PA 19044 (215) 542-7974 • (215) 542-7457 (fax) • camps@collegesettlement.org

THE COLORADO MOUNTAIN RANCH

General Camp • Colorado • Summer
www.coloradomountainranch.com

$ 🏠

Owned and operated by the Walker family since 1947, the Colorado Mountain Ranch summer camp provides a warm, friendly environment where individual growth and learning occur through confidence-building activities in an active outdoor setting. Adventurous programming abounds at the ranch, where campers can participate in everything from a ropes course to Western horseback riding, hiking, and camping.

YOUR SURROUNDINGS: Nestled in the pine and aspen forests and wildflower meadows of Colorado's Rocky Mountains, the ranch encompasses 180 acres at an elevation of 8,500 feet. The camp is bordered on the east by the mining town of Gold Hill, and to the west, Roosevelt National Forest rises to the magnificent snowcapped peaks of the Continental Divide. Days are generally sunny and warm, nights are cool, and the air is usually crisp and clear.

WHAT YOU'LL BE DOING: Summer seasonal staff are instrumental in creating and implementing every aspect of ranch programs, activities, facility use, food service, and maintenance. Every job (ranging from activity instructors to wranglers) involves inspiring and guiding campers, participating enthusiastically in all daily activities, and embracing the Native American philosophy of respect for self, others, and nature.

COMMITMENT: Staff training begins in early June, with camp finishing in mid-August. Only those who are available for the entire season will be considered.

PERKS AND REWARDS: Depending on the position, first-year staff members will earn $1,800 to $1,900 per season, along with meals, housing, leadership training, and future personnel references. Living with others and working together as a team, staff members will grow in love and understanding of themselves, each other, and life. The mountain climate and setting are also

Don't settle for less than your potential.
Remember, average is as close to the bottom as it is to the top. **149**
—ABIGAIL VAN BUREN

perfect for a full range of healthful outdoor activities, from swimming and hiking to camping and playing in the high-country snowfields.

THE ESSENTIALS: Applicants must be at least eighteen and have completed high school. Staff members are selected on the basis of abilities, enthusiasm, creativity, reliability, sincerity, sensitivity, and a commitment to guiding others toward their full potential.

YOUR FIRST MOVE: Applications can be downloaded from their website. Once you have submitted your application materials, you are encouraged to call for a personal telephone interview.

FOR MORE INFORMATION: Lynn, Gail, and Mike Walker, Owners, The Colorado Mountain Ranch, 10063 Gold Hill Rd., Boulder, CO 80302-9770 (800) 267-9573 • (303) 442-4557 • (303) 417-9114 (fax) office@coloradomountainranch.com

**⌐ INSIDER TIP: The ranch is a song; it is a song of happiness, of love, of peace, and of understanding. It is a song that had a beginning, but that can never die, for too many people have heard this song. The intertwining of the melodies will continue until the song has become a part of everyone who has come here. That song will go out from here in the hearts and minds of those who know it and spread itself and become a part of all it touches. Let your song reflect that which you are and will become here, and carry it with you when you leave.
—*The Colorado Mountain Ranch***

COLVIG SILVER CAMPS

General Camp • Colorado • Summer
www.colvigsilvercamps.com

$ ⛺

Located in the San Juan Mountains of southwest Colorado, Colvig Silver Camps (CSC) is a residential, wilderness-oriented summer camp serving children seven to seventeen years of age. The camp is a short drive or hike from high alpine regions (14,000-foot peaks), desert canyon areas (including Anasazi ruins), low alpine regions, mountain lakes and streams, raging rivers, and ponderosa pine forests. Their program is unique in that they offer a mix of traditional summer activities along with overnight backcountry wilderness trips.

WHAT YOU'LL BE DOING: This summer you could lead a climb up a 14,000-foot peak, guide a moonlight exploration of a desert canyon, or teach someone how

COLVIG SILVER CAMPS

With the help of summer staff members at Colvig Silver Camps, "outposters" take on a leadership role for expeditions throughout the mountains, rivers, lakes, deserts, and canyons of the Rockies.

to fish a mountain lake, raft a river, or set up camp in a ponderosa pine forest—and that's just for starters! Here's a quick overview of the possibilities: program coordinators organize and implement the camp's daily schedule; counselors are responsible for planning and leading in-camp activities and wilderness trips as well as living with a group of four to six campers; arts and crafts coordinators develop crafts programs for all age levels; wranglers are responsible for planning and teaching Western-style riding and tack care; the climbing coordinator supervises, plans, and instructs all climbing wall and natural rock climbing activities; and the expedition coordinator packs food and equipment for all expedition trips leaving camp.

COMMITMENT: The season begins with mandatory staff training in early June and continues through mid-August.

PERKS AND REWARDS: A salary of $1,200 to $1,825 is provided, along with room, board, laundry, training, and Wilderness First Aid certification for head counselors.

THE ESSENTIALS: Ideally, applicants should have completed one year of college and have first aid and CPR certifications.

YOUR FIRST MOVE: Visit their website for detailed job descriptions and an online application. After your application is received, they follow up on your references, then schedule an on-site or phone interview. Positions are filled on a first-come, first-served basis.

Embrace your uniqueness. Time is much too short to be living someone else's life.
—KOBI YAMADA

FOR MORE INFORMATION: Megan Weidmann and Lindsay James, Program Directors, Colvig Silver Camps, 9665 Florida Rd., Durango, CO 81301 (800) 858-2850 • (970) 247-2564 • (970) 247-2547 (fax) office@colvigsilvercamps.com

INSIDER TIP: I have been intimately associated with Colvig Silver Camps for seven years. I saw it in your book and just wanted to let you know that I think it is a wonderful place to work. I was a camper there for five years beginning when I was eleven; and later went back to work there as a counselor for two years. This camp was my initial introduction to outdoor recreation and obviously had some pretty amazing influences on me, being that I now want to pursue a career in that field. —Amie Podolsky, former program director of CSC

CYBERCAMPS

Computer Camp • USA • Summer
www.cybercamps.com
$ ♠♠

Attention computer geeks: do you have a passion for teaching and technology? Then you might want to consider a summer with Cybercamps. It's all the fun of a traditional camp, but without all the mosquitoes (that's not to say camp programmers never find "bugs"!). As a division of Giant Campus, Cybercamps is a progressive, innovative company that provides experience-based learning for boys and girls, ages seven to sixteen, at colleges and universities across the country. Summer staff—including camp directors, assistant directors, and computer camp counselors—provide hands-on learning and exposure to cutting-edge technologies, including web design, 3D animation, robotics, game design, programming, and digital arts. Both day and residential camp experiences are offered and vary by location. The average salary is $300 per week, along with meals. For residential locations, housing may be available; if not, Cybercamps does its best to help out. Applicants must be at least eighteen years old, have a knack for working with children, and know how to work in a team environment. A solid knowledge in web page design, programming, design software, robotics, hardware, 3D animation, or network maintenance is essential. Applications can be found online.

FOR MORE INFORMATION: Kat Fitzgerald, Director of Staffing, Cybercamps, Giant Campus, 2401 4th Ave., Suite 1110, Seattle, WA 98121 • (888) 904-2267 (206) 442-4500 • (206) 442-4501 (fax) • summerjobs@cybercamps.com

DROWSY WATER RANCH

Guest Ranch · Colorado · Summer
www.drowsywater.com

$ 🏠 ⊕

Nothing less than real down-home hospitality amid unforgettable mountain scenery—that's what you'll find at the Fosha family's home and six-hundred-acre working ranch called Drowsy Water. Each week fifty-five guests come to enjoy a true western ranch experience and "play" with the Foshas and seasonal staff who are there to feed them, house them, and entertain them. Summer positions include housekeepers, food servers, cooks, office workers, children's program counselors, and wranglers. Along with meeting people from all over the world, staff members will receive a monthly salary, room, meals, and gratuities. Applications can be obtained online.

FOR MORE INFORMATION: Ken and Randy Sue Fosha, Summer Staffing, Drowsy Water Ranch, P.O. Box 147, Granby, CO 80446-0147 • (800) 845-2292 (970) 725-3456 • (970) 725-3611 (fax) • whoadwr@aol.com

EAGLE'S NEST FOUNDATION

Outdoor Education · North Carolina · Seasonal
www.enf.org

$ 🏠 ⊕

With the mission of promoting the natural world and the betterment of human character, Eagle's Nest Foundation coordinates a children's summer camp (celebrating more than seventy-five years) and the Outdoor Academy of the Southern Appalachians, a semester school for tenth and select eleventh graders. This school-away-from-school focuses on environmental education, regional studies, and the arts, and centers students and faculty in a close community life. Pure and simple, the Eagle's Nest Foundation is about teaching and nurturing.

YOUR SURROUNDINGS: Nestled at the base of the Shining Rock escarpment in Pisgah National Forest, Eagle's Nest is situated on 180 acres of wooded land, where there are many places to rock climb, white-water paddle, and soak up the culture of the southern Appalachians. Evenings are cool; summer days are warm.

WHAT YOU'LL BE DOING: There are two facets to Eagle's Nest staffing opportunities: (1) Summer camp staff members teach activities in the arts, music, and drama (batik, West African drum and dance, pottery, making musical

Obstacles are placed in our way to determine whether we truly wanted something
or just thought we did.
—HAROLD SMITH

153

instruments, and raku—not your everyday arts and crafts classes), wilderness (white-water canoeing on a handful of rivers, rock climbing, and backpacking), and athletics (emphasizing skill and teamwork, not competition). Staff members also double as trip leaders: they develop, plan, and set goals for the courses, then take teenagers on intense wilderness experiences, such as hiking on the Appalachian Trail, mountain biking the Continental Divide Trail in Montana, participating in service and cultural-exchange projects in Mexico, and paddling the chilly waters of northern Ontario. (2) Outdoor Academy teachers emphasize a broad spectrum of knowledge, skills, and attitudes in a college preparatory curriculum of English, history, natural science, fine arts, foreign languages, and mathematics. The program combines classroom activities inside and out, with experiential learning as its strength.

COMMITMENT: The summer camp season runs approximately three months, while the Outdoor Academy season lasts from mid-August through mid-May. Some Outdoor Academy faculty members work the entire year, with the option of taking the summer off and returning in the fall. The hours are long but very rewarding, as the staff works with kids who are eager to learn and do. Camp staff members have one twenty-four-hour day off per week and at least two hours off per day; faculty time off varies.

PERKS AND REWARDS: A $170 to $350 per week salary, plus room and meals from the whole-foods kitchen (with options for vegetarians and vegans) is provided for the camp staff. Outdoor Academy benefits include year-round housing, full medical benefits, and a salary commensurate with experience. Fresh air, mountain music, laughter, and love abound at Eagle's Nest, and most thrive and live vivaciously in this community-empowering environment.

THE ESSENTIALS: Applicants with experience in outdoor and experiential education and who have a strong desire to teach and play in the outdoors are desired. A high energy level and creativity are a must.

YOUR FIRST MOVE: Staff applications can be found online (or call or email for one).

Summer instructors at Eagle's Nest Camp get their bearings prior to leading a group of campers on a three-week adventure along the Appalachian Trail.

EAGLE'S NEST FOUNDATION

FOR MORE INFORMATION: Paige Lester-Niles, Camp Director, Eagle's Nest Foundation, P.O. Box 5127, Winston-Salem, NC 27113-5127 • (336) 761-1040 (336) 727-0030 (fax) • Summer: (828) 877-4349 • (828) 884-2788 (fax) paige@enf.org

ECKERD YOUTH ALTERNATIVES

Therapeutic Camp • East Coast USA • 2 Years
www.eckerd.org

$ 🏕

Fresh air, open spaces, miles of blue sky above—you won't find them in a corporate cubicle. But as a youth counselor at an Eckerd Youth Alternatives (EYA) wilderness camp, the whole outdoors is your office. In fact, you'll live year-round in some of the most beautiful natural locations in the eastern U.S. (camps are spread out over eighteen sites in Florida, Georgia, New Hampshire, North Carolina, Rhode Island, Tennessee, and Vermont). Hike the Appalachians. Canoe the Suwannee. Sleep under the stars. Develop personal relationships. And help at-risk kids get back on track. It's an adventure that can change their lives—and yours—forever.

WHAT YOU'LL BE DOING: Over a two-year period, wilderness youth counselors supervise a group of ten to twelve at-risk youths twenty-four hours a day. Daily activities involve the construction and maintenance of the group's common living area. Additional activities vary, but can include leading the children in hiking, backpacking, low and high ropes work, playing outdoor games, and planning and preparing events such as cookouts and canoe trips. All activities are frameworks for problem solving and developing basic life skills.

PERKS AND REWARDS: The starting salary is $20,000 per year, with the opportunity to receive up to four pay increases and two promotions over a two-year period. Extensive paid training, along with room, board, relocation assistance, and comprehensive health benefits are provided.

THE ESSENTIALS: All candidates must be at least twenty-one years of age, and some state contracts require a four-year degree. Child care experience, paid or volunteer, is preferred, as well as diverse outdoor experiences and an interest in athletics and physical game activities.

YOUR FIRST MOVE: Resumes can be submitted by mail, fax, or preferably online. Phone calls are welcomed!

FOR MORE INFORMATION: Career Advisor, Eckerd Youth Alternatives, 100 N. Starcrest Dr., P.O. Box 7450, Clearwater, FL 33758-7450 (800) 222-1473 • (727) 461-4387 (fax) • recruiting@eckerd.org

Spirit has fifty times the strength and staying power of brawn and muscle. **155**
—MARK TWAIN

ELK MOUNTAIN RANCH

Guest Ranch • Colorado • Summer
www.elkmtn.com

$ 🏕

Sitting at almost 10,000 feet, Elk Mountain Ranch is situated in the midst of the San Isabel National Forest in a remote and secluded setting. For those who have a ready smile, are honest and willing to work long, hard hours, love the outdoors, and enjoy working with people, Elk Mountain might be a great fit! Fourteen staff members are hired for the summer season, with positions including cooks, housekeepers and waitstaff, a children's counselor, wranglers, and in maintenance (general ranch-hand work). Each staff member is given specific job duties and is also expected to help out wherever and whenever needed, six days per week. Staff members receive a monthly wage and tips, along with modest shared housing, meals, and laundry facilities. Staff also have the chance to participate in evening activities, including hayrides, square dancing, volleyball, games, and social events. Applicants must be at least eighteen years of age and willing to live on the ranch. Availability to work from mid-May to the end of August (with some positions that extend through the end of September) is an important hiring criteria. Applications are available online.

FOR MORE INFORMATION: Sue Murphy, Treasurer, Elk Mountain Ranch, P.O. Box 910, Buena Vista, CO 81211 • (800) 432-8812 • (719) 539-4430 info@elkmtn.com

FAIRVIEW LAKE YMCA CAMPS

Environmental Education • New Jersey • 3–4 Months
www.fairviewlake.org

$ 🏕

Fairview Lake YMCA Camps provide environmental education and conference programming for students in first through twelfth grades. The camps' mission is to improve the quality of life in the community by fostering healthful living, developing responsible leaders and citizens, strengthening the family, promoting the equality of all persons, protecting the environment, and utilizing community members and organizations to solve contemporary problems.

YOUR SURROUNDINGS: Located on six hundred acres of mountains and forests, the camps offer miles of trails for hiking, a 110-acre lake, athletic fields, a lighted tennis and basketball complex, cross-country skiing, boating, and canoeing.

WHAT YOU'LL BE DOING: Intern responsibilities include participation in staff training; planning and teaching environmental lessons on a variety of subjects that range from aquatic ecology to survival skills; providing instruction on the Action Socialization Experience Course; leading evening activities; assisting at dining hall orientation and meal service when needed; and completion of a project chosen in consultation with the director.

COMMITMENT: Internships are available beginning in March and September for three to four months.

PERKS AND REWARDS: Interns are paid a stipend of $275 per week, plus room and board. Staff housing includes a semiprivate room with a kitchen and living room complex.

THE ESSENTIALS: Lifeguard training, first aid, and CPR certifications are preferred; however, the camp may provide this training. Applicants are considered based on their love of the outdoors, the desire to influence young minds, and flexibility of their work schedule.

YOUR FIRST MOVE: Submit a resume and cover letter.

FOR MORE INFORMATION: Christina Hagan, Environmental Education Director, Fairview Lake YMCA Camps, 1035 Fairview Lake Rd., Newton, NJ 07860 (973) 383-9282 • (973) 383-6386 (fax) • fairviewlake@metroymcas.org

FARM AND WILDERNESS FOUNDATION

Farming Camp • Vermont • 2–8 Months
www.fandw.org

$ 🏠 🌐

Farm and Wilderness is a nonprofit educational organization that operates five residential camps for children ages nine to seventeen, a day camp, a family camp in late August, outdoor education programs in the spring through winter, a retreat center, and a spring and fall work crew. The essence of Farm and Wilderness can be found in the Quaker values of simplicity, honesty, self-reliance, and respect for all people. These values are woven into the fabric of the Farm and Wilderness community, creating an environment where people develop a deep regard for one another and explore a style of life that is simple, rugged, and exciting.

There is no shortcut to life. To the end of our days, life is a lesson imperfectly learned. **157**
—HARRISON E. SALISBURY

WHAT YOU'LL BE DOING: Each year, nearly three hundred staff members are hired for seasonal work (250 of them in the summer). Positions include camp counselors and administrators, carpenters, cooks, drivers, farmers, gardeners, maintenance workers, nurses, outdoor educators, special event coordinators, and trip leaders. There are no sharp lines between work and play in the camps because a cooperative group spirit enriches all the experiences of swimming and hiking, building and farming, dancing and music, crafts and cooking, and sharing thoughts and emotions. During the spring and fall, internships in outdoor education, maintenance, and organic farming are also offered.

PERKS AND REWARDS: Depending on the position, salaries range from $1,200 to $3,000 for the summer season ($155 per week for interns), plus housing, meals (with a strong emphasis on the use of fresh vegetables harvested from the organic gardens), and basic health insurance coverage.

THE ESSENTIALS: The staff is made up of "doers." They have backpacked in the Sierras, run food drives for the homeless, worked to clean up the environment, promoted the concept of world peace, played in bands, built houses, operated farms, and climbed in the Himalayas. In any given year, more than half are returning for another season.

YOUR FIRST MOVE: Applications can be found online, or call or email for more information. The hiring process for summer positions takes place from February through June.

FOR MORE INFORMATION: Staffing Coordinator, Farm and Wilderness Foundation, 263 Farm and Wilderness Rd., Plymouth, VT 05056-9434 (802) 422-3761, ext. 228 • (802) 422-8660 (fax) • staffinginfo@fandw.org

THE FRESH AIR FUND

General Camp • New York • Summer
www.freshair.org

$ 🏠 🌐

The Fresh Air Fund provides New York City youngsters with completely free camping programs, with fun away from the hot and noisy streets of the city as its priority. Serving boys and girls between eight and fifteen years old, the fund operates five camps on a three-thousand-acre preserve filled with forests, fields, lakes, and streams. In natural and rustic surroundings, campers learn to respect the environment and its wildlife. In addition, all activities are designed to provide challenges, build self-esteem, develop leadership and social skills, stimulate sharing and trust, encourage openness and cooperation, and create a sense of community.

WHAT YOU'LL BE DOING: During the summer months (from mid-June through mid-August) Fresh Air hires general counselors, waterfront staff, ropes-course facilitators, farm staff, nutritionists, and program staff who focus on everything from photography and woodworking to drama and outdoor living skills. Staff members at Fresh Air are important people in the eyes of boys and girls who have just been introduced to a new and exciting world. They'll act as guides and role models, teach new skills, answer questions about unfamiliar sights and sounds, and help plan days filled with fun and discovery.

PERKS AND REWARDS: Along with a wage ranging from $1,800 to $2,500 for the season, meals and housing are provided. A travel allowance is also provided for those who are traveling over three hundred miles to the camp.

THE ESSENTIALS: Applicants must be at least eighteen years of age, have completed their freshman year of college, and have previous experience with children. The most admirable quality is a sincere motivation to work with inner-city children.

YOUR FIRST MOVE: The Fresh Air website covers specific details and offers both online and downloadable applications. Additional questions can be directed to their camping department by phone or email.

FOR MORE INFORMATION: Camping Department, The Fresh Air Fund, 633 Third Ave., 14th Floor, New York, NY 10017 • (800) 367-0003 (212) 897-8979 • (212) 681-0147 (fax) • camping@freshair.org

JERRY SPEIER

Staff members at Fresh Air are important role models in the eyes of boys and girls who have just been introduced to a new and exciting world.

You get more joy out of giving joy to others and should put a good deal of thought into the happiness that you are able to give.
—ELEANOR ROOSEVELT

159

FRIENDSHIP VENTURES

Therapeutic Camp • Minnesota/USA • Seasonal
www.friendshipventures.org

$ 🏕 ⊕

Enriching the lives of children and adults with developmental disabilities
(from challenging behaviors to medical conditions), Friendship Ventures
offers a variety of programs, including a camp during the summer months
and Team Quest (a team-building adventure challenge course) throughout
the year. In addition to twenty-six full-time staff members, over 250 seasonal
and on-call employees—including nurses, dieticians, counselors, challenge-
course facilitators and interns, and specialists in nature, aquatic activities,
music, and art—work together to create an environment in which participants
can relax, learn, have fun, and gain self-confidence and independence. Most
resident camp staff members are required to live on–site and receive a weekly
salary, housing, and meals. For camp positions, a minimum commitment of
two weeks is required, and additional pay is offered for working four weeks
or more. Challenge-course facilitators are part-time, on-call positions, while
intern positions are available for an eight-week period in April and May or
September and October. Write, call, or email for more information.

FOR MORE INFORMATION: Laurie Tschetter, Program Director,
Friendship Ventures, 10509 108th St., NW, Annandale, MN 55302
(800) 450-8376 • (952) 852-0101 • (952) 852-0123 (fax)
jobs@friendshipventures.org

GUIDED DISCOVERIES

Ocean-Based Camp/Astronomy • California • Summer
www.guideddiscoveries.org

$ 🏕

Founded in 1978, Guided Discoveries is a nonprofit outdoor educational
organization providing hands-on science learning experiences for public
and private schools. Based on discovery, adventure, and an environmentally
conscious approach to learning, eight- to seventeen-year-olds have the opportunity to participate in the Catalina Island Marine Institute program, which
focuses on marine science and island ecology on Catalina Island; Tall Ship
Expeditions, with a focus on sailing and marine science training aboard a
156-foot schooner; and Astrocamp, a program that explores astronomy and
space technology in the San Jacinto Mountains near Idyllwild. Summer positions include counselors, marine science instructors, scuba and sail staff, and
astronomy instructors. While most staff work during the summer months,

transitioning into the year-round program in the fall is a possibility. All staff receive a weekly salary, plus room and board. Teaching experience with youth, flexibility, and the ability to work with others as a team and to live in a rural setting are desired. Certificates in first aid, CPR, and lifeguard training are the norm. Call for an application packet.

FOR MORE INFORMATION: Ross Turner, Executive Director, Guided Discoveries, Catalina Sea Camp/Astrocamp, P.O. Box 1360, Claremont, CA 91711 (800) 645-1423 • (909) 625-6194 • (909) 625-7305 (fax) info@guideddiscoveries.org

INSIDER TIP: **We look for employees who take pride in their work and are capable of thriving in a residential situation. The work can be hectic and difficult, but it is highly rewarding. Because the mountains and the ocean are such integral parts of the facilities, our employees often bring a love for the outdoors with them, or they quickly develop one.**

HIDDEN CREEK RANCH

Guest Ranch • Idaho • Seasonal
www.hiddencreek.com

$ 🏠 🌐

You'll find that horses, cowboys, and ranching traditions of the American West are front and center in many of the activities at Hidden Creek Ranch; however, they have a different philosophy on the dude ranch experience. Native American undertones resonate through all their unique offerings, whether it's participation in the holistic education program, a pipe and sweat lodge ceremony, the team-building challenge course, or the nature awareness course for children. Hidden Creek Ranch is about celebrating life, being fully alive, and connecting with Mother Earth.

WHAT YOU'LL BE DOING: When you begin working at Hidden Creek Ranch, you become an integral part of the ranch family. Whether working as a wrangler, kids' wrangler or counselor, baker or chef, waitstaff, housekeeper, maintenance staff, or massage therapist, you will have only one responsibility: to make each guest feel truly at home. To ensure that staff members have a frequent change of scenery, everyone will be cross-trained to help in other aspects of the ranch operation. Besides your main job, you might also be helping in the kitchen; serving meals and caring for the guests; assisting in some outdoor cooking; helping care for the animals; helping unload and stack hay; providing airport transportation; and doing general errands and maintenance.

A smile on your face is like a window to your heart that lets people know you are home. **161**
—PAULA LESLIE

Whether working as a wrangler, baker, or counselor, each staff member at Hidden Creek Ranch is cross-trained in all aspects of ranch operation.

CHRIS HOLLO

COMMITMENT: The guest season starts in the middle of April and ends in late September. Some positions start as early as February or begin as late as June, although you must be available to work June through August.

PERKS AND REWARDS: Along with a base salary, all staff will earn a bonus for successfully completing their contract. Benefits include three all-you-can-eat gourmet meals per day and housing in Wrangler's Haven, which Hidden Creek boasts is "the finest employee housing in the business"). Everything is provided, including fully furnished rooms (shared with one other person), laundry, recreation room, and satellite television—a place that certainly will provide that home-away-from-home feeling.

THE ESSENTIALS: Applicants must be at least eighteen years of age and have current standard first aid and CPR certification. International applicants must have a valid work visa and English-language fluency.

YOUR FIRST MOVE: Send a resume and cover letter denoting your earliest start and finish dates. An application, which you can submit through email, is available online. It is advised to get your application in as early as possible, as over one thousand are received each year. The hiring process begins in November.

FOR MORE INFORMATION: Laurie Melka, Human Resources, Hidden Creek Ranch, 11077 E. Blue Lake Rd., Harrison, ID 83833 (800) 446-3833 • (208) 689-3209 • (208) 689-9115 (fax) jobs@hiddencreek.com

HIDDEN VALLEY CAMP

General Camp • Maine • Summer
www.hiddenvalleycamp.com

$ 🏕 ⊕

Nestled in a valley near the coast, with a beautiful lake, rolling hills, and old farmhouses, Hidden Valley is an "amazingly creative community of children and adults." The camp offers a well-rounded blend of both artistic and outdoor adventure programming—everything from pottery, stained glass, batik, and photography to organic gardening, horseback riding, the challenge course, and outdoor living experiences. Creativity is definitely at the heart of the staff and campers alike.

WHAT YOU'LL BE DOING: Teaching a child to throw a pot. Greeting a camper at the top of the climbing wall for the first time. Hiking up Tipi Hill to paint wildflowers. Llama trekking to a picnic. That's right, summer staff are the role models who help campers explore, take risks, make choices, and have lots of fun. The staff is broken into two areas: cabin counselors/instructors and non-cabin professional staff. Up to four counselors care for their group (ages eight to thirteen), provide teaching in various areas, and plan events for the community. Established professional artists share their talents in one particular teaching area.

COMMITMENT: Counselors kick off the summer with two weeks of staff training in early June (are you ready to challenge yourself on the zip line in the high ropes course?), then participate in two four-week sessions through mid-August. Professional artist staff usually stay for one four-week session.

PERKS AND REWARDS: A salary, housing, healthy meals (rumor has it there's a lobster banquet), and generous amounts of time off are provided. Whether you want to grab a sundae at the Superscoop, climb Mount Katahdin, or canoe at sunrise, there are plenty of off-time activities to complement your work experience. Those anticipating a career working with children will find Hidden Valley a supportive learning environment with many opportunities to develop strengths and recognize limitations.

THE ESSENTIALS: Energetic, thoughtful people who have experience working with children make the best candidates.

YOUR FIRST MOVE: Applications are available online, or call or email for materials.

FOR MORE INFORMATION: Gi Reed, Program Director, Hidden Valley Camp, 161 Hidden Valley Rd., RR1, Box 2360, Freedom, ME 04941 • (800) 922-6737 (207) 342-5177 • (207) 342-5685 (fax) • summer@hiddenvalleycamp.com

The soul is healed by being with children. **163**
—FYODOR DOSTOYEVSKY

THE HOME RANCH

Guest Ranch • Colorado • Seasonal
www.homeranch.com

$ 🏠 🌐

The call of the West has always been strong in the hearts of Americans. No matter if they were raised on the romantic tales of Zane Grey, were thrilled by the heroics of matinee idols like Roy Rogers, or laughed at the antics depicted in *City Slickers*, it's a safe bet that people of every generation have longed for the opportunity to ride the range and conquer the mountains. Working at the Home Ranch is a chance to heed that call, if only for a little while. The 1,500-acre ranch accommodates over forty-two guests per week, with activities including wilderness hikes, horseback riding, or fly-fishing on the Elk River in the summer, and cross-country skiing, snowshoeing, and downhill skiing in the winter. Seasonal staff positions include children's counselors, kitchen helpers, cooks, dishwashers, waitstaff, housekeepers, front desk, maintenance personnel, hiking guides, fly-fishing instructors, and wranglers. All positions are offered with a graduated salary starting at $900 per month, plus room, board, and laundry facilities. The summer season runs from May through October, and the winter season extends from December through March. Applications are available online.

FOR MORE INFORMATION: Staffing Coordinator, The Home Ranch, 54880 Routt County Rd. 129, P.O. Box 822, Clark, CO 80428 • (970) 879-1780 (970) 879-1795 (fax) • info@homeranch.com

HORIZON CAMPS

General Camp • New York/Pennsylvania/West Virginia • Summer
www.horizoncamps.com

$ 🏠 🌐

Horizon Camps consist of three unique camps that work together to celebrate the growth and development of children. Camp Echo Lake is in the heart of the Adirondack Mountains; Indian Head Camp is in the Endless Mountains of northeast Pennsylvania; and Twin Creeks is in the Allegheny Mountains of West Virginia. All are in rustic, wooded settings with hundreds of acres to enjoy.

WHAT YOU'LL BE DOING: Being a camp counselor is a demanding and often difficult job. Counselors live, work, eat, sleep, and play with campers nearly all day, every day. Cabin specialists spend a majority of their time with their group of campers and benefit from a variety of activities throughout the course of a day. Activity specialists also live with campers, but their daytime focus is on a specific activity area. Additionally, there are some positions that allow staff members to become a jack-of-all-trades.

COMMITMENT: Depending on the camp and position, the camp season runs from approximately mid-June to mid-August, which includes a weeklong orientation.

PERKS AND REWARDS: All staff receive an unforgettable, powerful experience with children, along with a salary, shared housing in wood-frame cabins, and meals.

THE ESSENTIALS: Those who will thrive at Horizon Camps have high energy, are hardworking, and are committed to working with children. The average age of the staff is twenty-one; some are college students, some are teachers, and others have graduated and are looking for a fulfilling way to spend a summer. At minimum, one year of college is required.

YOUR FIRST MOVE: Applications are accepted from November through May, although early applications are encouraged, as positions fill quickly.

FOR MORE INFORMATION: Staff Recruiter, Horizon Camps, 3 West Main St., Elmsford, NY 10523 • (800) 544-5448 • (914) 345-2086 • (914) 345-2120 (fax) staff@horizoncamps.com

INSIDER TIP: If you are looking for a quiet, relaxed, laid-back environment, that's not what you'll find at our camps. However, if you are looking for a great life experience and a superb resume-building opportunity, a summer with Horizon might just be for you.

HUNEWILL GUEST RANCH

Guest Ranch • California • Seasonal
www.hunewillranch.com

$ ♠♠

Hunewill Ranch is situated in the Bridgeport Valley of California, in the heart of the eastern Sierras at 6,500 feet. Directly behind the ranch are snow-covered crags that mark the boundary of Yosemite National Park. Staff members come back year after year to work hard and meet vacationers from all over the world while spending free time in the Sierras, breathing fresh, clean air. Seasonal staff, who must be at least eighteen years of age, are hired to work from the end of May to early October, with duties that may include maintenance, child care, work in the kitchen, cleaning cabins, or wrangling. Applicants must be wholesome, robust, and cheerful employees who are willing to pitch in where needed. Benefits include a wage of $6.75 to $7.50 per hour (plus any tips), housing in employee cabins, and meals for a nominal fee (no cooking facilities are available in the cabins). Send a cover letter and resume to begin the application process.

A man can succeed at almost anything for which he has unlimited enthusiasm.
—CHARLES SCHWAB

FOR MORE INFORMATION: Betsy Hunewill Elliott, Personnel Director, Hunewill Guest Ranch, 200 Hunewill Ln., Wellington, NV 89444 (775) 465-2201 • (760) 932-7710 (summer) • hunewillranch@tele-net.net

LAKE MANCOS RANCH

Guest Ranch • Colorado • Summer
www.lakemancosranch.com

$ 🏠 ⊕

Saddle up and get in touch with nature in the heart of Mesa Verde country! Located thirty-five miles west of Durango, Lake Mancos Ranch promotes a true family atmosphere for its guests. To many, a job on a guest ranch sounds exciting and arouses images of cowboys riding the range, rodeos, and fireside sing-alongs. Yes, they have the cowboys, but working on a guest ranch is not glamorous—there are meals to cook, beds to make, toilets to scrub, floors to mop, yards to mow, and plumbing to unclog. Staff members are hired for specific assignments, including kitchen assistants, recreation counselors, dining room servers, maids, wranglers, and maintenance staff, but also share in chores related to community living. The summer season starts the first weekend of June and runs through September. Most staff arrive mid-May and stay through the end of August. Along with a weekly wage, meals and dormitory-style housing (one to two roommates) are provided. Applicants must be willing to put in long hours with great enthusiasm and be at least eighteen years of age. Application materials are available online.

FOR MORE INFORMATION: Todd Sehnert, Summer Staffing, Lake Mancos Ranch, 42688 County Rd. N, Mancos, CO 81328 • (800) 325-9462 • (970) 533-1190 (970) 533-7858 (fax) • info@lakemancosranch.com

LEGACY INTERNATIONAL— GLOBAL YOUTH VILLAGE

Global Camp • Virginia • Summer
www.globalyouthvillage.org

$ 🏠 🎓 ⊕

Every summer since 1979, a dynamic learning environment has been created at Legacy International's Global Youth Village that emphasizes experiential learning and challenges young people and staff to turn cross-cultural theory and skills into practical action. Each person contributes his or her own thread of education, thought, personality, and dreams to Legacy. Legacy's aim is to transform the legacy of prejudice, fear, confusion, and misunderstanding into a legacy of hope and to help future generations realize their capabilities.

WHAT YOU'LL BE DOING: Summer staff live and work with people from all over the world while developing a deeper understanding of community development issues, discovering the broader implications of daily actions and choices, and exploring the complexity of political and social situations. Very different from an academic environment, this experience is an intensive and fulfilling learning opportunity that requires active, responsible participation. A ten-day preprogram training enhances the diverse skills and perspectives represented within the staff team. The Global Youth Village experience offers a variety of staff positions—from leadership instructors and global-awareness trainers to lifeguards, art staff, counselors, and food-service staff.

COMMITMENT: The program extends from early July through early August, with most positions involving a six-and-a-half-day workweek, including twenty-four-hour on-site responsibility as live-in cabin counselors.

PERKS AND REWARDS: Benefits include a stipend (between $900 and $1,200 for the season depending on the position), housing, meals, and laundry service. Accommodations are in cabins with youth and/or other staff. In addition, Legacy offers a healthful rural environment including a whole-foods, vegetarian diet.

THE ESSENTIALS: Whether you are finishing college or in graduate school, the Global Youth Village experience offers an amazing learning opportunity. All applicants must have previous youth work experience, be at least twenty-one years of age, and seek to enhance professional youth work or teaching experience. In addition, applicants should have some previous experience of immersion in a culture different from their own, whether it be abroad or within one's own country. Smoking and alcohol use are not allowed during the term of employment.

YOUR FIRST MOVE: Explore the online staff center for details on the experience, a listing of available positions, and an application (available in January each year). It is suggested you contact Legacy by April 1 at the very latest, as positions fill quickly.

FOR MORE INFORMATION: Leila Baz, Staff Director, Legacy International— Global Youth Village, 1020 Legacy Dr., Bedford, VA 24523 • (540) 297-5982 (540) 297-1860 (fax) • staff@legacyintl.org

INSIDER TIP: We look for people who are really excited about the program and show the flexibility and maturity to work in an intense, multicultural setting with lots of challenges. An ability to work in a close team is essential! With these qualities, we'll sometimes overlook a person's lack of experience just because of their openness, idealism, and excitement, and we'll train them.

Do your little bit of good where you are;
it's those little bits of good put together that overwhelm the world.
—DESMOND TUTU

THE LIGHTHOUSE INN

Lighthouse • Massachusetts • Summer
www.lighthouseinn.com

$ 🏠 ⊕

Situated along the shore of Nantucket Sound in Cape Cod, the Lighthouse
Inn provides seclusion, relaxation, and fun for family vacationers from mid-
May through mid-October. The inn's team of seasonal staff provides all guest
and hospitality services. Positions are available in food and beverage (from
servers to chefs), the front office (from children's program staff to front desk
workers), and housekeeping. Along with a weekly wage, housing is provided
for those who can work through mid-October. Applications are available
online and a personal interview is required.

FOR MORE INFORMATION: Staffing Director, The Lighthouse Inn,
1 Lighthouse Inn Rd., P.O. Box 128, West Dennis, MA 02670 • (508) 398-2244
(508) 398-5658 (fax) • inquire@lighthouseinn.com

MOHONK MOUNTAIN HOUSE

Resort • New York • Seasonal
www.mohonkjobs.com

$ 🏠

One of the last of the great nineteenth-century Victorian castles, Mohonk
Mountain House is surrounded by thousands of acres of unspoiled forest and
winding trails (with trail signs that read "Slowly and Quietly Please"). This is
the essence of Mohonk (which means "lake in the sky")—a unique setting for
relaxation and renewal of the body, mind, and spirit in beautiful natural surroundings. Family-owned since 1869, the resort grounds feature gardens, a
greenhouse, picnic areas, a museum, stables, sports facilities, and an observation point known as Sky Top Tower. Seasonal and year-round staff members
have the opportunity to work in all resort areas, including food and beverage,
conference services, hotel operations, personnel, properties, retail, and guest
services. Most positions extend from April or May through mid-November.
Along with an hourly wage, there is limited dormitory-style housing available
for a modest fee, which also includes three meals per day. The resort prides
itself on offering use of the facilities and encourages employees to participate
in scheduled events. All applicants must be at least eighteen years of age, and
a personal interview is required for all positions. For more info on the resort
itself, visit www.mohonk.com.

FOR MORE INFORMATION: Personnel Director, Mohonk Mountain House,
1000 Mountain Rest Rd., New Paltz, NY 12561 • (845) 256-2089
(845) 256-2049 (fax) • info@mohonk.com

MOUNTAIN TRAIL OUTDOOR SCHOOL

Outdoor Education • North Carolina • 3–5 Months
www.kanuga.org

$ 🏕

Mountain Trail Outdoor School is the outdoor education wing of Kanuga
Conference Center, a nonprofit conference and retreat center affiliated with
the Episcopal Church. Kanuga also offers residential summer camp programs
for youth and adults. Mountain Trail is set on 1,400 acres in the beautiful
Blue Ridge Mountains, with many scenic vistas and an endangered species on
the property. After a training period, instructors and interns are responsible
for assisting with program development and teaching natural history classes,
environmental awareness, new games and initiatives, adventure activities, low
and high ropes, and rock climbing. Wages start at $200 per week, plus room
and board. The program runs February to May and August to December,
with several separate summer camp programs available from June through
August. Prior experience with children, nature studies, and the outdoors are
key assets for prospective applicants. It's best to send in all application materials by December 1 for the spring and July 1 for the fall.

FOR MORE INFORMATION: Paul Bockoven, Outdoor Education Director,
Mountain Trail Outdoor School, Kanuga Conference Center, P.O. Box 250,
Hendersonville, NC 28793-0250 • (828) 692-9136, ext. 240
(828) 696-3589 (fax) • mtos@kanuga.org

NORTH FORK RANCH

Guest Ranch • Colorado • Summer
www.northforkranch.com

$ 🏕 🌐

Experience the West, where the lifestyle of the American cowboy still lingers.
North Fork Ranch, a small, family-oriented ranch in the heart of the Rockies,
offers everything an outdoor enthusiast could want, including great horseback
riding, white-water rafting, overnight pack trips, hiking, trapshooting, terrific
fishing, and the unique opportunity to meet and make friends from all over
the world.

To put one's thoughts into actions is the most difficult thing in the world. **169**
—JOHANN VON GOETHE

WHAT YOU'LL BE DOING: Whether as a cook, wrangler, kid's counselor, or wait-person, summer staff members are the backbone of making guests feel right at home. Because the ranch is a people-serving business, they do not hire a person merely to get a job done. You will be expected to give totally of your-self, sharing with and caring for their guests.

COMMITMENT: The ranch is primarily interested in those who can arrive in May and stay through August.

PERKS AND REWARDS: Staff members receive $650 per month, plus room and great home-style meals. (Yes, there will be many barbecues and steak cookouts!) On your day off and after daily duties, you can enjoy all ranch activities.

THE ESSENTIALS: Simply stated, they seek dedicated, dependable, and dynamic individuals.

YOUR FIRST MOVE: Call for application materials. The ranch begins their review of applications starting in January and tries to have its entire staff hired by May 1.

FOR MORE INFORMATION: Dean and Karen May, Owners, North Fork Ranch, 55395 Hwy. 285, P.O. Box B, Shawnee, CO 80475 • (800) 843-7895 (303) 838-9873 • (303) 838-1549 (fax) • info@northforkranch.com

INSIDER TIP: Do you love people? Do you love to work? Are you willing to learn and do new things? Are you flexible and willing to help out anytime, anywhere, and do anything? Are you enthusiastic and excited about other people enjoying their vacation? Would you involve yourself in the ranch's basic objective of making the guests' stay at North Fork Ranch a great experience? If you answered yes to these questions, you are the type of person we are looking for!

OAKLAND HOUSE SEASIDE RESORT

Resort • Maine • 2–12 Weeks
www.oaklandhouse.com

$ 🏕 🌐

Life at Oakland House Seaside Resort is more "like it used to be," with guests and staff enjoying leisure hours and making creative use of time. At the turn of the nineteenth century, the first guests were the "Rusticators," who arrived on steamships from Boston, New York, and places beyond. They were writers, artists, and educators seeking respite from city bustle. Today

The Oakland House culinary staff meet in the organic gardens to discuss what herbs and vegetables will be harvested for the evening's five-course meal.

SALLY LITTLEFIELD

Oakland House offers a half mile of prime oceanfront, ocean and lakeside beaches, hiking trails, a dock, rowboats, and, of course, relaxation.

WHAT YOU'LL BE DOING: No matter their position, Oakland House staff members are there to make guests feel welcome in a family-style atmosphere. Positions include waitstaff, cabin stewards, housekeepers, first mate (for boat trips), and assistants for the office/reservation desk, kitchen, maintenance, and grounds and garden. Culinary internships with a seasoned culinary staff are also available. Interns will work with the executive chef to create five-course dinners that emphasize the use of locally harvested seafood and meat along with vegetables and herbs from their organic garden. At season's peak, you'll find thirty-five staff members working at various jobs on the property.

COMMITMENT: Positions begin in mid-May, with staggered completion terms through the end of October, and a few positions available into November. In addition, two- to eight-week culinary internships are available throughout the season. The normal workweek ranges from forty- to forty-eight hours per week, six days a week.

PERKS AND REWARDS: The pay varies with each position, and on-site room and board are available for $50 per week. On days off, staff members are welcome to use rowboats, recreational facilities, the lake, and ocean beaches. Assistance is also provided to get staff members off-site, including free boat excursions in the surrounding region.

THE ESSENTIALS: Applicants must be at least eighteen years of age and have a cheerful and positive attitude and a neat appearance. Because of the resort's rural location, it's recommended that you bring a car. Many staff members

There's always something to suggest you'll never be who you want to be. Your choice is to take it or keep on moving.
—PHYLICIA RASHAD

171

return year after year as they work through college. International applicants are hired only through student programs such as Resort America and CIEE.

YOUR FIRST MOVE: Detailed information and applications can be obtained online.

FOR MORE INFORMATION: Jim and Sally Littlefield, Innkeepers, Oakland House Seaside Resort, Herricks Landing, Brooksville, ME 04617 (207) 359-8521 • (207) 359-9865 (fax) • jim@oaklandhouse.com

🐾 **INSIDER TIP: English majors, artists, writers, and musicians! Besides being a beautiful rural coastal community, the area is a haven for the arts. You will find stimulation and like-minded people at Oakland House and in the local area.**

POINT REYES NATIONAL SEASHORE ASSOCIATION

Ocean-Based Camp • California • Summer
www.ptreyes.org

$ 🏠

Point Reyes offers a six-week residential science camp for kids aged seven to twelve, who explore the rich coastal environment and diverse habitats of the region, as well as a six-day adventure camp for teens aged thirteen to sixteen, who are led on a four-day backpack trip focusing on self-esteem, teamwork, and backpacking skills.

WHAT YOU'LL BE DOING: Naturalist interns/counselors primarily assist with guided natural history and environmental education programs, mealtime supervision, free-time activities, and cabin supervision for children attending the Science Camp. Not only will interns work with experts in the field of environmental and outdoor education, they will also have the chance to obtain training in educational and behavior-management techniques, natural history interpretation, and recreational-leadership skills. Other summer staff positions include six naturalists, a director, and three kitchen workers.

COMMITMENT: Summer positions start with staff training in mid-June and end in mid-August.

PERKS AND REWARDS: Naturalist interns/counselors are provided with a weekly stipend of $185 to $225, along with room and board; the weekly stipend for naturalists ranges from $375 to $425. This is a great way to experience the warmth and camaraderie of living and working with other staff members in a residential camp environment.

THE ESSENTIALS: All applicants should enjoy working with children and in the outdoors, have a knowledge of ecological concepts and ecosystems, and be certified in first aid and CPR. Preference is given to those who are in college (for intern positions); who are willing to work and live with campers in a rustic setting; and who are creative, enthusiastic, flexible, and self-motivated and have a sense of humor. Experience in supervising or teaching students is a bonus. Naturalists should have at least one year of experience working in a residential outdoor education program.

YOUR FIRST MOVE: Call for application materials. On-site interviews are preferred, but phone interviews are acceptable.

FOR MORE INFORMATION: Scott Wolland, Education Programs Director, Point Reyes National Seashore Association, Point Reyes Station, CA 94956 (415) 663-1224 • (415) 663-8174 (fax) • summercamp@ptreyes.org

RAMAPO ANCHORAGE CAMP

Therapeutic Camp • New York • Summer
www.ramapoforchildren.org

$ 🏠 🌐

Camp Ramapo fosters the development of positive social and learning skills for children who have a wide range of emotional, behavioral, and learning problems. Counselors work individually with children through educational and outdoor adventure programming, helping them to develop their school readiness and the communication skills necessary for healthy growth. The staff consists mostly of college students and recent graduates who have strong leadership and caring qualities that enable them to motivate and relate to young people. A stipend, room, and board are provided. Application forms can be found online. Ramapo also conducts Field Experience in Special Education, an on-site, year-round college course for which participants can receive academic credit.

FOR MORE INFORMATION: Scott Kemp, Director of Operations, Ramapo Anchorage Camp, P.O. Box 266, Rhinebeck, NY 12572-0266 (845) 876-8403 • (845) 876-8414 (fax) • office@ramapoforchildren.org

RESORT AT SQUAW CREEK

Resort • California • Seasonal
www.squawcreek.com

$ ⊕

Ideally situated at the base of Squaw Valley USA, the Resort at Squaw Creek offers more than four hundred rooms, five restaurants, a fitness center, a full-service spa, and unlimited recreation in the beautiful Sierra Nevadas. Whether you're looking for a summer, winter, or year-round job, positions are available as food servers, conference service attendants, retail sales clerks, fitness attendants, drivers, and spa hosts. It's always best to look for housing early, and keeping roommates in mind is a good idea. The average rent for a studio ranges from $550 to $700 a month, while houses start at about $1,000 a month. Specific job openings can be found online, or call or email for more information.

FOR MORE INFORMATION: Human Resources Department, Resort at Squaw Creek, 400 Squaw Creek Rd., P.O. Box 3333, Olympic Valley, CA 96146 530) 581-6642 • (530) 581-6681 (job hotline) • (530) 581-6648 (fax) info@squawcreek.com

SEACAMP

Ocean-Based Camp/Sailing • Florida • Summer
www.seacamp.org

$ ⚑ ⊕

Established in 1966, Seacamp is dedicated to the study of marine communities and island habitats, with courses led by academically trained marine science instructors. Over 7,500 teenagers have attended one of Seacamp's eighteen-day programs, which focus on everything from sailing, scuba, and kayaking to photography and arts and crafts. Although their backgrounds vary, participants share at least one common interest: the importance of oceans and marine life to their world.

YOUR SURROUNDINGS: With its beautiful location at Newfound Harbor, Seacamp is minutes from the most extensive living coral reef in North

America. Opportunities abound to explore the exciting waters of the Florida Keys, in both the Atlantic Ocean and the Gulf of Mexico. Indians, pirates, and Flagler's Railroad all contribute to the heritage of this subtropical area.

WHAT YOU'LL BE DOING: A variety of instructor positions are available, including in arts and crafts, boardsailing, photography, sailing, science, and scuba, as well as other positions as counselors and kitchen and maintenance staff. Whatever the position, each staff member participates in all camp activities. The camp experience is a unique learning environment that combines the living and working aspects of the staff member's life, and many times it becomes hard to distinguish between learning and teaching experiences.

COMMITMENT: The summer season runs from late May through late August. For those who would like to continue to teach young people about the sea, Newfound Harbor Marine Institute (a Seacamp program) provides workshops and residential programs from early September through late May. See their listing on page 284 for more information.

PERKS AND REWARDS: Benefits include a weekly salary, lodging, meals, and health insurance. A four-week precamp training program provides American Red Cross lifeguarding, first aid, and CPR certification, NAUI skin diving instruction, a forty-hour workshop in seamanship and boat handling, and if scuba certified, rescue-diver training.

THE ESSENTIALS: The minimum age for employment is nineteen years, and most candidates are either in college or have just graduated. With the heart of Seacamp's program focused on marine science education, the best applicants possess an interest in working with teenagers in a water-oriented setting.

YOUR FIRST MOVE: Call for application materials. Phone interviews begin in March and continue through April.

FOR MORE INFORMATION: Grace Upshaw, Camp Director, Seacamp, 1300 Big Pine Ave., Big Pine Key, FL 33043-3336 • (877) 732-2267 (305) 872-2331 • (305) 872-2555 (fax) • seacamp2002@aol.com info@seacamp.org

---

That which we obtain too easily, we esteem too lightly. It is dearness only which gives everything its value. Heaven knows how to put a proper price on its goods.
—THOMAS PAINE

WORKING AT A SKI RESORT

· ·

If you have a love for children, there are plenty of ski instructor opportunities with kid-friendly resorts.

The popular saying among employees at the Village at Breckenridge Resort is "you move here for the winters, but end up staying for the summers." This appears to be the common theme for thousands of snow enthusiasts who work seasonally at ski resorts all over the country. Beyond a work environment that provides breathtaking scenery, one of the biggest perks of becoming a "ski bum" for the winter is the coveted ski pass (along with free ski rentals and lessons and discounts on just about everything offered at the resort).

Most ski resorts offer the same types of seasonal jobs, which fall under the categories of administration, food and beverage, hospitality services, mountain operations, and ski services. So whether you want to become a snowboard instructor, teach children how to ski, serve meals to guests, or assist with marketing efforts, opportunities abound. In general, people from all walks of life are hired—from those who recently finished their college studies to those looking for a lifestyle change.

INSIDER TIP: For a directory of ski and snowboard related websites (including a great search engine and job page), check out **SkiCentral.com.**

SO YOU WANT TO BE A SKI INSTRUCTOR?

For those interested in ski and snowboard instructor positions, sometimes it's not enough to be an excellent skier. Certification in your specialty is often a requirement. Ski instructors should contact the Professional Ski Instructors of America (www.psia.org). For ski patrol positions, the National Ski Patrol (www.nsp.org) provides courses and certification. Similarly, the American Association of Snowboard Instructors (www.aasi.org) provides snowboarding certification. You'll also find that ski resorts look for those who are effective communicators and have a knowledge of teaching and learning theory, biomechanics and kinesiology, and human development.

CALIFORNIA

BEAR VALLEY MOUNTAIN RESORT

$ ⊕

Located in the Stanislaus National Forest between Lake Tahoe and Yosemite, Bear Valley boasts over thirty feet of snow each year with 1,280 acres of skiable terrain. In late November, hundreds of seasonal employees come to Bear Valley to work, learn, and play. Typical ski jobs can be found, ranging from lift operations and food service to ski and snowboard instruction, with positions generally running through April 15. Along with an hourly wage, benefits include generous ski and snowboard privileges, family and friends passes, and ski and snowboard lessons. Limited employee housing is also available. Applicants are encouraged to attend the resort's annual job fair in late October. Applications are available online, or call or write for more information.

FOR MORE INFORMATION: Human Resources, Bear Valley Mountain Resort, P.O. Box 5038, Bear Valley, CA 95223 • (209) 753-2301, ext. 105 (209) 753-6421 (fax) • work@bearvalley.com • www.bearvalley.com

The main thing in life is not to be afraid of being human.   177
—PABLO CASALS

DIAMOND PEAK SKI RESORT/ INCLINE VILLAGE GID

$ ⊕

Located on the beautiful north shore of Lake Tahoe, Incline Village General Improvement District (IVGID) facilities include Diamond Peak Ski Resort, two eighteen-hole golf courses, a recreation center, beaches, and parks—with seasonal employment opportunities available in each! During the winter, positions range from lift operators and instructors to food and beverage staff and ski patrol. Hourly wages vary and perks include food discounts, complimentary skiing and boarding, equipment rental and lessons, free or discounted use of the Incline Recreation Center (with an Olympic-size swimming pool, gym, weight room, and fitness classes), and the possibility of two free classes at Sierra Nevada College. During the summer, positions range from day camp leaders and lifeguards to recreation hosts and grounds staff. Perks include food discounts, access to private beaches, free or discounted use of the golf courses, Incline Recreation Center, and tennis complex, and the possibility of two free classes at Sierra Nevada College. Those who possess a good work ethic, enjoy the outdoors and beautiful mountain settings, are customer-service focused, and have a flexible schedule will thrive here. Specific job descriptions and applications can be found online.

FOR MORE INFORMATION: Lisa Hoopes, Human Resources Analyst, Diamond Peak Ski Resort/Incline Village GID, 893 Southwood Blvd., Incline Village, NV 89451 • (775) 832-1205 • (775) 832-1359 (fax) jobs@ivgid.org • www.diamondpeak.com • www.ivgid.org

HEAVENLY SKI RESORT

$ 🏠 ⊕

Spread over 4,800 acres of Tahoe's majestic terrain with the highest skiable peak rising to over ten thousand feet, the mountain itself certainly draws many to Heavenly Ski Resort. However, those who join the Heavenly team also join a community of people who share a common bond: a love for mountain living, outdoor adventuring, and, well, living life to the fullest. In addition to great alpine skiing, Heavenly offers a snowboard park (with a snowboard cross course and a half-pipe) and an adventure park at 9,100 feet that showcases a tubing run and wide-open terrain for snow play and sledding, cross-country skiing, and snowshoeing. Seasonal staff come from all over the world and work in every conceivable area on the mountain and at the resort. If working and playing at Heavenly aren't benefit enough, additional perks include a free ski pass for Heavenly and five other ski resorts

With panoramic views of California and Nevada, Heavenly's aerial tram takes guests and seasonal employees to Lake Tahoe's highest mountain—10,067 feet!

(Arapahoe Basin, Beaver Creek, Breckenridge, Keystone, and Vail), free ski and snowboard lessons, employee events and parties, medical and accident insurance (for a fee), and discounts galore on just about everything. For those who make at least a three-month commitment, limited employee housing is an option (units fit four to six people and are fully furnished). The majority of employees, however, live in the cities of South Lake Tahoe, California, and Stateline, Nevada. As a general rule, expect to pay $300 to $500 per month per person for rent. Current job openings are constantly updated online and an online application is available. Job fairs are generally held in late October.

FOR MORE INFORMATION: Personnel, Heavenly Ski Resort, P.O. Box 2180, Stateline, NV 89449 • (530) 542-5180 • (530) 541-2643 (fax) personnel@vailresorts.com • www.skiheavenly.com

KIRKWOOD MOUNTAIN RESORT

$ 🏠 ⊕

Over one hundred years ago, Zachary Kirkwood found himself in awe of a landscape of vibrant meadows surrounded by towering peaks. This High Sierra valley now bears his name and your reaction to this protected enclave may well be the same—that is, if you decide to explore the opportunities at Kirkwood Mountain Resort. As with most ski resorts, you'll find the usual seasonal employment opportunities—from lodging and housekeeping staff to skier services and ski and snowboard instructors. The ski season is always

When we do the best we can, we never know what miracle is wrought in our life, or in the life of another.
—HELEN KELLER

179

contingent on snow conditions, but usually runs from Thanksgiving through the end of April. Along with an hourly wage, there are a plethora of perks, including a free season pass, group ski and snowboarding lessons, cross-country trail use and lessons, lift tickets for family and friends, and an employee shuttle from surrounding towns (South Lake Tahoe, California, and Gardnerville, Nevada, are about forty miles from the resort). On-site housing is available for about 20 percent of the employees, so apply early! Rent for a fully furnished apartment runs $220 to $460 per month, including utilities. Applications can be obtained online, although it's best to apply in person at the hiring fair held in October.

FOR MORE INFORMATION: Human Resources Manager, Kirkwood Mountain Resort, P.O. Box 1, Kirkwood, CA 95646 • (209) 258-7310 (209) 258-7340 (job hotline) • (209) 258-7368 (fax) humanresources@kirkwood.com • www.kirkwood.com

MAMMOTH MOUNTAIN SKI AREA

$ 🏠 ⊕

As you drive along California's Highway 395 on the eastern side of the Sierra Nevadas, Mammoth Mountain is impossible to miss: its 11,053-foot summit dominates the skyline as the highway moves from desert to forest. One look at Mammoth any time between October and June will be explanation enough for Mammoth's claim to skiing fame: the mountain gets an average of 385 inches of snow per year! In addition to epic skiing at Mammoth Mountain, the resort also operates June Mountain, a smaller "boutique" resort, as well as a number of other recreational and lodging facilities. Seasonal positions are offered in four areas—skier services, outside operations, food services, and hotel operations—with the bulk of positions available during the winter from late November through April. Along with a weekly wage starting at $8 per hour, winter housing is provided for first-year seasonal employees who are part of the Mammoth entry-level staff or those participating in the foreign exchange program. Housing varies from private rooms to bunk beds at a cost of $9 to $16 per night (over six hundred beds in the Mammoth Lakes area are committed to employees). Yes, there are plenty of perks as well, including complimentary skiing, snowboarding, and cross-country skiing privileges and lessons. International applicants need to apply for winter employment by September 1 in order to ensure adequate time to process documentation and guarantee housing.

FOR MORE INFORMATION: Tim Vadheim, Recruiting Manager, Human Resources Department, Mammoth Mountain Ski Area, P.O. Box 24, Mammoth Lakes, CA 93546 • (800) 472-3160 • (760) 934-0654 • (760) 934-0608 (fax) personnel@mammoth-mtn.com • www.mammothmountain.com

NORTHSTAR-AT-TAHOE

$ ⊕

Located at Lake Tahoe in the majestic northern Sierra Nevada (where the sun shines 80 percent of the time), Northstar offers winter, summer, and year-round positions. The majority of opportunities are during the winter months (mid-December through mid-April), with a focus on mountain operations, food and beverage, housekeeping, ski rental, retail, and lodging. Along with a weekly wage, benefits include a complimentary ski and snowboard pass and skiing privileges at all Booth Creek Resorts (www.boothcreek.com), as well as participation in employee events, such as parties, ski races, and golf tournaments throughout the year. Most of the hiring is done at job fairs at the end of October, which gives applicants the chance to meet managers in person. Interviews can be arranged after the job fairs depending on what positions are still available. Employment packets for the winter season are available at the beginning of September and can be obtained by calling the job hotline.

FOR MORE INFORMATION: Holly Silverston, Employee Services, Northstar-at-Tahoe, P.O. Box 129, Truckee, CA 96160 • (800) 466-6784, ext. 3 (530) 562-3510 • (530) 562-2217 (job hotline) • jobs@skinorthstar.com www.northstarattahoe.com

ROYAL GORGE
CROSS COUNTRY SKI RESORT

$ 🏠 ⊕

With over nine thousand acres of private land and a network of ninety trails, Royal Gorge is the largest cross-country ski resort in North America. Guest services include two overnight lodges, a day lodge, and ten warming huts sprinkled throughout the track system on historic Donner Summit. From mid-November through mid-April, seasonal employees work in administration, mountain operations, resort services, the ski school, and the wilderness lodge. As in any ski area, work hours are entirely dependent upon the weather. Along with downhill skiing privileges at four neighboring resorts, perks include a free season pass, use of rental equipment, and ski school lessons, as well as discounted meals. For those who need housing, Royal Gorge has several furnished houses, mostly within walking distance of the resort, with rents ranging from $80 to $270 per month, plus utilities. Bunkhouse-style accommodations are also available for part-time employees. Send a resume and cover letter to begin the application process or attend the job fair in mid-October. Applications are available online.

Happiness resides not in possessions and not in gold.
The feeling of happiness dwells in the soul.
—DEMOCRITUS

DAVID MADISON

Seasonal ski instructors at Royal Gorge Cross Country Ski Resort help novices fine-tune their cross-country skiing abilities.

FOR MORE INFORMATION: Neil Erasmus, Director of Operations/Human Resources, Royal Gorge Cross Country Ski Resort, P.O. Box 1100, Soda Springs, CA 95728 (800) 500-3871 • (530) 426-3871 • (530) 426-9221 (fax) • hr@royalgorge.com www.royalgorge.com

SQUAW VALLEY USA

$ ⊕

Whether working as a children's ski instructor or as one of their cable car operators, winter seasonal staff at Squaw Valley are offered fun and recreation, lifetime friendships, personal achievements, and a valuable work experience. Flexible hours, competitive wages, and the benefits alone (a free ski pass, lessons, and discounts galore) make this a great way to spend a season in Lake Tahoe. It's always best to visit the personnel office in person or attend the job fair in November, where they'll be doing interviews and making job offers on the spot. However, if you won't be in the Tahoe area, either fill out the online application or call for an employment booklet.

FOR MORE INFORMATION: Personnel Department, Squaw Valley USA, P.O. Box 2007, Olympic Valley, CA 96146 • (530) 581-7112 (530) 581-7202 (fax) • personnel@squaw.com • www.squaw.com

SUGAR BOWL SKI RESORT

$ 🏠 🌐

Home to the first chairlift in California and the first gondola in the country, Sugar Bowl, with over 1,500 acres of challenging terrain, four picturesque mountain peaks, and three day lodges, is known for its rich history and deep powder. Those who come to work for Sugar Bowl are lured by the mountains, an enjoyable working experience, and an enriching lifestyle. Benefits include a season pass and complimentary lift tickets for friends and family, discounts on just about everything, and flexible schedules. Limited housing is also available: dorm rooms have two or three people per room, with community bathrooms down the hall, and are $225 to $250 per month, while semiprivate "hotel-style" rooms have two people per room, a private bath and TV, and run $275 to $300 per month. It's recommended that you attend the Sugar Bowl job fair, which is normally conducted the last two Saturdays of October. Applications are available online.

FOR MORE INFORMATION: Human Resources, Sugar Bowl Ski Resort, P.O. Box 5, Norden, CA 95724 • (530) 426-6730 • (530) 426-6731 (job hotline) (530) 426-3723 (fax) • personnel@sugarbowl.com • www.sugarbowl.com

COLORADO

CHALLENGE ASPEN

$ 🏠

Based in Snowmass Village, Colorado, Challenge Aspen is a year-round recreational program for people with disabilities. From December 1 through April 15, five interns and a program assistant will join the Challenge Aspen team for the winter ski season. Interns will spend a majority of their time helping with ski lessons as adaptive assistants on the ski slopes, with the remainder of their time spent helping in the schools and promoting disability awareness. The program assistant will mostly work alongside administration staff members, with duties ranging from phone communication and scheduling to personal relations with disabled skiers, families, and friends. Housing and a monthly living stipend are provided in exchange for all your work. If you have what it takes to help create possibilities for people with disabilities, zip on over to their website and fill out the online application.

*It is a good idea to obey all the rules when you're young just so you'll have
the strength to break them when you're old.*
—MARK TWAIN

CHALLENGE ASPEN

Helping those with disabilities gain the self-esteem and confidence necessary to lead fulfilling and productive lives, interns with Challenge Aspen use specially designed adaptive ski equipment on the slopes.

FOR MORE INFORMATION:
Stacey Berley
Internship Supervisor
Challenge Aspen
P.O. Box M
Aspen, CO 81612
(800) 530-3901
(970) 923-0578
(970) 923-7338 (fax)
stacey@challengeaspen.com
www.challengeaspen.com

COPPER MOUNTAIN RESORT

$ 🏠 🌐

Blessed with a nearly perfect mountain (naturally divided into a variety of terrain features for expert, intermediate, and beginning skiers), Copper Mountain Resort is both a local's choice and a popular destination resort for people who love the mountains. Winter seasonal employees begin their adventure in early November and work in a variety of on- and off-the-mountain positions. The average entry-level wage is $8 per hour, along with a season pass and free lessons. However, to keep your season filled with glades, half-pipes, parks, bowls, and cruisers, you'll also have unlimited skiing access at an additional fifteen ski areas in Colorado with the Real Deal reciprocal ski pass. An additional five free days of skiing at nine Intrawest resorts is also provided. Once you have secured a position with Copper, you can also apply for EDGE housing, which provides slope-side accommodations for up to five hundred people in shared rooms. Otherwise, most find housing in the surrounding towns of Frisco, Dillon, Silverthorne, Breckenridge, or Leadville, with the average cost of housing ranging from $350 to $650 per person per month. For those interested in booking short-term temporary housing (or maybe longer-term accommodations), one of these three hostels will get you started: Alpen Hutte (www.alpenhutte.com); Just Bunks (www.hostels.com/justbunks); and Leadville Hostel (www.leadvillehostel.com). Hostelling is one of the most affordable options in the area, averaging about $250 per month. If at all possible, apply in person—on-the-spot interviews are arranged whenever possible. You'll have a greater chance of securing a seasonal job (and housing!) faster. Phone calls are always welcomed!

FOR MORE INFORMATION: Human Resources Manager, Copper Mountain Resort, P.O. Box 3548, Copper Mountain, CO 80443 • (800) 458-8386 • (970) 968-3060 (970) 968-3165 (fax) • humanresources@coppercolorado.com www.coppercolorado.com

CRESTED BUTTE MOUNTAIN RESORT

$ ⊕

Known for its extreme skiing and its funky Victorian architecture, Crested Butte remains one of the last undiscovered ski towns in the West and is home to the U.S. Extreme Skiing and Snowboarding Championships. College students take note—in additional to seasonal employment opportunities, Crested Butte Mountain Resort also has a winter and summer internship program, with positions in business, early childhood development, food and beverage, hospitality management, sales, and ski area management. So while you're earning academic credit, you're also gaining experience in the field and making the same wages as other seasonal employees. Starting wages range from $7 to $8 per hour along with a Real Deal ski pass that gives you ski privileges not only at Crested Butte, but also at Aspen, Copper Mountain, Durango, Loveland, Monarch, Steamboat, Sunlight, and Winter Park! Check online for the latest openings, application details, and housing contact information.

FOR MORE INFORMATION: Kyndall Coffman, Human Resources, Crested Butte Mountain Resort, 12 Snowmass Rd., P.O. Box 5700, Mt. Crested Butte, CO 81225 • (970) 349-4069 • (970) 349-4777 (job hotline) (970) 349-2250 (fax) • jobs@cbmr.com • www.skicb.com

STEAMBOAT SKI AND RESORT CORPORATION

$ ⚑ ⊕

Steamboat Springs has the distinction of being the home of more winter Olympic athletes than any other town in North America (with forty-seven and still counting). Not only is this a great place to ski, averaging over three hundred inches of snow and 2,900 acres of skiing terrain, the town is rich in Western heritage, with a lifestyle that includes a true ranching community, many cultural events, great nightlife, and endless outdoor and sporting activities. Staff positions are available either indoors or out, and your new mode of transportation to work just may be a high-speed gondola with your skis attached! Close to a thousand full-time staff members are hired on the

It's never too late to be what you might have been.   **185**
—GEORGE ELIOT

mountain in these areas: accounting, competition services, courtesy patrol, mountain operations, food and beverage, kids' vacation center, lift ticket office, reservations, real estate and facilities, resort services, security, and ski and snowboard school, along with positions at the Steamboat Grand Resort Hotel. Winter staff are generally hired from Thanksgiving until mid-April. And don't forget about the summer months: summer operations normally begin in early June and go through Labor Day, with positions that range from adventure club counselors to mountain trail crew. Many jobs don't require that you know how to ski or snowboard, but if you'd like to learn, they'll be happy to teach you—just one of the many staff benefits. Others include competitive wages, a free ski pass (including dependents), access to a health insurance plan, and limited staff housing. Housing is maintained in two-bedroom, two-bath units located approximately one mile from the base area. These units are fully furnished, down to the pots and pans. Rent, based on two people per room (a total of four occupants in one unit), is $300 per month plus utilities, and units are filled on a first-come, first-served basis. Applications are available online and the resort's annual job fair is held in early November each year. Instructors and patrol candidates must attend a hiring clinic in late November or early December.

FOR MORE INFORMATION: Human Resources, Steamboat Ski and Resort Corporation, 2305 Mt. Werner Circle, Steamboat Springs, CO 80487 (970) 871-5132 • (970) 871-5130 (fax) • personnel@steamboat.com www.steamboat.com

TELLURIDE SKI AND GOLF COMPANY

$

In addition to your typical ski resort jobs that are available in the winter months and throughout the year, Telluride offers a twelve-week internship program that allows interns to work in different departments and perform varied tasks. For interns, a $1,000 stipend is provided, along with a free ski pass if you work during the winter months. Employee housing is limited; however, they will assist you in finding suitable accommodations (the local paper, the *Daily Planet*, is a good source of available rentals). To begin the internship application process, send a resume, a letter of reference, a copy of your school's internship manual, and a letter detailing your skills and internship goals. For seasonal employment, applications are available online.

FOR MORE INFORMATION: Heather Young, Human Resources Manager, Telluride Ski and Golf Company, 565 Mountain Village Blvd. Telluride, CO 81435 • (888) 754-1010 • (970) 728-7331 • (970) 728-7443 (fax) hyoung@tellurideskiresort.com • www.tellurideskiresort.com

VAIL RESORTS

$ 🏠 ⊕

Vail Resorts (www.vailresorts.com) owns and operates four ski resorts—Vail, Beaver Creek, Breckenridge, and Keystone—all located within a forty-mile radius of each other. That's good news for seasonal and year-round employees coming to the Rocky Mountains of Colorado, as your ski and snowboard pass is good at each of them. And that's just the beginning. In addition to free ski and snowboard lessons, health benefits, and resort-wide meal, lodging, and retail discounts, employee housing is available. All housing is furnished and cable ready, with dormitory- or apartment-style options and rents ranging from $250 to $490 per month.

Employment information can be found at www.skijob1.com, a searchable database of current employment opportunities; through the job hotline at (888) SKI-JOB1 (888-754-5621); or by contacting each resort individually.

Vail Mountain Resort

Most employees come to Vail for the skiing; however, the small-town atmosphere, active outdoor lifestyle, and friendly people lure them for more than just a season. Vail Mountain features the world-famous back bowls and the biggest network of high-speed quad lifts in North America.

FOR MORE INFORMATION: Human Resources, Vail Mountain Resort, P.O. Box 7, Vail, CO 81658 • (970) 479-3060 • (970) 479-3070 (fax) vailjobs@vailresorts.com

HOSPITALITY AND LODGING POSITIONS: The Lodge at Vail, Human Resources 174 E. Gore Creek Dr., Vail, CO 81657 • (970) 477-3751 • (970) 477-3746 (fax) lavjobs@vailresorts.com

Beaver Creek Resort

Located in the heart of Colorado's White River National Forest, Beaver Creek is one of the most spectacular ski mountains in the world. The 4,040 feet of awe-inspiring vertical slopes and 146 trails accommodate every level of rider, including those determined to win the World Cup on the legendary Birds of Prey downhill course. And if you love skiing with sunny skies, the area averages over 275 days of sunshine per year.

SKI AND HOSPITALITY/LODGING POSITIONS: Beaver Creek Resort, Human Resources, P.O. Box 7, Vail, CO 81658 • (970) 845-5270 • (970) 845-5284 (fax) beavercreekjobx@vailresorts.com

Vail/Beaver Creek Ski School employment information: www.vailbcsschools.com

Remember that the watcher learns it, but the doer lives it. **187**
—SCOTT LEWIS

Breckenridge Resort

Over 1,500 employees come to Breckenridge to enjoy alpine and Nordic skiing, snowboarding, and ice-skating during the winter months, while the summer is filled with white-water rafting, mountain biking, hiking, and a summer music festival on Maggie Pond. In addition to on-the-mountain ski positions, those who want to advance their careers in the resort and hospitality field will find plenty of opportunities at the Village at Breckenridge and the Great Divide Lodge.

FOR MORE INFORMATION: Breckenridge Resort, Human Resources, P.O. Box 1058, Breckenridge, CO 80424 • (970) 453-3238 (970) 453-3260 (fax) • breckjobs@vailresorts.com

LODGING AND HOSPITALITY POSITIONS: The Village at Breckenridge/ Great Divide Lodge, Human Resources, P.O. Box 8329, Breckenridge, CO 80424 (970) 453-3120 • (970) 453-3127 (fax) • breckhr@vailresorts.com

Keystone

With a naturally spectacular setting in the Arapaho National Forest, Keystone Resort offers a variety of year-round employment opportunities in addition to those on the slopes during the winter months. Keystone's best kept secret is its summer. More than 1,800 employees work year-round at the conference center, lodges, restaurants, or golf courses.

HELEN NORMAN

FOR MORE INFORMATION:
Human Resources
Keystone Resort
P.O. Box 38
Keystone, CO 80435
(970) 496-4157
(970) 496-4310 (fax)
keyjobs@vailresorts.com

Whether it's Glow Bug Skate Night or a pickup hockey game after work, Keystone's ice skating rink serves as a hub of winter activities for Keystone Village. The lake is the largest Zamboni-maintained outdoor rink in North America.

WINTER PARK RESORT

$ 🏕 🌐

Come enjoy the year-round beauty of the Rockies—and don't forget to bring your adventurous spirit with you. Winter Park is the fifth-largest ski area in Colorado, although it manages to avoid the mainstream crowds of the "rich and famous." Popular activities at Winter Park include skiing, snowboarding, snowshoeing, ice-skating, snowmobiling, tubing, mountain biking, climbing, rafting, hiking, camping, fishing, stargazing, hunting, and enjoying beautiful scenery (just to name a few). For those with a limited skiing or snowboarding background, seasonal positions are available in food service, facilities, grounds crew and parking, ticket and lesson sales, reservations, and children's center staff. If you have some basic skiing or snowboarding ability, there are numerous openings for lift attendants. Finally, advanced skiers and snowboarders may apply for positions as race crew members and ski and snowboard instructors. Wages start at $8.25 per hour for entry-level positions, with benefits including a free season pass (including the Colorado Real Deal—which means you can ski for free at eight other Colorado resorts), a five-day ski pass for all Intrawest Resorts, free ski and snowboard lessons, group health insurance, an employee shuttle, and many, many discounts. Employees can also use the Early Education Center (day care for employees' children) for a nominal fee. Winter Park offers a limited amount of subsidized employee housing in nearby condos. The winter season runs from mid-November through mid-April, and applications are available online.

FOR MORE INFORMATION: Cindy Newberry, Human Resources Director, Winter Park Resort, P.O. Box 36, Winter Park, CO 80482 • (888) 562-4525 (970) 726-1536 • (303) 892-5823 (fax) • wpjobs@skiwinterpark.com www.skiwinterpark.com

IDAHO

SCHWEITZER MOUNTAIN RESORT

$

Located in the northern panhandle of Idaho about ninety miles northeast of Spokane, Washington, Schweitzer Mountain Resort is one of those hidden treasures in the Northwest. However, it might be difficult to see how this enormous location remains hidden—Schweitzer has 2,500 acres of skiing

Life is like a game of cards. The hand you are dealt is determinism; the way you play it is free will.
—JAWAHARIAL NEHRU

terrain, sixty-one named trails, and Stella, Idaho's only six-person high-speed lift, which will take you to a spot where you can see Canada, Washington, and Idaho! Seasonal job opportunities abound at Schweitzer, with positions including food and beverage (at six outlets on the mountain), guest services (from providing guest information to selling lift tickets), hospitality services (from front desk clerks to housekeeping), and lift service operations, as well as work at the Source (a rental and retail center), Kinderkamp (a child care facility), and the Mountain Learning Center (ski, snowboard, telemark, cross-country, and snowshoe lessons for all ages). Benefits include an hourly wage, a free ski pass and lessons, an employee shuttle, and generous discounts on food, clothing, gear, and rentals. The normal winter season begins around Thanksgiving and ends in April, with most of the recruiting done at job fairs in late October and early November. Online applications can be filled out at www.harboremployment.com.

FOR MORE INFORMATION: Melanie Ball, Employee Services Supervisor, Schweitzer Mountain Resort, 10,000 Schweitzer Mountain Rd., Sandpoint, ID 83864 • (800) 831-8810 • (208) 263-9555, ext. 2203 (208) 263-0775 (fax) • ski@schweitzer.com • www.schweitzer.com

SUN VALLEY RESORT

$ ⊕

Nestled in the Idaho Rockies, Sun Valley Resort is home to Bald Mountain (also known as "Baldy"), with a perfect pitch and 3,400-foot vertical drop! It boasts great alpine and Nordic skiing as well as snowboarding during the winter months and incredible hiking and mountain biking during the summer. In addition to Baldy, Dollar Mountain caters to beginners and has been dubbed "the finest teaching mountain in the world." At this year-round destination resort, seasonal staff members can work in the summer, winter, or year-round. You'll find your typical resort positions available, and most first-year employees work in food and beverage, mountain operations, or retail. Wages start above minimum wage, with a slew of benefits, including access to the employee fitness center and pools, first-run movies at the Opera House, year-round ice-skating, bike rentals, discounts on just about everything, low-cost meals at the employee cafeteria, and dormitory-style housing for $150 per month. Current job opportunities can be found online, or call or email for more information.

FOR MORE INFORMATION: Human Resources Department, Sun Valley Resort, P.O. Box 10, Sun Valley, ID 83353-0010 • (800) 894-9946 • (208) 622-2061 (208) 622-2082 (fax) • svpersonnel@sunvalley.com • www.sunvalley.com

MAINE

SUNDAY RIVER SKI RESORT

$ ⊕

While sharing their guests' passion for great snow, Sunday River boasts superb skiing and snowboarding and offers a wide range of additional services—from the innovative Perfect Turn Ski and Snowboard Program to the mountaintop Peak Lodge. Each year more than 1,300 seasonal staff (including seventy-five internationals) come to the exciting and diverse work environment at the resort from mid-December to mid-April. With varied start and finish dates, positions include lift operators, housekeepers, snowmakers, food and beverage staff, ski and snowboard instructors, ticket sales, and lodging, retail, and maintenance staff. Typical workdays run from as early as 6:00 A.M. to after the lifts close, and most positions require working weekends and some holidays. Wages vary between departments, but range from $6.50 to $7.50 per hour, with housing options in the area found online. Benefits may include a free season pass valid at all American Skiing Company resorts around the country (www.peaks.com), discounts in the food and beverage outlets and retail stores, free ski and snowboard clinics, and free rental equipment when available.

DAVID NAGEL

Sunday River strives to hire energetic staff who are hard-working, dependable, flexible, and customer-service minded. Hiring begins in September, and application materials are available online. International staff who wish to be hired on an H-2B visa must begin the application process in June; those on a J-1 visa may apply in September.

FOR MORE INFORMATION:
Callie Pecunies
Human Resources Director
Sunday River Ski Resort
P.O. Box 450, Bethel, ME 04217
(877) 476-6956
(207) 824-5160
(207) 824-5110 (fax)
jobs@sundayriver.com
www.sundayriver.com

Don't love life, love the people in your life. After all, that's what makes your life.   **191**
—ANDREA STIER

MONTANA

BIG MOUNTAIN RESORT

$

Located in the Rocky Mountains of scenic northwest Montana, just thirty miles west of Glacier National Park, Big Mountain is one of the largest ski resorts in the U.S. and Canada, featuring three thousand acres of skiable terrain along with twenty miles of mountain bike trails. Whether you work seasonally during the winter or summer months (or both), Big Mountain is a great place to begin your mountain lifestyle. Seasonal positions are generally found in lift operations, ticket and ski lesson sales, hotel operations, retail sales, food and beverage operations, and parking. Since most are entry-level positions, no prior experience is required and training will be provided (although a smile is highly beneficial!). Limited ski patrol and ski school instructor positions are also available. The ski season typically opens on Thanksgiving Day and closes in mid-April, while the summer season opens the first Saturday in June and closes in early October. For students on winter holiday break, there is also a need for short-term employees from late December to early January. Entry-level wages range from $7 to $7.50 per hour along with great benefits. Most employees live in the nearby towns of Whitefish (eight miles from Big Mountain), Columbia Falls (sixteen miles), or Kalispell (twenty-five miles). Applications and detailed information can be found online.

FOR MORE INFORMATION: Human Resources Department, Big Mountain Resort Winter Sports, Inc., P.O. Box 1400, Whitefish, MT 59937 • (800) 858-3930 (406) 862-1937 • (406) 862-1998 (fax) • hr_wsi@bigmtn.com • www.bigmtn.com

BIG SKY RESORT

$ 🏠 ⊕

Home to the "huge, wonderful, uncrowded hill" in the winter, Big Sky Resort offers skiing and snowboarding on over 3,600 acres across three mountains. Winter opportunities include ski patrol, ski and snowboard instructors, guest services, lift operations, accounting staff, retail, food and beverage, hotel operations, and housekeeping. Look under Current Openings on their website for a complete list of seasonal and potential full-time year-round positions (along with downloadable application forms). Most positions pay between $7 and $7.50 per hour along with a ski pass in the winter or a golf pass during the summer. Dormitory-style housing is offered on a space-available basis either in the rustic Mountain Lodge ($200 per month) or in the dorms ($160 per month). In addition to the many outdoor activities in the area, Big Sky has an activities director who plans in-house activities for employees. Past activities have included dance parties, fly-fishing lessons, movie nights, golf tournaments, and group hikes. It's noted that the resort is looking for adventure-seeking outdoor enthusiasts who are not desiring much nightlife.

FOR MORE INFORMATION: Robert Jenni, Human Resource Director, Big Sky Resort, 1 Lone Mountain Trail, P.O. Box 160001, Big Sky, MT 59716 (406) 995-5812 • (406) 995-5001 (fax) • jobs@bigskyresort.com www.bigskyresort.com

OREGON

MT. BACHELOR

$ ⊕

Mt. Bachelor is nestled in the heart of central Oregon near Bend, where winter and summer collide in an explosion of exciting activities. From skiing, snowboarding, snowmobiling, and backwoods excursions to fishing, golfing, rafting, rock climbing, and mountain biking, there is always something to do. With a staff of over eight hundred team members working in your typical ski resort jobs, Mt. Bachelor is looking for reliable team members who are enthusiastic and like to have fun while they work. Winter seasonal positions run from approximately mid-November through April, and team members are expected to commit to a full season. The hiring process starts in mid-September, with a variety of job fairs scheduled in early November. Housing isn't provided, but there are ample options in Bend and the surrounding areas; for more information call *RENT Magazine* at (541) 617-1367. Applications can be found online, and in-person interviews are required.

FOR MORE INFORMATION: Human Resources Department, Mt. Bachelor, P.O. Box 1031, Bend, OR 97709-1031 • (800) 829-2442 • (541) 382-2607 (541) 382 6536 (fax) • jobs@mtbachelor.com • www.mtbachelor.com

UTAH

PARK CITY MOUNTAIN RESORT

$ ⊕

Located thirty-six miles from Salt Lake City, Park City Mountain Resort offers more than 3,330 acres of groomers, bumps, bowls, powder, and a number of top-rated terrain parks and pipes. The winter season generally

The child is both a hope and promise for mankind.
—MARIA MONTESSORI

runs from November through mid-April, with jobs that include lift operators, ski and snowboard instructors, food and beverage staff, rental shop employees, and a number of other opportunities. The resort doesn't offer housing, although it does offer good pay and great benefits. Prospective applicants are encouraged to attend one of the resort's job fairs, where you'll meet a variety of team members, interview for various positions, and see the resort in action. Applications and further details are available online.

FOR MORE INFORMATION: Linda Cooley, Human Resources, Park City Mountain Resort, P.O. Box 39, Park City, UT 84060 • (800) 222-7275 (435) 647-5406 • info@pcski.com • www.parkcitymountain.com

VERMONT

OKEMO MOUNTAIN RESORT

$ ⊕

Aside from Okemo's incredible terrain, it's the family-friendly atmosphere that sets this resort apart from the rest. Family owned and operated for over twenty years, Okemo Mountain Resort has fantastic snow conditions, southern Vermont's highest vertical drop, 95 percent snowmaking coverage, and a great team environment. Families can ski and ride together from virtually any lift or participate in instructional programs at the Learning Center, which features a staff of over four hundred professional (and young-at-heart) ski and snowboard instructors, with private and group instruction available. In addition to instructor positions, seasonal opportunities (indoors and out) exist in

OKEMO MOUNTAIN RESORT

Experiencing the "Okemo difference," this snowboarder enjoys the terrain at southern Vermont's family-owned mountain resort.

lift and mountain operations, rental and repairs, maintenance, housekeeping, reservations, sales, accounting, day care, guest services, culinary services, and more. A competitive salary and extensive benefits are provided, and a housing referral list is available upon request. Applicants are encouraged to attend one of the resort's job fairs in October or November; otherwise, applications are available online.

FOR MORE INFORMATION: Human Resources, Okemo Mountain Resort, 77 Okemo Ridge Rd., Ludlow, VT 05149 • (802) 228-1963 (802) 228-4558 (fax) • jobs@okemo.com • www.okemo.com

STOWE MOUNTAIN RESORT

$ ⊕

Since the ski area shares its name with the town, there's no confusion about where seasonal employees are headed when they come to Stowe Mountain. Beyond the great skiing and resort atmosphere, the unique thing about Stowe is their AAA philosophy: attitude, awareness, and accountability—that positive vibe and respect for others that they foster in their guests and employees alike. Seasonal jobs abound—housekeepers, repair and rental technicians, child care workers, food and beverage staff, lift and parking attendants, custodians, ski patrol and ski instructors—and so do the benefits! Full-time staff members receive free skiing and snowboarding privileges (as do spouses and children), lessons, rentals, and discounts on just about everything, including the fitness center. Although employee housing is not available, a two-bedroom apartment or condominium ranges from $400 to $700 per month. Send off a cover letter and resume to begin the application process.

FOR MORE INFORMATION: Kristen Kilbashian, Human Resources, Stowe Mountain Resort, 5781 Mountain Rd., Stowe, VT 05672-4890 (802) 253-3541 • (802) 253-3544 (fax) • jobs@stowe.com • www.stowe.com

WASHINGTON

STEVENS PASS WINTER RESORT

$ ⊕

Tucked between Mt. Baker–Snoqualmie and Wenatchee National Forest, Stevens Pass is part of the scenic Cascade Loop, a unique area filled with snow—and lots of it—during the winter months. Since the resort covers 1,125 acres of skiable terrain, alpine and telemark skiers have their choice of

Get your bearings and turn the crank.   **195**
—BOB LONEY

numerous bowls, glades, faces, and pristine areas, including the ominous Cowboy Mountain, which rises to 5,845 feet. Each winter, over eight hundred seasonal employees come to the mountain to work, play, and enjoy a plethora of benefits, with positions ranging from accounting and guest services staff to lift operators and snowboard instructors. Applications are available online.

FOR MORE INFORMATION: Joel Martinez, Director of Human Resources, Stevens Pass Winter Resort, P.O. Box 98, Skykomish, WA 98288 (206) 812-4510, ext. 283 • (206) 812-4517 (fax) humanresources@stevenspass.com • www.stevenspass.com

WYOMING

GRAND TARGHEE SKI AND SUMMER RESORT

$ ⊕

Grand Targhee is a small, family-oriented resort nestled in the pines at eight thousand feet on the west side of the spectacular Teton Mountain range. Over five hundred inches of annual snowfall provide some of the best skiing conditions anywhere during the winter, and miles of mountain bike trails are available during the summer, in addition to many other activities. For music lovers, Targhee is known for their great summer music festivals. Targhee offers typical resort jobs in these departments: accounting, food and beverage, guest services, lodging, mountain operations, retail, and the ski and snowboard school. The winter season runs from mid-November to mid-April; while the summer season runs from early June to Labor Day. Seasonal employees receive an hourly wage, a free season ski pass with reciprocal skiing privileges at Jackson Hole, Bridger Bowl, and Big Sky, and employee meal and retail discounts. Reasonable housing is available nearby in the Idaho towns of Driggs, Victor, and Tetonia, and the resort's free winter employee shuttle accommodates most work schedules. Hiring for the winter season begins in September, and for the summer, in March. Applications, additional information, and a listing of current openings are available online.

FOR MORE INFORMATION: Joni Dronen, Human Resources Office, Grand Targhee Ski and Summer Resort, Ski Hill Rd., Box Ski, Alta, WY 83414 (800) 827-4433 • (307) 353-2300, ext. 1310 • (307) 353-8148 (fax) info@grandtarghee.com • www.grandtarghee.com

SOL DUC HOT SPRINGS

Resort • Washington • Seasonal
www.solduchotsprings.com

$ 🏠 🌐

The Quileute Indians called it Sol Duc—a land of sparkling water. The original resort was built in 1912 and was conceived as a health spa in the European tradition. Today the main attraction to the area is the three hot spring mineral pools. These soaking pools are man-made circular pools supplied with all-natural, mineral-rich hot spring water. Staff opportunities during the summer months include your typical resort-type positions, from food and beverage staff to lifeguards. Wages start at $7.16 per hour, with coed, dormitory-style housing and three meals provided at $9 per day. The rooms vary in size, with the largest housing up to six staff members at peak season. The employee lounge has satellite TV, games, books, and a VCR. Accommodations for married couples are limited. The biggest perk is a lively family atmosphere and work environment, not to mention free use of the hot spring mineral pools and swimming pool. Those who have previous hotel or restaurant experience are preferred; however, it's even better if you have positive energy and a willingness to learn and put forward your best effort. Interviews are conducted by telephone.

FOR MORE INFORMATION: Candy Beckwith, Human Resources Manager, Sol Duc Hot Springs, Olympic National Park, P.O. Box 2169, Port Angeles, WA 98362-0283 • (360) 327-3583 • (360) 327-3593 (fax) sdrjob@aol.com

STANFORD SIERRA CONFERENCE CENTER

Conference Center • California • 2–3 Months
www.stanfordalumni.org/learningtravel/sierra/sierra-center/home.html

$ 🏠

With a lakefront property that includes guest and staff cabins, the main lodge, several docks, a fleet of boats, and volleyball, basketball, tennis, and horseshoe courts, Stanford Sierra Conference Center (SSCC) provides full-service lodging and meeting facilities for conferences, business retreats, weddings, and social events for groups ranging in size from twenty to two hundred people. Many of the conference guests return year after year for four-star meals, comfortable lodging, a beautiful location, and—above all—professional, efficient, and friendly service from the SSCC staff!

A life spent in making mistakes is not only more honorable but more useful than a life spent in doing nothing.
—GEORGE BERNARD SHAW

YOUR SURROUNDINGS: The center is located just five miles from South Lake Tahoe on the shores of Fallen Leaf Lake, a gorgeous Sierra lake with a breathtaking mountain backdrop. Behind the resort is the Desolation Wilderness Area, with some of the best hiking and scenery in the Sierras. The solitude of nature will certainly be right outside your back door.

WHAT YOU'LL BE DOING: Every spring and fall, SSCC forms a tight-knit community in their beautiful mountain environment. First-year staff members generally work in the kitchen or as all-purpose staff (with a majority of the workload in housekeeping and in the dining room). In addition, time is spent shuttling guests to the airport, monitoring the boat dock, washing dishes, cleaning the main lodge, and working in the center's store. Specialized positions are also available as office assistant, host/hostess, housekeeper, evening manager, and night watchman.

COMMITMENT: The spring conference season begins in mid-April and ends in mid-June; the fall conference season begins the first week in September and ends in mid-November. The workload varies widely according to conference size; however, plan on thirty to forty hours per week, with shifts spread throughout the day, and two days off per week. Opportunities for extended employment and increased responsibility may become available.

PERKS AND REWARDS: Wages start at $6.75 per hour, plus room and board, gratuities, and an end-of-season bonus of at least $150. Staff are housed in rustic lake-view cabins; some have roommates and a communal bathroom and shower area. The food is delicious, healthful, and plentiful, with vegetarian and vegan options available. You will eat what the guests do—everything from salmon and prime rib to burgers and the salad bar. One of the biggest perks is partaking of resort activities, including boating, sailing, waterskiing, tennis, volleyball, basketball, and hiking on miles of trails.

THE ESSENTIALS: Self-motivated, hardworking, and reliable people who have an excellent sense of professionalism, a warm personality, and a high level of maturity will thrive at SSCC. Applicants also must be able to handle the responsibilities of living and working in a diverse community. Staff members come from all walks of life—college students, professionals between jobs, experienced workers in the service industry, travelers, or people taking time off. Two years or more of college is preferred, but not required.

YOUR FIRST MOVE: Call or email for application materials. Phone interviews and hiring will occur during the week following the application deadline: mid-March for the spring; mid-August for the fall. Face-to-face interviews, if possible, usually work to the applicant's advantage.

FOR MORE INFORMATION: Andrew Dawson, Conference Staff Director, Stanford Sierra Conference Center, P.O. Box 10618, South Lake Tahoe, CA 96158-3618 (530) 541-1244, ext. 118 • (530) 541-2212 (fax) • afdawson@stanford.edu

SUNRIVER RESORT

Resort • Oregon • Seasonal
www.sunriverresort.com

$ ⊕

With over 3,300 acres in and around the Cascade mountain range, including Mount Bachelor, Sunriver Resort offers numerous recreational opportunities, including white-water rafting, canoeing, fishing, and swimming. The resort is surrounded by golf courses, tennis courts, pools, thirty miles of bike paths, a marina (with canoe, kayak, raft, and fishing rentals), a bike shop with over 450 bikes, and a complete stable operation.

WHAT YOU'LL BE DOING: Resort internship positions focus on social activities, youth programs, the bike shop, and the marina. Each intern will gain exposure to various departments to complete a well-rounded internship (such as sales and marketing, special events, the recreation department, management, and tours, just to name a few). Each intern will also be responsible for completing and presenting a special project beneficial to both the intern and Sunriver. In addition, over 250 seasonal positions are available, including youth program leaders, bike shop mechanics, marina program leaders, and food and beverage, front desk, recreation, housekeeping, and golf staff.

COMMITMENT: Most positions are twelve weeks, mid-June through Labor Day, with varying work schedules. Some year-round positions are available, and a few positions are available in May and June.

PERKS AND REWARDS: Interns receive a stipend of $950 per month; seasonal employees receive $7.05 to $7.50 per hour. Housing is not provided; however, efforts are made to help employees find adequate housing. Employees are welcome to take part in numerous free recreation amenities, and discounts are available in all the restaurants and resort shops, along with a 50 percent discount on accommodations for your immediate family. Your summer work attire is provided—Sunriver shirts and shorts. Oh, and don't forget your bike—it's the best way to get around.

THE ESSENTIALS: Applicants must be friendly and outgoing, enjoy working with people, and physically able to meet the demands of the job. Intern candidates must be college juniors or seniors studying recreation, physical education, elementary education, sports management, or hotel management.

Build a reputation on what you do, not all the things you intend to do. **199**
—JACKIE DOUGLASS

First aid and CPR certifications are required for all recreation employees. For those wanting a full-time job at Sunriver, get your foot in the door by working a summer seasonal job. The best employees receive offers to stay on through winter.

YOUR FIRST MOVE: Call for application materials or apply online. The best time to apply is generally in February or March, and a personal interview is a prerequisite to employment.

FOR MORE INFORMATION: Joyce Luckman, Human Resources Director, Sunriver Resort, P.O. Box 3609, Sunriver, OR 97707 • (503) 593-4600 (503) 593-4411 (fax) • personnel@sunriver-resort.com

SUPERCAMP

Academic Camp • Worldwide • 3–6 Weeks
www.supercamp.com

$ ♠♠

SuperCamp is an academic and personal-growth camp for teenagers. Each program teaches academic skills that help campers succeed in any subject, at any level, and also addresses life skills—to help develop friendships, resolve conflicts, and communicate more clearly. Camps are held on academic campuses across the country, including the Claremont Colleges, Colorado College, Hampshire College, Stanford University, University of Wisconsin, U.S. International University, and Wake Forest. SuperCamp also has international programs in Australia, Hong Kong, Indonesia, Malaysia, Mexico, Singapore, Switzerland, and Thailand.

WHAT YOU'LL BE DOING: Team leaders head up SuperCamp activities, supervise students, facilitate team meetings, and create camp spirit, as well as serving as a role model for teens. A team usually consists of two or three team leaders plus eleven to fourteen students. Facilitators set camp direction and tone, provide inspiration and guidance, and are the most visible leaders at camp. The curriculum they present consists of personal growth (communication, team building, relationships, and motivation) and academic growth (memory, creativity, power writing, quantum reading, and academic strategies). Other staff personnel include counselors, medical personnel, and office managers.

COMMITMENT: Staff members usually work three to six weeks during the summer; dates vary with each position and camp location.

PERKS AND REWARDS: An honorarium of $300 to $2,350 per camp session is provided, along with room and board. All staff members will attend a four-to five-day staff training session and learn accelerated-learning philosophies and techniques and communication and leadership skills, and gain experience working with teens.

THE ESSENTIALS: Applicants must be at least eighteen years of age, physically fit and energetic, comfortable relating to teenagers, highly committed to others, self-motivated, full of playful energy, and willing to work long hours and do whatever it takes to get the job done!

FOR MORE INFORMATION: Staffing Director, SuperCamp, 1725 South Coast Hwy., Oceanside, CA 92054-5319 • (800) 285-3276 (760) 722-0072, ext. 180 • (760) 722-3507 (fax) • staffing@supercamp.com

☞ INSIDER TIP: I started with SuperCamp on a whim, looking for something fun to do with my summer, and it was the most profound, life-changing experience ever. The benefits I've received from this experience are priceless. I've been working with SuperCamp for five years and have had the opportunity to travel and work in places like Colorado, Texas, Illinois, Massachusetts, Singapore, and Hong Kong—yes, I worked at a summer camp in Southeast Asia! These experiences not only boosted my self-confidence and self-esteem, but also gave me the satisfaction that I truly had made an impact on young people's lives (along with carving out my own career path).

If you care about making a difference for people by inspiring them to live up to their potential; if you want an experience that will have a lifelong impact on you; if you are interested in learning skills that will take your life to the next level, personally and academically, then grab on to this opportunity. You will come home not only with an incredible experience, but also with a fresh, new outlook on life. —*Contributed by Troy Stende, who use to spend his summers with SuperCamp and now inspires students from all over the world as a professional college speaker. Check out www.troystende.com to connect with Troy.*

SYLVAN DALE GUEST RANCH

Guest Ranch • Colorado • Seasonal
www.sylvandale.com

$ ♠

Nestled in a peaceful river valley at the mouth of Colorado's Big Thompson Canyon between Estes Park and Loveland, family-owned Sylvan Dale operates a working horse and cattle ranch and retreat center for guests to uncover their inner cowboy—and you can too! Seasonal job opportunities are available in administration, food service, housekeeping, support services, and grounds keeping, as well as positions as wranglers and youth counselors. A competitive wage is provided, and housing is limited. Applications are available online.

FOR MORE INFORMATION: Martha Brown, Staffing Coordinator, Sylvan Dale Guest Ranch, 2939 NCR 31D, Loveland, CO 80538 (877) 667-3999 • (970) 667-3915 • (970) 635-9336 (fax) employment@sylvandale.com

TUMBLING RIVER RANCH

Guest Ranch • Colorado • Summer
www.tumblingriver.com

$ ♠♠

Located in the middle of Pike National Forest at 9,200 feet (and just over an hour from southwest Denver), Tumbling River Ranch is a second-generation, family-run ranch serving fifty-five guests per week for a vacation of a lifetime. Summer staff have a tremendous opportunity to contribute to the guest experience through superb customer service and respect. Whether working as a cook, baker, housekeeper/waitperson, life guard/nanny, youth or teen counselor, or in the office or on the grounds, all staff members should be prepared to work hard and enjoy what they are doing. Benefits include a monthly salary, room, board, and a postseason bonus. Preference is given to those who can begin work in early May and finish their assignment in late August or September. Call or email for detailed job descriptions and an application. All completed applications must be sent through the regular mail.

FOR MORE INFORMATION: Megan Dugan, Staffing Director, Tumbling River Ranch, P.O. Box 30, Grant, CO 80448 • (800) 654-8770 (303) 838-5981 • (303) 838-5133 (fax) • info@tumblingriver.com

WYMAN CENTER

Experiential Education • Missouri • Seasonal
www.wymancenter.org

$ ♠♠ ⊕

Known for being the oldest continuously operating youth camp west of the Mississippi (for over one hundred years), Wyman is an innovative experiential education center serving youth and adults from diverse backgrounds. Programs focus on youth development, environmental awareness, group dynamics, diversity, and enhancing self-esteem. Throughout the year, seasonal staff members instruct and facilitate groups in environmental, life-skills, and adventure programs, including canoeing, river treks, high ropes challenge course, and the climbing wall. Along with extensive training, a $250 per week stipend, housing, and meals are provided. Applicants must be at least eighteen years of age and have interest in and experience working with children and youth, excellent communication and leadership skills, knowledge of ages and stages of youth development, flexibility, a strong work ethic, and a healthy sense of humor. Past staff members have said Wyman offers great training, a wonderful learning experience, and very rewarding work.

FOR MORE INFORMATION: Tami Renner, Director of Human Resources, Wyman Center, 600 Kiwanis Dr., Eureka, MO 63025 • (636) 938-5245, ext. 396 (636) 938-5289 (fax) • info@wymancenter.org

YMCA CAMP SURF

Ocean-Based Camp • California • Seasonal
www.ymca.org/camp
$ 🏠 ⊕

San Diego, California. A temperate climate year-round. Forty acres of beachfront property on the Pacific Ocean. The rhythmic sound of surf. Polynesian-theme cabins and bathhouses nestled in and around sand dunes. Young and old learning how to surf, body-board, kayak, or sculpt the sand. This is YMCA Camp Surf—outdoor and waterfront activities at their best.

WHAT YOU'LL BE DOING: Whether it be surfing or sailing, a science class on intertidal marine life or leadership development using the low ropes course, program instructors during the spring and fall are trained to lead and teach a variety of recreational activities. In addition, lifeguards and program coordinators are hired during this time frame. During the summer months, cabin counselors, program-specialty counselors, and camp coordinators come to Camp Surf to teach and impact children's lives through a traditional summer resident camp, day camp, and Castaway program for YMCA and other youth groups.

COMMITMENT: The spring and summer are definitely their busiest and longest seasons. Spring instructors generally begin in early March, with groups arriving mid-March through the first week of June; summer camp staff begin in early June and finish in late August; and instructors in the fall work from September through mid-November.

PERKS AND REWARDS: Base wages range from $180 to $270 per week depending on position and qualifications. Spring and fall staff are assigned to either a private or shared room in the waterfront facility. Yes, you'll sleep to the sounds of the pounding surf and start your day by stepping out the door into

The fool wonders, the wise man asks.   **203**
—BENJAMIN DISRAELI

the sand! Summer camp staff housing is in the cabins with campers. All staff receive meals with a vegetarian option.

THE ESSENTIALS: Strong water skills are needed for all positions. In addition, all staff must be certified in first aid and CPR prior to their arrival. Spring and fall staff should have a background in outdoor education, recreation, or leadership development, and a college degree is preferred. Summer staff should have experience working with children.

YOUR FIRST MOVE: Applications can be filled out online or submitted by mail. Their website also provides details on seasonal work opportunities at other YMCA camps in San Diego.

FOR MORE INFORMATION: Zayanne Thompson, Senior Program Director, YMCA Camp Surf, 106 Carnation Ave., Imperial Beach, CA 91932 (619) 423-5850 • (619) 423-4141 (fax) • campsurf@ymca.org

☞ **INSIDER TIP: This camp gets a lot of applicants over the Internet. Mailing a resume and application to Camp Surf allows staff to get a more complete picture of your experience and qualifications.**

YMCA CAMP WILLSON

Outdoor Education • Ohio • Seasonal
www.ymcawillson.org

$ 🏕

With a focus on outdoor education activities, YMCA Camp Willson provides programs that include summer camp, weekend retreats, outdoor education, conference and group camping, adventure education, and horseback riding. The camp sits on 455 acres of land, with a forty-acre glacial kettle lake, 1860s log cabin, thirty-five-foot climbing wall, high ropes course, and winterized housing for two hundred. Year-round outdoor education naturalists and interns are responsible for teaching classes in natural science and history, team building, and early American curriculum, as well as leading recreational activities. During the summer months, camp positions are available, including outpost counselors, waterfront director, sports coordinator, western horseback riding instructors/counselors, and leadership/trip directors. A wage of $240 to $290 per week is provided along with room and board. Send a cover letter and resume to begin the application process.

FOR MORE INFORMATION: Outdoor Education Director, YMCA Camp Willson, 2732 County Rd. 11, Bellefontaine, OH 43311-9382 • (800) 423-0427 (937) 593-9001 • (937) 593-6194 (fax) • outdooreducation@ymcawillson.org

RECOMMENDED RESOURCES

CAMPS

The **American Camp Association** (www.acacamps.org/jobs.htm) highlights hundreds of nationwide job listings for day and resident camps as well as youth development programs. With updates provided throughout the year, the listings provide detailed descriptions, salary ranges, employment benefits, and contact information. In addition, the latest line on job fairs, career information, education and training programs is featured.

KidsCamps.com offers an extensive database of more than twelve thousand programs—from art camps to community service programs (just for starters!) in the U.S. and abroad. Most search results include direct links to the camps' websites. For job opportunities, head on over to **CampJobs.com**—their companion job site—listing hundreds of summer camp jobs.

For further exploration of summer camp job opportunities on the Web, be sure to check out these sites: **www.campchannel.com, www.campsearch.com,** and **www.campstaff.com.**

The **Western Association of Independent Camps** (www.waic.org) provides a directory of western U.S. camps, including those in Arizona, California, Colorado, New Mexico, Oregon, Utah, Washington, and Wyoming. Although there aren't any job opportunities posted on their site, you will find a brief description of each camp, including contact and website information.

LESSONS LEARNED AROUND THE CAMPFIRE
by Michael Eisner, Disney's CEO

Simply consider the lessons I was taught by the campfire. Every time I was on fire detail, the situation and challenge was different. But, every time the rich reward was the same as we simply sat and enjoyed our consuming creation. And, there was one aspect in particular that never failed to intrigue me, and that was the process of seeing the single small flame of the match spread to the kindling and then the twigs and then the smaller branches and finally the larger logs. It didn't dawn on me until years later, but this was the perfect metaphor for the creative process. In much the same way, the fragile spark of an idea can spread to become a great work of art or a movie or a political movement or an automobile or a space shuttle or a new communications technology. But, these blazing achievements can only happen if the initial idea is cared for, protected, and nurtured until it is ready to spread.

Never limit your view of life by any past experience.
—ERNEST HOLMES

DUDE RANCHES

To assist individuals seeking employment at a ranch, the **Dude Ranchers'**
Association (www.duderanch.org) provides a couple of great services. First
off, they publish *The Dude Rancher Directory,* listing contact information,
amenities, and services for more than one hundred member dude ranches
in twelve western states and two Canadian provinces. Dude ranches vary
from working cattle ranches to more luxurious resort-type facilities. Although
it doesn't list seasonal jobs at each ranch, it's a great resource for contact
information—plus it's free. In addition, they publish a monthly in-house
newsletter that is sent directly to all member ranches. For a $10 fee, you can
place an "employment wanted" ad in the newsletter. Simply send your name,
address, phone number, dates of availability, type of positions preferred, and
two to three sentences describing your experience or qualifications. Many
ranchers do use these ads when hiring. Of course, there are no guarantees,
but it is a good and inexpensive way to contact all the ranchers at one time.
On the Web (www.duderanch.org/employment.html), you can view a listing
of current ranch job opportunities. For more information contact the Dude
Ranchers' Association, P.O. Box 2307, Cody, WY 82414; (307) 587-2339.

> *Dude and guest ranching is more than a vacation; it is a spirit, a*
> *tradition of Western hospitality, warmth, honesty, family, and nat-*
> *ural beauty. It is, indeed, a ministry that touches lives and helps*
> *to make this a better world in which to live.*
>
> —GENE KILGORE

MEGHAN KEEFFE

Some "dudes" on a ranch in Colorado.

*Climb the mountains and get their good tidings. Nature's peace
will flow into you as sunshine flows into trees. The winds will blow
their own freshness into you, and the storms their energies, while
cares will drop off like autumn leaves.*
—JOHN MUIR

CHAPTER **6**

JOBS IN THE GREAT OUTDOORS

Have you ever marveled at the geysers of Yellowstone, explored
the verdant mountains of the Rockies, paddled a canoe in the
Boundary Waters of Minnesota, or walked across a glacier in
Alaska and wondered what it would be like to work in such
magnificent places? These are the types of opportunities that
thousands of seasonal workers enjoy with organizations such as
the National Park Service, hospitality services within the parks,
or groups that maintain thousands of miles of hiking trails.
From jobs as campground hosts and interpretative rangers to
trail-maintenance laborers and guest-services staff, this chapter
explores a broad range of possibilities for working in the wild.

UNIQUE OPPORTUNITIES TO EXPLORE IN THIS CHAPTER

- Outdoor expert Bill Borrie believes that those who will succeed in the future are those who learn how to make wonderful things happen with a can-do attitude, regardless of what the naysayers might suggest. Explore his get-up-and-go approach to kick-starting a federal agency career (page 211).

- From the architectural relics of the Anasazi in Mesa Verde to geysers bursting in Yellowstone, the National Park Service offers seasonal workers some of the most incredible places to work in the U.S. (page 236). Explore your working options at other public agencies, including the Bureau of Land Management (page 219) and the U.S. Forest Service (page 247).

- Can you see yourself patrolling a remote island wilderness in Alaska by kayak, or playing the role of an 1800s resident of historic Fort Laramie? These are just a few of the assignments participants enjoy with the Student Conservation Association (page 244).

STUDENT CONSERVATION ASSOCIATION

Incredible jobs in beautiful places. An SCA conservation internship (page 244) takes you there.

A GET-UP-AND-GO APPROACH TO KICK-STARTING A FEDERAL AGENCY CAREER

• •

Are you considering a career in one of the four federal land management agencies (National Park Service, Forest Service, Bureau of Land Management, Fish and Wildlife Service)? Good for you! What a great opportunity to get involved and make a difference!

Dr. Borrie in the "outback" of the Upper Missouri River Breaks National Monument in Montana.

But it's going to take a little dogged determination and careful thinking to get where you want to go. Briefly put, I believe that the federal agencies will always find a way to hire good people. The leaders of these agencies know that long-term effectiveness depends on the creativity and enthusiasm of their personnel. True leadership requires constantly energizing and reinventing the agency. And this requires younger, competent people with the drive to provide true public service and stewardship of the national estate.

However, you will still have to work hard to blast off your career. You may also need to shift some of your expectations and change your sights as to what you can achieve in the short term. For instance, you may have to reconsider the hope of immediately working in your favorite state. Instead, you may have to go somewhere new, such as Georgia, which does have some wonderful wilderness areas! Similarly, you might not get to live in the size of town that you prefer. Instead, you might have to consider living in Washington, D.C., or Sacramento, California, or Glendive, Montana. You might also have to work on projects that are not your obvious choice. But the more you learn about the agency and all of its missions, the more effective you become. You may even get to work for a different agency (for instance, the Bureau of Land Management). In each case, you should view each of these as stepping stones, learning opportunities, and necessary experiences. And, you never know, you might like what you see!

You guys and gals are training for careers that will require different skills than what many current employees have. You have new perspectives, new experiences, and new ideas. This can be threatening to older employees, and one of their strategies for coping with this is to discourage or disparage you. But you will be the ones guiding the agency in the future—with your abilities, knowledge, and get-up-and-go. Those who succeed in the future, I believe,

What we need are more people who specialize in the impossible.
—THEODORE ROETHKE

will be those who learn how to make wonderful things happen, regardless of what the naysayers are suggesting. A can-do attitude will win in the long run.

Part of what I think older employees are communicating to you is that some of the old assumptions within the agencies no longer hold. For instance, it could be said that you no longer have a job for life. Others will tell you that it is no longer who you know that matters. And it is no longer reasonable to expect the government to look after your career. In short, you now have much more responsibility for your career. It's no longer an automatic rise through the levels. This is unsettling for people who still believe in the old ways, and one way of communicating that is to warn new people not to enter into the organization.

But, if you really, really want to work for a particular agency, then I say go out and work for them! Don't let anybody tell you that you can't! If you believe

BOB CLEAVER

Do you have the determination of a wombat? This adolescent critter is cared for by wombat experts Jan and Bob Cleaver, who received an award for having achieved the first-recorded captive breeding of the southern hairy-nosed wombat in South Australia.

that what you should be doing is working for the government—and that is the best use of your skills and enthusiasm—then you are a good prospect to hire. And managers worth their salary will go out of their way to find a way to help you. They will give you a chance to show your worth, and if they like what they see, they will want to keep you on. The decision they face is how many chips to spend on your behalf—how much are you worth? So, work hard, be reliable and energetic, and show how much the public lands and public service mean to you.

Maybe I should be recommending that you think like a wombat! (Wombats are stocky Australian marsupials.) Once there was a young wombat that was being raised by a park ranger after its mom got hit by a car. Well, as it grew to be a solid adult wombat, the critter didn't quite understand the human concept of doors. As a result, the walls of the house it lived in (which were made of thin cement sheets) had little wombat-shaped holes in them! You just can't stop a determined wombat from getting where he or she wants to go!

So, set your sights high and work hard toward getting there. These are magnificent places to manage and important benefits to be providing to the American public. You should be honored to have the opportunity to serve but also congratulated on your decision to do so. Be proud of the small contributions you can make—those contributions will grow.

· ·

—Contributed by Dr. Bill Borrie, who recently received the Faculty Member of the Year Award in the School of Forestry at the University of Montana. Montana Public Radio also channels his voice across the airwaves of western and central Montana. To learn more about Dr. Borrie's work and passions, visit www.forestry.umt.edu/personnel/faculty/borrie.

ADIRONDACK MOUNTAIN CLUB

Conservation • New York • Seasonal
www.adk.org

$ ♨ ⊕

Known for its rugged mountains (with forty-six peaks over four thousand feet high), rivers, streams, lakes and bogs, and a profusion of wildlife, Adirondack Park covers over six million acres and is the largest U.S. park outside of Alaska. With a mission to protect and encourage responsible use of this extraordinary wilderness area, the Adirondack Mountain Club provides educational workshops, wildflower and birding field trips, guided hikes, kayaking, and winter cross-country skiing for nature lovers. Seasonal opportunities may include assisting with the maintenance and reconstruction of backcountry hiking trails, working in a backcountry information center, interpreting Adirondack regional natural history, or operating two mountain lodges. Pay is based on position, and meals and housing in tents or rustic wilderness cabins may be provided. Applicants must have a strong outdoor orientation and public service skills, and positions are often filled by outgoing, highly motivated, and independent individuals. Call for application materials (or download them online). Applications are due by February 15 for the summer; other seasons have rolling deadlines.

FOR MORE INFORMATION: Applications, Adirondack Mountain Club, P.O. Box 867, Lake Placid, NY 12946-0867 • (518) 523-3441 (518) 523-3518 (fax) • adkinfo@adk.org

ALASKA STATE PARKS

State Park • Alaska • Seasonal
www.dnr.state.ak.us/parks

$ ♨

Created in 1970, Alaska State Parks manages more than 120 state park units with more than six million visitors each year. These park units range in size and character from the half-acre Potter Section House State Historic Site to the 1.5-million-acre Wood-Tikchik State Park. In general, state parks are accessible by road and offer a host of visitor facilities including campgrounds, boat launches, hiking trails, and visitor centers.

WHAT YOU'LL BE DOING: The majority of volunteer positions are as campground hosts, who assist rangers with campground maintenance and visitor contact. Other typical volunteer and internship assignments include archaeological assistant, backcountry ranger assistant, natural history interpreter, park caretaker, ranger assistant, and trail crew.

I only went out for a walk, and finally concluded to stay out until sundown; for going out, I found, was really going in.
—JOHN MUIR

213

COMMITMENT: Most positions are full-time during the summer; however, a few positions are part-time, and a handful of positions are offered during the winter. Time off is usually given during the middle of the week.

PERKS AND REWARDS: Most positions offer an expense allowance of $100 to $300 per month, uniforms, rustic housing (RV/trailer hookups for campground hosts), and, of course, the state's beauty. Transportation to and from Alaska is the responsibility of the volunteer.

THE ESSENTIALS: Applicants must be eighteen years or older and have U.S. citizenship.

YOUR FIRST MOVE: Their website provides current volunteer opportunities and an application; however, you are welcome to call for the volunteer program catalog that becomes available each October. Applications are accepted between November 1 and April 1 (with some exceptions), and you may apply for as many positions as you like.

FOR MORE INFORMATION: Lynn Wibbenmeyer, Volunteer Coordinator, Alaska State Parks, 550 W. 7th Ave., Suite 1380, Anchorage, AK 99501-3561 (907) 269-8708 • (907) 269-8907 (fax) • volunteer@dnr.state.ak.us

➳ **INSIDER TIP: Many positions are filled before April 1, so it is best to send your application in as soon as possible. Some of our rangers work seasonally, so do not be concerned if you do not receive an immediate reply, particularly from November through January.**

AMERICAN HIKING SOCIETY

Trail Maintenance • USA • 1–2 Weeks
www.americanhiking.org
♥ ⊕

The American Hiking Society (AHS) is a national nonprofit organization dedicated to establishing, protecting, and maintaining foot trails in America. Serving as the voice of the American hiker in our nation's capital, AHS works to educate the public about the benefits of hiking and trails, to increase the following for trails, and to foster research on trail issues.

WHAT YOU'LL BE DOING: AHS Volunteer Vacations offer an inexpensive way to visit a new part of the U.S., work with your hands, and help conserve and revitalize America's trails. Vacationers rake, shovel, trim, lop, and chop hundreds of trail miles in America's national parks, forests, and rangelands.

Participants on a volunteer vacation with the American Hiking Society help construct a footbridge.

Volunteering affords you an opportunity to whip some trail miles—and your mind and body—into shape. You'll spend your days performing rewarding trail work. During late afternoon and evening hours, you'll explore the countryside, photograph wildlife, relax by a mountain stream, or simply enjoy the fellowship of people who share your passion for the outdoors. Most projects require a hike into a remote base camp; some offer bunkhouse or cabin accommodations. For each project, American Hiking Society chooses an experienced volunteer team-leader to serve as the liaison between your crew and the host agency. If you are interested in serving as a leader, just indicate that on your registration form.

COMMITMENT: On a typical day, after a hearty breakfast, you will be on the trail at 9 A.M., work for six to eight hours, and return to base camp by 4 P.M., just in time to enjoy the long summer afternoons. On two-week vacations, you will get the weekend off.

PERKS AND REWARDS: Host agencies provide tools, safety equipment, workers' compensation, and project leaders. Most agencies also provide food; however, for some projects, volunteers may be asked to donate an additional $40 per week. Registration requires a nonrefundable $100 registration fee, which includes a one-year membership to American Hiking Society. AHS members pay $80 for the first trip, and each additional trip costs $60.

THE ESSENTIALS: Participants should possess a desire to improve America's trails and be in good physical condition (able to hike five miles or more a

Those who contemplate the beauty of the earth find reserves of strength that will endure as long as life lasts.
—RACHEL CARSON

day) and at least eighteen years of age. Volunteers supply their own camping equipment (tent, sleeping bag, personal items) and arrange their own transportation to and from the trailhead or work site (although many agencies provide pickups at major airports near the work sites).

YOUR FIRST MOVE: Call to receive a project schedule and registration form, or check out their website for complete details.

FOR MORE INFORMATION: Shirley Hearn, Volunteer Vacations Coordinator, American Hiking Society, 1422 Fenwick Ln., Silver Spring, MD 20910 (800) 972-8608 • (301) 565-6704, ext. 206 • (301) 565-6714 (fax) volunteer@americanhiking.org

☞ **INSIDER TIP: I have no right to set foot on any trail that someone else worked and sweated over if I don't work and sweat over some trail that someone else will hike on.** —*Joe Burton, AHS member and volunteer*

ANASAZI HERITAGE CENTER

Museum • Colorado • Summer
www.co.blm.gov/ahc

$ 🏠

Come spend eight weeks any time during the year in beautiful southwestern Colorado working in a "hands-on" museum committed to the preservation and interpretation of the northern San Juan Anasazi. Interns in collections management, interpretation, heritage education, and cultural resources management are provided with a realistic and well-rounded experience in a federal museum setting. Interns are expected to be self-motivated and able to work with a minimum amount of supervision once the task is understood. Interns receive a $100 per week stipend, plus communal housing. Send a resume and cover letter to begin the application process.

FOR MORE INFORMATION: Susan Thomas, Internship Coordinator, Anasazi Heritage Center, Bureau of Land Management, 27501 Highway 184, Dolores, CO 81323 • (970) 882-5622 • (970) 882-7035 (fax) susan_thomas@co.blm.gov

APPALACHIAN MOUNTAIN CLUB

Conservation · Northeast USA · Seasonal
www.outdoors.org

$ ⚑ ⊕

Appalachian Mountain Club (AMC), the nation's oldest and largest recreation and conservation organization, offers a smorgasbord of projects for volunteers, interns, and seasonal workers. Seasonal crews have the opportunity to work in the White Mountain National Forest in New Hampshire, Mount Desert Island in Maine, or in the hiking/canoeing center at the Delaware Mountain Gap in New Jersey—to name just a few. Crews generally work in base camps, shelters, huts, or roadside visitor centers with positions ranging from backcountry staff and trail crew to educational instructors. The average weekly pay for seasonal workers ranges from $250 to $340 after deductions for room and board. Interns get more involved in the business end of operations—everything from working on their website to assisting with the *AMC Outdoor* magazine. Volunteers for AMC help maintain more than 1,300 miles of recreational trails, including 350 miles of the Appalachian Trail. Volunteers also lead nature hikes, fill in for hut crews, and give public information talks. Call for a copy of the annual *Trail Volunteer Opportunities* catalog, which lists more than seven hundred opportunities. Specific job descriptions and details about the application process can be found online.

FOR MORE INFORMATION: Pat McCabe, Human Resources/Seasonal Employment, Appalachian Mountain Club, Pinkham Notch Visitor Center, P.O. Box 298, Gorham, NH 03581 · (603) 466-2721, ext. 145 · (603) 466-2822 (fax) amcemployment@outdoors.org

APPALACHIAN TRAIL CONFERENCE

Trail Maintenance · East Coast USA · 1–6 Weeks
www.appalachiantrail.org

♥ ⚑ ⊕

Help build a piece of the Appalachian National Scenic Trail, one of the most famous footpaths in the world. Winding along the peaks of the Appalachian chain from Georgia to Maine, this trail exists thanks to dedicated volunteers who planned, constructed, and now maintain and manage the trail by participating in ATC's Volunteer Trail Crew Program. In cooperation with the U.S. Forest Service, National Park Service, and trail-maintaining clubs, the crews design and build new trail segments, shelters, and bridges, rehabilitate

The world is a sacred vessel, which must not be tampered with or grabbed after.
To tamper with it is to spoil it, and to grasp it is to lose it.
—LAO-TZU

damaged trails, improve wildlife habitat, and preserve open areas. Food, accommodation, equipment, and on-the-job training are provided. Participants must be at least eighteen years of age, and no prior experience is necessary. Crews operate from May through October from base camps in Tennessee, southern Virginia, south-central Pennsylvania, Vermont, and Maine. Participants may volunteer for up to six weeks. Although coed crews are the norm, ATC also sponsors two-week all-women crews.

FOR MORE INFORMATION: Crew Program Coordinator, Appalachian Trail Conference, 1280 N. Main St., Blacksburg, VA 24060 (540) 961-5551 • crews@appalachiantrail.org

BADLANDS NATIONAL PARK

Natural Resources • South Dakota • Summer
www.nps.gov/badl

Badlands National Park consists of 244,000 acres of fossil-rich eroded sedimentary formations and mixed-grass prairie. In the summer, the weather is hot and dry and always windy. To hint at the beauty of the park, it was recently voted as having the best sunrises and sunsets in the world by International Nature Photographers. Summer interns staff park visitor centers; provide interpretive walks, children's hikes, and slide show presentations; patrol the backcountry; or engage in research and writing programs. Positions begin in mid-May and continue for twelve weeks. Applicants must be friendly and have strong public speaking skills and the ability to work in a high-stress environment and/or extremely remote setting. Shared housing is provided just a short walk from the visitor center, as is reimbursement of food and travel expenses up to $1,000.

FOR MORE INFORMATION: Marianne Mills, Resource Education Chief, Badlands National Park, 25216 Ben Reifel Rd., P.O. Box 6, Interior, SD 57750 (605) 433-5245 • (605) 433-5248 (fax) • badl_internships@nps.gov

WORKING FOR THE BUREAU OF LAND MANAGEMENT

The Bureau of Land Management (BLM) is responsible for managing about one-eighth of the land in the U.S. Most of these public lands are located in the western U.S., including Alaska, and are dominated by extensive grasslands, forests, high mountains, arctic tundra, and deserts.

VOLUNTEERING AND CAREER OPPORTUNITIES

Volunteers help the BLM educate others and instill a pride in the public lands that is crucial if these lands are to be held in trust for future generations. Volunteers improve the health of the public lands by restoring riparian areas across the West, building and repairing fences to protect special areas, planting trees, controlling weeds, and helping in many other ways.

Many students—from high school through college—can participate in one of two paid seasonal programs offered by the BLM: the Student Career Experience Program and the Student Temporary Employment Program. Positions are in natural resources, wildlife, cultural resources, recreation, information resources, and administration.

BUREAU OF LAND MANAGEMENT

Maintenance crews repair a BLM cabin along the Iditarod National Historic Trail. Extending from Seward to Nome, Alaska, the trail is famous for the annual dogsled race.

Be glad of life, because it gives you the chance to love and to work and to play and to look at the stars.
—HENRY VAN DYKE

Firefighting jobs are mostly seasonal positions during the months of May through September, depending upon the fire season in a particular area. Jobs include not only firefighting (hand crews, engine crews, smoke jumpers) but also many support positions in dispatching, warehousing, and equipment operations. Once they have become experienced wildland firefighters, many opt for the coveted smoke jumper position (a wildland firefighter who parachutes into remote areas to provide initial attack on wildfires). Smoke jumpers usually travel for 100 days out of a 120-day fire season (and it's noted that candidates should keep up a year-round physical fitness program to complete four weeks of rookie training—one of the hardest training programs to go through to get a job).

For further information on student, seasonal, temporary, and welfare-to-work opportunities call (202) 501-6723 or visit ww.blm.gov/careers; for volunteer opportunities call (202) 452-5078 or visit www.blm.gov/volunteer.

A BLM plant specialist gives a young student a hands-on lesson about one of Utah's many wild plant species.

BUREAU OF LAND MANAGEMENT

THE COLORADO TRAIL FOUNDATION

Trail Maintenance • Colorado • Summer
www.coloradotrail.org

♥ ⊕

The Colorado Trail Foundation recruits and trains over 350 volunteers to help maintain five hundred miles of trails stretching from Denver to Durango—and across eight mountain ranges and six national forests! Volunteers can participate in weeklong or weekend trail crew work (usually from mid-June through early August) with teams made up of twenty individuals. Trail crews are highly participatory, and all volunteers are encouraged to join in daily camp life. Volunteers bring their own tents, sleeping bags, and personal gear, but all meals, tools, and instruction are included for a nominal fee of $50 per week ($25 per weekend). Crews generally fill by April, so it's best to get on the mailing list by February 1. It's also noted that participants should establish an exercise program prior to their arrival on the crew to minimize sore muscles. Application materials and registration forms can be obtained online.

FOR MORE INFORMATION: Suzanne Reed and Marian Phillips, Volunteer Coordinators, The Colorado Trail Foundation, 710 10th St., Suite 210, Golden, CO 80401-5843 • (303) 384-3729 • (303) 384-3743 (fax) • ctf@coloradotrail.org

CUSTER STATE PARK RESORT COMPANY

Guest Services - South Dakota • Seasonal
www.custerresorts.com

$ 🏠 ⊕

In the summer of 1874, Major General George Custer led a scientific expedition through the Black Hills of Dakota Territory. When word spread that the expedition had discovered gold near the present-day city of Custer, prospectors and settlers soon followed. After the turn of the twentieth century, visionaries like South Dakota Governor Peter Norbeck realized that our environment was more precious than gold. In 1919, he urged the South Dakota State Legislature to preserve our natural resources and designate forty-eight thousand acres near Custer as a permanent state park. Today Custer State Park spreads across a total of seventy-three thousand acres. Seasonal employees have the opportunity to work in one of four resorts that are managed by Custer State Park Resort Company: the State Game Lodge and Resort, Blue Bell Lodge and Resort, Legion Lake Resort, or Sylvan Lake Resort. Typical seasonal positions are available; the more unique positions

---

Behold the turtle; for he makes no progress unless his neck is stuck out.   221
—JAMES CONANT

include entertainers, jeep drivers, interpretive guides, and wranglers. They also have a management-trainee internship program, with interns trained in all areas of resort operations. A monthly salary is provided, along with meals (and housing, if needed). An end-of-season bonus is also available to all who finish their agreements.

FOR MORE INFORMATION: Human Resources Department, Custer State Park Resort Company, HC 83, Box 74, Custer, SD 57730 • (800) 658-3530 (605) 255-4772 • (605) 255-4706 (fax) • e-mail@custerresorts.com

DENALI PARK RESORTS

Guest Services • Alaska • Summer
www.denaliparkresorts.com

$ ⛺ ⊕

Denali National Park has more than six million acres of pristine wilderness with some of the most awe-inspiring scenery and wildlife in North America, including Mount McKinley, which rises over twenty thousand feet into the Alaskan sky. If you prefer the water, employees at Glacier Bay National Park (spanning over three million acres and offering some of the best sea kayaking in the world) have an opportunity to see more marine wildlife than they could ever imagine. Denali Park Resorts operates the McKinley Chalets and the McKinley Village as well as Alaska Raft Adventures, Tundra Wilderness Tours, Natural History Tours, and the Visitor Transportation System; while Aramark/Huna Totem operates Glacier Bay Lodge and day boat tours into Glacier Bay.

WHAT YOU'LL BE DOING: Adventure awaits in the heart of the last frontier with Denali Park Resorts! Whether working as a hospitality staff member, a living history interpreter, or a tour or river guide, those who enjoy a busy work environment with extensive guest contact will thrive here. Over fifty types of positions are available, and each summer over 900 seasonal staff come to Alaska to work, play, and explore.

COMMITMENT: The season runs from May through mid-September, with preference given to those who can work the entire season.

PERKS AND REWARDS: Most first-year employees earn $7.15 to $10 per hour with an end-of-season bonus of approximately $300. Room and board are available for $12.50 to $15 per day, and if you serve as a resident assistant, a reduced housing fee is offered. A variety of rustic, dormitory-style company housing units (shared rooms with one or two others) with a central bathhouse and free use of the laundry facilities is provided. Perks include a hodgepodge of employee activities, high-speed Internet access, complimentary transportation from Fairbanks to Denali, free rafting and sea kayaking, and discounted tours, flightseeing, and retail purchases. And don't forget about your new playground—millions of acres of pristine Alaskan wilderness to hike, climb, bike, fish, kayak, and explore.

THE ESSENTIALS: Applicants must be at least eighteen for housing, and many jobs require that you be at least twenty-one. Local services are limited in Denali, which is 120 miles from Fairbanks, the nearest city. Therefore applicants should have a strong desire to enjoy and discover the wilderness.

YOUR FIRST MOVE: Most interviewing and hiring is done from January through April.

FOR MORE INFORMATION: John Tsoutsouvas, Regional Director of Human Resources, Denali Park Resorts, Aramark Parks & Resorts, P.O. Box 87, Denali National Park, AK 99755 • (907) 683-8286 • (907) 683-8275 (fax) denalihr@aramark.com

EVERGLADES NATIONAL PARK

Guest Services • Florida • Seasonal
www.flamingolodge.com

$ 🏠 ⊕

Seasonal positions at Flamingo Lodge (in the heart of Everglades National Park) range from food and beverage and hotel services to marina staff and accountants. The summer season runs from May 1 through the end of October, with the winter season spanning from November 1 through the beginning of May. Generally, the earlier you can start and the later you can stay, the better your chances will be of receiving an offer of employment. Wages for most positions start at $6 per hour and include low-cost dormitory-style housing or full RV hookups. Other benefits include complimentary Florida Bay and back country boat cruises and rental of canoes, kayaks, and skiffs. Applicants must be at least eighteen years of age.

FOR MORE INFORMATION: Human Resources Office, Everglades National Park, Xanterra Parks & Resorts, #1 Flamingo Lodge Highway, Flamingo, FL 33034-6798 (239) 695-3101, ext. 285 • (239) 695-3921 (fax) • jobs-flamingo@xanterra.com

*Now I know the secret of making the best persons; it is to grow in the open air
and to eat and sleep with the earth.*
—WALT WHITMAN

FLAGG RANCH RESORT

Guest Services • Wyoming • Seasonal
www.flaggranch.com

$ 🏠 ⊕

Centrally located between Yellowstone and Grand Teton National Parks, Flagg Ranch is a privately owned company that operates visitor services for the National Park Service. Seasonal positions are available in all areas of hospitality management from mid-May through the end of September. An hourly wage is provided (the base pay rate is $6 per hour), along with room and board for a nominal cost deducted from your paycheck. The ranch also has a limited number of full hookup sites for employees with their own trailers or motor homes (pets are allowed with this option!). Applicants must be at least eighteen years of age and applications are available online. Note that Flagg Ranch conducts its recruiting efforts from Tempe, Arizona.

FOR MORE INFORMATION: Jennifer Anderson, Human Resources Coordinator, Flagg Ranch Resort, 3207 S. Hardy Dr., Tempe, AZ 85282 • (800) 224-1384 (480) 829-7600 • (480) 829-7460 (fax) • jennifer@flaggranch.com

FLORISSANT FOSSIL BEDS NATIONAL MONUMENT

National Monument • Colorado • Summer
www.nps.gov/flfo

$ 🏠 ⊕

Florissant Fossil Beds National Monument sits at an elevation of 8,400 feet and preserves fossil remains and geologic evidence of a far different world from thirty-five million years ago. The fossil beds are named after a nearby small town, Florissant, which takes its name from the French word for "flowering" or "blooming."

WHAT YOU'LL BE DOING: Interpretive interns provide information on natural and cultural resources, explain the significance of the area, and communicate National Park Service philosophy to the visiting public. Paleontology interns are involved with projects relating to the geological or paleontological resources of the park, including resource management, museum collection curation, and technical assistance with excavating and monitoring of paleontological sites. All interns participate in a one-week orientation session, and throughout the twelve-week program (beginning in May), training is provided in park operations as well as natural and paleontological resources monitoring.

PERKS AND REWARDS: A weekly stipend of $150 is provided, along with housing and uniforms.

THE ESSENTIALS: Interpretive applicants must have effective communication skills, the ability to work comfortably with a variety of people of all ages, the ability to work independently and as part of a team, and an interest and ability to work outdoors. Paleontology applicants must have completed basic undergraduate course work in geology or biology. Since there is no public transportation in the area and housing may be several miles from the park, a personal vehicle is highly recommended.

YOUR FIRST MOVE: Send a cover letter, stating your interest in the position, and a resume with two references (with contact information) by mid-March.

FOR MORE INFORMATION: Volunteer/Intern Coordinator, Field Internship Program, Florissant Fossil Beds National Monument, P.O. Box 185, Florissant, CO 80816-0815 • (719) 748-3253 • (719) 748-3164 (fax)

FURNACE CREEK INN AND RANCH RESORT

Guest Services • California • Seasonal
www.furnacecreekresort.com

$ 🏠 🌐

Imagine working at 200 feet below sea level while being surrounded by a vast and arid desert region with mountains that rise to 11,500 feet. Yes, this is the desolate landscape of Death Valley National Park, where Furnace Creek Inn and Ranch Resort provides a contrasting lush oasis for guests and staff alike. Seasonal guest services and hospitality opportunities abound at Furnace Creek throughout the year—from guest room attendants and groundskeepers to front desk clerks and accountants. Staff will work at one of four properties: Furnace Creek Inn, a 68-room historic inn; Furnace Creek Ranch, a 224-room resort; Stove Pipe Wells Village, an 82-room motel; and Scotty's Castle. All staff receive an hourly wage along with housing and meals available for a nominal fee. Rustic double-occupancy cabin or dormitory-style housing is provided at $25 per week, which includes bedding, towels, utilities, and cable TV hookups (don't forget your TV!). Breakfast and lunch are provided at no cost; dinner is $2.50 per day. RV spaces are also available at $30 per week. For those who love the outdoors, the biggest perk may well be exploring the three million acres of Death Valley. Staff also have free rein on ranch activities, including tennis, volleyball, and basketball courts, the golf course, spring-fed swimming pools, a new employee fitness/weight room, and horseback riding October through May. Applicants must be at least eighteen years old and willing to work any day of the week (shifts may include weekends and holidays). Applications can be obtained online.

FOR MORE INFORMATION: Cyndi Harris, Human Resources Director,
Furnace Creek Inn and Ranch Resort, P.O. Box 187, Death Valley, CA 92328
(760) 786-2311 • (760) 786-2396 (fax) • jobs-fc@xanterra.com

THE GLACIER INSTITUTE

Outdoor Education • Montana • 2–7 Months
www.glacierinstitute.org

$ 🏠 🌐

The Glacier Institute is based at two facilities in and adjacent to Glacier
National Park in northwest Montana and is governed by a working board
of directors who aren't afraid to get dirty. Outdoor enthusiasts will enjoy
that most of their work is conducted outside in this rugged and beautiful
mountainous region. The institute courses often bring in local natural
resource specialists and employees from Montana Fish, Wildlife and Parks;
Flathead National Forest; Flathead Valley Community College; Glacier
Natural History Association; and Glacier National Park.

YOUR SURROUNDINGS: Both their facilities are rustic, historic sites in spectacular settings. Opportunities for river floating, hiking, wildlife viewing,
and backcountry camping abound. During time off, the towns of Columbia
Falls, Kalispell, and Whitefish are close enough for movies, restaurants, and
shopping.

WHAT YOU'LL BE DOING: As an intern at the Glacier Institute, you become a
full-fledged staff member and are responsible for all facets of running a residential outdoor education center, both as a teacher of youth programs and
as an assistant during adult classes. At the Big Creek facility, you will help
with all organizational, programming, and facility aspects relating to on-site
operations. This includes cooking with students, teaching evening programs,
creating and implementing curriculum, and helping with facility upkeep. At
the field camp, you will fill a similar role. Responsibilities include staffing the
office, accompanying instructors on field trips, trail and first aid support, and
developing and teaching youth programs. As a teacher/naturalist at Big Creek,
your responsibilities increase as you serve as a mentor to interns.

COMMITMENT: Positions can begin as early as mid-March and run through the
end of October (interns can work two to seven months). The work schedule is
very irregular and busy. There may be times with no programs and times
when programs run nonstop.

PERKS AND REWARDS: Interns receive $200 to $300 per month; teachers/
naturalists earn $550 to $800 per month. Housing as well as food or a food

stipend are also provided. Because they are a small organization, they rely heavily on staff creativity and input, so there are many opportunities to become involved in program enhancement and development.

THE ESSENTIALS: Applicants should be at least nineteen years old and have two years of college or more and some prior experience teaching or working with youth. All staff must have CPR and first aid certification.

YOUR FIRST MOVE: Call for job descriptions and an application. Most interviews are done over the phone, but they prefer personal interviews if at all possible. It's best to apply by the end of January.

FOR MORE INFORMATION: Big Creek Program Director, The Glacier Institute, P.O. Box 1887, Kalispell, MT 59903 • (406) 755-1211 • (406) 755-7154 (fax) register@glacierinstitute.org

INSIDER TIP: Staff members really enjoy working and living with people of all ages, are enthusiastic and energetic, love learning and being outside, and are creative and flexible. We need people who can be happy working and living in a residential, remote setting with rustic accommodations. Self-directed people who can work without much supervision and are willing to do anything will do very well in our program.

GLACIER PARK BOAT COMPANY

Tour Boat Outfitter • Montana • Summer
www.glacierparkboats.com

$ 🏕

A bank teller turned boat builder started a family legacy in Glacier National Park. In the summer of 1937, Glacier Park Boat Company launched its first boat tours in the park with two classic-style wooden boats. Four generations later, this family-run operation has five locations throughout the park and boats that now carry from forty-five to eighty passengers. Seasonal staff captain the tour boats from June 1 through September 15, giving commentaries on the historic and natural aspects of "America's little Switzerland." Extensive preseason training in tour boat operation and regional history is provided (which also prepares each staff member for boat certification exams). Applicants must be at least eighteen years of age, possess current CPR and first aid certificates, pass a physical exam and drug test, enjoy working with the public, and have good communication skills—especially public speaking. Benefits include minimum wage pay, along with family-style housing and meals (for $8 per day). It's suggested you apply by January or February.

We sleep, but the loom of life never stops, and the pattern which was weaving when the sun went down is weaving when it comes up tomorrow.
—HENRY WARD BEECHER

FOR MORE INFORMATION: Susan Burch, Director, Glacier Park Boat Company, P.O. Box 5262, Kalispell, MT 59903-5262 • (406) 257-2426 (406) 756-1437 (fax) • gpboats@montanaweb.com

GLACIER PARK, INC.

Guest Services • Montana • Seasonal
www.gpihr.com

$ 🏕 🌐

Rising from the plains of northwest Montana and southern Alberta, the jagged peaks of the Rocky Mountains make up the heart of Waterton-Glacier International Peace Park. This serves as the backdrop for seasonal employees at Glacier Park, which operates seven historic hotels, nine restaurants, five retail gift shops, a pro golf shop, four camp stores, and thirty-three famous (and recently restored) 1930s red tour buses. Whether you work as a baker, waiter, bellhop, accounting clerk, guest services agent, or tour driver, Glacier Park is a great place to begin your budding hospitality career.

PERKS AND REWARDS: Wages range from $5.15 to $7.25 per hour, depending on the position and whether you work in the U.S. or Canada. Housing in Glacier is extremely rustic. The "structures" are located in remote Rocky Mountain settings, weathering extreme winter elements and hundreds of new tenants each season. All housing is dormitory-style, with triple or quad accommodations. There is also limited trailer/RV space. Housing is charged at $2.50 per day, and meals are $7.50 per day.

THE ESSENTIALS: The minimum working age is sixteen; employees living on-site must be eighteen; and bartenders and drivers must be at least twenty-one. Applicants will be considered based on their work availability dates (a full season is preferred), qualifications, and relevant experience.

YOUR FIRST MOVE: More information and application materials can be found online, or call for a brochure and application. Most positions are filled by May 1, although midsummer opportunities, which begin as early as June 15 or as late as August 15, are available. General information about the park can be found at www.glacierparkinc.com.

FOR MORE INFORMATION: Dana Connell, Human Resources Director, Glacier Park, Inc., 774 Railroad St., P.O. Box 280, Columbia Falls, MT 59912 (406) 892-6739 • (406) 892-1140 (fax)

May through September: P.O. Box 147, East Glacier, MT 59434; (406) 226-5634, (406) 226-4176 (fax) • jobs@glacierparkinc.com

GRAND CANYON NATIONAL PARK LODGES, SOUTH RIM

Guest Services • Arizona • Seasonal
www.grandcanyonlodges.com

$ 🏠 🌐

Grand Canyon National Park Lodges, located on the South Rim of the
Grand Canyon, is the authorized concessionaire providing hospitality services
for the park. There are no easy jobs at Grand Canyon—the staff are known
to work hard and play ferociously. Positions include food and beverage, retail
sales, housekeeping, front desk, and accounting. Many employees start in
entry-level positions and advance during the season. Positions are offered
year-round or on a seasonal basis, beginning as early as March and ending
as late as mid-October. Preference is given to those who can work at least a
three- or four-month period. Wages start at $6 per hour for non-tipped posi-
tions. Dormitory-style housing (two to a room) is provided for $16 per week,
and RV spots are available for $90 per month. A low-cost employee meal plan
is also offered. Applicants must be eighteen years of age to live in company-
provided housing. Deadlines are rolling; however, it's best to apply in early
January.

FOR MORE INFORMATION: Staffing Manager, Grand Canyon National Park Lodges,
South Rim, Xanterra Parks & Resorts, P.O. Box 699, Grand Canyon, AZ 86023
(888) 224 0330 • (928) 638-2631, ext. 6280 • (928) 638-0143 (fax)
jobs-gcsr@xanterra.com

GRAND TETON LODGE COMPANY

Guest Services • Wyoming • Seasonal
www.gtlc.com

$ 🏠 🌐

Grand Teton Lodge Company manages three unique resorts in the heart
of Grand Teton National Park. Jackson Lake Lodge is their largest hotel
resort, situated on a bluff overlooking Jackson Lake and the skyline of the
Tetons; Colter Bay Village, on the shores of Jackson Lake, is a family resort
offering cabins, tent cabins, and RV park accommodations; and Jenny Lake
Lodge is a small, elegant resort located in the shadow of the towering Tetons.

WHAT YOU'LL BE DOING: Whether for a summer or many seasons, employment
with Grand Teton provides a unique experience in one of the most beautiful
and rugged areas in the world. (The first time you get a glimpse of the Tetons,
you'll truly be amazed.) While the work is demanding and the summer cannot

Teach us love, compassion, and honor that we may heal the earth and heal each other.   229
—OJIBWA PRAYER

be considered a vacation, Grand Teton Lodge Company offers employees an opportunity to live in an area that annually attracts well over three million visitors. Hospitality-type jobs run the gamut here and include accounting, employee services (including recreation staff and personnel clerks), food and beverage, guest activities (wranglers, river guides, and van/bus drivers), hotel services, maintenance, and retail.

COMMITMENT: The Grand Teton season runs from May through October. Depending on the position, various starting and ending dates can be accommodated. Preference will be given to applicants who can work through Labor Day (or the end of the season), and positions beginning in July and August are also available. Work schedules vary but in most cases are six days, forty-eight hours per week.

PERKS AND REWARDS: Entry-level salaries begin at $7.15 per hour, and dormitory-style housing is provided at no charge (RV sites are $4.75 per day). There is a $50 per week fee for employee services, which include cafeteria meals, laundry facilities, and laundered linens. Employee recreational activities, such as dances and sporting events, are scheduled throughout the summer.

THE ESSENTIALS: A minimum age of eighteen is required for all employees housed in company-maintained facilities.

YOUR FIRST MOVE: Applications can be filled out online.

FOR MORE INFORMATION: Personnel Manager, Grand Teton Lodge Company, P.O. Box 250, Moran, WY 83013 • (800) 350-2068 • (307) 543-3068 (307) 543-3139 (fax) • personnel@gtlc.com

GREAT SMOKY MOUNTAINS INSTITUTE AT TREMONT

Environmental Education • Tennessee • 3–12 Months
www.gsmit.org

$ 🏠 🌐

Located deep in the heart of the largest mountain wilderness in the eastern U.S., the Great Smoky Mountains Institute (GSMI) offers residential, hands-on environmental education programs for children, adults, teachers, and people of all ages and walks of life. Using its classroom of 522,000 acres of forest, field, and stream in the Great Smoky Mountains National Park, GSMI is dedicated to creating "environmentally literate" students who want to help preserve and protect places like the Smokies for the future. Year-round offerings include Elderhostel programs, teacher-training weeks, backpacking courses, summer youth camps, and weekend to weeklong adult workshops on topics from wildflowers to local culture and history.

WHAT YOU'LL BE DOING: For those who are excited about environmental education and want to gain practical experience in the field, GSMI offers a variety of summer and year-round opportunities. Summer teaching staff work in all aspects of the GSMI youth camps, including developing and teaching daily natural history activities, coleading backpacking trips, conducting evening programs, supervising campers in the dormitory, and a variety of other summer camp–related activities. A number of internships are also available for the summer season and those from abroad can participate in the International Volunteer Work Study Program (six-month to one-year positions beginning in January and June).

PERKS AND REWARDS: A $100 to $250 per week stipend (depending on position and experience) is provided, along with housing and meals.

THE ESSENTIALS: Teaching staff must have experience and training in environmental education and natural history, and experience working with children and adults in outdoor educational settings. A minimum of two years of college in a related field, a summer camp experience, and first aid and CPR certification are required.

YOUR FIRST MOVE: Call for application materials. Naturalists and interns must apply by February 1. International applicants must apply through the National Park Service's Office of International Affairs at (202) 565-1293.

FOR MORE INFORMATION: Education Director, Great Smoky Mountains Institute at Tremont, 9275 Tremont Rd., Townsend, TN 37882 • (865) 448-6709 (865) 448-9250 (fax) • mail@gsmit.org

GREEN MOUNTAIN CLUB

Trail Maintenance • Vermont • Seasonal
www.greenmountainclub.org

$ 🏕

Midway between Waterbury and Stowe, Vermont, you'll find the headquarters for the Green Mountain Club along with its thousands of members and volunteers who preserve, protect, and maintain Long Trail, Vermont's "footpath in the wilderness" and the oldest long-distance hiking trail in America. Seasonal opportunities on the trail include maintenance activities, working with the Long Trail Patrol trail crew, volunteering as a caretaker, or leading interpretive hikes. Off-the-trail volunteers can get involved in everything from

However much you knock at nature's door, she will never answer you in comprehensible words. 231
—IVAN TURGENEV

publications and grant writing to membership development. Stipends range from $40 to $400 per week, and some positions include meals and/or rustic housing.

FOR MORE INFORMATION: Greg Western, Field Supervisor, Green Mountain Club, 4711 Waterbury-Stowe Rd., Waterbury Center, VT 05677
(802) 244-7037, ext. 18 • (802) 244-5867 (fax) • gmc@greenmountainclub.org

ISLE ROYALE NATIONAL PARK

National Park • Michigan • Summer
www.nps.gov/isro

In Lake Superior's northwest corner sits a wilderness archipelago, a roadless land of wild creatures, pristine forests, refreshing lakes, and rugged, scenic shores accessible only by boat or floatplane. The place? Isle Royale National Park. Volunteer positions are available in the park library, *Ranger III* ship, resource management, backcountry campground, interpretation, park museum, and park wildlife and vegetation monitoring projects. A food stipend of $60 to $70 per week and comfortable dormitory-style housing is provided.

FOR MORE INFORMATION: Liz Valencia, Volunteer Coordinator, Isle Royale National Park, 800 E. Lakeshore Dr., Houghton, MI 49931
(906) 487-7153 • (906) 487-7170 (fax) • liz_valencia@nps.gov

LAKE POWELL RESORTS AND MARINAS

Guest Services • Arizona • Summer
www.lakepowell.com

Located in a magical place filled with towering mesas, long and twisting canyons, and clear mirrors of water, Lake Powell Resorts and Marinas operates five marinas and resort properties as well as Wilderness River Adventures. Over 1,200 people are employed by Lake Powell at the peak of summer season, with positions available at the marina (from boat instructors to rental attendants), food and beverage (waitstaff to bartenders), hotel (front desk clerks to van drivers), and retail positions. Seasonal wages start at $6 per hour and dormitory-style housing (with single and double occupancy options) or RV space is offered for a monthly fee. The biggest perks, however, are use of company powerboats and water toys, complimentary boat tours and float trips, and a seven-day houseboat vacation for your family. Call or email for further details and an application.

FOR MORE INFORMATION: Carol Mehler, Director of Human Resources, Lake Powell Resorts and Marinas, Glen Canyon National Recreation Area, P.O. Box 1597, Page, AZ 86040 • (928) 645-1081 • (928) 645-1016 (fax) lprm-hr@aramark.com

LAKE TAHOE BASIN MANAGEMENT UNIT

Natural Resources • California • Seasonal
www.r5.fs.fed.us/ltbmu

$ 🏠 🌐

Coordinated by the U.S. Forest Service at Lake Tahoe, the interpretive services program provides informational and interpretive materials through a visitor center, stream profile chamber, self-guided trails, brochures, displays, and guided activities. Year-round opportunities abound for seasonal interpretive naturalists. Summer naturalists assist with campfire programs, environmental education activities, living history programs, display exhibits, natural history information, recreational activities, and various special projects; fall naturalists teach third and fourth graders about the life cycle of the Kokanee salmon, which spawn in a creek near the visitor center; and winter naturalists serve fifth and sixth graders, interpreting Lake Tahoe's winter environment in a classroom setting and outdoors on snowshoes. A subsistence allowance, training, and complimentary government housing (on the shores of Lake Tahoe in a historic estate) are provided.

FOR MORE INFORMATION:
Michael St. Michel
Visitor Center Director
Lake Tahoe Basin
Management Unit
USDA Forest Service
35 College Dr.
South Lake Tahoe, CA
96150-4500
(530) 543-2600
(530) 543-2693 (fax)
mstmichel@fs.fed.us

MICHAEL ST. MICHEL

A summer naturalist with the Lake Tahoe Basin Management Unit helps children collect aquatic insects on a creek walk.

Forget not that the earth delights to feel your bare feet and the winds long to play with your hair.
—KAHLIL GIBRAN

LAND BETWEEN THE LAKES

Natural Resources • Kentucky • 3–12 Months
www.lbl.org/Internships.html

$ ⚑ ⊕

Located in western Kentucky and Tennessee, Land Between The Lakes (LBL) offers 170,000 acres of wildlife, history, and outdoor recreation opportunities, wrapped by three hundred miles of undeveloped shoreline. Interns and apprentices work closely with professionals and receive firsthand experiences in everything from recreation and environmental education to history and photography. Work locations might be in a family campground, a resident group camp, a living history farm, a nature center, or the LBL administrative office. Internships last from twelve to sixteen weeks, while apprenticeships are available for up to one year. A weekly stipend of $150 to $200 is provided along with housing in a fully-furnished home or house trailer. Prospective interns must have completed at least two years of college course work, while apprentice applicants must have at least a bachelor's degree. Someone with the ability and enthusiasm to work with a variety of people in the outdoors has as good a chance as someone with all the experience in the world. Call for application materials.

FOR MORE INFORMATION: Greg Barnes, Intern/Apprentice Coordinator, Land Between The Lakes, U.S. Forest Service, 100 Van Morgan Dr., Golden Pond, KY 42211 • (270) 924-2089 • (270) 924-2060 (fax) gmbarnes@fs.fed.us

MAINE APPALACHIAN TRAIL CLUB

Trail Maintenance • Maine • Seasonal
www.matc.org

$ ⚑ ⊕

Volunteer opportunities abound in the Maine Appalachian Trail Club. More than five hundred members and volunteers help maintain 261 miles of the Appalachian Trail in Maine, from Mount Katahdin to Route 26 in Grafton Notch, including thirty-seven lean-tos and tent sites. Trail crew leaders, assistants, and interns provide everything from logistical support to path reconstruction. Positions begin as early as May and include a travel grant, stipend (up to $400), lodging, and meals. Caretaker positions are available at various campsites throughout Maine from mid-May to late October. Duties include greeting and registering hikers, performing maintenance tasks, and guiding overnight backpacking trips. A stipend of $350 to $390 per week is provided along with housing, cookstove, work tools, and gear. Applications are accepted in late fall for the following season. View the club's website for a listing of positions and where to send your application materials.

FOR MORE INFORMATION: Dick Doucette, Corresponding Secretary, Maine Appalachian Trail Club, P.O. Box 283, Augusta, ME 04332-0283 (207) 265-6282 • ddouce8554@aol.com

MINNESOTA CONSERVATION CORPS

Conservation • Minnesota • Summer
www.conservationcorps.org

$ 🏕

The Minnesota Conservation Corps summer program provides the chance for Minnesota youth, ages fifteen to eighteen, to work on various natural resource projects while learning basic work skills. The summer staff—site directors, work-project coordinators, crew leaders, and education coordinators— supervise and work with the youth corps members, while also instructing them in environmental awareness, life skills, and career development. Past projects have included erosion control, building and maintaining hiking trails, historical restoration, tree planting, and building bridges. Depending on the position, a weekly stipend of $290 to $440 is provided, along with room, board, and transportation while on the job. Applicants who thrive in these positions aren't afraid of mosquitoes, rain, heat, and other challenges that the outdoors presents. Individuals who are sign language interpreters or skilled in American Sign Language are highly encouraged to apply. In addition, those who are deaf or hard-of-hearing are needed for leadership roles. Application materials must be received by mid-March.

FOR MORE INFORMATION: Pete Bonk, Youth Programs Manager, Minnesota Conservation Corps, 1200 Warner Rd., St. Paul, MN 55106 (651) 772-7985 • (651) 793-3889 (fax) • pete.bonk@conservationcorps.org

A pond-frog cannot imagine the ocean, nor can a summer insect conceive of ice.
Remember, you are restricted by your own learning.
—CHUANG-TSU

WORKING FOR THE NATIONAL PARK SERVICE

• •

Many Americans have had love affairs with the national parks since Yellowstone, the first national park, was created in 1872. Today the National Park Service preserves and manages more than 370 sites across the U.S. (including Guam, Puerto Rico, and the Virgin Islands). From the architectural relics of the Anasazi in Mesa Verde and the historical treasures of Gettysburg Battlefield to the fossil reefs of Carlsbad Cavern, the awesome coastal forest in Redwood National Park, and the geysers bursting in Yellowstone, National Park Service personnel are there to protect these awe-inspiring places and to teach and educate the millions of people who visit. All national park employment opportunities can be found online at www.nps.gov/personnel.

✦ **INSIDER TIP: The NPS manages more than just our national parks—the National Park system (encompassing more that 83.6 million acres!) is broken down by a variety of unique designations, including monuments, preserves, historic sites, memorials, battlefields, cemeteries, recreation areas, seashores, lakeshores, rivers, parkways, and trails—more than 370 national sites in all! To find out more information about a specific park, including job and volunteer opportunities, use the NPS Park Guide at www.nps.gov/parks.html.**

JOHN SPRING

A conservation intern with the Student Conservation Association (page 244) involved in a surveying assignment at Olympic National Park (page 241).

SEASONAL JOBS

Seasonal workers are hired every year to help permanent staff, especially during peak visitation seasons. Jobs range from carpenters, campground hosts, fee collectors, firefighters, historians, laborers, landscape architects, and naturalists to law enforcement rangers, lifeguards, park rangers, tour guides, visitor-use assistants, and so much more. Seasonal jobs are very competitive, although competition is usually less keen at smaller, lesser-known parks and for jobs in the winter season. Application forms, including a list of parks hiring for a particular season, are available from any regional office. The filing period for winter employment is June 1 through July 15 (postmarked); the summer employment filing period is November 15 through January 15 (postmarked). Applicants are encouraged to use the seasonal employment website at www.sep.nps.gov, and questions can be directed to nps_sep@nps.gov.

VOLUNTEERS IN PARKS (VIP) PROGRAM

VIPs work in almost every park in the National Park System and perform varied duties that might include working at information desks, presenting living history demonstrations in period costume, serving as campground hosts, leading guided nature walks and evening campfire programs, or maintaining and patrolling trails. All VIPs are given special training, and some parks reimburse volunteers for some out-of-pocket expenses, such as local travel costs, meals, and uniforms. Visit www.nps.gov/volunteer, where you'll find an extensive list of volunteer and artist-in-residence program opportunities, or call the VIP coordinator at the national park where you would like to volunteer. Be sure to ask for the Volunteers in Parks brochure, which provides a nifty map of all the national parks (with contact information) and application materials.

Earth gives life and seeks the man who walks gently upon it.   **237**
—HOPI LEGEND

The tools of the trade for SCA interns.

INTERNSHIP OPPORTUNITIES

Whether you are a college student or a retiree, the Student Conservation Association (SCA) is one of the best ways to land a paid seasonal internship with the National Park Service, as well as other federal agencies, like the Bureau of Land Management and U.S. Forest Service. Throughout the year, SCA publishes a catalog of opportunities that range from educating people to save the Florida manatee to providing guided nature and historic talks at a national monument. More information on SCA can be found on page 244, or visit them on the Web at www.thesca.org.

A variety of current opportunities can also be viewed in the volunteer section of the NPS employment website at www.nps.gov/volunteer; however, it's best to contact the SCA or each park for specific information.

PARK CONCESSIONAIRES

Hotels, lodges, restaurants, stores, transportation services, marinas, and many other visitor facilities in the National Park System are operated by private companies that hire their own employees. This chapter of your guide features the details for many—from Denali Park Resorts (page 222) to Furnace Creek Inn and Ranch Resort (page 225).

NORTHWEST SERVICE ACADEMY

Conservation • Washington • 6–11 Months
www.northwestserviceacademy.org

$ 🏠

As an AmeriCorps program that addresses critical environmental and educational needs of Oregon and Washington, the Northwest Service Academy hires field team members during the spring and fall for a six-month period. Participants restore and protect wild lands and rivers through projects ranging from trail maintenance to wildlife habitat restoration or lead youth programs with an environmental focus. Seven-person teams will live and serve with fellow field team members in the outdoors for periods up to a month, learning new skills and enjoying backcountry adventures. Benefits include a $5,200 stipend, room and board, a $2,363 education award, and many certification and training sessions. Applicants must be at least eighteen years old, possess outdoor living skills, be keen on leadership and positive group dynamics, and have an environmental bent with some college or a degree. Applications are available online.

FOR MORE INFORMATION: Bonny Cushman, Recruitment & Outreach Coordinator, Northwest Service Academy, ESD 112—National Service Programs, 2500 NE 65th Ave., Vancouver, WA 98661 • (360) 750-7500, ext. 378 (360) 694-2491 (fax) • nwsa.recruitment@esd112.org

NORTHWEST YOUTH CORPS

Conservation • Pacific Northwest • 2–4 Months
www.nwyouthcorps.org

$ 🏠 🌐

Known as the only fully mobile conservation corps in the country, the Northwest Youth Corps (NYC) is an education and job-training program for high school youth. Youth crews work on projects for government agencies and private landowners in a format stressing environmental education and development of basic job skills. Crews typically live and work in remote locations throughout Oregon, Washington, and Northern California, as well as parts of Arizona and Idaho. During the week, crews set up primitive camps near their job sites, live in tents, and cook their own meals over a campfire or campstove. On weekends, three to four crews rendezvous for recreational outings and educational activities.

I shall tell you a great secret, my friend. Do not wait for the last judgment,
it takes place every day.
—ALBERT CAMUS

WHAT YOU'LL BE DOING: More than seven hundred youth crew members maintain wilderness trails, build fences, pull debris from creeks, restore wildlife habitat, plant trees, enhance fisheries, or work to save endangered species. Crew leaders and assistants work shoulder to shoulder with their crew while also supervising the successful completion of a wide variety of manual labor projects, providing environmental education programs, and passing on leadership and growth skills to corps members. Most crews move to new project locations each week—it's not unusual to see three states and explore varied ecosystems during a six-week session.

This crew learns how to use a crosscut saw through teamwork and leadership skills taught by Northwest Youth Corps leaders.

COMMITMENT: Positions, with various start and finish dates, begin in late February and continue throughout the summer months into October. The program requires working long days, high energy, and a love for challenge. Time off is limited.

PERKS AND REWARDS: Crew leaders average $4,700 to $5,300 per summer (about $70 to $84 per day), and meals and rustic housing are provided. In addition, staff and youth alike walk away from NYC with skills—from technical project know-how to skills in wilderness travel, living, and teaching—that they can take into the "real" world. Many alumni have moved onto jobs with land management agencies or as teachers or outdoor leaders.

THE ESSENTIALS: The ideal candidate has a youth leadership background, experience in professional positions, a solid environmental ethic, and a diverse set of conservation skills. Current Wilderness First Aid and CPR certifications are required, and lifesaving certification is desirable.

YOUR FIRST MOVE: Applications can be filled out online. In addition, a cover letter, resume, and four references are necessary.

FOR MORE INFORMATION: YouthCorps Program Director, Northwest Youth Corps, 2621 Augusta St., Eugene, OR 97403 • (541) 349-5055 • (541) 349-5060 (fax) work@nwyouthcorps.org

OLYMPIC NATIONAL PARK

National Park • Washington • 2–6 Months
www.nps.gov/olym

$ 🏠 🌐

Olympic National Park, occupying nearly one million acres in Washington State, was established to preserve primeval forests and the largest natural herd of Roosevelt elk. In 1976, it was designated a biosphere reserve, and soon thereafter, it was designated a world heritage site. The park consists of a rugged and spectacular glacier-capped mountainous core penetrated by deep valleys, some with lush temperate rain forests, a separate fifty-seven-mile-long coastal strip, and some one hundred offshore islands.

WHAT YOU'LL BE DOING: In addition to a variety of volunteer opportunities (ranging from campground hosts to backcountry rangers), Olympic National Park has an extensive internship program for the budding outdoor enthusiast. Whether working as an interpretive ranger on Hurricane Ridge, at the visitor center at Lake Crescent, or at the Port Angeles wilderness information center, interns have the chance to work behind the scenes and develop the necessary skills to further their career with the National Park Service. A two-week training program is provided for most positions.

COMMITMENT: Positions are generally available throughout the year, including the summer months. Visitor center internship positions vary seasonally, although plan on two or three months or longer. A minimum commitment of two-and-a-half months is generally needed.

PERKS AND REWARDS: Interns receive a stipend of $50 to $100 per month, along with shared bunkhouse or dormitory-style housing. Housing or RV/trailer hookups are provided for volunteers.

THE ESSENTIALS: Applicants should have a strong background in natural science, park management, or interpretation. Some knowledge of ecological processes and natural history is desirable as is the ability to work independently and with people.

YOUR FIRST MOVE: Call for application materials and details of all their internship and volunteer opportunities. (They are extensive!) Phone calls are welcomed, and it is suggested you send your application one to three months before the season begins.

FOR MORE INFORMATION: Maurie Sprague, Volunteer Coordinator, Olympic National Park, 600 East Park Ave., Port Angeles, WA 98362-6798 (360) 565-3000 • (360) 565-3015 (fax) • maurie_sprague@nps.gov

Life is a succession of lessons which must be lived to be understood. **241**
—RALPH WALDO EMERSON

OREGON DUNES NATIONAL RECREATION AREA

Forest Service • Oregon • 1–6 Months
www.fs.fed.us/r6/siuslaw

This is sand dune country! Oregon Dunes National Recreation Area is unique in that it is one of only a few areas where windswept open dunes, some towering over four hundred feet high, are bordered by the beach to the west and coastal forest to the east. Volunteer and intern positions include overlook hosts, headquarters hosts, interpreters for guided field trips and nature walks, campground hosts, recreation (including off-road vehicle) assistants, fish and wildlife assistants, writers, illustrators, photographers, graphic designers, and office help. If you have a special skill or talent you think is valuable in managing the Oregon Dunes, let them know. Work one month or six, a few hours a week or full-time! Help is generally needed most from May through September. A small stipend and uniforms are provided, and housing is available to volunteers who work at least twenty-four hours per week. Housing, complete with kitchen, bathroom, and laundry facilities, is located two miles north of where you will be working. Campground hosts receive a campsite with hookups.

FOR MORE INFORMATION: Bill Blackwell, Volunteer Coordinator, Oregon Dunes National Recreation Area, Siuslaw National Forest, 855 Highway 101, Reedsport, OR 97467 • (541) 271-3611 (541) 271-6019 (fax) • bblackwell@fs.fed.us

SAGAMORE INSTITUTE

Historic Site • New York • 4–5 Months
www.sagamore.org

Built in 1897 as the wilderness retreat of the Vanderbilt family, Sagamore's twenty-seven rustic buildings include the architectural prototype for many National Park Service designs. Mostly a U.N.–designated biosphere reserve, the park is a historic laboratory for evolving land-use policy. Offered to the public during the summer and fall seasons, a two-hour guided tour engages guests in a twenty-five-minute slide presentation followed by a walking narrative of the grounds and many of the buildings.

WHAT YOU'LL BE DOING: After intensive training, historic preservation interns conduct tours that interpret the institute's socioeconomic and architectural history in light of American cultural and land-use history, as well as the history and uncertain future of Adirondack Park. Outdoor/environmental education interns deliver programs involving canoeing, hiking, swimming, and nature interpretation to residential guests. Other opportunities include actors and a technician as well as a museum/café intern. A weekly seminar with readings and guest speakers is also provided.

COMMITMENT: Summer interns begin residence between mid-May and mid-June and continue through Labor Day; fall residencies run September through October. Sagamore welcomes those who can work the entire season.

PERKS AND REWARDS: A weekly stipend of $150, along with room and board, is provided. Interns also have the opportunity to participate in residential programs, which might include workshops on Adirondack ecology, history, arts and crafts, or education and professional development, and may also engage in outdoor programs ranging from backpacking to llama trekking.

THE ESSENTIALS: Interns often come fresh out of college or on summer break, in a period of career change, or on sabbatical; some are retired professionals who have taken an Elderhostel course at Sagamore.

YOUR FIRST MOVE: Their website outlines detailed application materials that are required. During June through August, address correspondence to P.O. Box 146, Raquette Lake, NY 13436; (315) 354-5311, sagamore@telenet.net.

FOR MORE INFORMATION: Michael Wilson, Internship Director, Sagamore Institute, 174 Kiwassa Rd., Saranac Lake, NY 12983 • (518) 891-1718 (518) 891-2561 (fax) • mwilson@northnet.org

SHENANDOAH NATIONAL PARK

Guest Services • Virginia • Seasonal
www.visitshenandoah.com

$ 🏠 ⊕

Known as Virginia's mountain playground, Shenandoah National Park is situated close to Washington, D.C., and is encompassed by the Blue Ridge Mountains and the historic Appalachian Trail. From April through November, seasonal staff converge on the park and work in the lodges, dining facilities, camp stores, craft and gift shops, and stables. Competitive wages are offered (based on your experience), along with health insurance benefits. Dormitory-style housing in shared rooms with common or private bath are provided for a fee of $20 per week (three meals can run up to $10 per day). All applicants must be at least eighteen years of age; email for further details.

Thunder is good, thunder is impressive; but it is lightning that does the work. 243
—MARK TWAIN

FOR MORE INFORMATION: Debbie Zinn, Human Resources Department, Shenandoah National Park, ARAMARK, P.O. Box 727, Luray, VA 22835 (540) 743-5108 • (540) 743-7883 (fax) • zinn-debbie@aramark.com

SIGNAL MOUNTAIN LODGE

Guest Services • Wyoming • Seasonal
www.signalmountainlodge.com

$ ⛺ 🌐

Signal Mountain Lodge is a privately owned company that operates visitor services in spectacular Grand Teton National Park, with over two hundred miles of hiking trails and some of the best rock climbing in North America. Located directly on Jackson Lake, just thirty miles from the town of Jackson Hole and twenty-five miles from the south entrance of Yellowstone National Park, their operation includes seventy-nine guest units, two restaurants, two gift shops, a bar, a grocery/gas station, and a marina, along with Leek's Pizzeria and Marina, just ten miles north of the lodge. From early May through mid-October, over 150 seasonal workers come to Signal Mountain and work in a variety of hospitality-related positions. Hourly wages vary, and all employees live and eat on the property (which runs $250 per month). Benefits include free Internet access, a variety of sporting events, and outdoor recreation at its best! Applicants with retail, food-service, or hotel experience, and a genuine, enthusiastic desire to work with the public are most likely to get hired. Those with the longest dates of availability will be given first consideration. Hiring begins in January.

FOR MORE INFORMATION: Megan Dorr, Personnel Manager, Signal Mountain Lodge, Grand Teton National Park, P.O. Box 50, Moran, WY 83013 • (800) 672-6012 • (307) 543-2831 • (307) 543-2569 (fax) personnel@signalmtnlodge.com

STUDENT CONSERVATION ASSOCIATION

Conservation • USA • 3–12 Months
www.thesca.org

$ ⛺ 🌐

With a mission to create the next generation of conservation leaders through active stewardship of the environment, the Student Conservation Association (SCA) is the nation's largest and oldest provider of conservation service opportunities. SCA does this through a tuition-free summer volunteer program for high school students as well as through a three- to twelve-month expense-paid internship program for those eighteen and older. Nearly three thousand SCA members complete more than 1.25 million hours of conservation service annually.

WHAT YOU'LL BE DOING:

Can you see yourself kayaking through a remote island wilderness in Alaska? Assisting with desert tortoise research in Nevada? Leading educational canoe trips in the Boundary Waters of northern Minnesota? Re-creating the role of an 1800s resident at historic Fort Laramie? As a SCA conservation intern, these images are reality. Interns will also have the chance to live and work in America's spectacular

STUDENT CONSERVATION ASSOCIATION

As a national park visitor center intern through the Student Conservation Association, Brandy Brooks maps out the perfect trail for hiking enthusiasts.

national parks, wildlands, and historic sites, ranging from California's Joshua Tree to the Great Smoky Mountains. For those aged twenty-one and over, SCA also offers paid leadership positions, working with fifteen- to nineteen-year-old volunteers through their summer conservation crew program.

COMMITMENT: Depending on your availability and background, opportunities range from twelve weeks to twelve months.

PERKS AND REWARDS: Benefits include a basic living allowance (generally $50 to $160 per week), free housing and related expenses, travel to and from position site, free or low-cost health insurance, student loan deferment, possible academic credit, and valuable training packages and professional certification. Most positions also carry an AmeriCorps education award of $1,000 to $4,725 for future tuition or student loan repayment. Training in conservation work skills, environmental education, curriculum development, Wilderness First Aid, Wilderness First Responder, GIS/GPS technology, leadership, and conflict resolution may also be provided dependent upon position.

THE ESSENTIALS: A majority of participants are college students or recent graduates; however, teachers, career changers, and retirees join SCA each year. (There's a minimum applicant age of eighteen.) In general, applicants

Be able to be alone. Lose not the advantage of solitude.
—SIR THOMAS BROWNE

are seeking real-life experiences in the conservation field to further academic, career, or personal goals. International candidates can apply for positions lasting three to four months only.

YOUR FIRST MOVE: SCA publishes *Get Real,* a catalog of opportunities (including application materials) printed on a quarterly basis. In addition, a searchable database of available positions (updated on a weekly basis) and an online application can be found through the SCA website. The extensive application (which includes a $25 fee) is forwarded to various hiring agencies based on your choices. SCA accepts applications throughout the year; however, to enhance your chances of being selected for one of your top four choices, you should apply four months prior to your requested start date.

FOR MORE INFORMATION: Recruitment Office, Student Conservation Association, 689 River Rd., P.O. Box 550, Charlestown, NH 03603-0550 • (603) 543-1700 (603) 543-1828 (fax) • realinternships@thesca.org

U.S. ARMY CORPS OF ENGINEERS VOLUNTEER CLEARINGHOUSE

Conservation • USA • 1 Day–6 Months+
www.lrn.usace.army.mil/volunteer

♥ ⛺

The U.S. Army Corps of Engineers, the steward of almost twelve million acres of land and water, offers many volunteer opportunities in recreation and natural resources management—from one day to six months (and more). Positions include trail building and maintenance, campground hosting, wildlife habitat construction, educational interpretation, visitor center staffing, photography, and dozens of other unique and challenging opportunities. Along with working in beautiful parts of our country, helping people and the environment, meeting new people, and gaining valuable skills, benefits include a free campsite and full hookups. To learn about these opportunities, call their nationwide, toll-free hotline number. Before you call, you should be ready to provide information about your interests, talents, and the locations where you may want to volunteer. The clearinghouse, in turn, will provide you with contact information for the area you have requested, as well as written information about volunteer opportunities there. An application and details about opportunities are also available online.

FOR MORE INFORMATION: Volunteer Coordinator, U.S. Army Corps of Engineers, Volunteer Clearinghouse, P.O. Box 1070, Nashville, TN 37202-1070 (800) 865-8337 • (615) 736-2234 • (615) 736-7643 (fax) volunteer.clearinghouse@lrn02.usace.army.mil

WORKING FOR THE
U.S. FOREST SERVICE

• •

If you've heard of Smokey Bear or Woodsy Owl, you're familiar with the Forest Service. With thirty thousand permanent employees and a temporary workforce that typically exceeds fifteen thousand workers in the summer, the Forest Service is one of the government's major conservation organizations. The agency manages 192 million acres of federal lands, assists state and private landowners, conducts research, and works with international organizations and other countries to build a better world. Employees are stationed at more than nine hundred separate work locations—most of which are in national forests; however, many work on college campuses, at research laboratories, or in office buildings in cities or towns.

Although the largest number of jobs are in forestry, there's something for everybody. Here's a snapshot of some of the most sought-after seasonal and volunteer positions:

- Archaeologists help inventory national forest lands for prehistoric and historic sites (Native American burial grounds and hunting sites, old mining camps, or homesteads). Fieldwork varies but may involve inventory surveys, photography, mapping, and test excavation.

- Backcountry rangers are jacks-of-all-trades. In addition to educating the public to practice sound land ethics, fire prevention, and camping ethics, they also maintain fire lookouts, inventory campsites, record wildlife observations, and assist in clearing and maintaining trails.

- Campground hosts serve as picnic ground or campground resource people—greeting visitors, providing information, and maintaining the area.

- Wilderness rangers meet wilderness visitors and provide information on proper wilderness use and ethics. These rangers are usually in the field for one week to ten day periods.

- Other seasonal and volunteer opportunities include positions in administration, cartography, education, firefighting, guard stations, historical research, human resources, hydrology, interpretation, range management, recreation, research, visitor centers, and wildlife and fish management. As many Forest Service employees reach retirement age, employment opportunities will increase over the next couple years, especially in the fields of conservation, wildlife, and communications.

The game of life is a game of boomerangs.
Our thoughts, deeds, and words return to us sooner or later with astounding accuracy.
—FLORENCE SCOVEL SHINN

TIPS ON GETTING IN
WITH THE FOREST SERVICE

Contact local Forest Service offices to learn what types of seasonal positions are available, how best to find out about them, and what skills and abilities you need to develop. Although the regional offices are the forest hubs, there are more than nine hundred separate work locations across the U.S. Most regional offices publish volunteer opportunity directories that you can obtain for free.

Summer job opportunities begin approximately mid-May and end September 30, with applications typically accepted from December through April 15. Applicants must be at least sixteen years of age and qualify for a position based on work experience and/or education. Beyond the summer, positions can last a couple months or as long as four years.

JOB CONNECTIONS
WITH THE FOREST SERVICE

All temporary employment opportunities (including fire, nonfire support, resource technicians, internships, and student programs) can be found online at www.fs.fed.us/fsjobs. Further information can be obtained by calling (877) 813-3476 or sending an email to fsjobs@fs.fed.us.

VERMONT YOUTH CONSERVATION CORPS

Conservation · Vermont · Seasonal
www.vycc.org

$ 🏠

The Vermont Youth Conservation Corps (VYCC) is a nonprofit service, conservation, and education organization that strives to instill the values of personal responsibility, hard work, education, and respect for the environment in young adults. Corps members, who are between the ages of sixteen and twenty-four, work, live, and study together in small groups, completing priority conservation and park management projects throughout Vermont under the guidance of highly trained leaders. Projects focus on a daily integrated cycle of reading, discussion, writing, and team-building activities, with assignments that may include trail construction and maintenance, watershed restoration, bridge construction, park management, and facility improvement.

A diverse team is a key component to the VYCC experience. Corps members may be high school dropouts, economically disadvantaged, college-bound, or learning-disabled youth. This extraordinary diversity helps break down traditional social and economic barriers and provides a rich and challenging environment where participants can learn from one another.

Crew leaders with the Vermont Youth Conservation Corps learn the ropes of trail maintenance before leading their teams.

WHAT YOU'LL BE DOING: With a variety of field staff opportunities available, each staff member will co-lead groups of four to ten corps members in completion of their work project. In addition, each staff member will train, motivate, supervise, and support corps members, facilitate VYCC's daily education program, and create a sense of community within a diverse crew of young people. Park managers (and assistants) will manage all aspects of a Vermont State Park and campground and perform park ranger duties, such as leading nature and recreation programs, enforcing park regulations, and managing facilities and park finances. Crew leaders will complete high-priority conservation projects throughout Vermont, including stream bank stabilization, trail maintenance, bridge construction, and carpentry projects.

COMMITMENT: Park manager positions run from late April to mid-September or mid-October; assistant positions run from early May to late August or early September; and crew leader positions run from mid-May to late August.

PERKS AND REWARDS: Park manager and crew leader wages range from $360 to $480 per week; assistant wages range from $330 to $350 per week. Most positions include room and board, and all staff receive nationally recognized training and are eligible for an AmeriCorps education award.

THE ESSENTIALS: Candidates must have a strong desire to change young people's lives, a high level of maturity, a strong work ethic and self-confidence, and the ability to actively motivate young adults. Outdoor leadership experience, knowledge of trail work or natural resource management, and experience with group facilitation techniques are very helpful. The minimum age for park managers and crew leaders is twenty-two and for assistants is twenty.

YOUR FIRST MOVE: Applications are available online, or request a complete job description and application by phone or email.

FOR MORE INFORMATION: Recruitment Coordinator, Vermont Youth Conservation Corps, 92 S. Main St., Waterbury, VT 05676 • (800) 639-8922 (802) 241-3699 • (802) 241-3909 (fax) • info@vycc.org

WILDERNESS VOLUNTEERS

Wilderness Education • USA • 1 Week
www.wildernessvolunteers.org

From the Trinity Alps Wilderness to Hawaii Volcanoes National Park, Wilderness Volunteers organizes over fifty one-week volunteer service adventures with public land agencies across the U.S. Following a "leave no trace" (www.lnt.org) philosophy of outdoor-living skills and ethics, trips (with active, strenuous, and challenging options) are limited to twelve or fewer participants and are led by volunteers in cooperation with land agency representatives. Tools for the work project are provided and each adventure gives ample time to explore and enjoy the surrounding region. Participants must be at least eighteen years of age (the average age is forty-five) and all trips require regular conditioning for at least two months prior to the trip. Program fees for mainland trips run $219; for Hawaii and Alaska, $239. Food is provided for all trips, along with cooking gear, and participants are responsible for any travel costs. Specifics on all trips can be found online, or call for further information.

FOR MORE INFORMATION: Volunteer Coordinator, Wilderness Volunteers, P.O. Box 22292, Flagstaff, AZ 86002-2292 • (928) 556-0038 (928) 779-6339 (fax) • info@wildernessvolunteers.org

WIND CAVE NATIONAL PARK

National Park • South Dakota • 3–4 Months
www.nps.gov/wica/Internships.htm
$ 🏠

Located in the southern Black Hills (also known as Custer Country), Wind Cave National Park features some of the most pristine mixed-grass prairies found in the U.S. and a world-renowned cave with over one hundred miles of passages. Large herds of free-roaming bison, elk, pronghorn, and deer inhabit the grasslands and forest. Three- or four-month seasonal positions are available year-round in interpretation, visitor services, and resource management and as campground hosts. In addition, students with at least two years of college have the opportunity to participate in the park's summer park ranger/interpretation internship program (with an application deadline of early March). Experience in interpretation, public speaking, environmental education, or caves would be helpful, but is not required. Benefits for all opportunities include training, rent-free shared housing, and a $75 weekly stipend. Interns also receive up to $150 for round-trip travel to the park. Call for application materials.

FOR MORE INFORMATION: Phyllis Cremonini, Assistant Chief of Interpretation, Wind Cave National Park, RT 1, Box 190, Hot Springs, SD 57747-9430 (605) 745-1131 • (605) 745-4207 (fax) • phyllis_cremonini@nps.gov

YELLOWSTONE NATIONAL PARK LODGES

Guest Services • Wyoming • Seasonal
www.yellowstonejobs.com
$ 🏠 ⊕

Imagine watching Beehive Geyser shoot its hot water and steam hundreds of feet into the air, fly-fishing for acrobatic rainbow trout on the Firehole River, hiking on the Hayden Pass Trail and spotting a herd of buffalo, or trekking to the top of Mount Washburn (from which you can see the Grand Teton on clear days). Well, these are just some of the things you can do in your new backyard—that is, you can if you join the 3,500 other adventurous workers in Yellowstone National Park this summer. Of course it's not all play; however, time will be well spent working for Xanterra Parks and Resorts (www.xanterra.com), who operates the major visitor services concession facilities in Yellowstone National Park, including lodging, restaurants, shops, boat and horse activities, campgrounds, and transportation services.

WHAT YOU'LL BE DOING: Yellowstone must be approached with a "work hard, play hard" mentality. You'll definitely work hard in the position you take on; however, you'll also have the opportunity to play hard in time off. Seasonal staff come from all over the world and are hired in practically every conceivable resort-related field, from lodging services to employee recreation. A majority of the staff works at one of six major locations around the park— Mammoth Hot Springs, Roosevelt Lodge (the dude ranch of Yellowstone), Canyon Village, the Lake Area, Grant Village, and Old Faithful—each with its own unique charm and features. For many, a summer in Yellowstone is an unforgettable and once-in-a-lifetime experience.

COMMITMENT: Applicants who can work from mid-April or early May to October are preferred; however, shorter terms are available. Yellowstone also offers positions during the winter months (with many filled by summer employees).

PERKS AND REWARDS: The pay for entry-level positions begins at $6.15 per hour and some positions are salaried. Cafeteria-style meals, shared lodging, and laundry facilities are provided at a cost of about $285 per month. Employee residence facilities range from rustic cabins to a typical dorm complex. (Note that you can request to live with a friend or, perhaps, someone that you meet in your orientation seminar.) Summer employees who choose to return for a winter season can become eligible for health insurance, paid vacation and holidays, and other benefits. The biggest perk, however, is the employee recreation program, with activities that include outdoor adventure programs (from white-water rafting to fly-fishing trips), outdoor equipment rental, slide shows and seminars, live bands, sports leagues, video rental, a photography and T-shirt design contest, and a year-end talent show.

THE ESSENTIALS: People who are willing to work hard, who enjoy working with and for others, and who take pride in a job well done make the best employees.

YOUR FIRST MOVE: Applications are available online; however, you can also call to request one. Positions fill very quickly, so it is best to apply by early February. Note that applications are accepted into the summer, especially for those who can arrive in August (when many students go back to college) and work through September or October.

FOR MORE INFORMATION: Human Resources, Yellowstone National Park Lodges, Xanterra Parks & Resorts, P.O. Box 165, Yellowstone National Park, WY 82190 (307) 344-5324 • (307) 344-5441 (fax) • info@yellowstonejobs.com

INSIDER TIP: After spending twenty years working in corporate America, I realized that my most rewarding experiences inside work were guiding, educating, and mentoring others. Those outside of work were my artistic pursuits, travel, health and fitness, and environmental projects. Changes in my personal life have made it possible for me to change direction now and integrate my career with the real passions in my life. My resume outlines specific skills, but cannot possibly convey the positive energy, enthusiasm, and creativity I bring to my work. Coming to Yellowstone was just a step in breaking away from the mind-set that money and possessions are the measure of a person and their success in life. Being here has shown me that some people value other things and live a totally different way. Now I seek people who are doing what they really love, filled with creative force, shaping their own lives, and having a positive influence on the lives of others. —*Sandra Aldrich, a reader working at Old Faithful in Yellowstone National Park*

YOSEMITE NATIONAL PARK

Guest Services • California • Seasonal
www.yosemitepark.com

$ 🏔 🌐

El Capitan, one of the largest exposed monoliths in the world. The awe-inspiring Half Dome. Beautiful hikes to Mirror Lake or Yosemite Falls. Nordic skiing at Badger Pass. This is Yosemite National Park—a place that John Muir spoke about with passion: "a landscape that after all my wanderings still appears as the most beautiful I have ever beheld." As the host for the park, DNC Parks & Resorts provides all the guest services to the park's nearly four million annual visitors—ranging from the impressive National Historic Landmark Ahwahnee Hotel to guided tram and horseback tours, rafting along the Merced River, or the renowned Yosemite Mountaineering School (which offers rock climbing lessons, guided climbs, and backpacking trips in both Yosemite Valley and the High Sierra of Tuolumne Meadows).

WHAT YOU'LL BE DOING: First-season staff members are generally given an "unassigned" hire, which means they're given a current job opening that's available upon their arrival at Yosemite. Entry-level positions include hotel (housekeeping to front desk), guest recreation, food and beverage staff, support service (drivers to tour guides), and retail. Management and professional positions are also offered to those with more experience.

COMMITMENT: Seasonal and year-round schedules are available, with most positions available from the week before Easter through mid-September (over

---

If you put off everything until you are sure of it you'll get nothing done. 253
—NORMAN VINCENT PEALE

eight hundred positions are filled in this time frame). A minimum two-month commitment is needed; however, longer terms are preferred.

PERKS AND REWARDS: Wages begin at $7.38 per hour. Employee housing consists of shared rustic tents or wooden cabins and a limited number of dormitory rooms for $15 to $20 per week. A fifty percent discount is provided at most eating establishments and all housing areas have a community kitchen where employees may prepare their meals. One of the biggest perks during time off is participation in Yosemite's employee recreation program. A variety of activities and facilities are available to staff, including a fitness and wellness center, organized sports and hikes, craft classes, rafting trips, dances, movies, and barbecues. Yosemite also supports and encourages employee involvement in GreenPath, an internationally certified environmental management program.

THE ESSENTIALS: Employees must be at least eighteen years of age to room in employer-provided housing, and foreign applicants must possess the right to work in the U.S. prior to applying.

YOUR FIRST MOVE: Applications are available online, or call or email for more information.

FOR MORE INFORMATION: Human Resources Director, Yosemite National Park, DNC Parks & Resorts, P.O. Box 578, Yosemite, CA 95389 • (209) 372-1236 (209) 372-1050 (fax) • yoshr@dncinc.com

YOUTH CORPS OF SOUTHERN ARIZONA

Conservation • Arizona • 4–5 Months
www.ycosa.org

$ 🏠

Enhancing life, employment, and educational opportunities for youth and young adults, the Youth Corps of Southern Arizona (YCOSA) forms teams of ten corps members (aged sixteen to twenty-three) and two experienced crew leaders who live, work, and learn in rustic wilderness settings. Crew leaders provide the direction and supervision for their team, including leading the crew in conservation work projects, implementing a daily education program, developing the crew's work skills, coordinating camp life, and preparing reports. Positions are available throughout the year and a two-session (about five-month) commitment is preferred. Benefits include a $65 to $100 per day salary, primitive housing, and meals. Positions are also available for YCOSA's four-month leadership training program, which begins in January and August. Benefits include a bimonthly stipend of $200, housing, tent and food in the field, health insurance, and an AmeriCorps educational award ($2,363 or $4,725). Details for all job opportunities can be found online.

FOR MORE INFORMATION: William Drabkin, Director, Youth Corps of Southern Arizona, 2245 N. Flores Dr., Tucson, AZ 85705 • (520) 884-5550 (520) 791-7729 (fax) • william@ycosa.org

RECOMMENDED RESOURCES

To explore a variety of job opportunities and essential resources for working at state or national parks, check out **About.com's Guide to U.S./Canadian Parks** (www.usparks.about.com/cs/jobs), hosted by park expert Darren Smith.

The National Association for Interpretation (www.interpnet.com) publishes the biweekly newsletter *Interpretunities: Jobs in Interpretation,* which provides listings of internships, seasonal jobs, and career opportunities in the natural and cultural interpretation field (about eighty listings per issue). Members of the association ($15 for students, $45 for professionals) receive the newsletter for free by email ($4 per issue for hard copy). The four most recent issues can be downloaded as a PDF file online. To connect more with others in the interpretation field, don't miss the National Interpreters Workshop, their annual conference held each November. For more information contact the National Association for Interpretation, P.O. Box 2246, Fort Collins, CO 80522; (888) 900-8283, membership@interpnet.com.

Passport in Time Clearinghouse (www.passportintime.com), commonly known as PIT, invites you to share in the thrill of discovery through archaeological and historical research on national forests and grasslands throughout the U.S. Forest service archaeologists and historians guide volunteers in activities ranging from excavating sites to restoring historic buildings. Many projects involve backcountry camping in which volunteers supply their own gear and food. Some projects offer meals for a small fee; others might provide hookups for your RV. Project length ranges from a weekend up to a month, and there is no registration fee or cost for participating. The *PIT Traveler,* a free newsletter and directory, announces current projects every March and September (however, see their website for late-breaking project opportunities). For more information contact Passport in Time Clearinghouse, P.O. Box 31315, Tucson, AZ 85751-1315; (800) 281-9176, pit@sricrm.com.

Imagine banding birds at a national wildlife refuge, raising fish at a national fish hatchery, conducting wildlife surveys, leading a tour, or assisting in laboratory research. You can engage in these exciting opportunities by volunteering at national wildlife refuges, fish hatcheries, research stations, and administrative offices—nearly seven hundred **U.S. Fish and Wildlife Service**

There are two ways of spreading light—to be the candle or the mirror that reflects it.   255
—EDITH WHARTON

sites across the nation. The work may be hard, the conditions harsh, and living quarters primitive, but it is well worth the experience—and a commitment made by more than thirty-six thousand volunteers each year, who are helping to meet the challenges of pollution, deforestation, and the continued loss of wetlands and other vital wildlife habitat. The U.S. Fish and Wildlife website provides general employment information, specifics on volunteer positions in certain geographic locations, and a searchable database of current opportunities. Many volunteers receive room and board, and sometimes travel expenses. Summer employment applications generally need to be submitted sometime between January and April. Connect with the U.S. Fish and Wildlife Service online (http://volunteers.fws.gov), by email (volunteers@fws.gov), or by calling (800) 344-9453.

Have you ever wanted to explore Colorado's mountains, parks, trails, and open spaces? With the **Volunteers for Outdoor Colorado VOC Network** of volunteer opportunities, you can spend some quality time getting dirty, working your muscles and mind, meeting people, and giving something back to Colorado. Each April VOC publishes a guide profiling more than four hundred volunteer opportunities around Colorado with agencies including the U.S. Forest Service, the Bureau of Land Management, Colorado's state parks, and various other state programs. From building rock walls to developing new trails, projects focus on backcountry monitoring, environmental education and interpretation, fieldwork, forestry, gardening, recreation, trail construction and maintenance, visitor information, wildlife studies, and Youth Corps opportunities. Projects can range from a few hours per month up to full-time for one year. For some projects, training, housing, and a stipend are provided. Listings of current opportunities can be found by clicking on the VOC Network section of their website (www.voc.org), and the *VOC Guide* can be downloaded as a PDF file (or call for your complimentary copy). For more information contact Volunteers for Outdoor Colorado, 600 S. Marion Parkway, Denver, CO 80209-2597; (800) 925-2220, voc@voc.org.

ASPEN CENTER FOR ENVIRONMENTAL STUDIES

Nature Center • Colorado • Summer
www.aspennature.org

$ 🏕 🎓

Since its founding in 1968 by Aspen resident Elizabeth Paepcke, the nonprofit Aspen Center for Environmental Studies has been educating people to be environmentally responsible. Managing the 25-acre Hallam Lake sanctuary and another 175-acre natural area, the center offers hikes and nature classes to children and adults. It also runs the Environmental Learning Center, which houses the Scott Field Laboratory, Pinewood Natural History Library, Gates Visitor Center, and a bookstore informally known as "the Den."

WHAT YOU'LL BE DOING: Summer naturalist interns get involved in just about everything that has to do with maintaining the center—landscaping, giving talks on the birds of prey program, providing wildlife information, teaching natural history classes to children and adults, and leading nature walks. Interns teach all the summer programs, from leading a troop of adults on a sunset walk by the lake to teaching children about the rich diversity of insects in the area. After spending a summer leading interpretive walks, learning to handle birds of prey for educational programs, and teaching children about the environment, interns are sure to leave with a newfound appreciation of nature.

COMMITMENT: Mandatory staff training begins in early June with the season continuing through Labor Day.

PERKS AND REWARDS: A weekly stipend of $125 and housing are provided. Interns often cook and eat dinners together, forming friendships that the center's communal atmosphere encourages. Interns are also allowed to take at least one class for free from the center's naturalist field school. Following the internship, summer naturalists have the opportunity to apply for winter-naturalist and academic-year educator positions.

THE ESSENTIALS: College juniors, seniors, graduate students, and recent graduates are eligible, although the bulk of interns have received college degrees by the start of the internship. The center strongly prefers students who have studied the natural sciences or environmental studies and have experience working at other nature centers. First aid certification is required.

YOUR FIRST MOVE: Submit a completed application (which can be found on their website), a resume, and three letters of recommendation (the letters are suggested, but not required) by March 1. Top candidates are interviewed over the phone.

Use the talents you possess, for the woods would be very silent if no birds sang except for the best. **261**
—HENRY VAN DYKE

FOR MORE INFORMATION: Interpretation Director, Summer Naturalist Internship, Aspen Center for Environmental Studies, 100 Puppy Smith St., Aspen, CO 81612 • (970) 925-5756 • (970) 925-4819 (fax) aces@aspennature.org

AUDUBON NATURALIST SOCIETY

Natural History • Maryland • Summer
www.audubonnaturalist.org

$ 🏕 🌐

Spend the summer just outside Washington, D.C. Founded in 1897, the Audubon Naturalist Society (not to be confused with the National Audubon Society) pioneered the linking of natural history studies with conservation activities. Environmental education interns co-teach and assist teachers with all aspects of the summer day camp nature programs, which are geared for children ages four to fourteen and include nature activities, games, hikes, arts and crafts, and stories and music. The internship kicks off with a one-week training program beginning in mid-June (covering topics relative to child care and natural history), followed by nine weeks of day camp programs. Requirements include enthusiasm, energy, kindness, and experience with children. A $2,000 stipend and housing (if needed) is provided. Teachers/environmental educators are also needed for the summer, with responsibilities that include the design and implementation of summer camp curricula for nature-based day camps. Programs run one to two weeks, with a compensation package of $550 per week. Send or fax your cover letter, resume, and a list of references to begin the application process.

FOR MORE INFORMATION: Summer Camp Director, Audubon Naturalist Society, 8940 Jones Mill Rd., Chevy Chase, MD 20815 • (301) 652-9188, ext. 15 (301) 951-7179 (fax) • contact@audubonnaturalist.org

AUDUBON SHARON

Nature Center • Connecticut • 2–4 Months
www.audubon.org/local/sanctuary/sharon

$ 🏕 🌐

Spread over one thousand acres with protected ponds, streams, forests, fields, and wildlife, Audubon Sharon offers hands-on education experiences for people of all ages, wildlife rehabilitation, live animal exhibits, a children's adventure center, a nature store, and a natural history library.

WHAT YOU'LL BE DOING: During the spring and fall, environmental education interns get involved in all aspects of the center's operation, with a primary focus of developing educational materials and teaching a wide variety of topics—discovery walks, pond exploration, birds of prey, insect investigation, and maple sugaring—to audiences of all ages. Summer naturalist interns primarily oversee the weeklong Summer Explorers (ages two to eleven) and Eye on Nature (ages twelve to fourteen) programs for children. In addition, a bird banding internship (with two weeks of intensive training) and a research apprenticeship are offered from May through August.

PERKS AND REWARDS: A weekly salary of $245 is provided. In addition, each intern receives a furnished suite in the main building, with a private bedroom and shared kitchen, bath, and living area.

THE ESSENTIALS: Some teaching experience or curriculum development is desired; however, the most important assets include a strong natural history background, enthusiasm, commitment, a desire to learn, flexibility, and the ability to work well with others (especially children). Completion of at least two years of college course work in environmental studies is required.

YOUR FIRST MOVE: Send a cover letter, resume, and three references with contact information to Jeff Weiler. For bird banding internships, contact Scott Heth (sheth@audubon.org); for research apprenticeships, Mike Dudek (mdudek@audubon.org).

FOR MORE INFORMATION: Jeff Weiler, Environmental Education Specialist, Audubon Sharon, 325 Cornwall Bridge Rd., Sharon, CT 06069 • (860) 364-0520 (860) 364-5792 (fax) • jweiler@audubon.org

AULLWOOD AUDUBON CENTER AND FARM

Environmental Education/Farming • Ohio • 10–20 Weeks
http://aullwood.center.audubon.org

$ 🏠 ⊕

Aullwood Audubon Center and Farm is one of the five original environmental education centers in the U.S. owned and operated by the National Audubon Society. With over seventy-five thousand visitors per year, they reach far with their message about "promoting awareness of the relationships within natural and agricultural systems, with humans as an integral element." Environmental education and organic agriculture interns are involved in an extensive orientation and then gradually assume the same kinds of responsibilities as full-time staff, with a concentration on education and farming activities. All facets of an environmental education center and organic farm

It is not the strongest of the species that survive, nor the most intelligent, but the one most responsive to change.
—CHARLES DARWIN

are explored, including work with the public in program presentation, animal care at the nature center and farm, store operations, and maintenance. Positions are offered in January for twenty weeks; June for ten weeks; and September for fifteen weeks. A weekly stipend of $120 and furnished housing (including utilities) on the Aullwood property are provided, along with field study and visits to similar organizations. All interns must be high school graduates; however, having finished at least the sophomore year of college works out to the applicant's advantage. Call or email for further information and application materials.

FOR MORE INFORMATION: Alison Verey, Intern Coordinator, Aullwood Audubon Center and Farm, 1000 Aullwood Rd., Dayton, OH 45414-1129 (937) 890-7360 • (937) 890-2382 (fax) • averey@audubon.org

BRUKNER NATURE CENTER

Nature Center/Wildlife • Ohio • 3–9 Months
www.bruknernaturecenter.com

$ ♠♠ ⊕

Surrounded by 165 acres of rolling hills accessed through six miles of hiking trails, Brukner Nature Center endeavors to provide meaningful experiences that emphasize natural history and the environment. Over sixty permanently injured native Ohio animals and birds are housed on the property and used for educational programming.

WHAT YOU'LL BE DOING: Interns assist in planning, preparing, and conducting natural history, historical, and native wildlife programs for school-age children and the public. Extensive work is also done with the wildlife, including daily husbandry and care of the animals and birds as well as work with injured and orphaned native wildlife in the wildlife rehabilitation unit. This is a great program for those who want an in-depth experience at a nature center.

COMMITMENT: A commitment of three months is required; however, longer terms, from six to nine months, are preferred.

PERKS AND REWARDS: Housing and a $75-per-week food stipend are provided.

THE ESSENTIALS: A background in natural history or animal husbandry and previous experience working with wildlife, planning educational programs, and guiding interpretive hikes are preferred.

YOUR FIRST MOVE: Send a cover letter and resume. Opportunities are offered year-round; however, there is less competition for openings in the school year.

FOR MORE INFORMATION: Debbie Brill, Administrative Director, Brukner Nature Center, 5995 Horseshoe Bend Rd., Troy, OH 45373 (937) 698-6493 • (937) 698-4619 (fax) • info@brukernaturecenter.com

CAMP HIGH TRAILS
OUTDOOR SCIENCE SCHOOL

Outdoor Education • California • 4–9 Months
www.camphightrails.com

$ 🏕 🌐

If you have a college degree, a healthy amount of experience both with kids and the outdoors (or a strong and eager desire to learn), and the willingness to work and live in a small, close-knit staff community, Camp High Trails Outdoor Science School is a perfect place to begin new adventures. Located in the mountains of Southern California, this residential center gets sixth graders connected to nature. As an outdoor education instructor, you'll have the opportunity to create fun, educational, and meaningful experiences with classes and activities such as climbing, low ropes, archery, forest ecology, water study, outdoor living skills, astronomy, and nighttime wildlife. The benefits are also great—room, board, health insurance, and a nice paycheck! Four- to nine-month seasonal contracts begin in either September or January. Check out their website first to explore all the opportunities, then send your resume, cover letter, and three references.

FOR MORE INFORMATION: Chris Hoyt, Program Director, Camp High Trails Outdoor Science School, 4650 Jenks Lake Rd. East, Angelus Oaks, CA 92305 (909) 936-3240 • (909) 752-5414 (fax) • work@camphightrails.com

CAMP MCDOWELL
ENVIRONMENTAL CENTER

Outdoor Education • Alabama • 4 Months
www.campmcdowell.com/cmec

$ 🏕

Share Camp McDowell's nine hundred acres of secluded forests, streams, waterfalls, and canyons in northwest Alabama with groups of up to twelve students (mostly in grades four through eight). Environmental education instructors teach hands-on classes with subjects and activities including forest ecology, earth and water science, insects and wildlife, canoeing, map and compass, low and high ropes, Native American history, arts and crafts,

Adopt the pace of nature, her secret is patience.   **265**
—RALPH WALDO EMERSON

astronomy, fishing, and field games. Programs run from late February through May and late August through late November. Staff receive a weekly stipend of $200, meals, and private rooms in a newly renovated house, complete with kitchen, living room, laundry, and screened porch with rocking chairs. To apply, send a cover letter, resume, and references.

FOR MORE INFORMATION: Maggie Wade Johnston, Director, Camp McDowell Environmental Center, 105 DeLong Rd., Nauvoo, AL 35578 • (205) 387-1806 (205) 221-3454 (fax) • mwade@campmcdowell.com

🐾 **INSIDER TIP: We're seeking applicants who have maturity, enthusiasm, initiative, a sense of humor, flexibility, and team spirit. In addition, applicants must have a demonstrated respect and affinity for children and a desire to help them learn and grow, as well as a desire to work outside and be a member of a friendly and supportive team.**

CENTRAL WISCONSIN ENVIRONMENTAL STATION

Environmental Education • Wisconsin • 9–12 Months/Summer
www.uwsp.edu/cnr/cwes

$ 🏕

As a field station of the University of Wisconsin Stevens Point's College of Natural Resources, the Central Wisconsin Environmental Station (CWES) is a three-hundred-acre teaching and environmental learning center for youth and adults. Through hands-on environmental education activities, the station provides a foundation for the study of ecological principles and concepts as they relate to people and their environment.

CENTRAL WISCONSIN ENVIRONMENTAL STATION

An environmental education intern with the Central Wisconsin Environmental Station shows Natural Resource Careers Camp participants how to locate invertebrates through the muck.

WHAT YOU'LL BE DOING: Throughout the year (for nine to twelve months), environmental education/ interpretation interns serve as regular staff members and provide instruction in environmental studies for groups of students in kindergarten through twelfth grade, as well as outside groups who contract CWES for programming. During the summer months, staff counselors are responsible for carrying out overall camp operation, with an emphasis on environmental and outdoor education. Programs include a variety of residential camps for youth aged six to seventeen and a Natural Resource Careers Camp for high school students.

PERKS AND REWARDS: Interns received a stipend, on-site housing, and partial board. The wage for summer staff ranges from $170 to $195 per week (dependent on experience and certifications), which includes room and board.

THE ESSENTIALS: Intern applicants must have reached at least their junior year in college and have completed course work in methods of environmental education and interpretation, education, environmental studies, or a related major. Previous practical experience in environmental education, outdoor education, or natural history interpretation is desirable. Summer staff applicants should have training or experience in one or more of the following areas: recreation, environmental education, water or field sports, backpacking, canoeing, or arts and crafts. Preference will be given to applicants with a college background.

YOUR FIRST MOVE: Call or email for additional information.

FOR MORE INFORMATION: Bobbi Kubish, Director, Central Wisconsin Environmental Station, 10186 County MM, Amherst Junction, WI 54407 (715) 824-2428 • (715) 824-3201 (fax) • cwes@uwsp.edu

THE CONSERVANCY OF SOUTHWEST FLORIDA

Conservation · Florida · 3–9 Months
www.conservancy.org

$ 🏠 🛖

Since 1964, the Conservancy has served as the region's environmental leader, spearheading the conservation of more than 300,000 acres of environmentally sensitive land. In addition to an environmental policy, advocacy, and scientific research division, this progressive organization includes a nature center and wildlife rehabilitation center.

YOUR SURROUNDINGS: The climate of this region is subtropical, with a strong marine influence from the Gulf of Mexico. The average annual temperature is approximately seventy-five degrees and rainfall averages about fifty-four inches annually, with most precipitation occurring during the summer.

The old Lakota was wise. He knew that man's heart, away from nature, becomes hard;
he knew that lack of respect for growing, living things soon led to lack of respect for humans too.
—LUTHER STANDING BEAR

WHAT YOU'LL BE DOING: Whether leading interpretive canoe, boat, and beach programs for children and adults, implementing weeklong environmental specialty day camps for students, teaching ecology of south Florida to school children, working with the environmental policy staff to monitor development and environmental governance boards, or assisting the science staff in research projects such as monitoring sea turtles, this is an ideal place for interns to gain knowledge and experience in the field. Approximately fifty interns are hired throughout the organization each year.

COMMITMENT: Positions are available year-round, although a three-, six-, or nine-month commitment is necessary.

PERKS AND REWARDS: Besides receiving a very hands-on educational experience, a scholarship equivalent to $100 per week of service is awarded (with selective payment options). Perks include optional free housing, uniform shirts, accident insurance, and Conservancy membership.

THE ESSENTIALS: Applicants must be at least a junior in college (or be a recent graduate) with a background in biology, ecology, conservation, wildlife, research, teaching, elementary education, environmental education/science, or marine science. Those who are quick and eager learners and enjoy being outdoors are preferred.

YOUR FIRST MOVE: Details on each internship and applications are available online, or email or call for more information.

FOR MORE INFORMATION: Sharon Truluck, Human Resources Director, The Conservancy of Southwest Florida, 1450 Merrihue Dr., Naples, FL 34102 (239) 403-4214 • (239) 263-0067 (fax) • internships@conservancy.org

DELAWARE NATURE SOCIETY

Nature Center • Delaware • Seasonal
www.delawarenaturesociety.org

$ 🎓

Created by a handful of concerned people in 1964, the Delaware Nature Society fosters understanding, appreciation, and enjoyment of our natural world. Interns at the Ashland Nature Center teach and coteach children's classes, and have the opportunity to work with people of all ages and interests, design curriculum, work with farm and wild animals, and develop their own special skills and interests. A stipend of $2,000 helps to alleviate the costs of housing, food, and transportation. Applicants must have completed their junior or senior year in college and be pursuing a career in environmental education or natural sciences. Send a cover letter, resume, and two letters of recommendation by March 15 for summer positions. For other times during the year, applications are accepted on a rolling basis.

FOR MORE INFORMATION: Karen Travers, Member Programs Coordinator, Delaware Nature Society, Ashland Nature Center, P.O. Box 700, Hockessin, DE 19707 • (302) 239-2334, ext. 115 • (302) 239-2473 (fax) karen@dnsashland.org

EAGLE BLUFF ENVIRONMENTAL LEARNING CENTER

Environmental Education • Minnesota • 9 Months
www.eagle-bluff.org

$ ⚑ ⊕

Eagle Bluff Environmental Learning Center is a nonprofit environmental school dedicated to developing and fostering educational opportunities that will create universal awareness of, enhance respect for, and promote personal responsibility for the natural world. Twelve participants in the naturalist fellowship program spend nine months (beginning in late August) developing teaching, public relations, and many other skills related to residential environmental education. Fellows kick off the program with a two-week training period, then coordinate, teach, and lead residential and day-use naturalist programs for visiting groups. Fellows live in private rooms with a communal living area, dining room, and kitchen (the center's website has some great photos). In addition to room and board, a monthly stipend of $600 is provided. Applicants must have a bachelor's degree, experience working with children, and CPR and first aid certification. Applications are accepted year-round with hiring beginning on March 1.

FOR MORE INFORMATION: Sara Krebsbach Sturgis, Naturalist Fellowship Coordinator, Eagle Bluff Environmental Learning Center, 1991 Brightsdale Rd., Route 2, Box 156A, Lanesboro, MN 55949 (507) 467-2437 • (507) 467-3583 (fax) • fellowship@eagle-bluff.org

☞ **INSIDER TIP: Imagine learning every day and helping others discover all that they can; this in itself is part of the magic everyone should experience at one time in their life. —*Ilena Berg, Naturalist***

Plan for gradual improvements, not spectacular leaps.
A slow and steady stream of water, will, in time, erode the hardest rock.
—DAVID CAMPBELL

FERNWOOD BOTANICAL GARDEN AND NATURE CENTER

Nature Center/Gardens • Michigan • 8 Months
www.fernwoodbotanical.org

$ 🌲

Fernwood is a combined one-hundred-acre nature center, botanic garden, and arts and crafts center that provides a sense of environmental awareness, cultural appreciation, and education for the community. Seasonal naturalists (from late March through mid-November) develop and conduct natural history programs for school groups and weekend visitors, maintain and design educational displays, supervise care of animals, supervise and assist in the daily operations of the nature center, and provide grounds maintenance. A $6-per-hour wage is provided, along with housing, workshops, classroom training, and discounts in gift shops and the cafeteria. Applicants should have an interest and training in natural history, ecology, or biology. Previous experience (paid or volunteer) in environmental education or work with children improves your chances tremendously. Also, a good knowledge of plant and animal identification is very helpful. Send a cover letter, resume, and references to begin the application process.

FOR MORE INFORMATION: Wendy Jones, Head Naturalist, Fernwood Botanical Garden and Nature Center, 13988 Range Line Rd., Niles, MI 49120-9042 (269) 695-6491 • (269) 695-6688 (fax) • nature@remc11.k12.mi.us

FIVE RIVERS METROPARKS

Natural History/Farm Education • Ohio • 3 or 12 Months
www.metroparks.org

$ 🌲

Internships and apprenticeships at Five Rivers MetroParks provide practical on-the-job experience in outdoor and farm education, natural history, and park management. Positions are available in the following areas: Carriage Hill (historical farm restoration), Cox Arboretum (horticultural education); North MetroParks (natural history); Wesleyan MetroPark (urban youth programming); and Wegerzyn Horticultural Center (horticulture education). Although some positions are available for the summer, most are twelve-month positions that begin when the previous one is vacated, with an average thirty-two-hour workweek. An hourly wage of $7.61 is provided, along with limited housing at several work sites for those relocating to Dayton. With summer positions being so highly sought after, it's recommended that you apply for a twelve-month apprenticeship. Detailed information for each park and job opportunities can be found online. Call or email for application materials. Onsite interviews are required.

FOR MORE INFORMATION: Lyn Modic, Chief of Education and Programming, Five Rivers MetroParks, 1375 E. Siebenthaler Ave., Dayton, OH 45414 (937) 278-8231 • (937) 278-8849 (fax) • email@metroparks.org

FOOTHILL HORIZONS OUTDOOR SCHOOL

Outdoor Education • California • Academic Year
www.foothillhorizons.com

$ 🏕

During the school year, sixth-grade students spend an entire week at Foothill Horizons Outdoor School. During this time, the students participate in a variety of activities to increase their knowledge and awareness of nature, and take part in nature classes, campfires, dancing, free play, night hikes, and field trips. A garden and a cob and straw-bale greenhouse give students the opportunity to see where food comes from, to study insects in the butterfly garden, and to learn how their lunch scraps are turned into soil in the compost and worm bins.

WHAT YOU'LL BE DOING: Beginning in August, interns spend the first three weeks of their ten-month internship training, observing naturalists, and team teaching. From the fourth week on, interns lead groups of students on hikes, teaching them about ecology, conservation, Native American history and culture, and sensory awareness. After several weeks of teaching, interns rotate through other support positions. The head naturalist will observe each intern twice each semester to help refine the intern's teaching technique. Interns are encouraged to use any and all resources available to improve their teaching, including Project Learning Tree and Project Wild workshops, regularly scheduled in-services, conferences, curriculum guides in the library, and, of course, the knowledge of the naturalists.

COMMITMENT: Foothill honors a forty-hour workweek; however, the nature of an internship requires study and preparation beyond scheduled work hours. A commitment for the full school year (ten months) is essential.

PERKS AND REWARDS: A daily stipend of $54 is provided, along with room, board, and a health fund. Lucrative weekend and overtime work as a site host and counselor trainer is also available on an optional basis. Beyond the extensive training interns receive, the biggest perks are paid site visits to other outdoor schools, paid admission to professional conferences and fairs, and career support and guidance during and after the internship.

The frog does not drink up the pond in which he lives.
—INDIAN PROVERB

THE ESSENTIALS: Applicants must be college graduates who have concentrated in the areas of natural and environmental sciences, resource management, parks and recreation, child development, or education. Beyond that, Foothill is looking for people who are passionate about making a positive impact on kids' lives.

YOUR FIRST MOVE: The application process requires either an on-site visit and mini teaching demo or a phone interview and a videotaped lesson presented by the applicant to a group. Positions are filled between the months of January and May.

FOR MORE INFORMATION: Dan Webster, Head Naturalist, Foothill Horizons Outdoor School, Stanislaus County Office of Education, 21925 Lyons Bald Mountain Rd., Sonora, CA 95370 (209) 532-6673 • (209) 533-1390 (fax) • foothill@sonnet.com

INSIDER TIP: As a young teacher who wasn't sure of the exact path I wanted to take, working at Foothill Horizons has given me the opportunity to teach outdoor education and helped me with the decision of where I belong in the world. I learned about science, nature, Miwuk Indians, and classroom management skills from experienced naturalists. I have never worked in an environment where I have received so much support and enthusiasm from coworkers who love their jobs. I can already feel that my experience has helped me to stay on a path with heart, guiding me to whatever comes next—whether it be teaching or doing something completely different. I consider it a great gift to have spent a year of my life at Foothill Horizons. I am already a better person because of the time I have spent here. —*Jacob Sackin, former intern*

4-H ENVIRONMENTAL EDUCATION PROGRAM

Environmental Education • Georgia • 3–4 Months
www.georgia4h.org

$ 🏠 🎓 🌐

The 4-H Environmental Education Program, the largest residential environmental education program in the nation, is part of Georgia's 4-H and Youth Program (first implemented at Rock Eagle 4-H Center in 1979). More than 400,000 students from five hundred different schools have participated in the program.

WHAT YOU'LL BE DOING: Do you enjoy working outside and have an interest in teaching children? The 4-H Environmental Education Program hires forty to forty-five enthusiastic, creative, and motivated seasonal instructors and interns to join their staff in teaching science and outdoor education to grades three through eight. If selected, you will work at one of four 4-H state facilities: Rock Eagle (central Georgia piedmont), Jekyll Island (coastal barrier island), Wahsega (north Georgia mountains), or Tybee Island (coastal barrier island).

COMMITMENT: The spring season runs from mid-February to late May; the fall season runs from early September to late November.

PERKS AND REWARDS: Seasonal staff will receive a stipend of up to $240 per week, housing, meals, a limited health insurance policy, and extensive training in environmental education.

THE ESSENTIALS: Applicants should have a genuine interest in children, a dynamic personality, well-developed communication skills, creativity, and leadership abilities. A bachelor's degree in education, natural science, environmental education, or outdoor recreation is preferred.

YOUR FIRST MOVE: To begin the application process, submit a resume with references and a cover letter. Details on specific positions for each facility can be found on their website or by calling the contacts listed below.

FOR MORE INFORMATION: State 4-H Specialist,
4–H Environmental Education Program,
Rock Eagle 4-H Center, 350 Rock Eagle Rd., NW,
Eatonton, GA 31024-6104
(706) 484-2872 • (706) 484-2888 (fax) • ddavies@uga.edu

Jekyll Island: Melanie Biersmith, Jekyll Island
201 S. Beachview Dr., Jekyll Island, GA 31527
(912) 635-4117, ejekyll@uga.edu

Rock Eagle: Environmental Education Coordinator, Rock Eagle
350 Rock Eagle Rd., NW, Eatonton, GA 31024-6104
(706) 484-2836, 4henved@uga.edu

Tybee Island: Angela Bliss, Burton 4-H Center
9 Lewis Ave., Tybee Island, GA 31328; (912) 786-5534, acbliss@uga.edu

Wahsega: Cathy Bodinof, Wahsega 4-H Center
77 Cloverleaf Trail, Dahlonega, GA 30533; (706) 864-2050, cathyb@uga.edu

*Some trees grow very tall and straight and large in the forest close to each other,
but some must stand by themselves or they won't grow at all.*
—OLIVER WENDELL HOLMES

GARDEN IN THE WOODS

Gardens • Massachusetts • 3–6 Months
www.newfs.org

$ 🏠

On a forty-five-acre landscape of rolling hills, ponds, and streams emerges Garden in the Woods, with over 1,600 kinds of plants grown in a naturalistic fashion. As the headquarters for the New England Wild Flower Society, Garden in the Woods offers educational programming and garden walks and operates a native plant nursery that produces over thirty-five thousand plants for garden displays and sale to the public. The society also owns and manages several sanctuaries throughout New England and a native plant nursery in western Massachusetts.

WHAT YOU'LL BE DOING: With a focus on the practical aspects of propagation and nursery management or native plant horticulture, each intern is trained in their respective field and assigned a small special project based on their area of interest, which might include nursery sales, interpretation, design, or writing. Regular on-site activities for horticultural interns are supplemented by field trips to nearby gardens, arboretums, nurseries, and natural areas. Additional opportunities include a unique conservation fellowship program that begins each spring for six months (contact Chris Mattrick, cmattrick@newfs.org, ext. 3203) and environmental education internships working with youth and adult education programs (contact Erin Walsh, ewalsh@newfs.org, ext. 3304). Expanded job descriptions and application instructions for all positions are available online.

COMMITMENT: Programs typically run for six months beginning in March; environmental education positions have different start dates and length.

PERKS AND REWARDS: A weekly stipend of $230 and off-site shared housing within walking distance of the garden are provided. Perks include participation in selected field trips and a wide range of optional natural history classes provided by the education department, including a native plant certificate program.

THE ESSENTIALS: Preference is given to applicants who are highly motivated and who have career aspirations and at least two years of educational course work in plant-related fields, previous work experience, and the ability to engage in rigorous outdoor work.

YOUR FIRST MOVE: Reach the specific contact person for more information or download application materials online. Applications are due the first week of February for six-month positions beginning in the spring. Depending on distance, applicants may be interviewed in person or over the phone.

FOR MORE INFORMATION: Tom Smarr, Horticulture Internships/Fellowships, Garden in the Woods, New England Wild Flower Society, 180 Hemenway Rd., Framingham, MA 01701-2699 • (508) 877-7630, ext. 3404 (508) 877-3658 (fax) • tsmarr@newfs.org

HAWK MOUNTAIN

Conservation • Pennsylvania • 4 Months
www.hawkmountain.org

$ 🏠

Hawk Mountain is a private, nonprofit organization with programs in research education and conservation policy that are national and international in scope. Established in 1934, Hawk Mountain is the world's first sanctuary for hawks, eagles, and other birds of prey. Science education interns learn how to guide field trips and present on-site and off-grounds interpretive programs to schoolchildren and the general public; ecological research interns learn how the sanctuary studies raptors and Appalachian mountain fauna and flora; and biological interns assist with censuses of songbirds, raptors, and other flora and fauna, and maintain databases. Positions are available for four months beginning either in April or mid-August. A monthly stipend of $600 and free housing on the grounds (including access to a wireless computer network) are provided. Applications are available online.

FOR MORE INFORMATION: Dr. Keith Bildstein, Director of Conservation Science, Hawk Mountain, Acopian Center, 410 Summer Valley Rd., Orwigsburg, PA 17961 • (570) 943-3411, ext. 108 • (570) 943-2284 (fax) bildstein@hawkmtn.org

HEADLANDS INSTITUTE

Environmental Education • California • Seasonal
www.yni.org/hi

$ 🏠 🎓 🌐

Headlands Institute, operating out of historic Fort Cronkhite in the Marin Headlands (north of San Francisco), is an educational nonprofit organization that provides field-based science programs in nature's classroom to inspire a personal connection to the natural world and responsible actions to sustain it. Educational adventures engage students in interactive learning through outdoor activities, games, team-building exercises, and classroom instruction.

WHAT YOU'LL BE DOING: Field instructors develop a set of activities and hikes for ten to fifteen students (a majority are in the fourth through sixth grade) that meld the clients' needs with the instructor's unique strengths and the

The moment one gives close attention to anything, even a blade of grass,
it becomes a mysterious, awesome, indescribably magnificent world in itself.
—HENRY MILLER

275

institute's core themes. The three broad core themes are sense of place, inter-connections, and stewardship. In addition, each instructor is expected to attend weekly staff meetings and present a one-hour evening program once or twice a week for groups of up to eighty students. Education interns will have a rotating schedule that includes observing instructors in the field, working on administrative projects in the office, delivering promotional slide presenta-tions, and developing an educational project.

COMMITMENT: Field teaching positions begin in late August, early January, and mid-June. Internships begin in January and June for a duration of six months.

PERKS AND REWARDS: Instructor positions start at $70 per day and include housing, partial board, medical and dental insurance, retirement benefits, paid training, and vacation benefits. Part-time and substitute instructor posi-tions are also available. Education interns receive room, partial board, and a small stipend of $150 per week.

THE ESSENTIALS: Candidates for either position must have at least a four-year degree in a related field and current first aid and CPR certification. Success-ful candidates for field-instructor positions generally have a minimum of two years' experience teaching. Intern applicants must have demonstrated interest (education or experience) in natural science and experience working with children. Although not required, applicants are encouraged to complete a Wilderness First Responder, EMT, or other advanced first aid training.

YOUR FIRST MOVE: Applications are accepted on a rolling basis, but priority is given to those received by October 15 for positions starting in January and March 15 for summer and fall positions. Top candidates are invited to Headlands for an interview and an opportunity to observe a field program.

FOR MORE INFORMATION: Duffy Ross, Education Director, Headlands Institute, GGNRA, Building 1033, Sausalito, CA 94965 • (415) 332-5771
(415) 332-5784 (fax) • hi@yni.org

THE HOLDEN ARBORETUM

Gardens • Ohio • 3–12 Months
www.holdenarb.org

$ 🏠 🎓 🌐

As a nonprofit museum with over 3,500 acres of horticultural collections and natural areas, the Holden Arboretum connects people with nature for inspira-tion and enjoyment, fosters learning, and promotes conservation.

WHAT YOU'LL BE DOING: The internship program is designed to give a balance of hands-on experience and educational programming. The educational aspect of the program has four parts: an arboretum orientation that combines lectures and tours; educational sessions; field trips to other horticultural institutions in northeast Ohio; and demonstrations, which give interns an opportunity to learn additional skills on equipment they might not otherwise use during the summer. Internships are available in horticulture, horticulture maintenance, landscape gardening, conservation, horticulture therapy, and education.

COMMITMENT: The internship is a full-time position offered during the summer with terms up to one year. Interns spend between five and ten hours each week in educational programs—most of them taking place during work hours.

PERKS AND REWARDS: Along with housing, interns receive wages starting at $7 per hour. The intern campus promotes bonding on a social level through activities including picnics, ball games, and nights out.

THE ESSENTIALS: Applicants must be studying horticulture, natural history, or related fields. Current students and recent grads receive first consideration.

YOUR FIRST MOVE: Submit a cover letter, resume, and three references by February 1.

FOR MORE INFORMATION: Greg Wright, Intern Coordinator, The Holden Arboretum, 9500 Sperry Rd., Kirtland, OH 44094-5172 (440) 946-4400 • (440) 602-3857 (fax) • gwright@holdenarb.org

KEYSTONE SCIENCE SCHOOL

Science School • Colorado • 11 Months/Summer
www.keystone.org

$ 🏠

Whether through hiking to the top of a 14,000-foot peak in the summer or cross-country skiing in the winter, Keystone Science School (KSS) teaches and inspires students in grades two through twelve about respect for science and the environment through hands-on, fun, and interactive teaching methods in an outdoor setting.

WHAT YOU'LL BE DOING: For those looking to teach in the outdoors, increase their skills with different ages of students, and gain more experience designing their own teaching lessons, KSS is a place where staff members are given

If you give a person a fish, you feed him for a day.
If you train a person to fish, you feed him for a lifetime.
—CHINESE PROVERB

the opportunity to learn, grow, and be a part of a community. With a focus on earth science, forest ecology, environmental issues, aquatic ecology, and snow science, each instructor will work with a group of ten students from program start to end.

COMMITMENT: Field instructors must be available from August through the end of June; summer staff begin in June and finish in August.

PERKS AND REWARDS: Benefits include a monthly stipend of $950, private room or cabin, meals, and Internet access. The quaint, homey, and rustic housing is two miles from Keystone Resort skiing, and free transportation within the resort is a little bonus on powder days.

THE ESSENTIALS: Enjoyment of being outside with kids of all ages and teaching them about the science of the natural world is essential—as is flexibility and the willingness to adapt. A mixture of experience with youth and a strong science background or a strong background in education with a desire to learn more science are a great fit for KSS.

YOUR FIRST MOVE: Current job opportunities and applications are usually posted online by January of each year.

FOR MORE INFORMATION: Andy McIntyre, Program Director, Keystone Science School, 1628 Sts. John Rd., Keystone, CO 80435 (800) 215-5585 • (970) 468-2098 • (970) 468-7769 (fax) • hr@keystone.org

LONG LAKE CONSERVATION CENTER

Environmental Education • Minnesota • 3 Months+
www.llcc.org

$ ⛺ ⊕

Each year thousands of students and adults explore Long Lake Conservation Center's 760-acre outdoor classroom and learn about the environment and conservation of natural resources through programs during the school year, a summer camp, retreats, and public programs.

WHAT YOU'LL BE DOING: Interns will be at the heart of the Center's environmental education, through both learning and teaching. You'll learn by interacting with the center's creative and dynamic year-round staff. You'll teach by sharing knowledge with students and bringing fresh expertise to the community and gain hands-on proficiency teaching a wide variety of activities that change with the seasons. General topics include aquatic biology, wildlife natural history, predator-prey relationships, forest ecology and bog ecology,

This naturalist brings a fresh perspective about woodland ecology to a group of students at Long Lake Conservation Center.

as well as canoeing, archery, cross-country skiing, and many other activities. Summer camp counselors are also needed to supervise and assist campers during six day summer sessions, including Tadpole Day Camp, Junior Naturalist sessions, Ecology Exploration, and the Wild River Trip.

COMMITMENT: Internships are available September through May, with a three-month minimum commitment. Camp counselor positions are available from late June through late August.

PERKS AND REWARDS: Interns receive a weekly stipend of $100, as well as housing, meals, regular feedback, and diverse learning opportunities. The staff apartment provides private sleeping quarters, communal kitchen, lounge, and two bathrooms. Counselors receive a weekly stipend of $180, including housing and meals.

THE ESSENTIALS: Candidates seeking experience in teaching, environmental education, outdoor education, and natural resources interpretation are ideally suited for Long Lake internships. Applicants must be graduates or current students in a related field. Recent high school graduates will be considered based on extensive experience and recommendations. Counselor applicants must be at least high school seniors and enjoy working with children and

Look deep, deep into nature, and then you will understand everything better.
—ALBERT EINSTEIN

adolescents in the outdoors. Certified lifeguards are strongly encouraged to apply.

YOUR FIRST MOVE: Request an application packet. Applications are considered on a first-come, first-served basis, and many candidates apply nine to twelve months in advance.

FOR MORE INFORMATION: Todd Roggenkamp, Executive Director, Long Lake Conservation Center, 28952 438th Ln., Palisade, MN 56469 (800) 450-5522 • (218) 768-4653 • (218) 768-2309 (fax) • llcc@llcc.org

LONGWOOD GARDENS

Gardens • Pennsylvania • 3–24 Months
www.longwoodgardens.org

$ 🏠 🌐

Located in the culturally rich and historic Brandywine Valley, Longwood Gardens is one of the world's premier display gardens, with nearly four acres of greenhouses and conservatories, flower gardens, fountain gardens, century-old trees, and natural areas encompassing one thousand acres. Longwood offers six training programs geared for high school and college students as well as professional gardeners. In general, interns and trainees specialize in one work area, such as curatorial, arboriculture, greenhouse display, green-

L. ALBEE

house production, research, education, or performing arts, supplemented by seminars, workshops, continuing education courses, and field trips over a period ranging from three months to two years. All participants receive a stipend and may live rent free on the grounds of the former estate of industrialist Pierre S. du Pont. The student

The philosophy of "learning by doing" is the best teacher for interns at Longwood Gardens.

houses are furnished and include kitchen utensils and dishes, laundry facilities, study areas, and nearby garden space. Their website provides all the details, including job openings and an application form.

FOR MORE INFORMATION: Mark Richardson, Student Programs Coordinator, Longwood Gardens, 409 Conservatory Rd., P.O. Box 501, Kennett Square, PA 19348-0501 • (610) 388-1000, ext. 508 (610) 388-2908 (fax) • studentprograms@longwoodgardens.org

MISSION SPRINGS CONFERENCE CENTER

Outdoor Education/Ministry • California • Academic Year/Summer
www.missionsprings.com

$ 🏠

Mission Springs Conference Center hosts an outdoor education program in the redwoods for students in grades five to eight from both Christian and public schools. The program is affiliated with the Pacific Southwest Conference of the Evangelical Covenant Church and serves sixty schools with about three thousand students annually. The proximity to Santa Cruz, the beach, and many other natural attractions makes this a great place to work, live, and learn.

WHAT YOU'LL BE DOING: Over ten naturalists lead natural science classes, Bible studies, field trips, and other activities throughout the school year. Naturalists have the opportunity to gain work experience in outdoor education, camping, and youth ministry; obtain training in natural history interpretation and recreational leadership skills; and enjoy living in a tight-knit Christian community. Check out their website for other employment opportunities, including summer camp counselors and guest services positions.

COMMITMENT: Naturalists work full-time weekly from September to June, with a two-month winter break. In general, summer opportunities begin in early June and continue through Labor Day.

PERKS AND REWARDS: A stipend of $250 per week is provided, along with room, meals (when groups are being served), and limited health insurance. Lodging is also provided during the winter break.

THE ESSENTIALS: Individuals with emotional maturity, excellent physical health, enthusiasm, teaching experience, enjoyment of the outdoors, ability to teach Bible classes, concern about environmental issues, a bachelor's degree, and current first aid certification are desired.

YOUR FIRST MOVE: Submit a cover letter and resume, then follow up with a phone call or email.

FOR MORE INFORMATION: Scott Smithson, Outdoor Education Director, Mission Springs Conference Center, 1050 Lockhart Gulch Rd., Scotts Valley, CA 95066 • (800) 683-9133 • (831) 335-3205 (831) 335-7726 (fax) • outdooreducation@missionsprings.com

To the attentive eye, each moment of the year has its own beauty, and in the same field, it beholds, every hour, a picture which was never seen before, and which shall never be seen again.
—RALPH WALDO EMERSON

☞ **INSIDER TIP: I'm looking for solid Christians interested in teaching environmental education. Previous youth ministry and teaching experience are desirable. Guitar players and bilingual applicants are strongly encouraged.**

MONTSHIRE MUSEUM OF SCIENCE

Museum • Vermont • 15 Weeks
www.montshire.org

$ 🏕

Located a stone's throw from Dartmouth College, Montshire Museum of Science serves as a hands-on education center that creates its own natural history, physical science, and technology exhibits. The museum conducts a variety of programs, trips, and other activities for children and families, as well as courses, workshops, and forums for community groups.

WHAT YOU'LL BE DOING: Throughout the year, fifteen-week internships are available with options including science education programming, exhibit design and fabrication, membership and development, public relations, Internet and education, land management, and exhibit maintenance and reconstruction. During the summer months, Montshire offers extensive summer environmental and science programming for children of preschool, elementary, and middle school age with most programs taking place entirely outdoors. Summer staff positions (which range from environmental educators to museum exhibit hosts) begin with a week of training that includes a variety of sessions ranging from leadership skills to ecology to group management.

PERKS AND REWARDS: For interns, a $1,000 stipend is provided, and if desired, Montshire will provide free housing hosted by local families. Summer staff wages range from $300 to $400 per week.

THE ESSENTIALS: Prerequisites include an interest in science and a desire to work with people. Familiarity with natural and physical science, communications, and education is useful.

YOUR FIRST MOVE: Applications are available online. Upon receiving your application, a staff member will call or send a letter to arrange an interview. In-person interviews are held with applicants who live nearby and telephone interviews with more distant applicants.

FOR MORE INFORMATION: Amy VanderKooi, Intern Coordinator, Montshire Museum of Science, One Montshire Rd., Norwich, VT 05055 (802) 649-2200 • (802) 649-3637 (fax) • montshire@montshire.org

NATURE'S CLASSROOM ATOP LOOKOUT MOUNTAIN

Experiential Education • Alabama • 3 Months
www.naturesclassroom.com

$ 🏠 🌐

Started as an experiential education program with an environmental foundation, Nature's Classroom is designed to support traditional classroom learning by teaching creative and practical applications of subjects taught in school. Students enjoy the informal outdoor atmosphere, opening themselves to new growth experiences.

YOUR SURROUNDINGS: The facility, in the northeast tip of Alabama bordering Tennessee and Georgia, is located on picturesque and rural Lookout Mountain, on the Little River, one of only two rivers that begin and end on a mountain.

WHAT YOU'LL BE DOING: Teachers work with third- to ninth-graders from public schools, private schools, and homeschool environments, teaching hands-on classes in all curriculum areas as well as leading field hikes. Small-group activities are designed to foster cooperation, communication, and team-building concepts using group initiatives and a low-ropes challenge course. A large-group activity may include a simulation of the Underground Railroad, an environmental hearing, or a night hike.

COMMITMENT: Contracts are available from mid-February through the end of May and/or early September through early December. The staff generally works four thirteen-hour days per week, with some five-day workweeks.

PERKS AND REWARDS: Along with a private cabin or room, meals, phone, Internet access, and training, teachers receive a weekly stipend of $200 ($150 for interns). With many three-day weekends, staff members are able to take full advantage of activities in the region, including caving, climbing, mountain biking, hiking, backpacking, and paddling.

THE ESSENTIALS: Teachers must have a four-year degree and be at least twenty-one, while interns must be at least eighteen and working on a college degree. A sense of humor is very helpful and appreciated, and being able to put the needs of the program and children first is a must. Although individuality and diversity are celebrated, a professional appearance (woodsy professional, that is) is just as important. Emotional maturity is needed to be a success and have fun.

YOUR FIRST MOVE: Call or email for application materials. On-site interviews are preferred; however, phone interviews will be conducted when necessary. Candidates are welcome to stay for a few days during an on-site interview.

In this world, nothing is permanent except change.
—AMERICAN PROVERB

FOR MORE INFORMATION: Adam Goshorn, Program Director, Nature's Classroom Atop Lookout Mountain, P.O. Box 400, Mentone, AL 35984-0400
(800) 995-4769 • (256) 634-4443 • (256) 634-3601 (fax) • natures@hiwaay.net

NEWFOUND HARBOR MARINE INSTITUTE

Marine Science/Sailing • Florida • Academic Year
www.nhmi.org

$ 🏠 🎓

Newfound Harbor Marine Institute, sponsored by the Seacamp Association (see their listing on page 174), offers programs in marine science and environmental education to school groups (from elementary to high school). Designed to awaken the senses and gain a better understanding of the natural features of the ocean and its ecosystems, the institute allows participants to explore the dynamics of natural communities in a variety of habitats, including the opportunity to snorkel and wade with instructors as they experience the wonders of the Florida Keys. More than eight thousand students participate in the program annually.

YOUR SURROUNDINGS: The institute is located 120 miles southwest of Miami—an ideal site for exploring the subtropical marine and terrestrial habitats of the Lower Keys—and is within the boundaries of the Florida Keys National Marine Sanctuary, where the year-round temperature averages seventy-nine degrees.

Newfound Harbor Marine Institute instructors help participants gain a better understanding of the natural features of the Florida Keys and its ecosystems.

WHAT YOU'LL BE DOING: Instructor positions and internships are designed to provide college students and preprofessionals with a variety of experiences— from developing their ability to lead interpretive programs to snorkeling among coral reefs with visiting school groups. Over six to eight weeks of intensive training are provided; staff learn boat-handling skills and U.S. Coast Guard boating rules to captain their twenty-six-foot oceanic research vessels. Seminars and hands-on training workshops are conducted on topics including mangrove ecology, reef fish ecology, coastal ecology, shark biology, coral reef ecology, and field techniques. Staff also participate in teaching techniques seminars, program observations, and team-teaching sessions. Other seasonal opportunities exist in photography, marketing, maintenance, food service, and support staff.

COMMITMENT: Interns and instructors work eight to ten hours per day, five or six days per week throughout the academic year. For those who would like just a summer experience teaching youth about the sea, the Seacamp Association offers a residential program from late May through late August.

PERKS AND REWARDS: A monthly stipend (interns start at $50 per week), room and board, a travel bonus, and access to staff boats are provided. American Red Cross certification in advanced first aid, CPR, and lifeguarding is also provided.

THE ESSENTIALS: Applicants should have an interest in children and the marine environment, boating and waterfront experience, and a college degree (or current study) in biology or environmental science.

YOUR FIRST MOVE: Send your cover letter, resume, transcripts, and three letters of recommendation to receive an application. Deadlines: fall—July 1; spring—October 15.

FOR MORE INFORMATION: Intern Coordinator, Newfound Harbor Marine Institute, 1300 Big Pine Ave., Big Pine Key, FL 33043-3336 • (305) 872-2331 (305) 872-2555 (fax) • info@nhmi.org

NYS DEPARTMENT OF ENVIRONMENTAL CONSERVATION

Environmental Education • New York • 10–12 Weeks
www.dec.state.ny.us/website/education/5river.html
$ ⚑ ⊕

The New York State Department of Environmental Conservation operates three centers: Five Rivers Environmental Education Center (Delmar), Rogers Environmental Education Center (Sherburne), and Stony Kill Farm

How wonderful it is that nobody need wait a single moment before starting to improve the world. **285**
—ANNE FRANK

Environmental Center (Wappingers Falls). With programming for teachers, school groups, youth groups, conservation organizations, and the public, the three state-run centers promote an understanding of natural history, ecology, environmental science, and natural resources.

WHAT YOU'LL BE DOING: Working at one of the three centers, intern naturalists receive training in a wide variety of education-center programs, the operations and activities of a nature center, and principles of environmental interpretation. Duties range from leading environmental activities to designing educational exhibits.

COMMITMENT: Positions are available for ten to twelve weeks with sessions beginning in January, April, June, and September.

PERKS AND REWARDS: Each center provides a weekly stipend of $200 and housing with private bedroom, furnished living room, and fully equipped kitchen.

THE ESSENTIALS: Applicants must be at least eighteen and have a love for the outdoors and a desire to enthusiastically work with people. Two years of college study in environmental education, science education, or natural resources is recommended.

YOUR FIRST MOVE: Send your completed application three months before your desired start date. It's noted that summer is ten times as popular as other seasons and the spring session (April through June) is actually the most interesting.

FOR MORE INFORMATION: Anita Sanchez, Naturalist Intern Program Coordinator, NYS Department of Environmental Conservation, Five Rivers Environmental Education Center, 56 Game Farm Rd., Delmar, NY 12054 • (518) 475-0291 amsanche@gw.dec.state.ny.us

PEACE VALLEY NATURE CENTER

Nature Center • Pennsylvania • 10–12 Weeks
www.peacevalleynaturecenter.org

$ 🏕

Peace Valley Nature Center began in 1975 with a mission to educate schoolchildren and the general public about the natural world. The nature center features nine miles of trail winding through five hundred acres of diverse natural communities, including fields, deciduous forests, thickets, streams, ponds, coniferous forests, and a portion of Lake Galena. The center is home to a solar building that houses displays, a shop, and a Clivus Multrum composting toilet.

WHAT YOU'LL BE DOING: Interns are required to observe and teach programs, complete and present a project, write a natural history article, attend a board meeting, participate in bird walks, keep a daily diary, and attend staff meetings.

COMMITMENT: Positions run ten to twelve weeks during the spring, summer, and fall, with occasional work during the evenings and weekends.

PERKS AND REWARDS: A wage of $5.15 per hour is provided, along with housing and the opportunity to gain experience teaching and observe various teaching styles and methods.

THE ESSENTIALS: Preference is given to applicants with two years of study in environmental education, biology, or environmental studies. Applicants must be interested in teaching children of all ages about the natural world.

YOUR FIRST MOVE: Send a resume, references, and cover letter requesting an application. Candidates within a two-hour drive are interviewed on-site; others are interviewed by phone. Applying for the spring or fall internship increases the candidate's chances of employment.

FOR MORE INFORMATION: Gail Hill, Environmental Education Director, Peace Valley Nature Center, 170 Chapman Rd., Doylestown, PA 18901 (215) 345-7860 • (215) 345-4529 (fax) • peacevalleynaturecenter@co.bucks.pa.us

POCONO ENVIRONMENTAL EDUCATION CENTER

Environmental Education • Pennsylvania • 6–10 Months
www.peec.org

$ ♠ ⊕

Located in the Delaware Water Gap National Recreation Area, Pocono Environmental Education Center's (PEEC) outdoor classroom consists of a thirty-eight-acre campus with access to over 200,000 acres of public land— fields, forests, ponds, waterfalls, and scenic hemlock gorges. Throughout the year, PEEC hosts school groups, religious organizations, universities, professional conferences, and workshops. PEEC also sponsors Elderhostel programs, family nature-study vacations, and professional development workshops on topics ranging from ornithology and wildflowers to photography and Native American studies.

Look at everything as though you were seeing it either for the first or last time.
Then your time on earth will be filled with glory.
—BETTY SMITH

WHAT YOU'LL BE DOING: Environmental education instructors and interns teach outdoor living skills, orienteering, and recreational activities and also lead interpretive hikes and group initiative activities; program-planning interns assist in scheduling, implementing, and coordinating educational programs; and public relations interns focus on the publications and marketing efforts of PEEC.

COMMITMENT: Six- to ten-month staffing assignments begin in February, June, or September.

PERKS AND REWARDS: A $500 to $800 per month stipend is provided, along with lodging in a heated cabins with private bath (usually shared with one roommate), a shared staff lounge, and meals served in the dining hall.

THE ESSENTIALS: Enrollment in or completion of a degree program in English, communications, environmental or outdoor education, natural sciences, or related fields is required. Applicants must demonstrate experience working with people and interest in working in a residential setting. Certification in lifeguarding, first aid, or CPR is preferred.

YOUR FIRST MOVE: Submit your resume, cover letter, and two references. Selected candidates will have on-site interviews to observe the typical operation of the center.

FOR MORE INFORMATION: Mike Brubaker, Assistant Director of Education, Pocono Environmental Education Center, RR 2, Box 1010, Dingmans Ferry, PA 18328 • (570) 828-2319 • (570) 828-9695 (fax) peec@ptd.net

RIVER BEND NATURE CENTER

Environmental Education • Minnesota • 3 or 9 Months
www.rbnc.org

$ 🏠 🎓

Home to active wetlands, maple and basswood forests, and restored prairies, River Bend helps people "discover, enjoy, understand, and preserve the incredible natural world that surrounds us." Intern naturalists develop and teach programs, providing hands-on learning experiences for children from preschool through age twelve in environmental day camps during the summer and for school groups throughout the academic year. In addition, interns design and teach weekend public programs for all ages, including youth, families, seniors, and special-needs groups. Academic-year interns receive a $165 weekly stipend, two weeks' paid vacation, and housing; summer interns

This naturalist intern shows a youngster the art of banding a bird for River Bend Nature Center research.

receive a $185 weekly stipend plus housing. A minimum of three years of college study is required. Send off a cover letter, resume, and list of three references.

FOR MORE INFORMATION: John Blackmer, Chief Naturalist, River Bend Nature Center, 1000 Rustad Rd., P.O. Box 186, Faribault, MN 55021-0186 (507) 332-7151 • (507) 332-0656 (fax) • rbncinfo@rbnc.org

RIVERBEND ENVIRONMENTAL EDUCATION CENTER

Environmental Education • Pennsylvania • Summer
www.riverbendeec.org

$ 🏕 🌐

Housed in a converted 1923 barn and surrounded by thirty-one acres of forest, fields, and streams, Riverbend provides a unique setting for educational activities designed to establish an awareness and understanding of the principles upon which our natural world is based. Spend time at Riverbend using your creative abilities and love of natural history while sharing the joy of discovery with children. Environmental education interns prepare and teach

What I hear, I forget; what I see, I remember; what I do, I know.   **289**
—CHINESE PROVERB

classes to schools, organized groups, and the public while gaining an orientation to environmental education, a working knowledge of ecological and environmental concepts, and experience developing and implementing educational goals and lesson plans. Environmental educators and camp staff work at the Exploration Camp and are directly responsible for the creation and implementation of hands-on, exploration-based activities. Benefits include $150 to $275 per week and housing if needed.

FOR MORE INFORMATION: Jen Wanisko, Education Director, Riverbend Environmental Education Center, 1950 Spring Mill Rd., Gladwyne, PA 19035-1000 • (610) 527-5234 • (610) 527-1161 (fax) jwanisko@riverbendeec.org

RYERSON WOODS

Environmental Education • Illinois • 10–48 Weeks
www.ryersonwoods.org

$ 🏕

As the environmental education headquarters of the Lake County Forest Preserve, Ryerson Woods is home to several rare species, including the blue-spotted salamander, wood frog, eastern Massasauga rattlesnake, red-shouldered hawk, and purple-fringed orchids. The visitor center houses an extensive natural science library and is punctuated with changing art exhibits depicting the beauty and wonder of nature. As paraprofessional naturalists, environmental education instructors are exposed to all operations of the center. A large portion of time is spent developing, preparing, and presenting programs to youth and adults throughout the year and to the nature and adventure camps during the summer months. Other responsibilities may include participation in volunteer- and teacher-training programs or special events. Positions run from ten to forty-eight weeks with start dates in February, March, May, June, and September. Stipends range from $2,700 for summer camp instructors on up to $15,862 for forty-eight-week instructors. Furnished housing can be arranged for a fee of $100 per month. Ideally, applicants should have at least two years of course work in biology or education along with an enthusiasm and respect for both people and the environment. Call or email for application materials.

FOR MORE INFORMATION: Mark Hurley, Education Instructor Coordinator, Ryerson Woods, Lake County Forest Preserve, 21950 Riverwoods Rd., Deerfield, IL 60015 • (847) 968-3324 • mhurley@co.lake.il.us

SALISH SEA EXPEDITIONS

Marine Science/Sailing • Washington • 3 Months
www.salish.org

$ 🏠

Salish Sea Expeditions provides three- to five-day longboat-based research expeditions to groups of students ranging from fifth to twelfth grade. Aboard the research ship, a sixty-one-foot yawl, students rotate through tasks such as helping handle sail, cooking meals, launching and recovering scientific gear, evaluating data, plotting a course, and standing a watch. In the classroom, marine science educators help students develop their itinerary and research plan; then, while aboard the ship, they double as watch leaders and scientific-study teachers. Other seasonal staff include captain and mate (who must both be U.S. Coast Guard licensed), galley coordinator (onboard supervision of food prep), and logistics coordinator (onshore food and supply shopping, organizing, and delivering). Prior to working with students, all staff members participate in a two-week training period (beginning in March) that focuses on Puget Sound ecology, program methodology, safety procedures, and ship operations, then work through mid-June, with some staff offered summer contracts. Along with room and partial board, base salaries range from $1,000 to $1,600 per month, based on experience. Marine science applicants must have a college degree and a demonstrated ability to teach, design, and implement scientific research projects. Basic first aid and CPR certificates are required, and advanced EMT or Wilderness First Responder certification is highly encouraged. To begin the application process, submit a cover letter, resume, and contact information for three references by December 1.

FOR MORE INFORMATION:
Lori Midthun Mitchell, Education Director, Salish Sea Expeditions
647 Horizon View Place
Bainbridge Island, WA 98110
(206) 780-7848
(260) 780-9005 (fax)
lori@salish.org

SALISH SEA EXPEDITIONS

A staff member helps students deploy research equipment for hands-on experiments aboard the Salish Sea Expeditions yawl.

MAKING A POSITIVE IMPACT ON MY LIFE AND THE SALISH TEAM

It's one o'clock in the afternoon on our second day out. The *Lavengro* is coasting smoothly over moderate swell, her bow plowing a gurgling path through the dark blue water. I have my arms crossed on the rail and am leaning comfortably over the edge, watching the very tip of the bow—that exact point where this mass of wood and steel and twenty-five people meets a patch of water for the first time and begins to displace it.

Scattered around the deck of the boat are students, chaperones, and Salish staff. We're taking fifteen minutes out of a busy day to sail silently and observe the movement of the boat, to hear the creaking of the rigging, and maybe to get a glimpse of a sea lion sunning itself on a buoy or a bald eagle gliding along the shoreline. I've chosen this spot where I can see the bow ride through the waves because it always makes my spine tingle to think how much power is generated by just a light breeze. Perhaps that same feeling of wonder is affecting some of these students who, nervous and excited, boarded the boat just a day ago and are now relaxed and comfortable with their surroundings, letting their eyes settle on salt water or a faraway shoreline, almost as if they've been at sea for ages.

I can't remember what I expected when I called Salish last fall and asked if they needed any help with, well, anything. I had recently moved to Seattle. I rattled off my qualifications that I thought might be of use to Salish—experience as a copywriter, a stint as a youth camp director, two years studying marine science in college, an enthusiasm for sailing, and lots of time on my hands. I guess I envisioned them calling me when a crewmember was out sick and the boat needed to be moved. I never would have guessed that Salish would so profoundly shape my first year in the Pacific Northwest.

Part of making an organization like Salish thrive is having the ability to effectively use a group of volunteers. That takes a tremendous amount of energy and creativity on the part of the permanent staff. After I did some copywriting work for Salish, Lori and Alison invited me to participate in the spring staff training. Like most of my involvement with Salish, it was an intense experience, and I learned much from Lori and Alison, as well as from the extremely talented group of seasonal staff. I learned enough to help out on some spring trips, and I continued trying to be aboard whenever I could during the summer session.

Now, nearly a year since I first asked how I could help out, I feel a strong bond to the people I've met and to the organization itself. I've made a lot of good friends through Salish, and I am still thrilled every time I have the opportunity to go out on a trip. Whether I am teaching a group of students how to tie a bowline or trim the mainsail of the *Carlyn,* I feel proud to be a part of an organization that I know so positively impacts students.

—Contributed by Eric Thomas, Salish Sea Expeditions volunteer

SCICON

Outdoor Education • California • 10 Months
www.tcoe.org/scicon

$ ♨ ☗ ⊕

Experiencing nature and science firsthand, more than eleven thousand students each year participate at the Clemmie Gill School of Science and Conservation (SCICON), a residential outdoor education school operated by the Tulare County Office of Education. With community involvement as SCICON's backbone, every acre has been acquired through donations, and every building and facility built through volunteers and contributions. A museum of natural history, planetarium, observatory, raptor rehabilitation center, and over seventeen miles of trails are just some of the highlights of this beautiful 1,100-acre campus.

WHAT YOU'LL BE DOING: The internship program kicks off with an in-depth orientation, which includes guest speakers, field trips, and an intensive training workshop. Interns then gain experience in every facet of outdoor school operation and learn to teach basic concepts in all areas of natural history. In addition, interns gain skills in large-group management, program scheduling, and administration. There is also a California teaching credential program in which you can enroll concurrently with the internship.

COMMITMENT: Internships begin in mid-August with two weeks of staff training and continue with program operation through mid-June (a ten-month commitment). Interns can expect long days with irregular hours, Monday through Friday.

PERKS AND REWARDS: A stipend of $60 per day is provided, along with room, board, and health insurance. Intern housing (located in the heart of the SCICON campus) consists of private rooms, a comfortable lounge, dining area, kitchen, laundry room, phone, and computer with Internet access.

THE ESSENTIALS: Applicants with a bachelor's degree in science, education, or recreation are preferred (although upper-division students will also be considered). Applicants must have a high energy level, a professional appearance, and a real love for children and the outdoors. The program is ideal for those considering careers and leadership roles in outdoor education.

YOUR FIRST MOVE: Send off your resume and cover letter before May 1; an application packet will be sent to you upon receipt.

FOR MORE INFORMATION: Rick Mitchell, Administrator/Director, SCICON, P.O. Box 339, Springville, CA 93265-0339 • (559) 539-2642 (559) 539-2643 (fax) • rickmit@tcoe.org

The future must be seen in terms of what a person can do to contribute something, to make something better, to make it go where he believes with all his being it ought to go.
—FREDERICK KAPPEL

These students, interns, and faculty travel in Kenya to help protect our environment for future generations of plant, animal, and human life.

THE SCHOOL FOR FIELD STUDIES

Environmental Education • Worldwide • 1 Year
www.fieldstudies.org

$ 🏕🏠

The School for Field Studies (SFS) is the country's oldest and largest educational institution exclusively dedicated to teaching and engaging undergraduates in environmental problem solving. Students will learn about environmental issues and work to solve them by actually living within affected ecosystems and communities. In recent projects, students at the Center for Rainforest Studies in Australia assisted the communities there with planting more than twenty thousand trees as part of an experiment in rainforest restoration; at the SFS Mexico field station, students held a Sea Turtle festival to educate local children about the importance of conserving these endangered animals.

WHAT YOU'LL BE DOING: Interns will provide support in the areas of program delivery, academics, research, group dynamics, logistics, program safety, risk management, and site maintenance. Placements are offered in Australia, Costa Rica, Kenya, Mexico, and the Turks and Caicos Islands.

COMMITMENT: Interns must make a commitment of one year, with start dates in late January, June 1, and September 1.

PERKS AND REWARDS: Benefits include a stipend of $750 for each semester and $500 for both summer sessions ($2,000 total), along with on-site room and board, evacuation/repatriation insurance coverage, and reimbursement for any required visas or work permits. Half of the direct round-trip airfare is also reimbursed at the conclusion of service. Interns must have adequate, internationally valid health insurance for the entire internship period.

THE ESSENTIALS: Applicants must be college graduates and have valid certification in first aid and CPR (lifeguard certification preferred), as well as experience in group dynamics, leading groups, or teaching. Ideal candidates are energetic, motivated individuals who are willing to work flexible hours and live on-site at a field station with a small team of permanent staff, groups of U.S. undergraduate students, and visiting researchers or programs. Some programs also require specific language proficiency.

YOUR FIRST MOVE: Only online applications are accepted; click on the Jobs link on their website.

FOR MORE INFORMATION: Internship Coordinator, The School for Field Studies, 10 Federal St., Suite 24, Salem, MA 01970-3876 • (800) 989-4418 (978) 741-3567, ext. 204 • (978) 741-3551 (fax)

THE SCOTT ARBORETUM
OF SWARTHMORE COLLEGE

Gardens · Pennsylvania · 3–12 Months
www.scottarboretum.org

$ ⊕

The Scott Arboretum is uniquely situated on the campus of Swarthmore College, a small, outstanding coed liberal arts college with a student population of 1,375. The arboretum was established in 1929 for the purpose of cultivating and displaying trees, shrubs, and herbaceous plants suited to the climate of eastern Pennsylvania and which are suitable for planting by home gardeners.

WHAT YOU'LL BE DOING: Summer internships offer a broad range of practical work experience to those interested in the ornamental horticulture field. Interns work with the staff and volunteers in gardening, plant propagation, plant records, educational programs, and special events. In addition, a yearlong curatorial internship is offered, with duties including supervision of volunteers and summer interns along with assisting in educational events.

COMMITMENT: Summer internships are available for a minimum of ten weeks, April through September; the yearlong position begins in June.

Many things are clarified only with the passage of time.
—ANSEL ADAMS

PERKS AND REWARDS: Summer interns receive an hourly wage of $9, while the yearlong curatorial intern receives $1,500 per month plus full benefits.

A curatorial intern leads a tour at the Scott Arboretum on Arbor Day.

Assistance with locating housing will be provided, though the expense will be your responsibility. Swarthmore is a college community, so you shouldn't have a problem here. Other perks include free admission to college events, such as concerts and plays, as well as free use of the college's sports facilities.

THE ESSENTIALS: Applicants must have a keen interest in horticulture and enjoy working with people and plants.

YOUR FIRST MOVE: Submit a cover letter, resume, and three references (with contact information) by March 1.

FOR MORE INFORMATION: Claire Sawyers, Director, The Scott Arboretum of Swarthmore College, Swarthmore College, 500 College Ave., Swarthmore, PA 19081-1397 • (610) 328-8025 (610) 328-7755 (fax) • csawyer1@swarthmore.edu

SEA EDUCATION ASSOCIATION

Marine Science/Sailing • Worldwide • 8–12 Weeks
www.sea.edu

The world's oceans cover upwards of 70 percent of the planet, but our understanding of the ocean as a physical system and as a vital element in human culture and history is still in its infancy. The mission of Sea Education

Association is to give students the practical and theoretical experience necessary to contribute to our understanding of the ocean environment.

WHAT YOU'LL BE DOING: This is a uniquely challenging program. SEA Semester students spend six weeks at the Woods Hole campus (the world capital of ocean science) receiving intensive classroom instruction in oceanography, nautical science, and maritime studies. Each student works closely with the oceanography faculty to design a research project, using the resources of the nearby Marine Biological Laboratory. Upon successful completion of course work on shore, each student takes a berth as a crew member on one of SEA's two research vessels—120-foot blue-water "tall ships." Each vessel will then undertake its unique scientific mission during the second six weeks, to places as far as the shores of Venezuela. On board, students become active members of the ship's crew and conduct oceanographic research and gather data for research projects.

COMMITMENT: The semester program runs twelve weeks, five times per year. An eight-week summer class begins in early June.

PERKS AND REWARDS: The cost of SEA Semester is about the same as a semester at a private university—approximately $19,000 ($13,000 for the summer course). Financial aid is available. Housing is provided on shore; room and board are provided at sea. Students typically earn seventeen academic credits from Boston University, as well as 102 "sea days" toward the 180 days required to sit for a U.S. Coast Guard Able-Bodied Seaman's license.

THE ESSENTIALS: Previous sailing or marine science experience is not required. SEA Semester stresses problem solving, critical thinking, and teamwork. College-bound students seeking a rigorous academic experience prior to starting college, and college graduates seeking some practical experience before grad school or job hunting are welcome.

YOUR FIRST MOVE: Call or email for materials and a program video (which is also available online). Enrollment is limited to forty-nine spaces in each class, so it's best to apply early.

FOR MORE INFORMATION: Judith MacLeod Froman, Dean of Enrollment, Sea Education Association, SEA Semester, 171 Woods Hole Rd., P.O. Box 6, Woods Hole, MA 02543 • (800) 552-3633 • (508) 457-4673 (fax) admission@sea.edu

I often hesitate to say we own this land. How can a person own what he has not created?
The earth is the Lord's and the fullness thereof. We are only its custodians.
—JOSEPHINE DUVENECK

SEA TURTLE RESTORATION PROJECT

Conservation • Costa Rica • 1 Week–5 Months
www.tortugamarina.org

♥ ⌂ ⊕

Are you interested in saving sea turtles in the field? Searching the beaches at night for endangered nesting mothers? Counting baby sea turtle hatchlings and gently releasing them into the sea? Participating in community educational programs? With the Sea Turtle Restoration Project, you have the opportunity to help these gentle creatures on the Pacific coast of Costa Rica. Volunteers are needed from mid-July through mid-January for sea turtle conservation programs at San Miguel and Punto Banco (both situated on beautiful sandy beaches with warm ocean waters, and surrounded by tropical rain forests). It's definitely not all work while volunteering; leisure activities include jungle hikes, visiting waterfalls, swimming, surfing, snorkeling, teaching English, or just lounging in a hammock! Participants stay in the research station house and enjoy meals provided at the local restaurant. Several volunteers participate at a time and a one-month commitment is encouraged. Volunteers with enthusiasm and a positive attitude are highly desirable. Program fees vary depending on a multitude of factors; in general, a one-month commitment runs $800 (shorter and longer terms are available). Detailed information is available online or email for application materials.

FOR MORE INFORMATION: Randall Arauz, Central American Director, Sea Turtle Restoration Project, Costa Rica Volunteer Project, P.O. Box 400, Forest Knolls, CA 94933 • (800) 859-7283 • (415) 488-0370 (415) 488-0372 (fax) • info@tortugamarina.org

SHAVER'S CREEK ENVIRONMENTAL CENTER

Environmental Education • Pennsylvania • 3–6 Months
www.shaverscreek.org

$ ⌂ ⊕

Shaver's Creek, administered by Penn State's Continuing Education program, is an environmental education laboratory seeking to enhance the quality of life by providing exemplary outdoor learning opportunities. This multifaceted center offers environmental education programs for group visits, natural and cultural history exhibits, live amphibians and reptiles, hiking trails, herb gardens, and more. The raptor center, providing perpetual care and housing for eagles, falcons, hawks, and owls, is one of the few federally and state-licensed raptor facilities in Pennsylvania.

WHAT YOU'LL BE DOING: Environmental education interns become an integral part of the staff and are encouraged to participate in all aspects of the center's operation. A two-week orientation and training period is followed by seasonal program opportunities in both day and residential settings. Interns work with all ages, preschool to adult, as they lead natural and cultural history programs for school and community groups, families, and the general public. Interns also have the opportunity to contribute articles to the newsletter, lead adventure and team-building programs, participate in the care and handling of the live animal collection, and assist in the general operation of the center. Observations, recordings, and videotaping are used in evaluation, and interns are encouraged to keep a journal.

COMMITMENT: Positions are available year-round, from three to six months, with the opportunity to work multiple seasons.

PERKS AND REWARDS: A weekly stipend of $150 is provided, along with on-site housing nestled in the woods away from park visitors, with a private bedroom. Interns are encouraged to participate in professional development workshops and regional conferences, and each season includes a three-day staff trip to another environmental center or a facility of interest. Macintosh computers are used on-site, and access to the Internet is available. Career counseling, job-listing resources, and assistance with resume writing are also provided.

THE ESSENTIALS: Successful candidates have a strong desire to teach and share their knowledge and enthusiasm for the natural world. A background in education or the natural sciences is helpful but not necessary. International students are encouraged to apply, as the center can assist with the J-1 visa application process.

YOUR FIRST MOVE: Interested candidates can call, fax, or write for an application. Deadlines: winter/spring—November 1; summer—March 1; and fall—July 1. Interviews with top candidates are conducted in person or by phone.

FOR MORE INFORMATION: Doug Wentzel, Internship Coordinator, Shaver's Creek Environmental Center, Outreach Resource of Penn State, 3400 Discovery Rd., Petersburg, PA 16669-9317 • (814) 863-2000 (814) 865-2706 (fax) • shaverscreek@outreach.psu.edu

🖎 **INSIDER TIP: The most successful candidates have some experience working with children. A site visit and meeting with the intern coordinator is beneficial but not necessary. Many first-time undergraduate candidates who are not accepted mistakenly fail to reapply for an upcoming season.**

When we try to pick out anything by itself we find it hitches to everything in the universe.
—JOHN MUIR

SQUAM LAKES NATURAL SCIENCE CENTER

Environmental Education • New Hampshire • Summer
www.nhnature.org

$ 🏠 🌐

Located in the beautiful countryside of central New Hampshire, the Squam Lakes Natural Science Center is a unique outdoor classroom offering people of all ages the opportunity to discover and explore New Hampshire's natural world. Through the classroom and using the center's two-hundred-acre site, summer interns lead programs on natural history and environmental awareness. Interns are also involved in exhibit design and construction as well as care of the center's native wildlife collection. A $100-per-week stipend is provided along with on-site housing, including a private bedroom, shared bath, and kitchen use. College undergraduates with at least junior status or graduate students in the fields of natural sciences, education, or environmental education are most desirable. Enthusiasm, motivation, and a desire to work with people and animals are a must. Send your resume and a cover letter with three professional references.

FOR MORE INFORMATION: Beth Roy, Naturalist/Intern Coordinator, Squam Lakes Natural Science Center, P.O. Box 173, Holderness, NH 03245-0173 (603) 968-7194, ext. 18 • (603) 968-2229 (fax) • info@nhnature.org

TREES FOR TOMORROW

Natural Resources • Wisconsin • 8 Months
www.treesfortomorrow.com

$ 🏠 🎓 🌐

Trees For Tomorrow is one of the Midwest's oldest conservation education centers, with a "classroom" that includes miles of surrounding state and national forests, lakes and streams, and abundant wildlife. From their thirty-acre campus in Eagle River, participants travel to nearby demonstration areas to learn firsthand about forest management, wildlife habitat, water systems, and conservation practices. Whether walking through a bog, collecting critters from a stream, or learning how to weave a snowshoe, a "learn by doing" approach resonates throughout their entire programming.

WHAT YOU'LL BE DOING: With ongoing training from seven full-time educators, naturalist interns will give evening naturalist programs, teach a variety of indoor and outdoor classes, and develop an interpretive display or environmental education curriculum. The changing seasons offer additional duties ranging from teaching cross-country ski techniques to leading bog studies and orienteering classes.

COMMITMENT: Four naturalists are hired from late August through May.

PERKS AND REWARDS: A monthly stipend of $700 is provided, along with full room and board. Perks include catastrophic health insurance, paid holiday and vacation days, a staff jacket, curriculum guides, and the chance to tour other nature centers and network with professionals in the field.

THE ESSENTIALS: A willingness to learn coupled with good people skills and the ability to teach others about natural resources are the key ingredients for the ideal intern. Recent graduates in biology, forestry, environmental education, or natural resource management are preferred, although students at the junior or senior level are also welcome.

YOUR FIRST MOVE: Send your cover letter, resume, and three references by May 15. Telephone interviews are given to the most promising applicants.

FOR MORE INFORMATION: Sandy Lotto, Intern Coordinator, Trees For Tomorrow, Natural Resources Education Center, P.O. Box 609, Eagle River, WI 54521-0609 (800) 838-9472 • (715) 479-6456 • (715) 479-2318 (fax) learning@treesfortomorrow.com

UGA MARINE EDUCATION CENTER AND AQUARIUM

Marine Science • Georgia • 1 Year
www.uga.edu/aquarium

$ 🏠 🎓 🌐

Located on scenic Skidaway Island, the University of Georgia's Marine Education Center and Aquarium (MECA) includes a nineteen-thousand-square-foot education center with a teaching aquarium, classrooms, exhibit space, a sixty-bed dormitory, a cafeteria, and three research vessels. Each year, over thirteen thousand students from Georgia and adjacent states receive formal education from programs here.

WHAT YOU'LL BE DOING: Over the course of a one- to two-month intensive training period, interns will learn how to teach and convey marine-related content to children of all ages and adults using methods such as lectures, labs, coastal field studies, and distance learning. Interns are also in charge of maintaining touch-tank animals and assisting staff in other specialty areas. Each intern will also complete an education project for the MECA facility.

COMMITMENT: This is a full-time, fifty-week program that begins in early September. In the months of June and July, interns work with several week-long science camp programs for children.

Let us not look back in anger or forward in fear, but around in awareness.
—JAMES THURBER

PERKS AND REWARDS: A weekly stipend of $287 is provided along with single-occupancy studio apartments in the dormitory and free meals whenever

KAREN ROEDER

groups are scheduled to eat in the cafeteria. Perks include access to the on-site research library and the nearby Skidaway Institute of Oceanography, and the opportunity to attend local workshops and educational meetings.

A UGA Marine Education Center intern introduces some muddy students to a salt marsh snail.

THE ESSENTIALS: Internships are geared for recent graduates who would like some teaching experience in the marine realm and have not yet decided whether to go to graduate school or take a full-time permanent position. A degree in science or science education is required; however, university seniors may apply before graduation if their degree will be awarded before the internship begins. Marine science experience is not necessary; however, experience or coursework in invertebrate zoology and ichthyology are very helpful. Applicants must be physically fit and able to do fieldwork; previous work experience with children is looked upon favorably; and cheerfulness and flexibility are very important.

YOUR FIRST MOVE: Consult their website for detailed application instructions. All application materials must be received by April 15 for internships beginning the following September.

FOR MORE INFORMATION: Dr. Maryellen Timmons, Internship Coordinator, UGA Marine Education Center and Aquarium, 30 Ocean Science Circle, Savannah, GA 31411 • (912) 598-2496 • (912) 598-2302 (fax) • mare@uga.edu

UP YONDA FARM

Environmental Education • New York • Summer
www.upyondafarm.com

$ 🏠 🎓

With a spectacular view of Lake George, Up Yonda Farm sits upon a seventy-two-acre property surrounded by beauty (and lots of butterflies during the summer months). The environmental education center features wildlife exhibits and nature trails and offers a variety of interpretive programs to schools and the general public. During the summer months, naturalists are the backbone of the programming for visitors. Typical activities include providing information to visitors; conducting interpretive walks; developing presentations; designing and creating exhibits and displays; preparing and distributing promotional materials; and providing routine grounds and trail maintenance. Candidates must have great communication skills, the ability to work with the public, and degree studies in interpretation or environmental science. Housing is available along with a wage of $8.65 per hour ($1 more if you have your own housing). To apply, send your resume, references, and a college transcript. A personal interview is required for placement.

In hot pursuit of monarch butterflies for a tagging and identification research project at Up Yonda Farm, a summer naturalist explains catching techniques to two energized workshop participants.

MICHAEL LANDES

FOR MORE INFORMATION: Matt Sprow, Internship Coordinator, Up Yonda Farm, P.O. Box 1453, Bolton Landing, NY 12814 • (518) 644-9767 (518) 644-3824 (fax) • info@upyondafarm.com

YMCA CAMP WIDJIWAGAN

Adventure Education • Minnesota • 3–9 Months
www.widji.org

$ 🏕 🌐

Located at the edge of the Boundary Waters Canoe Area Wilderness, Widjiwagan is a place of beauty, solitude, and peace. Instructors use the boreal forest as their classroom to engage students in hands-on learning about the environment, outdoor skills, and teamwork. Residential programs are offered throughout the year and focus on wilderness adventure trips for twelve- to eighteen-year-olds and hands-on environmental education experiences for school groups.

WHAT YOU'LL BE DOING: Each year Widjiwagan hires over eighty summer trail staff and, during the school year, up to fifteen environmental education instructors. Summer wilderness trail counselors primarily lead canoe and backpack trips ranging in length from five to twelve nights, while support staff

Let no one be deluded that a knowledge of the path can substitute for putting one foot in front of the other.
—M. C. RICHARDS

(including trail-building coordinators, office staff, cooks, and maintenance assistants) are the "grease" of the in-camp programs. Instructor naturalists have the opportunity to work with small groups and exercise their own creative style in developing a range of lesson plans. Responsibilities might include leading a variety of instructional hikes, leading team-building exercises, or chaperoning a student cabin at night. Finally, interns in the wilderness or environmental education program receive extensive training in all aspects of the program while developing their abilities in natural history programming, wilderness skills, and youth leadership.

PERKS AND REWARDS: Wilderness trail staff wages range from $1,500 to $1,900 per summer; instructors, $650 to $700 per month; and interns receive a stipend. All staff receive room and board as well as expert staff training in leadership, teaching and outdoor skills, and wilderness medicine.

THE ESSENTIALS: Applicants must have experience teaching in an outdoor setting, skills in wilderness canoeing or backpacking, or training in the natural sciences. Interns must have a desire to develop youth leadership skills, have confidence working in an outdoor setting, and be pursuing (or have) a degree in an environmental field. Current certification in CPR and first aid is required (lifeguarding and Wilderness First Responder may also be needed).

YOUR FIRST MOVE: Applications can be found online. Inquire early as staff are hired on a rolling basis.

FOR MORE INFORMATION: Alissa Johnson, Summer Program Director, YMCA Camp Widjiwagan, 2125 East Hennepin Ave., Suite 150, Minneapolis, MN 55413 (612) 465-0450 • (612) 646-5521 (fax) • info@widji.org

YOUTH LEARNING INSTITUTE

Environmental Education • South Carolina • Seasonal
www.clemson.edu/yli

$ 🏠

Teaching Kids About the Environment (Teaching KATE), sponsored by the Youth Learning Institute and Clemson University, is an exciting, fun-filled program that gives students (grades four through eight) an opportunity to develop a sense of appreciation for our natural resources through three days of learning, recreation, and group activities. With KATE, participants will really get to see, feel, and smell what they're learning while gaining an understanding of the relationship between humans and the cycles of life in the wild. The Youth Learning Institute also has a handful of other unique programs,

NUANAARPUQ

How often do you find yourself taking extravagant pleasure in being alive? As we hike over the crest of a snowy ridge in the heart of the vast wilderness, the world seemingly unfolds in front of us. At once, we can embrace endless miles of ridges, peaks, and valleys. An inner joy bubbles up within each of us. Overtaken with the beauty of the moment, one of us spontaneously shouts out, "Nuanaarpuq!"

Is it possible to express the feelings of such special moments in words? We used to be skeptical, feeling that the joy of the moment alone would suffice. That was until we learned the Alaskan Inuit expression "Nuanaarpuq." Those who live by this expression live with a deep respect for the natural world and have learned to appreciate and celebrate all the wonders of nature. It is expressed with both reverence and pleasure.

Are you aware of such moments of extravagant pleasure?

Do you share this with others?

Nuanaarpuq is about awareness, about finding and celebrating beauty in the simple things in life. It is the key word for opening up eyes and creating an excitement for life. It is a way to express our celebration of the present moment and for expressing deep joy. Begin making this newfound awareness a daily part of your life and extend your joy to others. After all, excitement for life is contagious.

—Contributed by Christian Bisson and Julie Gabert, who work as outdoor educators at Northland College in Wisconsin during the academic year and teach seasonally for the National Outdoor Leadership School in Wyoming. Through these experiences, they find many moments of Nuanaarpuq!

including those that focus on at-risk kids, outdoor education, foster families, and faith-based groups, as well as a variety of summer camps.

YOUR SURROUNDINGS: Instructors will work at either the Robert M. Cooper Leadership Center in Summerton or the W.W. Long Leadership Center in Aiken. (Staff usually get a choice where they want to go.)

WHAT YOU'LL BE DOING: Environmental education instructors will use the outdoors as a hands-on living laboratory by teaching morning, afternoon, and evening classes to students in the four disciplines of forestry, soils, wildlife, and water, along with facilitating team initiatives and games. In addition, instructors will lead students in daily program activities and assist with the Portable Starlab and Portable Teams Course (where students learn to help each other through seemingly impossible activities).

The more you learn what to do with yourself, and the more you do for others,
the more you will enjoy the abundant life.
—WILLIAM J. H. BOETCKER

COMMITMENT: Fourteen to sixteen instructors are hired in the spring; five to six in the fall. Twelve instructors are hired for their specialty camps in the summer.

PERKS AND REWARDS: A $400 to $440 biweekly stipend is provided, along with room, meals, accidental/sickness insurance, and training in program curriculum and adventure education.

THE ESSENTIALS: A bachelor's degree in environmental education, natural sciences, forestry, geology, or education is preferred. Candidates must have a genuine interest in children and the patience, understanding, flexibility, and energy to work and live with staff and students twenty-four hours per day (meaning the ability to work long hours!).

YOUR FIRST MOVE: Send a cover letter, resume, and application (which can be found online), or call or email for more information.

FOR MORE INFORMATION: Chad Jones, Program Director, Youth Learning Institute, 698 Concord Church Rd., Pickens, SC 29671 (864) 878-1103 • (864) 878-5985 (fax) • crjones@clemson.edu

RECOMMENDED RESOURCES

Do you have a green thumb? Membership in the **American Association of Botanical Gardens and Arboreta** (www.aabga.org) is one way to further your career goals and keep you in touch with what's happening at public gardens throughout the U.S. and Canada. Their annual internship directory, available for $15, lists more than one hundred gardens that offer summer jobs and internships in fields including horticulture, conservation, education, collections, children's programs, historic garden restoration, horticultural therapy, and zoo horticulture programs. For more information contact the American Association of Botanical Gardens and Arboreta, 100 W. 10th St., Suite 614, Wilmington, DE 19801; (302) 655-7100, resources@aabga.org.

If you are a birding enthusiast looking for an interesting life experience or a new way to spend your vacation, explore the possibilities with the **American Birding Association.** Each January they publish *Opportunities for Birders,* listing more than 650 volunteer projects for birders in the U.S., Canada, and an ever-increasing list in other countries. Short- and long-term opportunities are available, and some offer a stipend. A copy of the directory is sent to each ABA member in February (membership is $25 for students; $45 for individuals); listings can also be viewed through www.americanbirding.org/opps/voldintr.htm, which is updated regularly. For more information contact the American Birding Association, P.O. Box 6599, Colorado Springs, CO 80934-6599; (800) 850-2473.

Whether you want to intern at a drive-through safari zoo, a freshwater aquarium, or a three-thousand-acre wildlife center, the **American Zoo and Aquarium Association** has hundreds of opportunities to explore at www.aza.org/joblistings.

EnviroEducation.com provides everything environment, including career advice, job listings and links, and colleges in the field.

The Job Seeker is a biweekly newsletter that provides extensive listings of environmental and natural resource work opportunities—from internships to career-track jobs—throughout the U.S. The newsletter is a perfect complement to your job search and can be received through either regular mail or email. Email subscriptions are available for three months ($19.50), six months ($36), or one year ($60). Subscriptions through regular mail are slightly higher in price. For more information contact *The Job Seeker,* 403 Oakwood Street, Warrens, WI 54666; (608) 378-4450, www.thejobseeker.net.

The Massachusetts Audubon Society (www.massaudubon.org) provides an online directory of seasonal employment, internship, and volunteer opportunities at Audubon sanctuaries throughout the state—from Cape Cod to the Berkshires. Typical assignments range from environmental education and naturalist internships to camp counselors and shorebird nesting monitors.

TREES
by Joyce Kilmer

I think that I shall never see
A poem lovely as a tree.

A tree whose hungry mouth
is pressed
Against the Earth's sweet
flowing breast;

A tree that looks at God all day,
And lifts her leafy arms to pray.

A tree that may in Summer wear
A nest of robins in her hair;

Upon whose bosom snow has lain;
Who intimately lives with rain.

Poems are made by fools like me,
But only God can make a tree

Do you need to make vital contacts with influential nature lovers? The **National Wildlife Federation** (NWF), the nation's largest member-supported conservation education and advocacy organization, offers an internship program for college graduates with an interest and knowledge in environmental issues. Each intern is given a responsible role and becomes an essential part of NWF's conservation and education efforts. Typical assignments are programs with backyard and schoolyard wildlife habitats, campus ecology, climate change, mercury and public lands, as well as in the communications,

I frequently tramped eight or ten miles through the deepest snow to keep an appointment with a beech tree, or a yellow birch, or an old acquaintance among the pines.
—HENRY DAVID THOREAU

legal, and publications divisions. The internship length varies from a summer on up to a year, with stipends ranging from $300 to $350 per week. Opportunities are available at their national headquarters in Virginia and at offices all over the U.S., with destinations as far as Anchorage, Alaska! Internships are posted online and removed once filled—thus, it's to your advantage to keep an eye on their website. Applications are available as a PDF download and resumes are accepted only for posted positions. Due to the large size of the organization, don't expect any correspondence from the NWF unless they're interested in you. For more information contact the National Wildlife Federation, 11100 Wildlife Center Dr., Reston, VA 20190-5362; (703) 790-4545, internopp@nwf.org, www.nwf.org/careergateway.

Are you interested in helping the environment while working with others who share your love for nature? The **Nature Conservancy** (www.nature.org/volunteer) provides hands-on conservation internships and volunteer opportunities at nationwide field offices and preserves. You can search for opportunities by state online, or call (800) 628-2860 for the latest information on opportunities and application materials. Each office conducts its own recruiting, so it's best to apply to the state office that interests you.

It is thus with farming; if you do one thing late, you will be late in all your work.
—CATO THE ELDER

CHAPTER 8

SUSTAINABLE LIVING AND FARMING OPPORTUNITIES

In a world focused on technology and getting ahead at all costs, it might be time to look at life in a different way and focus on what's really important. This chapter is about the simple life and living more sustainably. It's for those who want to transform their world into something completely different by learning to become more self-reliant, connecting with the earth, integrating skills from the "good old days" that many of us take for granted, and leading a more balanced, harmonious, and holistic lifestyle. It is the same spirit referred to by the poet Gary Snyder when he advised, "Find your place on the planet and dig in." This chapter will give you the tools to do just that.

UNIQUE OPPORTUNITIES TO EXPLORE IN THIS CHAPTER

- As you dig into the organic farming opportunities in this chapter, the overviews of Community Supported Agriculture (page 313) and Rudolph Steiner's biodynamic method of farming (page 318) will provide insight in your new journey.

- Are you in search for some food for the soul? The importance of the whole—the balance of the mind, body, and spirit—is essential for anyone who wants to make a personal commitment to self-exploration, growth, and sustainable living. Come indulge in a variety of retreat centers with a holistic twist (page 325) as well as Catharine Sutherland's captivating story of her Hawaiian experience at Kalani Oceanside Retreat, which offers the promise of a new direction, a new adventure, and a new way of life (page 329).

- Is it true that we can live out our dreams by creating our own realities? Find out how Cori Stennett's internship at Hidden Villa unlocked her door of opportunity (page 349).

- Working in exchange for your keep is the basis of Willing Workers on Organic Farms. As a short-term volunteer, you'll help with organic farming, gardening, homesteading, or other environmentally conscious projects in exchange for room and three wholesome meals. Check out the special section beginning on page 374 for ideas on how to job hop all over the world.

GUIDESTONE FARM AND CENTER FOR SUSTAINABLE LIVING

The lifestyle at Guidestone Farm (page 342) centers around healthy habits through recycling, composting, eating healthful food, practicing alternative healing methods, celebrating life, and taking time to replenish (as these interns do with their pet lambs on the porch).

WHAT IS COMMUNITY SUPPORTED AGRICULTURE?

Community Supported Agriculture, commonly known as CSA, is an innovative program connecting local consumers with a local farmer for fresh and sustainably produced food. With its roots reaching back some forty years ago in Japan, the CSA concept soon traveled throughout Europe and was formally introduced in the U.S. in 1985 at a farm in Massachusetts.

One has to wonder why the CSA movement didn't start sooner than it did. Just turn to your parents or grandparents to uncover these answers. You'll find that most families lived more sustainably in years past—growing their own vegetables or raising chickens as a way of putting food on the table. But as supermarkets emerged as an easy way of getting these staples, the small family gardens of the U.S. soon diminished. Today you only have to bite into a tasteless tomato purchased from a supermarket to understand why there's nothing like indulging in the sweet taste of a locally grown one.

With over one thousand CSA farms in the U.S. alone, CSA shareholders make a commitment to support the farm throughout the season, assuming the costs, risks, and bounty of the harvest along with the farmer. In this way, farmers and members become partners in the production, distribution, and consumption of locally grown food.

A season's share generally amounts to about $50 per month, and in return, a weekly bag of fresh vegetables, herbs, fruits, milk, eggs, meat, flowers, and/or crafts is provided, depending on the season and the farm. Many farms also include newsletters filled with recipes and unique activities and events at the farm. This community-spirited CSA concept forms the framework for most internships and apprenticeships at farms in this chapter.

AMERICAN HORTICULTURAL SOCIETY— RIVER FARM

Gardens • Virginia • 3–6 Months
www.ahs.org/river_farm

$

River Farm serves as the headquarters of the American Horticultural Society (AHS), and is situated on a historic twenty-five-acre property along the Potomac River. Throughout the property, visitors will find several home demonstration gardens, plant collections, perennial gardens, a wildlife habitat

There is a tremendous strength that is growing in the world through sharing together, praying together, suffering together, and working together.
—MOTHER TERESA

garden, boxwood hedges, theme gardens, fruit orchards, and shade gardens. Horticultural interns assist with renovation, restoration, and maintenance of the gardens and grounds, and help with the children's gardening program and other special projects. Editorial interns work with the staff of *The American Gardener* magazine and gain experience in all facets of the editorial and production processes. Primary duties include researching and writing short articles, proofreading and fact-checking, and coordinating author and photographer submissions. All interns will also participate in society programs and projects, such as their annual seed program, open house events, lectures, and seminars, as well as guided field trips to sites such as the U.S. National Arboretum, Dumbarton Oaks, and Mt. Vernon. Internships of three to six months are available, with various start dates throughout the year. An $8-per-hour wage is provided and AHS will recommend housing in a local neighborhood. Applications are available online.

FOR MORE INFORMATION: Internship Coordinator, American Horticultural Society—River Farm, 7931 E. Boulevard Dr., Alexandria, VA 22308 (800) 777-7931 • (703) 768-5700, ext. 114 • (703) 765-8700 (fax) Horticulture: tgibson@ahs.org • Editorial: editor@ahs.org

ANANDA MARGA LAKE HUGHES PEACH FARM

Farming/Yoga/Meditation • California • Seasonal
www.peachfarm.amps.org

♥ ⚑ ⊕

Situated within the Angeles National Forest at an elevation of 2,500 feet, Ananda Marga Lake Hughes Peach Farm is a nonprofit yoga/meditation, ecological, and social service organization. More than 2,500 peach trees and 400 Asian pear and pluot trees are intercropped with forty thousand Japanese and globe eggplants, okra, fava beans, and melons. Interns are welcome year-round and participate in all activities of the farm, which may include transplanting, mulching, weeding, harvesting, packing, marketing, and transport. The hours are flexible, but usually six to eight hours per day, and conditions range from intense to laid-back depending on the time of the year or day of the week. Benefits include a shared room in a large house, vegetarian meals, and a yoga/meditation lifestyle (including free instruction). They also have a good supply of spiritual and farming/gardening reading material. Send a resume and letter including such things as educational background, work experience, farming experience, hobbies and interests, and background in meditation, yoga, or other spiritual disciplines.

FOR MORE INFORMATION: Allen Thurm, Internship and Volunteer Program, Ananda Marga Lake Hughes Peach Farm, 880 Elyria Dr., Los Angeles, CA 90065 (323) 225-3290 • (661) 724-1161 (farm) • amurtla@igc.org

APROVECHO RESEARCH CENTER

Organic Farming/Sustainable Education • Oregon • 10 Weeks
www.aprovecho.net

♥ ⚏ ⊕

Aprovecho, which means "make best use of" in Spanish, is the central theme of the center—to learn how to live together sustainably and ecologically and to help others around the world to do the same. The center is located in the abundant ecosystem of Oregon's Willamette Valley. Culturally rich Eugene is just thirty minutes away.

WHAT YOU'LL BE DOING: Groups of up to fourteen interns join ten resident staff members for an intensive ten-week learning experience. Daily classes and activities teach interns basic principles of sustainable forestry, organic gardening, indigenous skills, and appropriate technology. Classes take a holistic approach, combining lecture and discussion formats with practical, hands-on activities. Readings, independent projects, and field trips supplement other course work. Applying newly learned skills, interns will cook with food from the garden, heat and build with wood from the forest, make use of native plant species for food, medicine, and crafts, and utilize resource-conserving technologies to build a solar oven.

COMMITMENT: Internships span ten weeks, beginning in early March, June, and September. Classes typically run from 8 A.M. to 5 P.M., Monday through Friday. Weekends are open so interns can take advantage of Oregon's beautiful coastline, mountain ranges, and lakes and rivers.

PERKS AND REWARDS: The sliding scale tuition of $2,000 to $3,000 covers room, board, and instruction for the term. Interns generally need only a small amount of spending money, as most necessities are provided on-site. All interns live in an eco-friendly straw-bale dormitory.

THE ESSENTIALS: Acceptance into the program is based on enthusiasm, a sincere interest in the subjects of study, and a willingness to join in a cooperative learning experience. Participants come from varied backgrounds and have ranged in age from seventeen to sixty-four. Interns who want to learn to live in ways that are more ecologically and socially sustainable and to acquire specific practical and intellectual skills that will aid them on this path will thrive in this program.

Don't judge each day by the harvest you reap, but by the seeds you plant. 315
—ROBERT LOUIS STEVENSON

YOUR FIRST MOVE: Call for a brochure and application. Internships are offered on a space-available basis to qualified applicants.

FOR MORE INFORMATION: Interns Coordinator, Aprovecho Research Center, 80574 Hazelton Rd., Cottage Grove, OR 97424 • (541) 942-8198 • apro@efn.org

ARCOSANTI

Sustainable Education • Arizona • 3 Months
www.arcosanti.org

♥ ⚒ ⊕

Back in the early 1970s, an experimental town called Arcosanti emerged in the high desert of Arizona. Developed as a model for how the world might build its cities in an energy-efficient way, Arcosanti intends to house seven thousand people living and working together. Designed with the concept of "arcology" (the synthesis of architecture and ecology), Arcosanti hopes to demonstrate ways to improve urban conditions, prevent the spread of suburban sprawl, and lessen our destructive impact on the earth while simultaneously allowing interactions with the surrounding natural environment.

WHAT YOU'LL BE DOING: Arcosanti's five-week workshop introduces participants to building techniques and takes an intensive look at Paolo Soleri's concept of arcology by incorporating independent, creative thinking and a "learn by doing" approach. The first week is dedicated to seminars, lectures, and tours of the facility. The rest of the time is spent experientially working on projects, participating in cultural events, and taking a field trip to Phoenix to see sites of architectural interest. Completion of the Arcosanti workshop qualifies individuals to be considered for a three-month internship, with positions in archives, agriculture, construction, facilities and maintenance, graphics, landscaping, and planning and drafting.

PERKS AND REWARDS: There is a fee of $1,175 for both the five-week workshop and the internship program. The fee covers tuition, housing, meals during the workshop period (plan on an extra $280 for meals during the intern period), and use of site facilities. Workshop participants generally stay in a camp equipped with electricity, toilets, showers, and simple living shelters. There is potential for interns to move to an apartment on-site.

THE ESSENTIALS: Although there is a need for skilled workers, most participants are novices. Participants younger than eighteen years of age must be accompanied by a parent.

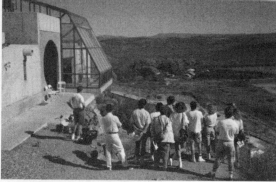

After exploring the energy-efficient structures of Arcosanti, prospective interns and guests view the organic garden area off in the distance.

MICHAEL LANDES

YOUR FIRST MOVE: Applications must include a cover letter outlining your interests and long-term goals, resume, portfolio (if applicable), and three letters of recommendation. A nonrefundable registration fee of $50 is required with the application, but it will be applied to the workshop fee total.

FOR MORE INFORMATION: Workshop Coordinator, Arcosanti, HC 74, Box 4136, Mayer, AZ 86333 • (928) 632-6233 • (928) 632-6229 (fax) workshop@arcosanti.org

ARCTIC ORGANICS

Organic Farming • Alaska • 4–7 Months
www.arcticorganics.com

$ 🏠

Arctic Organics, a twenty-acre farm set at the base of the Chugach Mountains in Alaska, focuses on intensive organic vegetable production. Interns interested in small-scale organic farming are needed from as early as March through early October, with varied start dates While fulfilling the general work needs of the farm, interns also take on individualized projects that focus on the greenhouse, field maintenance, planting, handy work, or harvesting. Benefits include a monthly food stipend, farm vegetables, lodging in the farm's bunkhouse, kitchen privileges, skills workshops, and weekly discussion groups. Applications will be reviewed and selections made as early as possible to accommodate those who will be traveling long distances.

FOR MORE INFORMATION: River and Sarah Bean, Owners, Arctic Organics, HC04, Box 9043, Palmer, AK 99645 • (907) 746-1087 • beans@alaska.com

The reason a lot of people do not recognize opportunity is because it usually goes around wearing overalls looking like hard work.
—THOMAS EDISON

BENEFICIAL FARM

Biodynamic Farming • New Mexico • 1 Week–1 Year+
www.beneficialfarm.com

As an off-the-grid homestead in the piñon-juniper wilderness at seven thousand feet near Santa Fe, Beneficial Farm uses biodynamic preparations and the Stella Natura calendar for growing vegetables, herbs, and flowers and raising seven hundred hens. A variety of short-term opportunities are available: apprentices work anywhere from three to twelve months (or more); working visitors have three-week to three-month stays; and working guests can come to the farm for five days to three weeks. Rustic housing, common meals, phone/Internet access, farm vehicle use, and weekly classes and activities are provided. Apprentices may receive a modest stipend depending on the duration of their stay (and their ability to learn and implement farm practices), while working guests are encouraged to make a donation for their farm experience. Santa Fe has a Waldorf school, an anthroposophical members group, and an active farmers' market. Call for more information.

FOR MORE INFORMATION: Steve Warshawer, Program Director, Beneficial Farm, 286 Arroyo Salado, Santa Fe, NM 87505 • (505) 422-2238 stevew@plateautel.net

BIODYNAMIC FARMING AND RUDOLF STEINER

When you begin your journey with biodynamic farming, you don't get very far into it before you are confronted with the philosophies from the forefather of the movement—Rudolf Steiner. Based on a series of lectures given by Dr. Steiner, the biodynamic concept centers around an organic method of agriculture that actively works with the health-giving forces of nature and the cosmic rhythms of the Stella Natura calendar. In essence, this means growing food with a strong connection to a healthy, living soil, and recognizing the basic principles at work in nature as well as those "from above."

Obviously the biodynamic concept has a jargon of its own and, perhaps, is best learned experientially from a farmer practicing these methods. (You'll find plenty of opportunities in this chapter!) A good introduction to these philosophies can also be found in the book *Gardening for Health and Nutrition: An Introduction to the Method of Biodynamic Gardening,* by John and Helen Philbrick (Garber Communications, $9.95).

> *In the seed we have an image of the whole universe. Each single time a seed is formed, the earthly organizing process is led to its end, to the point of chaos. And each time, within the seed-chaos, a new organism is built up out of the whole universe.*
>
> —RUDOLF STEINER

BROOKFIELD FARM

Biodynamic Farming · Massachusetts · 8 Months
www.brookfieldfarm.org

$ 🏠

As a living-learning center dedicated to promoting the development of healthy agriculture, Brookfield Farm is a 120-acre biodynamic farm that raises produce and meat for over four hundred CSA subscribers. Seasonal festivals, social events, and educational opportunities for children and adults provide a unique opportunity to create a community of people connected to each other through their connection to the earth. In 1986, Brookfield Farm was one of only three CSA farms in the U.S. Now there are over one thousand CSAs breathing new life into American farming.

WHAT YOU'LL BE DOING: If you are looking for an apprentice program that will teach you how to manage a mixed organic and biodynamic farm, not just how to go out and hoe, Brookfield is the place for you. During the course of the full season, apprentices work in all aspects of the farm's production, from soil preparation to harvest, tractors to hand hoes, and administration to marketing farm products. In addition, all apprentices may take part in the Collaborative Regional Alliance for Farmer Training (CRAFT) program, which offers in-depth tours to a wide variety of organic and biodynamic farms in the Northeast.

COMMITMENT: The program begins April 1 and concludes the day before Thanksgiving (no partial-season apprenticeships are possible). The work schedule is Monday through Friday, 6 A.M. to 5 P.M. (with one-hour breaks for breakfast and lunch) and Saturdays until noon.

PERKS AND REWARDS: A stipend of $500 per month, housing with a private room (with shared kitchen, living room, and bathroom), farm produce (vegetables, fruits, flowers, and herbs), weekday lunches at the farmhouse, and full health insurance (if needed) are provided. Apprentices can also purchase Brookfield Farm meat for half price and take up to fifty pounds of produce per year as gifts for family and friends.

THE ESSENTIALS: Anyone with a serious interest in agriculture and the physical ability to work the long hours of a farming schedule will be considered— from inexperienced city folks looking to explore agriculture as a career option to experienced farmers looking for a new approach to agriculture.

YOUR FIRST MOVE: To start the application process, send a letter of intent and resume. All interested applicants are encouraged to set up a time to visit and work on the farm. All hiring decisions will be made on a first-come, first-served basis.

Watching something grow is good for morale. It helps you believe in life.   **319**
—MYRON KAUFMANN

FOR MORE INFORMATION: Dan Kaplan, Apprenticeship Program, Brookfield Farm, 24 Hulst Rd., Amherst, MA 01002 • (413) 253-7991 info@brookfieldfarm.org

COLD POND COMMUNITY FARM AND LAND TRUST

Biodynamic Farming • New Hampshire • 1 Year/Seasonal

$ 🏠

Cold Pond Community Farm and Land Trust, a biodynamic, horse-powered intentional farm community in the hills of New Hampshire, offers a yearlong apprenticeship for singles or couples as well as seasonal internships throughout the year. The farm community depends on a year-round cycle of activities for their own food and for income to meet expenses. The emphasis is on producing high-quality food and crafts for themselves and for their shareholders, and on developing an ecologically sustainable community that will continue to be productive in years to come. Apprentices and interns are involved in this year-round cycle of activities, with work that is highly dependent on the seasons and the weather and that may involve the CSA and market garden, maple syrup, honey bees, food preservation, orchard and berries, dairy cows, poultry, logging, woodshop, and pottery. A small rustic cabin, a share of all produce, and a stipend are provided in exchange for labor in the fields and woodlot five days a week. The farm is specifically looking for motivated and energetic individuals interested in learning the skills needed to work on a sustainable farm or making a career out of farming. Call or email for more information.

FOR MORE INFORMATION: Steve Davis, Owner, Apprentice/Intern Program, Cold Pond Community Farm and Land Trust, P.O. Box 95, Cold Pond Rd., Acworth, NH 03601 • (603) 835-2403 • cpclt1@email.com

COMMON GROUND ORGANIC FARM

Organic Farming • Pennsylvania • Seasonal
www.commongroundfarm.com

$ 🏠 🌐

As an eighty-two-acre diversified organic farm in the Appalachian Mountains of central Pennsylvania, Common Ground raises vegetables, flowers, and lamb for two local farmers' markets. Each year three to six volunteers have the opportunity to gain experience in what it takes to create a successful organic farming system. Volunteers work with the farmer and farm manager, performing a variety of tasks determined by the season and weather (from livestock care and vegetable harvesting to selling produce and giving farm tours). Housing (in a cabin, camper, or farmhouse) and meals are provided. Educational activities include field trips to other farms, conferences, seminars, and workshops. Applications are available online.

FOR MORE INFORMATION: Leslie Zuck, Volunteer Program, Common Ground Organic Farm, 176 Zuck Rd., Spring Mills, PA 16875 (814) 364-9171 • (814) 364-2330 (fax) • commongro@aol.com

DAWN INSTITUTE GARDEN

Farming • California • 6 Weeks–6 Months

$ 🏠

Just a short walk from swimming holes and miles of forested trails, as well as the Bucks Lake Wilderness, Feather River, and the small "bustling" town of Quincy, the Dawn Institute Garden practices small-scale sustainable agriculture and sells a variety of vegetables and fruits at farmer's markets, grocery stores, and restaurants. In addition, Dawn offers models of sustainable agriculture and alternative energy as well as facilities for educational and social gatherings. From May through October, with flexible arrival and departure dates, interns will work fifteen hours per week in the gardens and three hours per week at the Dawn Community House (with ample time for self-motivated study and personal rejuvenation). Garden work includes everything from cultivating and compost making to harvesting and work at the farmer's markets. A minimum stay of six weeks is necessary to get a taste of garden work in each stage of the season. Benefits include a daytime communal space in a renovated farmhouse, a campsite to sleep under the Sierra sky, produce from the garden, a monthly stipend of $50, hands-on training, and weekly readings and discussions. The internship is best suited to beginning or intermediate gardeners who are willing to work hard and have a fun-loving attitude. Send off a cover letter and resume to begin the application process. An on-site visit is strongly encouraged before committing to a position.

FOR MORE INFORMATION: Garden Manager, Dawn Institute Garden, P.O. Box 32, Crescent Mills, CA 95934 • (530) 284-6036 • digarden@hotmail.com

Let us be grateful to people who make us happy; they are the charming gardeners who make our souls blossom.
—MARCEL PROUST

EDUCATIONAL CONCERNS
FOR HUNGER ORGANIZATION

Farming/Ministry/Hunger Awareness • Florida/Haiti • 12–15 Months
www.echonet.org

$ 🏠 🌐

Educational Concerns for Hunger Organization (ECHO) cultivates one of the largest collections of tropical food plants in the U.S. The fifty-acre farm serves as a training facility for interns, as an educational tool for public tours, and as a production farm for seeds and nursery plants.

WHAT YOU'LL BE DOING: Interns spend twelve months in Florida engaging in hands-on, experiential learning activities related to sustainable agriculture in the tropics. Common activities include growing tropical foods (including underexploited plants and fruit and multipurpose trees), caring for animals, and maintaining the various demonstrations. All interns help harvest, process seed orders, supervise the work of local volunteers, and lead educational tours for visiting individuals and groups. The climax of the internship is an optional three-month, cross-cultural experience in Haiti, which gives interns an opportunity to live and work in an actual third-world setting while working with farmers or urban gardeners.

PERKS AND REWARDS: Benefits include housing in apartment-style dorms, a $350 to $450 monthly stipend, health insurance, and travel expenses to Florida. Interns must raise their own support for the three months in Haiti, which is usually done through churches, friends, and relatives. ECHO provides a monthly stipend for each intern and often has matching funds available for up to 50 percent of the expenses.

THE ESSENTIALS: A bachelor's degree is required, although a degree in agriculture or previous farm or gardening experience is not mandatory (albeit helpful). A sincere Christian commitment and a strong body able to do manual work are essential. Most interns come to ECHO right after getting their bachelor's degree.

YOUR FIRST MOVE: Application materials can be found online, or call or email for more information. Completed applications must be received by September 15 for positions opening January through May, and by February 1 for positions opening June to December.

FOR MORE INFORMATION: David Balsbaugh, Educational Programs Director, Educational Concerns for Hunger Organization, 17391 Durrance Rd., North Fort Myers, FL 33917 • (239) 543-3246 • (239) 543-5317 (fax) dbalsbaugh@echonet.org

EMANDAL—A FARM ON A RIVER

Organic Farming/Sustainable Education • California • 2–10 Months
www.emandal.com

$ 🏕

Emandal—A Farm on a River, a thousand-acre organic mountain ranch, has been home to three generations of the Adams family. In addition to operating as a family camp since 1908, the farm hosts an environmental education program, destination weddings, and group rentals. Fine jams, syrups, hot cereals, and baking mixes are produced on-site and sold through mail order, while baked goods, brick-oven sourdough bread, and cut flowers are sold at a local farmer's market. The farm's philosophy is one of self-sufficiency, both mental and physical, as an individual and as part of a community, to ensure viability in our changing world.

YOUR SURROUNDINGS: Emandal is located in the heart of Mendocino County, on the main fork of the Eel River. This is a land where biomes of the arid Southwest and rainy Northwest overlap and interact, creating an incredible diversity of plants and wildlife. Set into this wilderness is Emandal, with its acres of fruits and vegetables that feed all who experience life on the farm.

WHAT YOU'LL BE DOING: Emandal provides a learning environment and a chance to do something constructive while pondering life's choices. Throughout the changing seasons, assistant gardeners, cooks, farmworkers, and naturalists converge on the farm to develop their talents while encouraging goodwill among the guests and staff alike. Typical job assignments include trail building, firewood gathering, painting cabins, fixing fences, planting

An organic farm instructor teaches participants about the wonders of growing vegetables at Emandal—A Farm on a River.

EMANDAL—A FARM ON A RIVER

seeds, washing clothes, making jam, packing mail-order boxes, feeding animals, butchering chickens, building compost, constructing rock walls, gardening, or creating meals.

COMMITMENT: Positions are full-time (forty hours per week for most positions, except naturalists, who work up to fifty hours per week) and range from two to ten months. Days and time off change dramatically with the seasons.

PERKS AND REWARDS: Most stipends range from $180 to $250 per week, plus a private room in shared employee housing and delicious family-style meals.

THE ESSENTIALS: The farm is ideal for transitioning from one life experience to another—whether at the end of school, between jobs, before a trip around the world, or while making a decision about a career change. Those who want to make a positive difference in people's lives while at the same time connecting with the earth and finding "the Zen" in manual labor will thrive here.

YOUR FIRST MOVE: Detailed information and application materials can be found online.

FOR MORE INFORMATION: Tamara Adams, Owner, Emandal—A Farm on a River, 16500 Hearst Post Office Rd., Willits, CA 95490 • (707) 459-5439 (707) 459-1808 (fax) • info@emandal.com

FOOD BANK FARM

Organic Farming • Massachusetts • 1–8 Months
www.foodbankwma.org/farm

$ 🏠

Located in the "five college area" of western Massachusetts (also known as the "happy valley"), Food Bank Farm grows and harvests organic vegetables, flowers, and small fruits for over six hundred CSA shareholders. But they don't stop there—the farm also donates almost half of its production to the nonprofit Western Massachusetts Food Bank. The farm is a constant bustle of community activity. From sunup to sundown, shareholders can be found picking up veggies, using the farm as a personal retreat, or participating in the full-moon potlucks at a bonfire under the stars. Meanwhile, apprentices are hard at work learning about all aspects of the farm's operation—from planning and land preparation to harvesting and planting of cover crops. Apprentices have the option of a full-season apprenticeship (from April or May to December 15) or a summer "planting" apprenticeship (from mid-May to mid-June). A stipend of $550 to $750 is provided, along with housing in a renovated eighteenth-century farmhouse, all the organic produce you can eat, and weekly yoga classes. Those who have an interest in both agriculture and feeding those in need, who have plenty of stamina and spirit, and who enjoy working with others will thrive at Food Bank Farm. Send off a cover letter, resume, and three references, or call or email for more information. It's best to apply between the months of December and March.

FOR MORE INFORMATION: Michael Doctor, Apprenticeship Coordinator, Food Bank Farm, 121 Bay Rd., Hadley, MA 01035 • (413) 582-0013 foodbankfarm@yahoo.com

FOOD FOR THE SOUL: RETREAT CENTERS WITH A HOLISTIC TWIST

· ·

The journey to wholeness requires that you look honestly, openly, and with courage into yourself, into the dynamics that lie behind what you feel, what you perceive, what you value, and how you act. It is a journey through your defenses and beyond, so that you can experience consciously the nature of your personality, face what it has produced in your life, and choose to change that. Words lead to deeds. They prepare the soul, make it ready, and move it to tenderness.

—GARY ZUKOV

Meditation—aerobic conditioning for the mind.

In the silence of meditation, the soulful songs of Sufi dance, the vitality and healthful benefits of yoga, the study of ancient disciplines of the East, or the healing techniques of Gestalt therapy, holistic retreat centers are providing something that's missing in so many people's lives—food for the soul. From ecovillages and monasteries to yoga institutes and Zen centers, this special section offers unique opportunities for hard work, personal growth, reflection and rejuvenation, spiritual exploration, and community building. The work component at each center is generally basic and rudimentary (from working in the gardens to housekeeping); however, the real draw is participation in a collection of stimulating classes and workshops, connecting with inspiring and supportive people, and indulging in fresh, organic meals. With a one-month commitment for most programs, this may be the hiatus you need to reawaken your soul.

The whole soul is composed into a kind of real harmony the instant one sets oneself to work.
—THOMAS CARLYLE

BIRCH CREEK ARTS AND ECOLOGY CENTER AT TRILLIUM FARM

Intentional Community • Oregon • 3 Months+
www.deepwild.org

♥ ⛺

Birch Creek Arts and Ecology Center at Trillium Community is a wilderness sanctuary and ecovillage in the Siskiyou Mountains of southern Oregon. Internships are a unique opportunity to spend a season or more (usually a three-month minimum from spring through autumn) at their rustic wilderness homestead and college campus, immersed in intentional community and beautiful natural surroundings. Learn about organic gardening, alternative building methods, permaculture, natural history, environmental ethics and activism, hosting large events and gatherings, wilderness homesteading, harmonizing with the seasons, living in place, creating beauty, and celebrating community, spirituality, and land stewardship. Benefits include shared or single living space in a rustic cabin and use of the center's facilities. All residents share in community food staples, to which all contribute. There are also opportunities to earn academic credit through self-directed, experiential courses offered by the Dakubetede Environmental Education Programs (through Antioch University) for an extra fee. Highly motivated vegetarian folks who love the natural world and approach life with an attitude of integrity and optimism, and who are willing to learn new ways of living, working, and serving will thrive here. Call or email for more information or find details online.

FOR MORE INFORMATION: Internship Coordinator, Birch Creek Arts and Ecology Center at Trillium Farm, P.O. Box 1330, Jacksonville, OR 97530 (541) 899-1712 • deep@deepwild.org

DHARMA PUBLISHING

Buddhist Studies • California • 6 Months+
www.dharmapublishing.com

♥ ⛺ 🌐

Founded by Tarthang Tulku, a Tibetan lama who came to the U.S. in 1968, Dharma Publishing prepares and prints traditional sacred Tibetan texts and art for Tibetan refugees in India. For those who have an interest in Buddhist studies, meditation, and the application of Buddhist practice in a work environment, Dharma offers a six-month work-study program. Volunteers work full-time in positions such as production, sales, mailing, shipping, and finance while taking four classes a week in subjects that include meditation, Kum Nye

(Tibetan relaxation techniques), Buddhist philosophy and psychology, skillful means, and classical Tibetan language study. Participants can also take part in two weekend workshops each quarter. Shared rooms at the Nyingma Institute (www.nyingmainstitute.com) and meals are provided. Individuals who are willing to view work as a source of learning and who possess a strong commitment to personal growth will thrive in this environment. Applications are available online.

FOR MORE INFORMATION: Work Study Program Coordinator, Dharma Publishing, 2910 San Pablo Ave., Berkeley, CA 94702 • (800) 873-4276 • (510) 548-5407 (510) 548-2330 (fax) • dp@dharmapublishing.com

ESALEN INSTITUTE

Holistic Learning/Yoga/Meditation • California • 1–3 Months
www.esalen.org

♥ ⛺ ⊕

Founded in the early 1960s, the world's first alternative education and holistic center has flourished, continually pushing the envelope of human potential. Esalen is situated on twenty-seven acres along the spectacular Big Sur coastline, once home to a Native American tribe known as the Esselen. Many

ESALEN INSTITUTE

In addition to learning about holistic practices—from massage to meditation—Esalen work-study students spend time working together in the laundry facility.

first-timers to the center opt for the "Experiencing Esalen" workshop, which provides an introduction to holistic practices, such as Gestalt therapy, massage, sensory awareness, creative arts, and meditation. For those interested in a more intense and complete involvement in the center, Esalen offers a four-week work-study program. Participants work thirty-two hours per week in one of Esalen's departments—kitchen, housekeeping, garden/farm, maintenance, or grounds—along with staff and long-term students. During most evenings and one weekend intensive, students are together with assigned leaders in groups exploring different practices and approaches available at the center. The program fee of $895 also covers shared housing, healthful food, participation in regularly scheduled movement classes, use of the Art Barn, and enjoyment of round-the-clock access to the Esalen baths. Work-study participants may be invited to remain for a second or third month (with lower fees) depending on space availability and community needs. Applications and specific details about each session can be found online, or email Esalen for more information.

FOR MORE INFORMATION: Mary Anne Will, Work Study Coordinator, Esalen Institute, 55000 Highway 1, Big Sur, CA 93920-9616 • (831) 667-3010 (831) 667-3069 (fax) • workstudy@esalen.org

KALANI OCEANSIDE RETREAT

Retreat Center/Yoga/Meditation • Hawaii • 1–3 Months
www.kalani.com

♥ ⋔ ⊕

Surrounded by thermal springs, orchid farms, tidal pools, waterfalls, botanical gardens, historic villages, and spectacular Volcanoes National Park, Kalani treats guests to Hawaii's aloha comfort, offering personal retreats that encompass adventure, wellness, natural steam baths, yoga, Hawaiian dance, music, art, and food for the soul.

WHAT YOU'LL BE DOING: Throughout the year, volunteers at Kalani support the day-to-day activities of the center and provide assistance in maintenance, food service, housekeeping, and landscaping. Upon arrival at the center, each volunteer is provided with a journal to capture his or her own growth and lessons learned, through writing and artwork—a necessary tool to prepare for life's next adventure.

COMMITMENT: Resident volunteers must commit to a three-month period, volunteering thirty hours per week in an assigned department, while volunteer scholars commit to a one-month period and assist twenty hours per week.

PERKS AND REWARDS: A participation fee ($900 for a one-month program; $1,200 for a three-month program) includes organic and locally grown vegetarian meals (with a fish or poultry option at dinner), community living in A-frame structures, a week of free time (for personal relaxation, exploration, or intensive study), and the option of instruction in a Level I Kalani Wellness Practitioner certification. Ongoing activities and instruction include volcano and native plant treks, dolphin swims, snorkeling, hula, Lauhala weaving, massage, Hawaiian mythology and language classes, ecstatic dance, shiatsu, and yoga.

THE ESSENTIALS: Strong and self-motivated individuals will thrive at Kalani. Volunteers must provide their own medical insurance to cover their entire stay and proof of a return airline ticket.

YOUR FIRST MOVE: Applications can be found online, or call or email for more information.

FOR MORE INFORMATION: Resident Volunteer Coordinator, Kalani Oceanside Retreat, RR2, Box 4500, Beach Rd., Pahoa, HI 96778-9724 • (800) 800-6886 (808) 965-0468, ext. 117 • (808) 965-0527 (fax) • volunteer@kalani.com

THE PROMISE OF A NEW DIRECTION, A NEW ADVENTURE, AND A NEW WAY OF LIFE

When I arrived at Kalani Oceanside Retreat on the Big Island of Hawaii one warm, rainy November afternoon, I thought my story would be startlingly unique. I mean, how many people in the world quit their jobs, pack their lives into storage units, and fly to Hawaii to spend their days peeling carrots at a tiny resort tucked into a tropical jungle—with no idea of what they'll do next, or even where they'll live when three months are up? At age twenty-five, I'd recently quit my job as an assistant editor at a successful publishing house to test the waters of freelance writing. After six months, I was ready to kiss my keyboard good-bye, leave the mountains for the sea, and get my fingernails dirty. "Why was I working? What, other than paying the light bill, was I accomplishing?" I thought, frustrated. I sought a life with meaning and direction, and I had no qualms about leaving job and home security to find it.

Much to my surprise, neither did anyone else at Kalani! My first evening dining on the *lanai,* or outdoor patio, I quickly discovered that I was surrounded by fellow work-scholars who had come to Kalani for exactly the same reasons I had: to escape the push-button, digitized,

I am beginning to learn that it is the sweet, simple things of life which are the real ones after all. 329
—LAURA INGALLS WILDER

ATM-everything, mile-a-minute lifestyle that has become so rampant in the world and the computer-keyboard-phone-desk-chair routine of daily office existence; to find a place where nature's sweet and soothing song could be savored one fragrant *pau-kini-kini* blossom at a time; and, most of all, to become quiet enough to hear our inner voices speak, and to slow down enough to listen to them. For many of us, Kalani held the promise of a new direction, a new adventure, and a new way of life.

Kalani's work-scholar volunteer program, as it turned out, was a magnet for individuals in life transition—as well as those who simply desired a sabbatical from fulfilling careers or a three-month vacation in the sun. From burnt-out New York City "dot-commers" to carefree Kansas retirees, the staff I grew to know and love was home to all kinds. We'd found our way there through friends who had visited, Internet searches, and, in my case, this guidebook! I worked in the kitchen, putting my interest in culinary school to the test. Slicing pineapples and bananas as the sun rose over coconut palms and doing dishes by candlelight when the generator shut down was unlike any other restaurant experience I'd had. I also helped on the waitstaff, coaxing tiny geckos away from the sugar bowl and serving bountiful plates of whole-food meals to delighted guests hungry after a day of yoga or snorkeling. Other volunteers toted their weight in sheets and towels on the housekeeping crew or built new A-frame huts as grounds maintenance staff.

When I wasn't working, I walked or rode a staff bike a mile and a half down the Red Road (a two-lane road that retains its familiar name, despite a recent coat of black asphalt) to Kehena Beach, a secluded strip of black sand accessible only by descending a winding, stairstep path along the black lava cliffs. Clothing on the beach was optional and the water sparkled, brilliantly blue and clear. I swam with dolphins in the small bay twice during the winter months, and once, pedaling home, a friend and I stopped and stared, awestruck, at a humpback whale a short distance offshore. She was slapping her huge tail against the water over and over, as if in a greeting to us. We hardly breathed until she disappeared beneath the blue water, and even then we looked at each other so full of joy and amazement we couldn't speak; instead, we whooped and sang all the way home.

I spent early mornings, late afternoons, and moonlit nights on the point, a grassy knoll perched above thrashing white foam where the sea crashed into black cliffs. It was the perfect spot to watch the sun rise out of the ocean or to gather for a drum circle after dark. Riding bikes to the tidal pools and thermal baths, we often stopped to pick fresh guava from the lush green foliage on the roadside. The fruits were bright yellow like lemons, with a pink, succulent flesh full of seeds. I trekked across a lava field to see hot, flowing, orange lava, and placed a red leaf in its path—an offering to Pelé, revered goddess of the volcano, who hungrily engulfed and accepted it. Lying in bed in my open-air A-frame hut after such full days, I could hear the waves of the ocean and see banana trees silhouetted in the moonlight.

In the midst of captivating beauty and activity, I learned many new things: the basics of Zen Buddhist meditation, Reiki healing techniques, the songs of Sufi dancing. Yet the most important thing I brought home from Kalani was a strong certainty about something I already suspected: that the universe operates perfectly, and that by trusting my inner guidance and a higher universal power, I will be guided along the path I am to walk in this lifetime. There is no need to worry. I am a wonderfully powerful being, capable of creating my own reality with my thoughts and actions—for better or for worse. The most magical part of my Hawaiian experience was being surrounded by people who embraced this view of the world in everyday life.

I left Kalani in May, two months later than planned, but at exactly the right time. My homeward journey was a complete test of the faith I'd strengthened during my sun- (and rain-) drenched days on the Big Island. I had to have faith; I had no job, no money, and nowhere to call home! I was not disappointed. Thanks to my family, my college degree, and the infallibility of the universe, I followed my path to a job in college public relations and a perfect apartment just blocks from my childhood home in a city I never dreamed I'd return to. It all fell so beautifully into place that I now feel sure of a truth I didn't even realize I was seeking: I'm in the writing business for a reason greater than paying the light bill. And, my curiosity piqued, I plan to stick around and see what it is.

—Contributed by Catharine Sutherland, who is enjoying a return to professional life that involves shoes, earrings, and deodorant! In addition to her work as a public information specialist at Greensboro College in North Carolina, Catharine practices yoga daily (along with teaching yoga classes for children), cohosts a kids' poetry club, happily creates art, and treads softly upon the earth. You can reach Catharine at yippeecat_2000@yahoo.com.

Catharine Sutherland outside her open-air A-frame hut at Kalani, just a short walk from the black sands of Kehena Beach.

A talent is something given, that opens like a flower, but without exceptional energy, discipline, and persistence will never bear fruit.
—MAY SARTON

331

If I could have my way about it, I would go back there and remain the rest of my days. It is paradise! If a man is rich, he can live expensively and his grandeur will be respected as in other parts of the earth. If he is poor, he can herd with the natives and live on next to nothing; he can sun himself all day long under the palm trees, and be no more troubled by his conscience than a butterfly would. When you are in that blessed retreat, you are safe from the turmoil of life. The past is a forgotten thing, the present is forever, the future you leave to take care of itself.

—MARK TWAIN, ON HAWAII

KRIPALU CENTER FOR YOGA AND HEALTH

Yoga/Meditation • Massachusetts • 1–12 Weeks
www.kripalu.org

♥ 🏠 🌐

Located in a former Jesuit seminary in the Berkshires of Massachusetts, Kripalu guest programs serve up every possible permutation of yoga—ranging from yoga camps for adults and Thai yoga massage to exploring your life's mission and meditation retreats. A day at Kripalu is filled with workshops, daily yoga, meditation, DansKinetics classes, relaxation in whirlpools and saunas, and healthful vegetarian food choices (animal protein available as needed). This is a true sanctuary for your body and soul.

WHAT YOU'LL BE DOING: Based on the yogic principle of *seva*, or selfless service, Kripalu volunteers serve in "off the mat" karma-yoga programs by sharing their time and energy—a lifestyle that supports the discovery of new ways to express each participant's energy and reveal his or her highest potential. With programs available throughout the year, the most popular is the one- to four-week Seva Program, where participants live a balanced spiritual lifestyle while serving forty hours per week alongside the staff. Be prepared to engage in an active, vigorous workweek that may involve chopping vegetables, cleaning bathrooms, washing dishes, or performing basic maintenance tasks. Those who desire a more in-depth transformation at all levels (physical, emotional, mental, and spiritual) opt for the intensive, three-month Spiritual Lifestyle Program.

KRIPALU CENTER FOR YOGA AND HEALTH

Along with a day filled with yoga, meditation, and healthful vegetarian meals, a volunteer with Kripalu shares her time and energy in an "off the mat" work assignment.

PERKS AND REWARDS: Volunteers receive dormitory-style housing and three healthy vegetarian meals per day (with a fresh salad bar and homemade breads). When not serving, volunteers can attend daily yoga and meditation classes, workshops, and evening concerts, and have access to the sauna, whirlpool, and weight room. Some yoga and evening workshops are required.

THE ESSENTIALS: Although practically every age and professional background is represented in Kripalu programs, volunteers all have a strong personal intention to learn and practice techniques that bring transformation and inner harmony. Participants must be at least eighteen, and a willingness to serve others is essential.

YOUR FIRST MOVE: It's strongly recommend that you attend a guest program or come for two days of rest and renewal before volunteering. The Seva Program runs weekly from Sunday to Sunday; the three-month Spiritual Lifestyle Program is offered each month. It's suggested that you apply at least two to three months prior to your anticipated start date, and at least four months in advance for the Spiritual Lifestyle Program.

FOR MORE INFORMATION: Volunteer Programs, Kripalu Center for Yoga and Health, P.O. Box 793, Lenox, MA 01240-0793 • (413) 448-3123 (413) 448-3384 (fax) • (800) 546-1556 (job hotline) • longterm@kripalu.org

Each dawn holds a new hope for a new plan, making the start of each day the start of a new life.   **333**
—GINA BLAIR

LOSANG DRAGPA CENTRE

Buddhist Studies/Yoga/Meditation · United Kingdom · Seasonal
www.losangdragpa.com

♥ ⌂ ⊕

Losang Dragpa Buddhist Centre, located in an unusual and picturesque Victorian castle surrounded by twenty-four acres, is a college and retreat center that is home to thirty-five (and growing) lay and ordained Buddhists of all ages and backgrounds. The center provides a place where people can learn about the Buddhist way of life through meditation classes, study programs, and retreats. The activities of the community reflect the Buddhist principle of leading a pure and simple way of life. In exchange for thirty-five hours a week on projects including gardening, decorating, and building, participants receive food, warm and cozy dormitory-style accommodations, and meditation sessions and evening classes.

FOR MORE INFORMATION: Working Visits Program, Losang Dragpa Centre, Buddhist College and Meditation Centre, Dobroyd Castle, Pexwood Rd., Todmorden, West Yorkshire OL14 7JJ, United Kingdom · (011) 44-1706-812247 (011) 44-1706-818901 (fax) · info@losangdragpa.com

Work-exchange participants at Losang Dragpa Centre learn about the Buddhist way of life at this unusual and picturesque Victorian castle.

MEDITATION AT LOSANG DRAGPA

Meditation is a method for changing our state of mind from a negative to a positive one—from anger to love and compassion, emotional turmoil to peace and contentment. If we wish to experience happiness (and we recognize that happiness is a state of mind), we can see that if we want to be happy, then we need to change our mind. That's what meditation helps us to do.

There are many different types of meditation available nowadays. In Buddhist meditation we begin with breathing meditation to calm our mind. Then we meditate on specific qualities, or attitudes, such as cherishing others, love, and compassion.

The more familiar we are with positive, peaceful states of mind, the calmer we become. Eventually, by training our mind to become peaceful, we will be happy all the time, even in the most difficult circumstances. The opposite is also true—if our mind is not peaceful, then even when we experience wonderful external conditions, we will not be happy.

MAHO BAY CAMPS

Sustainable Education · Virgin Islands · 1–6 Months
www.maho.org

♥ ⛺ ⊕

Maho Bay Resorts combines an environmental consciousness and green philosophy—pioneering the latest techniques in sustainable resort development, conservation, recycling, and site restoration, along with close-to-nature experiences and economy. Environmentally designed tent-cottages, which are surrounded by Virgin Islands National Park and the turquoise waters and white sandy beaches of the Caribbean, provide plenty of creature comforts without disturbing the creatures that were there before we were. Activities on the premises range from sailing and snorkeling to educational programs and yoga. For those who wish to blend a vacation adventure along with some work, Maho provides a work-exchange program. Volunteers contribute four hours per day of work to the Maho community, and in return receive a low-cost Caribbean vacation with free lodging and a nonoptional meal plan at $55 per week. No experience is necessary; however, volunteers must be at least eighteen years of age, and stay a minimum of one month between May 1 and October 15. Work assignments might include housekeeping, maintenance,

Meditate. Live purely. Be quiet. Do your work with mastery.
Like the moon, come out from behind the clouds. Shine!
—BUDDHA

food services, store assistance, or guest registration. Applications are accepted online from December 15 through April 15.

FOR MORE INFORMATION: Residential Manager, 4-Hour Worker Program, Maho Bay Camps, Box 310, Saint John, VI 00830 • (800) 392-9004 (340) 776-6226 • (340) 776-6504 (fax) • work@maho.org

OMEGA INSTITUTE FOR HOLISTIC STUDIES

Holistic Learning/Yoga/Meditation • New York • 2–7 Months
www.eomega.org

$ 🏠 ⊕

Omega Institute began in the mid-1970s, when holistic health, psychological inquiry, and new forms of spiritual practice were just budding in American culture. Since then, they have become one of the country's largest alternative education and retreat centers, focusing on every imaginable aspect of mind, body, and spirit. More than twelve thousand guests come to Omega each year to participate in workshops and professional training seminars in diverse areas such as psychology, health, spiritual studies, communication, sports, the arts, the environment, and social action. The Rhinebeck campus is spread over 150 acres of rolling hills, an inviting waterfront, and garden areas in the Hudson Valley (just two hours north of New York City).

WHAT YOU'LL BE DOING: A season at the institute offers a unique opportunity for hard work, personal growth, spiritual exploration, and community building. Each year four hundred staff members from all ages and backgrounds join together to work and grow alongside like-minded people. The work itself is basic and rudimentary, with a majority of jobs focusing on maintenance, housekeeping, food service, and luggage handling. There are also a number of jobs in administration, as well as lifeguard and first aid staff, and a limited number of supervisory positions. The real draw, however, is participation in a collection of stimulating staff classes taught by respected faculty, with a curriculum designed to support the process of self-discovery within the context of community life. Topics include bodywork, yoga, tai chi, alternative health, psychological studies, performing and visual arts, sports and play, and esoteric studies.

COMMITMENT: Participants must commit to at least one work period (approximately seven weeks) or stay for the entire seven-month season, which begins in April and continues through October.

PERKS AND REWARDS: Benefits include a weekly stipend of $50 (for full-time work), housing in the dorms or tents, wholesome meals, and use of the facilities.

THE ESSENTIALS: Whether you are in career transition, a college student looking to gain work and life skills over the summer, or an active retiree who wants to participate in community living and could offer mentoring to younger staff, anyone over the age of eighteen is considered for seasonal opportunities.

YOUR FIRST MOVE: Applications are available online (or by fax, phone, or email). It's important that you read the Myths and Realities form (which is online) prior to submitting your application. Hiring starts in early February.

FOR MORE INFORMATION: Toni Sinopoli, Staff Manager, Omega Institute for Holistic Studies, 150 Lake Dr., Rhinebeck, NY 12572-3252 (845) 266-4444, ext. 304 • (845) 266-8691 (fax) • sdd@eomega.org

THE OPTION INSTITUTE

Happiness Center • Massachusetts • 1–2 Months
www.option.org

♥ 🏠 ⊕

Imagine making a conscious commitment to help yourself and others live happier, more successful, and more peaceful lives! The Option Institute offers a two-month residential volunteer program six times each year, where you'll work on various community service projects and at the same time experience a lifestyle that fosters personal happiness. The service component entails support staff work in food service, housekeeping, office support, and grounds maintenance. You'll also be serving people—oftentimes people who are experiencing challenges and have come to the institute to reconstruct their lives. In weekly classes that challenge you to choose how you want to be in this world, you'll learn tools and ideas that participants have used to profoundly improve the quality of their lives. Volunteers also support the work of the Son-Rise Program, a unique method of working with children with special needs and their families. Room, vegetarian meals, weekly classes, "Option Process" dialogues, and a personal "happiness coach" are the biggest perks, not to mention being located in one of the most beautiful regions of New England—the Berkshires in western Massachusetts. Applications can be found online.

FOR MORE INFORMATION: Matthew Wheeler, Volunteer Supervisor, The Option Institute, International Learning and Training Center, 2080 S. Undermountain Rd., Sheffield, MA 01257-9643 • (800) 714-2779 (413) 229-2100 • (413) 229-8931 (fax) • volunteer@option.org

When you are content to be simply yourself and don't compare or compete,
everybody will respect you.
—LAO-TZU

✒ **INSIDER TIP: We seek enthusiastic, energetic individuals who want to wholeheartedly serve others, and who want to explore the idea of learning through service.**

SHAMBHALA MOUNTAIN CENTER

Yoga/Meditation • Colorado • 1 Week–6 Months+
www.shambhalamountain.org

♥ ⛪

Located on six hundred acres in northern Colorado, Shambhala Mountain Center offers hundreds of programs on Buddhist meditation, yoga, and other contemplative disciplines. Tamed by thirty years of use as a contemplative retreat center, Shambhala Mountain is a place where one of the basic truths of Buddhism—that people can be profoundly open to the wisdom of the present moment—is always readily available. Throughout the year there are many opportunities to join the community as a volunteer or work-study-intensive participant for a week, a month, or more. Positions include helping with tent village setup in the spring, working in the kitchens, housekeeping, and apprenticing in the botanic gardens. The basic schedule includes six hours of work each day (six days a week), daily group meditation, weekly instruction and discussion of meditation, and activities ranging from volleyball to movie nights. Room and hearty meals are provided, along with ongoing classes in Buddhism and Shambhala Training. Those willing to make a longer-term commitment may receive a stipend. Call or email for more information.

FOR MORE INFORMATION: Human Resource Manager, Shambhala Mountain Center, 4921 County Rd., 68C. Red Feather Lakes, CO 80545 (970) 881-2184, ext. 308 • (970) 881-2909 (fax) • hr@shambhalamountain.org

TASSAJARA ZEN MIND TEMPLE

Monastery/Yoga/Meditation/Zen Center • California • Summer
www.sfzc.com/zmcindex.htm

♥ ⛪ ⊕

Set in the wilderness of California's Santa Lucia Mountains behind Big Sur, Tassajara Zen Mind Temple is a working Zen Buddhist monastery that invites guests who wish to participate in some Zen practice along with the students and monks who live there. You'll rise with the residents (and the sun) around

5:30 A.M., then join them for a period of zazen meditation, morning service, temple cleaning, and breakfast, followed by three and a half hours of community work, then lunch. Afternoons and evenings are free to enjoy hiking, swimming, relaxing at the baths, and simple vegetarian cuisine for dinner. The program also includes an invitation to attend classes, lectures, and community discussions. There is a fee of $55 per person per day, with a minimum stay of three days. From April through September, Tassajara offers a work-practice program, where volunteers get the chance to assist with the maintenance of the facilities and follow the daily resident schedule of meditation and work. A minimum commitment of five days is required and applicants must be at least eighteen years of age. A $70 application fee covers room and board, as well as lectures and classes on Buddhism. Participants may also return in following years free of charge. For those planning on staying at least five months, a small stipend is available.

FOR MORE INFORMATION: Guest Practice Program Coordinator, Tassajara Zen Mind Temple, 39171 Tassajara Rd., Carmel Valley, CA 93924 (415) 865-1899 • tassrcz@sfzc.org

TREE OF LIFE REJUVENATION CENTER

Retreat Center/Yoga/Meditation • Arizona • Seasonal
www.treeoflife.nu/employ.html

$ 🏠 🌐

Using the metaphor of the "tree of life"—working with all the forces in our lives such as air, earth, sun, water, love, wisdom, joy, peace, right livelihood, and the Divine Presence—is at the heart of this spiritual eco-retreat center. Employment with the Tree of Life Rejuvenation Center offers the opportunity to live in a spiritually based community, serve others who are on the path of awakening, join in spiritual practices and celebrations, and enjoy organic meals. Full-time exchange positions in housekeeping and maintenance offer classes in yoga and meditation, with ample time available for quiet reflection and development of a healthy, holistic, and sustainable lifestyle. Dormitory-style lodging and "live-food" vegan meals are provided. Apprenticeships are also available in the café and gardens, with stipends that start at $700 per month. Applications are available online and in-person interviews are required.

FOR MORE INFORMATION: Susan Miller, Employment Coordinator, Tree of Life Rejuvenation Center, P.O. Box 1080, Patagonia, AZ 85624 (520) 394-2520, ext. 207 • (520) 394-2099 (fax) • healing@treeoflife.nu

As we cultivate peace and happiness in ourselves,
we also nourish peace and happiness in those we love.
—THICH NHAT HANH

FULL BELLY FARM

Organic Farming • California • Summer/1 Year
www.fullbellyfarm.com

$ 🏕

Just about an hour north of Sacramento, California, you'll find Full Belly Farm, a two-hundred-acre certified organic farm producing fruits, nuts, flowers, and every conceivable vegetable that can be grown in a Mediterranean-style climate. Four partners (all of whom live and work on the farm with their families), a crew of year-round hourly workers (most of whom are Mexican immigrants—Spanish speakers will feel right at home!), and up to five apprentices grow and harvest crops year-round for a five-hundred member CSA, three farmers' markets, and a wholesale unit. The rhythm of the farm varies with the seasons—and so does the work of the apprentice. One day you might be working in the packing shed (washing, packing, and organizing produce), and the next, delivering produce to the farmers' market or writing the weekly note for CSA boxes. This is not a job for someone who is uncomfortable around hard work! A one-year commitment is encouraged to get a sense of farmwork and farm life. Shorter stays only work if they span the summer, for example, from June through October. Benefits include a stipend, room (with shared living spaces), and plenty of great food; one meal a day is shared by all, with apprentices creating this meal once per week. Applications are available online, and an initial phone call is necessary as is a visit to the farm.

FOR MORE INFORMATION: Apprentice Program Coordinator, Full Belly Farm, P.O. Box 251, Guinda, CA 95637 • (530) 796-2214 • belly@fullbellyfarm.com

GARDEN HARVEST

Organic Farming/Hunger Awareness • Maryland • 1–8 Months
www.gardenharvest.org

$ 🏕 ⊕

Garden Harvest is a one-hundred-acre organic farm that also doubles as an educational center working to alleviate hunger and improve nutrition of the disadvantaged. One hundred percent of the organic fruit, vegetables, and eggs produced are distributed fresh to soup kitchens and emergency food pantries in the area. Apprentices will receive extensive training and education in organic farming and sustainable agriculture (including animal husbandry with chickens, goats, geese, and sheep), develop leadership and supervisory skills, gain experience in the operation of a nonprofit organization, and have exposure to issues of hunger and homelessness. Duties range from planting, growing, harvesting, and composting to beekeeping, delivery of produce, and supervision of volunteers. Positions are available from mid-March through mid-November (forty to fifty-five hours per week), with a one-month minimum commitment. No previous farming experience is necessary; however, applicants must be at least eighteen years of age, have a sincere interest in organic farming or helping humanity, and be capable of strenuous physical work outside in various weather conditions. Room, meals, and a stipend are provided. Applications are available online.

FOR MORE INFORMATION: Jim Dasher, Executive Director, Garden Harvest, 14045 Mantua Mill Rd., Glyndon, MD 21071 • (410) 526-0698 (866) 362-3644 (fax) • garharvest@aol.com

GARDENS OF EAGAN

Organic Farming • Minnesota • 4–6 Months
www.frontiernet.net/~atinagoe
$ 🏠

As a fifth-generation family farm located in a rural community forty-five minutes south of Minneapolis/St.Paul, the Gardens of Eagan farms over one hundred acres and provides organic vegetables to nine natural food stores, two wholesalers, and their very own roadside stand. Apprenticeships are available from mid-April through November 1 (with various start dates) and will provide a hands-on educational experience in organic vegetable production and marketing. Throughout the changing seasons, apprentices will have responsibilities in the greenhouse, weed control, field site selection, soil preparation and care, planting and harvesting, pest management, marketing, and equipment maintenance. Readings, discussions, and informal group meetings augment the work component. Benefits include a monthly stipend of $800 (plus a $200-per-month bonus if you can stay through November 1), private rooms in simple cabins (including electricity, heat, and hot water), shared kitchen space, produce from the farm, and use of the farm library. It is not necessary to have previous experience in farming, although applicants should enjoy physical work and being outside all day, have a positive attitude with a passion for learning, and be in good health (with a strong back!). Detailed information is available online, or call or email for more information.

FOR MORE INFORMATION: Atina Diffley, Owner, Gardens of Eagan, 25498 Highview Ave., Farmington, MN 55024 • (952) 469-1855 (952) 469-2504 (fax) • atinagoe@frontiernet.net

The harvest is plenty, laborers are few. Come with me into the fields. **341**
—MATTHEW 9:37-38

GREEN GULCH FARM AND ZEN CENTER

Organic Farming/Zen Center • California • 6 Months
www.sfzc.com/ggfindex.htm

Green Gulch Farm and Zen Center, nestled in a valley bordered by the Pacific Ocean, Golden Gate National Recreation Area, and Mount Tamalpais, offers a residential apprenticeship in organic gardening and farming from mid-April through mid-October each year. Along with hands-on experience and instruction in organic gardening and farming methods, the apprenticeship also emphasizes Zen meditation practice and study and instruction in Buddhist teachings. Daily work includes harvesting, sowing, transplanting, compost making, tractor cultivation, raised-bed flower and vegetable gardening, fruit cultivation, craft production, and opportunities to market the produce at the farm and regional farmers' markets. Room, board, and weekly classes and seminars with resident and visiting teachers are provided. As part of the application process, a two-week stay as a guest student is required (at a cost of $15 per day). Call or write for further information or to inquire about a guest student visit. The application deadline is January 15.

FOR MORE INFORMATION: Liz Milazzo, Farm Manager, Green Gulch Farm and Zen Center, 1601 Shoreline Hwy., Sausalito, CA 94965 • (415) 381-0253 (415) 383-3134 • (415) 383-3128 (fax) • farmandgarden@sfzc.org

GUIDESTONE FARM AND CENTER FOR SUSTAINABLE LIVING

Organic Farming • Colorado • 3–12 Months
www.guidestonefarm.com

Located one hour north of Boulder and one-half hour south of Fort Collins, Guidestone Farm and Center for Sustainable Living includes a 150-acre organic farm, a diversified livestock program (raising sheep, pigs, laying hens, and turkeys and working with three draft horses), a four-acre vegetable garden, and a small-scale cow dairy that provides raw milk for shareholders. The farm also sponsors a summer farm camp for children, educational programs, and adult workshops relating to alternative energy and natural home building.

WHAT YOU'LL BE DOING: Interns have the opportunity to focus on organic gardening, animal husbandry, creating a farm business, or farming. Although a specific area is chosen, everyone has an opportunity to learn and experience organic vegetable production, working with the animals, baking in a wood-fired brick oven, running a CSA farm, teaching educational programs to children, natural home building and alternative energy technologies, and various skills, such as tree grafting and permaculture.

COMMITMENT: The length of internships can range from three months to a year. The growing season is from April to November, while animal care and milking are year-round activities.

PERKS AND REWARDS: A stipend of $150 per month is provided, along with housing and food from the farm. Accommodations are simple and range from a three-person cabin to yurts overlooking the pond. Kitchen and bathroom facilities are also available and include solar showers, an innovative solar moldering outhouse, and a semi-outdoor kitchen. All facilities were built using alternative methods such as straw-bale or cob construction.

YOUR FIRST MOVE: Call for a detailed internship packet. If possible, prospective interns should visit Guidestone prior to committing to a position in order to make sure that the program and living situation is right for them.

FOR MORE INFORMATION: David Lynch, Internship Program, Guidestone Farm and Center for Sustainable Living, The Stewardship Community, 5943 N. County Road 29, Loveland, CO 80538 • (970) 461-0271 farmerlynch@msn.com

HAWTHORNE VALLEY FARM

Biodynamic Farming/Teaching • New York • 3–12 Months
www.vspcamp.com

$ 🏕

Hawthorne Valley Farm was founded in 1972 by a group of experienced educators and farmers who recognized a growing need to create a place where children and young people might experience life in its wholeness and gain the inner strength and practical abilities they would need as adults. At Hawthorne Valley, farmers, artists, and teachers working out the insights of Rudolf Steiner have joined together to create such a place. The four-hundred-acre biodynamic farm is home to a K–12 Waldorf day school, a children's residential school and summer camp program, a cheese and yogurt production dairy (with a sixty-head dairy herd), a full bakery, and a ten-acre market garden supplying a 225-member CSA program, a Green Market stand in New York City, and a retail natural foods and grocery store on the premises.

WHAT YOU'LL BE DOING: Whether you work as a Visiting Students Program intern, a summer camp counselor, or a farm apprentice, the farm provides ample opportunities to learn in new and exciting ways. As the Waldorf

Remember that your work comes only moment by moment,
and as surely as God calls you to work, he gives the strength to do it.
—PRISCILLA MAURICE

HAWTHORNE VALLEY FARM

Hawthorne Valley Farm summer campers and staff make their way to the biodynamic gardens to help out the farm team with the day's harvest.

educational arm of the farm, the Visiting Students Program brings students and teachers from public and private schools to spend a week on the farm. Interns and staff host the classes and conduct activities such as animal feeding, gardening, barn cleaning, sourdough bread baking, butter making, and seasonal projects including apple cider pressing and maple syrup making. During the summer months, camp counselors teach either in the House Camp for nine- to eleven-year-olds or the Field Camp for teens aged twelve to fifteen. A field camp director, houseparent, and assistant cooks are also needed during this time frame. These programs seek to build reverence for life and community awareness through living, playing, and working together on an active farm. Farm apprentices do whatever needs to be done during their on-the-job training—milking the cows, haying, caring for the livestock, cleaning the dairy barn, repairing machinery, planting or tending the garden crops, harvesting vegetables, or driving to the Green Market in New York City. Interactive sessions on biodynamic farming practices, informative talks with local geology and nature experts, and field trips to other farms round out the apprentice experience.

COMMITMENT: Internships begin with a two-week training period and are available during the spring (mid-January to early June) or the fall (late August to late November). Camp counselors kick off the summer in mid-June with a one-week training and work through mid-August. The apprentice program runs from February through November with the option to stay through the winter.

PERKS AND REWARDS: Interns receive a monthly stipend of $300; camp counselor stipends range from $1,500 to $1,700 for the summer; camp cooks receive $2,250 for the summer; and apprentices receive $400 per month. While on the farm, all staff members live as a community and eat family-style meals (consisting of whole foods, grains, and fresh vegetables). Home is a comfortable nineteenth-century farmhouse (some counselors have private tents).

YOUR FIRST MOVE: Call or email for details. Additional information and applications for all positions can be found online. For more information on the apprentice program, contact Rachel Schneider at (518) 672-4465, ext. 105. General information about the farm can be found at www.hawthornevalleyfarm.org.

FOR MORE INFORMATION: Helen Enright, Program Director, Hawthorne Valley Farm, 327 Route 21C, Ghent, NY 12075 • (518) 672-4790 (518) 672-7608 (fax) • vsp@taconic.net

NOWHERE ELSE I'D RATHER BE

When I was first considering a farm apprenticeship at Hawthorne Valley, I was still teaching in Brooklyn. I had spent four months at a farm in Kentucky before moving to New York City to study and teach in the inner city, and by my third year there, the concrete hurt. It was difficult to find a common language with children who were taught from the beginning to be removed from the sources of their sustenance. And I, too, was growing disconnected: if I wanted to eat mindfully, my choices seemed limited to organic foods grown by California migrant workers and trucked thousands of miles. I began to research CSA. I realized that my work with children needed to happen within the context of farming, not only so that I could be sustained, but also so that I could contribute to the making of a sustainable world.

As a farm apprentice for the past two seasons, I've had my share of long, hot, hard days. (Also long, cold, hard days!) I have grown strong and have felt a certainty deep in my bones that I have found a calling. I love hearing the cows coming in early in the morning and knowing that it's about time for me to rise too. I love harvesting out in the garden as the sun rises and knowing that, if the cows are going back out to pasture, it must be 7:15.

This year I have learned more about tractor operation, and recently, I spent the day raking hay on a big Belarus. I have witnessed the birth of three calves and saw one stillborn. The cycles of life and death are immediate, tangible, and an intimate part of what we do every day. Grass and hay become manure, which becomes compost, which is added to the soil to nourish more pasture or vegetables, which are, in turn, consumed or (through the process of feeding hay to the cows) used to create milk, and on and on.

This morning I transplanted our fall beets. Now, this afternoon, I am about to go milk the cows. Children from the summer camp will probably be in and out of the barn as they do afternoon chores and help us bring in the heifers. We'll all fan ourselves and comment on the weather and pray for rain, and I will feel grateful, for this will be a time when there is nowhere else I would rather be.

—Contributed by Rebecca Nellenback, former Hawthorne Valley Farm Apprentice

HEARTWOOD SCHOOL

House Building • Massachusetts • 1–7 Weeks
www.heartwoodschool.com

Heartwood teaches the skills and knowledge it takes to build an energy-efficient house as well as offering workshops on all aspects of the home-building crafts, including timber framing, cabinetmaking, and finish carpentry. Those who come to Heartwood range from students to retirees, and most have little or no previous construction experience. However, they all share a "clear determination to empower their hands, to train their eyes for quality and beauty in the design of things, and to question and explore the ways we might live in a more honest relation with our planet."

WHAT YOU'LL BE DOING: In addition to being a workshop participant, Heartwood invites four apprentices-in-residence who help with workshops and maintain tools and facilities in exchange for reduced rates in tuition. Apprentices will gain not only a comprehensive knowledge of house building and timber framing, but also a clear, concise methodology of problem solving and training of the eyes and hands for quality and beauty—yes, true craftsmanship! Note that the main purpose of the apprenticeship program is to train individuals who are interested in timber framing as a career. Upon conclusion of the program, apprentices must agree to continue working with a member timber company for a minimum of eight months. Heartwood arranges this and you will receive a stipend.

COMMITMENT: One- to two-week workshops are offered from early May through mid-October, and enrollment averages ten students. Apprentices must commit to at least seven weeks of residency (from mid-June through early August). This time period coincides with their core timber framing curriculum and also includes the two-week house-building workshop.

PERKS AND REWARDS: Those participating in one-week workshops pay a tuition fee of $550 ($1,000 per couple); the two-week house-building course runs $1,050 ($1,900 per couple). The fee include materials and hearty lunches. Special weekly rates at nearby hotels, bed-and-breakfasts, and campgrounds are offered. Apprentices pay a fee that averages $250 per week, which includes housing, lunch, and attendance at all Heartwood courses and Timber Framers Guild events (www.tfguild.org). Housing consists of use of a kitchen and bath and one of four sleeping areas: two lofts in the schoolhouse and two cabins behind it.

YOUR FIRST MOVE: Call for application materials. The apprentice application deadline is March 15 (with notification by April 15).

FOR MORE INFORMATION: Will and Michele Beemer, Workshop/Apprentice Coordinators, Heartwood School, Johnson Hill Rd., Washington, MA 01223 (413) 623-6677 • (413) 623-0277 (fax) • info@heartwoodschool.com

HEIFER INTERNATIONAL RANCH

Hunger Awareness • Arkansas/California/Massachusetts • Seasonal
www.heifer.org

$ 🏠 ⊕

Heifer International is a nonprofit development organization working in forty-eight countries (including the U.S.) to help alleviate world hunger. Their three learning centers (in California, Arkansas, and Massachusetts) are hands-on campuses that teach the public about the root causes of hunger and poverty and the way animals and people can make a difference. Volunteers are needed to work in the organic gardens and with the livestock, as well as to assist with office work, maintenance, and the education program, which includes field trips for children, alternative spring break, and tours. Volunteers receive a monthly stipend and on-site housing. Applicants must be at least eighteen, and applications are accepted year-round.

FOR MORE INFORMATION: Volunteer Manager, Heifer International Ranch, 55 Heifer Rd., Perryville, AR 72126 • (800) 422-0474 • (501) 889-5124 (501) 889-1574 (fax) • ranchvol@heifer.org

HIDDEN VILLA

Farming Camp/Teaching • California • 3–12 Months
www.hiddenvilla.org

$ 🏠 ⊕

Connecting children to the earth and instilling a sense of responsibility for their environment, Hidden Villa engages participants in innovative hands-on programs promoting environmental awareness, multicultural understanding, and humanitarian values. Located in the foothills of the Santa Cruz Mountains on a sixteen-hundred-acre wilderness preserve and organic farm, Hidden Villa features a multicultural summer camp (for ages six to eighteen), a school-year environmental education program for elementary school children, a youth hostel, a CSA program, and a variety of community programs. For many visitors, Hidden Villa provides an opportunity to walk in the woods, come face-to-face with a large, friendly farm animal, and see where milk and eggs come from.

The craftsman does not always build toward a prior vision.
Often images come in the process of working. The material, his hands—together they beget.
—M. C. RICHARDS

WHAT YOU'LL BE DOING: Environmental education interns spend one day each week working on the farm and studying agriculture and animal care with the ranch staff. The other four weekdays are dedicated to teaching.

HIDDEN VILLA

Duties include giving short tours of the farm for preschoolers, educating and working with elementary school-children on the farm, or giving presentations to classrooms at surrounding schools. With an emphasis on fun and interactive education, interns will learn leadership skills as well as hands-on and creative teaching techniques using slides, puppets, music, role-playing, and storytelling. Practical living skills, organic gardening, and the realities of life on a small farm round out the learning experience. Note that opportunities also exist at Hidden Villa during the summer months, with positions ranging from residential counselors and trip leaders to ropes-course and rock climbing coordinators to garden and farm staff—and much more!

An environmental education intern inspires children through Hidden Villa's science-based teaching curriculum.

COMMITMENT: Internships begin in September for nine months; camp positions are offered during the summer months.

PERKS AND REWARDS: Interns receive a monthly stipend of $525, shared housing, seasonal food from the farm, and full medical benefits. Summer wages start at $250 per week; rustic housing and meals are provided. One of the biggest perks is the chance to live in a beautiful place, meet inspiring people, and receive lots of experience with children, teaching, and farms.

THE ESSENTIALS: Those who have an interest in organic farming, the outdoors, and children and can show how an internship might benefit their career path are preferred. It's also helpful to have experience in teaching, counseling, or working with children in other ways. Traits found in their interns include a fun-loving spirit, maturity, and energy over the long haul.

YOUR FIRST MOVE: Call, email, or write for application materials. Internship applications must be received by mid-April. All applicants are interviewed by telephone.

FOR MORE INFORMATION: Intern Coordinator, Environmental Education Program, Hidden Villa, 26870 Moody Rd., Los Altos Hills, CA 94022-4209

Environmental Education: (650) 949-8643, hveep@hiddenvilla.org

Summer Camp: (650) 949-8641, camp@hiddenvilla.org

General: (650) 949-8643, hveep@hiddenvilla.org

THE REALITY OF DREAMS

Upon discovering a special place called Hidden Villa, I became enthralled by the opportunity to live on a farm and help children connect with nature. I realized this was the job I had been preparing for without knowing it: an internship experience representing a unique integration of the mind, body, and soul through work and recreation.

Imagine a long, narrow valley surrounded by lush tree-covered mountains glowing under a cloud-studded sky. Lichen and mosses ensure the air is crisp and pristine, as fragrant smells swim through the atmosphere, invigorating the lungs and spirit. Waterfalls gliding down the mountains soothe the mind under a canopy of green hues. Birds are chirping, frogs croaking, and in the distance the sounds of sheep ring through the valley.

As an intern at Hidden Villa, days are spent outside in the foothills of the Santa Cruz Mountains guiding children around the farm and wilderness preserve, fostering their connection to nature. For many children, Hidden Villa becomes their first exposure to a farm: eating food grown directly from the gardens, appreciating worms for making dirt, or, perhaps, seeing and touching a pig, chicken, sheep, cow, or goat— something only previously seen in storybooks or on television, yet such an integral part of our lives. We hike the trails of a mossy enchanted forest, exploring and sharing its awe and wonder.

Experiencing nature with children as they foster connections with their roots is an amazing journey. Today, many children are being raised with no concept of the interconnectedness and balance of all living things. Our intricate relationship with and reliance on the earth's energies for survival and happiness have become something we buy in a box on a shelf in a building. We cannot endure this disconnection and expect our children to clean up the environmental and social destruction that has been created. Healing begins now—by the way we live each day and by the way we teach our children that we are interconnected with all life that surrounds us.

When you work, you fulfill a part of earth's fondest dream assigned to you when that dream is born.
—KAHLIL GIBRAN

Working at Hidden Villa has been far more than a job—it has been a remarkable adventure of life. Challenges, truths, and realizations have been crucial contributors along this pathway for me. Existing in a new environment, developing new relationships with people and animals, and opening up to the myriad of possibilities has invigorated my soul. Living a lifestyle that offers a connection to the earth while devoting energy to an enjoyable job and meaningful purpose have helped me evolve toward the person I want to be. And the journey has just begun!

JUSTIN HALGREN

Using Hidden Villa's hands-on approach to learning, Cori Stennett and her team of children pause and reflect upon our links to the earth.

This experience has unlocked many doors of opportunity and many more positive situations to discover, learn, share, play, live, and evolve; much like *The Back Door Guide* unlocked the door to Hidden Villa for me. Beyond each description Michael Landes has given each of us in this book lies a world of pure imagination. As the Great Willy Wonka would say:

> If you want to view paradise,
> Simply look around and view it.
> Anything you want, you do it.
> Want to change the world?
> There's nothing to it.

Fortunately, we have the ability to make conscious decisions influencing our growth, discovery, and purpose. Where we position ourselves on this earth and the energies with which we come into contact create the scenes of our lives. Choosing a pathway that positively impacts the environment and human conscience is a dream of interdependence. Each of us can live our dreams by creating our own realities. What are yours?

—Contributed by Cori Stennett, Hidden Villa intern

HOLCOMB FARM CSA

Organic Farming • Connecticut • 3–7 Months
www.holcombfarmcsa.org

$ 🏠 ⊕

As a project of the Hartford Food System (www.hartfordfood.org), Holcomb Farm CSA grows twenty acres of organic berries and vegetables for over three hundred households as well as ten community organizations that provide food to low-income residents. From April through early November each year, the farm offers farming apprenticeships so participants can gain the skills and experience to run their very own farm. Using organic principles, apprentices will participate in every aspect of growing varied crops, including greenhouse management, transplanting, field preparation and fertilizing, tractor work, direct seeding, and cultivation, as well as distribution of produce to CSA members. One season of commercial vegetable farming experience is required for these positions. Summer internships are also available, with duties that focus on harvesting, transplanting, weeding, and hoeing. Apprentices receive a monthly stipend of $1,400 ($1,050 for interns), fresh produce from the farm, Internet access, and free registration and participation in the Northeast Organic Farming Association summer conference; you also have the option of renting a private room in the farmhouse for $150 per month. Plan on working about fifty hours per week over a five-and-a-half day period. To apply, send your resume and a letter stating educational goals, reasons for seeking the apprenticeship, and three references. Applicants are strongly encouraged to visit the farm before making a commitment to the position.

FOR MORE INFORMATION: Sam Hammer, Farm Manager, Holcomb Farm CSA, 111 Simsbury Rd., West Granby, CT 06090 • (860) 653-5554
sam@holcombfarmcsa.org

HOWELL LIVING HISTORY FARM

Sustainable Farm • New Jersey • 3–12 Months
www.howellfarm.com

$ 🏠 ⊕

Howell Living History Farm is a 130-acre farm where the techniques that farm families used to feed and clothe themselves at the turn of the nineteenth century are practiced and demonstrated to thousands of visitors each year. Hand, horse, ox, and steam- and gas-engine power are used to operate field, barn, and other equipment. As a working farm, Howell Farm offers recreational and educational opportunities to its visitors, involving them in the work and play of a traditional family farm.

Bloom where you're planted. 351
—MARY ENGELBREIT

WHAT YOU'LL BE DOING: The internship program at Howell Farm is designed to teach participants skills for interpretation of turn-of-the-century farm life. These skills may be useful to those working with small-scale farmers in developing countries or working at other living history farms or agricultural museums, or to the twenty-first-century homesteader. The internship program is integrated with the overall needs of a historical farm, which include cropping, equipment restoration and repair, site maintenance, an introduction to woodworking and metalworking, and educational programs for schools and the general public. The program is designed to involve participants in as many of the seasonal activities as possible.

COMMITMENT: Program dates vary from year to year, but generally the twelve-week sessions start in March, June, and September. The yearlong program is designed as an advanced program, so a college degree related to agriculture or farming experience is necessary.

PERKS AND REWARDS: A stipend, living quarters, hands-on training, and farm products are provided. Living accommodations are modest, with each intern having a private room and access to a shared kitchen, living room, and bathroom.

THE ESSENTIALS: Past interns have been returned Peace Corps volunteers looking to continue in the field of international agriculture, college students exploring careers related to agriculture, and people of all ages interested in sustainable agriculture.

FOR MORE INFORMATION: Rob Flory, Intern Coordinator, Howell Living History Farm, 101 Hunter Rd., Titusville, NJ 08560 (609) 737-3299 • (609) 737-6524 (fax) • internprogram@howellfarm.com

INTERNATIONAL AGRICULTURAL EXCHANGE ASSOCIATION

Farming • Worldwide • 4–12 Months
www.agriventure.com

$ 🏠 ⊕

Do you have an agricultural or horticultural background? Have you always dreamed of working abroad? The International Agricultural Exchange Association (IAEA), along with a strong international network of past trainees and host families, connects participants to farming and agriculture jobs in Australia, Canada, Japan, New Zealand, western Europe, the United Kingdom, and the U.S. There is more to life than what you can see out your back door!

WHAT YOU'LL BE DOING: Experience the thrill of herding cattle in the outback of Australia, milking two hundred cows in less than two hours in New Zealand, or working in the flower market in Amsterdam—not to mention the adventures you can experience on your days off. IAEA is a great way to meet people from all over the world, to experience a different culture, and to live as a member of a host family.

COMMITMENT: Departure dates are in March, April, July, August, September, October, and November, and programs range in duration from four to twelve months. "Flex" programs can be arranged to accommodate most schedules, and longer programs can combine work and travel in two countries.

PERKS AND REWARDS: In addition to providing room and board, host families generally pay trainee allowances once per month. Program fees range from $2,595 to $5,895 and cover work visas, medical and travel insurance, a round-trip airline ticket, an orientation seminar in the host country, supervision, and a two-year membership with IAEA.

THE ESSENTIALS: Candidates must be citizens of one of the member countries (the U.S. is one of them!); have the desire to work overseas; be eighteen to thirty years old; have practical experience in agriculture, horticulture, or home management; have a valid driver's license; have no criminal record; have no dependent children; be in good mental and physical health; and have a basic understanding of the English language.

YOUR FIRST MOVE: Call or write for more information, an application, and current program fees.

FOR MORE INFORMATION: Program Coordinator, International Agricultural Exchange Association, Agriventure, 105, 7710-5 St., SE, Calgary, Alberta T2H 2L9, Canada • (403) 255-7799 • (403) 255-6024 (fax) usa@agriventure.com

KEITH'S FARM

Organic Farming • New York • 6–8 Months

$ 🌲🏠

Growing over one hundred varieties of certified organic vegetables and herbs on twelve acres, Keith's Farm sells its produce at Union Square Greenmarket in New York City twice a week from June through December. The farm itself spans eighty-eight acres and includes woods, pastures, ponds, and a creek, and is rich in animal and bird life. Interns are involved in all aspects of farm operation, including seeding in the greenhouse, field preparation, transplanting, watering, weeding, mulching, harvesting, and selling. Learning is mostly hands-on and interns are expected to take responsibility for many tasks and individual projects. Benefits include housing in private rooms, bath, kitchen facilities, produce from the farm, and a weekly stipend of $200 for the first ten weeks (after that, it goes up an additional $50 per week). People with outdoor and physical work experience who don't mind real work and have a strong interest in learning about and practicing sustainable agriculture are preferred. Send off your resume and a cover letter providing reasons why you want to work on an organic vegetable farm and relevant work and educational experience.

FOR MORE INFORMATION: Keith Stewart, Intern Program, Keith's Farm, P.O. Box 146, Westtown, NY 10998 • (845) 856-4955 • keithsfarm@frontiernet.net

LINNAEA FARM
ECOLOGICAL GARDENING PROGRAMME

Organic Farming • Canada • 8 Months
www.linnaeafarm.org

♥ ⚐

Situated on the edge of a small lake on Cortes Island, British Columbia, and spread over three hundred acres of rich forests, fields, gardens, and orchards, Linnaea Farm operates a small organic farm, an alternative elementary school, and short-term workshops in sustainable living skills. In addition, an eight-month residential Ecological Gardening Programme provides students with a thorough grounding in organic gardening and small-scale farming

LINNAEA FARM ECOLOGICAL GARDENING PROGRAMME

Students with Linnaea Farm prepare produce for the market stand.

through experiential learning and classroom work for a fee of $2,100 (plus a registration fee of $100 and $75 for the textbook). The work component includes experience in the market garden, orchards, and a personal garden plot, while classroom and hands-on lessons cover topics including practical permaculture, herb use and culture, native plants, wildcrafting, woodworking, blacksmithing, and seed saving. The course operates through a full growing season from March 1 to October 31, with three term breaks. Private rooms with a shared kitchen are available for a monthly fee of $150 to $190, which includes utilities and firewood. Students are expected to make their own arrangements for food purchasing and preparation and will be free to share in fresh garden produce as available. The course is geared to those who see their future in small-scale farming or market gardening, or for urban dwellers seeking a fulfilling avocation that can help reduce their dependence on expensive, energy intensive, and chemically treated foods. Applications and references must be received by November 1 (with details found online).

FOR MORE INFORMATION: David Buckner, Coordinator, Linnaea Farm Ecological Gardening Programme, Box 98, Manson's Landing, British Columbia V0P 1K0, Canada • (250) 935-6717 • (250) 935-6413 (fax) garden@linnaeafarm.org

LOST VALLEY EDUCATIONAL CENTER

Intentional Community • Oregon • 1–8 Months
www.lostvalley.org
$ 🏠 🌐

Structured as an intentional community, Lost Valley is a nonprofit educational center that organizes and hosts conferences, workshops, and retreats focusing on personal growth and sustainable living. Committed to the pursuit of a more sustainable lifestyle, twenty to thirty adults and children live year-round on the grounds, located on eighty-seven acres in the foothills of western Oregon's Cascade Range and eighteen miles from Eugene.

WHAT YOU'LL BE DOING: Interns and work-exchange participants have the opportunity to work in the organic gardens using biointensive, permaculture, and "wild" gardening techniques. Garden activities vary depending on the season, but may include sheet mulching, soil preparation, sowing and saving seed, transplanting, composting, weeding, plant propagation, harvesting, food preservation, and greenhouse management. In addition to gardening positions, internships are also available in sustainable building and maintenance, vegetarian cooking and kitchen coordination, service and sacred space, and child care. An eight-week Ecovillage and Permaculture Certificate program provides a holistic introduction to creating ecovillages and sustainable communities, integrating the physical and social elements of ecovillages and including many hands-on and experiential opportunities. Visitor programs, community experience weeks, and other workshops are also available for those interested in exploring life in community.

COMMITMENT: A minimum three- to six-month commitment is suggested for interns; work-exchange visitors may come for any length of time, dependent on mutual needs. Both interns and work-exchangers work thirty hours per week in their areas of focus and spend five to ten additional hours participating

Sow an action and you reap a habit; sow a habit and you reap a character;
sow a character and you reap a destiny.
—WILLIAM JAMES

in community kitchen shifts, chores, and biweekly well-being meetings. Other programs vary in length, require a fee, and do not include the same work requirements.

PERKS AND REWARDS: Interns receive food and lodging or a campsite in exchange for work and may receive a small monthly stipend depending on time commitment and level of responsibility. Short-term work-exchange visitors pay a small fee to cover their food costs. Most other programs involve fees.

THE ESSENTIALS: As a community with a strong commitment to the technical skills of ecological living and open communication and personal growth, Lost Valley desires those who share these interests. Qualified interns will have previous experience in their areas of focus and be comfortable guiding volunteers, coordinating projects, and working cooperatively. Work-exchangers don't need previous experience but must have a willingness to work hard and be open to the multifaceted learning that occurs in the community.

YOUR FIRST MOVE: Program details, current opportunities, and application materials are available online. Qualified applicants are accepted on a first-come, first-served basis. For specific gardening inquiries, contact Chris Roth at garden@lostvalley.org.

FOR MORE INFORMATION: Tammy Davis, Intern Coordinator, Lost Valley Educational Center, 81868 Lost Valley Ln., Dexter, OR 97431 (541) 937-3351 • internship@lostvalley.org

☞ INSIDER TIP: A "journal of our evolving ecological culture," *Talking Leaves* **is filled with feature articles, essays, and other writings contributed by people working to restore healthy human relationships with the natural world, with one another, and with self. Published quarterly, each issue also includes an extensive book and music review section, announcements, poetry, and art. More information can be found at www.talkingleaves.org.**

MAST INTERNATIONAL EXPERIENCE ABROAD

Farming • Worldwide • 3–12 Months
http://mast.coafes.umn.edu

🏕️

MAST International offers those between the ages of eighteen and thirty the opportunity to participate in three- to twelve-month training assignments in agriculture, horticulture, or forestry in eighteen countries around the globe.

Applicants must have a minimum of six months practical or work experience in a related field, and knowledge of the host country's language is required in Argentina, France, Morocco, and Spain. Participants generally receive an allowance plus room and meals. There is a program fee of $400 (airfare, insurance, visa, personal expenses, and in-country program fees are additional). Apply a minimum of three months prior to your preferred start date; four months for Germany and Denmark.

FOR MORE INFORMATION: Susan Von Bank, Program Coordinator, MAST International Experience Abroad, University of Minnesota, R395 VoTech Bldg., 1954 Buford Ave., St. Paul, MN 55108-6197 • (800) 346-6278 • (612) 624-3740 (612) 625-7031 (fax) • mast@umn.edu

MAYSIE'S FARM CONSERVATION CENTER

Organic Farming • Pennsylvania • Seasonal
www.maysiesfarm.org

$ 🏠 🌐

Pure and simple, Maysie's Farm is dedicated to increasing the public's understanding of ecological living and the importance of communities based on local, sustainably produced food supplies. The unique educational activities at Maysie's sixty-five-acre farm include a CSA with 120 subscribers, school and youth programs, a community learning series, and sustainable agriculture internships.

WHAT YOU'LL BE DOING: Since the farm is based on education rather than solely dedicated to production, interns have the opportunity to really learn and understand soil fertility practices, crop rotation principles, organic pest control, and other aspects of the art and science of growing great vegetables. Additionally, interns will participate in the development of a community focused on a local food supply and can observe firsthand the benefits of the community's spirit. Maysie's also founded the Sustainable Agriculture Internship Training Alliance of Southeastern Pennsylvania (SAITA), which brings interns, farmers, and volunteers together for a weekend workshop and farm tour at one of fourteen farms each month.

COMMITMENT: Typically interns work at least forty hours per week, with longer hours in the spring and summer months. The internship term varies to meet personal or academic needs, with four to six interns at the farm at any given time.

PERKS AND REWARDS: Housing is provided in a renovated farmhouse near the farm. A local university professor (who is also on the board of directors) lives

*Work is not always required . . . there is such a thing as sacred idleness,
the cultivation of which is now fearfully neglected.*
—GEORGE MACDONALD

in the house to ensure a healthfully functioning communal home and a model of ecologically responsible living. Interns also receive a moderate stipend and food from the garden.

THE ESSENTIALS: Individuals who have an interest in sustainable agriculture, are in good health, and have the ability to work independently and in groups will thrive at Maysie's.

YOUR FIRST MOVE: Call or email for more information.

FOR MORE INFORMATION: Sam Cantrell, Internship Director, Maysie's Farm Conservation Center, 15 St. Andrew's Ln., Glenmoore, PA 19343 (610) 458-8129 • (610) 469-9662 (fax) • sam@maysiesfarm.org

MERCK FOREST AND FARMLAND CENTER

Organic Farming • Vermont • Seasonal
www.merckforest.org

$ 🏕

As a 3,150-acre preserve located in the Taconic Mountains of southwestern Vermont, Merck Forest and Farmland Center is a nonprofit conservation and education organization. Facilities include a small, diversified organic farm, working forest, maple sugar operation, rustic cabins and shelters, group camping area, solar-powered visitor center, and twenty-eight miles of trails for hiking and skiing. Internships in sustainable farm and forest resources are offered throughout the year. Depending on seasonal needs and intern interests, responsibilities may include animal care, organic farming (everything from planting to harvesting), use of power tools and tractors, firewood and Christmas tree harvest and production, sugaring, and marketing. Interns receive a stipend of $75 per week, housing at the lodge (which has running water, shower, gas lights, stove, and refrigerator, and is a one-mile hike from the farm), and complimentary farm produce, maple syrup, and meat as available. Interns must have an interest in sustainable forestry and farming, a willingness to work hard, and a positive attitude. Submit a cover letter, resume, and three letters of reference to begin the application process.

FOR MORE INFORMATION: Debra Fuller, Staffing Coordinator, Merck Forest and Farmland Center, Route 315, Rupert Mountain Rd., P.O. Box 86, Rupert, VT 05768 • (802) 394-7836 • (802) 394-2519 (fax) merck@vermontel.com

MICHAEL FIELDS
AGRICULTURAL INSTITUTE

Farming • Wisconsin • 2–7 Months
www.michaelfieldsaginst.org

♥ 🏠

Up at dawn for orders of the day at 6 A.M. Muscle-straining, perspiration-dripping, back-aching work—all day long. Knock off when the mosquitoes or darkness drive you inside. And follow this routine for seven months. It's a training ground in organic garden and field. It's a hands-on program of instruction in lessons ranging from hand-to-hand combat with weeds to planting and cultivation by tractor. "It" is Michael Fields's Garden Student Program, which teaches a broad range of fundamental skills in a working CSA and market garden.

WHAT YOU'LL BE DOING: Each year a variety of students come to Michael Fields to participate in this self-imposed boot camp for the mind, body, and soul. Along with learning the fundamentals of organic gardening (on twenty-eight acres of French-intensive raised garden beds and field sites) and building relationships with communities and markets, students will also learn about traditional farm-life skills.

COMMITMENT: The program runs seven months from early April to the end of October. Two- to four-month placements are also available.

PERKS AND REWARDS: Students learn, work, and live together. There is a tuition fee of $1,875 for the seven-month program (with the possibility of tuition assistance); two and four month positions run $275 per month. All students are also required to carry health insurance (which the institute does not cover).

A pair of garden students pause to display freshly harvested onions as they make their way to the washing and packing station at Michael Fields.

TONY ENDS

Gardening is an active participation in the deepest mysteries of the universe. **359**
—THOMAS BERRY

THE ESSENTIALS: Those who love the outdoors, revere nature, and appreciate both the spiritual and physical qualities of intensive organic vegetable production will thrive at Michael Fields. Applicants must also be willing to take on individual responsibility for completing scores of specific garden tasks as well as working well in a team on group tasks.

YOUR FIRST MOVE: An application can be downloaded through their website, or you can request a student handbook, brochures, and application by mail, phone, or email.

FOR MORE INFORMATION: Therese Philipp, Registrar, Garden Student Program, Michael Fields Agricultural Institute, W2493 County Rd. ES, East Troy, WI 53120 • (262) 642-3303, ext. 117 • (262) 642-4028 (fax) tphilipp@michaelfieldsaginst.org

MICHAELA FARM

Organic Farming • Indiana • 1 Day–2 Weeks+
www.oldenburgfranciscans.org

$ 🏠

Begun by the Sisters of St. Francis in 1854, Michaela Farm provides a center for organic food production, ecological education, and spiritual renewal. Farm resources and facilities include vegetable and flower gardens, a greenhouse, a pump house (which has been renovated into a hermitage), a retreat cottage, and a herd of beefalo that helps create a more "whole" farm system. Farm volunteers work on the gardens and grounds (or any other special interest)

Michaela Farm provides volunteers with the opportunity to experience all aspects of farm life, including a lifestyle that fosters simple and holistic living.

for a minimum of four hours per day in exchange for lodging in a private bedroom with community kitchen, bathroom facilities, laundry, and living quarters. An abundance of produce, when in season, is also shared; however, meals and additional expenses are the volunteer's responsibility. Focused individuals with an exuberant love of the land and willingness to work hard and learn will thrive here. To begin the application process, call or email Michaela with the details of your interest and availability. A cover letter, resume, and references are helpful, and a previsit to the farm is ideal.

FOR MORE INFORMATION: Ann Marie Quinn, Volunteer Program, Michaela Farm, P.O. Box 100, Oldenburg, IN 47036 • (812) 933-0661 • (812) 933-6403 (fax) michaelafarm@seidata.com

MOUNTAIN GARDENS

Organic Farming • North Carolina • 7 Months
www.mountaingardensherbs.com

♥ ⚶

Located at the foot of the Black Mountains in western North Carolina, Mountain Gardens features the largest collection of organically grown and sustainably wildcrafted Chinese and native Appalachian medicinal herbs in the eastern United States. Classes at this botanical garden center around the sustainable environmental philosophy of "paradise gardening"—both a place to live and a way to live, and, above all, a "visionary social theater." Four to five full-time apprenticeship opportunities are available from mid-March through late October, with shorter-term stays available for WWOOFers and college students on break, although you may have to bring your tent to sleep in! The apprenticeship is extremely varied and creative, with work in herb growing, seed saving, medicinal preparations, vegetable gardening, food preservation, rough carpentry, cob, bamboo and rockwork, maintaining and upgrading photovoltaic and irrigation systems, wildcrafting, library research, mapping and record-keeping, and all the varied tasks that compose a "simple" lifestyle. New ideas and projects reflecting the interests and skills of each apprentice are always encouraged. Neoprimitive lodging in a rustic environment and basic staples are provided; the botanic garden, research library and apothecary, and adjacent natural environments add up to a unique educational opportunity. Be prepared to "rough it" in a gentle way. Ideal candidates are fun-loving, hardworking, and creative individuals. To begin the application process, send an email with your intentions and work dates. A required visit prior to making a seven-month commitment is best for all, except in unusual circumstances.

FOR MORE INFORMATION: Joe Hollis, Head Gardener, Apprentice Program, Mountain Gardens, 546 Shuford Creek Rd., Burnsville, NC 28714 (828) 675-5664 • joehollis@excite.com

A man's accomplishments in life are the cumulative effect of his attention to detail.
—JOHN FOSTER DULLES

NEW MORNING FARM

Farming • Pennsylvania • 9 Months

$ 🏠

As a family organic farm located in the rural ridges and valleys of south-central Pennsylvania, New Morning Farm grows over forty crops—including berries and herbs—spread over twenty-five acres. In addition to selling produce at farmers' markets in Washington, D.C., they have founded and actively participate in a successful wholesale marketing cooperative, representing a community of twenty farms. Six apprentices are hired each year for a full-season stay (usually beginning sometime in April and finishing in late November), with a primary role of assisting in management of crops, equipment, and marketing. A $600 to $900 monthly stipend is provided, along with training, all-inclusive board, and private rooms in one-person cabins with shared cooking and washing facilities. Besides providing on-the-job training, New Morning Farm always takes time for orderly discussions and seminars on topics of interest to apprentices. After their tenure with New Morning, many apprentices have gone on to farm on their own. Call to begin the application process.

FOR MORE INFORMATION: Jim Crawford, Apprenticeship Program, New Morning Farm, HCR 71, Box 168, Hustontown, PA 17229 • (814) 448-3904 (814) 448-2333 (fax) • moiec@hotmail.com

OLD MILL FARM

Organic Farming • California • 3–6 Months+
www.oldmillfarm.org

♥ 🏠 🌐

Since 1974, the Old Mill Farm has been familiarizing city folk with both the work and the wonders of farm life. Surrounded by fifty thousand acres of state forests, the farm is an active, working homestead that places an emphasis on alternative energy and solar heat; growing organic vegetables in biointensive beds, fruit trees, and herbs on forty acres; tending and utilizing sheep, swine, and fowl; and sustainable forestry of redwoods and fir on an additional 280 acres. Also available on the property is a vacation rental cabin.

WHAT YOU'LL BE DOING: The farm offers an alternative form of education to interns desiring to become familiar with and experience the chores required to maintain both a general farm and a sustainable lifestyle, as well as to become aware of the natural, organic relationship to the land and animals utilized. Working with guests, gardening, animal husbandry, and sustainable forestry and assisting with various workshops will occupy most of the intern's time.

PERKS AND REWARDS: Room and some farm-raised food are provided. Apprentices live in a bunk cabin with a wood-heat cookstove and solar/propane oven.

THE ESSENTIALS: The position requires a person who has organic gardening experience, is self-motivated, works well with others, and is interested in small-scale animal care and sustainable forestry. Interns must make a three- to six-month commitment.

YOUR FIRST MOVE: To pursue an internship further, send an email or letter about yourself—your interests, experiences, skills, what time period you are interested in, and anything else they should know about you—as well as two work character references. After your letter has been reviewed, someone from the farm will contact you.

FOR MORE INFORMATION: Cas Sochacki, Intern Program Coordinator, Old Mill Farm, P.O. Box 553, Mendocino, CA 95460 • (707) 937-3047 (707) 937-0244 (fax) • inquiry@oldmillfarm.org

INSIDER TIP: With the philosophy of early to bed, early to rise, we are a diversified farm expecting those with us to appreciate hard work and generate good ideas to improve our sustainability and the environment. Farm life is twenty-four hours a day, seven days a week. Time off is possible and encouraged, but specific times are subject to change. Living over thirty minutes from the nearest town, the intern must be able to incorporate working and living in the same place.

QUIET CREEK HERB FARM & SCHOOL OF COUNTRY LIVING

Organic Farming • Pennsylvania • 1 Week–1 Year
www.quietcreekherbfarm.com

♥ ⛺

If you're looking for a place to experience community building and a healthy, sustainable lifestyle, you will enjoy all that Quiet Creek Farm has to offer. Spread over thirty acres (and located two hours north of Pittsburgh), the farm uses organic methods to grow over two hundred species of herbs, flowers

Real development is not leaving things behind, as on a road, but drawing life from them, as from a root.
—G. K. CHESTERTON

(many edible!), and vegetables. Throughout the year, over sixty community workshops are provided, including papermaking, herbal soap making, organic gardening, ethnic cooking, holistic health classes, and an environmental kid's camp. A CSA program, gift shop, and special events round out life at the farm. Apprentices are needed throughout the changing seasons to learn about every aspect of the farm—from organic farming and medicinal use of herbs to bread making and practicing yoga. Benefits include organic meals, lodging, free classes at the farm, and unlimited mentoring. Those who are healthy, strong, and motivated will thrive at the farm. A phone call is your first step in becoming an apprentice; a farm visit is required.

FOR MORE INFORMATION: Claire Orner, Apprentice Program, Quiet Creek Herb Farm & School of Country Living, 93 Quiet Creek Ln., Brookville, PA 15825 (814) 849-9662 • quietcreek@usachoice.net

RAPHAEL GARDEN

Biodynamic Farming • California • 1 Year
www.steinercollege.edu/biodynamics.html
$ 🏠

As one of America's leading Waldorf teacher education colleges, Rudolf Steiner College offers a variety of teacher and training programs based on the innovative ideas and discoveries of Rudolf Steiner as well as an anthroposophical training center. Raphael Garden serves as the training ground for many activities at this thirteen-acre campus, including a one-year apprenticeship for those looking for a vocation in teaching, gardening, or small-scale farming. A combination of practical and theoretical skills in biodynamic and CSA farm production comprise this unique program. There is no fee for the training; however, it does involve hard work (from seven to ten hours per day, with occasional weekend chores). Housing in a new dormitory, vegetables, four weeks of vacation, and a monthly stipend of $200 are provided. An application consists of a biographical sketch that addresses why you'd like to become an apprentice and your future aspirations, two references, and when you are able to start the program. Further details can be found online or by calling.

FOR MORE INFORMATION: Harald Hoven, Farmer, Apprenticeship Training Program, Raphael Garden, 3937 Bannister Rd., Fair Oaks, CA 95628 (916) 965-0389 • (961) 961-2662 (fax) • rsc@steinercollege.edu

☞ **INSIDER TIP:** Born in Austria in 1861, Dr. Rudolf Steiner studied modern science and philosophy, edited Goethe's scientific works, and developed anthroposophy—the science of the spirit. Echoing the ancient Greek axiom "Man, know thyself," Dr. Steiner described anthroposophy as an "awareness of one's humanity." Humanity *(anthropos)* has the inherent wisdom *(sophia)* to transform both itself and the world. Anthroposophy is a path in which the human heart, hand, and especially the capacity for thinking are essential— and at the heart of Rudolf Steiner College and the apprenticeship experience at Raphael Garden.

THE RODALE INSTITUTE

Farming • Pennsylvania • 6–9 Months
www.rodaleinstitute.org

$

Rodale-style farming has changed over the years—from organic and low-input to sustainable and regenerative—but the intent is unchanged: to provide more healthful food by creating and maintaining healthy soil. Each year more than twenty-five thousand visitors see the results of health-based growing techniques firsthand in both the field crops and the demonstration garden. It is hoped that each visitor will rediscover that the food they eat is a primary tool in achieving optimum health and avoidance of illness and disease. At the experimental farm, interns assist the staff in a variety of projects while gaining hands-on study and educational experience. Internships are generally available in the following departments, subject to change due to funding: creative-education team; farm operations (a complete view of what it takes to run and profit from an organic farm); international programs (developing self-sustaining organic models within other countries); and soil health. Interns receive an hourly wage and generally work for six to nine months between March and November. Priority will be given to applications received prior to February 15. Unpaid internships are available year-round and can be arranged in cooperation with a college or university for credit or with funding from a scholarship or other grant. Detailed information can be found online.

FOR MORE INFORMATION: Sandra Strausser, Human Resources, Internship Program, The Rodale Institute, 611 Siegfriedale Rd., Kutztown, PA 19530-9749 (610) 683-1428 • (610) 683-1431 (fax) • sandra.strausser@rodaleinst.org

Do not wish to be anything but what you are, and try to be that perfectly.
—ST. FRANCIS DE SALES

ROXBURY FARM

Farming • New York • 1–9 Months
www.roxburyfarm.com

$ ⚐ ⊕

Roxbury Farm, an eight-hundred-member CSA farm in upstate New York, is located on 250 acres in the Hudson Valley and serves CSA members locally, in the Capital District (Albany), Westchester County, Harlem, and Manhattan. Prior to the beginning of the farm season each year, members contribute toward the operating costs of the farm. In return they receive freshly harvested organic produce for twenty-five weeks.

WHAT YOU'LL BE DOING: Each season the farm looks for three to four apprentices to learn about farming while they take part in all aspects of the operation—from field preparation and greenhouse work to harvesting and distribution. While apprentices are exposed to all aspects of the farming operation, each apprentice also takes on the responsibility of one specific area: greenhouse production, field seeding and cultivation, member outreach, or work as the assistant harvest manager. This gives apprentices the opportunity to learn all the ins and outs of one specialized area of farm management.

COMMITMENT: The season runs from April until December; however, apprenticeships can be arranged for all or part of the season. During the peak of the season, apprentices can figure on ten hours of work per day; during the spring and late fall, the workload falls to eight to nine hours a day. Every other Saturday apprentices travel to a Collaborative Regional Alliance for Farmer Training (CRAFT) farm visit.

PERKS AND REWARDS: A stipend reflecting experience and responsibility is paid monthly. On-farm housing with full facilities and vegetables and fruit produced on the farm are also provided. Each week the apprentices and farmers take a farm walk to discuss the work for the upcoming weeks and talk about soil fertility, crop rotations, disease and insect management, and many other topics related to sustainable agriculture. Many agricultural resources such as harvest manuals, seeding schedules, and biodynamic farming resource books are available for use.

THE ESSENTIALS: Candidates should have some farming experience as well as the desire to learn how to farm efficiently in order to produce affordable food. Those who are self-motivated and have good organizational skills and a love for hard work do best. Many of Roxbury's past apprentices have gone on to have their own successful farm operations.

YOUR FIRST MOVE: Send a letter of interest, including a short description of past agricultural experiences, future goals, and what you are looking for in apprenticeship at Roxbury Farm, along with a resume and two references, by either email or regular mail. Candidates are asked to visit the farm before a final commitment is made to get a good feeling for the farm, the people, and the work.

FOR MORE INFORMATION: Jean-Paul and Jody Courtens, Owners, Roxbury Farm, 2501 State Route 9H, Kinderhook, NY 12106 • (518) 758-8558 (518) 758-8559 (fax) • info@roxburyfarm.com

SHELBURNE FARMS

Organic Farming/Teaching • Vermont • 3–6 Months
www.shelburnefarms.org

$ 🏠

Located in Vermont's Champlain Valley, Shelburne Farms is a 1,400-acre working farm and dairy known for their incredible farmhouse cheddar cheese. They offer year-round conservation education programs and events for students, teachers, and people of all ages. Organic gardening apprentices work alongside a master gardener in the two-acre market garden, where organic vegetables, herbs, and fruits are also grown for the Inn (the farm's historic guesthouse). Six-month positions begin in April, and job responsibilities range from planting and cultivating to assisting with animal care and educational garden programs. Education apprentices instruct and assist with the development of agricultural and natural resource education programs for preschool children through adults throughout the year (usually one or two seasons). Individuals holding a degree in environmental studies, education, or agriculture are preferred. All apprentices receive a living expense reimbursement of $180 per week, along with participation in orientation and training events, on-site housing, and access to in-season garden produce, cheddar cheese, and free-range, organic chicken eggs. Send a cover letter and resume to begin the application process.

FOR MORE INFORMATION: Christine Durant, Work and Learn Coordinator, Shelburne Farms, 1611 Harbor Rd., Shelburne, VT 05482 (802) 985-8686, ext. 21 • (802) 985-8123 (fax) • cdurant@shelburnefarms.org

SLIDE RANCH

Sustainable Education • California • 11 Months
www.slideranch.org

$ 🏠 ⊕

As a nonprofit education center, the 134-acre Slide Ranch uses hands-on experience to teach respect for the human role in the web of life. Educational programs encourage participants to touch, taste, smell, hear, and observe plants, sea life, and the earth. Whether milking a goat, searching for worms, turning compost, making solar ovens, or exploring the tide pools, visitors will gain an understanding of organic food production, animal husbandry, recycling, open space conservation, and the responsibility each of us has for sustaining a healthy environment.

YOUR SURROUNDINGS: As a park partner with the Golden Gate National Recreation Area, Slide Ranch is nestled in the rugged coast on the ocean side of Highway 1 just north of San Francisco. A short hike from the farm and residential areas of Slide Ranch bring visitors to the shore itself, where an abundance of coastal marine life thrives in the intertidal zone tide pools. Most people who come here feel they've discovered something very special.

WHAT YOU'LL BE DOING: Upon arrival, teachers-in-residence participate in a three-week intensive training program, and throughout the program they receive ongoing support, supervision, staff development, and enrichment. Under the guidance of the program manager and with the support of the entire staff, teachers gain valuable outdoor education teaching experiences by teaching groups of all ages. Beyond responsibilities in the teaching programs, teachers-in-residence are also responsible for a chore area, which includes caring for the garden and compost or one of the many animals on the ranch.

COMMITMENT: Positions begin in early February and end in mid-December. Living at the ranch is more than a nine-to-five job; it's a full-time commitment. Operating as a small community that works, lives, and plays together, all residents are expected to take part in the shared decision making and domestic responsibilities that go along with being part of a community.

PERKS AND REWARDS: A monthly stipend is provided. While each teacher is provided with an individual room and full board, cooking and dining space is shared, and all residents help in the preparation of food and the maintenance of the facilities. A three-week break between summer and fall is given as well as flexible vacation days. Many former Slide Ranch teachers now teach professionally, while others work in social services, community-development organizations, sustainable agriculture, and environmental organizations.

THE ESSENTIALS: Candidates must have a keen interest in environmental education and community spirit.

YOUR FIRST MOVE: Call for a brochure and application guidelines. Speaking other languages or having experience working with low-income or special populations is pertinent information that should be included in your application.

FOR MORE INFORMATION: Program Director, Slide Ranch, 2025 Shoreline Highway, Muir Beach, CA 94965 • (415) 381-6155 • (415) 381-5762 (fax) admin@slideranch.org

SOLAR LIVING INSTITUTE

Sustainable Education • California • 3–9 Months
www.solarliving.org

♥ ⚐

As a spin-off from Real Goods Trading Company (www.realgoods.com), the nonprofit Solar Living Institute promotes sustainable living through inspirational one- to nine-day workshops on renewable energy (solar, wind, water), green building, sustainable living, ecological design, and alternative construction methods. Visited by over 200,000 people annually, this twelve-acre demonstration site features northern California's largest solar arrays, an organic garden site, and a self-contained demonstration tree home and is home to SolFest, a festival held each August. The Institute also offers a unique intern program with positions in nonprofit management, festival production, site maintenance, workshop coordination, and permaculture farming. Positions are offered year-round; however, the greatest need falls between March and October. Although positions are unpaid, interns will be able to attend workshops for free and work on research projects of interest. Primitive camping, food from the gardens (supplemented with a weekly food allowance), a community cooking area, and solar-powered hot showers are provided. Those who are flexible, eco-minded, interested in making a difference in the world, and have completed at least one year in college are welcome to apply. Application materials and current positions details are available online.

FOR MORE INFORMATION: Workshop and Intern Coordinator, Solar Living Institute, 13771 S. Highway 101, P.O. Box 836, Hopland, CA 95449 (707) 744-2017 • (707) 744-1682 (fax) • sli@solarliving.org

🖝 **INSIDER TIP: In the end, we will conserve only what we love. We will love only what we understand. We will understand only what we are taught. —*Baba Dioum***

TERRA BELLA FARM

Organic Farming • Missouri • 3–7 Months
www.terrabellafarm.net

$ 🏕

Located about twenty minutes from Columbia, Missouri, Terra Bella Farm is a twelve-acre certified organic vegetable, herb, and flower operation supporting both a CSA program and sales to local farmers' markets, natural food stores, and restaurants. During the mid-April to early November growing season, apprentices have the opportunity to work and learn about all aspects of organic gardening—from production and marketing to bed preparation and harvesting. A monthly stipend of $100 to $350, housing, and fresh produce are provided. After filling out the online application, all candidates must make a visit to the farm.

FOR MORE INFORMATION: DeLisa Lewis, Farmer, Terra Bella Farm, 1303 State Road M, Auxvasse, MO 65231 • (573) 387-4949 apprentice@terrabellafarm.net

TILLERS INTERNATIONAL

Farming • Michigan • 3–9 Months
www.wmich.edu/tillers

$ 🏕 🌐

Tillers Training Center offers learning opportunities in traditional farming and crafting techniques, including classes in alternative energy, animal power, blacksmithing, farming, rope and broom making, and woodworking, as well as old-time barn raising. Classes and activities are available year-round, with fees ranging from free to $310. In addition to classes, Tillers offers internships in farming and woodworking. Two to four interns help with the farm, wood shop, and organizational work over a three- to nine-month period. While the pay is modest, most of the compensation comes from the opportunity to learn rare skills. On the farm, interns learn to drive oxen and horses in an array of tasks from manure spreading to hay making. In the wood shop, interns learn to shape ox yokes, bend bows, and construct joinery for timber frames. A farmhouse serves as a guesthouse for students and interns working at Tillers. Breakfasts and lunches are provided during classes; there is a kitchen to prepare evening meals. Contact Tillers for their most recent catalog and application materials.

FOR MORE INFORMATION: Dick Roosenberg, Program Organizer, Tillers International, 10515 East OP Ave., Scotts, MI 49088 • (800) 498-2700 (269) 626-0223 • tillersox@aol.com

WILLOW POND FARM

Organic Farming • Maine • 6 Months
www.willowpf.com

$ 🏠

Located just a half hour's drive from Portland, Maine, Willow Pond Farm has six acres of certified organic vegetables and raspberries for their 110-member CSA, eight acres of pick-your-own apple orchards, a children's garden, and several acres to support turkeys, chickens, pigs, sheep, and work horses. From May through October, apprentices help with the entire operation while learning organic vegetable production and livestock care. Duties may include seeding and transplanting, greenhouse maintenance, harvesting, organization and operation of the CSA, food preservation, tractor operation, horse-powered cultivation, tending to the animals, and carpentry work. A monthly stipend of $300 to $500 is provided, along with housing in heated cabins, produce from the farm, a fully-equipped outdoor community kitchen for meals, and a composting toilet. Applicants must be community minded, punctual, and self-motivated and have the ability and desire to do strenuous physical labor. Applications are available online or call for more information.

FOR MORE INFORMATION: Jill Agnew, Apprentice Program, Willow Pond Farm, 395 Middle Rd., Sabattus, ME 04280 • (207) 375-6662 • willowpf@aol.com

WOLLAM GARDENS

Flower Farming • Virginia • 10 Weeks
www.wollamgardens.com

$ 🏠 🌐

At Wollam Gardens, three apprentices have the opportunity to learn all aspects of a cut-flower growing operation—from seeding, planting, and weeding to cutting and bouquet making. Most of the flowers are propagated in a small greenhouse and grown outdoors on over six acres. Flowers are sold to florists and at three large farmers' markets in the Washington, D.C., area. A

$150-per-week stipend is provided, along with a private room in a historic colonial farmhouse, meals, laundry facilities, and an Internet connection. Note that life on the farm is a communal-living experience—all share in the chores of cooking, shopping, and cleaning. Positions are available beginning mid-March and continue through October. Most apprentices make a commitment of ten weeks, although shorter or longer time frames are possible. To begin the application process, review the details online, then contact them by phone or email.

FOR MORE INFORMATION: Bob Wollam, Owner, Wollam Gardens, 5167 Jeffersonton Rd., Jeffersonton, VA 22724 • (540) 937-3222 (540) 937-8290 (fax) • wollamgardens@earthlink.net

WORLD HUNGER RELIEF INC.

Organic Farming/Ministry/Hunger Awareness • Texas/Haiti • 15 Months
www.worldhungerrelief.org

♥ ⚎

At the heart of World Hunger Relief Inc. (WHRI) is the philosophy to live simply and to help those who struggle to meet their basic needs by sharing and investing into others what God has given us. At their forty-acre demonstration farm and training center in Texas (which includes a straw-bale visitor and education center), WHRI runs a CSA and farm market, offers seminars on intensive organic gardening and hunger awareness, and works with low-income, elderly, and disabled individuals on community garden projects. WHRI also supports a twenty-two-acre training center in northeastern Haiti.

WHAT YOU'LL BE DOING: Each year, WHRI selects up to a dozen interns to participate in a twelve-month sustainable farming and development program followed by an optional three-month field experience in Ferrier, Haiti. From day one, interns become a major part of the farm and are involved in every aspect of running it—from planning and production to research and marketing. Along with the daily (and intensive) labors of producing organic vegetables and pecans, as well as milk, eggs, and meat for sale at the local market, interns are also involved in leading school tours, teaching classes, and speaking to church and community groups. The facilities are to be used as a training tool for the interns to practice all aspects of development work for developing countries. For those who wish to earn income beyond room and board, assistantships are also offered in one of their income-generating areas: fresh market vegetable production, livestock, pecan orchard, village store, and local education.

PERKS AND REWARDS: Dormitory-style housing with a communal kitchen, fresh organic produce (including vegetables, fruit, grains, legumes, meat, eggs, milk, cheese, and yogurt), and bicycles to explore the surrounding area are provided. Those who take on assistantship responsibilities also receive a monthly stipend of $300. Field trips are organized to other farms, and interns are encouraged to attend short courses at other facilities in Texas and beyond.

MATTHEW LESTER

THE ESSENTIALS: Candidates must be eager, creative, industrious, committed, willing to be taught, and able to work independently when needed.

YOUR FIRST MOVE: Call or email for more information. A visit to the farm for an interview is welcomed.

FOR MORE INFORMATION:
Dale Barron
Development Director
World Hunger Relief Inc.
P.O. Box 639
Elm Mott, TX 76640
(254) 799-5611
whrieducation@hot.rr.com

With hoe in hand, a World Hunger Relief intern prepares for his three-month field experience in Haiti.

Individuality is the salt of common life. You may have to live in a crowd but you do not have to like it, nor subsist on its food. You may have your own orchard. You may drink at a hidden spring. Be yourself if you would serve others. —HENRY VAN DYKE

WILLING WORKERS
ON ORGANIC FARMS

• •

*WWOOF (wuf), v. [O.E. woef, to travel in search of organic
farms; to pull weeds in exchange for alms.]*

—FROM *THE SHORTER OXFORD DICTIONARY*

Established in the United Kingdom in the seventies, Willing Workers on
Organic Farms (commonly known as WWOOF) was initially designed to
allow people from the city to experience rural areas of the U.K. Today its purpose is to promote the organic agricultural movement in the global village in
which we live. Working in exchange for your keep is the basis of WWOOFing.
As a short-term volunteer, you'll help with organic farming, gardening,
homesteading (animal care, weeding, harvesting, and construction projects),
or other environmentally conscious projects in exchange for room and board
(usually three wholesome meals a day). A half-day's work for a full-day's keep
seems to be a good rule of thumb, with the length of stay varying from a few
days to several months, and sometimes longer. Of course, this varies with
each country and farm.

This type of lifestyle affords the opportunity to obtain firsthand experience in organic and biodynamic growing methods by working with experts in
the field; a chance to meet, talk, learn, and exchange views with others in the
organic movement; the ability to learn about life in the host country by living
and working with a family; and the opportunity to travel in areas of a country
that might have been overlooked.

GETTING INVOLVED

Details of farms registered with WWOOF in each country are available
through the various programs listed on the following pages. Each organization publishes a directory of opportunities that you can obtain for a fee that
generally ranges from $20 to $40 (cash), plus one or two International Reply
Coupons (IRCs) for programs outside the U.S. Fees for each program are
listed in U.S. currency unless otherwise noted.

Once you have received the WWOOF listings, it's then your responsibility
to contact the farm directly and arrange a mutually convenient time and
period of work. Telephoning or emailing the host seems to be the most convenient method. For those with families, some farms are prepared to take
children, with meal and supervision arrangements agreed upon between the
WWOOF member and host beforehand.

If you'll be working in a country other than your own, be sure to read through the visa requirements. According to most immigration departments, WWOOFing is seen as voluntary work and therefore can be done by holders of a regular or tourist visa, provided that it is not the main reason for coming to a country.

🖎 INSIDER TIP: The acronym IRC stands for International Reply Coupon, which serves as a form of payment for sending a twenty-gram letter anywhere in the world. IRCs are available at most post offices and cost slightly more than an international stamp (generally $1).

WWOOF CONNECTIONS AROUND THE WORLD

North America

HAWAII

Ever heard of *lilikoi* or *awapuhi*? As an apprentice on a Hawaii Organic Farmers Association (HOFA) farm on the Hawaiian Islands, apprentices will plant, harvest, and taste these and hundreds of other tropical fruits and vegetables. And what's unique about the Hawaiian Islands is that they contain eleven of the thirteen microclimates found throughout the world. Thus, apprentices have the opportunity to work in dry, wet, coastal, or mountainous regions. HOFA provides all the details of farm opportunities—including contacts and a short description of each farm—for a fee of $20. Most farms offer room and board, a stipend, or both. Positions are available year-round; however, if you're interested in a particular crop, be sure to do some research. Some crops, like pineapples, are generally harvested in July and August, while bananas and papayas can be harvested year-round. Call or email for more information or fill out the questionnaire that's found online. By the way, *lilikoi* is a wild passion fruit and *awapuhi* is edible root ginger.

FOR MORE INFORMATION: Farm Apprentice Program Director, Hawaii Organic Farmers Association, P.O. Box 6863, Hilo, HI 96720 • (877) 674-4632 (808) 969-7789 • (808) 969-7759 (fax) • hofa@hawaiiorganicfarmers.org www.hawaiiorganicfarmers.org

We are not human beings on a spiritual journey.
We are spiritual beings on a human journey.
—STEPHEN COVEY

375

MAINE

The Maine Organic Farmers apprenticeship program places individuals on one of forty sustainable farms in Maine. Participants learn rural skills and gain firsthand experiences in market growing, livestock management, marketing techniques, food preservation, homesteading, and dairy farming. Opportunities are available year-round; however, most farmers look for apprentices from March through October. In addition, a summer education series will complement your on-farm experience. Room, board, instruction, practice, and a stipend are provided in exchange for your labor.

FOR MORE INFORMATION: Andrew Marshall, Education Programs Director, Apprenticeship Program, Maine Organic Farmers and Gardeners Association, P.O. Box 170, Unity, ME 04988-0170 • (207) 568-4142 • (207) 568-4141 (fax) education@mofga.org • www.mofga.org

VERMONT

Certified Organic. This is at the heart of the Northeast Organic Farming Association of Vermont (NOFA-VT). Along with summer workshops, a winter conference, and certifying over 225 organic farms each year, NOFA-VT programs include getting organic produce into elementary school lunch programs (and agriculture education into the curriculum!), making organic food more accessible to limited-income individuals, and apprenticeship and WWOOF opportunities. Each year Vermont farmers provide exciting opportunities for young farmers interested in learning about mixed vegetable production, greenhouse tomato operations, maple syruping, haying, growing berries or apples, raising poultry or beef, or producing cheese. For a nominal fee, NOFA-VT will send you a directory (published each year in February) of over sixty-five farmers looking for apprentices and willing workers, as well as information that will help you locate the appropriate apprenticeship. In addition, discounts on books and free admission to all NOFA-VT training sessions and workshops are provided. Applications for apprenticeships are accepted year-round, although most placements are made March through October.

FOR MORE INFORMATION: Apprenticeship Coordinator, Northeast Organic Farming Association of Vermont, P.O. Box 697, Richmond, VT 05477 (802) 434-4122 • (802) 434-5154 (fax) • info@nofavt.org • www.nofavt.org

USA

As a project of the Ecological Farming Association (www.eco-farm.org), WWOOF USA produces a directory of over three hundred organic farmers in the United States (including Hawaii) who are willing to host volunteers on their land. The directory provides descriptions of each farm, including the type of land, crops being grown, personality of the farm family and community, and current farm projects. A preview of the directory can be found online; one-year memberships run $20.

FOR MORE INFORMATION: Coordinator, WWOOF USA, P.O. Box 510, Felton, CA 95018 • (831) 425-3276 • info@wwoofusa.org • www.wwoofusa.org

CANADA

John Vanden Heuvel states that WWOOF Canada continues to grow (organically and sustainably) and now has over five hundred hosts all across Canada, with two hundred of these in British Columbia. In addition, they have introduced WWOOF opportunities in Hawaii, with forty-five farm listings (check out www.wwoofhawaii.org for more info and application fees). Most opportunities are offered spring through fall; however, volunteers are needed year-round. A membership fee of $35 (plus appropriate postage from your home country) includes a booklet listing farms, with descriptions and contact information. Application materials are available online.

FOR MORE INFORMATION: John Vanden Heuvel, Coordinator, WWOOF Canada, 4429 Carlson Rd., Nelson, BC V1L 6X3, Canada • (250) 354-4417 wwoofcan@shaw.ca • www.wwoof.ca

Asia

JAPAN

For $40, you can obtain online access to the WWOOF Japan host list, with text in both English and Japanese, which consists of detailed program and contact information for over seventy-five programs, including farms, pensions in ski resort areas, healing centers, martial arts studios, tea rooms, and environmental centers.

FOR MORE INFORMATION: Coordinator, WWOOF Japan, Honcho 2-jo, 3-chome, 6-7, Higashi-ku, Sapporo 065-0042, Japan • info@wwoofjapan.com www.wwoofjapan.com

The appearance of things change according to the emotions, and thus we see magic and beauty in them, while the magic and beauty are really in ourselves.
—KAHLIL GIBRAN

WWOOFING IN NEW ZEALAND: HAPPILY SWEATING IN THE SUNSHINE WITH LIKE-MINDED PEOPLE

My choice to WWOOF in New Zealand was impulsive and uninformed, at best. Upon learning of the WWOOF program, I quickly visited the WWOOF New Zealand website (see page 381), saw a beautiful picture of a young WWOOFer working proudly in a garden, and was hooked. I sent in my $15 and became a member of WWOOF New Zealand. I envisioned roaming the picturesque New Zealand countryside, living cheaply on farms, and spending my days happily sweating in the sunshine with like-minded people. Having just graduated from college and feeling completely unready to do the real-world thing, this seemed like a great adventure and the right thing to do at the time. Though I was by no means a farmer (my parents love to remind me of my total disinterest in their large garden and my amusing inability to discern the spinach patch from the beet greens), I had raked blueberries and detasseled corn with enthusiasm, and I knew that I would enjoy any task that involved getting dirty and being outside. So I was off to New Zealand.

My first WWOOFing site was with a family on an ecovillage. Arranging this couldn't have been easier—I sent them an email (the address obtained from my WWOOF–NZ directory) while I was still in the U.S., then called them once I arrived in Auckland. They were extremely kind and hospitable and even picked me up from my hostel in Auckland and brought me to their home in Northland. Their generosity was shocking (nearly uncomfortably for this American)! They gave me the first few days off to rest up; set me up in their daughter's bedroom while she moved onto a cot in the parents' bedroom; took me to beaches and museums; and refused to let me help with anything. It was strange. The experience was new to both of us; they had never hosted a WWOOFer before, and I had never WWOOFed before, so we were both on uncertain ground, and I often felt they didn't know exactly what to do with me. As it worked out, I worked about six hours each day doing odd jobs around the house (brush clearing, weed pulling, painting, sanding, and even babysitting) and then would have the rest of the day off. It was a fair arrangement and I was treated wonderfully, but I was quite lonely, being miles from anything with no email or phone and never seeing anyone else my own age. I stayed there for three weeks, then called another WWOOF host and arranged to move on.

My next WWOOF experience was radically different from my first. Radically. I ended up at a beautiful bed-and-breakfast and horse farm, where I was expected to work all day riding horses and cleaning the guests' rooms. The work was not particularly hard and I loved riding the horses, but it was not a fair arrangement and I encountered many other very disgruntled WWOOFers there. I must say that I had a lot of good and interesting experiences at this farm, and for the most part enjoyed the work, but would not have been able to deal with the constant work (and the incredibly zany host) if I had not maintained a strict "go with the flow" attitude about it. Most other WWOOFers stayed for only a day or two before leaving in a huff. After a few weeks, I, too, was glad to leave.

The third, and last, farm I WWOOFed at ended up being the best. I felt very fortunate to have found it, and WWOOFing there helped me to understand what WWOOFing should really be like. The hosts were exceptionally nice and fair, the work arrangement was clearly defined, and there were always at least five other WWOOFers working there. Upon arriving, I became instant friends with the other WWOOFers (we still keep in touch) and felt very comfortable with the whole situation. Our duties were to keep the house clean, care for and ride the horses, and do various tasks in the garden. After our work was finished, we were encouraged to go off on our own horse rides, explore the town, or just relax in front of the television. The combination of enjoyable hard work and meaningful friendships made this experience memorable and fulfilling. This, truly, was what I had envisioned WWOOFing to be.

My advice for future WWOOFers—at least those going to New Zealand—is to be ready for anything. Of course, everyone has an image of what WWOOFing will be, and while this image should be used as a guide, be careful not to reject any experience that doesn't measure up to your expectations. Even my worst WWOOFing moments taught me something, and if nothing else, make for really interesting stories to tell people back at home. I do suggest, however, trying to get a feel for a place before agreeing to WWOOF there. Every WWWOF host is different, and there is really no way of knowing, via one phone call, what the realities on that farm will be.

Here are some good questions to ask a prospective host:

- What kind of work will I be doing?

- How many hours will I work per day?

- Will I get a day off?

- Do you often have WWOOFers? If so, how long do they usually stay?

- Will you have any other WWOOFers during my stay?

We grow in time to trust the future for our answers. **379**
—RUTH BENEDICT

I highly recommend going to farms with other WWOOFers—not only will you have more fun, but you are also less likely to be exploited. Farms that depend on WWOOF labor will be well set up to host WWOOFers and will probably have a clearly defined and fair work arrangement. Also, be sure to ask about the diet of the host—some farms do not like vegetarians and will not provide vegetarian fare, while others only accept people willing to give up meat. Finally, you may want to ask about any nearby town and about your access to it. Lots of hosts will provide bikes and even cars for WWOOFers, but some are very isolated, meaning you should stock up on shampoo and chocolate before arriving!

All in all, I was very happy with my time WWOOFing. It enabled me to travel all of New Zealand for little money, helped me to sharpen my horse-riding skills, and introduced me to many great people. Though I still have trouble telling spinach from beet greens, I know a whole lot more about New Zealand and the world. I don't know if I'll ever WWOOF again, but I am glad to have done it once, and I think that for a hasty and impulsive decision, it turned out to be amazing.

—Contributed by Rebecca Morey

Australia/New Zealand

WWOOF Australia publishes two WWOOF books that include their network of hosts in Australia and throughout the world. Their flagship list, *The Australian WWOOF Book,* includes more than 1,600 participating hosts who are mainly pursuing a simple, sustainable lifestyle. Also included are nurseries, schools, and people running home businesses such as guesthouses, publishers, and writers, who have a willingness to host visitors for a cultural exchange experience. The list runs AUS$55 (which includes shipping) and is updated in January and July each year. For those looking beyond Australia, *WWOOF Australia's Worldwide Book* includes more than five hundred programs covering forty-eight countries for AUS$27. See their website for details and payment options in other currencies, including secure credit card payments.

FOR MORE INFORMATION: Garry Ainsworth, Director, WWOOF Australia, WWOOF Pty Ltd, Mt. Murrindal Co-op, Buchan, Victoria 3885, Australia (011) 61 03 5155-0218 • wwoof@wwoof.com.au • www.wwoof.com.au

LIFE ON THE KIWI FARM

From mango and wine-grape picking to orange and peach harvests, there is a way to continually be employed in Australia. Sponsored by Australian JobSearch (www.jobsearch.gov.au/HarvestTrail), visitors can choose various harvest trail options to explore the opportunities, complete with contact information and dates of harvest.

Farm Helpers in New Zealand (FHiNZ) began out of the Grady family's decision to offer free New Zealand farmstays for visitors at their own farm in exchange for room and meals. The idea was to treat visitors like members of the family so that they could experience the real Kiwi farming way of life and join in both the highs and lows of living on a farm. Now over 160 farms have opened their doors to thousands of working guests. You choose the farm type and location and the host family generally picks you up at the nearest town. Stays on the farm range from a minimum of three days on up to a year. Those who are interested in animals, family fun, and having "a go" at anything will particularly enjoy this way of life. A one year membership in FHiNZ runs NZ$25 for up to two people traveling together. Application details are available online. You'll receive a farm booklet providing details of active guest farms, visitors' reporting on their experiences, and ratings for each farm.

FOR MORE INFORMATION: Warwick and Heather Grady, Coordinators, Farm Helpers in New Zealand, 16 Aspen Way, Palmerston North, New Zealand (011) 64 6 355-0448 • info@fhinz.co.nz • www.fhinz.co.nz

The WWOOF New Zealand membership fee of $26 covers a booklet of eight hundred properties (including farms, permaculture properties, market gardens, communities, and ventures in self-sufficiency in which organic growing plays some part), access to the online version, and postage.

FOR MORE INFORMATION: Andrew and Jane Strange, Directors, WWOOF New Zealand, P.O. Box 1172, Nelson, New Zealand • (011) 64 3 544-9890 support@wwoof.co.nz • www.wwoof.co.nz

🐾 **INSIDER TIP: It's the good, the bad, and the ugly: accommodations can range from a tipi to a retreat center to a biodynamic farm in the hills.** —*Alona Jasik on her experience at organic farms in New Zealand*

Happiness must be cultivated. It is like character.
It is not a thing to be safely let alone for a moment, or it will run to weeds. 381
—ELIZABETH STUART PHELPS

Europe/United Kingdom

AUSTRIA

Looking to get into the Austrian countryside? A one-year membership with WWOOF Austria provides a detailed listing of over 140 farms along with four newsletters throughout the year. The fee runs $25 plus two IRCs. Check out a sample of farm descriptions online.

FOR MORE INFORMATION: Hildegard Gottlieb, Director, WWOOF Austria, Einödhofweg 48, A 8042 Graz, Austria • (011) 43-(0) 316-464951 wwoof.welcome@telering.at • www.wwoof.welcome.at.tf

CZECH REPUBLIC

Membership in WWOOF Czech Republic offers a printed brochure of farms or access to their Internet database, including regular email updates, for a fee of $15.

FOR MORE INFORMATION: Jana Lojkova, Program Director, WWOOF Czech Republic, AREA viva, Dubecno 50, 28902, Knezice, Czech Republic (011) 420 776 226 014 • areaviva@quick.cz • www.wwoof.ecn.cz

ITALY

The WWOOF Italia list includes about two hundred biodynamic and organic farms all over Italy, with a large concentration in Tuscany and Umbria. Host farms range from large farms (where a living is made by farming and selling products) to small-scale family holdings (where self-sufficiency in their food is the primary aim), with organic as the common thread. WWOOFers work up to six hour per day over five to six days (one-week stays are the minimum). Even though skills in farming are not necessary, WWOOFers are expected to work hard in a variety of jobs and have the ability to adapt and fit into the family's lifestyle. The work is diverse and may include rounding up sheep on horseback, cultivating bamboo, helping with school visits, making bread and pasta to sell at local organic markets, picking olives or grapes, or making salami and sausages, alongside all the other mundane tasks such as gardening, weeding, harvesting, and working in the fields. Although most farms take WWOOFers year-round, the best time to go is in autumn for the grape and olive harvests and spring for preparation of vegetable gardens, pruning, and manuring. Membership runs EUR$25 (a nifty currency converter is provided online), which includes an official membership card, insurance coverage for a twelve-month period while on a registered farm in

Italy, and the most current listings, which you can receive through either email or mail. Regular updates are also provided through email.

FOR MORE INFORMATION: Bridget Matthews, Coordinator, WWOOF Italia, via Casavecchia 109, 57022, Castagneto Carducci Livorno, Italy (011) 39 0565-765001 • info@wwoof.it • www.wwoof.it

🐾 **INSIDER TIP:**
- **Always telephone or write before visiting a farm, and if you expect a reply, enclose an IRC or stamp. Try to plan your travels well in advance and keep hosts informed of changes in your plans. Never turn up unexpectedly on a host's doorstep expecting to be made welcome.**
- **Before you arrive, make sure that you have a clear agreement with your host as to the basis of your stay—working hours, food, accommodations, facilities, arrangements if you take children with you, and so forth.**
- **Always take working clothes, such as gloves and good shoes or boots. Sometimes it may be necessary to take a sleeping bag.**
- **It would be a good idea to make sure you and your host have a language in common!**

SWITZERLAND

Details of organic farms, from big to small and rural to urban, that are registered with WWOOF Switzerland can be obtained for $20 plus $2 postage. Membership requirements can be found online.

FOR MORE INFORMATION: Director, WWOOF Switzerland, Postfach 59, CH-8124 Maur, Switzerland • wwoof@gmx.ch • www.wwoof.org/switzerland

UNITED KINGDOM

WWOOF UK publishes a newsletter every month, which contains details of longer stays, events, developments, training and opportunities in the organic movement and includes members' contributions and advertisements. For an annual membership fee of $30 you will receive six issues along with a detailed listing of farm hosts in the UK.

FOR MORE INFORMATION: Fran Whittle, Coordinator, WWOOF United Kingdom, P.O. Box 2675, Lewes, East Sussex BN7 1RB, England, United Kingdom (011) 44 1273 476 286 • hello@wwoof.org • www.wwoof.org.uk

🐾 **INSIDER TIP:** Check out the International WWOOF Association at www.wwoof.org to see what's new in the WWOOF movement.

A society grows great when old men plant trees whose shade they know they shall never sit in.
—GREEK PROVERB

RECOMMENDED RESOURCES

Every December the Alternative Farming Systems Information Center publishes *Educational and Training Opportunities in Sustainable Agriculture,* a resource listing hundreds of opportunities in organic, alternative, or sustainable agriculture work, education, and training. The majority of listings are in the U.S. and Canada, although a handful are overseas. Call for your free copy—(301) 504-6559—or view the listings at www.nal.usda.gov/afsic (click on the Publications link or type in www.nal.usda.gov/afsic/afsic_pubs/edtr.htm). Each listing is verified with the organization every year, with changes and additions incorporated throughout the year on their Web version.

Appropriate Technology Transfer for Rural Areas, commonly known as ATTRA, provides an extensive online database of programs offering internships and apprenticeships on farms, sustainable living centers, and the like (www.attrainternships.ncat.org). Self-updated by the actual farmers throughout the year, the listings are a gold mine of opportunities for the budding farmer, with program details broken down by four regions in the U.S. and Canada.

The Biodynamic Farming and Gardening Association provides an abundance of information on the biodynamic movement as well as a quarterly magazine of opportunities for biodynamic apprenticeships. Single copies cost $6, or an annual subscription runs $45 (which includes a one-year membership). You can also explore current and ongoing internships and apprenticeships through www.biodynamics.com. For more information contact the Biodynamic Farming and Gardening Association, 25844 Butler Rd., Junction City, OR 97448; (888) 516-7797, biodynamic@aol.com.

Through a special online matching service, the **Ohio Ecological Food and Farm Association** (www.oeffa.com) links prospective apprentices with farmers looking for assistance. After submitting application materials (by January 15), applicants will receive mailings of potential hosts. Farmer and apprentice applicants contact each other for mutual "sizing up," farm visitations, and making arrangements. Apprentices must be eighteen or older and no previous farm experience is necessary.

As a matchmaking service for those looking for an apprenticeship, internship, or employment in the organic farming movement in the U.S., **OrganicVolunteers.com** offers hundreds of opportunities that cover everything from programs in ecotourism and education to gardening and construction.

The Robyn Van En Center for CSA Resources (www.csacenter.org) provides a searchable directory (by zip or state) of CSA farms throughout the U.S., as well as an extensive list of organizations involved in the CSA movement.

The Rural Heritage Good Farming Apprenticeship Network (www.ruralheritage.com/apprenticeship) is designed to link future farmers with experienced handlers of working draft horses, mules, and oxen to ensure that animal-powered farming and logging practices are passed down through the generations. The participating farmers—in locations ranging from British Columbia to Tennessee and from California to Nova Scotia—offer a broad range of learn-by-working experiences. Participating farms can be viewed online. For more information contact the Rural Heritage Good Farming Apprenticeship Network, 281 Dean Ridge Ln., Gainesboro, TN 38562-5039; (931) 268-0655, editor@ruralheritage.com.

The Seattle Tilth Association (www.seattletilth.org) promotes the art of organic gardening in an urban setting and maintains gardens at the Good Shepherd Center in Seattle's Wallingford district. Volunteers and interns (one position is funded) are an integral part of the group's operations, making involvement with the association a great way to learn organic gardening through hands-on experiences. In addition, a free online listing of Washington organic farms looking for seasonal workers and apprentices is available through their sister organization, Tilth Producers (www.tilthproducers.org/placement.htm). For more information contact Seattle Tilth Association, Tilth Placement Service, 4649 Sunnyside Ave. N., Room 1, Seattle, WA 98103; (206) 633-0451, tilth@seattletilth.org.

FURTHER READING

We're living in a society where more and more people take things for granted and don't learn important skills for leading a self-reliant and simple lifestyle. *Back to Basics* (Reader's Digest, $30) provides practical and useful information that brings you back to the "old-fashioned" way of doing things—such as converting trees to lumber and building a home from them, growing and harvesting your own vegetable garden, learning traditional crafts and homesteading skills, or enjoyable activities that don't hurt your pocketbook. The pages are filled with ideas for building a new way of life.

Nothing could be more fundamental to the needs of an increasingly crowded world than food. Based on biointensive gardening techniques, *How to Grow More Vegetables* (Ten Speed Press, $19.95) will show you how to raise enough fresh, healthy, organic vegetables for a family of four on a parcel of land as small as eight hundred square feet. John Jeavons provides the ultimate how-to manual for sustainable gardening with results that are more bountiful.

A FARMER'S CREED

(written for the New Holland America, originally published in 1975)

I believe a man's greatest possession is his dignity and that no calling bestows this more abundantly than farming.

I believe hard work and honest sweat are the building blocks of a person's character.

I believe that farming, despite its hardships and disappointments, is the most honest and honorable way a man can spend his days on this earth.

I believe my children are learning values that will last a lifetime and can be learned in no other way.

I believe farming provides education for life and that no other occupation teaches so much about birth, growth, and maturity in such a variety of ways.

I believe many of the best things in life are indeed free: the splendor of a sunrise, the rapture of wide open spaces, the exhilarating sight of your land greening each spring.

I believe true happiness comes from watching your crops ripen in the field, your children grow tall in the sun, your whole family feel the pride that springs from their shared experience.

I believe that by my toil I am giving more to the world than I am taking from it, an honor that does not come to all men.

I believe my life will be measured ultimately by what I have done for my fellow men, and by this standard I fear no judgement.

I believe when a man grows old and sums up his days, he should be able to stand tall and feel pride in the life he's lived.

I believe in farming because it makes all this possible.

A musician must make his music, an artist must paint, a poet must write if he is to ultimately be at peace with himself.
—ABRAHAM MASLOW

CHAPTER

ARTISTIC AND LEARNING PURSUITS

No one can tell you how to live your life. You are the artist and must shape your experiences with your own hand. Whether working as an accomplished artist or just starting out in the field, creative-minded painters, writers, photographers, actors, musicians, dancers, crafters, filmmakers, architects, exhibit designers, museum enthusiasts, living history performers, archaeologists, historians, and researchers will find a supportive arts environment to learn and grow from in this chapter. Come take your career to new heights, explore your options, and learn what it takes to do what you love and make enough money to support your creative passions.

UNIQUE OPPORTUNITIES TO EXPLORE IN THIS CHAPTER

- Recognizing the need for artists and writers to set aside periods of time to work intensively on projects away from the distractions of everyday life but still have a social connection, artist communities and resident programs offer a unique way to foster your creative pursuits virtually expense free (page 395).

- Whether you'd like to gain more experience in stage management, artistic design, or any other facet of professional theater, the Seattle Repertory Theatre's training program has something for each budding artist (page 423)—as do plenty of other theaters, playhouses, and festivals profiled in this chapter.

- The Smithsonian Institution is the world's largest museum and, quite possibly, has the world's largest museum internship program. The Center for Education and Museum Studies coordinates the central referral service for all internship programs, including those in sixteen museums and galleries, and the National Zoo (page 424).

- At some point in our life, we all come to a place where we long to uncover our mission—a lifelong "assignment" that evolves from deep within our soul. Join David Lyman, the founder of the Workshops, in his journey of uncovering a deeper calling and building his place in the world (page 431).

PHIL GRANT

The chamber music class with Eagle's Nest Foundation (page 153) performs barefoot as their music lifts through the trees.

AMERICAN CONSERVATORY THEATER

Theater • California • 2–10 Months
www.act-sf.org
$

San Francisco's Tony Award–winning American Conservatory Theater (ACT) is one of the largest and most active of the nation's resident professional theaters. In their magnificently restored Geary Theater, ACT presents a season of the classics of dramatic literature and outstanding works of modern theater. In addition to housing a prestigious actor training program, ACT employs more than eight hundred people annually, including actors, directors, teachers, designers, administrators, technicians, and craftspeople.

WHAT YOU'LL BE DOING: Since 1976, ACT has provided in-depth training for individuals seeking a career in theater arts by offering internships in theater production and administration. These programs provide students and other interested people the opportunity to work closely with top professionals in the field. The production department includes positions in stage management, production management, properties, technical design, sound design, lighting design, costume rentals, costume shop, and wig construction and makeup. The artistic and administrative departments offer positions as assistant directors and artistic staff and in marketing/public relations, literary/publications, arts management, and development.

COMMITMENT: Production department internships are full-time positions that parallel the Geary season, approximately August to June. Due to the variable hours of the program and the intense nature of the work, it is impossible to hold an outside job during the internship period. Artistic and administrative internships are generally flexible, lasting from two to six months throughout the year, and work schedules that accommodate outside employment may be arranged.

PERKS AND REWARDS: A small hourly wage is available to all interns. ACT will provide housing assistance, but securing housing is the responsibility of each intern. Perks include complimentary tickets to ACT productions (and other local theater productions), monthly intern roundtables with guest speakers, and a resume/portfolio workshop.

THE ESSENTIALS: Most departments require previous experience in their area of production, but a sincere and enthusiastic personality may compensate for lack of experience in some cases. Due to the high costs of living in the Bay Area, all applicants must have additional independent funding for living expenses while in residence.

Love is the spirit that motivates the artist's journey. The love may be sublime, raw, obsessive, passionate, awful, or thrilling, but whatever its quality, it's a powerful motive in the artist's life.
—ERIC MAISEL

YOUR FIRST MOVE: Visit ACT's website for complete details and an application, or call for a brochure. Production department internship applications are due April 15. Notification of acceptance will be made by June 1, after an in-person or telephone interview. Artistic and administrative internship applications are accepted anytime.

FOR MORE INFORMATION: Internship Coordinator, American Conservatory Theater, 30 Grant Ave., San Francisco, CA 94108-5800 • (415) 439-2447 (internship hotline) • (415) 834-3200 • (415) 423-2711 (fax) • hr@act-sf.org

AMERICAN DANCE FESTIVAL

Dance Festival • North Carolina • Summer
www.americandancefestival.org
$ ⊕

Here's a chance to become part of an exciting community of dancers, students, choreographers, teachers, performers, critics, body therapists, dance medical specialists, scholars, and arts managers from all over the U.S. and around the world. Held for six weeks each summer at Duke University, the American Dance Festival offers internships in the box office, facilities services, food and housing, merchandising, performances, press, schools and workshops, and production. In addition to a $950 or $1,100 stipend, interns will receive one complimentary ticket to one night of each performance. Interns may also take one dance class per day and can observe panel discussions, seminars, and lectures by distinguished visitors as the work schedule permits. Apartments and shared housing are conveniently located near the festival site. Those needing help with housing are encouraged to seek the festival's assistance. Applications must be received by February 15. International applicants must have a U.S. social security number.

FOR MORE INFORMATION: Kimberly Quick, Intern Coordinator, American Dance Festival, Box 90772, Durham, NC 27708-0772 • (919) 684-6402 (919) 684-5459 (fax) • adf@americandancefestival.org

APERTURE FOUNDATION

Photography • New York • 6 Months
www.aperture.org
$ ⊕

Devoted to photography and the visual arts, the Aperture Foundation promotes the development of photography as one of the most powerful forms of human expression, helping to illuminate important social, environmental, and cultural issues. While working with a small, committed staff and some of the greatest living photographers and photography writers, work-scholar program participants engage in all facets of Aperture activities—from writing and design to production and traveling exhibitions. A monthly stipend of $250 is provided along with discounts on books, magazines, and prints. Positions are available for six months beginning in either January or July. Applicants are selected on the basis of their interest and motivation in working for Aperture, their ability to contribute significantly to the program, and their openness to gaining a meaningful work experience. Send a resume, a short writing sample, and a cover letter describing your background, special skills, and personal objectives. Detailed information can be found online.

FOR MORE INFORMATION: Work-Scholar Program Manager, Aperture Foundation, 20 E. 23rd St., New York, NY 10010-4463 • (212) 505-5555, ext. 312 (212) 598-4015 (fax) • reddey@aperture.org

🐦 **INSIDER TIP: Be concise in your letter: please let us know what positions you are most interested in and exactly when you can start. Enthusiasm and interest are the most important qualities for getting accepted into the program. Staff members want to know that you are interested and that you will work hard once you arrive.**

APPEL FARM ARTS AND MUSIC CENTER

Performing Arts • New Jersey • 3–9 Months
www.appelfarm.org

$ 🏠

Appel Farm is renowned for its evening concerts and family matinee series, annual Arts and Music Festival and country music events, summer camp, arts classes, and community arts outreach program—programs that provide people of all ages a supportive environment in which to study, appreciate, and present work in the creative and performing arts.

WHAT YOU'LL BE DOING: Interns work side-by-side with Appel Farm staff either in marketing/box office, arts education, or outreach/event coordination. Summer camp staff positions are available in theater, music, fine arts, media, dance, and sports/swimming. Along with specific projects, interns will be expected, as is everyone at Appel Farm, to pitch in where help is needed. Everyone will do their share of envelope stuffing, data entry, filing, and other office work.

COMMITMENT: Interns should plan to make at least a three-month commitment, although positions may be extended up to six to nine months and are

The only way to make sense out of change is to plunge into it, move with it, and join the dance.
—ALAN WATTS

available September through June. Summer camp positions span from late June through late August.

PERKS AND REWARDS: Interns receive a monthly stipend of $500 along with meals and on-site housing in Appel's original farmhouse. Summer staff wages vary based on experience, with meals and on-site housing in bunkhouses provided. Since the farm is located in a quiet country setting, most staff bring along a car to explore the surrounding region. (Philadelphia is just a half hour away.)

THE ESSENTIALS: If you want to gain administrative experience in the arts while being in a supportive atmosphere, contribute to a growing arts center, and thrive on being given responsibility and hard work, then Appel is an ideal place to work and learn. Camp staff must be at least twenty-one years of age, available for the entire camp season, and nonsmokers.

YOUR FIRST MOVE: Applications and detailed staff descriptions can be found online. An application, resume, and three references are required.

FOR MORE INFORMATION: Matina Lagakos, Office Manager, Appel Farm Arts and Music Center, 457 Shirley Rd., P.O. Box 888, Elmer, NJ 08318-0888 (800) 394-1211 • (856) 358-2472, ext. 100 • (856) 358-6513 (fax) appelarts@aol.com

ART WORKSHOPS IN GUATEMALA

Art Education • Guatemala • 10 Days
www.artguat.org

♥ 🏠 ⊕

Art Workshops in Guatemala offers a wide variety of ten-day workshops for those who want to add an educational component to their travel experience. Known as "the Land of Eternal Spring" because of its year-round seventy-degree weather, Guatemala is the kind of place travelers fall in love with and never want to leave. The pace is slower, less hectic. Cobblestone streets and colorful bougainvillea spilling over rocks of century-old ruins provide daily inspiration. The range of workshops is perfect for those who want to expand their creative horizons, with classes that extend from creative writing and photography to backstrap weaving. The price for each educational travel package averages $2,000 and includes airfare from most major U.S. cities, lodging in a beautiful old colonial home, hearty breakfasts, ground transportation, and interesting field trips.

FOR MORE INFORMATION: Liza Fourré, Director, Art Workshops in Guatemala, 4758 Lyndale Ave., South, Minneapolis, MN 55409-2304 • (612) 825-0747 (612) 825-6637 (fax) • info@artguat.org

ARTIST COMMUNITIES AND RESIDENT PROGRAMS: SPECIAL PLACES TO CREATE

• •

If you're looking for an inspiring setting that's rich in stimulation and fellowship to encourage and nurture your creative pursuits, this section will provide you with a variety of creativity-stirring colonies, communities, and resident programs. Geared to both the emerging and the established artist, residence programs generally run from one week on up to nine months throughout the year. Undoubtedly, the biggest lure for many artisans is the ability to create without interruption in beautiful and unique surroundings. Most programs also take care of all your daily needs—including housing, meals, studio space, equipment, and even supplies—while providing common areas to socialize and collaborate with other talented people.

> *Creation is a peculiar process. It is something that happens between the earth, sun, and the human mind. . . . In creation we must have both leisure to think and dream and means to execute.*
> —MARY CROVATT HAMBIDGE

ARROWMONT SCHOOL OF ARTS AND CRAFTS

Traditional Crafting • Tennessee • 2–5 Weeks or 11 Months
www.arrowmont.org

$ 🏕 ⊕

Arrowmont School of Arts and Crafts, located adjacent to the Great Smoky Mountains National Park, serves as a cultural and educational center for visitors and students. Workshops lure those who wish to learn traditional and contemporary crafts, with classes in ceramics, wood turning, woodworking, fine metals, enameling, glass, fibers (weaving, surface design, quilting, basketry), photography, papermaking, drawing, and painting.

WHAT YOU'LL BE DOING: Each spring, summer, and fall, Arrowmont sponsors a two- to five-week work-study and studio assistantship program. Successful applicants will receive one week of class study for one week of work. Work-study individuals assist the full-time support staff in the kitchen, housekeeping, maintenance, gardens, or office, while studio assistants (who must have four

> *It is the function of art to renew our perception. What we are familiar with we cease to see. The writer shakes up the familiar scene, and as if by magic, we see new meaning in it.*
> —ANAÏS NIN

years of completed course work in a specific media) work alongside the support staff assisting with the studios, gallery installations, book and supply store, and clerical functions. In addition, Arrowmont selects five artists each year to participate in their eleven-month artist-in-residence program (beginning mid-June), where artists work both in their private studios and in workshops, special media conferences, seminars, retreats, Elderhostel classes, and ten hours per week for Arrowmont.

PERKS AND REWARDS: Room, board, and tuition for classes are provided for work-study/studio assistants. Resident artists receive a monthly stipend of $300, two workshops, and a private room with bath, meals, and private studios in the spacious resident-artist studio complex. Several paid teaching opportunities are also available for artists-in-residence. College credit is offered through the University of Tennessee for select workshops for a per-credit-hour fee.

YOUR FIRST MOVE: Work-study/studio assistant applicant deadlines: spring—January 15; summer—April 1; and fall—August 1. Artist-in-residence program applicants must apply by February 15. Applications are available online.

FOR MORE INFORMATION: Bill Griffith, Assistant Director, Arrowmont School of Arts and Crafts, P.O. Box 567, Gatlinburg, TN 37738-0567 • (865) 436-5860 (865) 430-4101 (fax) • info@arrowmont.org

CENTRUM

Artist Retreat • Washington • 1 Week–1 Month
www.centrum.org

♥ ⛺

For over thirty years, creative people have been gathering at historic Fort Worden State Park (a 445-acre park and Victorian seaport) for Centrum's music festivals (from fiddle to jazz), writers conference, and life-changing workshops, where students of all ages share their passion for the arts while learning from gifted instructors. If you are an artist, thinker, composer, activist, writer, visual artist, performer, or involved in creative endeavors, participation in Centrum's creative residency program will provide you with the time and space to grow. Whether for a week or a month, a residency may serve as a reflective retreat or involve active engagement with other programs, artists, and communities. Benefits include housing in small cabins (some with small studios and upright pianos), studio space, Internet access, use of the facilities, and, of course, time. Application materials and detailed information are available online; there is a $20 application fee. Note that residencies are not available from mid-June through mid-August.

FOR MORE INFORMATION: Sally Rodgers, Creative Residencies Coordinator, Centrum, P.O. Box 1158, Port Townsend, WA 98368-0958 • (360) 385-3102 (360) 385-2470 (fax) • sally@centrum.org

DORSET COLONY FOR WRITERS

Artist Retreat • Vermont • Seasonal
www.dorsettheaterfestival.org/html/colony.html

♥ ⚶

Recognizing the need for writers to set aside periods of time to work intensively on projects away from the distractions of everyday life but still have a social connection, Dorset Colony for Writers provides a quiet working retreat for writers and other artists. September through November and April through May, eight private rooms, along with public areas where conversation and fellowship are encouraged, are available for a fee of $150 per week. Residency lengths vary and rooms are filled as requests come in. To apply, submit a letter with requested dates of residency, description of the project to be worked on while in residence, and a resume of publications. More information about Dorset can be found on page 408.

THE HAMBIDGE CENTER
FOR CREATIVE ARTS AND SCIENCES

Artist Retreat • Georgia • 2–8 Weeks
www.hambidge.org

♥ ⚶

Nestled within the lush forests of northeast Georgia's Blue Ridge Mountains and covering six hundred acres, the Hambidge Center's natural environment provides the atmosphere and connections that encourage human creativity—and the foundation for their resident artist program. Writers, poets, visual and environmental artists, photographers, composers, performers, and dancers are housed in eight individual cottages (which double as studios), complete with bath and kitchen facilities. The Rock House serves as a communal place for residents and includes a laundry area, phones, and dining room where dinner

The art of life lies in a constant readjustment to our surroundings.
—KAKUSO OKAKURA

is served February through December. The center offers a warm-weather clay studio (with electric and kick wheels and two electric kilns), a performance studio with a Steinway grand piano, an artists' gallery, and a working gristmill. Various nature trails on the property lead to streams, waterfalls, and wildflower coves. Residents can stay from two to six weeks for a fee of $125 per week. An application (with a $20 processing fee), samples of work, and letters of recommendation are due on the fifteenth of either January, May, or September. The review process usually takes from six to eight weeks.

FOR MORE INFORMATION: Fran Lanier, Residency Director, The Hambidge Center for Creative Arts and Sciences, 105 Hambidge Ct., P.O. Box 339, Rabun Gap, GA 30568 • (706) 746-5718 • (706) 746-9933 (fax) center@hambidge.org

KALANI OCEANSIDE RETREAT

Artist Retreat • Hawaii • Seasonal
www.kalani.com/reside/artist.htm

♥ 🏠 ⊕

Located on over one hundred acres on Hawaii's Big Island, Kalani Oceanside Retreat provides resident artists with the impetus to complete works in progress, strike out in new directions, or simply exchange ideas with other resident artists from varied disciplines, backgrounds, and cultures. Living accommodations and working/performance space are provided for visual, literary, folk, and performing arts. Kalani's monkeypod tree houses, wooden lodges, and private cottages provide simple but comfortable accommodations. Lodging runs $105 to $210 per night; however, half-off lodging cost stipends are available during the less busy periods (May to July and September to December). Healthful and delicious meal options are also available for a fee. More information about Kalani can be found on page 328.

THE MACDOWELL COLONY

Artist Retreat • New Hampshire • 4–8 Weeks
www.macdowellcolony.org

♥ 🏠 ⊕

Founded in 1907, the MacDowell Colony offers a place where emerging and well-established creative artists can find freedom to concentrate on their work. Architects, composers, filmmakers, photographers, printmakers, visual artists, interdisciplinary artists, and writers come to the colony each year for a four- to eight-week period (with twenty to thirty artists-in-residence at any given time). Most artists come to the colony to take advantage of uninterrupted time and seclusion in which to work as well as the experience of living in a community of gifted artists. Undoubtedly friendships established among artists-in-residence often lead to collaborations and connections beyond the colony. There are no residency fees, and each participant is provided with a private room and studio as well as three meals per day. Grants for travel to and from the colony are available based on need. Financial aid for writers is available through a special grant from an anonymous foundation. A two-page application form, work sample, project description, two references, and an application fee of $20 are required. Deadlines: summer—January 15; fall—April 15; and winter/spring—September 15. Residence notification is given eight weeks after the application.

FOR MORE INFORMATION: Admissions Coordinator, The MacDowell Colony, 100 High St., Peterborough, NH 03458 • (603) 924-3886 • (603) 924-9142 (fax) admissions@macdowellcolony.org

MILLAY COLONY FOR THE ARTS

Artist Retreat • New York • 1 Month
www.millaycolony.org

♥ 🏠 🌐

The Millay Colony offers one-month residencies to talented writers, visual artists, composers, and performance artists in a setting that is designed to foster creativity. Whether you are just starting out in your career, an accomplished artist, or need a place to be refreshed, the colony accepts six to seven artists each month from April through November. A private studio and separate living quarters are provided in the renovated Millay Barn, which includes a kitchen (food for meals is included), dining room, living room, library, and a sitting darkroom. Call for information and an application.

FOR MORE INFORMATION: Nikki Hayes, Residency Director, Millay Colony for the Arts, 454 East Hill Rd., P.O. Box 3, Austerlitz, NY 12017-0003 • (518) 392-3103 application@millaycolony.org

To affect the quality of the day, that is the highest of arts.
—HENRY DAVID THOREAU

WATERSHED CENTER FOR THE CERAMIC ARTS

Artist Retreat • Maine • 2 Weeks–9 Months
www.watershedceramics.org

♥ ⚏ ⊕

If you are a serious artist and need the time and space to create in clay, Watershed offers an intimate communal approach and peaceful environment for experimentation, exploration, collaboration, and growth. The studio is housed in a spacious old brickworks barn that provides ample, flexible studio space. Equipment includes propane car kilns, a wood and soda kiln, various electric kilns, potter's wheels, clay mixers, and slab rollers. While a hillside of local earthenware brick clay is free and abundant, standard clay and glaze materials are available for a fee. A separate residence building provides dormitory-style housing for residents, including a central living area for conversation and a dining room where healthful meals are prepared by staff artists. Fully funded and partially funded residencies run from two weeks on up to nine months. Call for application materials and deadlines.

FOR MORE INFORMATION: Lynn Thompson, Executive Director, Watershed Center for the Ceramic Arts, 19 Brick Hill Rd., Newcastle, ME 04553 • (207) 882-6075 (207) 882-6045 (fax) • director@watershedceramics.org

ARTISTS' ALLIANCE

Whether located in a pastoral setting or in the middle of an urban warehouse district, the artist communities listed with the Alliance of Artists Communities (www.artistcommunities.org) are a great starting point for your research. Over one hundred member programs are profiled on their website, where you can search for programs by architecture and design, film/video and media, interdisciplinary, music/dance/performance, scholarship, visual arts, and writing. The alliance also has a handful of great publications, including Artists Communities (Allworth Press, $24.95), which is a must for those needing a creativity-stirring change of pace. The guide details 360 residencies and retreats in the U.S. and abroad, with descriptions of facilities, history, stipends and fees, selection processes, odds of acceptance, special programs, admission deadlines, and contact information. In addition, contact information for nearly one hundred residency programs is provided. For more information contact the Alliance of Artists Communities, 255 S. Main St., Providence, RI 02903; (401) 351-4320, aac@artistcommunities.org.

BERKELEY REPERTORY THEATRE

Theater • California • 11 Months
www.berkeleyrep.org

$ 🏠 🌐

Since its founding in 1968, Berkeley Rep has focused on the development of a resident company of theater artists, including actors, playwrights, directors, designers, and artisans. The sense of community, shared growth, and knowledge that now exists within Berkeley Rep is one of its real strengths. Its national reputation draws theater artists from around the country to work on a variety of productions from September through July.

WHAT YOU'LL BE DOING: With positions available in every conceivable area of the theater, interns have the opportunity to work closely with an accomplished company of artists, administrators, guest directors, and designers. The program includes regularly scheduled informal seminars every month throughout the season as the production schedule allows. The partnership between the theater and the intern is intended to fulfill as many career-building goals and objectives as possible and to provide the intern with a variety of professional contacts and craft-building experiences.

COMMITMENT: Internships usually begin in August or September and are full-time over an eleven-month period.

PERKS AND REWARDS: A monthly stipend of $400 is provided, plus local housing for most positions.

THE ESSENTIALS: Applicants should have already acquired basic training and experience in the theater and be ready for the next step toward a career in professional theater. Candidates should be willing to engage in the creative process and test the limits of their own ingenuity. Serious-minded and highly motivated applicants are most often hired.

YOUR FIRST MOVE: Applications are accepted from January 1 through April 1 for positions beginning the following August. Telephone and in-person interviews are generally held in late April and early May. Additional interviews will be held if openings occur during the season.

FOR MORE INFORMATION: Internship Coordinator, Berkeley Repertory Theatre, 2025 Addison St., Berkeley, CA 94704 • (510) 647-2900 • (510) 647-2929 (fax) internship@berkeleyrep.org

It's not what we have, but what we are, that makes the poverty or richness of our life. **401**
—PHILLIP BROOKS

CAREER DISCOVERY PROGRAM

Design • Massachusetts • 6 Weeks
www.gsd.harvard.edu/professional/career_discovery

♥ ⚶ ⊕

Whether you are considering a design career in architecture, landscape architecture, or urban planning and design, the summer Career Discovery Program at Harvard University can help you experience what it's like to be in these professions. Students participate in a core program of morning lectures and panel discussions, with most of the time devoted to studio work. Short, intensive projects simulate typical first-year experiences in a professional design program. Drawing and computer workshops, one-on-one instruction, and field trips and tours throughout the Boston area round out this six-week intensive program. The tuition of $2,200 includes a kit of basic studio supplies; there is also $30 application fee. On-campus housing is available for a fee starting at $1,050, although you can look for shared living possibilities that may be less expensive. The Harvard Square subway stop makes it easy to live just about anywhere in the Boston area. The program is open to anyone who is seriously considering a career in the design professions. At a minimum, applicants must be high school graduates. Application materials are due in early May.

FOR MORE INFORMATION: Program Coordinator, Career Discovery Program, Harvard Design School, 48 Quincy St., Cambridge, MA 02138 • (617) 495-5453 (617) 496-8306 • (617) 495-8949 (fax) • discovery@gsd.harvard.edu

CARIBBEAN VOLUNTEER EXPEDITIONS

Restoration • The Caribbean • 1–2 Weeks
www.cvexp.org

♥ ⚶

"Preservation in paradise" is the theme for volunteers who venture off to the islands with Caribbean Volunteer Expeditions (CVE). Having skills in preservation, architecture, history, carpentry, photography, or teaching, volunteers are typically those who are not satisfied by merely visiting an island, but are driven to record its architecture, document its heritage, and preserve its history. Working with local preservation leaders, volunteers generally measure and document historical plantations, windmills, and other structures to help local agencies keep a record of their architectural heritage. Typical expeditions last one to two weeks and volunteers should be prepared for thorns, mosquitoes, and other Caribbean conditions. But don't worry, the beach is never far away. CVE charges a fee to cover room, board, tours, and local transportation; airfare is the responsibility of each volunteer.

FOR MORE INFORMATION:
Anne Hersh
Program Director
Caribbean Volunteer Expeditions
P.O. Box 388
Corning, NY 14830
(607) 962-7846
ahershcve@aol.com

A National Park Service archaeologist discusses the day's game plan with his Caribbean Volunteer Expeditions team in the Virgin Islands.

CENTER FOR PHOTOGRAPHY AT WOODSTOCK

Photography • New York • 3–6 Months
www.cpw.org

$ ⊕

Founded in 1977, the Center for Photography at Woodstock provides year-round programs in education, exhibition, publication, residency, and services for artists. The workshop intern experience is unlike traditional classroom education. In a matter of months, interns have the opportunity to meet an average of twenty different guest teachers and hundreds of students. An entire range of topics—from teaching strategies to professional image making—is presented in a relatively short span. Interns facilitate events Fridays through Sundays, providing general hospitality and support for guest artists. In addition to the four workshop internships that are available, Woodstock also offers an arts administration internship with training opportunities ranging from exhibition design to fund-raising strategies.

COMMITMENT: Workshop internships are available full-time from June through October; arts administration positions are available year-round (one to three days for three to six months).

PERKS AND REWARDS: In addition to a stipend of $250, workshop interns have the opportunity to participate in workshops and the photography lecture series tuition free; arts administration interns are on a volunteer basis. A fully equipped professional darkroom and use of the library are also available free of charge.

THE ESSENTIALS: Individuals who have displayed a commitment to the photographic arts and who are curious, highly motivated, technically skilled, and

Determine that the thing can and shall be done, and then we shall find the way. **403**
—ABRAHAM LINCOLN

able to handle a diverse audience and a fast-paced work environment are encouraged to apply.

YOUR FIRST MOVE: Workshop intern applicants are required to contact the center directly to schedule a personal interview; interviews take place on Fridays at 2 P.M. during the last two weeks of March or in the month of April. A personal portfolio (ten prints), resume, and three references with phone numbers are required for the interview. Deadlines for arts administration interns are rolling and require an in-person interview.

FOR MORE INFORMATION: Kate Menconeri, Program Director, Center for Photography at Woodstock, 59 Tinker St., Woodstock, NY 12498 (845) 679-9957 • (845) 679-6337 (fax) • info@cpw.org

CENTERSTAGE

Theater • Maryland • 9–10 Months
www.centerstage.org

$ 🏕🏠

CENTERSTAGE strives to explore a wide range of dramatic literature and production approaches, from fresh visions of the classics to active support of contemporary writing. Production internships are available in stage

Working from a sketch board, a production intern at CENTERSTAGE adds her artistic touches to a background scene for an upcoming show.

404

management, scenic carpentry, painting, properties, costumes, electrics, and sound. Administrative interns work in development, publications, audience development, dramaturgy, education and community programs, production and patron services, or company management. Positions begin in late August for a nine- to ten-month period. A stipend of $90 per week is provided along with a fully-furnished efficiency apartment in one of three refurbished row houses close to the theater. Perks include tickets to all productions at CENTERSTAGE (and often to other local theaters and concerts) as well as participation in biweekly seminars. Applicants should have a proven ability in their area of specialization and a willingness to work hard. It's best to apply by March for the following season. Application instructions can be found on their website in the Community section.

FOR MORE INFORMATION: Internship Coordinator, CENTERSTAGE, 700 N. Calvert St., Baltimore, MD 21202-3686 • (410) 986-4000, ext. 4060 (410) 539-3912 (fax) • info@centerstage.org

CENTRAL CITY
OPERA HOUSE ASSOCIATION

Music Festival • Colorado • Summer
www.centralcityopera.org

$ 🏠

Built in 1878 by Cornish and Welsh miners, Central City Opera House hosts one of the oldest opera festivals in the U.S. The 550-seat theater, a historic landmark in an old mining town (just forty-five minutes northwest of Denver), affords an intimate experience with opera. Summer festival staff positions include interns in public relations, house management, special events, stage management, props, costumes, music library, gardening, the gift shop, and office administration. A weekly salary of $237 is provided, along with housing (with kitchen and laundry facilities) and a one-time travel stipend. It's best to request an application by January as materials are due by the end of February (although applications will be taken until positions are filled). Applicants must be at least nineteen years of age and exude a positive attitude. An interest in opera is helpful, but not required.

FOR MORE INFORMATION: Karen Federing, Festival Manager, Central City Opera House Association, 400 S. Colorado Blvd., Suite 530, Denver, CO 80246 (303) 292-6500 • (303) 292-4958 (fax) • info@centralcityopera.org

Originality does not consist in saying what no one has ever said before,
but in saying exactly what you think yourself.
—JAMES STEPHENS

405

CHESAPEAKE BAY MARITIME MUSEUM

Museum • Maryland • 10–13 Weeks
www.cbmm.org

$ 🏠 🐖

Enter a fully restored 1879 Hooper Strait lighthouse and feel what it must have been like to guide ships to safety. Or climb aboard the skipjack *Rosie Parks* and experience the daily drudgery of sailing a large wooden boat while hauling up heavy oysters in freezing temperatures and wind. With engaging exhibitions, boatbuilding classes, and outdoor summer concerts, the Chesapeake Bay Maritime Museum explores how the bay has shaped the lives of everyone who has lived around it.

WHAT YOU'LL BE DOING: The museum's internship program is an integral part of its educational activities. Interns will have the opportunity to develop and support on-site and family interpretive programs, assist in the documentation of folklife and folk arts, work with museum collections, or assist in public relations. Internships are available in the research/curatorial, education, exhibits, boatyard, marketing and public relations, membership, and museum advancement departments.

COMMITMENT: Internships span thirteen weeks during the summer months (with the exception of curatorial and education positions, which are also available in the winter and spring for ten to thirteen weeks).

PERKS AND REWARDS: A weekly stipend of $125 plus housing is provided. Interns will also have exposure to the entire museum through attendance at staff meetings, rotation through the institution, opportunities to shadow key staff, and field trips or independent visits to other museums.

THE ESSENTIALS: Individuals working toward undergraduate or graduate degrees in museum studies or history are encouraged to apply.

YOUR FIRST MOVE: Application information can be found through their website, or call for more information. Applications must be in by February 28 for summer positions.

FOR MORE INFORMATION: Leigh Ann Gay Schaefer, Internship Program Coordinator, Chesapeake Bay Maritime Museum, P.O. Box 636, St. Michaels, MD 21663-0636 • (410) 745-2916, ext. 122 • (410) 745-6088 (fax) lschaefer@cbmm.org

CREEDE REPERTORY THEATRE

Interns at Creede Repertory Theatre will enjoy the pedestrian-friendly downtown that's been transformed from a roaring mining town of yesteryear to a place now rich in the arts and outdoor activities.

CREEDE REPERTORY THEATRE

Theater • Colorado • 4 Months
www.creederep.org

$ 🏛

Established as a silver-mining town over one hundred years ago, the town of Creede is situated at 9,000 feet near the headwaters of the Rio Grande. This incredible backdrop along with dramatic weather conditions make for a unique living experience for interns and staff at Creede Repertory Theatre. Four-month internships are available in business, costume design, light and sound, shop set, and stage management. A $180 weekly stipend is provided as well as double-occupancy housing in the newly refurbished historical Rio Grande Hotel (where all staff live), which overlooks the amphitheater. Opportunities are available during the summer and fall months.

FOR MORE INFORMATION: Maurice LaMée, Artistic Director, Creede Repertory Theatre, 124 N. Main St., P.O. Box 269, Creede, CO 81130 • (866) 658-2540 (719) 658-2541 • (719) 658-2343 (fax) • crt@creederep.com

The world is moving so fast these days that the man who says it can't be done is generally interrupted by someone doing it.
—HARRY EMERSON FOSDICK

DORSET THEATRE FESTIVAL CONSERVATORY PROGRAM

Theater Festival • Vermont • Summer
www.dorsettheaterfestival.org

$ 🏠

American Theatre Works presents the Dorset Theatre Festival each summer at the Dorset Playhouse, built from two pre-Revolutionary barns in the historic village of Dorset. The festival's conservatory program adheres to the traditional sense of the word "conservatory": learning a craft by working closely with professionals for an intense and extended period of time. The program focuses on performance, production, a series of seminars, and contact with professionals. For those with more experience, internships are available in arts management, technical theater, and the acting apprentice company. A weekly stipend of $125 and housing are provided. A one-time fee of $150 covers housing supplies, maintenance, trash removal, and repairs.

FOR MORE INFORMATION: John Nassivera, Producing Director, Dorset Theatre Festival Conservatory Program, American Theatre Works, P.O. Box 510, Dorset, VT 05251-0510 • (802) 867-2223 • (802) 867-0144 (fax) theater@sover.net

EUREKA SPRINGS SCHOOL OF THE ARTS

Art Education • Arkansas • 1–6 Weeks
www.esartschool.com

♥ 🏠

Nestled in a small village in the Ozark Mountains, Eureka Springs School of the Arts is home to over two hundred working artists. Artists in their respective fields teach small intensive classes that include ceramics, painting, drawing, and techniques for working with wood, fiber, metal, paper, and other mediums. In addition, ongoing classes in art, dance, music, and writing are available to the community. For up to six weeks throughout the year (twenty to thirty hours per week), studio assistants provide help with studio maintenance and photography, work with the artists and their teaching needs as well as with the executive and program director during class sessions, and act as ambassadors for school participants. There is an application fee of $50 and housing runs $100. Benefits include the ability to take classes during the week, use of the studio, and the possibility of staying with local artists in their studios. Applicants should be students who are in a BFA or MFA program or committed artists; all must be willing to work with teachers and students on their projects. Happy people are encouraged to apply. Send a letter of intent to begin the application process.

FOR MORE INFORMATION: Jacqueline Wolven, Executive Director, Eureka Springs School of the Arts, P.O. Box 657, Eureka Springs, AR 72632 • (479) 253-5384 director@esartschool.com

FLAT ROCK PLAYHOUSE

Theater • North Carolina • Summer
www.flatrockplayhouse.org
♥ 🏠

From building and running shows to attending classes, assisting patrons, or performing on the main stage and at the Sandburg Home (a national historic site across the street), apprentices are constantly on the move. Flat Rock Playhouse believes that hands-on professional training is essential to any drama student's education. That's why they expose each apprentice to as many facets of theater as possible. Daily master classes range from acting and improvisation to costume design and professional preparation. Other opportunities exist in weekly technical crew assignments and performing in as many as five venues. Apprenticeships run for ten to twelve weeks and start in early June. The room and board fee of $400 includes three meals a day and on-site dormitory-style housing. Apprentices must be at least high school graduates with prior theatrical experience and committed to development of the art form. Applications (available online) are due by March 15.

FOR MORE INFORMATION: Apprentice Program Director, Flat Rock Playhouse, P.O. Box 310, Flat Rock, NC 28731-0310 • (828) 693-0403, ext. 18 (828) 693-6795 (fax) • design-education@flatrockplayhouse.org

GEORGE WASHINGTON'S MOUNT VERNON

Living History • Virginia • Summer
www.mountvernon.org
$ 🏠

Mount Vernon is a nonprofit organization created to preserve George Washington's home. Located just outside Washington, D.C., the estate welcomes more than one million visitors each year.

WHAT YOU'LL BE DOING: After completion of a short training program, which includes several field trips to related historic sites, interns act as living history guides, teaching visitors about Washington's innovative approach to farming and his stature as a progressive leader in early American agriculture. Interns also demonstrate Washington's farming practices, working with livestock

People are like stained-glass windows. They sparkle and shine when the sun is out; but when the darkness sets in, their true beauty is revealed only if there is a light from within.
—ELIZABETH KÜBLER-ROSS

JINNY FOX

A pioneer farming intern at George Washington's Mount Vernon demonstrates hoeing practices of years past for a group while teaching them about the historical relationship between farmers and slaves.

(horses, mules, and sheep), using period-style farm tools, and discussing such things as Washington's crop rotation schemes, his use of fertilizers, and the diet of the field workers.

COMMITMENT: Internships run ten weeks during the summer months and begin in June.

PERKS AND REWARDS: Interns are provided round-trip travel to Mount Vernon, a weekly stipend of $200, housing on the Mount Vernon estate, and period attire (eighteenth-century field-hand clothing).

THE ESSENTIALS: Mount Vernon recruits as many as six graduating high school seniors and undergraduate students (aged eighteen to twenty-two) who have a strong background in agriculture and history as well as good public speaking skills.

YOUR FIRST MOVE: Applications are available online and are due by February 15.

FOR MORE INFORMATION: Supervisor of Interpretation, Pioneer Farmer Internships, George Washington's Mount Vernon, P.O. Box 110, Mount Vernon, VA 22121 • (703) 799-8611 • (703) 799-8609 (fax)

✎ INSIDER TIP: Mount Vernon also offers four-week, unpaid internships for retired agricultural teachers, who receive compensation for round-trip travel to Mount Vernon, as well as free housing on the estate. (Spouses are welcome!)

HISTORIC DEERFIELD

Museum • Massachusetts • Summer
www.deerfield-fellowship.org

$ 🏠 🎓

Art and history. This is at the heart of Historic Deerfield (www.historic-deerfield.org). Carefully preserved eighteenth- and nineteenth-century houses, the Flynt Center of Early New England Life, and the decorative art pieces within them allow visitors to see what life once was like in this unspoiled village.

WHAT YOU'LL BE DOING: Attention college students: every year since 1956, Historic Deerfield has offered summer fellowships for those who desire a rare behind-the-scenes view of the workings of a museum, and a thorough investigation of early American history and material life. The unique "learning and living" fellows program provides hands-on research into daily life and the cultural history of New England, a chance to interpret the American past through objects, and the opportunity to meet visitors from throughout the U.S. and around the world. Along with seminar sessions in a classroom setting, on walking tours, and in the museum houses, fellows also go on weekly field trips to other museums in New England, including Old Sturbridge Village and Plimoth Plantation. Near program's end, fellows take a weeklong trip to the South, visiting the Winterthur Museum in Delaware, the city of Annapolis, and Colonial Williamsburg in Virginia. Fellows have the opportunity to work with museum staff in every department at the museum—from curatorial, archives, and collections management to architectural conservation, development, and research.

PERKS AND REWARDS: The $7,500 fellowship award covers tuition, books, field trip expenses, housing, and meals for nine weeks. In addition, a limited number of $500 to $1,500 awards to offset lost summer income will be given to students of exceptional promise and with demonstrated financial need. Historic Deerfield can also arrange academic credit through the history department at the University of Massachusetts at Amherst.

THE ESSENTIALS: Fellows must have completed two years of college, have a background in history, art, American studies, museums, or public history, and still be in school.

YOUR FIRST MOVE: Call for application materials, which are due in late February; there is a nonrefundable $15 application fee. Decisions will be announced in early April.

FOR MORE INFORMATION: Jessica Neuwirth, Director of Academic Programs, Historic Deerfield, P.O. Box 321, Deerfield, MA 01342-0321 • (413) 775-7207 (413) 775-7224 (fax) • sfp@historic-deerfield.org

No one can whistle a symphony. It takes an orchestra to play it. 411
—HALFORD LUCCOCK

JACOB'S PILLOW DANCE FESTIVAL

Dance Festival • Massachusetts • Seasonal
www.jacobspillow.org

$ 🏠 ⊕

"How fitting that many in the dance world refer to Jacob's Pillow as the Dance Farm, for it is indeed a place that nurtures." As America's oldest dance festival, Jacob's Pillow presents summer dance performances (modern, ballet, jazz, and cultural dance); provides over two hundred free talks, exhibits, and showings; conducts a professional dance school; and offers intern, artist residency, and community dance programs. Professional-track dancers, choreographers, and students from all over the world come together to create a unique and exciting environment.

A documentation intern with Jacob's Pillow videotapes a summer outdoor performance.

YOUR SURROUNDINGS: Located in the Berkshire Hills of western Massachusetts, the campus includes over 160 acres of woodlands, two theaters, three studios, and an outdoor stage.

WHAT YOU'LL BE DOING: Working closely with staff members in all aspects of festival operation, audience enrichment, and educational programs, interns receive extensive on-the-job training and experience. Visiting artists and professionals offer additional insights and the opportunity to make valuable contacts. Thirty summer positions are available in archives/preservation, business, development, editorial, education, general management, graphic design, operations, photojournalism, press, production, technical theater, ticket services/house management, and videography. A lesser number of interns are needed during the fall through spring.

COMMITMENT: Summer positions begin in late May and finish in early September. During the fall through spring, internship dates and times are flexible.

PERKS AND REWARDS: For summer internships, a stipend of $500, shared housing in the Pillow's rustic wood-framed cottages, meals at the hand-built dining room, and workshops by staff members are provided. Beyond living and working with a diverse community of artists, faculty, students, and staff, interns may also attend performances, community and master classes, and festival events without charge. Housing may be provided for nonsummer interns.

THE ESSENTIALS: Enthusiastic, self-motivated workers who are excited about the arts will thrive at Jacob's Pillow.

YOUR FIRST MOVE: Call or view the application details online. For priority consideration, summer interns must apply before February 15. Applications for internships in other times of the year are accepted on a rolling basis. Applicants are welcome to apply for more than one position.

FOR MORE INFORMATION: Intern Program, Jacob's Pillow Dance Festival, P.O. Box 287, Lee, MA 01238 • (413) 327 1234 • (413) 243-4744 (fax) info@jacobspillow.org

THE JOHN F. KENNEDY CENTER FOR THE PERFORMING ARTS

Performing Arts • Washington, DC • 3–4 Months
www.kennedy-center.org

$ 🎓

The Kennedy Center is one of the country's foremost performing arts institutions and runs an admirable array of educational programs and competitions for students of all ages. Founded in 1971 as a memorial to JFK, the center not only was a sorely needed addition to Washington's cultural scene but also quickly became an arts center of national and international importance. Today, the center attracts an international array of some of the finest music, dance, and theater companies, while also providing a home to the National Symphony Orchestra, the American Film Institute, and the Washington National Opera. The center's grand marble exterior inspires a sense of awe enhanced by the red-carpeted foyer and eighteen-foot bust of JFK.

WHAT YOU'LL BE DOING: Up to twenty students are selected each semester to participate in the Kennedy Center's Vilar Institute for Arts Management internship program. Positions may be available in advertising, development, education (local and national programs), the National Symphony Orchestra, press, production, programming, special events, and volunteer management. In addition to creating a list of learning objectives and goals with their supervisor,

It's never too late—in fiction or in life—to revise.
—NANCY THAYER

interns will develop a special project that they will complete during their time at Kennedy. Interns also submit a weekly journal, maintain a working portfolio, attend required intern events, and participate in midsemester and final evaluations. In addition, interns will attend the weekly Executive Seminar Series, which involves presentations by executives of the center and other major arts institutions in Washington, D.C.

COMMITMENT: Internship assignments are full-time and available during the fall (September to December), winter/spring (January to May), and summer (June to August).

PERKS AND REWARDS: A stipend of $800 per month is provided to help defray housing and transportation costs. Interns also have the chance to attend performances, workshops, classes, and courses presented by the center free of charge.

THE ESSENTIALS: Internships are designed to offer meaningful learning experiences for those interested in careers in performing arts administration or arts education. Upper-level undergraduate students (juniors and seniors), graduate students, and students who have graduated but have not been out of school for more than two years are eligible.

YOUR FIRST MOVE: Information on application requirements and deadlines can be found online, or call or email for more information. Phone interviews may be conducted.

FOR MORE INFORMATION: Caitlin Albers, Internship Program Coordinator, Education Department, The John F. Kennedy Center for the Performing Arts, 2700 F St., NW, Washington, DC 20566 • (202) 416-8821 (202) 416-8853 (fax) • rcalbers@kennedy-center.org

JULLIARD SCHOOL

Theater • New York • Academic Year
www.juilliard.edu

$

The Juilliard School has various facilities that serve various types of theater productions. The Juilliard Theatre, seating more than nine hundred people, and with a sixty-foot proscenium stage, houses Juilliard's opera and dance productions, concerts, recitals, and special events. The Drama Theatre contains a large thrust stage that supports drama productions ranging from classical Greek to modern avant-garde plays, as well as lectures, workshops, and spring repertory. Juilliard also has black box studios for performance, drama, and opera.

WHAT YOU'LL BE DOING: Technical theater internships are available in costumes, electrics, production, props, scene painting, stage carpentry, stage management, and wigs and makeup. The arts administration internship covers a variety of areas and departments, including concert office, dance division, drama division, facilities management, and chamber music management. Many former interns now work at Juilliard as administrators or as theater technicians.

COMMITMENT: Full-time internships begin in September and end in May. Although reasonable working hours are generally maintained, the interns' weekly schedules will vary with their duties and the requirements of the overall production schedule.

PERKS AND REWARDS: A stipend of $253 per week is provided in addition to basic student medical coverage. Keep in mind that you will be living in New York and may need more income in order to cover living expenses. Housing in New York is expensive and requires careful consideration.

YOUR FIRST MOVE: Call for application materials, which are due by June 1.

FOR MORE INFORMATION: Helen Taynton, Professional Intern Program Director, Juilliard School, 60 Lincoln Center Plaza, New York, NY 10023-6588 (212) 799-5000, ext. 7102 • (212) 724-0263 (fax) • htaynton@juilliard.edu

KENTUCKY SHAKESPEARE FESTIVAL

Theater Festival • Kentucky • Summer
www.kyshakes.org

$ ♠

As the oldest independently operated professional Shakespeare company in North America, the Kentucky Shakespeare Festival produces a variety of summer plays in Central Park (in a thousand-seat outdoor amphitheater), which are free of charge to the public. In addition, the festival offers an assortment of summer youth activities, including Camp Shakespeare, Globe Players, and Kids' Globe, and during the academic year, an educational outreach program for grades K–12 entitled Will on Wheels. The festival's professional internship program offers participants the opportunity to make the transition from their training program to the rigors of the professional world. Positions are available in acting, carpentry, costuming, design, education, electrics, promotions/marketing, props, scenic painting, and stage and production management. A stipend of $100 per week and shared dormitory-style housing are provided. Acting interns participate in free workshops led by members of the resident acting company and other theater professionals from the Louisville arts community. Send a current headshot and resume to begin the application process; all internships require an audition and/or interview. For acting positions contact Curt Tofteland, producing artistic director (tofter@aol.com); technical positions—Michelle Bombe, head of design (mgbombe@aol.com); administrative positions—Steven Renner, executive director (steven@kyshakes.org); and education positions—Regan Wann, assistant director of education (regan@kyshakes.org).

FOR MORE INFORMATION: Professional Internship Program, Kentucky Shakespeare Festival, 1387 S. 4th St., Louisville, KY 40208 • (502) 583-8738 (502) 583-8751 (fax) • info@kyshakes.org

LA SABRANENQUE

Restoration • France/Italy • 1 Week–3 Months
www.sabranenque.com

♥ 🏠 ⊕

La Sabranenque programs offer the chance to discover French village life "from the inside" through dynamic and genuine immersion in regional life and historic preservation. As a grassroots, nonprofit organization created in 1969, La Sabranenque has won several national awards for its restoration work and its international cultural activities.

YOUR SURROUNDINGS: Most activities are based in the restored old quarter (with full modern comfort) in the village of Saint Victor la Coste (near Avignon, southern France), considered to be one of the most beautiful villages in France. Projects are also conducted in various hamlets in Italy.

WHAT YOU'LL BE DOING: Volunteers have the opportunity to become actively and directly involved in preservation and reconstruction work on sites and monuments often dating back to the Middle Ages. Volunteers learn the traditional construction techniques on the job from experienced technicians and, in a short period, experience the satisfaction of making a lasting contribution to the preservation of the villages of southern France. Work is shared with a diverse multinational team and can include stonemasonry or stonecutting, tile floor or roof restoration, or construction of vaults or drystone walls. This is a different and unique way to see the beautiful villages of southern France and, at the same time, participate in a creative experience.

COMMITMENT: Projects range from one week to three months and take place in March through October.

La Sabranenque volunteers spend their days restoring a medieval castle in an Italian hamlet.

PERKS AND REWARDS: Participants pay a $690 program fee for a two-week session, which includes all activities, meals, and shared housing in the restored village site.

THE ESSENTIALS: Applicants must be at least eighteen years of age.

FOR MORE INFORMATION: Jacqueline Simon, Restoration Projects Coordinator, La Sabranenque, 124 Bondcroft Dr., Buffalo, NY 14226-3427 • (716) 836-8698

In France: Marc Simon, La Sabranenque, rue de la Tour de l'Oume, 30290 Saint Victor la Coste, France, (011) 33 466 500 505 info@sabranenque.com

LIVING HISTORY FARMS

Living History • Iowa • Summer
www.lhf.org

$ 🎓

Telling the amazing story of how Iowans transformed the fertile prairies of the Midwest into some of the most productive farmlands in the world, Living History Farms offers visitors the opportunity to explore this six-hundred-acre, four-farm living history museum. With up to twenty-five positions

Only those who attempt the absurd can achieve the impossible.
—ROBIN MORGAN

available in historical interpretation, public information, marketing, and as day camp counselors, interns kick off the summer program with an intensive orientation session (counselors receive three weeks of training). Throughout the summer, all interns will attend four evening seminars that explore some aspect of history, museum operations, or a related topic, and will write three short papers and complete a special project. Along with a $2,000 stipend, six hours of tuition-free credit is provided by the History Department of Graceland University (www.graceland.edu). Candidates must have completed one year of college and have an interest in history, agriculture, museum studies, leisure studies, folk art, child development, or education. Applications are due by March 1, with in-person interviews conducted in March.

FOR MORE INFORMATION: Internship Program Coordinator, Living History Farms, 2600 111th St., Urbandale, IA 50322 • (515) 278-5286 • info@lhf.org

THE METROPOLITAN MUSEUM OF ART

Museum • New York • Summer
www.metmuseum.org

$ 🎓 ⬦

The Metropolitan Museum of Art (the Met) is the largest and most diverse museum in the western hemisphere, containing two million pieces that cover nearly five thousand years of history. Summer interns are placed in a variety of areas, including conservation, library, education, administration, or one of their nineteen curatorial departments. The program begins with a two-week whirlwind orientation, where interns visit each curatorial department. This prepares college students to give gallery talks and work at the visitor information center. Graduate students begin work on projects related to the museum's collections or to a specific exhibition. The Met also sponsors other programs, including a six- or nine-month internship program, fellowships, and a nine-week summer internship program at the Cloisters (a branch of the Met that resembles a twelfth-century monastery and is devoted to the art of medieval Europe). Both volunteer and paid positions exist; honorariums range from $2,500 on up to $22,000 depending on position and term. Applicants must be college or graduate students. Specific details on all the opportunities can best be viewed on their website (just type "internship" into the search box). Electronic applications are encouraged.

FOR MORE INFORMATION: Internship Program Coordinator, Education Department, The Metropolitan Museum of Art, 1000 Fifth Ave., New York, NY 10028-0198 • (212) 570-3710 • (212) 570-3872 (fax) mmainterns@metmuseum.org

NAVAL HISTORICAL CENTER

History • Washington, DC • Seasonal
www.history.navy.mil

$ ⊕

Tired of condescending internships? The Naval Historical Center treats its interns well. (Admittedly, they must perform herculean amounts of work, but isn't that the nature of the position?) Internships here excite people about history. With a staff of less than one hundred, the center produces books, exhibits, and brochures. The museum and art gallery have less than a tenth of the National Air and Space Museum's annual visitors, but they provide their interns with greater insight into museum operations. The center serves a large branch of the federal government and is the only organization dedicated to the history of all aspects of the U.S. Navy. Internships here consistently garner good reviews, and many former interns return as volunteers. It is no platitude to say that an internship at the center enhances one's academic and employment prospects.

WHAT YOU'LL BE DOING: Each intern works on a personal project, with possibilities in archives, editing, design, historical research and writing, collections management, curation, education, publicity, documentary editing, and library science. Archival and collections management interns catalog new material and assist with accounting for items already in the collection. Editing interns help with the publication program. In design, interns work on invitation and exhibit layouts and silk-screening. Research and writing form the backbone of work in the branches dealing with post-1945 history, ships, and naval aviation, but interns also learn about museum curation. Library interns work in one of the oldest federal libraries. All interns, just like the paid staff, cover the more mundane tasks, such as answering inquiries, addressing mass mailings, short bursts of office work, assisting with public programs, and organizing educational tour materials.

COMMITMENT: Interning hours are Monday through Friday, excluding federal holidays, so you'll have your weekends free. You won't make a fortune at the Naval Historical Center, but you will be able to arrange a schedule convenient for your academic or employment needs.

PERKS AND REWARDS: A small stipend is offered, and you will receive sound information on housing options. When intern numbers warrant (generally in the summer), the coordinator arranges field trips and intern T-shirts are designed and produced in-house. Interns have the social cachet of inviting their friends to public programs and private exhibit openings. In addition, each branch sends off its interns with a farewell lunch, and each intern will receive the services of excellent reference writers.

You can't change the music of your soul. **419**
—KATHARINE HEPBURN

THE ESSENTIALS: The center wants everybody to have the opportunity to work in naval history. Past interns have included history majors (naturally) but also those in museum studies, studio art, anthropology, English, French, political science, computer science, international relations, and geography.

YOUR FIRST MOVE: Application materials are available online. Completed applications (which include a writing sample, unofficial transcripts, and an academic letter of reference) should be sent electronically or by fax. Design interns must submit a portfolio (call for specifics). Interviews by telephone or in person form part of the application process.

FOR MORE INFORMATION: Edward Furgol, Curator, Naval Historical Center, The Navy Museum, 805 Kidder Breese St., SE, Washington Navy Yard, Washington, DC 20374-5060 • (202) 433-6901 • (202) 433-8200 (fax) edward.furgol@navy.mil

NEW STAGE THEATRE

Theater • Mississippi • 9 Months
www.newstagetheater.com

$ 🏠 🌐

Founded in 1965, New Stage Theatre is the only fully professional theater in the state of Mississippi. Under the leadership of its staff, the theater operates year-round, offering an ambitious season that includes six main-stage productions, two second-stage shows, the premiere of a new play, and a main-stage production for young audiences.

WHAT YOU'LL BE DOING: Acting intern company members tour the state of Mississippi with two arts-in-education productions for a variety of audiences. Interns also teach creative dramatics for children, conduct theater workshops in area schools, assist with teacher workshops, and help coordinate equity auditions. When not performing or rehearsing, acting interns assist in the daily operation of the theater, including technical and administrative duties as well as the strike of all productions. Technical interns participate in the building of all New Stage productions by assisting in design, carpentry, scenic painting, props, lighting, sound, and costuming.

COMMITMENT: Internships run nine months, starting in September. Interns usually work an average of forty hours per week with one day off.

PERKS AND REWARDS: Stipends range from $6,000 to $7,000, and limited housing is available within walking distance of the theater.

THE ESSENTIALS: New Stage prefers recent college graduates with theater experience, although others may apply. Applicants must have a good attitude, dedication to the theater, and the ability to adapt and get along with others.

YOUR FIRST MOVE: Call for application materials, which are due in mid-April.

FOR MORE INFORMATION: Patrick Benton, Artistic Director, New Stage Theatre, 1100 Carlisle St., Jackson, MS 39202-2127 • (601) 948-3533, ext. 224 (601) 948-3538 (fax) • newstage@netdoor.com

NORLANDS LIVING HISTORY CENTER

Living History • Maine • 2 Months+
www.norlands.org

$ ⚒ ⊕

Emphasizing the frugal lifestyle of the northern New England farm family as expressed in a "use it up, wear it out, make it do, or do without" philosophy, Norlands Living History Center offers the visitor an in-depth experience of nineteenth-century rural life. The programs are unique and innovative, encouraging visitors to participate in history with the hope of developing an appreciation of the present! Thus, visitors might bake cornbread on a woodstove, drive a team of oxen in the fields, or worship in church while learning from "local characters."

WHAT YOU'LL BE DOING: With the goal of making the sights, sounds, smells, and citizens of the nineteenth century come to life, interns will portray a local character while educating guests. Prior to choosing a character, interns receive a thorough training period on local history and everyday lifestyles of the area. In addition, interns will assist with or participate in daily programs, living history techniques, historic agriculture, archives and research, outreach programs, public festivals and meals, hayrides, site maintenance, and special projects (not to mention learning about business aspects of running a nonprofit museum).

COMMITMENT: The program is offered year-round with flexible start dates; however, due to the training required to fully participate in an internship, a two-month minimum requirement is necessary.

PERKS AND REWARDS: A weekly stipend of $50 is provided ($75 per week after three months), along with on-site staff housing in a Cape Cod–style house by the lake. Each intern has a private sleeping room and shares a kitchen, living room, and bath; meals are provided while participating in

The notes I handle no better than many pianists.
But the pause between the notes—ah, that is where the art resides.
—ARTUR SCHNABEL

a program. In addition, interns attend one of Norlands' Live-In programs (a three-day, two-night experience of nineteenth-century rural New England life) free of charge.

THE ESSENTIALS: As interpreters of a rural lifestyle, interns should be comfortable with barns and livestock, dirt paths, outhouses, kerosene lamps, and cooking and heating with woodstoves. Those with a high energy level, initiative, enthusiasm, and the willingness to communicate the heritage of rural Maine to people of all ages and backgrounds will thrive here.

YOUR FIRST MOVE: Applications are available online, or call or email for further information.

FOR MORE INFORMATION: George Lyons, Executive Director, Norlands Living History Center, 209 Norlands Rd., Livermore, ME 04253 • (207) 897-4366 (207) 897-4963 (fax) • norlands@norlands.org

ORLANDO-UCF SHAKESPEARE FESTIVAL

Theater Festival • Florida • 6 Weeks–10 Months
www.shakespearefest.org

$ 🏠

With a new three-hundred-seat Elizabethan-inspired thrust theater and newly renovated 120-seat theater, the Orlando–UCF Shakespeare Festival, in partnership with the University of Central Florida, produces six mainstage productions and a staged workshop and reading series from September through May. As the festival's training wing, the education department teaches Shakespeare in over ninety central Florida classrooms each year and also offers a summer camp for middle school students, a training program for high school students, and an internship and apprenticeship program. Over a nine-month period (forty to sixty-five hours per week), interns work in performance, education, stage management, and/or administration/box office. Interns are usually offered main-stage roles and participate in a variety of classes and workshops. Apprentices work in a more specific capacity for a shorter-term contract (six weeks to ten months). A stipend of $125 per week along with housing is provided (add $50 per week if you have your own housing), and you'll have Disney, Universal, Sea World, and the beach in your own backyard. Auditions and interviews are held locally and at the Southeastern Theatre Conference (www.setc.org).

FOR MORE INFORMATION: Sarah Hankins, Internship Coordinator, Orlando–UCF Shakespeare Festival, 812 E. Rollins St., Suite 100, Orlando, FL 32803 (407) 447-1700, ext. 214 • (407) 447-1701 (fax) • sarahh@shakespearefest.org

🐋 INSIDER TIP: We are looking for hardworking, creative, and dedicated individuals who can work well with a variety of supervisors in a fast-paced environment. We especially appreciate challenge-seeking self-starters with a positive attitude and time-management skills. Our internships are adjustable to all levels of training: from beginners to recent undergraduate students to MFA graduates.

SEATTLE REPERTORY THEATRE

Theater • Washington • 9 Months
www.seattlerep.org

$

Producing plays that excite the imagination and nourish a lifelong passion for the theater, the Seattle Repertory Theatre is America's largest professional, nonprofit theater. Receiving international renown for its consistently high production and literary standards, the Rep is in a unique position to offer aspiring theater professionals top-notch training through its Professional Arts Training Program.

WHAT YOU'LL BE DOING: Interns participating in the Professional Arts Training Program will undertake responsibilities as members of the staff, contribute ideas, participate in department and staff meetings, and complete projects under the guidance of their supervisors. Staff members guide the work of each intern to help prepare them for a career in professional theater. Internships are available in the artistic department, communications, costume shop, education, production management, properties, scenic art (paints), scenic and lighting design, stage management, and technical production. The Seattle Rep also provides a unique learning opportunity to all interns through a series of professional workshops. These workshops provide a chance for interns to learn more about the many different departments and connect with theater staff, guest artists, and members of the Seattle arts community—along with enjoying a late morning snack!

COMMITMENT: Internship start dates range from late summer into early fall and continue through the following May on a full-time basis. Please note that you must be available for the complete duration of the internship. (However, on rare occasions, there may be some flexibility on your time commitment.)

PERKS AND REWARDS: Interns will receive a weekly stipend of at least $160, and college students may also arrange academic credit through their internship department. Although housing is not provided, the Rep is happy to provide information regarding housing options and other resources. Check

It is your work in life that is the ultimate seduction.   **423**
—PABLO PICASSO

out the Living in Seattle link on their website for housing information and other resources.

THE ESSENTIALS: The Rep seeks bright, creative, reliable, and self-motivated individuals with basic training and experience in theater who are committed to strengthening their skills and talents.

YOUR FIRST MOVE: The application process for the September season-opener begins on January 1 and concludes on March 15. To apply, send off the following in one packet: a resume of theater and related experience; a letter of intent listing internship desired (you may choose up to three areas) and how you heard about the program; and two letters of recommendation from people who know your work. A photo is optional.

FOR MORE INFORMATION: Internship Coordinator, Seattle Repertory Theatre, P.O. Box 900923, 155 Mercer St., Seattle, WA 98109 • (206) 443-2210 (206) 443-2379 (fax) • interns@seattlerep.org

☞ **INSIDER TIP: The Rep's tech people don't seem to have a limit to what they can do. When you have ideas at other theaters, you get excuses why they can't be done. But when you have an idea at the rep, the tech people think about it for a while and then say, "Yes, we can do that." —*Actor, director, and inspired clown Bill Irwin***

SMITHSONIAN CENTER FOR EDUCATION AND MUSEUM STUDIES

Museum • Washington, DC • 2–12 Months
http://museumstudies.si.edu
♥ ⊕

The Smithsonian Center for Education and Museum Studies (SCEMS) coordinates a central referral service for all internship programs at the Smithsonian Institution. Incorporating sixteen museums and galleries plus the National Zoo, the Smithsonian is the world's largest museum complex and offers, quite possibly, the world's largest museum internship program.

WHAT YOU'LL BE DOING: Interns at the Smithsonian develop job skills, expand expertise in academic disciplines, learn about museum careers, and see the workings of a major institution from the inside out. Smithsonian interns learn by doing, working closely with an internship supervisor in a tutorial setting. Interns are placed in one of forty museums, administrative offices, and research programs—there is truly something for everyone. Remember that the Smithsonian Institution is more than just the science, art, and history museums. The great size of this cultural institution means that there are many interns here doing a wide variety of work, from exhibit design to research to conservation to public programs and education. There are also internships in areas not normally associated with a museum, such as photography, computer science, public affairs, administration, product development, and library science. Most museums also have enrichment programs for interns, which include career seminars, behind-the-scenes tours, and the like.

COMMITMENT: Most interns work at the Smithsonian for a period of two months to one year, for a minimum of twenty hours per week.

PERKS AND REWARDS: Unless otherwise noted, internships at the Smithsonian do not carry a stipend. Perks include enrichment events and a 20 percent discount at museum gift shops.

YOUR FIRST MOVE: Visit SCEMS online for many links to institution-wide programs, or email for information and an application. Applicants can apply directly to each museum or office or through the Central Referral Service. For the latter, you must submit five sets of application materials for each museum or office where you wish to be considered for an internship. This includes a completed application form, a two- to three-page essay, two letters of recommendation, and transcripts. Deadlines: spring—October 15; summer—February 15; and fall—June 15. No interviews are conducted.

FOR MORE INFORMATION: Tracie Spinale, Internship Coordinator, Smithsonian Center for Education and Museum Studies, A&I Room 2235, MRC 427, P.O. Box 37012, Washington, DC 20013-7012 • (202) 357-3102 (202) 357-3346 (fax) • interninfo@scems.si.edu

🐾 **INSIDER TIP: Make sure you find out about the internship program you are applying for. A good way to get information is to contact the intern coordinator for each specific program; and it is better to ask any questions you might have about the process before you apply. Don't ever think a question is stupid or irrelevant. Some of us were interns before and probably had the very same question. The most important thing to remember when applying is being yourself and letting you and your interests be apparent in your application. This way the project you may be selected for will truly match your interests and help you to fulfill your goals. The application essay gives you the opportunity to do this.**

Creativity is inventing, experimenting, growing, taking risks, breaking rules, having fun. **425**
—MARY LOU COOK

WHAT DO MUSEUM PROFESSIONALS DO?

Not only are museums a powerful source of knowledge, they are also exciting places to work. People who work in this environment find that many of the rewards come from disseminating their knowledge to others. The museum field encompasses a variety of opportunities that include interpretive specialists and docents, collections managers and exhibition researchers, and writers and designers, along with administrative positions ranging from membership coordinators to public-relations specialists. Potential employers are especially attracted to applicants who possess solid practical museum experience and can demonstrate a strong academic background. Many people secure practical, on-the-job training through internships or working as a museum volunteer. For a listing of museum-related website links, visit www.aam-us.org.

SPOLETO FESTIVAL USA

Music Festival • South Carolina • 4–6 Weeks
www.spoletousa.org

$ 🏠 ⊕

The Spoleto Festival produces and presents world-class opera, dance, theater, chamber music, symphonic and choral music, jazz, and literary and visual arts—more than 120 events in seventeen days, playing to an international audience of more than seventy-five thousand in a variety of theaters and other performance sites throughout historic Charleston.

WHAT YOU'LL BE DOING: In what is called "a short-term, intensive, and exciting opportunity to learn about the world of the performing arts," apprentices work with arts professionals to produce and operate this extravagant event (from mid-May to mid-June, full-time). Apprenticeships are available in artist services, media relations, development, finance, box office, office administration, merchandising, orchestra management, education, and production (including stage carpentry, stage electrics, wardrobe, properties, sound, stage management, and production administration).

PERKS AND REWARDS: A weekly stipend of $250 and housing at the College of Charleston is provided. Out-of-town apprentices also receive $50 toward travel expenses. Other perks include a welcoming party, a participant badge (open access to all events), and excellent career training in the arts.

THE ESSENTIALS: Applicants should have excellent organization, communication, and administrative skills. Familiarity with the arts is a plus.

YOUR FIRST MOVE: Applications are available online and are due by February 1. Applicants must also submit a resume, cover letter, and two letters of recommendation. Three writing samples are also necessary for media relations applicants.

FOR MORE INFORMATION: Apprentice Program Coordinator, Spoleto Festival USA, P.O. Box 100, Charleston, SC 29402-0100 • (843) 722-2764 (843) 723-6383 (fax) • apprentice@spoletousa.org

WESTPORT COUNTRY PLAYHOUSE

Theater • Connecticut • Summer
www.westportplayhouse.org
$ ⚶

Each summer since 1931, a series of comedies, dramas, and musicals has been presented in the Westport Country Playhouse. One feels the history and charm of the playhouse just by walking through the lobby, where the walls are covered with posters advertising shows dating from the beginning of the theater's history.

WHAT YOU'LL BE DOING: Each intern will work directly under a department head, with positions in administration, company management, artistic, marketing/public relations, development, front-of-house, electrics, properties, scenic construction, scenic painting, stage management, and wardrobe. To supplement their experience, interns may get involved with workshops designed to provide a look into the inner workings and operations of a regional summer theater while connecting with playhouse staff, guest artists, and members of the local arts community. For those who are in high school and between the ages of sixteen and nineteen, the playhouse also offers an eight-week volunteer apprenticeship program. The program is designed to provide an in-depth exposure to the theater with a chance to rotate through various work assignments and performance responsibilities.

COMMITMENT: Internships begin mid-May and continue through mid-September. A minimum commitment of twelve weeks is required.

PERKS AND REWARDS: Housing and a weekly stipend of $100 are provided.

THE ESSENTIALS: The internship is best suited for those who have already acquired basic training and experience in the theater and are ready for the next step toward a career in professional theater. Applicants must be serious-minded, highly motivated, and at least nineteen.

YOUR FIRST MOVE: Application materials are available online, or call for more information. Applications are due by the beginning of March.

We don't see things as they are, we see things as we are.   427
—ANAÏS NIN

FOR MORE INFORMATION: Hyla Crane, Education Coordinator, Westport Country Playhouse, P.O. Box 629, Westport, CT 06881 • (203) 227-5137, ext. 16 (203) 221-7482 (fax) • hcrane@westportplayhouse.org

INSIDER TIP: Interns must be willing to engage in the creative process, test the limits of their own ingenuity, and work hard. In return, interns are treated as members of the professional staff, receive the intensive hands-on experience crucial to a professional resume, and make professional contacts that will help get that "foot in the door."

WILLIAMSTOWN THEATRE FESTIVAL

Theater Festival • Massachusetts • Summer
www.wtfestival.org

♥ ⛺ 🌐

Once a small summer company, the Williamstown Theatre Festival (in northwest Massachusetts) has grown into a major theatrical event and has acquired a national reputation for the artists it attracts and the gifted young actors, designers, and directors it sends out into the world. Interns concentrate in one of the following areas: box office, design (sets, costumes, lights, and sound), directing, general/company management, literary management, photography, producing, production management, publications management, publicity, stage management, or technical production. Interns work from early June through the end of August and are responsible for their own daily living expenses, including $500 for Williams College housing. An acting apprentice program is offered as well as a few fellowships and paid staff positions.

FOR MORE INFORMATION: Michael Coglan, Company Manager, Williamstown Theatre Festival, 229 West 42nd St., Suite 801, New York, NY 10036-7205 (212) 395-9090 • (212) 395-9099 (fax) • wtfinfo@wtfestival.org

WOLF TRAP FOUNDATION FOR THE PERFORMING ARTS

Performing Arts • Virginia • Summer
www.wolftrap.org

$ 🎓 🌐

Known as America's national park for the performing arts, Wolf Trap's mission since its inception in 1971 has been to "enrich, educate, and provide enjoyment to the widest possible audiences through a broad range of accessible,

Operated in partnership with the National Park Service, Wolf Trap's Filene Center offers a magical outdoor venue for world-class performances of every genre.

high-quality activities in the performing arts." To reach the community, the country, and the world, Wolf Trap not only presents outstanding perform-ances, including world premieres, national radio and television broadcasts, and events that preserve culturally diverse art forms, but provides educational opportunities in the arts to people of all ages and backgrounds.

YOUR SURROUNDINGS: Just a half hour from Washington, D.C., Wolf Trap is situated on an expanse of Virginia farmland complete with an open-air amphitheater with thousands of lawn seats.

WHAT YOU'LL BE DOING: Wolf Trap's Internship Program provides meaningful hands-on training and experience in the areas of arts administration, educa-tion, and technical theater, with the opportunity to work side-by-side with professionals producing, promoting, and administering the full spectrum of the performing arts. Positions are available in every conceivable area of the theater—from stage management, directing, and costuming to graphic design, Internet programs, and catering. A complete list can be found online.

COMMITMENT: Internships are available for twelve weeks, full-time (forty hours per week) during the summer, and part-time (twenty-four hours per week) in the fall and spring.

PERKS AND REWARDS: Summer interns receive a stipend of $210 per week, while fall and spring interns receive up to $126 per week. Housing is the responsibility of each intern, although guidance is available. Perks include the

If you do not express your own original ideas, if you do not listen to your own being, you will have betrayed yourself.
—ROLLO MAY

429

opportunity to attend a variety of performances and events (two complimentary tickets for each), field trips and facility tours, and educational seminars on topics relating to careers in arts management, as well as participation in "brown-bag lunch" presentations by department heads and guest speakers.

THE ESSENTIALS: Internships are designed for students who have completed a minimum of one year of undergraduate study, as well as graduate students and recent graduates. Wolf Trap is not accessible by public transit, thus interns must have a reliable mode of transportation.

YOUR FIRST MOVE: Specific application materials can be found on their website, or call for a brochure. The majority of interviews take place over the phone, but in-person meetings can be arranged. Deadlines: spring—November 1; summer—March 1; and fall—July 1. An early application is advised.

FOR MORE INFORMATION: Internship Program, Wolf Trap Foundation for the Performing Arts, 1624 Trap Rd., Vienna, VA 22182 • (800) 404-8461 (703) 255-1933 • (703) 255-1924 (fax) • internships@wolftrap.org

WOMEN'S STUDIO WORKSHOP

Art Education • New York • 6 Months
www.wsworkshop.org

$ 🏠 🎓 🌐

Founded in 1974, the Women's Studio Workshop (WSW) is a nonprofit artists' space founded and run by women to serve as a supportive working environment for all people interested in the visual arts. WSW staff artists coordinate grants, fellowships, internships, exhibition opportunities, and the Summer Arts Institute—WSW's primary education program for visual artists.

YOUR SURROUNDINGS: Located in the beautiful Hudson Valley, in the foothills of the Shawangunk and Catskill Mountains, WSW is surrounded by acres of marsh and woodlands. It is housed in the Binnewater Arts Center, a hundred-year-old mercantile building that has been completely renovated to accommodate specialized studios for printmaking, papermaking, photography, and book arts. The five thousand square feet of studio space has been carefully designed, localizing work and printing areas, all with plenty of natural light and direct access to the outdoors.

WHAT YOU'LL BE DOING: Interns work alongside the artist staff on projects in papermaking, printmaking, book arts, and arts administration, as well as assist in the artists-in-residence program, work with artists and educators in the Art in Education program, and participate in the Summer Arts Institute classes as studio assistants. Tasks vary throughout the internship, but may include preparing studios, designing brochures and posters, assisting in all aspects of the exhibition program, preparing the apartment for visiting instructors, setting up for evening programs, managing the setup and break-down of lunch each day, staffing the annual fund-raising auction, and assisting in the day-to-day running of the organization.

COMMITMENT: Interns have the option of working from January through July (Session I) or August to December (Session II).

PERKS AND REWARDS: A monthly stipend of $150 is provided along with housing, a communal staff potluck lunch each workday, and unlimited access to studios after hours.

THE ESSENTIALS: Ideal applicants enjoy working at a variety of tasks and have an undergraduate degree, experience in studio arts, and an ability and willingness to work in a close-knit community. Applicants must understand that their internship experience does not serve as an artist's residency program.

YOUR FIRST MOVE: Send a cover letter, resume, ten to twenty slides of your work, and three letters of reference. Postmark deadlines: Session I—October 15; Session II—April 1.

FOR MORE INFORMATION: Internship Coordinator, Women's Studio Workshop, P.O. Box 489, Rosendale, NY 12472 • (845) 658-9133 • (845) 658-9031 (fax) info@wsworkshop.org

INSIDER TIP: Do not send old recommendation letters. We would rather hear from a friend who knows you well than a professor who does not. In your cover letter, address why you want to come here, specifically how we will benefit from having you here, as well as how a WSW internship can help further your professional ambitions. A strong body of work is essential, as shown through good-quality slides.

THE WORKSHOPS

Photography • Maine • 7 Weeks+
www.theworkshops.com

$ 🏠 ⊕

The picture-perfect Maine coast village of Rockport serves as a backdrop for inspiration and subject matter for one of the nation's leading educational centers for photography, film and video, and creative writing. Referred to by students as the "Outward Bound School of Photography," more than 250 one-week workshops, master classes, and expeditions are conducted by some of the most successful visual minds in the field. The curriculum is designed for everyone from budding enthusiasts to professional actors, filmmakers, photographers, storytellers, and writers.

WHAT YOU'LL BE DOING: The Workshops hires nearly one hundred energetic people each summer to help run their "creative community of visual artists." Interns and staff members work as teachers and teaching assistants, technical and lab assistants, office and kitchen help, studio and darkroom assistants, video and computer technicians, gardeners, store clerks, drivers, administrative assistants, and publicity people. Another option you might consider is the highly praised seven-week work-study program (offered twice during the summer), which includes a comprehensive course in black-and-white photographic craft and vision, along with practical assignments, critiques, classes, field trips, lectures, slide presentations, and a term-end group exhibition in the Workshops' gallery. Students attend this course in exchange for twenty hours per week of work in a variety of roles.

PERKS AND REWARDS: Interns receive room and board, and paid staff start at $7 per hour. There is a fee of $2,195 for the work-study program, which covers tuition, lab, and production fees. Work-study students work twenty hours a week around the campus to cover shared room and board for seven weeks. All participants have access to darkrooms, editing suites, studios, and the library and gallery.

THE ESSENTIALS: In addition to experience and practical skills in darkroom work and film and video technology, characteristics of the summer staff include high energy, enthusiasm, responsibility, and punctuality. They are people who want to make a contribution as well as improve their career options.

YOUR FIRST MOVE: Write or call for a listing of openings and positions. A majority of the positions are filled at the three-day summer job fair, held the first weekend of April (provided it's not Easter).

FOR MORE INFORMATION: David Lyman, Founder and Director, The Workshops, 2 Central St., P.O. Box 200, Rockport, ME 04856 • (877) 577-7700 (207) 236-8581 • (207) 236-2558 (fax) • info@theworkshops.com

☞ INSIDER TIP: In addition to their summer staff opportunities, you may want to participate in one of the one- to three-week learning vacations, photographic expeditions, or workshops that can take you to all corners of the world! These unique programs focus on travel photography, documentary photography, documentary film, documentary video, and photojournalism.

IN SEARCH OF A MISSION—
A DEEPER CALLING

David Lyman teaches creative people to become better at what they do at a total-immersion workshop.

At some point in our lifetime, we come to a place where we long to uncover our mission—a lifelong "assignment" that evolves from deep within our soul. Here's David Lyman's story about his journey of uncovering a deeper calling and building his place in the world:

My father, the son of a New England minister, described one's mission in life as a "calling." However, a calling is not exactly a job. That was something you did to support your lifestyle. Nor was a calling exactly a profession, which is earning a living by doing something you like to do. A calling was more. It was something you had to do, loved doing, and loved doing for others.

For me, it began as photography. After a year covering the war in Vietnam as a navy journalist, I went to work for a variety of adventure and sports magazines. By the age of thirty-two, I was feeling pretty good about my achievements, but I'd become bored. I longed to make photographs and tell stories that made a difference. When I learned that Robert Gilka, then director of photography at *National Geographic* magazine, was to teach a workshop at the Center of the Eye in Aspen, I signed up, was accepted, and arrived at the workshop with portfolio in hand. To work for *National Geographic* and to travel the world making photographs of my adventures were lifelong dreams.

It was the summer of 1972, and I was thrilled to be among twenty other would-be photojournalists, all hoping to be discovered. Appearing before Gilka at the workshop, I presented my portfolio. He opened my book, turned

*If you keep following your own footprints, you will end up where you began,
but if you stretch yourself your artwork will flourish.* —DONNA BASPALY

433

a few pages, closed it, and pushed it back across the table. Then, in his famous drill sergeant's voice he said, "You earn a living with this stuff?"

I left the room in disillusionment and spent the remainder of the day in shock. I finished the workshop with thoughts racing through my mind about my future. However, I realized that if I were to make a statement with my photography, I would need to learn from the best. All fall I thought about what to do. The Center of the Eye went out of business. My research turned up only a few other workshops and none that fit my requirements. Jokingly I said to myself, "Why don't I start my own workshop right here on the coast of Maine?"

Soon thereafter, with the help of a photographer and designer, the Workshops became a reality. One hundred and fifty students attended twelve workshops that first summer. It all started with $1,000 in my pocket and a $3,000 loan. I lost money the first summer, and again after the second, but the realization of what was happening drove me on. During the winters I recouped my losses by photographing ski races, sports personalities, and resorts. Sooner than I could imagine, I was surrounded by the greatest minds in photography.

Twenty-five years later, we have a new campus with eight buildings, a summer enrollment of 2,700, and have become a well-established international center. As I look back over the years, I see that Gilka had given me just the right assignment after all—not the glamorous one I sought but an assignment that answered a deeper calling. It has been a gift to be able to build not only a place where creative people can come and learn but also a place that provides support and encouragement for those developing their own "calling." That is what I intended to do all along.

• •

—Contributed by David Lyman, director and founder of the Workshops

THE WORKSHOPS

Work-study students learn new processes, tools, and techniques for mastering the craft of black-and-white photography at the Workshops.

RECOMMENDED RESOURCES

The American Association of Museums (AAM) represents the entire scope of museums, including art, history, science, military and maritime, and youth museums, as well as aquariums, zoos, botanical gardens, arboretums, historic sites, and science and technology centers. Museum Careers (http://museumcareers.aam-us.org), AAM's online career center, provides listings for museum positions and internships. AAM also sponsors a job placement center, resume review, and mentoring opportunities forum at its annual meeting held in mid-May each year. For more information contact the American Association of Museums, 1575 Eye St., NW, Suite 400, Washington, D.C. 20005; (202) 289-9122, www.aam-us.org.

Have you always wanted to participate in an archaeological dig? With the *Archaeological Fieldwork Opportunities Bulletin,* you just might find the perfect project. Researched and edited by the Archaeological Institute of America (and updated for release each year in January), this comprehensive guide lists over two hundred excavations, field schools, and special programs with openings for volunteers, students, and staff throughout the world. The majority of the opportunities listed take place over the summer (and generally have late spring or early summer application deadlines). The guide can be purchased for $19.95, or you can explore all the opportunities through their online searchable database (www.archaeological.org/fieldwork).

"An organization of people who bring history to life," the **Association for Living History, Farm, and Agricultural Museums** (ALHFAM) has more than nine hundred members who work in living history sites as volunteers or paid staff. Their website provides a listing of more than two hundred national and international sites with living history programming, as well as a job directory. For more information contact ALHFAM, Brownwood Farm, 8774 Route 45 NW, North Bloomfield, OH 44450-9701; (440) 685-4410, www.alhfam.org.

If you are a storyteller, musician, magician, puppeteer, speaker, or theater artist, you might consider taking to the road and performing at school assemblies across the nation. To get the inside scoop on developing a program, marketing yourself, and presenting at schools, check out *How to Make Money Performing in Schools* (Silcox Productions, $18.95) or just start doing it: contact schools locally and see what opportunities come forth. **Schoolgigs.com** and **SchoolShows.com** offer more information and links.

Need to feel empowered about your career as an artist? *How to Survive and Prosper as an Artist* (Owl Books, $17) will provide you with optimistic and helpful information to assist you in taking control of your career while creating a successful livelihood as an artist. As an author, sculptor, and veteran

To create one's own world in any of the arts takes courage. **435**
—GEORGIA O'KEEFFE

arts career counselor, Caroll Michels (www.carollmichels.com) provides advice and information on selling from a studio, working with galleries, generating exhibition opportunities, and understanding grants. She also offers thousands of resources—from art colonies and internships to online galleries and studios. If you're looking for further information, contacts, links, guidance, and advice on artist resources, stop by the author's latest creation, the **Artist Help Network** (www.artisthelpnetwork.com).

The New England Conservatory (NEC) *Job Bulletin* is one of the most comprehensive resources for music-related jobs around. Listings include teaching positions in higher education and K–12; orchestral, choral, church, and military jobs; and arts administration opportunities. The newsletter also includes interesting information on grants, festivals, and competitions as well as helpful career information. Once every two weeks you can have the newsletter delivered to your email box for a subscription fee of $45 (twenty-four issues total). To take a peek at a newsletter sampler along with other features of the NEC Career Services Center, visit their website at www.newenglandconservatory.edu/career.

Shaw Guides (www.shawguides.com) provides continually updated information on educational travel and creative career programs throughout the world, and access to all the content is free. Their online database contains more than five thousand programs ranging from cooking schools and writer retreats to arts and crafts workshops and language vacations.

Theatre Directories, the publishing wing of American Theatre Works (see page 408 or visit www.dorsettheaterfestival.org/html/directories.html), provides some great directories that include information on apprenticeship, internship, and short-term employment opportunities throughout the U.S. The *Summer Theatre Directory* is filled with summer employment and training opportunities in summer stock theaters, Shakespeare festivals, theme parks, outdoor dramas, performing arts camps, and cruise ships. Or to find a job or an internship as an actor, designer, technician, or staff in a professional regional or dinner theater across the U.S., the *Regional Theatre Directory* provides endless leads ($29.95 for either book).

CHAPTER 10

HEARTFELT WORK

The pay is modest. The work is important. The satisfaction is
incredible. Whether working in soup kitchens or family shelters,
teaching and inspiring at-risk youth, ministering to the abused
or mentally ill, building houses for the poor, empowering people
through ministry work, assisting the elderly, helping the fight
against hunger or AIDS, or working to keep the world's population in check, this chapter has plenty of options to choose from.
Your efforts may not immediately change the world or solve
deep-rooted problems, but they will help others in need while
promoting the integrity of creation. If you have a passion for
service and are willing to go the extra mile to help a good cause,
it's time to start making a difference—the world needs you!

UNIQUE OPPORTUNITIES TO EXPLORE IN THIS CHAPTER

- We all know the heartfelt work Habitat for Humanity provides—bringing people from all walks of life together to make affordable housing and better communities a reality for everyone. But did you know you can experience the work of Habitat around the globe? From joining an RV Care-A-Vanner program to volunteering at their national headquarters, the special section beginning on page 460 explores all your options.

- Finding a community to thrive in is a little harder to come by these days—unless you stumble upon Innisfree Village. Read about how Innisfree helped Lisa Gerlits find a new way to move through the world while volunteering again and again and again (page 465).

- All of us experience brief periods of confusion, anxiety, or sadness as a normal part of our everyday lives. However, there are many who are unable to cope with the daily struggles—not because of choice but because of mental illness. Programs such as Gould Farm (page 458) or Spring Lake Ranch (page 478) offer hope and a place for volunteers to help those in need.

- Just because you've reached your golden years doesn't mean there isn't a world of opportunities to explore. It's only too late if you don't begin your journey now. Those who are beyond the age of fifty will uncover some unique opportunities and resources in the special section beginning on page 485.

ALICE MCGAREY MARTIN

A celebration of life and community best captures the heart of Spring Lake Ranch (page 478)—a place where people can work on life's emotional challenges with a supportive and skilled staff.

AMERICORPS

Service Learning • USA • 10–12 Months
www.americorps.org

$ 🏕

AmeriCorps is a national service movement that engages thousands of Americans of all ages and backgrounds in a domestic Peace Corps—that is, getting things done across America by meeting our education, public safety, environmental, and human needs. The work will be tough and AmeriCorps members won't solve all of America's problems, but those who join this effort will definitely make a difference.

WHAT YOU'LL BE DOING: AmeriCorps*VISTA has been helping to meet the needs of low-income communities since 1965, when it was first established as Volunteers in Service to America (VISTA). Members make a full-time, full-year commitment and are assigned to local public and private nonprofit organizations to work toward meeting the community needs determined by the community itself. VISTA members might mentor teens, teach elementary schoolchildren, walk the beat with community police officers, renovate low-income housing, help the homebound and disabled achieve self-sufficiency, or tackle one of the thousands of projects other VISTA members are conducting right now to help their communities. AmeriCorps*NCCC, the National Civilian Community Corps, is a ten-month residential national service program for those between the ages of eighteen and twenty-four. The program takes its inspiration from the Depression-era Civilian Conservation Corps (CCC), which put thousands of young people to work restoring our natural environment. Today corps members in NCCC work on environmental projects but also in disaster relief, education, and public safety; they also help address other unmet human needs.

COMMITMENT: VISTA members serve one year, with opportunities available year-round. NCCC members begin with a three-week training class starting in October and continue with a ten-month commitment.

PERKS AND REWARDS: All AmeriCorps members receive a modest living allowance, health coverage, travel expenses, and after completing one year of full-time service (from ten to twelve months), an education award of $4,725 ($2,362 for part-time service). NCCC members live on one of five campuses that serve five separate regions of the U.S., ranging from a closed military base in San Diego to the Veterans Administration Medical Center in Maryland.

THE ESSENTIALS: Along with having a deep desire to make a difference, VISTA applicants must be at least seventeen years of age and U.S. citizens or permanent residents; NCCC members must be between eighteen and twenty-four.

I would have you learn this great fact—that a life of doing right is the wisest life there is. **441**
—PROVERBS 4:11

YOUR FIRST MOVE: Call for an information kit (plenty of info is also available online, including a searchable database of projects). Joining AmeriCorps is a highly competitive process. Members are selected through a review process involving an initial screening of the application, an interview, and a review of references. Once an applicant qualifies for service, a placement officer attempts to locate a suitable assignment, taking skills and preferences into account. This process may take a few months, so an early application is advised. The deadline for NCCC is March 15 for positions beginning in October.

FOR MORE INFORMATION: Recruitment Administrator, AmeriCorps, 1201 New York Ave., NW, Washington, DC 20525 • (800) 942-2677 (202) 606-5000 • (202) 565-2789 (fax) • questions@americorps.org

> *I will get things done for America—to make our people safer, smarter, and healthier.*
>
> *I will bring Americans together to strengthen our communities.*
>
> *Faced with apathy, I will take action.*
>
> *Faced with conflict, I will seek common ground.*
>
> *I will carry this commitment with me this year and beyond.*
>
> *I am an AmeriCorps member, and I will get things done.*
>
> —AMERICORPS PLEDGE

BRETHREN VOLUNTEER SERVICE

Service Learning/Ministry • USA/Worldwide • 1–2 Years
www.brethrenvolunteerservice.org

$ 🏠 ⊕

Sponsored by the Church of the Brethren, Brethren Volunteer Service (BVS) volunteers give their time and skills to help a world in need. It is a way for people to work at issues greater than themselves, recognizing that their efforts may not immediately solve deep-rooted problems but can be a part of ongoing work for justice, peace, and the integrity of creation.

WHAT YOU'LL BE DOING: Volunteers can choose from a variety of programs— more than 150 are available in twenty-four states in the U.S. and in seventeen nations abroad. Whether you want to help the disabled, senior citizens, or the homeless, or, perhaps, work in community organizing, education and teaching, or camping ministries, BVW has a heartfelt project for you. A booklet describes the specifics of each position. Volunteers begin their term of service with ten to thirty other volunteers in a BVS three-week orientation (scheduled four times per year), which examines a wide range of topics, including peace and justice issues, hunger, cross-cultural understanding, and poverty.

COMMITMENT: Positions in the U.S. require a one-year commitment; overseas positions require two years.

PERKS AND REWARDS: Volunteers receive room, board, medical coverage, life insurance, transportation to and from the project, a monthly allowance of $60, and an annual retreat for those in the U.S. and Europe. Possible living environments include community-style with other volunteers, in an apartment (sometimes shared), with a family, or on the project site. The financial costs include transportation to the orientation and an overseas travel fee of $500 for those going abroad. Some projects qualify for an AmeriCorps education award.

THE ESSENTIALS: BVS seeks those who are willing to act on their commitment and values. BVS challenges individuals to offer themselves, their time, and their talents to work that is both difficult and demanding, yet rewarding and joyful. The minimum requirements: eighteen years of age, sound physical and mental health, willingness to examine and study the Christian faith, and commitment to the goals of BVS. A college degree or equivalent life experience is required for overseas assignment.

YOUR FIRST MOVE: Call for application materials. Applications are accepted year-round, although applicants are encouraged to apply four to six months prior to their availability.

FOR MORE INFORMATION: Dan McFadden, Recruitment, Brethren Volunteer Service, 1451 Dundee Ave., Elgin, IL 60120-1694 • (800) 323-8039 (847) 742-5100 • (847) 742-0278 (fax) • bvs_gb@brethren.org

INSIDER TIP: It is essential that each volunteer bring a willingness to grow and a desire to serve. Important work toward peace, justice, and meeting the needs of humanity and the environment calls out for people willing to serve.

CAMPHILL ASSOCIATION OF NORTH AMERICA

Therapeutic Community • USA/Canada/Worldwide • 3–12 Months+
www.camphill.org

$ 🏠 🌐

After fleeing the Nazi invasion of his own country, Dr. Karl Koenig (an Austrian pediatrician and educator) settled in Aberdeen, Scotland, to develop a community focused on the abilities, talents, and gifts of each person—not their limitations. Inspired by Rudolf Steiner's philosophy of "anthroposophy" (see page 365 for details), Camphill attempts to foster and support lively, viable communities that celebrate the individual while making educational, social, cultural, and environmental contributions to society. Today, the international Camphill movement consists of more than one hundred communities in twenty-two countries. In the U.S. and Canada alone, there are ten independent communities that are home to over eight hundred people.

WHAT YOU'LL BE DOING: Camphill is a way of life. It is not a job. There are no shifts, no salaries, no relative values placed on people according to the nature of the work they do. But it is certainly a life full of jobs to be done. There are meals to cook, floors to sweep, fields to mow, cows to milk. There are children in need of special care. Tasks are undertaken for the good of the whole, out of a sense of commitment and responsibility. To be able to do real, meaningful work gives purpose and dignity to life. The arts are also an important aspect of life in Camphill, with each center hosting concerts and other cultural activities. Thus, there are many participatory artistic activities, such as orchestra, choir, drama groups, community newspapers, weaving, candlemaking, and study groups.

COMMITMENT: Whether you are looking for an internship opportunity, a formal training program, a short-term volunteer experience, or a new, fully committed lifestyle, Camphill offers a variety of time frames and commitments for its coworkers. In general, most coworkers are asked to make a commitment of one year.

PERKS AND REWARDS: There is no salary in the usual sense. Coworkers receive room, board, and a monthly stipend for personal expenses. Most of the Camphill centers offer formal courses on social therapy, and there are opportunities to learn many transferable and practical skills, including a variety of crafts, biodynamic gardening, farming, pruning fruit trees, baking, cooking, caregiving, and homemaking. Those who provide a year of service may be eligible for an AmeriCorps educational award of $4,725.

THE ESSENTIALS: Camphill coworkers come from different countries and age groups and have a variety of interests and professional and educational backgrounds; those with families are also welcome. Prospective coworkers with a genuine interest in others, a willingness to do what is needed, flexibility, tolerance, and cheerfulness are eagerly sought by each community. Coworkers are expected to share their lives with others, especially those with developmental disabilities.

YOUR FIRST MOVE: Call or email for more information. All current opportunities in North America can be found online; those outside the U.S. can be viewed at www.camphill.org.uk.

FOR MORE INFORMATION: Lauren Bratburd, Coworker Development, Camphill Association of North America, P.O. Box 1008, Hudson, NY 12534 (518) 671-6832 • (518) 671-6783 (fax) • coworker@camphill.org

INSIDER TIP: When I come here, I see the coworkers and the villagers in this kind of mutual "us," which, I have to say, is a quite unusual thing in the world. I come here not only to play concerts for people, but to feel a sort of spiritual refreshment that being here makes me feel. It's not very often that you feel this kind of harmoniousness in the world. It's a wonderful experience. —Richard Goode, pianist

THE CARTER CENTER

Social Justice • Georgia • 15 Weeks
www.cartercenter.org
♥ 🎓

In partnership with Emory University, and headquarters for Jimmy Carter's postpresidential activities, the Carter Center primarily focuses on alleviating human suffering throughout the world. The center's work includes resolving conflicts, monitoring elections, fighting disease, reducing poverty, seeking justice for political prisoners, and increasing equity for the mentally ill. Each year over one hundred students intern at the center, with positions primarily offered in the peace program. Responsibilities include reporting on activities with assigned countries, planning international conferences, and occasional short-term travel with the full-time staff. Other internship opportunities are offered in public information, finance, development, art services, and events. A minimum commitment of twenty hours per week for at least fifteen weeks is required. Graduate students may be eligible for a $3,000 stipend during the summer session (for a fifteen-week, forty-hour-per-week term); otherwise positions are unpaid. Benefits include lectures, career sessions, and field trips. Applicants must be undergraduate juniors or seniors, recent grads, or graduate students. Application materials are available online. Deadlines: spring—October 15; summer—March 15; and fall—June 15.

FOR MORE INFORMATION: Dr. Peter Mather, Educational Programs Director, The Carter Center, 453 Freedom Parkway, One Copenhill, Atlanta, GA 30307 (404) 420-5179 • (404) 420-5196 (fax) • carterweb@emory.edu

The healthy social life is only found when in the mirror of each human soul the whole community finds its reflection and when in the community the virtue of each one is living.
—RUDOLF STEINER

CATHOLIC NETWORK OF VOLUNTEER SERVICE

Social Justice/Ministry · Worldwide · 2 Weeks–2 Years+
www.cnvs.org

$ 🏠 🌐

The Catholic Network of Volunteer Service (CNVS) publishes *Response*, an annual directory of volunteer opportunities that includes over two hundred faith-based, full-time volunteer programs in the U.S. and more than one hundred countries worldwide. Volunteers of all ages, committed to social justice, spirituality, and a simple lifestyle, work in soup kitchens or family shelters, direct programs for at-risk youth, teach in schools, minister to the abused, provide health care, build houses, or offer service to refugees—to name just some of the many opportunities. Programs vary in length from a few weeks to a few years, although the average length of a domestic placement is one year, and an international program, two years. Each program has its own combination of benefits and compensation; most include a stipend, room and board, and health insurance. All provide orientation and training, and some may offer retreats or language training. Call for your free copy of the directory, or view the most current listings (including urgent opportunities) on their website. Long-term, full-time administrative volunteers are also needed at the CNVS office in Washington, D.C. Benefits include a stipend, health insurance, and housing in a Christian community setting.

FOR MORE INFORMATION: Volunteer Coordinator, Catholic Network of Volunteer Service, 6930 Carroll Ave., Suite 506, Takoma Park, MD 20912-4423 (800) 543-5046 · (301) 270-0900 · (301) 270-0901 (fax) · volunteer@cnvs.org

🐟 **INSIDER TIP: The Catholic Network is a wonderful resource for finding a well-rounded, faith-based volunteer program. Each program in the network has something different to offer and each is run by an incredible staff that carries such a passion for the work that they do. I have never worked in an environment where the people I corresponded with every day [the program directors] were so understanding, loving, and full of energy for their daily work. If you are looking to begin or enhance your spiritual journey while participating in a wonderful, yearlong volunteer experience, the Catholic Network is an ideal program. —*Therese Strasser, participant***

Small class sizes and dynamic hands-on service learning experiences enrich Center for Purposeful Living students of all ages and backgrounds.

CENTER FOR PURPOSEFUL LIVING

Service Learning • North Carolina • 1 Year
www.purposeful.org

♥ ⛪ 🌐

With their beginnings as an all-volunteer organization providing free care for the terminally ill, respite care for children with disabilities, and health and wellness programs for hundreds of individuals, Human Service Alliance has evolved into something very special, now called the Center for Purposeful Living (CPL). People of all ages have the opportunity to participate in the yearlong Soul-Centered Education for a Lifetime program. What's really unique to the program is that there are no fees for tuition, room, and board, and all faculty are volunteers who do regular service tasks alongside the students.

WHAT YOU'LL BE DOING: Self-discovery. A sense of purpose. Roadblocks removed. The joys of group work and living. Lessons learned—some unexpected and some from surprising sources. These are just some of the experiences students at CPL can expect. Each day students participate in various combinations of learning experiences: class work, group development,

Through an awakened spirit we find the place where meaning grows;
we commit to work vision and life with purpose.
—MARILYN MASON

cooperative living, project creation, reflection and journaling, recreation, and hands-on service in several laboratory settings, including the popular restaurant California Fresh Buffet (where guests will find fresh food and inspiration on the menu, with all profits going to charities), as well as through the video, audio, and graphics production studio. The program combines the three elements of service, study, and reflection, and centers around four tracks: the totally responsible person, science of the soul, service entrepreneurship, and practical spirituality (which brings all the learning together).

COMMITMENT: Students may enter the program at any time during the year at the discretion of the faculty. The weekly schedule runs forty-five hours over six days in classroom work with one unscheduled day per week dedicated to applied service learning.

PERKS AND REWARDS: Students receive room, meals, and tuition at no charge—even your laundry detergent is provided!

THE ESSENTIALS: People of all faiths, backgrounds, and ages (ranging in age from eighteen to eighty-two) come to CPL to discover a common ground through their spiritual connection with the goodness or soul within. If you are ready for the challenge of a lifetime—ready to do what it takes to hone, refine, and polish yourself to be more of what you can really be—this just might be the place for you.

YOUR FIRST MOVE: To get a real sense of the program, prospective students are invited to a "Come and See" weekend preview. An application (available online), three letters of reference, a full-length photo, and a personal interview are required. "Come and See" dates can be found online.

FOR MORE INFORMATION: Joanna White, Coordinator of Admissions, Center for Purposeful Living, Human Service Alliance, 3983 Old Greensboro Rd., Winston-Salem, NC 27101 • (336) 761-8745 • (336) 722-7882 (fax) inquiry@ufhg.org

> *In the midst of gathering doubt, there is a light for all to see. It's the light of loving service given selflessly. Let our hands be joined in joy, let our actions speak of love, guided by the greater wisdom from above. From every corner of the earth, the light of loving service blazes forth and warms the chill inside those who need a hand. Groups working in joyful harmony to build a planet united in love, so all may know the feel of the "fire of life." Serving joyously is the goal. Open your heart to the light of your soul.*
>
> —EXCERPT FROM THE CENTER FOR
> PURPOSEFUL LIVING'S "SONG OF
> SERVICE," WRITTEN IN 1991

CENTER FOR STUDENT MISSIONS

Ministry • USA/Canada • 3–11 Months
www.csm.org

$ 🏠

If you're interested in youth ministry and want to participate in an urban short-term mission experience, the Center for Student Missions can provide you with an extraordinary opportunity. As a city host, you'll be responsible for bridging the gap between suburban/rural people and city people. Duties include facilitating groups of youth and adults (from junior high to college), while making a profound impact on their relationship with God. Lasting from three to eleven months, and with various start dates throughout the year, over seventy positions are available in seven major cities throughout the U.S. (Chicago, Houston, Los Angeles, Nashville, San Francisco, Washington, D.C., and Philadelphia) and in Toronto, Canada. A monthly stipend, housing, food while hosting, training, and supervision are provided. Applicants must be from either the U.S. or Canada, at least eighteen years old (preference is given to those over twenty-one), and certified in first aid and CPR, and have excellent people and leadership skills and the desire to be a servant and leader. Applications may be filled out online.

FOR MORE INFORMATION: Kyle Becchetti, VP Operations, Center for Student Missions, P.O. Box 900, Dana Point, CA 92629-0900 • (949) 248-8200 (949) 248-7753 (fax) • jobs@csm.org

CHOATE ROSEMARY HALL

Teaching • Connecticut • Summer
www.choate.edu/summer

$ 🏠 🎓

Choate Rosemary Hall, a secondary school spread over four hundred acres, offers one of the oldest summer enrichment programs in the country. Each summer thirty to thirty-five teaching interns are hired as members of the faculty, with senior teachers serving as mentors. Whether in the classroom, on field trips, or in the dorms, interns become engaged, stimulated, and supported in every facet of resident school life. Applicants must have completed three years of college and have a strong interest in exploring teaching as a potential career. A salary of $2,500 ($2,600 for graduates) is provided, along with room and board. It is advised that you submit application materials by the end of January. Selected candidates will be invited to Choate Rosemary Hall for a campus tour and interviews.

The greatest challenge of the day is how to bring about a revolution of the heart,
a revolution which has to start with each one of us.
—DOROTHY DAY

FOR MORE INFORMATION: Jim Irzyk, Director of Summer Programs,
Choate Rosemary Hall, 333 Christian St., Wallingford, CT 06492-3800
(203) 697-2365 • (203) 697-2519 (fax) • summer@choate.edu

CHRISTIAN APPALACHIAN PROJECT

Service Learning/Ministry • Kentucky • 3 Weeks–1 Year
www.christianity.com/cap

$ 🏠

The Christian Appalachian Project serves economically, socially, and/or
physically challenged people in eastern Kentucky through programs including
child and family development centers, adult education, elderly services, housing and home repair, youth/teen centers, outreach services, disability services,
educational programming, and other various professional placements. Volunteers live together and share household duties, meals, and prayer as they
support each other through their strong motivation to serve people. One-year
volunteers receive room and board, a monthly stipend, health insurance, loan
deferment information, and a potential AmeriCorps educational award.
Summer-camp counselors, medical personnel, and lifeguards, who must be
eighteen and older, are needed to staff two summer camps in eastern
Kentucky (room, board, orientation and training, and daily prayer are provided). A limited number of short-term opportunities are available for three
weeks to eight months. Call for specific details and an application.

FOR MORE INFORMATION: Kim Otto, Manager of Volunteer Recruitment,
Christian Appalachian Project, Route 6, Box 43, Mt. Vernon, KY 40456
(800) 755-5322 • (606) 256-0973 • (606) 256-5942 (fax)
volunteer@chrisapp.org

A CHRISTIAN MINISTRY
IN THE NATIONAL PARKS

National Park/Ministry • USA • 3–15 Months
www.acmnp.com

$ 🏠

A Christian Ministry in the National Parks is an interdenominational movement recognized by over forty Christian denominations. It extends the
ministry of Christ to the millions of people who live, work, and vacation in
our national parks. This ministry serves government personnel and their families who live in these areas, students and professional resort workers who are

employed to operate resort facilities, and the millions of tourists visiting the parks. This ministry cooperates with support committees in each area to provide regular interdenominational services, religious education, and Christian fellowship.

WHAT YOU'LL BE DOING: Worship, work, and wilderness! This theme pervades the whole meaning of the ministry as it provides opportunities for Christian witness and service. Each member of the staff has a full-time job with a park company. Participants work as desk clerks, housekeepers, bellhops, store clerks, tour guides, or wait staff. Participants also plan and lead interdenominational services of worship and Bible studies throughout the week. An important aspect of the program is being a positive Christian witness in the workplace. All staff leaders are encouraged to attend one of ten regional spring orientation conferences throughout the U.S.

RICHARD P. CAMP JR.

From Rocky Mountain National Park (shown here) to Acadia in Maine, participants with A Christian Ministry in the National Parks lead interdenominational worship services.

COMMITMENT: A three-month commitment is necessary. Most participants arrive at the parks between late May and mid-June and stay through Labor Day, although some parks are open from May 1 through November 1. Year-round and winter placements are available for those who are able to commit to periods of six to fifteen months, depending on the area assigned.

PERKS AND REWARDS: The park concessionaires pay participants for their work, with most earning between $1,800 and $2,400 (after room, board, and taxes) for a three-month period. Of course, having a national park as your backyard is the biggest perk to many.

THE ESSENTIALS: The program seeks individuals who are least eighteen years of age, imaginative, dedicated, and open to creative service. The ministry demands maturity of thought and conduct, and applicants must have the ability to understand and live amiably with other people and other faiths.

YOUR FIRST MOVE: Applications are accepted year-round, although early applications are given first preference. Offers for summer positions are sent to qualified applicants starting in January.

Grant me the serenity to accept the things I cannot change, courage to change the things I can, and wisdom to know the difference.
—SERENITY PRAYER

451

FOR MORE INFORMATION: Rev. Richard Camp Jr., Director, A Christian Ministry in the National Parks, 10 Justin's Way, Freeport, ME 04032 • (800) 786-3450 (207) 865-6436 • (207) 865-6852 (fax)• info@acmnp.com

☛ **INSIDER TIP:** You will meet new friends, deepen your personal faith, grow in leadership abilities, explore a truly awesome national park, and learn more about yourself. —*Steven Hamrick, ACMNP participant at Yellowstone National Park*

CITY YEAR

Service Learning • USA • 10 Months
www.cityyear.org
$

Ever since their beginning in Boston in 1988, the vision of City Year has remained the same: the hope that one day the question most commonly asked of an eighteen-year-old will be "Where are you going to do your service?" Each year, beginning in September, City Year unites diverse groups of young people, ages seventeen to twenty-four, for a full year of rigorous community service, leadership development, and civic engagement in communities from coast to coast. Teams of corps members work in a variety of service opportunities, from teaching social issues on topics such as HIV/AIDS and domestic violence prevention to running after-school programs and organizing and leading out-of-school programs such as Camp City Year and Young Heroes (a service-learning corps for middle school students). Corps members receive a weekly stipend, health insurance coverage, student loan deferment, and, upon graduation, are eligible for a postservice AmeriCorps education award up to $4,725, job training, and other life-changing opportunities. Application materials are available online. Four decision-making periods for completed applications span from November 30 through May 31.

FOR MORE INFORMATION: Recruitment Department, City Year, 285 Columbus Ave., 5th Floor, Boston, MA 02116 • (888) 424-8993 • (617) 927-2500 (617) 927-2510 (fax) • info@cityyear.org

☛ **INSIDER TIP:** While browsing the City Year website, be sure to take a look at the history of their logo, which will provide you with interesting information for your interview. For instance, did you know the seven triangles in each segment of the logo represent the days of the week and the American Indian belief that we should consider the impact any major decision will make on the next seven generations?

CONFRONTATION POINT MINISTRIES

Youth Development/Ministry • Tennessee • Summer
www.confrontationpoint.org

$ 🏠

Confrontation Point Ministries offers opportunities to lead weeklong mission trips with youth groups doing repairs on the homes of poverty-stricken people or on outdoor adventure trips designed to teach leadership development. The programs run from late May to early August, with training provided for the adventure staff. Besides having a solid Christian faith, applicants must have group leadership skills, maturity (not necessarily age, but twenty or over is better), and a valid driver's license, and be hardworking, fun loving, and adventurous. Leaders receive a salary of $1,500 and half of all partnerships that they raise (a partnership-raising packet will be provided to help you raise partners effectively), plus room and board. Over forty positions are offered each summer; applications can be found online.

FOR MORE INFORMATION: Randy Velker, Summer Staff Coordinator, Confrontation Point Ministries, P.O. Box 572, Crossville, TN 38557 (800) 884-8483 • (931) 484-7819 (fax) • randy@confrontationpoint.org

CONGRESSIONAL HUNGER CENTER

Hunger Awareness • USA/Worldwide • 1 Year
www.hungercenter.org

$ 🏠

Did you know that more than one billion people throughout the world are denied the most basic of human rights—access to food? In the U.S. (the richest country in the world), one in ten people suffer from hunger and malnutrition. The Bill Emerson Hunger Fellows Program, a program of the Congressional Hunger Center, helps to make an impact by developing leaders in the fight against hunger.

WHAT YOU'LL BE DOING: Each year a select group of twenty-four participants are chosen to be fellows in this twelve-month program (beginning in late August). After an intensive ten-day orientation and training period in Washington, D.C., fellows are placed for six months, in teams of two, in grassroots organizations at sites throughout the U.S. to learn about hunger and poverty through hands-on experiences. The following six months are spent in Washington, D.C., at national nonprofit organizations working on hunger and poverty policy. During this time, fellows attend professional development seminars. Also inquire about their two-year international fellows program, with placements in South Asia, sub-Saharan Africa, and Latin America and the Caribbean.

PERKS AND REWARDS: Since the program is designed to experience living at the poverty level, fellows receive a modest living allowance that averages $10,000 for the year. Benefits include health insurance, relocation stipends, and an end-of-service cash award of $3,500. Housing is provided in the host community during the six-month field placement and assistance in locating housing in Washington, D.C., is offered for the policy placement segment of the program. Travel to and from training sessions and placements are also provided.

THE ESSENTIALS: Applicants are chosen on the basis of their commitment to social change, diversity of experience and perspective, vision for the future, demonstrated leadership potential, and willingness to learn and have their lives changed by this experience. All applicants over the age of eighteen will be considered.

YOUR FIRST MOVE: Call, email, or visit their website for application materials, which are due in January. Openings may occur late in the hiring process, so qualified candidates are encouraged to contact the center after the priority deadline.

FOR MORE INFORMATION: John Kelly and Kristin Anderson, Codirectors, Congressional Hunger Center, Bill Emerson National Hunger Fellows Program, 229½ Pennsylvania Ave., SE, Washington, DC 20003 • (202) 547-7022 (202) 547-7575 (fax) • fellows@hungercenter.org

CO-OP AMERICA

Social Justice • Washington, DC • Seasonal
www.coopamerica.org

$ ⊕

As a nonprofit membership association of individuals and organizations working to build a more cooperative and socially responsible economy, Co-op America strives to educate their members to use their buying power more effectively to create change. They also serve as a link between socially conscious consumers and responsible businesses by providing a variety of benefits, including a quarterly publication and the *Green Pages* to their members.

WHAT YOU'LL BE DOING: While at Co-op America, interns are exposed to the world of marketing and development in the nonprofit, social change sector. Internships are available in these departments: corporate accountability, executive, foundation fund-raising, Internet marketing, magazine and publications, marketing analysis, media, national *Green Pages* advertising, research, and socially responsible business research. All positions involve work in developing programs, research and writing, and general organizational strategy. Co-op America has a progressive office, treats interns as part of the team, and encourages interns to participate in all staff activities.

COMMITMENT: Internships are offered year-round, although preference is given to those who can work a minimum of two months. Schedules and length of internships vary depending on the project and the intern's availability.

PERKS AND REWARDS: A stipend of $230 to $300 per month is provided. All interns receive a two-year membership to Co-op America, a number of "intern appreciation lunches" (free food!), and every so often they close the office to do something fun together (such as tubing or bowling).

Our deepest fear is not that we are inadequate.

Our deepest fear is that we are powerful beyond measure.

It is our light, not our darkness, that most frightens us.

We ask ourselves, Who am I to be brilliant, gorgeous, talented, and fabulous?

Actually, who are you not to be?

You are a child of God.

Your playing small doesn't serve the world.

There's nothing enlightened about shrinking so that other people won't feel insecure around you.

We were born to make manifest the glory of God that is within us.

It's not just in some of us; it's in everyone.

And as we let our own light shine, we unconsciously give other people permission to do the same.

As we are liberated from our own fear, our presence automatically liberates others.

—FROM NELSON MANDELA'S
INAUGURAL SPEECH IN 1994,
ORIGINALLY WRITTEN BY
MARIANNE WILLIAMSON

The greatest mistake you can make in life is to be continually fearing that you will make one.
—ELBERT HUBBARD

THE ESSENTIALS: Those who are hardworking, interested in the environmental and social change movement, able to work independently and as part of a team, and willing to work in a cooperative environment make ideal candidates.

YOUR FIRST MOVE: Detailed position descriptions can be viewed on their website, or call for more information. Send your resume and cover letter stating why you want to work for Co-op America and which position you are interested in and why.

FOR MORE INFORMATION: Internship Coordinator, Co-op America, 1612 K St., NW, Suite 600, Washington, DC 20006 • (800) 584-7336 • (202) 872-5307 (202) 331-8166 (fax) • internships@coopamerica.org

 INSIDER TIP: Let us know which internship you would like. Don't make us guess. Make sure there are no typos in your letter and resume. Be clear and concise about what you are looking for and what your skills are. Know something about the organization you are writing to. Let us know why you want to work at Co-op America rather than some other organization.

FARM SANCTUARY

Animal Rights • California/New York • 1–3 Months
www.farmsanctuary.org

♥ ♠ ⊕

Dedicated to ending the exploitation of animals used for food production, Farm Sanctuary (located both in the heart of upstate New York and in a small farming community in Northern California) serves as a refuge for hundreds of abused or badly injured farm animals—a haven where "food animals" come to live, not die. More than three hundred animals reside in twelve shelter barns at the farms. A "People Barn" functions as a learning center where visitors can find out more about factory farming and the harsh realities of the "food animal" industry.

WHAT YOU'LL BE DOING: The sanctuaries' well-established internship program allows volunteers to learn firsthand about the day-to-day responsibilities of farm work, farm animal care, educational programming (from staffing and maintaining the visitor center to conducting tours), and the practical applications of grassroots participation.

COMMITMENT: Full-time positions are available year-round, so volunteers can join the sanctuary any time. It's preferred that volunteers make a commitment of at least one month, and two- or three-month internships are encouraged.

PERKS AND REWARDS: Interns receive shared housing, with access to kitchen facilities.

THE ESSENTIALS: Anyone who has a strong commitment to animals and wants to experience the joy of doing outdoor work is welcome.

YOUR FIRST MOVE: Fill out the online application, or call or write for more information. Summer interns should apply by February; otherwise, send applications at least two months prior to your desired start date.

FOR MORE INFORMATION: Erin Flowers, Intern Coordinator, Farm Sanctuary, P.O. Box 150, Watkins Glen, NY 14891-0150 • (607) 583-2225 (607) 583-2041 (fax) • intern@farmsanctuary.org

GOOD SHEPHERD VOLUNTEERS

Community Service/Ministry • USA/Mexico/Paraguay/Peru • 1–2 Years
www.goodshepherdvolunteers.org

$ 🏠

Founded by the Sisters of the Good Shepherd (www.goodshepherdsistersna.com), Good Shepherd Volunteers is a faith-based volunteer program that places Christian men and women in jobs working with children, teens, and women in social service agencies.

WHAT YOU'LL BE DOING: Volunteers live together in communities that focus on simplicity, spirituality, and social justice, with typical service placements that include teaching (ranging from an inner-city junior high to a domestic violence center), child care, outreach coordination, youth development, activities coordination, and counseling. Programs are offered in the U.S. in Los Angeles, New Jersey, New York, Philadelphia, and Washington, D.C., and abroad in Paraguay, Peru, and Mexico.

COMMITMENT: Placements begin in late August with an initial weeklong orientation and continue for one to two years. Throughout the year, there are four weekend retreats as well as opportunities for work-related training and workshops.

PERKS AND REWARDS: Benefits include professional support and supervision, a $100 monthly stipend, assistance with travel costs, full medical coverage, deferred student loans, and an AmeriCorps education award for most positions. A private room in community-style housing and a monthly food stipend of $80 is also provided.

THE ESSENTIALS: Most volunteers are between the ages of twenty-two and twenty-five and have either just graduated from college or graduate school or have graduated in the past couple of years; others have taken a break from school to volunteer or were working and decided that they really wanted to try something else with their lives. At minimum, applicants must be high school graduates at least twenty-one years of age and have two years of work experience or some college education.

YOUR FIRST MOVE: Applications are available online and are accepted on a rolling basis; however, many people submit their application materials starting in January.

FOR MORE INFORMATION: Michele Gilfillan, Director, Good Shepherd Volunteers, 337 E. 17th St., New York, NY 10003 • (888) 668-6478 • (212) 475-4245, ext. 718 (212) 979-8604 (fax) • gsv@goodshepherds.org

GOULD FARM

Therapeutic Community • Massachusetts • 9–12 Months
www.gouldfarm.org

$ 🏠

Gould Farm is a compassionate, respectful family environment where people with mental illness learn to build more meaningful lives for themselves. The services at the farm remain rooted in the belief that every person has something to contribute despite mental or emotional limitations. Central to the farm model is a structured, supportive work environment for clients. Volunteers, staff, and clients work together to run the six-hundred-acre farm, whether tending to the gardens or roadside store, pasteurizing milk, or preparing the meals. Volunteers generally work in one specific area of the farm, such as gardening, farming, forestry, dairy management, livestock, cooking, child care, administration, or clinical work. Serving as informal counselors, work team leaders, and role models, most volunteers lead a small group of people through work tasks that are required to run the farm and maintain the community. Volunteer positions are usually filled throughout the year, along with occasional summer opportunities based on housing availability. Preference is given to those who can commit to one year. Benefits for those who commit for one year include a monthly stipend of $250, a private bedroom in shared staff housing on the grounds, farm-fresh meals, full medical coverage, and the possibility of an AmeriCorps Education award. One of the biggest perks may be the spirit that resides in this rural, community lifestyle, which is filled with lots of work along with singing, crafts, music, art, weaving, and the celebration of nature and life!

FOR MORE INFORMATION: Cynthia Meyer, Human Resources Manager, Gould Farm, 100 Gould Farm Rd., P.O. Box 157, Monterey, MA 01245-0157 (413) 528-1804, ext. 17 • (413) 528-5051 (fax) • humanresources@gouldfarm.org

GREEN CHIMNEYS CHILDREN'S SERVICES

Farming/Therapeutic Community • New York • 3–5 Months
www.greenchimneys.org

$ 🏠 ⊕

Green Chimneys is dedicated to the development of basic education and daily living skills for children and adults to restore and strengthen their emotional health and well-being. The main campus is situated on a 150-acre farm where injured animals also have the chance for rehabilitation through help from participants. The lessons learned from the animals become the stepping-stone for human connection and healing.

WHAT YOU'LL BE DOING: A typical day at Green Chimneys includes special education classes, vocational education, life skills training, therapy, therapeutic activities, and recreation. Internships are available in the farm program, as well as the special education, recreation, and child care departments. Farm interns work with children who are participating in daily barn chores and special projects (such as grooming animals, painting signs, or creating educational displays). Interns are offered the chance to participate in a variety of activities, including public programs and tours, teacher workshops, and weekend events.

COMMITMENT: Programs vary in length from three to five months, with start dates beginning in January, June, and September.

PERKS AND REWARDS: A small stipend is provided, along with room and board. Interns are housed in shared rooms in a residence located across the street from the campus.

THE ESSENTIALS: Applicants must have a keen interest or background in children, animals, farms, and outdoor education, and must be at least twenty years of age (at least a junior in college or equivalent).

YOUR FIRST MOVE: Email or call for application materials and further information; to hear a recorded message of current employment opportunities, dial extension 501 when calling.

FOR MORE INFORMATION: Jackie Ryan, Internship Coordinator, Green Chimneys Children's Services, 400 Doansburg Rd., P.O. Box 719, Brewster, NY 10509-0719 (845) 279-2995, ext. 158 • (845) 279-0496 (fax) • info@greenchimneys.org

The shoe that fits one person pinches another; there is no recipe for living that suits all cases. **459**
—CARL JUNG

WORKING OPTIONS WITH HABITAT FOR HUMANITY INTERNATIONAL

• •

*Love without limits. Build without limits. That's what we do in
the work of Habitat for Humanity*

—MILLARD FULLER, FOUNDER

Putting faith into action, Habitat for Humanity brings people from all walks
of life together to make affordable housing and better communities a reality
for everyone. Habitat volunteers provide their construction and administrative
skills for the vision of eliminating poverty housing from the face of the earth.

Volunteers with Habitat's RV Care-A-Vanners program "take five" from their "Building on Faith" housing
project in Seattle.

OPPORTUNITIES IN GEORGIA

Something new to Habitat's campus in Americus is the creation of the Global
Village and Discovery Center—and they need plenty of volunteers to help
out! Phase one of the village began in 2002 and calls for fifteen replica homes
to be built, representing fifteen of eighty-three countries in which Habitat

works. The village will be built in five phases over the course of five years; and once completed, the village will be an interactive museum where visitors can wind their way through multimedia displays on world housing and then wander through a village to see replicas of houses from places such as such as Tanzania, Kenya, and Sri Lanka.

Volunteers work to build the homes, starting with the first step of making each brick by hand with the aid of a manual machine. The experience is unique in that you'll learn just how difficult it is for people in other countries, who do most of the labor themselves, to have a home of their own. A one-month, full-time commitment is necessary, and volunteers can stay on up to three months. Construction skills are not a prerequisite as Habitat will teach you—if you have the will to learn! Fully furnished housing (with shared kitchen, bath, and living area) is provided; food expenses are additional.

Other volunteer opportunities in Americus include positions in administration, child care, fund-raising, graphic arts, information systems, language translation, photography, or public relations. Internships are also available for college students. Furnished housing and a food stipend are provided for all volunteer programs (and some positions include health insurance). Check out www.habitat.org/hr for more information.

ATTENTION RVERS—ROAD TRIP USA?

Do you want to blend the fun of RV travel with a fulfilling Habitat for Humanity experience? Habitat's RV Care-A-Vanners organize caravans of six to ten RVs whose owners have a commitment to eliminate substandard housing and a willingness to learn from and partner with local affiliates and homeowner families. In general, these nationwide projects run two weeks, with a typical workday beginning with devotions and lasting about seven hours. Each volunteer must own a recreational vehicle (motor home, trailer, or van), along with a few basic tools, and have energy and a spirit of enthusiasm and flexibility. A caravan is time for growth and fellowship, as well as for service and hands-on experience. Activities may include work at any stage of new home construction, occasionally the renovation of an older home, or building awareness of Habitat's mission at churches, civic groups, or the local media. Participants must be financially able to travel to the project site and cover personal expenses while there; host affiliates provide a safe place to park your RV (with water and electrical hookups and waste disposal). To get the wheels of your RV turning, call for an information packet or visit www.habitat.org/gv/rv.html.

It's not what's out there in the world that you have to worry about.
It's what's in your heart and your head.
—JOSEPH M. MCINTYRE

GLOBAL VILLAGE PROGRAM

The Global Village Program (www.habitat.org/gv) provides participants with a unique opportunity to become active partners with people of another culture. Team members work alongside people of the host community, raising awareness of the burden of poverty housing and building decent, affordable housing worldwide. As partners, team members help build a true "global village" of love, homes, communities, and hope! Unlike tour groups, Global Village hosts offer team members a "back door" welcome to their community and encourage teams to visit nearby cultural and national treasures. One- to three-week itineraries are balanced with plenty of work, recreational activities, and free time. In addition to short-term missions in the U.S., Mexico, and Canada, over sixty international destinations include Africa (Ethiopia, Ghana, and Tanzania), Asia and the Pacific Rim (Fiji, India, Nepal, New Zealand, and Sri Lanka), Central America and the Caribbean (Honduras and Nicaragua), and South America (Bolivia, Brazil, Ecuador, and Guyana). Program fees vary depending on the country and length; however, in general they range from $1,200 to $1,800, plus airfare. The fee covers room and board, travel insurance, and a donation toward the construction cost of houses built in the host country. Habitat provides simple, respectful ideas for fund-raising efforts. Applicants include individuals, couples, groups, and families.

Global Village volunteers from the U.S. work alongside local volunteers to gather raw material for making soil bricks in Urubamba, Peru.

DON'T SKIP THE TRIP

• •

I am still surprised when I hear from people who are not aware that Habitat for Humanity is an international ministry. They ask, "Do you mean that Habitat builds houses in Nepal too?" I am even more surprised when I think that people might not realize that Habitat started as an international ministry. Yes, houses were built on a no-profit, no-interest basis by Millard and Linda Fuller in Africa before the program ever began in the United States.

My own personal experience with Habitat has had an international focus for over eighteen years, so my first thoughts always run to the international work. I often have to pause to think that hundreds of thousands of people may only be aware of Habitat's work in their own hometown. Perhaps that's what makes this Global Village work so much fun. Every single day we invite people to experience Habitat in another part of the world. We encourage them to go to Mongolia, to Tanzania, to El Salvador. We encourage them to taste and feel and smell the work of Habitat around the globe.

We also encourage them to help raise money to build more houses internationally. Some folks take the fund raising challenge very seriously. The unstoppable Cynthia Kersey—a nationally acclaimed writer and speaker—recently used a team experience to raise funds for one hundred homes in Nepal! Amazing! And she committed to a similar effort in Guatemala shortly thereafter. Yet I know that if I asked any of Cynthia's team members what was most important about their experience, they would say the trip itself.

Global Village brings people together in a spirit of partnership and camaraderie. We connect people who would never otherwise meet. We expose people to God's work with God's people in a powerful and meaningful way. No matter what your experience with Habitat is to date, I encourage you to get out and experience Habitat anew. Experience Habitat in another land. Don't skip the trip!

• •

—Contributed by David Minich, director of the Global Village Program, who together with his family served as an international partner in Papua New Guinea

FOR MORE INFORMATION: Habitat for Humanity International, 322 W. Lamar St., Americus, GA 31709 • (800) 422-4828 • (229) 924-6935 • www.habitat.org

Human Resources: Extension 2377 • hrstaffing@hfhi.org • www.habitat.org/hr

Global Village and Discovery Center Volunteering: Extension 2655
vsd@hfhi.org • www.habitat.org/GVDC/volunteer.html

RV Care-A-Vanners: Extension 2466 • rvinfodesk@hfhi.org
www.habitat.org/gv/rv.html

Global Village Program: David Minich, Director • Extension 2549 • gv@hfhi.org
www.habitat.org/gv

Both tears and sweat are salty, but they render a different result.
Tears will get you sympathy; sweat will get you change.
—JESSE JACKSON

INNISFREE VILLAGE

Therapeutic Community • Virginia • 1 Year+
www.innisfreevillage.org

$ 🏠 🌐

Set in the foothills of the Blue Ridge Mountains (and only seventeen miles from Charlottesville, Virginia), Innisfree Village is a life-sharing community for adults with mental disabilities. Sixty-five people live and work together on a six-hundred-acre farm in a model therapeutic environment emphasizing empowerment, interdependence, and mutual respect of all community members.

In the community of Innisfree Village, staff members and those with mental disabilities share in meaningful life and work experiences.

WHAT YOU'LL BE DOING: Volunteers and coworkers live together in family-style homes throughout the village. Generally two to four volunteers are assigned to each house and serve as "houseparents." After a one-month orientation period, responsibilities include cleaning, cooking, laundry, shopping, and finances of the house as well as caring for the personal needs of each coworker. Volunteers are also engaged in therapeutic and meaningful work in the bakery, gardens, weavery, woodshop, and kitchens.

PERKS AND REWARDS: One-year volunteers receive a private room, board, a monthly stipend of $215, fifteen paid vacation days, medical insurance, and two consecutive days off per week.

THE ESSENTIALS: Fifteen to twenty people between the ages of twenty-one and sixty, all with various backgrounds and nationalities, are needed each year. Volunteers must be at least twenty-one years of age and able to commit for one year, although shorter-term positions are offered each year. The desire to live with adults with disabilities in a rural community is a must, as are patience, a sense of humor, flexibility, and common sense.

YOUR FIRST MOVE: Call for application materials (which are accepted year-round).

FOR MORE INFORMATION: Nancy Chappell, Recruitment Director, Innisfree Village, 5505 Walnut Level Rd., Crozet, VA 22932 • (434) 823-5400 (434) 823-5027 (fax) • innisfreevillage@prodigy.net

A WHOLE NEW WAY
TO MOVE THROUGH THE WORLD

· ·

Innisfree changed my life—in jolts and bolts and slow rolling waves. After college I found myself in a corporate job that seemed to suck the life out of me.

I needed change. I needed challenge that involved more meaning than designing a marketing campaign for a product I didn't really care about. I came to Innisfree seeking something new, something fun. What I found was a whole new way to move through the world. I volunteered for a year and then another. I went away, and like many other volunteers I have come back.

With a smile as wide as the community she has uncovered, Innisfree volunteer Lisa Gerlits (she's on the right) takes a break with a participant while working in the weavery shop.

Mornings are especially lovely here, when patches of mist still crouch among the trees, and the edges of the mountains blur into the sky. A whippoorwill calls. A woodpecker answers. A hummingbird zooms into view and zooms away again. The sun crests the mountains to the east, and a sliver of light appears on the mountains to the west. The light spreads down and down. All that was purple and blue and deep green slowly becomes yellow and orange and bright green. All around the air is charged with life—buzzing insects, birdcalls. The guinea hens yodel; the cows moan; Joe's tractor purrs in the distance. A spider's web that appeared overnight outside your window is laced with dew. And you have never seen anything so delicate and permanent in all your life.

You take a walk. You breathe the impossibly clean air. You pass the garden, see the tomato plants climbing, smell basil on the breeze, and hear the bees already working the blooms. And then you return to your house. Someone has already started the coffee. Someone has set the table. Someone has taken out the compost. And you glide into your place in the morning bustle. You help Angelica shower and dress for the day. You wake up Nicky. You all eat breakfast together and head out the door and down the hill. You work. You share life. You live in community, where everyone's talents and offerings are picked into the same basket.

The amazing thing about Innisfree is the unconditional love and support that you get from the community. You feel it the moment you arrive. You are reminded of it every day with hugs and smiles and laughter. This is community. This is the way we ought to live. It's so simple really. When you leave, you wonder why the rest of the world doesn't operate this way.

In this time when much of the world seems to close in around us—the airplane seats move closer together, the cubicles get smaller and smaller, time is always in short supply—Innisfree offers a place to expand, to breathe deeper than you thought you could, to spill over the edge of yourself and into a community that requires the fullness of your experience and compassion.

· ·

—Contributed by Lisa Gerlits, Innisfree volunteer

You will find as you look back upon your life that the moments when you have truly lived are the moments when you have done things in the spirit of love.
—HENRY DRUMMOND

465

JESUIT VOLUNTEERS INTERNATIONAL

Service Learning/Ministry · USA/Worldwide · 1–2 Years
www.jesuitvolunteers.org

$ 🏠

In the mid-1980s the first team of volunteers with Jesuit Volunteers International (JVI) began their service with the people of Belize in Central America. Since then, over six hundred men and women have committed themselves to walking with people in marginalized communities around the world. JVI volunteers currently work in countries as diverse as Belize, Bolivia, Nepal, Nicaragua, Micronesia, Peru, South Africa, and Tanzania. In the U.S., JVI's sister organization, Jesuit Volunteer Corps (JVC), works with hundreds of grassroots organizations across the country who count on volunteers to provide social justice work to those who have few options.

WHAT YOU'LL BE DOING: Volunteers abroad have the opportunity to teach a variety of subjects (from the social sciences to dance classes), coach sports teams, provide pastoral support, counsel children and families, and work in a variety of other placements. In the U.S., volunteers serve the homeless, the unemployed, refugees, people with AIDS, the elderly, street youth, abused women and children, the mentally ill, and the developmentally disabled. At the cornerstone of the volunteer experience are the four values of community, simple living, social justice, and spirituality. To assist volunteers in integrating these values into their daily lives while in the field, a series of retreats and workshops are offered throughout their tenure.

COMMITMENT: International placements require a two-year commitment (with a two-week orientation); domestic volunteers must make a one-year commitment (with a one-week orientation). Most placements begin in the late summer or fall.

PERKS AND REWARDS: Housing, utilities, a food stipend, transportation to and from work (such as a bus pass or bicycle), medical insurance, and a small monthly stipend are provided. JVI also provides travel from the orientation site to the placement site (in the U.S. or abroad), transportation to and from retreats during the year, and transportation home upon conclusion of the program. Housing is community style with other volunteers—a place to share in meals, conversation, and prayer while encouraging each others' ministry.

THE ESSENTIALS: JVI welcomes those who are at least twenty-one years old, have a college degree (or applicable work experience), and are self-motivated, mature, and genuinely interested in living out all four values. Some job placements require specific credentials or licenses; however, most can be done by people who have a general educational background and a willingness to learn new skills.

YOUR FIRST MOVE: Contact information for domestic and international offices as well as application materials are available online. JVI and JVC share common values; however, application requirements, length of commitment, benefits, and job placements differ. Review each region carefully.

FOR MORE INFORMATION: Programs and Services Director, Jesuit Volunteers International, P.O. Box 3756, Washington, DC 20007-0256 • (202) 687-1132 (202) 687-5082 (fax) • jvi@jesuitvolunteers.org

> ## If you're looking for a volunteer experience abroad, be sure to explore more options found in the next chapter!

LANDMARK VOLUNTEERS

Community Service • USA • 2 Weeks
www.volunteers.com

♥ ⚒

Landmark Volunteers is a nonprofit summer service organization for placing high school students who are looking for an opportunity to do something for others through community service. Under the supervision of an adult leader, volunteers are placed in teams of thirteen at host organizations ranging from Colonial Williamsburg in Virginia to the Grand Teton Music Festival in Wyoming. In return for lending a hand (primarily manual labor) to accomplish much needed work for other worthy environmental, cultural, historical, and social service nonprofits over a two-week period, participants receive an exceptional learning opportunity and a chance to understand how voluntary service functions as an essential element of the American experience. Volunteers are admitted on a competitive basis with purpose, diligence, and responsibility as determining factors. Applicants must be at least fourteen and a half by June and be entering at least the tenth grade (sorry, no high school graduates). A program fee of $875 covers the cost of placement as well as food and housing for the two-week program.

FOR MORE INFORMATION: Program Director, Landmark Volunteers, P.O. Box 455, Sheffield, MA 01257 • (413) 229-0225 • (413) 229-2050 (fax) landmark@volunteers.com

LITTLE BROTHERS— FRIENDS OF THE ELDERLY

Aging • Illinois/Ireland/France • 3–12 Months
www.littlebrothers.org/chicago

$ 🏠 🌐

No one plans to grow old alone, but it happens. Little Brothers—Friends of the Elderly serves lonely and isolated elderly over the age of seventy who live within the city of Chicago. These people most often lack a social network of family and friends, or have few social skills to build friendships, and identify themselves as lonely. Little Brothers' motto of "flowers before bread" points to their belief that hearts starve as well as bodies. Chicago is the original home of Little Brothers in the U.S., but programs also exist in eight other U.S. cities and in Canada, France, Germany, Ireland, Mexico, Poland, and Spain.

WHAT YOU'LL BE DOING: Summer interns will be part of a team of helpers who, together with the elderly, organize and go to their vacation home, a fifteen-room house set on seven acres just two hours outside of Chicago. Interns will have constant interaction with the elderly, prepare and assist with various group activities, help with personal hygiene, assist with meal preparation, and drive passenger vans. Although challenging, vacations are often the most rewarding intern experience at Little Brothers. Program assistants in Chicago make a one-year commitment and assist the program coordinators to ensure that every elderly "friend in the family" has a relationship with Little Brothers. This may include personal visits to nursing homes, assistance in helping the elderly meet their daily needs to live independently, or working with program coordinators to plan and carry out celebrations of life. Finally, there are also three- to twelve-month internships available in France (activities assistant) and six- to twelve-month internships in Ireland (program coordination).

COMMITMENT: Positions are offered during the summer or for one year and are full-time with a flexible schedule, including some evening and weekend work.

PERKS AND REWARDS: Program assistants receive $600 per month, plus lodging and health insurance; summer interns in Chicago receive $200 for a seven-week period along with room and board; and interns abroad receive approximately $100 per month, with room, board, and health insurance (for at least a six-month commitment in France). All interns will receive excellent training and experience in the field of aging, while working under the guidance of experienced volunteers and staff.

THE ESSENTIALS: Applicants must have sensitivity to the needs of elderly people who are growing old alone, a personal values system that emphasizes respect for the individual, a belief that friendship is essential in the lives of elderly people, and strong communication and interpersonal skills. Bilingual English/Spanish skills are welcomed for Chicago positions; applicants for positions in France must be fluent in French.

YOUR FIRST MOVE: Applications and additional details can be found online.

FOR MORE INFORMATION: Christine Bertrand, Internship Coordinator, Little Brothers—Friends of the Elderly, 355 N. Ashland Ave., Chicago, IL 60607-1019 (312) 455-1000 • (312) 455-9674 (fax) • cbertrand.chi@littlebrothers.org

☞ INSIDER TIP: Before I started volunteering with Little Brothers, I believed the world would be a better place if we focused on friendship and celebrating life, but now I am convinced. I realized that friendship takes time to develop but that everyone needs it. I learned that through celebrating life, chronic pain can disappear, at least for a second, and that even death loses its sting. —David Scott, volunteer

LOCH ARTHUR COMMUNITY

Therapeutic Community • Scotland • 1 Year
www.locharthur.org.uk/home.htm
♥ ♠ ⊕

Loch Arthur is a working community of seventy people in the southwest of Scotland, where volunteers live with, support, and work with adults who have learning disabilities. The five hundred acres include an organic farm using bio-dynamic practices, market gardens, a large creamery (for cheese making), a bakery, a weaving workshop, and seven large households. A sense of home, community, spirituality, cooperation, emotional support, relationship building, and encouragement are the key ingredients of this shared lifestyle. The work component is about cooperation rather than competition and provides a sense of responsibility and satisfaction. Most volunteers make a one-year commitment (although shorter stays are possible), with flexible schedules and time off for "holidays." Applicants must be at least eighteen, physically and mentally healthy, and open to new challenges. Pocket money, lodging, and board are provided.

FOR MORE INFORMATION: Lana Chanarin, Volunteer Coordinator, Loch Arthur Community, St Bride, Loch Arthur, Beeswing, Dumfries DG2 0JQ, Scotland (011) 44 1387 760621 • admin@locharthur.org.uk

LUTHERAN VOLUNTEER CORPS

Service Learning • USA • 1 Year
www.lvchome.org
$ ♠

The Lutheran Volunteer Corps provides the opportunity for participants to work full-time in nonprofit agencies over the course of a year. Volunteers commit to exploring their spirituality while working for social justice, living in

Imagine what a harmonious world it could be if every single person, both young and old, shared a little of what he is good at doing. —QUINCY JONES

an intentional community, and simplifying their lifestyles. More than one hundred opportunities in a variety of organizations are available, including working with children and youth, counseling rape survivors and AIDS patients, organizing for better health care, advocating on behalf of refugees, staffing shelters for the homeless, tutoring adults, or working to preserve the environment. Life together with other volunteers includes sharing meals, chores, weekly community time, and monthly faith nights. In addition, LVC schedules four regional retreats each year that provide time for personal reflection, recreation, and exploration of the program's beliefs in the day-to-day lives of volunteers.

COMMITMENT: The program year begins with a five-day orientation at the end of August, followed by the work placement that continues through late August of the following year. Positions are available in the inner cities of Baltimore, Chicago, Milwaukee, Minneapolis/St. Paul, Oakland/Berkeley, Seattle, Tacoma, Washington, D.C., and Wilmington.

PERKS AND REWARDS: The biggest perks include a great work experience, new friends, urban living, and the opportunity to make a difference! Volunteers also receive a monthly stipend, room and board, medical insurance, transportation money, and two weeks of vacation. In addition, volunteers may be eligible for forbearance on student loans and an AmeriCorps education award of up to $4,725.

THE ESSENTIALS: Applicants must be at least twenty-one years of age (with no upper age limit) and willing to commit to exploring their spirituality while working for social justice, living in an intentional community, and simplifying their lifestyle. Volunteers do not need to be Lutheran—individuals of all faith backgrounds are encouraged to apply. Married couples and committed partners are also welcome to apply. Volunteers often find themselves in new and unexpected situations, so flexibility, openness, and a sense of humor are essential. Most volunteer placements can be done by people who have a general educational background and a willingness to learn new skills.

YOUR FIRST MOVE: Program information and applications are available upon request or on their website. Applications are accepted from February 1 through mid-May for positions beginning in the fall. Get your application in by February 1 for the best selection of cities and agencies.

FOR MORE INFORMATION: Jen Moore, Recruitment Coordinator, Lutheran Volunteer Corps, 1226 Vermont Ave., NW, Washington, DC 20005 (202) 387-3222 • (202) 667-0037 (fax) • lvcrecruitment@lvchome.org

COMPOSTING
THE FRUITS
OF THE SPIRIT

• •

My LVC housemates and I designed a covenant to describe the most meaningful aspects of sharing this year together. We decided to build a compost
pile. Eggshells, banana peels, and other things that have lost all their value,
once composted, can turn into very fertile soil. I feel our compost pile is a
symbol.

Sometimes my life feels like it has lost its value. In the world we live in,
what difference do I make? I am working at a homeless shelter, but I see
only a little change day to day. Maybe I am not so different from compost.
Sometimes I may feel as insignificant as an eggshell, but if my gifts form a
compost pile, than I am creating fertile ground. Maybe, like the eggshell, I
won't see or understand the change I'm making, but creating that fertile
ground is the most important thing. It is the fertile soil that brings growth
and excitement. Every day I hope that, like the compost, I am making fertile
ground for someone else.

• •

—Samuel Strommen, LVC volunteer

> *It is not by accident that the happiest people are those who
> make a conscious effort to live useful lives. Their happi-
> ness, of course, is not a shallow exhilaration where life is
> one continuous intoxicating party. Rather, their happiness
> is a deep sense of inner peace that comes when they believe
> their lives have meaning and that they are making a dif-
> ference of good in the world.*
>
> —ERNEST FITZGERALD

*When our eyes see our hands doing the work of our hearts,
the circle of Creation is completed inside us, the doors of our souls fly open
and love steps forth to heal everything in sight.* —MICHAEL BRIDGE

471

MERCY SHIPS

Sailing/Ministry • Worldwide • 2 Weeks–2 Years
www.mercyships.org

Mercy Ships is a nonprofit Christian humanitarian organization committed to a threefold purpose of mercy and relief, training, and ministry. Mercy Ships has served the poor in over seventy-five port cities by providing medical care (surgeries along with medical, dental, and optical clinics and health care teaching), assisting through development projects, and fulfilling basic daily needs in order to demonstrate the message of hope through Jesus Christ. Whatever your interest or background, there could be a place for you in Mercy Ships—at sea or on land. Join Mercy Ships for as little as two weeks and up to two years (although many make a lifetime commitment). As a volunteer short-term crew member, you will have the opportunity to take a look at missions as well as at Mercy Ships. Openings are available in a variety of positions—from bakers and carpenters to translators and deckhands. Applicants must be at least eighteen years old and in good health (current physical required).

FOR MORE INFORMATION: Recruiting Manager, Mercy Ships, P.O. Box 2020, Garden Valley, TX 75771-2020 • (800) 882-0887 • (903) 939-7000 (903) 939-7114 (fax) • jobs@mercyships.org

MOBILITY INTERNATIONAL USA

Disability Awareness/International Education • Oregon/Worldwide
3–6 Months • www.miusa.org

Mobility International USA (MIUSA) is an innovative nonprofit organization that empowers people with disabilities around the world through international exchange, information, technical assistance, and training. MIUSA also serves as the National Clearinghouse on Disability and Exchange, which provides personalized information, referrals, and support for those who are disabled and interested in international exchange. Short-term exchange programs specialize in leadership training, community service, cross-cultural experiential learning, adaptive recreational activities, and volunteer service projects for youth, adults, and professionals. In the past, exchanges have taken place in Azerbaijan, Bulgaria, China, Costa Rica, eastern Asia, Germany, Italy, Japan, Mexico, Russia, and the United Kingdom. (For more information on these programs, send an email to exchange@miusa.org or fill out the online application.)

WHAT YOU'LL BE DOING: Interns will work directly with staff volunteers and have the opportunity to develop skills and gain direct work experience in disability rights, international educational exchange, leadership, travel and recreational opportunities, research, article and grant writing, program development, public relations, computer graphics and layout, and the day-to-day operation of a nonprofit organization. Interns are encouraged to work independently on their own projects as well as on assigned and supervised projects.

COMMITMENT: Internship programs usually last between three and six months.

PERKS AND REWARDS: For interns committed to six months or longer, a stipend of $125 per month is provided to help with living expenses.

THE ESSENTIALS: Interest in people with disabilities and promoting cross-cultural understanding is necessary. Preference will be given to applicants with international exchange or travel experience or who have career or master's project goals that mesh with the goals of MIUSA. People with disabilities are especially encouraged to apply.

YOUR FIRST MOVE: Along with providing a resume, cover letter, and two letters of recommendation, you will need to complete an application.

FOR MORE INFORMATION: Cerise Roth-Vinson, Intern Coordinator, Mobility International USA, P.O. Box 10767, Eugene, OR 97440 • (541) 343-1284 (541) 343-6812 (fax) • info@miusa.org

HELPFUL RESOURCE

Are you a disabled person about to embark on an international adventure? With adequate preparation, much of the world is accessible to a disabled traveler—especially with help from Mobility International. From spending a study-abroad year in Spain to working in Australia, *Survival Strategies for Going Abroad: A Guide for People with Disabilities* explores academic, volunteer, short-term work, and other types of cross-cultural exchange for people with disabilities. You'll also learn about choosing and applying to a program, preparing for your journey, adjusting to a new country, and returning home. The book runs $16.95 and can only be purchased through MIUSA. In addition, MIUSA publishes *A World Awaits You*, an annual journal of success stories about people with disabilities who have participated in international exchange. Call for your complimentary copy.

If you improve in one talent, God will give you more. **473**
—MOTHER ANN LEE

NATIONAL 4-H COUNCIL

Youth Development • Maryland • 3–5 Months
www.fourhcouncil.edu

$ ⌂ 🎓

Research confirms that our young people—the future citizens, workers, parents, and leaders of our society—face unprecedented challenges, making the business of growing up more complex than ever before. Obscured at times by statistics of youth violence, crime, substance abuse, and suicide is the equally tragic waste of our youths' creative talents and unique skills by the neglect or ineffective interventions of public and private institutions. The National 4-H Council embraces these challenges by offering community youth development, youth leadership, and experiential educational programs for the young citizens of our world.

WHAT YOU'LL BE DOING: Program assistants (PAs) become licensed tour guides and facilitate the National 4-H Council's educational programs by leading groups of all ages through Washington, D.C., and at the National 4-H Youth Conference Center. Using the city and its sites as a classroom for learning, PAs provide commentary and site interpretation, and also serve as role models for school groups and 4-H members. The Wonders of Washington (www.wowwashington.org) program offers groups the ultimate Washington experience, with a focus on museums and historical sites, and includes a study-track option. The Citizenship Washington Focus (www.cwf.n4h.org) helps teach youth how to become "better citizens today, better leaders tomorrow" for seven weeks in June and July. When not escorting groups, PAs work with various center teams in sales, planning, guest services, and other departments. In addition to PA opportunities, a hospitality internship offers participants the chance to participate in activities, projects, and programs of the entire operation.

COMMITMENT: The program lasts from three to five months during the spring (February to mid-May), summer (May to July), and fall (September to December). The workload averages between fifty and sixty hours per week (it's a long workday!), and may include evenings, weekends, and holidays.

PERKS AND REWARDS: A weekly stipend of $300, on-campus dormitory-style living quarters, and cafeteria meals are provided. Interns will reside in Warren Hall, a three-story coed house with all the amenities of home, including kitchen, TV room, washer/dryer, towel and linen service, and computer lab. The twelve-acre suburban campus is just one mile from Washington, D.C. and features a high energy recreation room, basketball and volleyball courts, a cyber café, and comfortable lounges.

THE ESSENTIALS: Applications are accepted from eighteen- to twenty-three-year-old students with U.S. citizenship and an interest in history, government, communication, education, and youth development. The ability to think critically and work in a team environment and under pressure, and excellent presentation, leadership, and public speaking skills, are essential.

YOUR FIRST MOVE: To download application materials, visit the Program Assistant portion of www.cwf.n4h.org or www.wowwashington.org, or email Lita Haarer. Deadlines: spring—November 1; summer—January 28; and fall—June 1. Additional information about the Youth Conference Center can be found at www.4hcenter.org.

FOR MORE INFORMATION: Lita Haarer, Program Assistant Internships, National 4–H Council, 7100 Connecticut Ave., Chevy Chase, MD 20815-4999 (800) 368-7432 • (301) 961-2898 • (301) 961-2894 (fax) careers@fourhcouncil.edu

☞ **INSIDER TIP:** My summer was about growing as a person. I moved out of Wisconsin to a place I knew nothing about to live with people I had never met. In this setting I truly learned about who I am and who I want to become. I know that when I return home I will never be the same, because I have worked and lived with twenty-four other people who have impacted my life in a way that cannot be described. It can only be experienced. —*Monica Monfre, participant*

POPULATION CONNECTION FELLOWSHIP PROGRAM

Population Activism • Washington, DC • 5½ Months
www.populationconnection.org

$ 🎓

At last count there were 6,460,120,369 people on this earth. That's a lot of people. This, of course, is creating a certain havoc in our circle of life: population growth disrupts a sustainable balance of the earth's people, environment, and resources. And this is the very premise of Population Connection, the committed folks who hand out condoms with the wrappers embossed "Save the world: Use a condom." Well, there's a lot more to keeping the world's population in check than getting people to use condoms. Population Connection deals with both the causes and the effects of overpopulation, addressing issues ranging from supporting international family planning to suburban sprawl to contraceptive coverage by insurance policies. Let's hope their message of action and hope won't come too late.

We are here not to get all we can out of life for ourselves,
but to try to make the lives of others happier.
—WILLIAM OSLER

WHAT YOU'LL BE DOING: Grassroots organizing, attending hearings and coalition meetings, contacting the media, developing teaching materials—these are just some of the activities that fellows engage in while participating in a broad range of activities for the organization.

COMMITMENT: Fellowships are full-time, last five-and-a-half months, and are offered in two sessions: from January to mid-June and July to mid-December. Full- and part-time unpaid internships may occasionally be available for periods less than six months, and you can always lend a helping hand on Volunteer Night, held every Tuesday.

PERKS AND REWARDS: Fellows earn $750 every two weeks and receive full medical and dental insurance coverage, but the real benefits come from the connections you'll be making in the nation's capital.

THE ESSENTIALS: Whether you are still in college or recently graduated, fellows must have an academic background and experience relevant to their work at Population Connection. You must also have excellent writing and communication skills and the ability to work independently, and be prepared to advocate the positions of Population Connection. Candidates with English/Spanish bilingual skills are encouraged to apply.

YOUR FIRST MOVE: Explore their website for details on each fellow position and application materials. Deadlines: January session—end of October; July session—April 15.

FOR MORE INFORMATION: Jay Keller, Fellowship Director, Population Connection Fellowship Program, 1400 16th St., NW, Suite 320, Washington, DC 20036 (800) 767-1956 • (202) 332-2200 • (202) 332-2302 (fax) activist@populationconnection.org

THE POPULATION INSTITUTE

Population Activism • Washington, DC • 1 Year
www.populationinstitute.org

$ 🎓

With its headquarters on Capitol Hill, the Population Institute is a small nonprofit organization working to increase public awareness of the world's constantly increasing population and to foster leadership that works on solutions to the overpopulation problem.

WHAT YOU'LL BE DOING: Many of the institute's accomplishments can be attributed to the hard work of the fellows participating in the Institute's Future Leaders of the World (FLW) program. The FLW program allows recent college graduates from around the world to develop interpersonal, organizational, public relations, and writing skills while learning about current problems faced by nations around the world, including the U.S., as a result of overpopulation. Besides their daily interactions with the institute's staff, the fellows also have ample opportunities to meet with staff members from other organizations working on population, environment, and women's issues.

COMMITMENT: Fellows kick off the program in July with intensive training and make a commitment of one year, full-time.

PERKS AND REWARDS: Participants receive a $2,000 per month stipend, along with medical benefits and paid vacation time.

THE ESSENTIALS: Applicants must have completed at least two years of college, be between twenty-one and twenty-five years of age, and demonstrate leadership qualities, international experiences and perspectives, a good academic record, and strong writing and oral skills. Knowledge of a foreign language is essential.

YOUR FIRST MOVE: Send your resume, cover letter, an official transcript, and three letters of recommendation (two from academic sources) by April 15. A personal interview in their D.C. office is required.

FOR MORE INFORMATION: Fatou Fall, Education Coordinator, The Population Institute, 107 2nd St., NE, Washington, DC 20002-7396 • (800) 787-0038 (202) 544-3300, ext. 121 • (202) 544-0068 (fax) • web@populationinstitute.org

ROSE RESNICK
LIGHTHOUSE FOR THE BLIND

Therapeutic Camp • California • Summer
www.lighthouse-sf.org

♥ ⛺ ⊕

Rose Resnick Lighthouse for the Blind serves blind, visually impaired, and deaf/blind persons of all ages by providing rehabilitation, social services, and recreational opportunities. During the summer, volunteers provide practical support services at Enchanted Hills Camp, located in the wine country of Northern California. Volunteers assist with arts and crafts, hiking, swimming, horseback riding, and a variety of special activities. Fun is the common theme for the camp experience; however, the most important goal is for campers to achieve independence and develop confidence in their abilities. Sessions run from mid-June through the end of August for four to twelve days. Volunteers receive room and board and training in sensitivity to blindness, and also benefit from the chance to test their own boundaries of giving and caring.

The best and most beautiful things in the world cannot be seen or even touched. **477**
They must be felt with the heart. —HELEN KELLER

FOR MORE INFORMATION: Donna Amburn, Volunteer Coordinator, Rose Resnick Lighthouse for the Blind, 214 Van Ness Ave., San Francisco, CA 94102-4508 (415) 431-1481, ext. 237 • (415) 863-7568 (fax) • volunteers@lighthouse-sf.org

SPRING LAKE RANCH

Therapeutic Community • Vermont • 6 Months–2 Years
www.springlakeranch.org

$ 🏠

Spring Lake Ranch is a small, therapeutic work community founded in 1932. Residents decide to come to the ranch because stress, breakdown, or illness has interrupted the normal progress of their lives. All share a need for time to identify and work on problems and to assess and develop abilities that can be a foundation for future life. It is much easier to make friends and focus on what one can do rather than what one can't when working together on a common task.

YOUR SURROUNDINGS: The ranch is situated in a small, rural New England town located in the Green Mountains of Vermont. The ranch covers six hundred acres, most of which is either farmland or forest, with the Appalachian Trail crossing the property and major ski areas nearby.

WHAT YOU'LL BE DOING: House advisor/work crew leaders are responsible for the residents with whom they share living space. They also lead or participate in a wide variety of manual tasks appropriate to the rural environment and dramatically changing seasons. These might include cutting wood, caring for

It's not all work at Spring Lake Ranch—the annual all-ranch canoe trip on the Battenkill River is one of the many perks while working as a house advisor.

animals, growing vegetables in the gardens for sale at the farmers' market in town, shoveling snow, maple sugaring, haying in meadows, and helping with ongoing chores of cooking, cleaning, sewing, and construction. The majority of people who have worked in the ranch community have found the experience both physically and emotionally demanding but intensely rewarding as well. Unlike many institutions for the chronically ill, the ranch program has little structure or job description and demands flexibility and emotional spontaneity from its staff.

COMMITMENT: There is a minimum six-month commitment. The time spent at Spring Lake Ranch is an extremely demanding life experience, requiring balance, stability, and an ability to set limits on one's involvement and the use of one's energy to achieve a positive end.

PERKS AND REWARDS: Interns receive a weekly stipend of $223, plus room and board. Acting as a house advisor, each intern will live in one of nine cottages, supervising from two to nine residents. Perks include two weeks of vacation during the first year, comprehensive health insurance, and personal use of the auto and woodworking shop, computers, and laundry facilities. Interns also have the opportunity to attend seminars and workshops and receive other benefits that only come from working and living in a small community.

THE ESSENTIALS: Applicants must be twenty years of age or older and show a willingness to share life with a community of diverse people. A basic knowledge of and experience in farming, gardening, carpentry, cooking, sewing, auto mechanics, landscaping, and recreational skills are not necessary but can be very helpful.

YOUR FIRST MOVE: Send a resume and cover letter. A twenty-four-hour visit is strongly recommended as part of the interview process.

FOR MORE INFORMATION: Lynn McDermott, Personnel Director, Spring Lake Ranch, Spring Lake Rd., Box 310, Cuttingsville, VT 05738 • (802) 492-3322 (802) 492-3331 (fax) • lynn@springlakeranch.org

SPROUT

Therapeutic Recreation • USA • 1 Week+
www.gosprout.org

$ 🏠 🌐

Are you ready for a personal challenge? With Sprout, you'll travel, have fun, and contribute to the lives of others by co-leading vacations throughout the U.S. for small groups of adults with developmental disabilities. Taking to

The ultimate measure of a man is not where he stands in moments of comfort and convenience, but where he stands at times of challenge and controversy.
—DR. MARTIN LUTHER KING, JR.

the road in Sprout's fifteen-passenger van (with ten participants and three leaders), leader responsibilities include safety monitoring, providing physical and emotional support, activity planning, budgeting, and, of course, enhancing fun! Training, a small stipend, and all trip-related expenses (food, accommodations, activities, and transportation) are covered. With opportunities available year-round, you can commit for one trip (three to ten days), for months at a time, or anything in between (provided you show dedication and responsibility). Between trips, leaders can enjoy New York City while staying at the International Youth Hostel (the Sprout office is located in the hostel). Applicants (from all over the world) must be at least twenty (most are between the ages of twenty and thirty), proficient in English, fun loving, responsible, enthusiastic about care for people with special needs, and, of course, must love to travel. Applications are available online, or call or email for more information.

FOR MORE INFORMATION: Santiago Bareiro, Director of Leadership, Sprout, 893 Amsterdam Ave., New York, NY 10025 • (888) 222-9575 • (212) 222-9575 (212) 222-9678 (fax) • leadership@gosprout.org

ST. ELIZABETH SHELTER

Homeless Shelter • New Mexico • 6–12 Months
www.steshelter.org

$ ⚑ ⊕

The St. Elizabeth Shelter is a homeless shelter providing services to more than one thousand homeless individuals and families each year. Six live-in interns are responsible for most of the hands-on operation of the shelter, ranging from assisting homeless guests, organizing meals, processing donations, and maintaining the facilities. Past interns have noted that time spent with the guests is both the most rewarding and the most challenging aspect of the job. A modest stipend of $60 to $85 per week and a fully furnished, private suite above the shelter (with shared kitchen privileges) is provided, along with a hands-on experience in crisis resolution, mediation, and nonprofit management. Positions are available from six months to one year, forty hours per week. Those willing to make a commitment of one year are eligible for health insurance and an exit stipend upon completion of the program. Spanish language ability and intercultural experience are a plus. Applications are available online.

FOR MORE INFORMATION: Maria Lopez, Program Manager, St. Elizabeth Shelter, 804 Alarid St., Santa Fe, NM 87505-3040 • (505) 982-6611 (505) 982-5347 (fax) • mlopez@steshelter.org

AN INTERN'S LIFE AT A HOMELESS SHELTER

· ·

It's 6:30 A.M. and I vaguely hear my alarm calling me into consciousness. After one or two hits of the snooze button, I roll out of bed, brush my teeth, pull on some clothes, and make my thirty-second commute to work. I am one of the St. Elizabeth Shelter interns.

From an outsider's perspective, my job may look deceptively simple. While working the day shift, the other interns and I are responsible for monitoring guests' chores and medication, running errands, and making sure the shelter gets put back together for the guests' return at 3:00 P.M. This consists of doing laundry, restocking supplies, and a significant amount of cleaning. The evening shift entails much more direct interaction with the guests and often requires that we make the weighty decision of who gets a bed and who must sleep outside. We also supervise dinner and chores, monitor medication, conduct new guest intakes, and complete any necessary paperwork. My job, however, is so much more than the sum total of the loads of laundry I wash and fold each day.

I, like many others, applied to become an intern with the shelter hoping to find an entrée into the social work field, learn about operating a nonprofit, and get some experience in case management. I will soon complete my internship with my expectations fulfilled beyond my wildest dreams.

I watched in amazement as two people, once perfect strangers, sat in the dining room and laughed together far into the night, neither knowing more than ten words of the other's language. I saw a fifty-year-old and an eight-year-old become best friends, each caring for the other with seemingly no regard to the chronological divide between them. In the midst of winter, I witnessed a police officer fetch his own down coat out of his cruiser and give it to a man wearing nothing but a thin T-shirt. During the holiday season, I went through literally hundreds of boxes of goods donated by the community in the hopes that our guests would have, if not a roof over their heads, at least a pair of new gloves on their hands come Christmas morning. I commiserated with young women who, like myself, were having "boy trouble" or problems with their parents. I lived in an apartment where young people from twenty to thirty-two years old came together from all across the country to live out their conviction that everyone deserves a warm bed, a hot meal, and the right to be treated with respect, kindness, and love.

These and the myriad of other experiences I've had have taught me when it's appropriate to trust others and when it's appropriate to trust my gut instincts. I know how to create boundaries and recognize when it's okay to let down my guard a bit. I've also learned to identify my own flaws, the situations that provoke them, and how best to surmount them.

In class, we study the big questions. At the homeless shelter, we live the big questions.
—ELAINE RANKIN

On a recent trip home to Washington, D.C., I saw a number of homeless people in the streets, soliciting donations or attempting to barter odd jobs in exchange for food or a place to stay the night. Whereas before my internship, I may have preemptively crossed the street or, at the very least, averted my eyes, I now found myself actually seeking eye contact because I knew these people. I spent the last twelve months with them—eating, chatting, sharing, living, and learning. They, in turn, will remain with me for the rest of my life, giving me a deeper sense of home, wherever that may be.

• •

—Contributed by Sarah Dolan, former intern at St. Elizabeth Shelter

A WORD ON ABUNDANCE

(notes from a sermon by the Reverend Peter Gomes
at the Memorial Church of Harvard University)

It is not "ask and it shall be given you," but "give and it shall be given to you." Generosity begets generosity. By giving what you even don't have, you will get that back with interest. If you don't give, that is what you will get back: nothing. You will respond and will be responded to in the same way. Open hands and open lives are contagious.

> *Good measure, passed down, shaken together, and running*
> *over, will be poured into your lap; for whatever measure*
> *you deal out to others will be dealt to you in return.*
>
> —LUKE 6:38

The key to abundance is generosity. Not God's generosity to us, but our generosity toward others. Instead of asking God to bless us so that we might receive, let us bless others, and ourselves, by giving and by sharing. Let us break the plane of territory and turf and priority. We must do the giving before we can do the receiving.

What is so interesting, so novel, or so brave about loving people who love you, who are supposed to love you? Like likes like. But you get no credit for liking people who like you. God is not running a bank here: you give not because you expect to get it back, but because the person who asks, needs it.

The key is neither asking nor saving, but in giving and in sharing, and in the remembrance of God's generosity to us. I must give much because I have been given so much. I am rich not by what I have, but by what I have shared.

TEACH FOR AMERICA

Teaching/Service Learning • USA • 2 Years
www.teachforamerica.org

$

As a senior at Princeton University in 1989, Wendy Kopp was troubled by the educational inequities facing children in low-income communities. She was also convinced that many of her classmates were searching for a way to assume a significant responsibility that would make a real difference in the world. Working on her senior undergraduate thesis, she developed a dream to create a national corps that would recruit talented, driven graduating seniors who would commit two years to teach in urban and rural public schools. The reality? The creation of Teach for America, a national corps that calls upon outstanding recent college graduates to teach in urban and rural public schools, ensuring that all our nation's children have an equal chance in life.

WHAT YOU'LL BE DOING: Today, close to three thousand Teach for America corps members (with over nine thousand alumni) are impacting student achievement in full-time teaching positions in twenty-one sites throughout the U.S. Corps members kick off their two-year program with a rigorous pre-service summer training program for five weeks in Houston, Los Angeles, or New York City. Here you'll participate in six courses, learn how to become a successful and highly effective teacher in low-income communities, teach in a summer school program, and receive feedback from experienced teachers. Once placed in your teaching assignment, you will work relentlessly to overcome immense challenges and ensure your students have the educational opportunities they deserve, while also gaining the insight, network, and credibility you need to effect long-term change.

PERKS AND REWARDS: Corps members are paid full-time teaching salaries ranging from $22,000 to $41,000 per year. In addition, an AmeriCorps education award of $4,725 per year is generally provided (dependent on Congressional funding) along with student loan forbearance eligibility.

YOUR FIRST MOVE: Applications can be found online, with deadlines in mid-February and late October.

FOR MORE INFORMATION: Alison Banks • Admissions Communications Manager, Teach for America, 315 W. 36th St., 6th Floor, New York, NY 10018
(800) 832-1230 • (212) 279-2080, ext. 225 • (212) 279-2081 (fax)
admissions@teachforamerica.org

THIRD WORLD OPPORTUNITIES

Community Service • Mexico • 1 Week
www.thirdworldopportunities.org

As a "developmental response" to poverty (rather than through charity), volunteers with Third World Opportunities become involved in work projects at Ranch San Juan Home for Boys in Tecate, Mexico. About thirty-six boys, aged six to nineteen, live at the ranch, most of whom have been abandoned by parents and later picked up off the streets. Although there are many construction and maintenance tasks to perform, the most important part of volunteering is building relationships with the boys and the community. Two field trips serve as learning ground to poverty and cross-cultural issues. For a fee of $250, participants are fed and housed at the project site. One of the highlights of the experience is the integration of work and worship, language development and play, and growth and fellowship with one another. The minimum age requirement is fifteen, and knowledge of Spanish and construction experience are helpful but not necessary. Prospective candidates must have a keen interest in the third world and a desire to learn about the root causes of hunger and poverty. Projects are generally for one week during spring break and summer.

FOR MORE INFORMATION: Rev. George S. Johnson, Program Coordinator, Third World Opportunities, 779 Fulton Rd., San Marcos, CA 92069 (760) 471-8240 • severinelaine@aol.com

The trails aren't always dry when adventuring in the wild, but the destination is definitely worth it.

THE GOLDEN YEARS:
IT'S ONLY TOO LATE
IF YOU DON'T START NOW

• •

I think the most important thing is when we reach the point of acknowledging that we are aging, whether it's at retirement or after, that we pause for maybe a week or two and consult with people in whom we have confidence, to inventory every possible element of life that we in the past have enjoyed but had to put aside because we didn't have time to pursue it. We need to determine what things are interesting to us, and then constantly explore new ideas and be willing to take a chance.

—JIMMY CARTER

Just because you're getting older doesn't mean that you have reached the end of the road. This life transition can serve as a challenging and exciting beginning—the chance to take advantage of opportunities that you never had time to explore. Obviously there are some restraints (Maslow's Hierarchy of Needs on page 12 comes to mind), but beyond these things, you have to determine if you'd like to look at the world through curious eyes or not. Realize that you have a lifetime of experiences and abilities that will assist you in a new career, volunteer work, learning a new trade, or making a difference in the world. It's only too late if you don't begin your journey now.

Throughout your guide you'll find plenty of opportunities for active retirees. Each summer hundreds of retirees work and live in Yellowstone National Park (page 251) and the average age of a Global Volunteers (page 517) participant is fifty—and that's just for starters. Beyond the opportunities presented throughout your guide, here are some special programs and resources specifically for those in their golden years.

Elderhostel (www.elderhostel.org) offers those age fifty-five and over inexpensive, short-term academic and volunteer opportunities around the world. Participants, known as "Elderhostelers," participate in "lively and social" one- to four-week adventures ranging from a jazz course in New Orleans to experiencing the works of Michelangelo in Florence. Those that shy away from an academically stimulating experience might choose to participate in one of their many service projects, affording the opportunity to contribute energy and experience to important causes throughout the world. These short-term volunteer projects (over ten

*Being human is difficult.
Becoming human is a lifelong process. To be truly human is a gift.*
—ABRAHAM HESCHEL

485

thousand per year in ninety countries) range from conservation work at national parks to building affordable housing with Habitat for Humanity. The all-inclusive program fee averages around $105 per night; overseas programs average $190 per night and include round-trip airfare in most cases. Hotels and motels, inns, college dormitories, rustic lodges, tents, and shipboard cabins serve as a home base and meals sample the local flavor. Add yourself to their mailing list, and you will receive their 175-page newspaper-sized catalog jam-packed with more than two thousand opportunities. You can also receive catalog announcements online with their monthly electronic news bulletin. For more information contact Elderhostel, 11 Avenue de Lafayette, Boston, MA 02111-1746; (877) 426-8056, registration@elderhostel.org.

The National Senior Service Corps (www.seniorservice.org) helps people aged fifty-five and older engage in community-based service opportunities right in their own backyard. Foster Grandparents offer emotional support to child victims of abuse and neglect, tutor children who lag behind in reading, or perhaps assist children with physical disabilities and severe illnesses. Senior Companions reach out to adults who need extra assistance to live independently in their own homes or communities. They provide companionship and friendship to isolated and frail seniors, assist with chores, provide transportation, and add richness to their clients' lives. Both these programs offer modest stipends and other benefits to help offset the cost of volunteering. Retired and Senior Volunteer Program volunteers choose how and where they want to serve—from a few hours to over forty hours per week. They might tutor children in reading and math, help to build houses, plan community gardens, or offer disaster relief to victims of natural disasters. Together, these programs involve over half a million seniors serving in tens of thousands of sites across the country. For the Web-savvy, all the opportunities can be viewed online, or call (800) 424-8867.

Work Options (www.aarp.org/money/careers/workoptions), provided by AARP, serves as a resource center for midlife and older workers. The online guide offers information on everything from job searching to staying employable to overcoming barriers to employment. You might also consider a membership with AARP, which is open to anyone age fifty or older, whether you are working or retired. Membership runs $12.50 per year. For more information contact AARP, 601 E. St., NW, Washington, D.C. 20049; (888) 687-2277, member@aarp.org.

RECOMMEND RESOURCES

Every day the **American Red Cross** (www.redcross.org) helps people in emergencies—whether it's a thousand disaster victims or one sick child who needs blood. Volunteers make up 97 percent of the Red Cross workforce—people of all ages carrying out vital humanitarian work. Current volunteer opportunities, including thousands of one-time and ongoing positions can be found through the searchable online database (redcross.volunteermatch.org).

What's your cause? With **Do Something** (www.dosomething.org), young people can make a difference and take action to change the world around them. You and your classmates identify the issues you care about and Do Something provides the resources and support to help you make your community projects happen.

Idealist.org, a project of Action Without Borders, is a nonprofit organization that promotes the sharing of ideas, information, and resources to help build a world where all people can live free, dignified, and productive lives. At one of the richest communities of nonprofit and volunteering resources on the Web, visitors can quickly find the information they need through a searchable database of current job, volunteer, and internship opportunities in the non-profit/social-service field. Over forty thousand organizations in some 150 countries are tucked away inside. If you're leaning toward the nonprofit field, you're bound to find something with Idealist. In addition, daily job/internship alerts and a monthly newsletter will definitely keep you in the know.

Everyone is disabled and everyone is employable. These encouraging words are at the heart of *Job Hunting for the So-Called Handicapped* (Ten Speed Press, $12.95)—and the very philosophy that will encourage anybody with a disability to find a job and meaning in his or her work. Career guru Richard Bolles and disability expert Dale Brown have teamed up to provide a new way to look at the world of work. In addition to explaining the ins and outs of the Americans with Disabilities Act (ADA), the guide provides fresh perspectives, helpful job-hunting ideas, and plenty of resources to get on the right path. Connect with Dale at www.ldonline.org/dale, where she hosts "Dialogue with Dale."

The Quaker Information Center (www.quakerinfo.org) provides an extensive listing of Quaker and non-Quaker opportunities including weekend work camps, volunteer service, internships, and alternatives to the Peace Corps, both in the U.S. and around the world. Detailed information and links to hundreds of listings for people of all ages are available for free on their website.

The time is always ripe to do what is right.   **487**
—DR. MARTIN LUTHER KING, JR.

A program of Youth Service America (www.ysa.org), **SERVEnet.org** specializes in volunteer opportunities for high school and college students. Along with an extensive database of opportunities (searchable by zip code, city, state, skills, interests, and availability), SERVEnet also highlights volunteer events, recommended reading, and inspirational quotes.

Get out. Do good. This is at the heart of **VolunteerMatch** (www.volunteermatch.org). Prospective volunteers can search their website for nonprofit and community service organizations according to interest, location, and age group. And if you don't want to leave the comforts of your home, be sure to check out the "virtual volunteer" opportunities.

The world only exists in your eyes. You can make it as big or as small as you want.
—F. SCOTT FITZGERALD

CHAPTER 11

TRANSITIONS ABROAD

For many, working, learning, living, and traveling abroad for extended periods of time becomes the adventure of a lifetime. Many venture to unknown lands to fill a gap of time in their lives, improve their fluency in a foreign language, meet new and interesting people, or build self-reliance. Whatever your situation, by traveling and working in a new land, you'll have the chance to immerse yourself in the culture and meet people on their own terms rather than experiencing it as a tourist would. This chapter will provide you with hundreds of work options to choose from along with the tools to shape your journey of self-discovery abroad.

UNIQUE OPPORTUNITIES TO EXPLORE IN THIS CHAPTER

- Whether you are just exploring your options abroad or are ready to pack your bags and go for it, global expert Elizabeth Kruempelmann provides an introduction and essential tips for adventuring overseas (page 495).

- Did you know that each chapter in your guide has a handful of programs offering opportunities abroad? So you don't miss a beat, a special page-by-page directory provides all the details—including information for applicants living outside the U.S. (page 496).

- Do you need the security of a prearranged job and living situation prior to going overseas? There are plenty of programs that will help you with your efforts. InterExchange (page 523) will take care of all your overseas arrangements, while BUNAC USA (page 502) or CIEE (page 506) will provide you with the coveted work permit to legally work in another country.

- Helping people help themselves is the heart behind volunteering abroad. A special section beginning on page 510 provides an overview of international volunteering, selecting the right program, ways to fund your life-changing pursuits, and essential resources.

- Is it possible that a honeymoon adventure can bring out one's calling in life? Find out how the founders of Global Volunteers turned a two-week vacation into their life's work (page 519).

KATE BUNDRA

Helping to make a meaningful contribution in developing countries, this WorldTeach (page 538) volunteer teacher takes time out to play with one of her students in Namibia, Africa.

THE THRILL OF EXPERIENCING THE WORLD

· ·

If you are like most people, you want to make the most of your life. You crave exciting adventures in intriguing places that get your heart pumping and mind racing. You long for life experiences that make you feel alive! For many people, the thrill of experiencing the world is what life is all about.

Since you have found your way to this chapter, I assume you are ready for your life journey to take you somewhere abroad—be it Brazil, China, or southern France—or on an adventure, like helping indigenous tribes of the rain forest, restoring a historic piece of the past, or working on a community development project. You probably don't know the specifics of "where in the world am I going" and "how in the world am I getting there," but you can rest assured that your life will be unique, out of the ordinary, and a very rewarding adventure. How do I know? Because I've been traveling, studying, and working abroad in various countries for ten years and know there is no life more fulfilling than the adventurous life of a global citizen. How do you know if you're ready for an adventure abroad and ultimately destined to lead a longer-term life living, studying, working, and traveling overseas? Just answer these questions:

- Are you amazed at students and professionals who seem to casually decide to put aside their studies and work for a while in favor of throwing on a backpack to spend six months working and traveling around the world?

- Do you feel great respect and admiration for the dedicated volunteers who make a real difference to folks in other parts of the world by building schools, roads, and houses, or teaching essential skills like farming, math, and English?

- Are you in awe of linguistically talented folks who speak Italian, German, and French fluently without even pausing to think about what they're saying?

- When someone's academic qualifications include studying abroad or a degree from a foreign university (in a foreign language), are you impressed and maybe even a slight bit envious?

- Do you want the life of the gal or guy whose international firm just sent her or him to live and work in Rome for a year with future opportunities to work in one of their other twenty offices in places like Tokyo, Mexico City, Melbourne, or Cape Town?

If you've said yep to at least one of these questions, or even if you have a slightly different vision of your life abroad, you're already thinking about how

Though we travel the world over to find the beautiful, we must carry it with us or we will find it not.
—RALPH WALDO EMERSON

to build a global life for yourself. Just imagining what you would love to be doing overseas is the first step to making your dream come true. Here are two tips to think about:

Define your passion: What is it that pulls you out into the world? Foreign languages, international business, global issues, the love of discovering new people and places, or something completely different? Defining your real passion will help determine the steps you need to take to develop those interests abroad.

Find a program (or another way) to fulfill your global dreams: It all starts with your first experience overseas. If you want a personally rewarding and professionally fulfilling adventure in a foreign country, the options are endless: intern, work on a farm, volunteer on a community development project, teach, take a language course, build bridges, get an international MBA, be a nanny, join the Peace Corps . . . and the list goes on and on. Throughout your guide you'll find a ton of unique, short-term adventures that serve as a starting point for nearly every global citizen's life journey.

PACK YOUR BAGS AND GO!

Ready to go for it now? If you're already living your dream life abroad mentally and just need to know how to get your physical body there ASAP, here's a quick rundown of what to do.

Applications and Essential Documents

Applications can take a few weeks or up to a year to process, depending on the program, so get them in early. Once you are accepted into a program, gather the documents you'll need for work permits, residency visas, scholarships, directions for lodging and accommodations, addresses of important contacts, and any other documentation that you'll need. If you'll be going abroad on your own to travel or look for a job, be aware of how long you are allowed to travel within that country. Also be sure to learn about the work permit regulations of that particular country.

Passport

Apply for your passport now as it could take up to six weeks to be delivered. Depending on your nationality and where you are headed, you may also need a visa to travel to that destination. Check with an embassy or consulate for further information.

Travel Arrangements

Buy your plane ticket and make other travel arrangements. Don't forget to sign up for frequent-flier miles and pay with a credit card that also adds miles to your account. Take advantage of discounted travel offers you might find by booking online or that you are eligible for because of your age. (Students and seniors often get a travel discount.)

Money

Arrange to bring traveler's checks, a bank card that can be used at ATMs worldwide, and a bit of cash. Many ATMs overseas accept only four-digit pin numbers, so check with your bank to ensure your card will work in ATMs everywhere.

Connections

Gather the names of the contacts you have in the country you'll be visiting. Even if you don't know a soul, you can easily make contact with foreigners living in your destination through "expat" communities online, such as EasyExpat.com. If you're going abroad on your own, it is good idea to have at least your first few days of lodging reserved.

Other than a few details that will naturally fall into place—like packing your bags and saying your last good-byes—you can be on the way to your next overseas adventure in no time. Bon voyage!

Elizabeth Kruempelmann creating an international way of life in Portugal.

—Contributed by Elizabeth Kruempelmann, who currently lives with her German husband and two children in Portugal. Her international experience includes studying international business for a year in Denmark, interning and teaching English in Germany, working as a partner and marketing manager in a small advertising company in Poland, and selling cross-cultural training programs in Portugal. You can reach her at ekruempe@hotmail.com or through the Global Citizen website at www.the-global-citizen.com.

The wonder of the world, the beauty and the power, the shapes of things, their colors, lights and shades. These I saw. Look ye also while life lasts.
—FROM AN OLD GRAVESTONE IN ENGLAND

DIRECTORY OF PROGRAMS ABROAD
IN EACH CHAPTER

In addition to the unique work-abroad opportunities found in this chapter, your guide is filled with plenty of other overseas short-term job adventures. This page-by-page directory provides all the specifics.

Chapter 7—A Walk in Nature—Jobs in the Natural World

Chapter 8—Sustainable Living and Farming Opportunities

Chapter 9—Artistic and Learning Pursuits

Chapter 10—Heartfelt Work

Chapter 11—Transitions Abroad

Dig in!

Live in New York City once, but leave before it makes you hard.
Live in Northern California once, but leave before it makes you soft. Travel.
—KURT VONNEGUT

INSIDE INFORMATION
FOR INTERNATIONAL APPLICANTS

If you're from the U.S. and want to work overseas, this chapter (along with many programs and resources listed throughout your guide) will provide you with the tools to make this happen. Otherwise, if you don't reside in the U.S., you'll want to pay close attention to programs in each chapter with a globe icon at the top of the listing. This icon denotes programs that hire international applicants; however, this doesn't always mean the organization will help you with all the details or pay for the proper working visa to legally work in the U.S. Your first move is to contact each organization that piques your interest and obtain more information about international applicant requirements. You'll find that some programs will help with the visa process, while others will refer you to many of the exchange programs mentioned below. As I'm sure you are aware, obtaining a visa is a little tougher than it used to be. Here are your options:

- The F-1 visa allows students to work while enrolled in school in the U.S., as well as for a period of fourteen months after graduation, for what is often referred to as "practical training."

- The J-1 exchange visitor visa allows internationals to enter the U.S. for cultural exchange work and travel for a specific period of time (generally from four months to two years). Applicants that fall under the J-1 status generally include students, teachers, scholars, camp counselors, au pairs, and participants in summer travel-work programs.

- The H-2B visa is strictly for seasonal or temporary work in the U.S. for up to one year. With this option, applicants must have a job offer from a U.S. employer, although the visa is not guaranteed until it is approved by USCIS (U.S. Citizenship and Immigration Services) and a consulate. Many ski resorts (see page 176) offer a limited number of H-2B visas each year; otherwise they are hard to come by. Check out Immigration Services of America (www.isaunited.com) for more information and ideas.

FINDING OUT MORE

BUNAC.org (see listing on page 502)

Camp Counselors USA (CCUSA.com)

CIEE.org (see listing on page 506)

InterExchange.org (see listing on page 523)

International Student Travel Confederation (ISTC.org)

VisaNow.com

Vacation Work (www.vacationwork.co.uk) publishes a handful of unique "short-term work" publications for those who reside outside the U.S.

AFS INTERCULTURAL PROGRAMS USA

Service Learning • Worldwide • 1–12 Months
www.afs.org/usa

♥ ⛪

Building a global community through student exchange for more than fifty-five years, AFS (American Field Service) Intercultural Programs sends students and volunteers (over ten thousand each year!) to more than forty countries for a semester, summer, or year. Those who are at least eighteen years of age and have graduated from high school can participate in the 18+ Community Service program. Participants volunteer in nongovernmental organizations in Belgium, Bolivia, Brazil, Costa Rica, the Dominican Republic, Ecuador, Ghana, Hungary, Panama, Paraguay, South Africa, Thailand, and the United Kingdom, with work that includes everything from education and the environment to childhood development and cultural preservation. Volunteers work with AFS staff and in-country volunteers to design a work experience that best meets all needs. Programs are also available for high school students (volunteering done as a group) and current and future educators (through a one-month intensive teaching program). Program fees vary, and cover transportation from the U.S. departure city to the host community, meals, lodging, twenty-four-hour support, and several orientations throughout the program. Fees for 18+ Community Service programs range from $5,000 for semester opportunities to $6,000 to $7,000 for one-year volunteer opportunities. Scholarships and financial assistance are available. Call or visit AFS online for details.

FOR MORE INFORMATION: Program Director, AFS Intercultural Programs USA, 198 Madison Ave., 8th Floor, New York, NY 10016 • (800) 237-4636 (212) 299-9000 • (212) 299-9090 (fax) • afsinfo@afs.org

AMERISPAN UNLIMITED

Service Learning • Latin America/Spain • 2–6 Months+
www.amerispan.com

♥ ⛪ 🌐

AmeriSpan's volunteer/internship program offers a wide variety of work opportunities for adults in Latin America and Spain. Two- to six-month placements are generally offered in social work, education and ESL teaching, health care, environmental programs, and student services, although customized placements are available in some countries. Prior to the work assignment, volunteers participate in a one- to four-week language and cultural component (dependent on language level). A homestay experience

The world we have created is a product of our thinking.
It cannot be changed without changing our thinking.
—ALBERT EINSTEIN

along with meals is offered for most placements; the cost runs from $77 to $125 per week (with longer term commitments, this may be provided). There is a fee of $350, plus the costs for language classes, housing, and airfare. Predeparture information, an in-country orientation, and travel insurance are provided. Applicants must be at least eighteen years of age, and most positions have additional requirements, such as relevant education, experience, or Spanish language proficiency. Their website provides a search engine that allows you to view placements by country or by type of work. A minimum two-month window is needed prior to your requested start date.

FOR MORE INFORMATION: Anne-Marie Dingemans, Volunteer/Internship Director, AmeriSpan Unlimited, 117 S. 17th St., Suite 1401, Philadelphia, PA 19103 (800) 879-6640 • (215) 751-1100 • (215) 751-1986 (fax) • info@amerispan.com

AMIGOS DE LAS AMÉRICAS

Service Learning • Latin America • 6–8 Months
www.amigoslink.org

♥ ⚒ ⊕

Through the unparalleled "Amigos experience," more than twenty thousand young volunteers have completed extensive leadership and community service training programs that prepare them to spend a summer volunteering in ongoing community health and environmental development projects throughout Latin America (including Brazil, Costa Rica, the Dominican Republic, Honduras, Nicaragua, Mexico, Panama, and Paraguay).

WHAT YOU'LL BE DOING: The program begins with an extensive six-month experience-based training program both in the U.S. and in Latin America. Once trained, volunteers are assigned to ongoing health, community-development, and environmental programs partnered with sponsoring agencies in the host countries, ranging from community sanitation and nutrition education to home improvement and family garden projects. Programs generally run from six to eight weeks during the summer months, although a Costa Rica program runs three and a half weeks beginning in January. Participants typically live with families in small communities in rural and semi-urban areas and are supervised by more experienced volunteers and officials of the host agency. Amigos volunteers who have participated actively in training programs and who excel in the Latin America program are always encouraged to apply for project staff positions.

PERKS AND REWARDS: The program fee of $3,650 ($2,500 for the three-and-a-half-week program in Costa Rica) includes round-trip international airfare, training materials, orientation, weekly training sessions (for chapter volunteers), project supplies, professional staff support, and host-country room, board, and transportation. Many participants are able to cover program fees through fund-raising efforts. Amigos has put together a fund-raising booklet with suggestions that have been proven successful by veteran volunteers. Participation-fee scholarships up to $800 are available to applicants with proven financial need.

THE ESSENTIALS: Volunteers must be at least sixteen years of age, have at least two years of Spanish or Portuguese study, and successfully complete the training requirements.

YOUR FIRST MOVE: Visit their website for more specifics, or call or email for an information packet.

FOR MORE INFORMATION: Glenn Bayron, Director of Volunteer Administration, Amigos de las Américas, 5618 Star Ln., Houston, TX 77057 • (800) 231-7796 (713) 782-5290, ext. 119 • (713) 782-9267 (fax) • info@amigoslink.org

INSIDER TIP: Amigos volunteers are flexible, motivated, able to live and work independently and as team members, energetic, adventuresome, enthusiastic, and interested in public health, quality of life, and community service.

AMIZADE

Community Service • USA/Worldwide • 1 Week–1 Year
www.amizade.org

♥ ⌂ ⊕

Amizade, the word for "friendship" in Portuguese, is a nonprofit organization dedicated to promoting volunteerism, providing community service, encouraging collaboration, and improving cultural awareness in locations around the world. Short- and long-term volunteer programs offer a unique cross-cultural experience woven into community service and personal exploration. Amizade program sites abroad include the Brazilian Amazon, Bolivian Andes, Australia's Hervey Bay, the Khumbu Region of Nepal, Ghana, Jamaica, Northern Ireland, and Poland/Germany; in the U.S., programs are offered in the Navajo Nation of Arizona, the Greater Yellowstone region, and Washington, D.C. Volunteers work with members of the local community to complete a community-identified project that addresses needs in education, environment, or health and well-being. Short-term programs run one to three weeks, while long-term volunteers must commit to at least two months. The program fee (ranging from $530 for one week in Yellowstone National Park on up to $2,110 for three weeks in Nepal) includes meals, housing (dorms,

Each friend represents a world in us, a world possibly not born until they arrive, and it is only by this meeting that a new world is born.
—ANAÏS NIN

tents, rustic cabins, or homestays), travel at the project site, project materials, and cultural and recreational activities. Airfare, visas, and immunizations are additional. Volunteers from all backgrounds and nationalities are welcome to participate, and no special skills are needed—just a willingness to help. Individuals twelve to seventeen years of age must be accompanied by a chaperone. Program details and an application are available online or by calling.

FOR MORE INFORMATION: Michael Sandy, Executive Director, Amizade, P.O. Box 110107, Pittsburgh, PA 15232 • (888) 973-4443 • (412) 441-6655 (fax) volunteer@amizade.org

BUNAC USA

Work Abroad • Worldwide • 1–12 Months
www.bunac.org

$ 🏠

The British Universities North America Club—commonly known as BUNAC—provides U.S. full-time students aged eighteen and upward with the coveted Blue Card, allowing participants to obtain paid work experiences for a maximum of six months in England, Scotland, Wales, and Northern Ireland. An orientation is provided in BUNAC's London and Edinburgh offices, where you'll receive vital information on jobs and accommodations, maps and student guides, advice and counseling, and government paperwork. After filling out an application, you'll receive a program handbook outlining general living and accommodation information, general advice, and employer listings ranging from pubtenders to "career-type" positions for a fee of $275. Beyond the U.K., programs are also offered in Ireland (up to four months; students only; $375 fee), Canada (up to six months; students between the ages of eighteen and thirty; $250), Peru (volunteer placement; up to three months; students or degree holders between the ages of eighteen and thirty-five; conversant in Spanish; up to $1,650), and South Africa (volunteer placement; up to two months; students or degree holders between the ages of eighteen and thirty-five; $1,230). In addition, for anyone (students and nonstudents) between the ages of eighteen and thirty, there is the opportunity to work in Australia (up to four months, $550) and New Zealand (up to one year, $495). It's suggested you bring along at least $1,000 to cover personal and living expenses prior to receiving a first paycheck. Applications and detailed information are available online.

FOR MORE INFORMATION: Director, BUNAC USA, P.O. Box 430, Southbury, CT 06488 • (800) 462-8622 • (203) 264-0901 • (203) 264-0251 (fax) info@bunacusa.org

CASA XELAJÚ

Language/Community Service • Guatemala • 1–6 Months
www.casaxelaju.com

♥ ⛺ ⊕

Casa Xelajú (pronounced "shay-la-hoo") provides Spanish and Mayan language study, internships and volunteer work experience, homestays, and tour and travel programs in Guatemala. Internships might include work in human rights, the medical field, education, social work, or vocational education. There is a weekly program fee of $50 for the internship program (a placement fee of $300 is also charged during the summer), which includes supervision, homestay experience, and three meals per day; the language program tuition of $170 to $200 per week includes five hours of instruction five days per week, daily social and cultural activities, free Internet access, a homestay in private room, and three meals per day. Visit their website, or call or email for more information.

FOR MORE INFORMATION: Julio Batres, General Manager, Casa Xelajú, 4701 Zenith Ave. South, Minneapolis, MN 55410 • (888) 796-2272 • (612) 281-5705 info@casaxelaju.com

CDS INTERNATIONAL

International Education • Worldwide • 3–18 Months
www.cdsintl.org

$ ⛺ ⊕

CDS (Carl Duisberg Society) International is a nonprofit organization dedicated to developing and enhancing opportunities for Americans to participate in meaningful, practical training opportunities in Argentina, Germany, Russia, Spain, and Switzerland. Geared toward students, those recently graduated, and young professionals, CDS provides visa sponsorship and internship placement services as well as study tours and seminars. While all programs contain an internship component, some have academic or language training elements as well. Programs also exist for international citizens to complete internship programs in the U.S.

WHAT YOU'LL BE DOING: CDS offers three unique programs for those who want to broaden their professional and life experience while living, working, and learning overseas. For participants between the ages of eighteen and thirty, the Placement Program provides paid and unpaid internship opportunities in Argentina, Germany, and Spain in business, engineering, and technical fields. The Work Authorization Program offers participants the necessary visa sponsorship and documents for employment in Germany and Switzerland once they have secured an internship position on their own. Finally, the Scholarship/Fellowship Program consists of four programs that range from three months to one year. Details on each can be found online.

A TRUE TRANSITION

Participating in CDS International's Work Authorization Program in Germany proved to be a turning point for my personal and professional growth. CDS provided me with the proper work and residency permits, a one-month language course, and a homestay experience with a family. Finding an internship and a permanent place to live was my own challenge. It was far from easy trying to secure a job with hardly any work experience; my rudimentary knowledge of the German language and a high unemployment rate in Germany made this difficult.

After several months of plugging away at the job search, I was happy to land an internship at a management consulting firm where I assisted with project presentations and proposal translations. As my internship came to an end and my German gradually improved, I decided to prolong my work and residency permits to get more out of my stay in Germany.

I had made it over the hardest part of adapting to the German culture and was finally starting to enjoy the language and social life. By securing a flexible and well-paying job teaching English at the local language institute, I was not only able to extend my stay but also had more time and money to travel and make friends with other foreigners and Germans alike. Together we enjoyed bike tours around the countryside, German festivals, boat cruises on the Rhine, and weekends in Paris and Amsterdam, among many other unforgettable travel adventures.

At the time, CDS provided me with a window of opportunity to learn a language, get international work experience, and travel relatively cheaply around Europe. However, as I reflect now on my total experiences of studying and working in four foreign countries, learning two foreign languages, and traveling to thirty lands, CDS was truly the catalyst for living out my dream of an international way of life.

—Contributed by Elizabeth Kruempelmann, who has a lot more to say about the international experience in the introduction to this chapter (page 493).

PERKS AND REWARDS: Many internship placements are paid, and compensation generally covers basic living expenses abroad. Scholarship/Fellowship Programs usually offer round-trip transportation and stipends. Fees range from $300 to $1,000 depending on the program. Additional services, such as housing or language courses, may also affect the total program cost.

THE ESSENTIALS: A high level of interest in working in and acclimating to a foreign culture is necessary. Most programs require at least intermediate language skills, as participants will be required to function in a German, Spanish, or Russian work environment.

YOUR FIRST MOVE: Application packets can be downloaded from their website, or call for more information.

FOR MORE INFORMATION: Program Officer, Internships Abroad, CDS International, 871 United Nations Plaza, 15th Floor, New York, NY 10017-1814 (212) 497-3500 • (212) 497-3535 (fax) • usabroad@cdsintl.org

CENTER FOR GLOBAL EDUCATION

Educational Travel • Worldwide • 1–3 Weeks
www.centerforglobaleducation.org

♥ ⚐ ⊕

The Center for Global Education takes participants around the world on short-term travel seminars, encountering the peoples and situations of the Caribbean, Central America, Mexico, and southern Africa. These one- to three-week educational trips bring participants face-to-face with people of other cultures—people struggling for justice and human dignity. Each day consists of two to four meetings with community representatives, ranging from grassroots organizers to business leaders and representatives of the ruling and opposition political parties, as well as visits to key historical or archaeological sites. The program attracts a broad range of participants, from ages eighteen to eighty, from all ethnic backgrounds, and from all professional areas. All have an interest in listening to and learning from people in the community. Seminar fees start at $900 and include meetings with community representatives, lodging, meals, translation, and local travel. (Airfare is additional.)

FOR MORE INFORMATION: Janeen McAllister, Travel Seminar Program Director, Center for Global Education, Augsburg College, 2211 Riverside Ave., Campus Box 307, Minneapolis, MN 55454 • (800) 299-8889 • (612) 330-1159 (612) 330-1695 (fax) • globaled@augsburg.edu

Once in a while it really hits people that they don't have to experience the world in the way they have been told to.
—ALAN KEIGHTLEY

CIEE

Work Abroad/Teaching • Worldwide • 2 Weeks–10 Months
www.ciee.org/isp

$ 🏠 🌐

Since its founding in 1947, CIEE (Council on International Educational Exchange) has been active in the development and administration of study, work, travel, and volunteer programs worldwide. Let's take a bird's-eye view of each program:

If you're a U.S. college student at least eighteen years of age or recent graduate who has three to six months to enjoy an unforgettable travel experience, you can take advantage of CIEE's Work Abroad Program in Australia, Canada, Ireland, and New Zealand. Most participants find short-term or seasonal service-industry positions, such as waiting tables, bartending, office temping, and retail sales. CIEE will provide you with job leads, apartment listings, and contacts to help you set up your working and living arrangements as well as give you an in-country orientation and handbook upon arrival. There is a program fee of $350 to $450 (depending on country), which includes the highly coveted work permit to legally work in another country. While working, most participants earn enough money to cover day-to-day expenses. Email contact: work@ciee.org.

A program with fewer restrictions is CIEE's Global Volunteer Projects, a two- to four-week work camp experience in Africa, the Americas, Asia, Europe, and the Middle East—from national parks and forests to inner-city neighborhoods and small towns. Volunteers may choose to build a playground, plant trees, restore a castle, organize a festival, or implement a recreation program for at-risk children. There is a $350 to $395 placement fee, which includes room and board. Placements primarily begin in May and continue on a first-come, first-served basis until September, by which time most summer projects have been filled. In addition, you can participate year-round in a two-, four-, or six-week environmental project with the Conservation Australia Experience. Volunteers travel around with a group and perform a variety of ecological tasks. Program fees range from $795 for the two-week program to $1,395 for six weeks. The average age of participants is twenty to twenty-five (although you must be at least eighteen and some countries have upper age limits). To learn more about these opportunities, a project directory is available at www.ciee.org/volunteer. Email contact: volunteer@ciee.org.

Finally, for those with a bachelor's degree, you might consider CIEE's Teach in China or Thailand programs. You don't need teaching experience or a

TEFL (Teaching English as a Foreign Language) qualification to apply—just a genuine interest in Asia and teaching, along with an appetite for adventure. You'll have the option of a full-year (ten months) or semester (five months) teaching contract (Thailand departures—May and October; China—February and August). A salary of about $250 to $400 per month (depending on country and exchange rates), furnished accommodations, work visa, and a weeklong training and orientation program are provided. Fees range from $1,250 to $1,500 plus international airfare. Email contact: teach@ciee.org.

FOR MORE INFORMATION: Program Coordinator, CIEE, 7 Custom House St., 3rd Floor, Portland, ME 04101 • (800) 407-8839 • (207) 553-7600 (207) 553-7699 (fax) • info@ciee.org

CONCERN AMERICA

Community Service • Africa/Latin America • 2–3 Years
www.concernamerica.org
$ 🏠 🌐

Concern America is an international development and refugee aid organization that has staffed development projects in more than a dozen countries since 1972. Healthy children, appropriate sanitation systems, potable water, public health systems, and lasting employment opportunities are a few of the results from the work of Concern America.

WHAT YOU'LL BE DOING: Through the work of volunteers, who are professionals in the fields of health, public health, nutrition, health education, adult literacy, sanitation, agroforestry, appropriate technology, and community organizing, Concern America assists impoverished communities and refugees in developing countries in their efforts to improve their living conditions. The program emphasizes empowering and training community members in order to impart skills and knowledge that remain with the community long after the volunteer is gone. Volunteers currently serve in development projects in Columbia, El Salvador, Guatemala, Honduras, Mexico, and Mozambique.

COMMITMENT: There is a minimum two-year commitment.

PERKS AND REWARDS: Concern America provides room and board, round-trip transportation, health insurance, a small monthly stipend of $250 per month, a repatriation allowance (first year—$50 per month, second year—$100 per month, third year—$150 per month), and support services from the home office.

Most people seek after what they do not possess and are enslaved by the very things they want to acquire.
—ANWAR EL-SADAT

THE ESSENTIALS: Applicants must have a degree or experience in public health, medicine, nutrition, nursing, agriculture, community development, education, or appropriate technology. Fluency in Spanish (except for the project in Mozambique, where Portuguese is required) or ability to learn Spanish at one's own expense is also required. All candidates must be at least twenty-one years of age.

YOUR FIRST MOVE: Send a cover letter and resume to begin the application process.

FOR MORE INFORMATION: Janine Mills, Recruitment Coordinator, Concern America, 2015 N. Broadway, P.O. Box 1790, Santa Ana, CA 92702 (800) 266-2376 • (714) 953-8575 • (714) 953-1242 (fax) concamerinc@earthlink.net

CROSS-CULTURAL SOLUTIONS

Service Learning • Worldwide • 2–12 Weeks
www.crossculturalsolutions.org

♥ ⚐ ⊕

With unique short- and long-term volunteer, intern, and study-abroad programs in Brazil, China, Costa Rica, Ghana, Guatemala, India, Peru, Russia, Tanzania, and Thailand, Cross-Cultural Solutions offers volunteers from all over the world the opportunity to come face-to-face with global issues and become part of productive solutions through community development.

WHAT YOU'LL BE DOING: Working side by side with local people on locally designed and driven projects, volunteers engage in vital humanitarian work. You might teach English to adults and schoolchildren, stimulate small business activities, initiate programming with women's empowerment groups, observe and assist local doctors, improve the quality of life for senior citizens, or act as a mentor to orphans. Yes, the types of work are limitless. While in the host country, volunteers are divided into small groups of two or three, which provides a more productive and meaningful experience.

COMMITMENT: Programs are offered year-round, begin on specific start dates, and last from two to twelve weeks.

PERKS AND REWARDS:

The program is entirely driven by each volunteer's contribution, which ranges from $2,279 (for two weeks) to $4,873 (for twelve weeks). Your contribution pays for all country-based expenses, including three meals per day, modest accommodations with shared-occupancy rooms, airport transfers and daily transportation, professional staff guidance and supervision, orientation, and program materials. Beyond the set program fee, you will also be responsible for your visa, shots, and international airfare. Those who need help with the program fee can access the Cross-Cultural Solutions Fundraising Kit online.

A Cross-Cultural Solutions volunteer makes a difference in India.

YOUR FIRST MOVE: All nationalities and backgrounds are welcome, and nearly every candidate is accepted into the program. Volunteers are encouraged to apply at least one month prior to the projected start date.

FOR MORE INFORMATION: Steve Rosenthal, Executive Director, Cross-Cultural Solutions, 2 Clinton Pl., New Rochelle, NY 10801 • (800) 380-4777 (914) 632-0022 • (914) 632-8494 (fax) • info@crossculturalsolutions.org

✥ **INSIDER TIP:** Three fundamental goals of international volunteerism shape Cross-Cultural Solutions' programs: providing service, learning about development work and the local culture, and educating volunteers' own communities upon their return home.

Imagination is more important than knowledge.
Knowledge is limited. Imagination encircles the world.
—ALBERT EINSTEIN

INTERNATIONAL VOLUNTEERING AND FUND-RAISING IDEAS

. . . .

> *Everybody can be great because anybody can serve. You don't*
> *have to have a college degree to serve. You don't have to make*
> *your subject and your verb agree to serve. . . . You only need a*
> *heart full of grace. A soul generated by love.*
>
> —DR. MARTIN LUTHER KING, JR.

Traveling as a volunteer departs from conventional adventure travel and cultural-immersion experiences in one very important way: the wondrous experience of giving. Volunteers live and work with local people who need assistance in fulfilling life's basic needs—food, shelter, clothing, education— development projects that help people to help themselves. Each volunteer's energy, creativity, and labor are put to use as he or she gains a genuine, first-hand understanding of other people.

First off, you must realize that for most programs, volunteering costs money. Many volunteer organizations are underfunded and understaffed (and their staffs are often overworked). They keep their efforts alive by the contributions volunteers provide in exchange for the experience. Program expenses, transportation costs, meals, rent, health insurance, and the cost of developing and maintaining volunteer placements all add up. To put this participation fee into perspective, think about the costs associated with running a local animal or homeless shelter in your community. Creative funding and the work of volunteers make it all possible. As you begin your search for a volunteer project, keep in mind that you will probably have to pay for many of these basic expenses.

Fees for volunteer projects can start as low as $300 for one- to three-week experiences and can grow to $4,500 or more for programs that take you to places further from the U.S. and that are longer in duration. Many programs offer all-inclusive fees, which include food, lodging, ground transportation, visas, and project materials.

Once you've compiled a list of possible volunteer programs that meet your criteria, your next step is to call the organizations for more information. First impressions are a big deal to me. Talking to a knowledgeable and experienced program coordinator will outweigh any glossy catalog that you receive in the mail. It's also important that you assemble a list of key questions for each organization:

• Are there specific projects you'll be working on, or will you just get involved where help is needed?

- How many volunteers work on a particular project?

- Will you be living with a family in the community or with other volunteers?

- What types of food will be available?

- Does the village have running water?

- How long do the projects last?

- Is there time for additional travel once the project ends?

- What does the program fee include and do you help with fund-raising efforts?

FUNDING YOUR ADVENTURE

For many, one of the biggest obstacles to international volunteering is the financial challenge. However, a lack of funds shouldn't diminish your dreams. With a little planning and hard work, you can definitely succeed in raising nearly all of your needed funds. Steve Rosenthal, the executive director of Cross-Cultural Solutions (see page 508), provides these essential fund-raising tips and activities.

Who Do You Know?

The cardinal rule of fund-raising is that if you don't ask, you won't get anything. Ask anyone and everyone you know and even those you don't know to contribute to your cause. One of the best places to start is to make a list of everyone you know.

Letter Writing

A letter-writing campaign is one of the most simple and effective fund-raising methods you can employ. Send letters to family and friends, employers and coworkers, clubs you belong to, churches or temples, local banks, foundations, and charitable organizations in your area. The Rotary, Lions, and Elks Clubs, Junior League, and United Way are some larger charitable organizations that may be interested in donating to your cause as well. When writing your fund-raising letter, keep it short and simple and demonstrate the immediate impact of your donor's dollars. Don't forget to mention that most donations are also tax deductible.

I just carry hope in my heart. Hope is not a feeling of certainty; that everything ends well. Hope is just a feeling that life and work have meaning.
—VACLEV HAVEL

Always Follow Up!

You have to get on the phone with the small businesses, the civic and religious groups, and your friends and relatives to let them know that you really do need their support. One follow-up phone call can make the difference between a donor sending a check or pushing the request to the back burner and never getting to it.

University Funds

If you are a student, a major source of funding is through your own college. Many school clubs are allocated a certain amount of funds through student activities. See if your club is eligible. Many departments also have discretionary funds for projects and programs. If your trip can be integrated into an academic or service learning course there may also be some funds that could be used for your program.

Grants

One of the most common ways to raise money is through grant proposals. Though a grant proposal is very simple to write, getting it accepted is difficult. The Ford Foundation receives over one thousand proposals per day requesting money! Also, grants are often time sensitive in that foundations have deadlines and funding cycles. One of the most comprehensive books on foundations is *The Foundation Directory,* which is available at most libraries. The directory lists the board members of all the foundations and the types of projects they fund.

Local Businesses

Local businesses are far more likely to support you than large corporations are. The key is to make a link between the owner of the business and you or someone close to you. You may want to approach the business with a letter first. Enclose all relevant material and a pledge form, then follow up with a phone call.

Service Clubs and Places of Worship

Service clubs, such as Rotary or Kiwanis; fraternal organizations, such as the Elk or Moose Clubs; and churches and temples are excellent sources for fund-raising. Follow the "Who Do You Know?" principle: is someone you know a member or the friend of a member? The best course of action is to contact as many clubs in your area as possible and ask to give a presentation to the club. Many clubs have breakfast, lunch, or dinner meetings where you can ask to speak for fifteen minutes to present your request and explain what you will be doing. This is your chance to sell the program while promoting a good cause. Remember, you are not asking for money for your vacation. You are asking for a donation to do volunteer work overseas and to make a difference in the world. Also, let them know that you are willing to come back and show them slides or a video of the program when you return.

After the meeting write a follow-up letter thanking them for letting you speak and reiterating your request for money. Be specific about how much money you are requesting and how it will be used. Be realistic about the amount you are requesting ($200 to $400 is a reasonable amount).

Events

From bake sales to dinner parties, planning an event can be very labor-intensive. Be careful how you structure it and be clear about your expectations. One of the traditional ways to raise money is through bake sales, candy sales, garage sales, and so forth. Alternatively, an event, such as a black-tie affair or simple pizza party, might help with your fund-raising efforts. Again, use the "Who Do You Know?" principle. Do you have a friend in a band? Do you know the owner of a bar or a restaurant? Some simple events include having a band play at a club and you get the cover charge or a percentage of the drink sales. Or perhaps a restaurant will allow you an evening offering an all-you-can-eat buffet for $15 where you and the restaurant split the proceeds.

Media

Perhaps one of the best ways to promote awareness about your upcoming adventure and to raise funds for it is through the local media. In fact, this is how Cross-Cultural Solutions has attained most of its popularity, having numerous articles published about their programs in major newspapers and magazines across the country. Having a short piece published anywhere can go a long way in your quest for funds.

> It is important to remember why you are raising the money. Be persistent. You might get a lot of rejections and become pretty discouraged at times, but there will also be a lot of people who will support and encourage you.

> —STEVE ROSENTHAL

The easiest challenges are the ones you dream up for yourself.
The tough ones are the ones you don't get to choose.
—LEE IACOCCA

THE EXPERIMENT IN INTERNATIONAL LIVING

International Education • Worldwide • Summer
www.usexperiment.org

$ 🏕 🌐

"High school students changing the world one friendship at a time"—this is at the core of the Experiment in International Living, where students (known as experimenters) challenge themselves to become immersed in different cultures, learn through adventure travel and language immersion, and celebrate the diversity of life. The Experiment's summer programs feature opportunities in Africa, the Americas, Asia, Europe, and Oceania. For three to five weeks, experimenters focus on themes such as community service, language study, travel, peace studies, ecology, the arts, or outdoor adventure as they enjoy daily life with their host families and participate in activities with their group.

WHAT YOU'LL BE DOING: Each summer, over ninety group leaders spread out all over the world and help facilitate the learning experience for program participants. From program start to finish, leaders guide experimenters in the ongoing acquisition of survival language skills along with discussion and reflection on experiences, while also conducting group excursions and remaining in close contact with all the host families. At program's end, leaders facilitate the evaluation process—with the realization that each participant's "experiment" has actually just begun.

COMMITMENT: Those selected as leaders are required to attend a training workshop in Brattleboro, Vermont, in late June, just prior to program departure.

PERKS AND REWARDS: The experience alone is reward enough to most leaders; however, the perks aren't bad: a weekly honorarium of $100, room and board, domestic and international airfare, health insurance, and orientation and training.

THE ESSENTIALS: A bachelor's degree is required. Other essential traits for leaders are demonstrated interest in intercultural and experiential learning, in-depth experience living abroad, competency in the language of the host culture, and experience working with young people.

YOUR FIRST MOVE: Call for a leadership application. All materials are due by February 15.

FOR MORE INFORMATION: Program Director, The Experiment in International Living, Kipling Road, P.O. Box 676, Brattleboro, VT 05302-0676 (800) 345-2929 • (802) 257-7751 • (802) 258-3428 (fax) • eil@worldlearning.org

FULBRIGHT TEACHER AND ADMINISTRATOR EXCHANGE PROGRAM

Teaching • Worldwide • 6 Weeks–1 Year
www.fulbrightexchanges.org

$ 🏠

The U.S. Department of State promotes national interests through a wide range of overseas information programs. One for teachers in particular is the Fulbright Teacher and Administrator Exchange Program. This program provides opportunities for qualified educators to participate in direct exchanges of positions with colleagues from other countries for six weeks, a semester, or a full academic year. In general, exchange teachers are granted a leave of absence with pay and use their regular salary to cover daily expenses while abroad. A number of country programs provide full or partial transportation awards as well as housing. Orientation costs, including one-way travel to orientation and two to three days of food and lodging at the orientation site, are paid by the Department of State. There is a deadline of October 15 for all programs that begin the following year.

FOR MORE INFORMATION: Director, Fulbright Teacher and Administrator Exchange Program, U.S. Department of State, 600 Maryland Ave., SW, Suite 320, Washington, DC 20024-2520 • (800) 726-0479 • (202) 314-3520 (202) 479-6806 (fax) • fulbright@grad.usda.gov

GLOBAL CITIZENS NETWORK

Community Service • USA/Worldwide • 1–3 Weeks
www.globalcitizens.org

♥ 🏠 🌐

Global Citizens Network sends teams of six to twelve people to rural communities around the world, including Guatemala, Kenya, Mexico, Nepal, and Tanzania as well as Arizona, New Mexico, and Washington State in the U.S. The teams, led by a trained team leader, spend one to three weeks in their

GLOBAL CITIZENS NETWORK

A Global Citizens Network volunteer and a local man from Kenya dig the foundation for a health clinic.

chosen community and become immersed in the daily life of the local culture. Community projects are initiated by the local people and may include planting trees, digging irrigation trenches, setting up a schoolroom, or building a health clinic. Each day consists of both work and learning. Volunteers stay in local homes or as a group in a community center, and meals are shared with the host family or communally prepared and shared with project hosts. No special skills or experience are required—only an open mind, open heart, and willingness to experience and accept a new culture. The tax-deductible fee ranges from $650 to $1,950. (Airfare is additional.) Volunteers under eighteen years of age must be accompanied by a parent or guardian.

FOR MORE INFORMATION: Jennifer Dirks, Program Director, Global Citizens Network, 130 N. Howell St., St. Paul, MN 55104 • (800) 644-9292 (651) 644-0960 • info@globalcitizens.org

GLOBAL SERVICE CORPS

Service Learning • Worldwide • 2 Weeks–6 Months
www.globalservicecorps.org

♥ 🏠 🌐

Do you have the desire for a life-changing volunteer vacation or internship? With Global Service Corps (GSC) you can experience a country from an insider's perspective while living with your own local family. Rewarding experiences in cultural immersion and learning through service are offered year-round in Tanzania and Thailand, with opportunities available in health care, education, HIV/AIDS prevention education, sustainable agriculture, and Buddhist immersion. Programs include short-term (two to four weeks), long-term (six weeks to six months), and student internships (ten weeks). Local counterparts assist with language translation and skills, and program fees cover airport pickup, in-country transportation, homestay, meals, travel excursions, and project administration. Airfare, visas, and inoculations are additional. In your spare time, you also have the opportunity to visit nearby temples, parks, hot springs, or volcanic lakes, depending on the country. For application materials, call, email, or visit GSC online. Applications are needed at least two months prior to departure date. GSC also offers internships at their headquarters in San Francisco.

FOR MORE INFORMATION: Rick Lathrop, Executive Director, Global Service Corps, Earth Island Institute, 300 Broadway, Suite 28, San Francisco, CA 94133-3312 • (415) 788-3666, ext. 128 (415) 788-7324 (fax) • gsc@earthisland.org

GLOBAL VOLUNTEERS

Service Adventures • Worldwide • 1–4 Weeks
www.globalvolunteers.org

♥ ⚿ ⊕

Since 1984, Global Volunteers has worked at the invitation and under the direction of local people on human and economic development projects worldwide. Now serving in more than eighty host communities in twenty countries on six continents, Global Volunteers mobilizes up to 150 service teams each year. "Travel that feeds the soul" sums up the volunteer experience, where each participant's energy, creativity, and labor are put to use as they gain a genuine, firsthand understanding of how other people live day to day. Global Volunteers also has special consultative status with the United Nations.

GLOBAL VOLUNTEERS

A Global Volunteers participant walks with children in rural Tanzania while helping to change the world in a positive way.

WHAT YOU'LL BE DOING: The work projects encompass six primary categories: conversational English instruction, caring for children, literacy, community infrastructure, health care, and environmental projects. Volunteers might teach conversational English to elementary classrooms in China, nurture mentally disabled children in Ecuador, assist with building houses or community gardens in Ghana, provide basic health services to communities in the Cook Islands, or help eradicate invasive plants in Hawaii. Volunteer programs are maintained year-round throughout Africa, the Americas, Asia, Australia, the Caribbean, Europe, and the Pacific.

COMMITMENT: Programs generally last one to four weeks, depending on the destination.

PERKS AND REWARDS: A tax-deductible program fee ranges from $750 to $2,850, with discounts for online processing, groups, students, families, and returning volunteers. The fee helps maintain the local development program and covers on-site volunteer costs such as food, lodging, ground transportation, team leader expenses, project materials, volunteer coordination, program development, volunteer materials, evacuation insurance, host communications, and consultants. Airfare, visas, and medical insurance are additional costs. Volunteers find community meals abundant, sometimes adventurous, and a refreshing change for the palate. Lodging is generally double occupancy in hotels, guesthouses, community centers, or private homes.

THE ESSENTIALS: Volunteers typically share common characteristics, such as flexibility, compassion, open-mindedness, a sense of adventure, and most important, the desire to work with and learn from local people in the host community. Volunteers generally come from the U.S. and Canada, are drawn from all occupations and backgrounds, and are typically between the ages of thirty and seventy-five (although the program is open to people of all ages). There are no language or professional requirements for participation in most programs.

YOUR FIRST MOVE: Call for a current brochure or visit their website for program information and the latest news (including subscriptions to a monthly online newsletter). Applicants must complete their application materials one to three months prior to their departure date.

FOR MORE INFORMATION: Volunteer Coordinator, Global Volunteers, 375 E. Little Canada Rd., St. Paul, MN 55117-1628 • (800) 487-1074 (651) 407-6100 • (651) 482-0915 (fax) • email@globalvolunteers.org

INSIDER TIP: If our national anthem weren't "The Star-Spangled Banner," it would be an infectious symphony of Tex-Mex polkas, mystical Lakota drumming, Mississippi Delta blues, cowboy soliloquies, and Appalachian reels. You don't need to cross the oceans to explore new worlds. Unique and powerful service opportunities exist within U.S. borders. From coast to coast, we can help as developing communities fight the challenges of high unemployment, substandard living conditions, racism, and low per-capita income.

FINDING A PLACE IN THE WORLD

• •

Twenty years ago, we had what my husband, Bud Philbrook, wryly refers to as "a properly balanced honeymoon." We spent five days at theme parks in Orlando, followed by five days in an impoverished Guatemalan village. This curious blending of Disney World and "the real world" was, I believed then, a statement of our commitment to keep our marriage balanced and focused on human values. But more, it was a harbinger of our work to afford others a new perspective on their place in the world.

Over twenty-five years ago, Global Volunteers' co-founders Bud Philbrook and Michele Gran discovered their life's work on their honeymoon in Guatemala.

The first week in Orlando was predictably captivating as we explored all the area attractions. At the week's end, I was eager, but also apprehensive, about the next leg of our journey.

One thought dominated my mind as we embarked on our journey to Conacaste, Guatemala: I was writing a new, significant chapter of my life. Our act of service would define who we were as individuals and as a couple in a world where humanity struggles to maintain human relationships. Bud's vision was clearer than mine. He believed it was each person's moral responsibility to work for human justice and equality. As a former state legislator, he often challenged me to question my personal role in waging world peace. But I felt ill-equipped to make a real difference outside my immediate area of influence. How would I make sense of the poverty and struggles of a life I knew nothing about?

Our warm welcome into Guatemala assuaged my worries. We were greeted by the American program directors and the local community leaders. One of my first thoughts was: "They're just like us." While we toured the village, I felt progressively comforted by the openness and hospitality of the villagers.

The little mountain hamlet housed some two hundred families, many descendants of indigenous Indian tribes. They opened their homes to us, welcomed us into their fields, and included us in their friendly conversations, allowing us a glimpse into their daily lives. I was awestruck by how utterly normal—albeit difficult—life here seemed. With minimal electricity, no running water, few books, and no stores for daily necessities, the villagers

Things turn out best for the people who make the best out of the way things turn out.
—ART LINKLETTER

accepted their formidable challenges not with resignation, but with pride. A nature-dominated flow of daily life seemed to guide their gentle spirits. Life was to be celebrated.

My comfort level in my temporary "home" grew as I became familiar with local residents. We were eager to become as much a part of the community as possible. Bud, with his background in human and economic development, was asked to help write a grant proposal, and I, with my journalism background, began work on a brochure explaining the community's needs to potential benefactors.

Every evening Bud and I joined project leaders to reflect on the day. The goals of their work were explained to us: Conacaste was a "demonstration" village for neighboring communities. The hope was to develop strategies in farming, health care, education, and commerce that other villages could replicate to improve their subsistence-level standard of living. Over several years, several innovations had been developed, including a bread-baking "industry" and basket-weaving center.

The project leaders explained that progress was slow, because as a demonstration project, the construction techniques used must be replicable with locally available resources. The American program directors knew that the initiative, as well as the strategies, must be the local people's themselves if the community's efforts would remain long-term. Therefore, construction practices that to me had first seemed awkward and unnecessarily labor-intensive gained greater relevance as I began to understand the meaning of "appropriate technology."

As I scanned the village square, I tried to imagine what this place would look like in twenty years. Would one-room, thatched-roofed homes be replaced by more spacious dwellings? Would the village build the educational and medical facilities needed to ensure its children's health and development? Would farmers develop agricultural techniques to raise the families' subsistence style of life? My heart swelled with hope and optimism.

Now, twenty years later, I have personally witnessed what is possible when local initiative and community self-determination join with catalytic assistance from committed "outsiders."

Like most people, Global Volunteers' team members are at first motivated to make a difference, to "give back" some of what they are grateful for in their own lives, and to know that in a small, personal way, they have altered the course of world history in a positive way. It is upon reflection they often realize, perhaps as they are packing their bags to return home, that they are the ones who have truly benefited from their act of service. Life will never be the same. They have their own story to tell.

• •

—Contributed by Michele Gran, codirector of Global Volunteers

I-TO-I VOLUNTEER TRAVEL

Volunteer Vacation • Worldwide • 1–24 Weeks
www.i-to-i.com

♥ ⚒ ⊕

If you're looking for a travel or work experience with a purpose, i-to-i offers volunteer vacations in more than twenty countries around the world. A variety of one- to twenty-four-week ventures are designed to provide unique and fulfilling experiences that give something back to the host community and ecosystem. Projects range from teaching and building to community development and environmental conservation work. For a fee (starting at $795 for one-week programs; $1,595 for four weeks), i-to-i arranges everything for you so you can make the most of your overseas break: the project, airport pickup, comprehensive insurance, food and accommodation, predeparture training, Teaching English as a Foreign Language (TEFL) certification (for teaching and community development placements), Spanish language training (for Latin American travelers), extensive arrival orientation, and in-country support from i-to-i's local coordinators. Volunteers of all ages and backgrounds have traveled with i-to-i: university and graduate students, professionals on sabbatical, career changers, retirees, or travelers looking for a more meaningful adventure. Life in the project countries is not always easy, so volunteers must be prepared for the living and working conditions as well as for the inevitable culture shock that will accompany them on their journey. The right person will not only have the desire to travel responsibly, but will also realize the importance of helping those in need. Call or email for more information, or fill out the online application a minimum of one month prior to your desired start date.

FOR MORE INFORMATION: i-to-i Volunteer Travel, 190 East 9th Ave., Suite 320, Denver, CO 80203, (800) 985-4864 • (303) 765-5327 (fax) • usca@i-to-i.com

INSTITUTE FOR CENTRAL AMERICAN DEVELOPMENT STUDIES

Language/Community Service • Costa Rica/Nicaragua • 4–14 Weeks
www.icads.org • www.icadscr.com

♥ ⚒ ⊕

The main focus of the Institute for Central American Development Studies (ICADS) is to teach first-world citizens about Central America from a third-world perspective. This is done by teaching Spanish and by offering for-credit

Become so wrapped up in something that you forget to be afraid. **521**
—LADY BIRD JOHNSON

study-abroad programs that help students gain insight into current social and economic realities and their effects on women, the poor, and the environment.

WHAT YOU'LL BE DOING: Throughout the year, ICADS offers a monthly, four-week Spanish language immersion program. During the spring and fall, a field course in resource management and sustainable development is offered, as well as a semester internship and research program. Finally, during the summer months, a ten-week internship/language program is provided. Each program generally begins with a rigorous orientation and four weeks of intensive Spanish training for four and a half hours per day, five days per week (in small classes). Then, depending on the program, students participate in an internship or fieldwork projects in Costa Rica or Nicaragua emphasizing the environment, agriculture, women's issues, development work, education, health care, public health, or sustainable development.

PERKS AND REWARDS: Program fees range from $1,700 to $8,500 depending on the program, and include airport pickup, intensive Spanish instruction, internship or fieldwork placement, a homestay experience that includes room, breakfast, and dinner (the main staple in Costa Rica is rice and beans), laundry service, Internet access, and group field trips and activities. (Airfare, health insurance, and visa fees are additional costs.) Students should also budget $400 to $600 per month for local travel, lunches, and other incidental expenses.

THE ESSENTIALS: Anyone with a serious desire to learn Spanish makes a good fit for the language immersion program, and undergrads in college (and gap-year students) with some Spanish language experience are ideal for the semester program. All applicants must have a working knowledge of Spanish upon arrival, and those who feel they would like to provide their labor, energy, and expertise to help further the goals of oppressed groups and social justice organizations in Costa Rica and Nicaragua will thrive in the program.

YOUR FIRST MOVE: Applications and specific deadlines can be found online. Since applications are considered on a space-available basis, it's best to get materials in early; decisions are announced within two weeks of each deadline.

FOR MORE INFORMATION: Program Coordinator, Institute for Central American Development Studies, Dept. 826, P.O. Box 025216 • Miami, FL 33102-5216 (011) 506-225-0508 • info@icads.org

INTEREXCHANGE

Work Abroad • Worldwide • 1–12 Months
www.interexchange.org

$ 🏠

In addition to helping arrange for any necessary work and residence permits, InterExchange prearranges work-abroad experiences for U.S. citizens. The security of a prearranged job and accommodation allows participants to integrate into their new life more easily, without the stress of having to find a position and a place to live. Living and working in another culture enables participants to develop foreign language skills and gain greater insight into another way of life, all while receiving a salary or stipend (or other payment in kind) to help offset living and traveling expenses.

WHAT YOU'LL BE DOING: Have you ever dreamed about ordering a croissant and café au lait in Paris or wanted to become part of a real Spanish family? If so, InterExchange might be the program for you. They have dozens of positions in dozens of countries worldwide. Typical jobs include picking rhubarb and blackberries, tending livestock, teaching English, being a camp counselor or an au pair, or working at a hotel.

COMMITMENT: Placements vary from one month to one year depending on program: teaching and au pair positions range from three months to a year; farm programs range from two to four months; and internships range from summer positions to yearlong ventures.

PERKS AND REWARDS: Program fees range from $350 to $1,600. Along with a self-sustaining work salary or other payment in kind (not all programs offer salaries), housing is offered with most programs.

THE ESSENTIALS: Participants must be at least eighteen years of age; some programs have an upper age limit or language and degree requirements. Additionally, all participants must be covered by health and accident insurance.

YOUR FIRST MOVE: Applicants are required to submit applications two to four months prior to their desired start dates. After the proper paperwork is completed, most participants receive word of placement anywhere from four to eight weeks before their requested departure date.

FOR MORE INFORMATION: Patsy Kng, Program Manager, InterExchange, Working Abroad Program, 161 Sixth Ave., New York, NY 10013 • (800) 479-0907 (212) 924-0446 • (212) 924-0575 (fax) • workabroad@interexchange.org

Once we believe in ourselves we can risk curiosity, wonder, spontaneous delight, or any experience that reveals the human spirit.
—E. E. CUMMINGS

THE INTERNATIONAL PARTNERSHIP FOR SERVICE-LEARNING AND LEADERSHIP

Service Learning • Worldwide • 1–12 Months
www.ipsl.org

♥ ⛪ 🌐

The International Partnership for Service-Learning and Leadership, a non-profit educational consortium of colleges, universities, and service agencies, develops programs that link college-level academic studies with volunteer service in international and intercultural settings. Programs are offered in the Czech Republic, Ecuador, England, France, India, Israel, Jamaica, Mexico, the Philippines, Russia, Scotland, Thailand, and in the U.S. with Native Americans in South Dakota.

WHAT YOU'LL BE DOING: The International Partnership fully integrates participants into a new culture through service, academics, and living arrangements. Participants work in a community service project up to twenty hours per week in schools and orphanages, educational and health care institutions, recreation centers, or community development projects. The rest of the week is filled with an academic component, integrating studies and service that range from education and social services to intercultural and health care studies at a local, accredited university. Finally, living arrangements are provided with a host family or college housing, providing a unique way to interact and learn from the new culture. Also inquire about their master's degree in international service.

COMMITMENT: A variety of terms are available, including a three-week session in India, along with summer, semester, and yearlong programs.

PERKS AND REWARDS: Program fees range from $3,700 to $11,200 (depending on location and time frame), and cover tuition, housing and meals, on-site orientation, service placement, field trips, and administrative fees. Students can earn up to fifteen college credits per semester (which are granted from the student's home college).

THE ESSENTIALS: Applicants from all nations and backgrounds are welcome. The minimum age is eighteen and some programs have language requirements. College students and graduates are encouraged to apply.

YOUR FIRST MOVE: Applications must be received at least two months prior to the program start date. Details can be found online, or call or email for an information packet.

FOR MORE INFORMATION: Linda Chisholm, President, The International Partnership for Service-Learning and Leadership, 815 Second Ave., Suite 315, New York, NY 10017-4594 • (212) 986-0989 • (212) 986-5039 (fax) info@ipsl.org

INTERNATIONAL VOLUNTEER PROGRAM

Service Learning • California/Worldwide • 3–12 Weeks
www.ivpsf.org

♥ 🏠 🌐

The International Volunteer Program (IVP) provides people from all countries with the opportunity to work in Costa Rica, France, Spain, and the United Kingdom, as well as California. Throughout the year, IVP volunteers are placed in full-time projects with a local nonprofit organization that matches their expressed interests and skill. Typical assignments are in tourism offices, summer camps, hospitals, environmental projects, museums, and homeless shelters. Over the three- to twelve-week program period, volunteers provide invaluable support to the host organization and their clients while learning about a new culture. Placements are limited and are assigned on a first-come, first-served basis (thus, applicants must be receptive to any assignment). The fee of $1,100 to $2,550 includes in-country orientation and transportation, airport transfers, meals, and housing with host families, in dorms, or on-site. Applicants must be at least eighteen years of age (no upper age limit) and have at least an intermediate level of French to volunteer in France, English to volunteer in California or the U.K., and Spanish to volunteer in Spain.

FOR MORE INFORMATION: Allison Phillips, Program Manager, International Volunteer Program, 678 13th St., Suite 100, Oakland, CA 94612 (866) 614-3438 • (510) 433-0414 • (510) 433-0419 (fax) • ivpsf@swiftusa.org

INTERNSHIPS INTERNATIONAL

International Education • Worldwide • 2–3 Months
www.internshipsinternational.org

♥ 🏠 🎓 🌐

With Internships International (II), you have the opportunity to add a foreign dimension to your college or graduate degree through carefully chosen "coat and tie" professional internship placements in many international cities.

Covering all disciplines and fields, participants are placed in a full-time, volunteer internship for two to three months.

WHAT YOU'LL BE DOING: Think about what you want to do, where you want to go, how long you want to intern, and when you want to start. Don't worry, because you'll get plenty of help. During the application process, the II staff works with you to figure out an internship that best fits your needs and qualifications. Once you've settled on the details, one of II's international partners does all the legwork and finds an internship that meets your criteria. At the same time, you'll also receive a list of possible housing sources. After that, the rest is up to you—you'll have time to create, learn, grow, and be exposed to whole new world. (Of course, in an emergency, your program director would be there as a safety net!)

COMMITMENT: A minimum commitment of eight weeks is necessary, with placements lasting up to three months.

PERKS AND REWARDS: There is a placement fee of $1,100, which covers all costs associated with your internship placement. If an appropriate internship is not found based on your qualifications, the fee is fully refundable. All living and travel expenses are additional expenses. Many students have found ways to moonlight to bring in extra money. A special eight-week summer program in the fields of journalism, business, premed, and engineering includes housing in the fee.

THE ESSENTIALS: The program is geared for rising seniors, college grads, or graduate students who want to expand their resume in order to become more competitive in the academic or professional world. Exceptions can definitely be made for mature college juniors who require an internship for graduation. In addition, applicants must be independent and self-sufficient.

YOUR FIRST MOVE: Application information can be found online, or call or email to obtain more details. In addition to the application form, you will need to provide a statement of purpose in English (and in the language of the country you will work in, if required), two references, your college transcript, a resume, two photos, and the program fee. Placements generally take three months after your application is complete.

FOR MORE INFORMATION: Judy Tilson, Director, Internships International, 1612 Oberlin Rd., #5, Raleigh, NC 27608 • (919) 832-1575 • intintl@aol.com

JAPAN EXCHANGE AND TEACHING PROGRAM

Teaching • Japan • 1–3 Years
www.us.emb-japan.go.jp

$ 🌐

The Japan Exchange and Teaching Program (commonly known as JET) seeks to enhance internationalization in Japan by promoting mutual understanding between Japan and other countries, including the U.S. The program's aims are to intensify foreign language education in Japan and to promote international contacts at the local level by fostering ties between Japanese youth and young foreign college graduates. More than six thousand participants are currently involved in the JET Program; nearly half of whom come from the U.S.

WHAT YOU'LL BE DOING: Assistant Language Teacher (ALT) participants are assigned to local schools and boards of education in various cities, towns, and villages throughout Japan as team teachers and engage in foreign language instruction. They may also be involved in language clubs, teachers' seminars, and judging speech contests. Coordinator for International Relations (CIR) participants engage in international activities carried out by local governments throughout Japan. These activities include receiving guests from abroad, editing and translating documents, interpreting during international events, assisting with the language instruction of government employees and local residents, and assisting with international exchange programs.

COMMITMENT: The duration for an individual contract is one year, beginning in late July or early August. JET contracts are generally renewable for up to three years, upon consent of both the participant and the host institution.

PERKS AND REWARDS: An annual remuneration of ¥3,600,000 (approximately $32,000 per year, or check out www.xe.com/ucc for up-to-date currency exchange) is provided to cover the cost of accommodations, living expenses, and mandatory health insurance. Round-trip airfare is also provided, although only from designated points within the U.S. The host institution in Japan will assist participants with finding accommodations, which cost about ¥30,000 to ¥60,000 per month.

THE ESSENTIALS: ALT applicants must have an interest in Japan and excellent English communication skills. Japanese language ability or teaching experience is not required. CIR applicants must have a functional command of Japanese and excellent communication skills. All candidates must have a bachelor's degree and U.S. citizenship and be under forty years of age. Those outside the U.S. should check out requirements for their country at www.mofa.go.jp/j_info/visit/jet.

The real voyage of discovery consists not in seeking new landscapes, but in having new eyes. 527
—MARCEL PROUST

YOUR FIRST MOVE: Call 1-800-INFO-JET for application materials. Applications for the following year's JET Program will be available beginning in late September. Completed application packets must be received by the Japanese Embassy in Washington, D.C., by the deadline in late November or early December. (Call for exact dates.)

FOR MORE INFORMATION: Program Coordinator, Japan Exchange and Teaching Program, Embassy of Japan, 2520 Massachusetts Ave., NW, Washington, DC 20008 • (800) 463-6538 • (202) 238-6772 • jet@embjapan.org

MONTEVERDE FRIENDS SCHOOL

Teaching • Costa Rica • 6 Weeks–2 Years+
www.mfschool.org

$ 🏠 🌐

Monteverde Friends School is an English-dominant, bilingual school in Costa Rica's rural mountains. Tuition is kept low for the eighty students (in multigrade levels) so that no child will be denied an education. Challenging teaching assignments for a minimum of two years allow teachers, who lovingly share their knowledge and skills, to serve as role models for these children. Classes are small, generally eight to twelve students, with a curriculum based on the sciences, math, social studies, history, English, Spanish, and religion, along with special awareness of the environment, community, and peace issues. An interest in or experience with bilingual education and conversational Spanish, and a willingness to develop curriculum while living in a rustic tropical setting, are required. Benefits include a modest salary, rustic housing, health insurance, and visa costs. Volunteers are also welcome for a minimum stay of six weeks.

FOR MORE INFORMATION: Jenny Rowe, Director, Monteverde Friends School, 5655 Monteverde, Puntarenas, Costa Rica • 011 (506) 645-5302 • mfschool@racsa.co.cr

OPERATION CROSSROADS AFRICA

Global Development • Africa/Brazil/The Caribbean • Summer
www.operationcrossroadsafrica.org

♥ 🏠 🌐

Since Operation Crossroads Africa's founding in 1957, more than ten thousand volunteers have made contributions to development in thirty-five

African and twelve Caribbean countries as well as in Brazil. The late President Kennedy paid special tribute to Crossroads for serving as the example and inspiration for the creation of the Peace Corps.

WHAT YOU'LL BE DOING: After a brief but intense cross-cultural training, Crossroads volunteers are teamed up with eight to ten other men and women and immersed into the culture of their host community (along with a team leader and an equal number of local volunteers). All projects are community initiated, and volunteers will live and work with hosts who have designed the project. The project work may entail construction of a school, an inoculation drive, or planting trees, and all projects fall into four categories: construction of community facilities, community health, agriculture, and education and training. Living conditions provide only the basic amenities and lack many of the modern conveniences many Westerners take for granted; often there is no electricity or running water, and participants eat a modest, high-starch, low-protein diet. Each season Crossroads also hires a handful of team leaders who are responsible for stimulating interest and cooperation among participants and for guiding them in attaining greater contextual understanding of the experience. Call for the specifics on these positions.

COMMITMENT: The program runs from mid-June to mid-August and consists of three orientation days in New York City, six weeks of work on a rural project, and one travel week in the host country.

PERKS AND REWARDS: There is a participation fee of $3,500, which covers all program expenses, including round-trip airfare. A majority of volunteers raise all or part of their fee. Crossroads provides fund-raising how-tos, contacts with others who have successfully raised their fee in the past, and consistent encouragement in the process.

THE ESSENTIALS: Though most Crossroaders are college students and young professionals (with a minimum age of seventeen), there are no set occupation requirements. Fluency in French or Portuguese is a plus, since these are the main languages of many host countries.

YOUR FIRST MOVE: Call for application materials and current deadlines. In general, all applications must be turned in by March 1.

FOR MORE INFORMATION: Program Services Director, Operation Crossroads Africa, P.O. Box 5570, New York, NY 10027 • (212) 289-1949 (212) 289-2526 (fax) • oca@igc.org

🖎 **INSIDER TIP: You will experience Africa from the inside out . . . this is not an African tour.**

The slower one travels, the more enriching the experience. 529
—SHEILA CUNNINGHAM

OTZMA

Kibbutz/Community Service • Israel • 10 Months
www.otzma.org

♥ 🏠

A great alternative to work or graduate school, OTZMA (the Hebrew word for strength) is a ten-month leadership development program in which North American young adults (aged twenty to twenty-six; college graduates preferred) contribute a year of service to Israel and the Jewish people and gain an in-depth understanding of the country and their own capacities to lead. Beginning in mid-August, volunteers initially live and work in large groups at immigrant absorption centers, then participate in an *ulpan,* a program of intense Hebrew language study. For the next three months, volunteers participate in community service projects, which range from building playgrounds to coordinating events for youth in the community center. During the final three months, participants can either live on a kibbutz or intern at a nongovernmental/nonprofit organization. The OTZMA year also includes numerous education days, seminars, group trips, and two vacations. Each participant is paired with an Israeli host family with whom to share holidays and weekends throughout the program. The financial obligation for participants is $2,000, plus airfare to Israel (which runs around $1,000) and food. The cost of the program helps pay for housing for the entire year as well as for educational seminars, speakers, and a small stipend. Applications are due March 1, with a rolling admissions policy on a space-available basis after that point.

FOR MORE INFORMATION: Reina Cohen, Recruitment Coordinator, OTZMA, United Jewish Communities, 111 8th Ave., Suite 11E, New York, NY 10011-5201 (877) 466-8962 • (212) 284-6786 • (212) 284-6988 (fax) • otzma@ujc.org

🦅 **INSIDER TIP: The intensity of my year on OTZMA enabled me to grow in ways that far exceeded my expectations. The opportunities that were presented to me, and those that I sought out for myself, led me to have one of the most rewarding adventures of my life. —*Brooke Gardberg, participant***

PEACE CORPS

Global Development • Worldwide • 2 Years+
www.peacecorps.gov

$ 🏠

Since 1961, Peace Corps volunteers have been sharing their skills and energies with people in the developing world, helping them learn new ways to fight hunger, disease, poverty, and lack of opportunity.

WHAT YOU'LL BE DOING: As a Peace Corps volunteer, you'll travel overseas and make real differences in the lives of real people. Whether you're helping people stay healthy, expand their businesses, or grow more-nutritious food, you will help change and improve the human condition at the grassroots level. There is a particular need for certified teachers, French-language speakers, and those interested in agriculture, environmental education, business development, and teaching English.

COMMITMENT: Assignments last for two years and begin after the successful completion of an intensive language, cultural, and technical training (which lasts from two to three months).

PERKS AND REWARDS: "Two years of service, a lifetime of benefits." It is often said that the Peace Corps is not simply something great; it is the beginning of something great. From practical benefits such as student loan deferment, to career benefits like fluency in a foreign language, to the intangible benefits that come with making a difference in people's lives, there are a variety of rewards for serving. During this serving time, volunteers receive a monthly allowance to cover housing, food, clothing, and spending money. Medical and dental care, transportation to and from their overseas sites, and twenty-four vacation days a year are also provided. Upon completion of service, volunteers receive a $6,075 readjustment allowance and job-hunting assistance.

THE ESSENTIALS: Any healthy U.S. citizen of eighteen years or older is eligible for consideration, with most assignments requiring at least a bachelor's degree or three to five years of substantive work experience. For many assignments, a language other than English is required. Previous knowledge of another language can be very helpful but is not always required. Perseverance, adaptability, creativity in problem solving, and sociability are traits important in volunteers.

YOUR FIRST MOVE: For more information, call the toll-free number to locate the recruitment office nearest you. Volunteers will be notified where they'll be serving as much as six months before they get on a plane.

FOR MORE INFORMATION: Director, Volunteer Recruitment and Selection, Peace Corps, 1111 20th St., NW, Washington, DC 20526 • (800) 424-8580 volunteer@peacecorps.gov

✄ INSIDER TIP: Not sure if you want to continue with graduate school or become involved with the Peace Corps? Now you can do both by participating in the Master's International Program. Through partnerships with more than thirty schools offering master's-level studies in a variety of subjects, individuals become Peace Corps volunteers as partial fulfillment of a graduate degree.

Your diamonds are not in far distant mountains or in yonder seas;
they are in your own backyard, if you but dig for them.
—RUSSELL H. CONWELL

SCI—INTERNATIONAL VOLUNTARY SERVICE USA

Work Camp • Worldwide • 2 Weeks–1 Year
www.sci-ivs.org

♥ ⛺ 🌐

SCI–International Voluntary Service is the U.S. branch of Service Civil International, which is celebrating over seventy-five years of promoting peace and international understanding through community service projects. The hallmark of SCI is the annual exchange of thousands of volunteers who work at short-term community service projects around the world.

WHAT YOU'LL BE DOING: Throughout the year, eight to fifteen volunteers of various nationalities and backgrounds come together to solve problems, work together in grassroots community service projects, and have fun. Volunteers might help teach solar technology in Denmark, renovate an ancient church in Russia, or work on an organic farm in the Swiss Alps. SCI-sponsored work camps have local sponsors in more than seventy-five countries around the globe.

COMMITMENT: Although there are some work camp opportunities available throughout the year, by far the largest number of camps are offered during the summer months and last from two to four weeks. Longer opportunities—from three months to one year—are also available.

PERKS AND REWARDS: The application fee for residents of the U.S. and Canada is $65 for domestic programs and $175 for most overseas programs. Sponsors of some camps in Africa, Asia, Eastern Europe, and Latin America may charge an additional fee, which varies by location. Participation in more than one camp runs an additional $40 to $80 (with a limit of three camps per year). SCI covers room and board and a supplemental health and accident insurance. (Airfare is additional.) Your fee also pays for a year's membership in SCI.

THE ESSENTIALS: U.S. and Canadian volunteers must be sixteen or older for U.S. camps and eighteen or older for overseas camps. (There is no upper age limit and retirees are welcome.) In general, there is no special experience required, except the ability to work in a team environment.

YOUR FIRST MOVE: Information regarding all camps and applications forms are available on their website. Summer opportunities are generally posted by mid-March. Summer volunteers are placed in work camps of their choice, beginning in mid-April on a first-come, first-served basis. (After June 15, it becomes more difficult to get your first choice.) Have patience, as applications are processed by a small group of volunteer staff across the country.

FOR MORE INFORMATION: Volunteer Exchange Coordinator, SCI—International Voluntary Service USA, 5474 Walnut Level Rd., Crozet, VA 22932 (206) 545-6585 • information@sci-ivs.org

STUDENTS PARTNERSHIP WORLDWIDE

Environmental Education/Service Learning • Africa/Asia • 4–9 Months
www.spw.org

♥ ⛺ ⊕

Are you prepared for the real challenges of grassroots sustainable development? Over eight hundred volunteers a year (aged eighteen to twenty-eight) work on SPW International's four- to nine-month environmental and health education programs in India, Nepal, South Africa, Tanzania, Uganda, Zambia, and Zimbabwe. Local volunteers from these countries work in partnership with volunteers from the U.S., Europe, and Australia. After four weeks of comprehensive training, local and international volunteers are placed in rural communities where they work with schools and community leaders to identify and resolve key health or environmental issues. The all-inclusive program fee of $5,400 to $6,000 covers training and travel, meals, housing, comprehensive health insurance, return airfare, and a stipend for yourself and your local volunteer partner. The application process is selective, and applicants are encouraged to apply three to twelve months prior to the program departure date.

FOR MORE INFORMATION: Robyn Munford, Program Director, Students Partnership Worldwide, 1401 New York Ave., NW, Suite 500, Washington, DC 20005-2150 • (202) 662-0714 • spw@worldpath.net

VIA

Teaching • Asia • 6 Weeks–2 Years
www.viaprograms.org

$ ⛺ ⊕

VIA (formerly Volunteers in Asia) traces its origins to a group of Stanford students who in 1963 saw volunteer work as an appropriate way to enter and better understand the non-Western world. Since its beginnings in the refugee settlements of Hong Kong, VIA has sent more than a thousand volunteers to a wide range of assignments in Asia. Current programs in China, Indonesia,

If the path be beautiful, let us not ask where it leads.
—ANATOLE FRANCE

and Vietnam continue to reflect the organization's original goals: to immerse Americans directly into the workplaces and neighborhoods of contemporary Asia and to provide Asian organizations with volunteer assistance.

WHAT YOU'LL BE DOING: As a small organization with limited resources, VIA focuses its efforts on one skill Americans can offer Asian organizations without displacing Asian workers—native English-language assistance. Volunteers either teach English primarily to university students (although some posts are with younger children and adults) or work as English-language resource helpers, providing translation and editing services with a local organization. Between thirty and forty volunteers are sent each year.

COMMITMENT: Summer programs are open to college undergraduates, while long-term programs are for college graduates of all ages. All volunteers participate in a predeparture training program in the Bay Area, which focuses on cross-cultural training, work role specifics, and language training. There are two mandatory training sessions in the spring and early summer. Participants generally depart for Asia in late June.

PERKS AND REWARDS: Participant fees run $975 to $1,975 for the summer program; $1,975 for the one-year program; and $975 for two years. This fee represents approximately ten percent of the cost of sending a volunteer into the field. VIA covers the cost of round-trip transportation, basic health insurance, cross-cultural training, and in-country field support. Living arrangements are provided in guesthouses, faculty apartment buildings, or dormitories. While on assignment, one- and two-year volunteers receive a monthly housing and living stipend. Scholarships are available.

THE ESSENTIALS: Applicants must be mature, responsible, native English speakers, and should hold a bachelor's degree. Due to the visa application process, applicants must be U.S. citizens or currently reside in the U.S. VIA does not require any specific educational background, prior language training, teaching, or overseas experience. Volunteers range in age from eighteen to eighty and come from many different walks of life.

YOUR FIRST MOVE: Applications are available starting in September and are due in mid-February. All prospective applicants are encouraged to attend one of VIA's informational sessions held during this time frame. Staff and former volunteers will be on hand to help you gain a clearer picture of the program and its philosophy and whether it meets your needs and interests. Acceptance into the program will be announced in early March.

FOR MORE INFORMATION: Kirsten Walsh, Outreach Director, VIA, P.O. Box 20266, Stanford, CA 94309 • (650) 723-3228 • (650) 725-1805 (fax) info@viaprograms.org

VISIONS IN ACTION

Service Learning • USA/Africa/Mexico • 6 Weeks–12 Months
www.visionsinaction.org

♥ 🏕 ⊕

Visions in Action is an international nonprofit organization founded in 1988 out of the conviction that there is much we can learn from and contribute to the developing world by working as part of a community of volunteers committed to social justice in the urban setting.

WHAT YOU'LL BE DOING: Visions in Action programs feature a monthlong orientation, including intensive language study, followed by a five- or eleven-month volunteer placement. Positions are offered in three African countries (South Africa, Tanzania, and Uganda) and Mexico, with projects that include business and community development, environmental issues, health care, housing and urban planning, human rights, journalism, nonprofit development, scientific research, and women's rights. For those who desire a shorter-term placement, a six-week summer program is also an option. In addition, intern positions are available on a continuous basis in the Washington, D.C., office and range from international administration to recruitment and public relations (with a minimum commitment of three months or more). Although internships are unpaid, an $800 credit toward a Visions in Action overseas program fee is provided.

PERKS AND REWARDS: Fees start at $3,200 for the summer program; $4,200 for six months; and $5,000 for one year. This includes housing, orientation and language training, medical insurance, overseas support, and a small monthly stipend to assist with daily living expenses. (Airfare is an additional cost.) Volunteers are normally housed in major urban areas in coed group houses, living in a supportive community. All funds donated toward your program are tax-deductible, and Visions in Action will help you with fund-raising ideas once you have been accepted as a volunteer.

THE ESSENTIALS: Volunteers of all nationalities must be at least twenty years of age (eighteen for the summer program) and have two years of college or equivalent work experience. Most volunteers are university graduates, the average age is twenty-seven, and married couples are encouraged to apply. The Spanish language is required in Mexico.

YOUR FIRST MOVE: Applications are due three months prior to departure, although it's suggested that you apply early so you have time to raise funds before you go. Materials are available online or call for more information.

Experience is a hard teacher because she gives the test first, the lesson afterwards.   **535**
—VERNON SANDERS LAW

FOR MORE INFORMATION: Shaun Skelton, Program Director, Visions in Action, 2710 Ontario Rd., NW, Washington, DC 20009 • (202) 625-7402 (202) 588-9344 (fax) • visions@visionsinaction.org

VOLUNTEERS FOR PEACE

Work Camp • Worldwide • 2–3 Weeks
www.vfp.org

♥ ⛺ ⊕

International work camps emerged in war-torn Europe back in 1920. More recently, work camps have become an affordable and meaningful way for people of all ages to travel, live, and work in a foreign country. Volunteers for Peace (VFP) coordinates more than 2,400 work camp experiences in ninety countries, including Africa, the Americas, Asia, and Eastern and Western Europe. Hundreds of field volunteers and office staff provide consultation and placement services for work camp hosts and volunteers.

WHAT YOU'LL BE DOING: As a fully internationalized short-term "Peace Corps," work camps are a way you can respond positively to the challenges we face in our world. Focusing on cooperation, caring, sharing, and group living, you'll have a fun-filled adventure, building bonds with people from diverse cultural backgrounds. Work camps are sponsored by an organization in the host country and coordinated by people in a local community. Agricultural, archaeological, construction, environmental, and restoration projects are common. In general, ten to twenty volunteers from four or more countries work together on each community-sponsored work project.

COMMITMENT: Programs vary as to their start dates and length but generally run two to three weeks from mid-June to mid-October. About 20 percent of the people they place abroad every year register for multiple work camps in the same or different countries and spend several months abroad.

PERKS AND REWARDS: Most programs cost $200, with room and meals provided. African, Russian, and Latin American programs may cost $300 to $500. You may be housed in a school, church, private home, or community center. Living arrangements are generally family style, with participants coordinating and sharing day-to-day activities, food preparation, work projects, and recreation. Travel expenses will be left up to the volunteer.

THE ESSENTIALS: You must be at least eighteen years old (although there are over 150 work camps for sixteen- and seventeen-year-olds in Belgium, Estonia, France, Germany, Italy, Latvia, Lithuania, Turkey, and the U.K.), and there is no upper age limit. (They've placed several folks in their seventies.) The most common age of participants is between twenty and twenty-five. In most areas, foreign language proficiency is not necessary.

YOUR FIRST MOVE: The *International Workcamp Directory,* which lists more than 2,400 opportunities, can be obtained for $20. Issued annually in April, it also contains registration information and VFP's free newsletter. Volunteers are placed on a first-come, first-served basis and are advised to register as soon as possible after receipt of the directory. Most volunteers register between mid-April and mid-May.

FOR MORE INFORMATION: Peter Coldwell, Director Volunteers for Peace 1034 Tiffany Rd. Belmont, VT 05730-0202 (802) 259-2759 (802) 259-2922 (fax) vfp@vfp.org

Volunteers for Peace participants restore ancient stairs in the Cinque Terre of Italy and enjoy views of the Mediterranean stretching as far as the eye can see.

INSIDER TIP: My work camp experience was one of the best of my life; in fact it changed my life. It was definitely a good experience to find out how well I function in a foreign environment, and it's definitely good for someone who is thinking of living abroad or joining a longer-term volunteer project. It is an experience that will live within me forever and which no one will understand unless they experience it themselves. —*Jill Zabloski, volunteer in Bolivia*

*To know what you prefer instead of humbly saying Amen
to what the world tells you ought to prefer, is to have kept your soul alive.*
—ROBERT LOUIS STEVENSON

WORLDTEACH

Teaching • Worldwide • 2–12 Months
www.worldteach.org

$ 🏠 🌐

WorldTeach provides opportunities for individuals who want to make a meaningful contribution to international education by living and working as volunteer teachers in developing countries. Opportunities are available for a full year in Chile, China, Costa Rica, Ecuador, the Marshall Islands, and Namibia; or during the summer (for eight weeks) in China, Costa Rica, Ecuador, Namibia, and Poland. Most volunteers teach English as full-time employees; however, in some countries (depending on the needs of the host community), subjects may include math, science, computer skills, and HIV/AIDS awareness. Finally, for those with an interest in the environment and ecotourism, an eight-month Nature Guide Training Program is also available in varied locales. Program fees range from $1,000 to $5,990 and include housing with a private room and meals (generally with a local host family), a small stipend, round-trip international airfare, health insurance, training, a teaching position, and field support. To help with fund-raising efforts, WorldTeach produces a fund-raising guide that is given to all volunteers; they'll also connect you with alumni who can provide personal fund-raising tips. Candidates must have a bachelor's degree and a sincere interest in education, international development, and/or cultural exchange. Summer program applicants must be at least eighteen years of age. The

HELEN CLAIRE SIEVERS

WorldTeach volunteer Sara Schmitt shares her enthusiasm with Costa Rican students.

ability to speak a foreign language or teaching experience is not necessary, but an open mind, adventurous spirit, and enthusiasm for intercultural learning are essential. Applications are available online.

FOR MORE INFORMATION: Molly Greene, Admissions Coordinator, WorldTeach, Center for International Development, 79 John F. Kennedy St., Cambridge, MA 02138 • (800) 483-2240 • (617) 495-5527 (617) 495-1599 (fax) • admissions@worldteach.org

INSIDER TIP: This year I have found, more than ever before, that everything always works out as it is supposed to. All of the situations, no matter how scary, surreal, or joyful, have proven to be just what I needed to experience. My coming to Costa Rica was a personal quest, to find a part of myself that I felt was missing. [I needed] to exhibit myself as an independent and resourceful person, able to handle negative situations that may arise. Also, [I needed] to acknowledge positive situations and recognize the special benefits I will receive because of them. I feel I have found a large piece of what I was searching for because I have learned that every experience happens for a specific reason: *to grow! —Jennifer Lamb, volunteer in Costa Rica*

YMCA INTERNATIONAL

Work Abroad • Worldwide • 2–12 Months
www.ymcagoglobal.org

♥ 🏠

The YMCA Go Global Program provides exciting opportunities for those over the age of eighteen to share their talents, interests, and culture with another country—including fifty YMCA sites throughout the world. Go Global fills a void for U.S. citizens wanting to develop a greater international knowledge and competence along with experiencing a completely different way of thinking, learning, and living. Volunteers typically work up to three months in the summer or winter in a wide variety of YMCA programs— everything from community development and education to English teaching, teen leadership, and camps. Some overseas YMCAs also look for volunteers who can stay for up to one year. In exchange for your volunteer service, room, board, and a small stipend are provided. Volunteers are responsible for their airfare, health insurance, and a $500 application fee, but don't let this discourage you, as scholarships are available. In general, applications are due two months prior to your desired placement date.

FOR MORE INFORMATION: Jean-Paul Sewavi, Director, YMCA International, Go Global Program, 5 West 63 St., New York, NY 10023 • (888) 477-9622 (212) 727-8800, ext. 4327 • (212) 727-8814 (fax) • sprogram@ymcanyc.org

A person who is looking for something doesn't travel very fast.
—E. B. WHITE

RECOMMENDED RESOURCES

Alternatives to the Peace Corps (Food First Books, $10.95) offers
many options for those who want to volunteer their time almost anywhere
in the world for a good cause. The guide provides listings of voluntary
service organizations, work brigades, and study tours that work to support
development as defined by the local people. A must for anyone dedicated to
grassroots work in their own backyard and in the Third World. Food First
also offers internships at their headquarters in California, with work dedicated to eliminating the injustices that cause hunger and poverty. For more
information contact Marilyn Borchardt, Internship Coordinator, Food First,
Institute for Food and Development Policy, 398 60th St., Oakland, CA
94618-1212; (510) 654-4400, foodfirst@foodfirst.org, www.foodfirst.org.

For anyone interested in teaching English as a Second Language or working
abroad, head to **Dave's ESL Café** (www.eslcafe.com). The café's Job Center
provides postings of hundreds of teaching and administration jobs throughout
the world, while the ESL Web Guide provides literally thousands of links
sorted by category.

Would you like to escape to a new country and restart your life? With
EscapeArtist.com, you can escape from the ordinary with extraordinary
ideas. Come explore thousands of resources and links—and be sure to sign
up for the free monthly eZine *Escape from America.*

If you decide that traveling, studying, volunteering, working, and living abroad
are going to be a way of life for you, *The Global Citizen* (Ten Speed Press,
$16.95) will lead you every step of the way. You'll find tips and resources for
uncovering your global passion, take a mini cross-cultural course to polish
your cultural skills, and complete a self-survey to plan your international life
and career. After this little bit of prep work, you'll be on your way to choosing
from over two hundred ways to travel, learn, volunteer, and work abroad—the
fabric of your global future. And once you know the next stepping stone in
your journey, the author, Elizabeth Kruempelmann, will help you out with
the practical to-dos of making it happen, funding your sojourns, and optimiz-
ing your time overseas. Finally, you'll discover how other global citizens got
started on their worldly paths and how you too can transform your international experience into a truly rewarding way of life.

If you're dreaming about living and volunteering abroad, *How to Live
Your Dream of Volunteering Overseas* (Penguin USA, $17) offers all the
necessary ingredients for success. The authors—all founders of volunteer
organizations—provide a unique insider's perspective on choosing the right

program, fund-raising efforts, and how to be an effective volunteer, and profile over one hundred volunteer organizations. For further information, turn to the companion website at www.volunteeroverseas.org.

Whether you want to intern, volunteer, study, or teach abroad, you'll find plenty of information, programs, and travel resources with the **GoAbroad.com** network.

If there is a program that sends volunteers, interns, or lay missionaries abroad, you'll find it in a searchable database of opportunities through the **International Volunteer Programs Association** (www.volunteerinternational.org). While exploring the IVPA site, be sure to sign up for their bimonthly email newsletter.

Written by two seasoned American journalists who lived and worked in Italy, *Living, Studying, and Working in Italy* (Owl Books, $17) is brimming with candid insider tips and practical advice on experiencing Italy as the locals might. Travis Neighbor and Monica Larner provide information on volunteer opportunities, internship programs, and language schools as well as information about freelance and professional employment opportunities for Americans. Essential for anyone interested in making Italy his or her home—at least for awhile.

Sprechen Sie Deutsch? Parla italiano? Parlez-vous français? A Middlebury summer prepares people of all ages for a much more successful study- or work-abroad experience by dramatically improving their language skills, deepening their cultural understanding, and strengthening their confidence and learning strategies. With a formal commitment of "No English Spoken Here," Middlebury students use their target language exclusively—in classes, dining halls, and dormitories, and throughout a range of co-curricular activities over a course of seven to nine very full weeks of intensive language learning! Whether studying Arabic, Chinese, French, German, Italian, Japanese, Spanish, or Russian, participants literally live the language at all hours of the day. One summer at Middlebury equals at least one full academic year of conventional language study. Tuition starts at $5,350, which includes room and board, for the six-week summer program. For more information contact **Middlebury College Language Schools,** Sunderland Language Center, Middlebury, VT 05753-6131; (802) 443-5510, languages@middlebury.edu, www.middlebury.edu/ls.

If you're thinking about joining the Peace Corps, Dillon Banerjee offers an insider perspective of his trials and tribulations before, during, and after his two-year volunteer experience in Cameroon. *So You Want to Join the Peace Corps* (Ten Speed Press, $12.95) is organized around seventy-three questions, starting with "What is the application process like?" and ending with "Would you go back and do the Peace Corps all over again?" Extensive information can be found on what programs currently exist, the requirements, and how to strengthen your own application.

StudyAbroad.com provides an online directory of study, language, internship, and volunteer opportunities abroad, along with valuable country-specific information.

With over thirty years' worth of experience in Teaching English as a Foreign Language (TEFL), Jeff Mohamed provides detailed information and how-to advice on successfully creating a new teaching lifestyle anywhere in the world. *Teaching English Overseas* (English International, $19.95) contains details of 450 schools and other organizations that hire more than ten thousand teachers every year. For further information and advice on teaching overseas, check out the author's companion website at www.english-international.com.

Anyone making plans to travel abroad should stop in first at **Transitions Abroad** (TA). Along with their companion website (www.transitionsabroad.com), TA publishes a handful of resources and directories that will have you fully engrossed in planning your new adventure. For those who need a constant stream of knowledge throughout the year, you might indulge in their bimonthly magazine, *Transitions Abroad*. Topics include short-term jobs, special interest and language vacations, an overseas travel planner, work abroad, and adventure travel ($28 per year, or $6.45 for a single issue or back issues, which includes shipping). For those who want the whole kit and kaboodle in one book, the *Alternative Travel Directory* focuses on travel, study, and living overseas; the *Work Abroad* guide provides the key contacts for landing an overseas job ($19.95 for either book). Stop by their website and sign up for the *Transitions Abroad eNewsletter,* a monthly email newsletter that will keep you updated about new travel websites, programs, recommended publications, and the latest line on their magazine.

Travelers who want to combine a little adventure and personal growth with service to others should include *Volunteer Vacations,* by Bill McMillon (Chicago Review Press, $17.95), in their research. This classic profiles more than two hundred organizations that need volunteers and offers vignettes from previous volunteers.

Get the real scoop on working overseas through the eyes of author Susan Griffith. Although geared mainly to the U.K. crowd, *Work Your Way Around the World* provides detailed information for the working traveler, with explicit country-by-country overviews that cover everything from picking olives in Greece to working as a tour guide in Peru. And for those who might want to "talk" their way around the world, *Teaching English Abroad* intertwines actual accounts of enjoyable and disappointing experiences by people who have taught abroad. You'll also find specific job vacancy information compiled from language schools from the south of Chile to Iceland. Finally, for a directory of volunteer gigs worldwide, be sure to check out *The International Directory of Voluntary Work,* by Louise Whetter. All titles are published by Vacation Work in the U.K. (www.vacationwork.co.uk) for $19.95 and distributed by Peterson's in the U.S. (www.petersons.com).

TRAVEL GUIDES

Researched, written, and produced entirely by students (over 250 of them from Harvard University) who know firsthand how to see the world on the cheap, **Let's Go** (www.letsgo.com) guidebooks provide information on the hippest backstreet cafés, pristine secluded beaches, the best routes from border to border, off-the-beaten-path cultural sites, and budget-conscious accommodations (starting from the least expensive and working up). The classic Europe handbook, *Let's Go Europe* (Let's Go Publications, $24.99), has been the bible for a generation of student travelers; however, fifty-five in-depth city, regional, and country guidebooks now crisscross five continents, with countries from the U.S. to China.

Lonely Planet (www.lonelyplanet.com) publishes down-to-earth, comprehensive, and practical guidebooks for independent travelers who "have an interest in things." There are over 650 guidebooks in print, all written in a straightforward, readable style with lots of firsthand tips and recommendations. Upgrades documenting significant changes to current editions for over sixty guidebooks can be found online as well as a variety of email newsletter subscription options.

For more than three decades, **Moon Handbooks** (www.moon.com) have appealed to an eclectic group of travelers—from backpacking students to solo adventurers to families on vacation with a budget. With expert authors delivering a mix of honest insight, street-savvy advice, and an essential dose of humor, Moon Handbooks ensure that travelers have an uncommon experience—and a few new stories to tell.

Author Rick Steves takes a lighthearted, personal approach to sharing with you everything you need to know to have a great trip in Europe. *Rick Steves' Europe through the Back Door* (Avalon Travel Publishing, $21.95) is full of practical travel advice—a must for anyone venturing to Europe who desires a more intimate feel for the places that locals patronize rather than hitting the main tourist stops. You can receive a free quarterly travel newsletter or monthly email dispatch providing information on Rick Steves's travel guides as well as tour information, money-saving travel tips,

Sometimes the road less traveled is less traveled for a reason.   **543**
—JERRY SEINFELD

and other great stuff (including the best deals on Eurail passes). Contact Rick at P.O. Box 2009, Edmonds, WA 98020-2009; (425) 771-8303, rick@ricksteves.com, www.ricksteves.com.

Rough Guides (www.roughguides.com) are aimed squarely at independent-minded travelers of all kinds, on all budgets—whether vacationers, business travelers, or backpackers. Thoughtful writing, painstaking research, and conscientiously prepared maps are fundamental to their commitment to provide you with the best possible guides—from Amsterdam to Zimbabwe, with almost two hundred more in between.

Traveling alone need not mean lonely. How about taking a gourmet cooking and language workshop in France? What about a three-week cycling tour in the Grand Canyon or hiking the hills of Tuscany? In *Traveling Solo* (Globe Pequot Press, $17.95), Eleanor Berman provides great ideas and advice for over 250 learning adventures for travelers doing it solo, along with plenty of advice on how to plan the perfect vacation. The book does have more of a female perspective, but don't worry guys, Berman's impressions will certainly help you make some great decisions.

INDEXES: YOUR COMPASS TO THE GUIDE

ALPHABETICAL LISTING OF PROGRAMS

CATEGORY INDEX

GEOGRAPHICAL INDEX

PROGRAM LENGTH INDEX

GENERAL INDEX

ALPHABETICAL LISTING OF PROGRAMS

This index is geared to all the programs and associations located throughout your guide. For a listing of resources, book, publications, and websites, check out the general index on page XXX.

The true measure of an individual is how he treats a person who can do him absolutely no good.
—ANN LANDERS

This country will not be a good place for any of us to live in   **551**
unless we make it a good place for all of us to live in. —THEODORE ROOSEVELT

Many of life's failures are people who did not realize how close they were to success when they gave up. —THOMAS ALVA EDISON

CATEGORY INDEX

From adventure education to Zen centers (and everything in between), this index is organized by the buzz words that describe the programs. Although specific categories have been assigned to each program, some programs cover such a wide spectrum of opportunities that they could be listed under many other categories. So become an explorer while perusing this index.

He who has a why to live can bear with almost any how.
—FRIEDRICH NIETZSCHE

Blessed is he who expects nothing, for he shall never be disappointed.
—JONATHAN SWIFT

If you're not failing every now and again, it's a sign you're not doing anything very innovative. —WOODY ALLEN

Change your thoughts and you change your world. **561**
—NORMAN VINCENT PEALE

GEOGRAPHICAL LISTING OF PROGRAMS

Are you looking for a program in a specific locale? This index gives you the tools to narrow your search to a specific state, country, or region. The U.S. is broken down by state, with the rest of the world grouped by country. You'll find programs that are offered in more than one state grouped under the heading "USA" and those offered in more than one country grouped under "Worldwide." The programs under these headings are not listed separately by their respective states or countries, so you'll have to get the specifics by referring to each listing.

Whether you think you can do a thing or not, you're right.
—HENRY FORD

There are things for which an uncompromising stand is worthwhile.   **567**
—DIETRICH BONHOEFFER

No sooner do we think we have assembled a comfortable life than we find a piece of ourselves that has no place to fit in. —GAIL SHEEHY

He who is afraid to ask is ashamed of learning. 571
—DANISH PROVERB

PROGRAM LENGTH INDEX

This index groups programs by length, with some programs appearing in multiple categories. Seasonal, summer, and winter programs can be found at the end of the index, followed by programs whose length varies.

*I have learned this: it is not what one does that is wrong,
but what one becomes as a consequence
of it.* —OSCAR WILDE

To make your ideas work for you, you first have to work for them. **575**
—THOMAS ALVA EDISON

The most exhausting thing in life is being insincere.
—ANNE MORROW LINDBERGH

GENERAL INDEX

Consult this index for general information on career change, life philosophies, books, publications, resources, or websites. If you want to find a specific program or association—whether by name, category, location, or program length—the previous four indexes will provide you with the information that you need.

Do not let what you cannot do interfere with what you can do.
—JOHN WOODEN

Don't look back. Something may be gaining on you.
—SATCHELL PAGE

DORRIE WILLIAMS

HAPPY TRAILS!